EXPLORING CHILD WELFARE

A Practice Perspective

Cynthia Crosson-Tower
Fitchburg State College

Allyn and Bacon
Boston   London   Toronto   Sydney   Tokyo   Singapore

Series Editor, Social Work and Family Therapy: Judy Fifer
Vice President, Social Sciences: Karen Hanson
Editorial Assistant: Jennifer Muroff
Marketing Manager: Susan E. Brown
Editorial Production Service: Chestnut Hill Enterprises, Inc.
Manufacturing Buyer: Megan Cochran
Cover Administrator: Suzanne Harbison

Library of Congress Cataloging-in-Publication Data

Crosson-Tower, Cynthia.
    Exploring child welfare : a practice perspective / Cynthia
Crosson-Tower.
        p.   cm.
    Includes bibliographical references.
    ISBN 0-205-14743-7
    1. Child welfare—United States.   2. Social case work with
children—United States.   3. Family social work—United States.
    4. Social work education—United States.   I. Title.
HV741.C76   1997
362.7'0973—dc21   97-28097
                                                                            CIP

Printed in the United States of America

10 9 8 7 6 5 4 3 2 1   02 01 00 99 98 97

Photo Credits:
Chapters 1, 2, 3, 4, 5, 6, 8, 11, 12, 13, 14—Robert Harbison; Chapters 7, 9, 10—Robert J.
Thomas; Chapter 15—© Mary Ellen Lepionka.

To Muriel, my mother and friend
who saw me through the tough times

CONTENTS

Services to Children outside of Their Homes

PREFACE

We cannot forget that children are our most important resource. It is through our children that we can touch the future. But childhood is a time when children must depend on all of us to protect and nurture them to meet that future. Usually that task falls to the parents of children. But what if they are unable, or even unwilling, to carry the burden themselves? Hillary Clinton, in her book *It Takes a Village,* expanded the African saying,"it takes a village to raise a child," and spoke of how it is the responsibility of every citizen to insure the well-being of children.

The tool that the "village" or society uses to care for the well-being of its children is epitomized in the services provided under the child welfare system. These services vary greatly in purpose, intensity, cost, and procedures. For one who is unfamiliar with the services for children and their families, it may seem like a maze. This book is designed to help potential practitioners to understand that maze and become comfortable in using it and working within a variety of fields. The emphasis in the following pages is placed on the practice perspective both from the vantage point of the professional as well as understanding the experience of the child or family that is being helped. Since the intent is to empower the individual and family, the term *consumer* has become increasingly popular as a way of referring to those using services. By seeing the person as a consumer rather than a "patient" or a "client," as they were seen in the past, the practitioner becomes more of a guide or support as the family seeks to help itself. Thus, the analogy of the "village" becomes stronger by bringing to mind a community that helps its members rather than disempowering them. Certainly, there are times when the family is not able to care for its children and society must step in, but today the hope is that this will not happen until the community's efforts to support and keep the family together have failed.

PLAN FOR THE TEXT

The text is designed to explore child welfare services from the least intrusive into family life to the more intrusive and finally those that substitute care for the family. The chapters are arranged so that, after a brief background of child welfare and the family, the reader will recognize the services that support family life, those that supplement the roles of the family, and those that substitute for what should be provided by the family.

Chapter 1 lays a framework for child welfare by considering the past…how children were perceived and treated, and the services available for them. Chapter 2 looks at the family, both traditional and nontraditional. The chapter explores the roles and rights of family members in diverse cultures. Further, internal and external stressors are outlined that may be responsible for bringing a family to seek help from the community.

Many children within our society live in poverty and this fact makes it difficult for them to develop normally. What are the implications of growing up in poverty? Chapter 3 answers this question. It also looks at the present methods of fighting poverty and speculates about some solutions in society's effort to reduce child poverty.

Poverty is not the only social problem that plagues today's children. Actually there are many issues with which they must deal. Three of the most prevalent are violence, addiction, and homelessness. Chapter 4 explores the problems facing children growing up in a violent society, children who are addicted to drugs or alcohol or whose parents are substance abusers, and children who have no place to call home.

The next two chapters, Chapters 5 and 6, acquaint the reader with the services provided for children through education and socialization. Chapter 5 outlines day care services and Chapter 6 explains the full range of services offered to children by the schools they attend. Counseling for children and their families is considered in Chapter 7. Chapter 8 discusses family-centered (more recently referred to as "family preservation") services that strive to keep families together in their own homes. Chapter 9 looks at situations in which families cannot parent properly and end up abusing or neglecting their children. Maltreated children and their families may end up in the court system. Court services for children are outlined in Chapter 10.

A problem of almost epidemic proportions today is teens, now, at a younger age than ever, having children and attempting the challenging role of parenting. Chapter 11 examines this phenomenon and its impact on both the teens and their children.

When families are unable to provide for their children, substitute arrangements must be made. The next three chapters explore these arrangements. Chapter 12 provides insight into the foster care system from entrance into the placement process to termination. The text describes the roles, feelings, and attitudes of both the birth parents and the foster parents. The role of the foster care social worker is also discussed. Chapter 13 outlines the adoption process from the ways children are released for adoption to the feelings of the adoptive parent or parents and the problems they face. But not every child is able to adjust to a home environment. Chapter 14 describes residential settings for children who may not have the family as a viable alternative.

The text concludes with Chapter 15, which explores the future for children and their families. What will the twenty-first century bring in the way of policy changes, resources, and new problems to be faced? These are topics of discussion for today and challenges to be faced by tomorrow's practitioners.

Case examples from field experience have been woven throughout the text to help the reader see the "faces" behind the words. Each chapter is followed by Exploration Questions, developed to help the student review and pick out important material, and by Activities for Applied Learning, which invite the reader to consider how the material can be applied or how professionals in the field view their roles or some practice-related issue. The Suggested Readings suggest materials that enable the student to read books in the area covered by each chapter.

Exploring Child Welfare: A Practice Perspective is a suitable text for both undergraduate and graduate students in the fields of social work, human services, psychology, sociology, counseling, or education.

ACKNOWLEDGMENTS

Numerous people have helped, either directly or indirectly, with the completion of this text. My thanks goes first to my family, my sons and my mother, who have stayed by my side through the turbulent and difficult moments during which this book was being written. They continue to be wonderful at understanding that "Mom needs to write" and giving her space to do just that. My thanks too to dear friends Kate Martin, Mary Ann Hanley, Pauline Carruli, and Sharon Brown who were there to listen. I thank Jim Harrington for his positive outlook and for reminding me to hope.

The contributors, Lloyd Williams, Dee Whyte, Mary Ann Hanley, Elaine Francis, Judy Noel, Jenny Savage, Pamela Saulsberry, Dave Whelan, and Matthew Porter, worked hard and I thank them for their perspectives. Ken Ayers, Lois Barry, Barbara Wentz, Charlene Recos, Janice Ouellette, and Diane Kaiser also offered valuable insights. I appreciate the typing efforts of my former students Michelle Rubin and Josie Gullifa in the days before I had a computer. Since I booted up my computer and entered the computer age (albeit kicking and screaming), I thank Laura Gurlie–Mozie for helping me to tame the difficult mechanical beast that often seemed to have a mind of its own.

The following reviewers made many helpful suggestions: Cheryl K. Sibilski, Lansing Community College; Thomas M. Collins, University of Scranton; Kinly Sturkie, Clemson University; Suzanne McDevitt, University of Northern Iowa; Krishna Samantrai, California State University, Sacramento; Gail Folaron, Indiana University; and Anthony N. Maluccio, the University of Connecticut, Hartford.

I appreciated the help of my students in my child welfare classes over the last few semesters who have made suggestions, added materials, and have been waiting anxiously for the publication of this text. And finally, my sincere thanks to my editors Karen Hanson and Judy Fifer, who have been supportive, patient, and hopeful and encouraging that the deadline at hand could be met.

ABOUT THE AUTHOR

Cynthia Crosson–Tower, M.S.W., Ed.D. is Professor of Behavioral Sciences and Director of the Child Protection Institute at Fitchburg State College in Massachusetts.

Dr. Crosson–Tower is the author of numerous publications, including *Understanding Child Abuse and Neglect, How Schools Can Combat Child Abuse and Neglect, The Educator's Role in Child Abuse and Neglect, Secret Scars: A Guide for Survivors of Child Sexual Abuse,* and *Homeless Students.* Most recently, she has authored a monograph, *Designing a School Reporting Protocol,* for the Children's Trust Fund in Boston.

Dr. Crosson–Tower brings to the writing of this text over thirty years of experience in child welfare practice. She has worked as a protective services worker, a foster care specialist, an adoption specialist, a juvenile court liaison, and a regional trainer for the Massachusetts Department of Social Services. Her career has included corrections, child guidance, family services, work with the homeless, drug abuse treatment, and counseling with a variety of other agencies.

Currently, in addition to her teaching, Dr. Crosson–Tower consults to various schools, residential treatment centers for teens and social agencies, and maintains a private practice, Harvest Counseling and Consultation, specializing in the treatment of adult and teen survivors of abuse and perpetrators of sexual abuse. She offers workshops and training both nationally and internationally for educators and other human service professionals.

INTRODUCING THE CONTRIBUTORS

As I began the writing of this text, with over 30 years in child welfare practice under my belt, it became evident to me that there are too many aspects of child welfare and too many varied services for me to know all of them in depth. It was for this reason that I enlisted the contributions of colleagues who are experts in their fields and who were anxious to help me present a positive picture of these services to the future practitioner. The following introductions will give the reader insight into these authors and their contributions to the field.

Elaine Francis, Ed.D. is Professor of Special Education at Fitchburg State College in Massachusetts. Dr. Francis has over twenty years experience in the teaching field and works closely with schools providing consultation services and advocacy for students with special needs. She is the author of "Teacher Evaluation and the Renewal of School Curriculum" in S. Nieto, *Renewing School Curriculum,* Amherst, MA: The Coalition for School Improvement (1986).

Mary Ann Hanley, Ed.D. is Associate Dean of Academic Affairs, at Fitchburg State College who comes to her position with over twenty years of teaching experience in psychology and human services. She co-wrote the curriculum for School Guidance at Fitchburg State College and continues to teach and supervise students in the field. Dr. Hanley sits on the statewide committee of school counselors and counselor educators and works with MMCEP, the state group that monitors continuing education units for Mental Health Counselors.

Judy A. Noel, Ph.D. is Associate Professor of Social Work and Head of the Social Work Program at Northeast Louisiana University in Monroe, LA. She came to her twenty-five-year teaching career in child welfare with a background in the juvenile court system. Dr. Noel was primary investigator for a child fatality grant from the State of Louisiana and the Children's Trust Fund, which served to provide data to develop a protocol to limit the number of deaths of children. She is also the author of "The Lower Income, Black Rape Victim: The Case for Hospital Based Services," *Journal of Alternative Human Services,* Autumn 1980, Vol. 6., No. 3, pp. 17–20.

Matthew D. Porter, M.Ed. is the co-owner of Horizon Schools with a twenty year background in teaching and administration for both profit and non-profit early childhood education programs. He consults to a variety of school settings and is an adjunct professor at Springfield Technical Community College in Springfield, MA.

Pamela Higgins Saulsberry, M.S.W. is Associate Professor of Social Work at Northeast Louisiana University. Ms. Saulsberry is the founder and director of Reach Adolescent Potential (RAP), a community-based prevention program for teens, and a therapist for Project REspect a community-based rehabilitative program for African American males ages 14–17. She is also the co-director of Family Encounters, a parenting program for residents of the Monroe Housing Authority. Ms. Saulsberry has over twenty years experience in working with families, children, and teens in a variety of other child welfare agencies.

Jennifer J. Savage, BCSW-BAS is Assistant Professor of Social Work at Northeast Louisiana University. She began her career in medical social work as a perinatal social worker specializing in family support and parent training activities. While teaching, Ms. Savage maintains a private practice as a parent instructor for families involved with public child welfare. She recently completed two large family preservation/family support projects for the State of Louisiana and has been involved in the development of the State's plan for implementation of federal family preservation and family support legislation.

David C. Whelan, Ph.D. is Assistant Professor in the department of Law and Justice Studies at Rowan University, Glassboro, New Jersey. He brings to his teaching an extensive background in urban law enforcement and is the author of "Organized Crime and Sports Gambling" in J. Albanese, *Contemporary Issues in Organized Crimes,* Willow Tree Press, 1995.

Dee L. Whyte, B.S. is the National Director of Government Relations for TMSI, a company that designs and implements innovative and unique public/private partnerships. Prior to holding this position, Ms. Whyte was Director of Programs and Evaluations for the Children's Trust Fund, the organization mandated to implement the child abuse prevention plan for the Commonwealth of Massachusetts. She has written and spoken extensively about childhood poverty and child abuse for many years and is an advocate for family support as a critical strategy to address both of these issues.

Lloyd T. Williams, M.S.W. is a clinical social worker in full time private practice with children, adolescents, and adults in Worcester, Massachusetts. He formerly served as staff clinician, intern and staff supervisor, and community consultant for Youth Opportunities Upheld, Inc. and as program director and clinician at the Worcester Youth Guidance Center, one of the oldest youth guidance centers in the United States. He is an expert in Jungian analysis, Sandtray therapy, and the interpretation of drawings and is presently in intensive training studying hypnoanalysis and hypnotherapy.

My thanks and appreciation to all of the contributors.

Cynthia Crosson–Tower

1

CHILDREN
Our Most Important Resource

There is only one child in the world and the child's name is All
Children… This child speaks our name.
—CARL SANDBURG

The fate of one child in the United States today can be the fate of all children. Likewise, we must seek, in the interest of serving all children, to help each individual child. It is this goal toward which the child welfare system strives.

Today's world is not necessarily a safe place for our children. Every nine seconds a child drops out of school. Every ten seconds a child will be abused or neglected. Every thirty-two seconds a child is born into poverty. Every minute a baby is born to a teen mother. Every three minutes a baby is born to a mother who received no prenatal care. Every fifteen minutes a baby dies. Every two hours a child is killed by firearms (Children's Defense Fund, 1996, x).

And children act out what they see around them. Every fourteen seconds a child is arrested. Every four minutes a child is arrested for a drug offense or a violent crime. Every four hours a child commits suicide (Children's Defense Fund, 1996, **x**).

And yet, these children are our future…our most important resource. It will be up to the adults in today's world to intervene so that children will have a better future. This is the challenge facing the child welfare system.

To understand how we view children and our responsibility to protect and provide for them, we must look into the past and what the history of children's services has been.

A BRIEF HISTORY OF CHILD WELFARE

The concept of childhood as we know it is relatively new. At one time, children were seen as miniature adults with many of the responsibilities, albeit few of the rights, given to the adults of that time. Bremner (1995) points out that the plight of children was often reflected in the novels of various periods. For example, Disraeli's novel, *Sybil: The Two Nations* (1845), describes how children were subjected to horrendous conditions (sleeping on "moldering straw in a damp cellar…a dung heap at his head, and a cesspool at his feet"). A child was given drugs by his nurse and eventually left on the streets at two years old to die. Charles Dickens writes of children apprenticed to cruel masters, and kept in poor houses that treated them very badly. (See *Oliver Twist*, Dickens, 1838 [1987].) David Copperfield was neglected by his stepfather and eventually sent to a dirty, dark warehouse to work (Dickens, 1849 [1981]). Numerous other accounts throughout literature speak of how children were treated as chattel, abused and neglected because adults saw them as expendable.

ABORTION, INFANTICIDE, AND ABANDONMENT

The concept of abortion is not unique to our current society, nor is contraception. If contraception were ineffective, abortion was the traditional solution. Kadushin and Martin (1988) report that numerous studies of ancient societies reveal that abortion was widely accepted in all of them. Unwanted children who were not aborted were often dealt with in early times by abandoning or killing them. Infanticide was not an uncommon practice. During the Roman Empire and the flourishing of the Greeks, infanticide, although prohibited by law, appeared to be one of the responses to poverty and the burden of too many female children. In fact, Sumner (1959) comments that "for the masses, until the late days of the Empire, infanticide was a most venial crime" (319).

Stone (1977) reports that the history of infanticide in Western Europe dates back to antiquity, when it was widely practiced. He further comments

How far it remained a common deliberate policy for legitimate children in the Early Modern period is still open to question, although it is suggestive that as late as the early nineteenth century in Anjou, priests were instructed to warn their congregations in their sermons every three months of the mortal sin of killing an infant before baptism (473–474).

We know too, from historical references and even popular ballads of early times, that infanticide was one solution for bearing children out of wedlock. The well-known old English ballad, "Mary Hamilton," tells how a lady-in-waiting to the Queen (believed to be Mary, Queen of Scots) became pregnant by the royal consort ("the highest Stewart of all") and was driven to solve her problem by drowning the baby at sea.

> She tyed it in her apron
> And she's thrown it in the sea;
> Says, "Sink ye, swim ye, bonny wee babe
> You'll ne'er get m'air o' me (Friedman, 1956).

Infanticide was used to control the population and to insure that the populace would remain a strong and healthy race. Langer (1974) reports that infanticide has "from time immemorial been the accepted procedure for disposing…of deformed or sickly infants" (354). In their early histories, such cultures as Hawaii and China used infanticide as a form of maintaining healthy populations. Hawaiians drowned sickly children and sometimes female children in the sea (Kempe and Helfer, 1968). Although outlawed by governments, some cultures still practice forms of infanticide today.

Sometimes infanticide took the form of abandonment. Parents who were unable to care for their children might leave them to die or be found by someone else. Kadushin and Martin (1988) cite Caulfield's (1931) assessment of England in the 1700s when "dropping [abandoning] infants was an extremely frequent occurrence …and was accepted by all classes without comment" (p. 31). Even during the late 1800s children were abandoned in the streets of New York City at an astonishing rate (Kadushin and Martin, 1988). Although we would like to think that abandonment is a practice of the past, the high incidence of drug addiction among parents of young children means that some continue to be abandoned and even killed.

CHILD LABOR AND EDUCATION

Children have always been expected to work along with their parents. Farm children in a largely agrarian society did chores to contribute to the family's livelihood. At one time children were also indentured to learn trades. *Indenture* was an arrangement whereby a child would be given over to an individual who could teach him (usually, though not always, the child was male) a trade. Some of these children were well treated but others were not. Dickens (1838) spoke of the plight of one such apprentice in *Oliver Twist*. Oliver was apprenticed to an undertaker who not only mistreated him, but exposed him to the fine points of death. Like Oliver's Master, many of those using apprentices made them work long hours and in unreasonable circumstances.

But with the industrial revolution came a new way of using children in the workforce. Not only were children more plentiful than adults, but they were able to do jobs, due to their small hands and bodies, that adults were too large or too cumbersome to do. For example, children were frequently used in mining and chimney sweeping due to their ability to get into tight places. Little thought was given to the effect of the soot or mine dust on their growing bodies. In addition, they could be paid very little, and because children were thought to have no rights, little would be said by anyone about the long hours they were expected to work, the conditions under which they labored, or their treatment in general. Even the parents often depended so much on the child bringing in an extra income that they dared not protest their maltreatment, if they even knew about it. Other parents felt that their children owed them the wages they earned no matter the conditions.

It wasn't until the late nineteenth and early twentieth centuries that child labor was addressed in any significant way. It was through the efforts of such reformers as Jane Addams, Homer Folks, and Grace Abbott that the *National Child Labor Committee* (NCLC) was organized in 1904 to undertake reforms in the interest of working children (Stadum, 1995). Through its numerous publications that reported field investigations, the NCLC appealed to church, women's, and college groups to advocate for the reformation of child labor laws. The message was a straightforward one. Reformers believed that children could help with tasks around the farm or the home, but that they should also be allowed a childhood free from "unhealthy and hazardous conditions," "unsuitable wages," and "unreasonable hours" that could interfere with their "physical development and education" (Trattner, 1970, 9–10).

The first White House Conference on Children in 1910 stimulated the establishment of the U. S. Children's Bureau in 1912. It was the role of the Children's Bureau to advocate for children and one of its first tasks became the furthering of reforms in the area of child labor. In reality the number of children in the workforce between ten to thirteen had dropped from 121 in 1,000 in 1900 to 24 in 1,000 by 1930 (Trattner, 1970), but large numbers of children were still being used as migrant labor and were often uncounted in the census. When the Fair Labor Standards Act of 1938 established rules governing both wages and hours for all workers, Grace Abbott of the Children's Bureau lobbied to extend the act to insure that children under sixteen could not be used in certain industries (Stadum, 1995).

The economic needs of World War II put a strain on the enforcement of child labor laws, however, and the NCLC changed its focus to vocational training for children leaving high school. This change in focus would eventually culminate in the NCLC becoming the National Committee on the Employment of Youth in 1957 (Trattner, 1970).

Despite the fact that it would seem that early child labor laws would be applauded by all, some families found that the prohibitions dictated by the laws meant that there was one less wage earner in the family. Social workers, recognizing the families' need questioned the stringency of the new legislation. At the same time, poor parents were often portrayed as lazy individuals who would prefer to send their children to work in factories than to become employed themselves. Rarely did the hardworking parents who labored along with their children to eke out a meager livelihood come to the attention of the media or the public (Stadum, 1995).

States began to allow children to be employed if a severe family need could be documented. The NCLC opposed such exceptions and in 1921 most states had eliminated this practice. In fact, argued the NCLC, allowing children to work for low wages actually contributed to family poverty by "driving down the pay for adults who should be the household supporters" (Stadum, 1995, 37).

Along with the argument against child labor came the push for mandatory school attendance. Thus school attendance laws piggy-backed on the child labor laws while some parents questioned the need for a formal education for the children who were needed more as wage earners. The first compulsory attendance laws in the 1920s addressed children under the age of fourteen; by 1927, most states had increased the age to sixteen. Still, if families could demonstrate an economic need, children were given a certificate that allowed an exception from school in favor of earning a wage. Even if a child did attend school, it was permissible for him/her to complete a full week's work after school hours (Stadum, 1995). It often fell to the Juvenile Courts to verify the family need to require their children to work. In some areas, this task fell to the Charity Organization Society (COS), which served as the first relief organization in the United States. It was the role of the COS (later to be called the Family Welfare Association) to coordinate services for families in need of assistance (Heffernan et al., 1997). When COS workers refused to grant the requests of parents to have their children work instead of attending school, tempers flared, and the debate became heated. To encourage children to stay in school, the COS began instituting "scholarships" for needy families, which equalled what the child would have earned in wages. Reformers discovered that these scholarships actually increased children's persistence in school. "Mother's Pensions" were also given to a select group of women who were raising their children on their own. It was these payments that actually became the forerunner of the later Aid to Families with Dependent Children (Stadum, 1995).

Today, most states decree that children must remain in school until the age of sixteen. More recent legislation protects children from unfair labor practices and insures that they have an opportunity for an education.

RESPONSIBILITY FOR CHILDREN

Out-of-Home Care

As children were originally considered the property of their parents so the responsibility for them was expected to lie with these parents unless they were unable to assume it. Poor parents took their children with them to suffer the degradation of the almshouses. Other children remained at home with their parents receiving "outdoor relief," a form of "in kind" assistance. Children who had no parents or could not be kept by these parents were cared for by others, originally church-sponsored organizations. The first established orphanage in the United States was the Ursaline Convent, founded in 1727. But orphanages were initially slow in developing. By 1800 there were only five orphanages in the United States, and seventy-seven by 1851. Once the idea took hold, however, orphanages multiplied quickly, with 400 in existence by the year 1900. By 1910, 110,000 children resided in 1,151 orphanages (Smith, 1995, 118). Orphan asylums, as they were sometimes known, might house few children or many, depending upon the facility. The late 1800s also saw the moving of children from orphanages to "placing out." This practice, instituted largely by Charles Loring Brace, gave children an opportunity to live with families in the Midwestern United States (Cook, 1995). (See Chapter 12 for more details).

For the children who remained in orphanages, life varied, depending on the type of institution, the administration, and the personality of the individual environment. Corporal punishment was the norm and little thought was given to the developmental needs of children. As Thurston (1930) described orphanage life,

> *Life for a typical boy in an institution…meant essentially shelter, the actual necessities in the way of clothes, and food which primarily served the purpose of preventing starvation, rather than scientific or, may I say, common sense nourishment. The attitude of those responsible for the institution was that the boys and girls were unfortunate objects of charity (70–71).*

Early child care institutions were also largely segregated. In fact, the only facilities for many African American children were jails or reform schools even when they were not delinquents. In the early twentieth century associations of African American women finally began to address the needs of African American children (Peebles–Wilkins, 1995). One such organization's first president, Mary Church Terrell (1899), described their mission:

> *As an Association, let us devote ourselves enthusiastically, conscientiously, to the children… Through the children of today, we must build a foundation of the next generation upon such a rock of integrity, morality, and strength, both of body and mind, that floods of proscription, prejudice, and persecution may descend upon it in torrents, and yet it will not be moved. We hear a great deal about the race problem, and how to solve it…but the real solution of the race problem, both so far as we, who are oppressed and those who oppress us are concerned, lies in the children (346).*

Institutions specifically for African American children, like the Colored Big Sister Home for Girls in Kansas City, Missouri and the Carrie Steele Orphan Home in Atlanta, began to emerge (Peebles–Wilkins, 1995). Like the African American child, little was provided for the Native American child. Native American children were often sent to boarding schools (whether or not they had parents to care for them) as a way of not only providing for their care, but also for enculturating them into the white society (Mannes, 1995). It was not to be until the mid-twentieth century that child care institutions would be fully integrated.

During the 1920s the institutions saw the need to modernize slightly. Increased recognition of the needs of children gave rise to attempts to provide more humane treatment and more "advantages" to the residents. Punishments continued to be, in some cases, severe, in spite of the reformers' criticisms of corporal punishment.

Another way to care for dependent children became the free boarding home. Here children were placed with families who agreed to assume their care, initially for no compensation. Eventually a fee was granted for room and board, and agencies began to study those wanting to provide homes. These "free homes" were a precursor of today's family foster homes (see Chapter 13).

It was expected that children in both orphanages and boarding homes would show how grateful they were for their care by being respectful, compliant, and generally well-behaved. Children who "misbehaved" were threatened with expulsion. Children who complied with the rules of the institution could remain there until their majority (Smith, 1995; Hacsi, 1995).

With the recognition that children needed families, the use of orphanages declined in favor of family foster care. During the 1940s and 1950s child welfare advocates spoke of the limitations of institutional care for children. Lillian Johnson, Executive Director of the Ryther Center in Seattle, likened an institution for a child to "a life jacket that holds the child above water but without putting solid ground beneath the child's feet" (Smith, 1995, 135). The numbers of children in child care institutions dropped from 43% in 1951 to 17.1% in 1989 (Wolins and Piliavin, 1964; Merkel–Holguin, as cited in Smith, 1995, 135).

Today it is rare to find an institution dedicated to the provision of care solely for dependent children. Instead children are cared for through the provision of assistance payments to their parents or in family or group foster care. Current institutions are reserved for emotionally disturbed or delinquent children (see Chapter 15).

Day Care

The daily care of children who had parents was also expected to be provided by them. During the years of the at-home mother, this was usually not a problem. But World War II and the advent of the mother who joined the workforce changed this picture considerably. Tuttle (1995) comments:

> *America's working mothers had to confront many obstacles during the Second World War, not the least of which was people's hostility to the idea of mothers working outside of the home, even in defense plants. Feeding this sentiment were not only longstanding gender roles, but also a slew of wartime magazines and speeches by Father Edward J. Flanagen of Boys Town, J. Edgar Hoover of the F.B.I., and other defenders of the father-led family in which the mother dutifully stayed at home (p. 93).*

The advent of these working mothers, many of whose husbands were fighting at the front, necessitated that new programs be instituted for the care of their children. The Lanham Act of 1940, signed by Franklin Roosevelt, provided, among other funds for communities, money for day care centers (Tuttle, 1995). Despite suppositions that the end of war would see mothers returning home to care for their children, "Rosie the Riveter" found that she enjoyed her new freedom and the family's increased income. Thus the era of working mothers had begun, and day care outside the home increased. That trend has continued until, today, many families depend on the income of the mother to survive. (See Chapter 5 for additional information on the history of day care.)

ADVOCACY IN THE PROVISION OF SERVICES FOR CHILDREN

Over the years, a number of agencies and individuals and pieces of legislation have actively advocated the provision of services for children. One of the earliest agencies to advocate for children was the New York Children's Aid Society, founded in 1853. It was through this organization that Charles Loring Brace began to address the needs of dependent children through "placing out" (see Chapter 13). If the numbers attest to success, this agency's efforts were extremely successful. By 1873 Brace's program had placed 3,000 children and, in the year 1875, the peak year, 4,026 children found new homes in this manner (Popple and Leighninger, 1996; Johnson and Schwartz, 1991; Zastrow, 1996; Heffernan et al., 1997).

The case of Mary Ellen Wilson in 1874 (see Chapter 10) brought with it the efforts of Henry Bergh, then director of the Society for the Prevention of Cruelty to Animals, and his colleague, Elbridge Gerry, who not only advocated for one child, but for all abused and neglected children by forming the Society for the Prevention of Cruelty to Children, the first agency with the specific mission of intervening in cases of child maltreatment.

Another group of advocates in the latter part of the nineteenth and early twentieth centuries were those individuals associated with the settlement house movement. Such figures as Jane Addams, Julia Lathrop, and others blazed the way for reform in child labor, the court system, and other matters affecting children.

In 1912, the United States Children's Bureau was established as a result of the first White House Conference on Children (1910). This marked the first recognition that the federal government had any responsibility in the provision of services for children. Julia Lathrop became the first director and led the efforts to institute programs to improve maternal infant care and decrease infant mortality. The Government Printing office still carries one of the Bureau's first publications, *Infant Care*, which has undergone over twenty revisions since its first printing (Johnson and Schwartz, 1991; Downs et al., 1996; Heffernan et al., 1997).

The years 1919 and 1920 saw the creation of the American Association for Organizing Family Social Work (which later became the Family Service Association of America) and the Child Welfare League of America. Both of these organizations established standards for the provision of children's services and assistance in encouraging research, legislation, and publications related to child welfare issues (Johnson and Schwartz, 1991; Heffernan et al., 1997).

Although it is not always thought of as specifically an advocate for children, the 1935 Social Security Act did establish mothers' pensions (later to become

AFDC and Transitional Assistance) as well as mandating that states strengthen their child welfare services. Further, the act encouraged the views that poverty is a major contributor to family problems, that children be kept in their homes whenever possible, that states be allowed to intervene to protect family life, and that the federal government should have more of a role in overseeing child welfare services (Popple and Leighninger, 1990; Heffernan et al., 1997).

The 1960s and the War on Poverty saw the development of Project Head Start. This program was based on the research being done on the development of children and the effects of stimulation and poverty on children's ability to learn in school. Head Start strived to insure that economically disadvantaged preschool children would receive the medical care, nutritional services, and educational preparation to help them succeed in school (Downs et al., 1996).

Another important advocacy agency for children was the Children's Defense Fund (CDF), founded by Marian Wright Edelman in 1973. Deeply involved in the civil rights movement of the 1960s, Edelman felt that there was a need to help children throughout the country regardless of their race or class. Thus the CDF encouraged parental involvement and change within the community. Early on, the CDF dedicated itself to several aspects of child welfare:

1. Fighting the exclusion of children from school;
2. Promoting classification and treatment of children with special needs;
3. Ending the use of children in medical (especially drug) research and experimentation;
4. Guaranteeing the child's right to privacy with the growth of computerization and data banks;
5. Reforming the juvenile justice system;
6. Recognizing the importance of child development and child care; and
7. Monitoring the treatment of children in foster care (Downs et al. 1996, 453).

Since its beginnings, the CDF has also addressed child abuse and neglect issues, teen pregnancy, homelessness, and parenting issues.

In 1975 both the Title XX amendments to the Social Security Act and the Child Abuse Prevention and Treatment Act made major contributions to the provision of services for children. Public Law 94–142 (as part of the Title XX amendments) insured the education of all handicapped children (see Chapter 6) and the Child Abuse Prevention and Treatment Act mandated reporting of child maltreatment, encouraged and provided funds for research, and mandated training for the recognition, prevention, and treatment of child abuse and neglect (Tower, 1996; Heffernan et al., 1997).

Perhaps a forerunner of the family preservation (see Chapter 8) and permanency planning emphasis of today, the 1978 Indian Child Welfare Act sought to protect tribal rights and stop the frequent removal of Native American children from reservations to Anglo homes, a practice that betrays their heritage and destroys their kinship networks. It may have been this act that impelled African American activists to insist that children from their cultural background also be kept within their own kinship and extended family systems (Downs et al., 1996).

The provision of services to Native American children was further extended by the 1991 Indian Child Protection and Family Violence Act (PL 101–630) that mandated reporting of child abuse on Native American reservations. Prior to this act, there was the potential for confusion as to whether abuse was handled by tribal councils or by the local child welfare agency. This discrepancy caused inconsistency in services (Pecora et al., 1992).

Permanency planning was further addressed by the Adoptions Assistance and Child Welfare Reform Act (PL 96–272) of 1980, which discouraged placement of large numbers of children in foster care and required case plans and reviews of services to be done every six months. Further, it provided federal funding to assist the adoption of special needs children. Following the institution of this law, the number of children in foster care dropped in the early 1980s, from an estimated 500,000 to an estimated 270,000. Unfortunately, some think that the numbers of abused and neglected children have also risen since the Act was instituted (Johnson and Schwartz, 1991; Heffernan et al., 1997).

During the 1980s and 1990s several pieces of legislation affected the provision of services for children although they were not always directed specifically toward children. The Public Health Act of 1987 addressed teen pregnancy by establishing programs for pregnant and parenting teens. The Special Education for Infants and Toddlers Act (1989) enables developmentally delayed young children to receive services. The Developmentally Disabled Assistance and Bill of Rights Act (1990) requires that developmentally delayed individuals, including children, receive services in the least restrictive setting. Despite the passing of such acts, the funds to implement them are not always available. In addition, there have sometimes been ceilings placed on the amount of funds allocated to meet client needs (Heffernan et al., 1997).

The Family Preservation and Support Services in the Omnibus Budget Reconciliation Act of 1993 was the first major piece of legislation concerned specifically with child welfare since 1980. This act was directed toward vulnerable families and attempted to strengthen the services to parents in order to enhance parental functioning and protect children. The act was designed to be culturally sensitive and family-focused with an emphasis on preserving the family unit (Downs et al., 1996). In addition to specific services, child welfare agencies were also encouraged to explore the resources of kinship and community care to meet the needs of children.

THE CURRENT PICTURE OF CHILD WELFARE SERVICES

Currently there are discussions about various issues of public policy that greatly affect the provision of child welfare services. In addition, children are exposed to a variety of social problems that affect their well-being. The high incidence of drug use among both parents and their children influences healthy child development. Along with drugs goes the threat of HIV/AIDS and children's exposure to the virus. Further, the increase of violence in our society makes children especially vulnerable to harm, and the fact that the highest number of our nation's homeless are women and their children means that even the basic needs of some children are not being met (see Chapter 4 for additional discussion).

In the provision of services to children, the minority child is still underserved. Prejudice and discrimination are as present in the field of child welfare as in any other area of public service. Johnson and Schwartz (1991) cite the provision of services to African American children as an area of concern, and point out that

> *only within the last fifty years have the needs of black children been considered. Prior to this time, the black community cared for its own children. Even though laws require that minority children receive the same standards of care as are given white children, such is not the case; widespread discrimination continues to exist within the system (175).*

The Native American community has been given the authority, under the Indian Child Welfare Act of 1978, to intervene in the care of children of their own culture, and therefore has more opportunity to protect its own children. It is the Asian community, however, that may be feeling some of the pressure of not having adequate services provided. Over the last few years, there has been an influx of Asian people to a variety of communities. The wide diversity of the cultures represented have created a challenge for the social service system. For example, one social worker in a large eastern city recounted the following story.

> *We have had a large number of Cambodian families in our city for several years. Because of this, our social workers received training in some of the cultural issues so that we would know how to deal with these families. Then quite a few Hmongs moved here. The Hmongs are Laotian hill people whose customs are quite different from the Laotians themselves. They have what we might consider somewhat archaic ideas of courtship and child-rearing and helping them to integrate into our culture has been a real challenge. Understanding these families, along with the Vietnamese parents, the several Chinese clients, and the families from India and Pakistan we serve has kept us very busy. The cultural variations among these folks is great and to treat them all the same does them a great disservice.*

Hispanic families too are increasing in many areas and, like the Asian population, cannot be assumed to share one specific set of cultural customs.

The emphasis today in child welfare services is first on family preservation (see Chapter 8) and on permanency planning. Child welfare advocates agree that, whenever possible, the best place for children is with their families. Thus the family must be given assistance in solving whatever problems make it difficult to deal with their parenting role. Kadushin and Martin (1988) cite eight factors that may affect the family's ability to care for and nurture its children adequately: parental role unoccupied; parental incapacity; parental role rejection; intrarole conflict; interrole conflict; role transitions; child incapacity and/or handicap; and deficiency of community resources (15).

Parental role unoccupied refers to the situation in which there is no parent in a particular role. This parent, either mother or father, might not be present due to death, physical or mental illness, imprisonment, migration, or because the child was born to an unwed mother. *Parental incapacity* describes the parent's inability to adequately provide for his/her children due to this adult's emotional immaturity, ignorance, illness, physical disability, mental retardation, or drug addiction. A parent is said to be involved in *role rejection* when she/he has neglected, abandoned, or physically abused her/his children. *Intrarole conflict* refers to parents who recognize their need to parent but are not clear about exactly how to do this. For example, parents may narrowly define their role, leaving some family needs unmet. One single father felt that as long as he provided for his children financially, his obligation was met. He therefore expected his ten-year-old daughter to be the caretaker of her younger sister and to take care of the house and meals. Or the parent may overly restrict the child, assuming that she/he is doing what is best for the child. *Interrole conflict*, on the other hand, occurs when the role of parent conflicts with another role expected by society. For example, working mothers may find it difficult to attend to the needs of their children while giving full attention to their jobs. Assuming both roles simultaneously often requires some adjustments, especially for single mothers.

Some parents find themselves in the midst of *role transition issues*. When a parent is suddenly disabled or his/her spouse dies, accommodations are necessary to fill the parenting role. Each developmental stage, for both parents and children, has the potential for creating a crisis within the family. And divorce and remarriage may also be challenges for all parties.

Children who have a disability (*child incapacity or handicap*) can be difficult for their parents, requiring the parents to seek help to meet this challenge. And finally, even though parents may recognize a problem, the *deficiency of community services* can prevent their ability to address the need adequately (Kadushin and Martin, 1988).

All of these issues may require the child welfare system to intervene. If the family cannot be helped to deal with these problems and, thereby, remain intact, substitute care, either temporary or permanent, may be necessary. When this is the case, the goal of the agency will be in favor of permanency planning or finding the best possible plan for the child as quickly as possible. The current emphasis on permanency planning originated with a study done by Henry Maas and Richard Engles, *Children in Need of Parents* (1959). These authors looked at nine communities and discovered that, of the 260,000 children in foster care at that time, only 25% of them would return to their parents. The remainder of these children appeared destined to remain in foster care throughout their childhood. Despite the fact that foster care was deemed a temporary arrangement, no permanent plans had been devised for them, and the authors recommended that the children be returned home, placed for adoption, or that another permanent plan be created for them. This study also prompted the writing of the landmark work, *Beyond the Best Interests of the Child* (Goldstein, Freud, and Solnit, 1973), which, in turn, alerted child welfare advocates to the need for permanent plans for children (Popple and Leighninger, 1990). The recognition of the need for permanency planning was the impetus for the Adoption Assistance and Child Welfare Act of 1980 (mentioned earlier).

In some instances, efforts to preserve the family are stymied by the controversy around getting families off welfare. Legislation that prevents unwed parents from receiving benefits under certain circumstances can serve to prohibit them from parenting. For example, in some states, an unwed mother cannot receive welfare unless she returns to or remains in her family of origin. For young mothers who have been abused at home, this plan is not safe for their baby or them. Other states propose that the birth of additional children should mean the cessation of benefits. In order for families to get off welfare and parent effectively, they will require additional social supports that are, at this point, not available. Despite President Clinton's emphasis in his re-election campaign on the strengthening of services for children, youth, and families, and the need for health and welfare reform, significant positive innovations are yet to be made. It is the Children's Defense Fund (1996) contention that the elimination of child poverty will go a long way toward eliminating the pressure on the child welfare system and enabling families to provide adequately for their children.

There is also an increased emphasis on serving children with special needs. Both in the educational setting (see Chapter 6) and for substitute care (see Chapters 12 and 14) practitioners recognize that the needs of children with a variety of disabilities require alternative methods of intervention.

SERVICES IN THE TWENTY-FIRST CENTURY AND BEYOND

The future brings challenges for the provision of child welfare services. In the 1995 Congressional session, it was proposed that specific child welfare programs be eliminated by collapsing them into noncategorical block grants. This Republican plan, publicized as the Contract with America, suggested that this solution would be more effective as it was holistic in nature and took into consideration the needs of various geographic areas. States and communities would have more flexibility in the allocation of these funds. Critics of the plan felt that this would also allow advocates for specific causes to lobby for funding for their plans, leaving the majority of child and family needs unaddressed. In short, the proposal of block grants would also mean that child welfare dollars would be reduced by over five billion dollars by the year 2000 (Heffernan et al., 1997).

The Republican proposals would eliminate twenty-three federal programs aimed at high-risk children and families. Among these would be child care for mothers on AFDC and those recently returning to work from welfare, programs for child abuse and domestic violence prevention, programs related to the provision of foster care and preparation for independent living, and a variety of others promoting family support. The Child Welfare Protection Block Grant would instead give the states large blocks of money to use as they saw fit. The concern is that such a plan would not only cut funds but would mean an uneven distribution of services from state to state (Heffernan et al., 1997).

What direction should child welfare services and policy-making relating to child welfare be taking in the twenty-first century? Lisbeth Schorr (1989), in a national review, found that many of the current child welfare programs were effective. She cited the efficacy of such programs as being based on several assumptions: Children who were consistently poor and lived in concentrated areas of poverty were more at risk for later damage; the issues that affect children are societal rather than related to individual children; and the knowledge of how to solve problems is available. What is required is the commitment to use the knowledge and resources (29). Further, the programs that were successful provided a large range of services involving concrete services as well as emotional and support services, the services were flexible in their ability to collaborate with other service networks and providers, the services treated the child in the context of the family system as well as the rest of the environment (neighborhood, community, and so on), the staff were caring and committed, which created trust and respect in their clients, and the services were easy for people to use (Schorr, 1989).

It is unfortunate that we seem to have lost the "personal touch" in the provision of services. Some argue that the personalization of services precludes responsible fiscal management. Yet, story after story of change attests to the fact that the human factor cannot be ignored. It may be that the hallmark of effective provision of services in the twenty-first century will necessitate recapturing the human side rather than the fiscal side of human services. The conundrum will be how to accomplish this in our high tech world.

PROVIDING SERVICES FOR CHILDREN TODAY

The child welfare worker assumes many different roles in the provision of services today. Each of these roles may require a different type of training. The first "child welfare workers" were volunteers and it wasn't until the 1900s that child welfare became a field as such (Heffernan et al., 1997). What might a child welfare worker do? This is largely dependent on the type of service or agency in which he or she is employed. Table 1-1, based on the chapters to follow, gives an idea of what roles one might perform. It is far from inclusive of all the possible roles.

The roles mentioned in Table 1-1 require different levels of education. Some agencies will hire residential counselors or aids without a college education, but most prefer an Associates or Bachelors degree. Although some agencies will hire people who have a degree in unrelated fields, most prefer that the degree be earned in such disciplines as human services, social work, or other subjects that prepare one for social service delivery. The more specialized the role, the more education required. For example, counseling often requires a Masters in Social Work or counseling.

What a child welfare worker does from day to day depends largely on the type of agency. The following descriptions illustrate some of the diverse tasks performed by such workers.

As a residential counselor in a home for unwed mothers, Sally has myriad tasks. She helps the teens accomplish their daily tasks as they adjust to the progression of their pregnancies. She gives training sessions on making decisions about keeping the baby versus adoption. For the mothers who choose to keep their babies, she leads discussions on baby care.

TABLE 1-1   Examples of Child Welfare Roles

Type of Service	Agency	Possible Job Title	Roles Performed
Family Services	Family Planning Clinic	Counselor	counsels on contraception, family planning, pregnancy, pre-natal care, and so on
	Early Intervention	Home Visitor	provides support for new parents, especially at-risk families
For Homeless	Homeless Shelter	Shelter Staff	provides support, counseling in budgeting, housing, child care, homemaking, advocacy for families in shelter
	Housing Agency	Advocate	provides support, advocacy or counseling for families seeking housing, and helps identify housing and places families
For Drug-Addicted	Various Drug Agencies		provides support and counseling for parents or teens who are drug addicted, and drug abuse prevention training in schools and the community
Day Care	Day Care Center (private or federal, e.g. Head Start)	Teacher or Aid or Family Worker	provides services for children in day care setting, and does outreach to parents
Education	Schools	School Counselor, Aid, Health Educator	provides a variety of services to remove barriers to children's learning, such as counseling, groups, aid to special needs children, and functions as a liaison to parents
Counseling	Family Service Agency	Counselor	provides counseling to families and children
Child Protection	Child Protective Services	Child Protection Social Worker	provides case management to families at risk for child maltreatment
Court Services	Juvenile Court	Social Worker Probation Officer	provides counseling or case management for children and families seen by the juvenile court
Teen Parents	Agency for Teens, Family Service Agency	Counselor Residential Staff	provides support, counseling or case management for teen parents and serves as residential staff in homes for unwed mothers
Foster Care	Child Protection Agency Family Service Agency	Social Worker	provides home studies of potential foster parents; places and supervises children in foster homes
Adoption	Adoption Agency Family Service Agency Child Protection Agency	Social Worker	provides home studies on potential adoptive parents; places and supervises children in adoptive homes
Residential Care	Residential Treatment	Social Worker Residential Staff	supervises children in residential settings and provides counseling for children in care

Vanessa is a placement worker for an adoption agency. It is her job to visit foster homes where children are awaiting adoption. She develops a profile of the children and readies them for placement. Once a couple is found, Vanessa calls them about a potential child, meets with them to discuss the child, and introduces them to the child. If the couple chooses to go forward with the adoption, Vanessa places the child in their home and visits on a monthly basis for six months to a year, depending on the child's age. When the time comes for the adoption to be finalized, she accompanies the family to probate court.

Herb is an outreach worker for a local family service center. He goes to the homes of high-risk families and helps to hook them up with the appropriate social services. He visits agencies that provide services to families in order to keep current on their programs. He helps families figure out budgets and aids them in planning transportation, child care, and a variety of other needs.

Most child welfare workers perform their roles in an agency or in some type of bureaucratic setting. This can add to the frustration of the job as many bureaucracies, in order to maintain themselves and insure quality, require that staff follow a great many procedures and document these through paperwork. "The paperwork can seem overwhelming at times," recounts a veteran worker, "but it all seems worth it when a child and his or her family are receiving the service they need."

Training is a vital part of child welfare. Unfortunately some agencies in the past have used the "learning by doing" method to train staff to the detriment, in some instances, of the clients. Currently the U. S. Department of Health and Human Services has available, under the Child Welfare Training Section 426 of the Social Security Act, funds for nonprofit agencies and educational institutions to train staff in public child welfare agencies (Johnson and Schwartz, 1991). Many professionals feel that it is also advisable to have college training in order to provide adequate services for families and children.

The field of child welfare can be a challenging one, but the role of the child welfare worker also has numerous rewards.

SUMMARY

The role of child welfare services is to provide a safety net for children. To better understand how today's services for children operate it is helpful to consider the past. Children have always been at the mercy of their caretakers. Unwanted children were dealt with from earliest times by abortion, infanticide, and even abandonment. Children were also required to work alongside adults who may have disregarded the fact that the children were not as strong and not as able to work long hours. An early form of child labor was indenture, a system whereby children were apprenticed to tradesmen to learn by doing. It was not until the late nineteenth and early twentieth centuries that such reformers as Jane Addams, Homer Folks, Grace Abbott, and Julia Lathrop sought reform in child labor laws. Several agencies have advocated for children over the years. The U.S. Children's Bureau (founded in 1912), the Family Welfare Association (formerly the Charity Organization Society), and the Children's Defense Fund all had a role in protecting children and advocating for their well-being.

The responsibility for children, originally, rested entirely with their parents. Children were expected to follow their parents even to almshouses in which the conditions could be unfit for adults let alone their offspring. Later, the care of orphaned children or children whose parents could not care for them shifted to orphanages. In the late nineteenth century, Charles Loring Brace, feeling that family life for children was preferable to an institutional setting, instituted "placing out" whereby children were sent by train to the Midwestern United States to find homes with farm families.

Minority children were excluded from the programs aimed at white children. For African American children, this could mean being sent to a reform school rather than an orphanage or a private home. Native American children were often sent to boarding schools so that they could be better assimilated into the white culture.

With advances in research about child development came the recognition that children needed a family environment, and placement in foster and adoptive homes became the priority. In addition, the well-publicized case of the maltreated Mary Ellen Wilson in 1874 gave rise to the Society for the Prevention of Cruelty to Children and the first formalized efforts to protect children from abuse and neglect.

Since the early 1900s there have been numerous advances in the provision of services for children. Today, the concepts of family preservation (that all reasonable attempts to maintain the family intact must be made) and permanency planning (finding a permanent arrangement for children whose parents cannot care for them as early as possible) are the key phases that characterize the provision of services.

Funding, always an issue in the provision of child welfare services, is a major concern. Critics of the move to collapse moneys into block grants contend that services to children would be cut substantially. Others argue that it is the "personal touch" that is lacking in today's agency efforts. The fact remains that children are our most important resource and strengthening the safety net that protects them from harm and enables them to develop safely and healthfully is the obligation of all adults.

EXPLORATION QUESTIONS

1. What problems characterize the lives of children today?
2. Why did early people practice infanticide?
3. What is meant by the term *indenture*? Why might it have not served the best interests of the child?
4. What efforts were made toward reform in child labor? Who were some of the main advocates?
5. Trace the history of services for children whose parents could not care for them.

6. How did the services for minority children differ from those provided for white children?
7. Cite some key agencies that advocate for children. What do they do?
8. What recent legislation has advocated for children?
9. What are the major trends in the provision of child welfare today?
10. What types of roles might a child welfare worker take in helping children?

ACTIVITIES FOR APPLIED LEARNING

1. Research the types of child welfare services in your community. Where are they listed? What is the function of each?
2. Invite representatives from various child welfare agencies to sit on a panel for a class presentation. Ask each not only about their jobs but also about their training.
3. Ask a local child welfare agency to put you in touch with an individual who has used child welfare services as a child and would agree to speak about the experience. Invite the person to speak in class.
4. What type of child welfare needs might your family have had when you were a child? Did they receive services or not?

SUGGESTED READING

Brown, R. (ed). *Children in Crisis.* New York: H. W. Wilson, 1994.

Children's Defense Fund. *The State of America's Children Yearbook.* Washington, DC: Children's Defense Fund, 1996.

Golden, R. *Disposable Children: America's Welfare System.* Belmont, CA: Wadsworth, 1997.

Goldstein, J., Freud, A., & Solnit, A. J. *Beyond the Best Interests of the Child.* New York: Free Press, 1973.

Mannes, M. "Factors and Events Leading to the Passage of the Indian Child Welfare Act," *Child Welfare,* 74(1), (1995), 264–282.

Schorr, L. *Within Our Reach: Breaking the Cycle of Disadvantage.* New York: Anchor, 1989.

Stadum, B. "The Dilemma in Saving Children from Child Labor: Reform and Casework at Odds with Families' Needs (1900–1938)," *Child Welfare,* 74(1), (1995), 33–55.

Trattner, W. I. *Crusade for the Children: A History of the National Child Labor Committee and Child Labor Reform in America.* Chicago: Quadrangle Books, 1970.

REFERENCES

Bremner, R. H. "Child Welfare in Fact and Fiction," *Child Welfare,* 74(1), (1995), 19–31.

Caulfield, E. *The Infant Welfare Movement of the Eighteenth Century.* New York: Paul Locker, 1931.

Children's Defense Fund. *The State of America's Children Yearbook.* Washington, DC: Children's Defense Fund, 1996.

Cook, J. F. "A History of Placing-Out: The Orphan Trains," *Child Welfare,* 74(1), (1995), 181–197.

Dickens, C. *David Copperfield.* Oxford: Oxford University Press, 1849 [1981].

Dickens, C. *Oliver Twist.* Oxford: Oxford University Press, 1838 [1987].

Disraeli, B. *Sybil: The Two Nations.* London: Oxford University Press, 1845.

Downs, S. W., Costin, L. B., & McFadden, E. J. *Child Welfare and Family Services.* White Plains, NY: Longman, 1996.

Friedman, A. B. *The Viking Book of Folk Ballads of the English-Speaking World.* New York: Viking, 1956.

Goldstein, J., Freud, A., & Solnit, A. J. *Beyond the Best Interests of the Child.* New York: Free Press, 1973.

Hacsi, T. "From Indenture to Family Foster Care: A Brief History of Child Placing," *Child Welfare,* 74(1) (1995), 162–180.

Heffernan, J., Shuttlesworth, G., & Ambrosino, R. *Social Work and Social Welfare.* St. Paul, MN: West, 1997.

Johnson, L. C., & Schwartz, C. L. *Social Welfare: A Response to Human Need.* Boston: Allyn and Bacon, 1991.

Kadushin, A., & Martin, J. *Child Welfare Services.* New York: Macmillan, 1988.

Kempe, C. H., & Helfer, R. *The Battered Child.* Chicago: Chicago University Press, 1968.

Langer, W. L. "Infanticide: A Historical Survey," *History of Childhood Quarterly,* 1 (1974), 353–365.

Maas, H. S., & Engles, R. E. *Children in Need of Parents.* New York: Columbia University Press, 1959.

Mannes, M. "Factors and Events Leading to the Passage of the Indian Child Welfare Act," *Child Welfare,* 74(1), (1995), 264–282.

Merkel–Holguin, L. A., with Sobel, A. *The Child Welfare Stat Book 1993.* Washington, DC: Child Welfare League of America, 1993.

Pecora, P., Whittaker, J. K., Maluccioo, A. N., with Barth, R. P. & Plotnick, R. D. *The Child Welfare Challenge.* New York: Aldine DeGruyter, 1992.

Peebles–Wilkins, W. "Janie Porter Barrett and the Virginia Industrial School for Colored Girls: Community Response to the Needs of African American Children," *Child Welfare,* 74(1), (1995), 143–161.

Popple, P. R., & Leighninger, L. *Social Work, Social Welfare and American Society.* Boston: Allyn and Bacon, 1996.

Schorr, L. *Within Our Reach: Breaking the Cycle of Disadvantage.* New York: Anchor, 1989.

Smith, E. P. "Bring Back the Orphanages? What Policymakers of Today Can Learn from the Past," *Child Welfare,* 74(1), (1995), 115–142.

Stadum, B. "The Dilemma in Saving Children from Child Labor: Reform and Casework at Odds with Families' Needs (1900–1938)," *Child Welfare,* 74(1), (1995), 33–55.

Stone, L. *The Family, Sex and Marriage in England, 1500–1800.* New York: Harper & Row, 1977.

Sumner, W. G. *Folkways.* New York: Dover, 1959.

Terrell, M. C. "The Duty of the National Association of Colored Women to the Race" *Church Review* (pp. 340–354). In Mary Church Terrell Papers. Washington, DC: Moorland–Spingarn Research Center, Howard University, 1899.

Thurston, H. W. *The Dependent Child.* New York: Columbia University Press, 1930.

Trattner, W. I. *Crusade for the Children: A History of the National Child Labor Committee and Child Labor Reform in America.* Chicago: Quadrangle Books, 1970.

Tuttle, W. M. "Rosie the Riveter and Her Latchkey Children: What Americans Can Learn about Child Day Care from the Second World War," *Child Welfare,* 74(1), (1995), 92–114.

Wolins, M., & Piliavin, I. *Institution or Foster Family: A Century of Debate.* New York: Child Welfare League of America, 1964.

Zastrow, C. *Introduction to Social Work and Social Welfare.* Pacific Grove, CA: Brooks/Cole, 1996.

2

THE CHANGING FAMILY

A family has traditionally begun when two people decide to join together for the purpose of sharing their futures and possibly bringing into the world or into their lives children whom they expect to raise. Throughout history, no one institution has had more impact on the forming of the values of the society than the family. Today, the family may look quite different than it did in previous generations. The model of the "intact nuclear household unit composed of a male breadwinner, his full-time homemaker wife, and their dependent children" (Walsh, 1993, 13) belongs, for the most part, to the past. Modern families may consist of a single adult, multiple generations, heterosexual or homosexual couples, or a mosaic of color, values, and culturally diverse variations (Walsh, 1993). Yet it is still some form of family which is responsible for imparting the mores of the society to the majority of America's children.

THE RESPONSIBILITIES AND RIGHTS OF THE FAMILY

In a world of flux, it is expected that the family will provide the context for the procreation, enculturation (imparting of society's values), and protection of children. When we think of the concept of family, we usually think of a group of people who choose to live together, or at least have regular contact, for the purpose of performing specific functions (Tower, 1996). These functions can be broken down into a series of responsibilities taken on by the family system. First, it is assumed that the family will be responsible for *procreation*. While biologically procreation may require a male and a female partner, it is not uncommon for these individuals to procreate but, for whatever reason, decide not to remain together to parent the child. Whatever the family unit involved, it is expected that the family will then be responsible for the *socialization* of the child, helping him or her to learn to relate to other members of society, both peers and adults. Families are also expected to teach children the values of the society, the process of *enculturation*. By verbalizing to and modeling for children, the parental figures let them know what is deemed appropriate by the culture in which they live. In addition, families model appropriate gender-linked and cultural roles (Kadushin and Martin, 1988; Hess et al., 1993). Male children learn from their male caretakers just as females learn from their female caretakers what is relevant to their gender.

Families are expected to provide *protection* for their offspring, insuring that these children are given as safe an environment as possible to grow into adulthood. Families also *provide both financial and emotional support* to their members. They are expected to *meet the child's other basic needs* such as food, shelter, clothing, and affection. Our culture also expects that the family will *provide for the child's medical and educational needs*. Finally, the family has the extremely important role of *interpreting the world to the child and the child to the world*. The following situation illustrates the interpretation of the child to the world.

Franz is a severely handicapped child of twelve, whose younger brothers protect and nurture him with diligence. Unable to speak, Franz uses a wooden board on which the alphabet is printed. To make his needs known, he has learned to point to the letters on the board and spell out his requests. At a very early age, each of his three younger brothers learned to read his words or understand the hand signals he uses. "It is not unusual," recounts his mother, "to see Franz talking to a stranger surrounded by his brothers who are eagerly interpreting. The children seem to find it a way of connecting that meets everyone's needs."

Families who meet the expectations society has of them are subsequently awarded the *right to privacy*, and they carry out their roles with a minimum of societal intervention. The functional family need only deal directly with society when it comes to the school and the medical community. It is the family that does not meet its obligations that comes to the attention of the services designed to provide a safety net for family functioning.

THE SETTING FOR TODAY'S FAMILY

It is not always easy for the family to meet its responsibilities, especially against the backdrop of the complexity of today's world. There are several major factors that affect family functioning and require accommodation on the part of each family system.

The *violence* that characterizes society today can significantly affect children and the family (see Chapter 4 for more discussion). Daily, children are exposed to violence in the streets as well as in the media. Family violence, too, is at an all time high. Whether the violence is within the family or external to the family, it will have an impact on the functioning of the family unit.

Divorce continues to threaten the stability of the modern home. While the divorce statistics appear to be leveling out to some extent, the reality is that many families still find themselves coping with the emotional and financial ramifications of this phenomenon. With it divorce brings an increase in *single parent households* while the supports available for these single parents continue to decrease (Downs, et al., 1996). In addition, two-parent families, as well as single-parent families, find it necessary for the *caretakers to work outside the home,* requiring more alternative care for children.

PROFILE OF TODAY'S FAMILY

The family is a complex system that constantly changes. Within the greater system are a series of subsystems. The *parent subsystem* is made up of caretakers who are responsible for making decisions and regulating the activities of the family unit. It is expected that parents will protect and nurture their children and teach them the values of the culture so that they might grow to take their place in society. To do this parents provide not only verbal cues to proper behavior but also model the behavior and attitudes that are expected socially.

The *sibling subsystem* is composed of the children in a given family and provides an arena for trying out relationships with peers. Children have an opportunity to compete, fight, negotiate, and learn from each other so that they can eventually transfer these skills to peers outside of the family (Minuchin, 1981). In the healthy family, there are clear boundaries between the parental and sibling subsystems. Parents have specific roles and children have their roles as well. Family dysfunction can occur when these generational boundaries become compromised. The sexually abusive family is characterized by a blurring of generational boundaries. Here the sexual relationship that is appropriate between adults crosses boundaries and involves the children. By the same token, generational boundaries must also be fluid enough to allow members to have appropriate interaction with each other. When boundaries are too rigid, children often feel abandoned and as if their parents are not available to them emotionally (Herbert, 1989).

In addition to these two main subsystems, families are composed of a variety of other units. For example, all the males of a particular family comprise another subsystem as do all the females. Extended families living together increase the possibilities for subsystem combinations. For example, there may be grandparent subsystems.

A family system must also maintain boundaries with the outside world. If these boundaries are poorly defined, the family may lose its identity as a family. If they are too rigidly kept, the family becomes isolated from the world in which it operates.

FAMILY ROLES AND RULES

Historically, family members have assumed a set of roles expected by society and an individualized set of roles dictated by the individual family. Often, these overlapped. For example, at one time the father figure in the home was expected to be the breadwinner while the female figure had the role of maintaining the home. Most families accepted these roles and governed themselves according to them. Certainly, some families deviated, based on their own needs to achieve homeostasis. Today, there have ceased to be these clear-cut, societally prescribed roles, partially due to the economic need for both parents to work outside the home. Therefore families are more apt to find their own way of taking care of the family tasks. For some, the mother is still the regulator of the household functioning while also maintaining a job outside. Still other families find ways to share the roles and tasks inherent in everyday life. The assignment of these roles can in itself create stressors. Increasingly, women are pointing to the need for parents to take on more equal responsibility for child-rearing so they are not overtaxed in their roles as wife and mother. New generations are increasingly conscious of this need to share in maintaining a home, but not always sure how to put it in practice. The way in which the family deals with these issues may be largely based on the personality structure of the adults (Swanson, 1993).

Some families find that their ethnic orientation imposes roles on them that they find difficulty in maintaining. For example, some cultures still see the man as the head of household and the primary breadwinner. Yet, it may be easier for the woman, who may not in their culture do so, to work outside the home. As a result, the male feels he is losing some of the respect previously given him.

The assignment of roles can be spoken or unspoken and is often quite complex. In addition, roles are not always functional. Children are sometimes cast into roles that do not benefit them in their healthy development. Parents who are themselves unable to accept responsibility and nurture may see their children as their caretakers, thus robbing children of their right to be taken care of.

Roles are often supported by family rules. Rules are "repetitive patterns of interaction that family members develop with each other" (Tower, 1996, 26). Rules are either spoken or unspoken and govern the way in which families communicate and perform. Rules that are unspoken in one family may be spoken in another. For example, in one family the females do the inside tasks, such as cleaning and cooking, while the men do the outside tasks, such as mowing the lawn. In some homes this is just understood while in others it is clearly stated.

Rules may also support or cover dysfunctional behavior. In an alcoholic family, it might be understood that family members stay out of Dad's way when he is drinking or make excuses for Mom when her drug problem impedes her functioning. In sexually abusive families siblings often know not to communicate with each other. This may actually be something impressed on them by the perpetrator, who recognizes that the secret of his abuse is best kept if family members do not talk to each other about it. Rules dictate how family members will behave, feel, and think. Conflict with these rules can also create conflict within the family.

COMMUNICATION PATTERNS

Communication within a family system often is at the root of how the family functions. Communication is not always on the surface nor do people always communicate through words. Gestures, postures, voice intonation, and facial expressions sometimes say more than the words spoken. Culture also has an impact on the way in which families communicate. Some ethnic populations use communication patterns that are hierarchical (Hutter, 1991). Elders are respected (as in Asian cultures) and the young must listen and learn from them. Some families express their emotions freely, given their cultural heritage, while in others the show of emotions denotes a lack of strength or self-control (Mass and Yap, 1992). Family rules differ from culture to culture. Many cultures see the father as the family head and his word is not to be disputed. In this case, rules like 'asking father before decisions are made' are paramount. In still other cultures, the mother may be in a pivotal position.

It is important for those working with particular cultural groups to be familiar with the mores and values of that group. Not to take the time to do so could result in an inability to help the family and even insult them, as the following event illustrates.

[handwritten marginalia: Perhaps more p.to impt to treat people individual]

A Muslim family was referred to a family service agency by their son's school when the boy had become too difficult for school personnel to handle. The family came reluctantly, the mother encased in her traditional garb, including a veil over the lower half of her face. Interested in knowing how the family was functioning, the worker, unfamiliar with Muslim custom, made eye contact with the mother and asked her how she felt about their child's acting out. The whole family's reaction was immediate and the worker quickly realized that he had somehow offended them. It was not until he talked with another worker that he learned the cultural error of making eye contact with a Muslim woman and not allowing her to go through her husband to communicate.

To be clearly effective communication patterns in families must be clear and open. With added stress on the family system, effective communication can often get lost in the demands of everyday life. It is often incomplete or unclear communication that brings families to child welfare agencies.

OBSERVATION OF THE FAMILY AS A SYSTEM

One highly effective method of looking at the family as a system with its roles, rules, and communication patterns is through the use of genograms. Genograms are a "schematic diagram of the family's relationship system, in the form of a genetic tree, usually including at least three generations" (Goldenberg and Goldenberg, 1991, 325). Specific symbols (see Figure 2-1) are used to represent family members and relationships between them. Anecdotal data can then be added.

One advantage of a genogram is that it can give both the helper and the family a quick and fairly comprehensive view of what is occurring in the family, what patterns are present, and how these are impacted by previous generations. Often, clients are helped to recognize that they are part of generations of dysfunction and that the patterns they now practice have been handed down from previous generations. When this becomes evident, individuals and families can more effectively strive to break these patterns for future generations.

The Hartowski family came to the attention of social services because Mr. Hartowski was sexually abusing his daughter. It is obvious from the genogram (see Figure 2-2) that child sexual abuse has been a part of several generations as well as other types of family dysfunction. From the overall view provided by a genogram, it would become clear that intervention is needed in this generation.

TYPES OF FAMILIES

The picture of family life differs greatly today. Acock and Demo (1994) studied 2,457 families to look at diversity and family well-being. Within this sample they identified four types of family configurations: First marriages (N = 1,085), Divorced (N = 677), Stepfamilies (N = 277), and Continuously single mothers (N = 418) (51–52). The sample represented all income levels and included 255 African American, 1,367 white, 150 Hispanic mothers, and 26 mothers of other ethnic origins (64). African American children were more likely to come from single-parent households (42.7%) while only 3.9% of white children and 18.0% of Hispanic children have single parents. White children were more likely to be in first

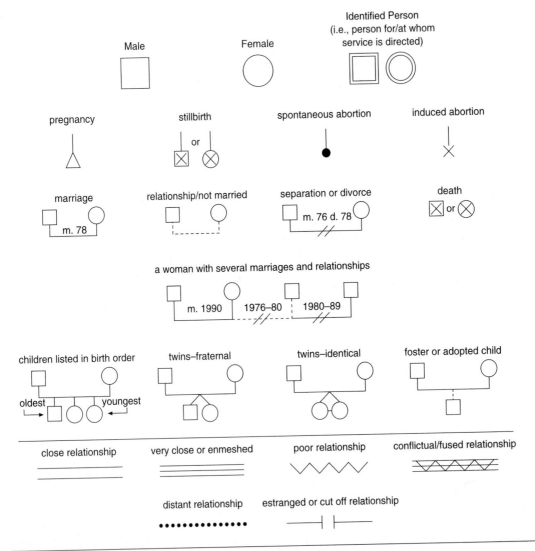

FIGURE 2-1   Symbols Used in Genograms

Adapted from M. McGoldrick and R. Gerson. *Genograms in Family Assessment*. New York: Norton, 1985.

married families (70.8%) or stepfamilies (11.1%). In contrast, only 31.8% of African American children are in first married families and 5.1% in stepfamilies. Thus it is expected that 70% of white children and 94% of African American children will be part of other than a two-parent family system before their eighteenth birthday (63).

Other authors (Walsh, 1993; Hess et al., 1993; Wells, 1991) divide the family into the two parent–dual wage earner family, the single-parent family, and the reconstituted family.

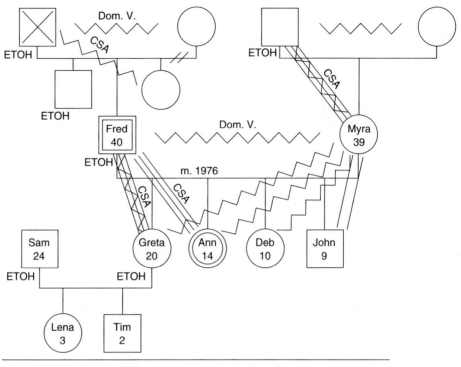

ETOH = alcohol abuse   CSA = child sexual abuse   Dom. V. = domestic violence

FIGURE 2-2   The Hartowski Family

The *two parent–dual wage earner* family is the closest remnant of earlier family concepts. Here two parents strive to raise their mutual children, but economic necessity has required the female parent to also enter the workforce. This family system grapples, not only with common family demands, but also with the time management and role assignment issues that are inherent in both parents being outside of the home for much of the time. It is the latter set of issues that have created the need for research and intervention and caused the family to seek help more often than any other. The pervading myth, despite the reality of today, is of father as breadwinner and mother as nurturer, and it is not uncommon for families to have difficulty adjusting these perceptions to meet their needs.

The *single-parent family* is usually headed by the mother (although fathers as single parents appear to be increasing as divorce laws attempt to cater to the best interest of the child) who tries to assume the role of both parents. The one-parent status of this family may have been created either by divorce, death, or because the mother/parents chose not to marry.

The *reconstituted family* refers to one in which there are two parents, one or both of whom have had children by another partner. These parents marry, bringing with them their respective families, which they then co-parent. They may also bring into the family children of their own. The definition of role, rules, and communication patterns for such families may be challenging. Each adult brings with them at least two sets of role expectations (their family of origin and their first marriage/relationship) and the children may compare what they have been used to between their biological parents and what has developed with the new family system.

In addition to these family types, Walsh (1993) identifies several others: families by adoption (see Chapter 14) and gay and lesbian families.

Rebecca had always felt more attracted to her own sex than to men. Rebecca Tanner and Freda Schultz have been partners for ten years. After Rebecca's divorce, she was concerned about raising her two small children alone. Her early marriage had been the result of a pregnancy and had never been very happy. When she met Freda at work, she was very attracted to her. Their relationship eventually became intimate and the two women had a commitment ceremony and settled down together to raise Rebecca's children.

Although gay and lesbian families have long been discounted as a viable family structure, there are an increasing number of them today. Laird (1993) comments that "'normalcy' [is] an idea located in the eye of the beholder" (283). While some argue that being raised by two parents of the same sex does not provide children with adequate gender models, others point out that having two parents gives the child more adult role models. Many children grow up in single-parent families with a myriad of stresses placed on their sole parent. On the significance of families created by same-sex couples, Laird further comments:

> Family theorists would do well to heed the lesbian and gay family, for it can teach us important things about other families, about gender relationships, about parenting, about adaptation to tensions in this society, and especially about strength and resilience. For in spite of the pervasive and profound stigmatization of gay life, gay men and lesbians are building stable and satisfying couple relationships and forming families that seem to be doing at least as well as other kinds of families in carrying out their sociologically defined family roles and tasks (284).

In years past, families often consisted of multi-generations. Today there are a few *extended or intergenerational family systems*, often more likely among minority or newly immigrated families. While the children of these groups have more adult models with whom to identify, they may also feel the pull of the greater society to become independent of their traditional cultures. This, in and of itself, can create stress within the family.

One family structure seen increasingly in today's society is *grandparents raising grandchildren.* There are numerous reasons (e.g., teen parents, career-oriented parents) why grandparents become the primary caretakers for their children's children.

Karpel and Strauss (1983) suggest that the family should be seen in several contexts:

> *The functional family,* whose members who share household tasks, activities, and child care;
>
> *The legal family,* which is bound together by its legal structure and altered by divorce or the legal removal of children;
>
> *The family by perception,* in which members see others as being part of the family (e.g., live-in partner, considered to be acting in the role of mate and second parent, compadres, and kinsfolk);
>
> *The biological family,* which is held together by blood relationships;
>
> *The family of long-term commitments,* in which long-term expectations encompassing trust, fairness, and loyalty are present (as cited by Tower, 1996, 23).

Obviously, some of these may overlap, but the framework provides an idea of how the family may see itself or be seen by others.

THE IMPACT OF CULTURE ON FAMILIES

Families may have totally different roles, rules, and communication patterns depending on the culture in which they reside. The most statistically prevalent cultures are discussed below, but the child welfare worker should become familiar with the variations present in his/her client population. For example, one can discuss generalized characteristics of Hispanic or Asian families, but within those two cultural groupings is a variety of individual orientations. Mexican families are not necessarily like Puerto Rican families, and Chinese families have different values from families whose origins are in India. Thus one should digest the generalizations but seek more detailed information as necessary.

How an individual family functions is influenced by several variables:

1. The family's culture of origin;
2. The subgroup of that culture and its particular values (for example, cultures with caste systems may have different expectations of individuals depending on their castes);
3. The relationship of the culture or the subgroup to the wider culture in which it functions (prejudice and stigma play a role in how well families are able to integrate into the larger society);
4. Individual family member characteristics;
5. The familys members' ability and strategies for adapting to the stresses of living in a family unit (Tower, 1996, 27).

Leiberman (1990) reflects on the fact that, while other cultures value collectivism, the culture of the United States emphasizes individualism, two social values that he contrasts in some detail.

> *An individualistic culture is one where a person's social behavior is shaped by primarily by personal goals and needs which do not necessarily overlap with the goals and needs of their in-group. Competition is stressed and cooperation is not. In contrast, in a collectivist culture the person's behavior is shaped primarily by the goals, needs, and values of the in-group, even when this involves giving up personal pursuits. These cultures tend to stress cooperation and avoid competition. There is also a high personal identification with the family and a sense of mutual obligation and responsibilities among extended family members. Personal sacrifices are expected on behalf of family welfare… In individualistic cultures, people who sacrifice important personal goals for the sake of others may be considered masochistic, immature or overly dependent… In a collective culture a person who fails to sacrifice personal goals for the welfare of others is often rebuked as selfish, disloyal, and untrustworthy (107).*

Because many families from collectivist cultures find this a difficult society into which to integrate, it must be assumed that at the root of the problem of an ethnically oriented minority family may be role confusion based on the differences between their cultures of origin and this one. Yet all families have at one time experienced the difficulties inherent in the fact that the United States is the "great melting pot" and therefore does not duplicate any one culture, including the Native American culture that settled it and the European cultures that colonized it.

FAMILIES WITH ANGLO-EUROPEAN ROOTS

When considering culture, there is often no discussion of early immigrants with European heritage and how their values influenced the greater society of today. Such platitudes as "if you don't succeed, try, try again," "where there's a will, there's a way," or "a penny saved is a penny earned" have become such an integral part of the thinking of so many people that we rarely stop to identify these sentiments as remnants of the philosophy of the early Anglo-European colonists (Hanson, 1992).

Reports of a rich, new world and disillusion with their native land brought early colonists from England, the Netherlands, Spain, Portugal, France, and Italy. They brought with them a desire to forge a new life and a set of values from their own lands. While they interacted with the Native people of their new land, they maintained their own traditions as they settled to hunt, farm, and trade. They possessed a pioneering spirit that was only enhanced by breaking from the rule of England in the 1700s. The westward expansion resulted from this desire to reach out and forge one's own way. With this need to settle and cope in the face of numerous odds came the strengthening of the rugged individualism that produced an undercurrent that still exists in many spheres today.

Values

The values of those with European heritage tend to include independence, self-directedness, assertiveness, acquisition, equality, freedom, and self-help (Hanson, 1992). In his guide to the United States for foreigners, Althen (1988) suggested the following as representative of American values: (1) individualism and privacy; (2) equality; (3) informality; (4) the future and progress; (5) goodness of humanity; (6) time; (7) achievement, action, work, and materialism; and (8) directedness and assertiveness (as cited in Hanson, 1992, 71).

The family is greatly affected by these values. Family *privacy,* for example, is a highly valued right among many individuals. It is expected that the family will be left to its own pursuits and allowed to raise its children as the parents see fit. Only when parents maltreat or fail to provide for their children is family sanctity threatened. Even then, some critics of current child welfare practices feel that agencies are too quick to intervene in family life.

Within the family context, everyone is encouraged to become an individual, and the sentiment is that all should be given the space, and in fact have the responsibility, to pursue what is best for their growth and enjoyment. Equality is valued and it is hoped that each individual will be given equal opportunity to achieve.

For many cultures, the American, as described by Althen, seems too informal to the point of being uncultured or uncouth. Slang, casual dress, and open discussions of almost any topic are the norm. The emphasis is on the future and what will happen tomorrow, as opposed to the historical or the happenings of today. Today is regarded in terms of how it will affect tomorrow (Hanson, 1992).

The tenor of communication and behavior is action oriented, direct, materialistic, and based on time constraints. Success is based on power and resources, especially money. Each individual is expected to do his/her best and is often thrown into the arena of fierce competition in which he/she is encouraged to flourish.

Communication Patterns

Communication among those with European roots is usually relatively open and direct. Warmth toward others is expected, although there is a lack of the ritual characterizing many other cultures in the way people are met and dealt with. People are expected to be seen as equal and therefore they have an equal right to express themselves. Personal space is prized and many individuals expect about an arm's length in their physical closeness to others. There is not an expectation of a great deal of physical closeness such as hand-holding on the street or open displays of affection in public. It is polite to be on time and to keep one's commitments at all cost (Althen, 1988; Hanson, 1992).

The family interprets these norms of communication in different ways, depending on the influence from other cultural groups and the individual upbringing of the parents. For example, while some families have little or no ritual in greeting or in their everyday lives, others have more. The Watson family greets relatives and friends with smiles and even handshakes, but it is not common to kiss or hug as a greeting. Their meals are taken informally and family members may come together at meals only if they happen to be there at the same time. The Whites, on the other hand, greet each other with a hug and a kiss, rarely a handshake. They make a practice of eating the evening meal together, and it is expected that each family member will be present unless otherwise arranged with Mrs. White.

Religion and Spirituality
Religion is seen as something that the individual has a right to espouse or not espouse. Because religion and one's spiritual beliefs are considered private, they are usually not discussed. It is also expected that there is a clear separation between church and state, giving rise to such issues as the cessation of prayer in public schools in many states.

The choice and practice of an organized religion is also up to the individual. Most families function within the framework of a Judeo-Christian belief system, with the majority ascribing to some type of Christianity. Although not everyone goes to church or synagogue, holidays that have religious origins, such as Christmas, Easter, and Chanukah, are celebrated by the majority of families (Hanson, 1992).

FAMILIES WITH NATIVE AMERICAN ROOTS

Native Americans have their roots in a time long before the European colonists arrived. Despite the changes brought on them over the years by immigrants, many Native American values and customs have survived and are actually seeing a revival as others become interested in the old world philosophy. Today, there are 400 distinct tribes, each with its own variation in customs and practices. While some live on reservations and live as much within old traditions as possible, many have been integrated into the larger society and may not be distinguishable from the general population. These families may practice a mix of their Native American rituals as well as hold the customs and beliefs of their non-Indian neighbors (Joe and Malach, 1992; Lum, 1992). The variations in their ways of life and customs are influenced largely by their geographic regions as well as the impact of non-Indian people on particular tribes. There are, however, some generalizations that can be made about Native American cultures.

Values
For Native Americans the concept of *sharing* is an integral part of the community and their way of life. Individuals share freely with others even to the extent that child-rearing is a shared and community experience. Children have the run of the community and each adult feels an obligation to interact freely with them through teaching, encouragement, or even discipline. Yet, learning among Native American children is largely experiential. For example, a child might be allowed to experience some minor harm (e.g., burning a finger to learn not to touch something hot) as a way of learning by experience (Joe and Malach, 1992; Tower, 1996).

Native Americans also believe in a oneness with nature that dictates an acceptance of natural happenings and their impact on the individual. Thus, suffering at the hands of natural happenings becomes an integral part of growth (Joe and Malach, 1992; LaFromboise et al., 1993; Thomason, 1993; Tower, 1996). Indian children are taught a respect for nature, natural events, and the land, and an intuneness with Mother Earth is at the core of many rituals and ceremonies.

Native American families also teach that it is important to control one's emotions. It is not unusual for Native Americans to seem stoic or even aloof to members of other cultures in the face of stressful events. The family keeps to itself, as does the individual, practicing the noninterference that has characterized Indian peoples for centuries. The Native American's form of protest is silence or withdrawal. Such behavior may actually confuse those in the child welfare field who often mistake this behavior on the part of Native American parents as indifference (Lum, 1992; Tower, 1996).

The Graywing family had moved off the reservation several months earlier when the father took a job fifty miles from their Reservation home. It was the first time in several generations that anyone from the Graywing family had lived off the reservation and the mother and her four children were most uncomfortable with the idea, though this would never have been verbalized to anyone outside the family.

The Graywing children first came to the attention of the local child welfare agency when the youngest child, age two, was found by a neighbor several blocks from the house. The child had been observed by another neighbor the previous day in an area even further away from the Graywing home. Talking about the events, the two women became concerned and felt that the agency should be notified.

When a social worker visited Mrs. Graywing, the mother seemed unconcerned. The next day, the neighbors again called the agency saying that the same child had been seen on the railroad tracks. The worker again went to the house and, finding the Graywing children (ages two, three, and five) alone, she took them into custody until the mother could be located. When the mother arrived home, she found a message from the worker asking her to contact the agency immediately. Assuming that her children were somewhere in the neighborhood and resenting the agency intervention, the mother discarded the note and did not call. The agency assumed that the children had been abandoned and placed them in foster care. It was not until a worker familiar with Native American custom was brought in on the case that the issues were resolved and the children were returned to their parents.

Native Americans view time differently than many other cultures. To them time is a "rhythmic, circular pattern" (Ho, 1987, 71, as cited in Joe and Malach, 101). For this reason issues like developmental milestones are difficult to determine.

Time is measured, not by the clock, but by the moon, the stars, and the seasons. Native Americans may also operate on their own time schedule, valuing congeniality more than a schedule, to the frustration of more punctual cultures or individuals (Joe and Malach, 1992).

Over the years, the values of the Native American have been greatly misinterpreted. In fact, there have been movements to alter that value system and force the Native American to conform to non-Indian values. Off-reservation boarding schools in the late 1800s were one attempt to separate Indian children and enculturate them into Anglo culture. These schools had a far-reaching impact on those who attended them, and have been much debated. Although today there may be more tolerance for ethnic diversity, Native American values may still come into conflict with those of other cultural orientations (Iglehart and Becerra, 1995).

Communication
Because the Native American believes that each individual has his/her own right to dignity, each person is respected and revered. As a result, there is little hierar-

---

BOX 2-1   Courtesies to Remember When Working with Native American Families

1. Many families believe that an abundance of compliments to their babies will bring harm to them. Therefore, it is acceptable to compliment babies but to a limited degree.
2. Native American families often place their babies on cradle boards. The family should be asked before removing the baby from the board.
3. Certain types of dolls or toys are considered to be bad luck by some tribes (e.g., for some, pictures of or representations of such animals as owls are bad omens). Therefore, the worker should talk with the family before presenting the children with toys or animals or pictures of these.
4. Some Native American healing ceremonies require that objects or markings be placed on the child's body. The family should be asked before these objects/markings are disturbed or washed as they may be considered sacred.
5. Many Native Americans live in rural areas and do not have phones. It is the custom to honk the horn when you arrive and to wait until someone comes out until you enter the house. Failure of anyone to appear may mean that the family does not wish to see you at this time, and, provided that this is not an urgent protective matter, this communication should be respected.
6. When guests enter the home, they should ask the family where to sit.
7. During visits, it is common for other members of the family to come and go, often choosing to enter into the conversation. If privacy is required, the agency office may be a better location for the interview.
8. All family members should be addressed during a visit as all have an equal role in Native American culture.
9. If food or drink is offered, it is respectful to accept unless you explain why you cannot.
10. All adults within a family may assume a parenting role. Do not be surprised if children are parented by all equally.
11. Patience is important for the worker as it is valued by the family.

(Adapted from Joe and Malach, 1992, 117–118.)

chical communication; rather everyone is considered to be on the same level. Cooperation is also valued and one tends to give in rather than compete.

Patience is also important to Native Americans, who believe that the universe is unfolding as it should. While some outside the Indian culture view this ability to rest and wait as laziness, the Native American is comfortable with the recognition that what should happen will do so in due time.

Religion and Spirituality

A new interest in Native American philosophy on the part of those outside the culture has made many people more familiar with the belief in the healing power of nature. The American Indian sees the need to remain in harmony with nature and from this union will come a kind of harmony that is much valued. Ceremonies and rituals dedicated to the reverence for nature punctuate the Native American's daily life (Tower, 1996).

When working with diverse populations, it is important to recognize their traditions. Lists of courtesies appropriate to each culture inserted after each section will help the child welfare worker to be familiar with some of the courtesies necessary within various populations.

FAMILIES WITH AFRICAN AMERICAN ROOTS

The customs and traditions of the African American family have been part of this country since its early history. The majority of African Americans came from slave ancestors who were brought to this country in the 1700s and 1800s. A small number of Africans also came over as free but indentured servants who were seeking a new life. Once freed, Southern slaves migrated north in search of more and better opportunities. These migrants were largely ignored and only some work in the settlement houses of the late 1800s furthered their integration into the mainstream culture (Willis, 1992).

During the 1900s African Americans have experienced much prejudice and much controversy has surrounded their integration into "white" areas. From school segregation and freedom marches to the efforts of the NAACP (National Association for the Advancement of Colored People) and other activist organizations the African American has sought to be more fully accepted by others in American society. Today, African Americans make up over 12% of the population of the United States (Willis, 1992; McGoldrick, 1993). Of the African American family's experience, McGoldrick (1993) comments:

> We cannot understand the context of a Black family without looking at the context of the larger system: less access to medical care, housing, education, employment, political power, and a general sense of powerlessness, and of not belonging to the larger society. All these will have their impact on African-American families, even across class lines. They influence how parents raise their children—knowing they will be exposed to hatred and discrimination (353).

In addition to other stresses, the African American family is more likely than its white and Hispanic counterparts to experience poverty. About 29% of all African American families live below the poverty line, in contrast to only 8% of white families and 24% of Hispanic families (Iglehart and Becerra, 1995, 26; Willis, 1992, 129; McGoldrick, 1993, 353). In addition, African American families are most likely to live in inner cities amidst crime, unemployment, and other stresses. Infant mortality is twice as likely to occur among African American infants as it is among whites (Willis, 1992, 129). Amidst these realities, the African American family continues to persevere.

Values

One value that has brought the African American through a myriad of stresses is reliance on each other and shared religious beliefs. Extended family and friends, often referred to as *kin*, provide mutual aid in a variety of situations, including such things as child care, financial aid, advice, and emotional support (Prater, 1992; Willis, 1992; Tower, 1996). It is not uncommon for extended family or friends to take children whose parents are unable to care for them. Children are prized among African American cultures and their well-being is seen as the responsibility of the total family and even the community. Perhaps this strong sense of kinship originated in early tribal tradition and has been passed down through the centuries.

Within African American families, work is expected of all members. Today it is African American women who are more able to enter the work force and, because they are often single parents, the children are expected to assume a substantial amount of the household tasks (Lum, 1992; Tower, 1996). The fact that African American children assume as much responsibility as they do has often been construed by white child welfare agencies as constituting neglect on the part of their parents. The reality is that, as is true for many minorities, African American parents recognize that it is only through hard work and perseverance that their children will survive in this world. Thus, this early training prepares their children for their later lot in life.

Because African Americans recognize that education can elevate one's status, they value educational opportunities. Elders are also seen as possessing knowledge that can be beneficial to the young and oral tradition plays a large part in the African American culture (Willis, 1992).

Communication

African American families are by nature closely knit. Children are given love and accepted into the family circle with warmth and understanding. Due to the emphasis on the extended family and friends, children move freely through the circle of adults and have a number of adult models with whom to identify. There is an emphasis on instilling in children a sense of pride in who they are. Communication is often abstract and analogies are used to express feelings without explicitly identifying the feelings themselves. Rather than being out of touch with feelings, the African American family is very much in touch with feelings but has a characteristic manner of expressing them.

Cora Lee Thomas and her six children are a common sight at the Stafford Street School playground. The mother's loud, deep voice is often raised in hearty laughter as she watches her children in play. She frequently brings her mother or one of several aunts who also encourage the children and chuckle about their antics. Despite the fact that the children remain largely independent of their mother, Cora Lee seems very much in tune with their feelings. A fall from the jungle gym usually results in the child being scooped up against his mother's big chest and hummed to while she continues to listen to her adult companions. In no time, the soothed child is off to play again with his siblings and peers.

Music often plays a part in the African American family's life. It is experienced rather than listened to and song may be used to sooth, to play, and to accompany work (Willis, 1992).

Religion and Spirituality

Historically, the church has played a significant role in African American life. Religion and family are closely linked and over the years the family has used its religious beliefs to protect it from the hostile white world. The church becomes a focal point, not only for emotional support, but also for socialization. Ministers are seen as teachers, counselors, spokesmen, and even kinsmen (Tower, 1996).

The organized African church began in the late 1700s in Philadelphia. Known originally as the Free African Society, the movement eventually gave rise to the African Methodist Episcopal Church (AME). About the same time, New York City

---

BOX 2-2   Courtesies to Remember When Working with Families with African American Roots

1. Do not use first names with African American clients unless you ask permission to do so. Calling someone by their first name without being asked is considered disrespectful.
2. Recognize that the client might have strong feelings about race and prejudice and do not tell them that they are "too touchy" about it.
3. Although much of the literature refers to African American households as headed by single females, do not make assumptions about the family and their functioning without a thorough individual assessment.
4. Do not use ethnic jokes even if they refer to your own ethnic group.
5. Remain professional with African American clients. Small talk about personal issues (e.g., vacations, own family, new car, and so on) with coworkers may be construed as unprofessional and they may therefore question your competence.
6. Poverty and dysfunction are not necessarily synonymous. Each family's functioning should be assessed individually.

(Adapted from Willis, 1992, 148.)

saw the development of the African Methodist Episcopal Zion (AMEZ). Over time, the Baptist churches began to attract African Americans in increasing numbers until today the Baptist churches represent a large percentage of the church-going population (Willis, 1992).

Whether associated with an organized church or not, the African American family holds a strong belief that "the Lord will provide." This assumption that life will unfold as it is meant to do may cause them to seem to those not familiar with African American philosophy as fatalistic or uninvolved in their own destiny. Nothing is further from the truth.

FAMILIES WITH HISPANIC ROOTS

To say that a family is Hispanic does not fully explain the diversity of the Spanish-speaking peoples. The term *Hispanic* includes numerous cultures, each with its own traditions and values. Mexicans represent the largest number (62.3%) of Hispanics in the United States today, followed by Puerto Ricans (12.7%), Central and South Americans (11.5%), Cubans (5%), and other groups (8%) (Zuniga, 1992, 151–2; Tower, 1996, 30).

Despite the cultural differences among these groups, it is possible to make some generalizations about families with Hispanic roots.

Values
The extended family plays a large part in the lives of the Hispanic community. In defining the extended family, however, one does not look at only blood relatives but also friends and anyone else who shares their living space. Godparents or sponsors (*padrinos*) play a major role in the lives of children. *Compadrazzo,* or the practice of using these compadres in a variety of ways, is integral to Hispanic life. Compadres, whether they be godparents, relatives, or close friends, maintain a close relationship with the children of the family, treating them almost as their own (Delgado, 1992; Zuniga, 1992).

The traditional Hispanic family believes in male supremacy, strict role delineations, and submissiveness on the part of the female. *Machismo,* or the male's sense of honor, courage, and responsibility to his family is extremely important in the Hispanic family, but a much misunderstood concept in the outside world (Delgado, 1992). It is the father's role to keep the family together and to provide for them. The economic realities of the present may make it easier for the woman in a two-parent family to find work, making the man feel less powerful and placing extreme stress on the family as their adopted homeland tests their traditional views (Zuniga, 1992). This family tension may lead to aggression and possibly violence as the male's machismo is threatened (Mizio, 1989). Today, some Hispanic families may also be headed by single females, changing the balance of power and the family's way of operating. Yet, as her male children grow, this mother may be more likely to recognize their power than mothers of some other cultures.

Also central to the value system of Hispanic families are the concepts of *dignidad, respecto,* and *personalismo. Dignidad* acknowledges the importance and worth of each individual. *Respecto* incorporates a hierarchical view of relationships in which elders must be respected and the young look to the older for decisions and teachings. *Personalismo* refers to the Hispanic reverence for individualized, warm, and close personal relationships. The feeling is that each individual deserves personal one-to-one attention and large impersonal bureaucracies are usually avoided by Hispanics for this reason (Zuniga, 1992; Mizio, 1989). Keeping these values in mind, workers dealing with the Hispanic family do best if they use a friendly, informal, but respectful manner that encourages trust on the part of the clients. Hispanic families need to see the helper as a professional whom they can respect, but one who does not look down on them or depersonalize them or their needs.

Communication

The concept of *respecto* governs much of the communication between family members in the Hispanic family. Males and elders are given higher status and therefore communication tends to take place with these individuals in key positions. Traditional roles are adhered to and both genders have particular things that are expected of them.

Children are considered to validate a marriage in this family and they tend to be pampered and overindulged. The parent–child relationship actually takes precedence over the marital relationship when the children are young. Male children are revered and daughters are protected. Hispanic mothers teach their sons that it is their role to protect and provide (Zuniga, 1992).

Strong negative emotions, such as anger and aggression, are not acceptable in the traditional Hispanic family. Family members maintain close emotional ties based on respect rather than the airing of personal grievances. For the Hispanic family, this tendency toward respecting and projecting congeniality toward others may cause them difficulty in the non-Hispanic world. Leiberman (1990) describes

---

BOX 2-3   Courtesies to Remember When Working with Families with Hispanic Roots

1. Because men are dominant in this culture, address the husband or male head of household in preference to the wife or female when both are present.
2. The male/father should be consulted as to whether he is in agreement with the plans or recommendations. Not to do so would imply disrespect.
3. Accept food or drink if it is offered. It is polite for them to offer, and would be rude to refuse this hospitality without good reason.
4. It is customary to begin with polite small talk in a relaxed manner. Beginning to talk immediately about tasks or plans is considered impolite.
5. Although the family expects you to be a professional and an expert, do not talk down to them or use an authoritarian or harsh tone.
6. Give the family your full attention without appearing hurried or needing to get on to the next client. It is a sign of respect to give all clients their time.

how Hispanic mothers may often agree graciously to appointments made by social workers, but then fail to keep them. It would be disrespectful to disagree.

Due to the fact that Hispanics are taught not to disagree or express negative emotions, they may turn stress inward and suffer from somatic ailments. Headaches, stomachaches, and other physical problems may indicate psychological distress (Derezotes and Snowden, 1990).

Religion and Spirituality

Catholicism is the predominant religion of the Hispanic population and plays an extremely important part in family life. In the *barrio* (the Hispanic community), the church is the focal point for both social and inspirational events. Many families use *mandas* (a promise or offering asking for God's intervention) to call on their faith to direct their lives. Prayers to the Virgin Mary are also a common practice within Hispanic households (Zuniga, 1992).

Although it may seem contradictory to outsiders, Hispanic families also rely on folk healers to cure their ills and intervene for them. Delgado (1992) points out that Hispanics' strong reliance on folk medicine and their belief in it make these practices especially effective.

FAMILIES WITH ASIAN ROOTS

Today, Asians are the fastest growing minority group in the United States, with a projected number of 10 million living in this country by the year 2000. This growth seems to be a result of the Asian refugees and immigrants who have entered this country since the Immigration and Nationality Act Amendments in 1965 and the influx of people after the United States left Vietnam in 1975 (Chan, 1992). Although Asians are usually grouped together, there are probably more differences from culture to culture than in any other grouping. Asia encompasses China, Japan, Vietnam, Cambodia, Laos, India, Thailand, Burma, Malaysia, Singapore, the Philippines, Sri Lanka, Pakistan, and Korea, and each of these represents vastly different traditions and ways of life. In fact, it would take volumes to consider many of these cultures in any depth, so complex are they (Mass and Yap, 1992). Here, we can only consider Asian cultures in the most superficial manner.

Values

Like the Hispanic family, the Asian family is one with clearly defined roles based on male dominance and a hierarchical structure. The older generation especially is revered. Parents command respect and must be obeyed. The family behaves as a unit, a closely knit group, and individuals are not expected to be autonomous. To do so would be a rejection of family values.

Shame plays a major role in dictating the behavior of adults and in disciplining and molding the behavior of children. Honor should be brought to the family at all cost, by doing one's best, behaving respectfully, and refraining from doing wrong. *Face* refers to the ability to hold one's head high knowing that one has behaved honorably. Asians talk of *saving face*, or maintaining one's honor, as paramount to the family. Family honor is greatly valued and family members will go to great lengths to save face. Shame is used so much in child-rearing that non-Asian agencies may question if this practice is emotionally abusive (Mass and Yap, 1992; Chan, 1992).

It would be unthinkable, for example, to sexually abuse children in Asian families, an attitude that makes the incidence of sexual abuse in this population extremely low. Such behavior would bring great dishonor to the family. In many types of Asian communities, the virginity of the female before her marriage is a high priority. The Vietnamese woman, for example, is expected to be a virgin when she marries and the loss of her virginity may mean that she is prohibited from marrying (Mollica and Son, 1989). Similarly, daughters from Indian families are married whenever possible to someone who will improve their families' social status. The young woman is expected to come to her new husband pure and virginal. Thus, a father would not sexually abuse his daughter lest he endanger her (and his) chances of attaining a higher social status or caste. This too would dishonor the family.

Harmony is highly valued in some Asian families, especially when the family operates under a Confucian philosophy. The group is paramount and the needs of the individual are secondary to the desires of the group. Self-esteem is dependent on how well one fits into and is accepted by the group and how well one avoids conflict with the group. Most Asians do not wish to stand out from others and will often take a seemingly benign or middle-of-the-road position to avoid being noticed as separate from the group (Mass and Yap, 1992).

Communication

Because of the need to be part of the group and the value of harmony, communication among Asians brings with it a rigid set of rules. Since the elder is held in highest regard, communication begins at the top and filters down to others. One is not expected to be direct, as in Western cultures, but calm, respectful, and congenial. Thus, a "yes" from an Asian family member may not mean that he/she will do as requested, but only indicates that the person has heard you. It may also mean that he/she would not dishonor you by disagreeing. This cultural value is especially difficult for the non-Asian to comprehend and can cause problems between Asians and workers in Western agencies who are not familiar with this fine point (Lum, 1992; Chan, 1992).

Among themselves, Asian family members practice respect and recognize that honoring the family is paramount, because their self-esteem is based on how honorable each family member is. Further, the Asian is not likely to conflict with other family members, so intent is he/she on the protection of harmony.

Religion and Spirituality

Religions among Asians differ greatly. Confucianism, Taoism, and Buddhism, as they are practiced in China and Korea, emphasize respect for one's ancestors, filial piety, and the avoidance of shame (Lum, 1992). Buddhism emphasizes "four noble truths": life is suffering; suffering exists because of people's overattachment to the world; suffering can be extinguished by giving up this attachment; and one does

---

BOX 2-4   Courtesies to Remember When Working with Families with Asian Roots (Chinese, Japanese, Korean, Vietnamese, Cambodian)

1. Age is revered in these cultures. Address the oldest family member first.
2. It is respectful to use Mr., Mrs., or Miss with the family name. Recognize that in many Asian cultures (e.g., Chinese, Korean, Cambodian, Vietnamese) the family name is first. For example, in the name Po Wang Do the last name is Po. Therefore the client should be addressed as Mr. Po.
3. Women often do not take their husband's name when they marry. Be aware of this before addressing a wife.
4. Women do not shake hands with men, nor do younger people offer hands to those much older than themselves. A bow is preferable to a handshake, even between men.
5. Direct physical contact (pat on back, hug, and so on) is considered inappropriate.
6. Direct eye contact between strangers and especially with women is inappropriate and even disrespectful.
7. Touching the head (even a child's) is considered threatening in some cultures.

---

this by attending to one's views, speech, thoughts, and through meditation (Chan, 1992, 188). Confucianism has no specific doctrine other than a belief that people must be in harmony with the world and others in it. Taoism seeks to cultivate inner strength, selflessness, and harmony, and to stress being on the "path" toward spiritual truth. Koreans also practice Shamanism, although this is more prevalent in the rural communities of Korea than in larger urban areas. Shamanism involves relationships among people, spirits, and the universe and how these interrelate in one's life (Chan, 1992).

Hinduism and Islam, which involve more of a moral code than actual worship of deities, are also practiced in some Asian countries. All of these Asian doctrines emphasize the concept of harmony with others and some form of fatalism or philosophical detachment. Possibly because of the fact that many Asian cultures have been buffeted by a variety of political events beyond their control, many Asian peoples treat events as if they are inevitable. This means that the Asian family may be less likely to seek help from outside agencies as family members assume that the crisis they are experiencing is their "lot in life" and therefore must just be endured (Ho, 1989; Tower, 1996).

FAMILIES WITH MIDDLE EASTERN ROOTS

The Middle East includes areas of Asia and Africa, which have distinct and different cultural orientations. These political states are usually identified as Iraq, Jordan, Saudi Arabia, Kuwait, Bahrain, Egypt, Sudan, Turkey, Iran, Oman, Yemen, and the United Arab Emirates (Sharifzadeh, 1992). These cultures are sometimes grouped with Asian groups, but to do so is to overgeneralize and do both types of cultures a grave disservice.

Immigration of people from the Middle East increased in the late 1800s when Arab tradesmen came to this country seeking new opportunities. From the 1890s to the 1930s Armenians, who were being persecuted by the Turkish government, fled to the United States for sanctuary. Since that time there continues to be an influx of Middle Easterners seeking refuge from a variety of political events as well as in search of freedom and opportunity.

Values

There is a marked difference among Middle Easterners between those who are educated and come from large urban areas and those from more rural settings. More highly educated people have more familiarity with Western culture and therefore an easier time assimilating in the United States. Many have learned English early and this also helps their integration into this culture.

The family is of primary importance in Middle Eastern cultures. Multiple generations, often as many as three generations, tend to live and work together. The family structure is patriarchal and the family adheres strongly to religious rules. The family values the collective achievement of its members and holds these achievements up in pride and as a form of identity. Those who have immigrated to the United States also try to bring kinsmen over and surround themselves with large families that provide support and encouragement. Having children is considered the essence of being. Boys are highly valued and the birth of a male child is a cause for celebration. Neglect of one's children is considered to be a serious violation in these cultures and the internal sanctions for such parents are more threatening than those of a protective service agency (Sharifzadeh, 1992).

Communication

Because Middle Eastern societies are patriarchal, the hierarchy of communication begins with the oldest males. Mothers are seen primarily as the nurturers of their children and their proximity to them is expected to be very close. Babies are usually kept in the same room, if not the same bed, as their mothers, and these mothers tend to be much more permissive with their children than their Western counterparts.

Metah Halvanian came to the attention of the protective service agency when the kindergarten her son attended reported that they were concerned that "there was something going on at home." The boy had few boundaries or inner controls and spoke of sleeping with his mother. When the worker investigated, she found an extremely devoted and overindulgent mother who was horrified that she had come to the attention of an agency. She openly told the agency that her five-year-old son still slept in her bed as her husband worked long hours and she felt that it was better for the boy. As the mother and worker talked the boy roamed freely about the house and interrupted frequently. It soon became obvious that he had as much, if not more control, than his mother. It took some time before the school guidance counselor, working with the family, was able to acclimate the child to the more structured school setting.

**BOX 2-5   Courtesies to Remember When Working with Families
with Middle Eastern Roots**

1. Remove shoes if the family members have removed theirs.
2. Do not sit with your back to any adult in the room.

3. Do not cross your feet or legs in the company of elders.

(Adapted from Sharifzadeh, 1992, 349.)

Individuation of children is an issue that may cause some problems for Middle Easterners as they attempt to integrate into their adopted culture. The emphasis on interdependence given to relationships may cause conflicts for children as they strive to acclimate to the Western school system (Sharifzadeh, 1992).

In communication, outsiders may find the Middle Easterner confusing. For example, a direct "no" is considered impolite. Instead, the Middle Easterner is likely to say "maybe" or a weak "yes," either of which can either indicate agreement or that he/she does not want to say no because that would be disrespectful. Some cultures of the Middle East also respect professionals to the point that it would be impolite to give the impression of being in conflict with a professional's opinion or recommendation. Therefore, the family may seem to comply when, in fact, they disagree. In addition, it is not acceptable to express one's own needs, and family members may actually deny that they want something (Sharifzadeh, 1992). It may require a worker who is familiar with the Middle Eastern culture to work successfully with a Middle Eastern family.

Religion and Spirituality

Religion to the Middle Easterner is not a private and personal issue. It occupies a central position socially, culturally, and politically. Islam was one of the earliest religions in the Middle East and continues to be the most widely practiced today. Judaism and Christianity are also part of the religious mosaic. The Eastern Orthodox and Catholic churches comprise the largest number of non-Muslims. Judaism is concentrated in Israel. Iran is also known for its populations of Bahais and Zoroastrians, now decreasing (Sharifzadeh, 1992). All of these faiths influence the customs of their followers and the way in which families carry on everyday life.

THE FAMILY LIFE CYCLE

Like every other system, families change continuously. They also may follow somewhat predictable and definable life cycles (Acock and Demo, 1994; Freeman, 1992; McCowan and Johnson, 1993). Carter and McGoldrick (1988) suggest that middle-class Americans, for example, have six stages within their developmental cycle:

1. *Single young adults* who are charged with accepting emotional and financial responsibility as they leave their families of origin and become independent;

2. *The new couple* who commit to joining together to form their own family and in so doing rework their relationships with their own families of origin and friends;

3. *Families with young children* who must accept new members into the family system, decide how they will raise these children, and realign their own relationships, between themselves and with others, to accomplish this;

4. *Families with adolescents* who must increase their flexibility in order to allow their offspring to grow and begin to move away from the family. In addition, this may well be a time when the couple is asked to care for their own aging parents and readjust their relationship to do this;

5. *The couple who is launching children and moving on* must learn to accept the emancipation of their children and adjust to the impact that it has on their relationships; they may also be faced with the deaths of their own parents;

6. *Families in later life* must accept the change in generational roles, make room for grandchildren, maintain their own functioning as a couple, and continue to cope with the losses of family friends and perhaps each other (18–19).

Families who experience a breakdown caused by something such as death or divorce will probably not follow this developmental process. Herbert (1989) outlines stages of transition that can be applied to families as well as individuals: immobilization, minimization of the experience, depression, testing, and, finally, finding meaning in the event. Families faced with acute stress may first *be immobilized.*

When Julia Higgins filed for divorce, the whole family, consisting of her husband and three children, seemed unable to respond. "It was as if we were all paralyzed," recounted Herb. "We had been having troubles but I couldn't believe it when I was served with papers. Neither could the girls, who were then fourteen, sixteen, and nineteen. I think they thought their mother had gone mad. They always thought we were so happy."

Families will often then *minimize the experience,* as the Higgins family did:

Our daughters kept telling me "Don't worry about it Dad! Mom will come to her senses. This is just a whim of hers." We all kept saying to ourselves that we didn't have to worry. Julia would realize that that was not what she wanted and drop the whole thing. But she didn't!

Once they realize that the crisis is real, families often *go into depression.*

> Once we realized that Julia really meant to leave, we all slumped into a kind of depression. We each appeared to be functioning okay, but there was this overtone of sadness and hopelessness. We bickered with each other and everyone seemed caught up in her/his own needs.

At some point, family members accept that the crisis is a reality and that they *must let go* of the concept of what they had hoped for, usually the idea of the happy, together family. There may be a period of testing when the family members strive to see if the new configuration is really what is wanted by all. This period is seen as a form of *testing.*

> There was a time, soon after I decided that the divorce was inevitable, that our children seemed to be trying to fix things up again. They would invite Julia and me places together, despite the fact that she had a new boyfriend. When Dianna, then 20, got her first apartment, she invited Julia and me to dinner together. It was awkward, but we both love her so we made the best of it. I finally had to talk to the kids and say that their mother and I would not get back together and they had to stay out of it. They finally got the message.

As the change completes itself, the family once again seeks homeostasis by *searching for the meaning* in the event. The Higgins girls spent long hours in discussion about what had driven their mother away. They talked about how their father had always made the decisions and that his need to control might have been a factor. And finally, each individual *internalizes the meanings* of the crisis, as does the family system (109–111).

> Each of my daughters seemed to have a different idea of why Julia had divorced me. I know that they thought my immigrant father's old world attitudes had made me into a bit of a tyrant too, but I think there was more to it than that. Each girl was also impacted differently by us being divorced. When they all eventually married, I could recognize in their choice of mates how they had interpreted what had happened in our family.

Families that experience the loss of a family member may join with other family units. Several years after the divorce, Herb Higgins remarried. His daughters, then sixteen, eighteen, and twenty-two, had a difficult time with his decision. The two youngest, still living at home, found the adjustment challenging. Their new stepmother came to the union with four boys, ages seven, nine, twelve, and fourteen. The girls feared that they would be placed in the role of babysitters. They also had comments about their stepmother's more permissive child-rearing standards. By the same token, their oldest stepbrother, used to being "the man of the house," resented being "bossed around" by two older girls. As is often common in blended families, the first several years were a challenge. For these families, the initial developmental task is to realign relationships so that the family can function relatively smoothly.

Culture, too, may have an impact on family development and change. Each culture has specific expectations of its members and the family system is affected by these. There may also be variations depending on when a particular ethnic group immigrated to America (Walsh, 1993; Lynch and Hanson, 1992). For example, the way in which families from different cultures deal with specific developmental tasks of their children can differ greatly. While white children usually learn to dress themselves at 3.7 years, African American children are 4 years old, while their Native American counterparts are only 2.8. Native American children are also allowed to stay alone in the evening earlier (9.2 years) than white children (14.4 years) and African American children (13.6). They also care for younger siblings at an earlier age (9.9 years for Native Americans; 13.1 years for whites; and 12.9 years for African Americans) (Joe and Malach, 1992, 104). Children from other immigrant cultures may be expected to tackle these tasks at earlier or later ages, depending on the values of the parents. These methods of dealing with children will affect the development of the entire family.

For the gay or lesbian family, the process of "coming out" to their families and friends may be construed as part of the family life cycle as well. When and how the parents disclose their lifestyle choice to individual families of origin impacts their intergenerational relationships. Parental experiences as children, who may have had to hide their true feelings from others, may result in families that strive to create different family rules and roles that influence how the family functions and develops (Laird, 1993).

STRESSES ON FAMILIES

PARENTAL/FAMILY DYSFUNCTION

Chapter 1 discussed Kadushin and Martin's (1988) suggestion of a framework for ascertaining why families must seek help. They say that services are required when there are difficulties in parental functioning in the following areas: *unoccupied parental role,* usually through death, illness, imprisonment, mental illness, or abandonment; *parental incapacity* due to illness, ignorance, emotional immaturity, mental retardation, or substance abuse; *role rejection,* when a parent chooses to neglect, abandon, or abuse the child; *interrole conflict,* when there is conflict in the family about roles; *transition issues,* when a family is trying to cope with some type of transition, either developmental or environmental; and *child incapacity* issues, such as a family trying to cope with a child's disability. Several other specific issues will be discussed shortly.

ROLE DEFINITION AND INEQUALITY

There has been much discussion about family roles in this era, when it is the norm in two-parent families for both parents to work outside the home. The dominant assumption, especially among higher socioeconomic groups, is that the father has assumed more in the way of house responsibilities to offset the stress on his partner of working and maintaining a home. The reality, based on a study of 2,457 mothers (Acock and Demo, 1994), appears different from what one might assume. These authors studied families in four categories: first-married (two-parent) families, divorced (single-parent) families, stepfamilies (reconstituted two-parent families), and continuously single families (in which the mother has had her children without being married and continues to remain so). A study of the distribution of household tasks found that mothers in all families do the household chores a disproportionate amount of the time: first married = 71.6%; divorced = 85.7%; stepfamily = 69.4%; continuously single = 84.4% (77). All mothers, regardless of the presence of a male partner, spent between 40–43 hours a week on household chores (79). Husbands performed between 6.2–7 hours on household tasks, excluding car maintenance, outdoor work, and driving (82). The amount of work done by children was also negligible. These data indicated that there was little difference in this division of labor whether women were in their first marriage or whether they had remarried. In addition, there appeared to be little reduction in the time spent on household tasks when the women worked outside of the home. Acock and Demo see the wife's perception that she is doing most of the work, contrasted with her husband's perception that he is contributing significantly, if not equally, as a major strain in family relations.

PARENT–CHILD RELATIONS

As the American family is threatened by economic strain and divorce, relations between parents and their children have come into increasing focus. As parents feel more stressed, they have less energy, time, and patience to give to their children. Rules and roles become more flexible and even less well-defined to cope with the changing demands on the family structure. Mothers in one study (Acock and Demo, 1994) complained that they had less time with their children, more disagreements, less enjoyable times with their spouses, and less involvement in their children's schools, sports, and other activities than their parents did with them (120).

Stepparent relationships are another issue that many families point to as stressful. Reconstituted families are faced with the joining of two families, both with different sets of rules and expectations. As the parents strive to negotiate their own relationship, parental roles may come into conflict. Who will discipline whose children is often a bone of contention. Who controls the family decisions and who does what tasks in the house create other areas in which negotiation is necessary. Not all families are able to weather these storms of adjustment successfully.

Another issue of parent–child conflict may confront the newly immigrated family. Parents who hold cultural expectations of their children that differ from what is expected of American children may discover that, as their children become integrated into the school system and form relationships with peers, they are influenced by a new set of values.

A family recently immigrated from Vietnam expected that their teenage daughter would respect the traditions under which she grew up. It was anticipated by the family that she would not see boys alone and would wait until the family believed that she should be allowed to have contact with the opposite sex. But the boys in her high school class found her attractive and appealing and were soon asking her to go out with them. Knowing her parents' feelings, she at first refused. But it was also important to her to fit in with her new friends and they all seemed to be dating. She began to see boys after school and to sneak out of the house when her parents were not aware. When her father discovered what his daughter had been doing, he was extremely upset and felt that the family had lost face.

DISABILITY

It is certainly obvious when discussing stresses placed on families that disability or illness on the part of the parent creates stress for the family. What many of us do not realize is how much stress the disability of a child within the family can place on the family system. As one older teen explained about living with his sister who was born with spina bifida:

The birth of Deborah changed our family's whole life. When she was first born Mom and Dad spent a lot of time in the hospital. We were left with grandparents and other relatives. We weren't neglected. Mom and Dad tried to explain to us and spend time with us but their priority had to be Deb. Even after she came home things were never the same. She always had to be the center of attention. She had so much medication and had seizures. We all learned to go into a "crisis mode." That meant that when she was in crisis and Mom and Dad had to be there for her, we kids learned to be very self-sufficient. One of my brothers really resented her though and that was hard for all of us. I think the stress destroyed my parent's relationship too because after about ten years they got divorced.

Families with special needs children learn to accommodate in a variety of ways, but often not without some type of support or outside intervention.

WHEN FAMILIES NEED HELP

Kadushin and Martin (1988) divide the services provided for families into three categories: supportive services, supplementary services, and substitute services. *Supportive services* refer to home-based services that help the family to perform its role in the care, protection, and nurturing of its children. They strive to use the family's own strength to empower them to help themselves. Such services might include counseling, early intervention, and protective services. The last category might be confusing as one often thinks of protective services as removing children from their parents. In reality, separation of children from parents is the last resort. The first goal of protective services is to discover and enhance parental strengths to help the parents cope and not abuse or neglect their children. Only when this is not possible are other interventions used. *Supplementary services* are used when the parent–child relationship has begun to be impaired or needs additional help. Financial assistance, day care, and homemaker services are examples of supplementary programs. *Substitute services* are used as a last resort. These services substitute the care that the family of origin is not able to provide either temporarily or permanently. Such services are adoption, foster care, and residential treatment.

Although this is one way to categorize services, some find that it is inadequate. Services may actually overlap or parts of service provision can be categorized in different ways. Services may also be divided into categories, depending on who provides them. There are public agencies under state, federal, or country governments, voluntary nonprofit agencies supported by community funds, private for-profit agencies supported by client fees, and industrially sponsored agencies (Kadushin and Martin, 1988).

How services to families are categorized is not as crucial as how well the families' needs are met by these services. It is vital in the study of child welfare services that the potential professional be familiar with the wide range of services available and how these can be used to benefit clients. The most important aspect of helping is to empower. Empowerment enables families not only to solve today's problems but gain insight in facing the problems of tomorrow.

TRENDS

When looking at the trends for something as woven into our thinking as the family, it is difficult to predict the future. One can only look at current trends with the expectation that they may continue.

ECONOMIC STRESSORS

It is evident that the family will continue to feel the stress that our current economic situation enhances. Family members will continue to be faced with the challenge of how to meet family needs while both parents work or, in the case of single-parent families, when the only adult must work outside the home. Parents will continue to be faced with the necessity of finding adequate day care arrangements in a market that is already overstressed. Both husbands and wives will need to find creative ways to negotiate with employers over such issues as maternity–paternity leave, flex time, and shared vacations. Families will continue the struggle of making decreasing paychecks meet the demands of increasing prices.

How these factors affect family dynamics will prove interesting. Already there is speculation and research on the influence the mother working has on the mother–child dyad (Moorehouse, 1993). For example, while Moorehouse found that mothers who work had a stronger and more positive association with their older children, this author expressed some concern about the attachment of infants, who experienced prolonged hours of nonmaternal care (269). Studies related to fathers who assumed more caretaking roles as a result of their wives' employment showed mixed results. On one hand, researchers felt that these fathers formed closer ties with their children, while still another study pointed to the fact that in this sample fathers who cared for children on a regular basis were more irritable toward them and demonstrated more marital dissatisfaction (Moorehouse, 1993). Certainly the effects on children of their parents' working warrant further investigation.

THE OPTIONAL STATUS OF MARRIAGE

Aerts (1993) points out that more than ever before marriage has become an option rather than an expectation in the lives of most young adults. Increasingly, couples choose either to live together or merely date while bringing a child into the world. If this relationship terminates, as is often the case, given the lack of expectation of permanence, children often become the total responsibility of their mothers. In addition, the model for permanence and negotiation to sustain a relationship is absent. Some would argue that this is preferable to the past when children may have been trapped in loveless and conflict-ridden marriages because the expectation was that one would remain married. The fact remains that the lack of permanence of today's relationships can also take its toll on children.

THE VANISHING FATHER

A trend of somewhat serious concern is the fact that fathers as a whole are assuming a different role in their children's lives. While, at one time, father was the head of the house, the primary breadwinner, and only a part-time support in his wife's child-rearing, divorce and single parenthood has changed the position of fathers in today's society. Perusal of a fast-food restaurant on a typical Saturday will attest to the fact that fathers are more likely to see their children on a limited basis and engage in activities that are less likely to contribute to their overall care. The introduction of the stepfather does not change this picture but rather complicates it. Now children are thrust into two or more roles with men who, although assuming a fathering role, are doing so on a limited basis (Aerts, 1993).

In addition to the impact of divorce on children's relationship with their fathers, more women are opting to become pregnant with the anticipation that the biological father of the child will not remain a part of the child's immediate home environment. Thus, we move more and more toward a matriarchal society in which women have the primary role for full-time parenting.

BLENDED FAMILIES

When we look at the previously mentioned trends, it is easy to recognize that the majority of children in the United States will not reside with both their biological parents for the entirety of their childhood. As the circle of divorce widens and people remarry, more and more families will be blended together. Inherent in this process is a myriad of complex attitudes, emotions, and tasks. The new parental subsystem will need not only to find its own balance but each adult will also need to forge a working relationship with each child, whether that child be his/her own or the new spouse's. Problems like who will discipline whom, who is responsible for meeting the needs of whom, and a variety of other issues will be of increasing focus in the lives of tomorrow's families.

RESOLUTION OF CHILDHOOD CONFLICTS

A paramount need, not necessarily met by the family, but rather by society as a result of the family, will be services to resolve the residual effects of family conflict. Divorce and family instability have a profound effect on children, who grow into adulthood with resulting scars that may make it difficult for them to form their own families. Thus, we in the helping professions are increasingly recognizing the importance of providing an opportunity for teens and adults to understand the role their families played in the emotional conflicts that create problems for them. Granted, family dysfunction has always been with us and many young adults have sought to make sense of traumatic childhoods. But as we recognize more fully the impact of family unrest on children's development, services and resources seem more vital.

Currently, groups dedicated to understanding family dysfunction, books on the subject, and therapists who specialize in helping adults to "make peace with the past" strive to meet this need.

CHANGES IN FAMILY CONTROL

At one time, the family could rely on controlling its own functioning. Only if members demonstrated gross inadequacies did societal institutions intervene. Often children were totally under the influence of the family until they went to school and then the family still exerted the major influence. Today that has changed. One of the most obvious factors in the decline of family control is in the case of divorce. Courts are now in the position of deciding with whom the children will reside and the amount of contact they will have with the noncustodial parent. Parents' freedom is significantly curtailed and their privacy is no longer sacred. The "best interests of the child" may be something that society rather than the parent is responsible for protecting (Aerts, 1993; Johnston, 1993).

Divorce is not the only factor affecting the family's ability to control its own functioning. As the traditional family disintegrates, and with it the supports provided by multiple adults, family members find themselves seeking outside help. Over half of all single-parent families have sought out some type of societal support, whether it be income maintenance, day care, legal assistance, or counseling (Aerts, 1993). It does not look as though this trend toward the invasion of family functioning by outside sources will subside in the future.

Families have long been the framework on which our society is based. As the picture of the family changes, the way that we help families will also need to change. As we review the services that currently exist, it is important to keep in mind the trends discussed above and how these trends will affect the family of tomorrow and the needs that they will have for services.

SUMMARY

The family provides the basic foundation for individuals in this and other societies. The functions of the family are procreation, socialization, enculturation, and protection. In addition, families provide financial and emotional support, meet the child's basic needs as well as providing for medical and educational needs, and serve to interpret the world to the child and the child to the world. Today's family must cope with a variety of barriers to functioning. Violence, both societal and intrafamilial, and the increase of divorce are two major factors.

The family is a system composed of a group of subsystems, each interrelated. This system operates through a series of roles and rules that govern how the family regulates itself and relates to the outside world. Communication refers to the manner in which family members relate to others within the family system as well as the outside world. Families may be two-parent, single-parent, reconstituted, or blended, or may be children with a parent who has chosen to never marry.

Culture plays a large role in the way families operate. The African American, Hispanic, Asian, Native American, and Middle Eastern groups are all comprised of smaller cultures, each with its own values, patterns of communication, and spiritual beliefs.

Every family, no matter the cultural background, has a life cycle from the time the parents first come together until their death. Each member of the family is affected by developmental milestones even after the adult children begin their own nuclear families.

The major stresses on today's families are role definition and inequality, a variety of problems in parent–child relations, and the family's ability to cope with the disability of one of its members. The future of family life in this country appears to be influenced by the continued economic stressors on families, the likelihood that many couples will never marry, the fact that the role of the father is changing dramatically, the role of blended families, the resolution of childhood conflicts, and the fact that families do not have as much control over their own functioning and resources as did their predecessors. How the family as a system will meet these challenges remains to be seen.

EXPLORATION QUESTIONS

1. What are the primary responsibilities of a family?
2. What are the influences that negatively affect the family in today's world?
3. What are family rules and what part do they play in a family's functioning?
4. What are genograms and why are they useful in studying families?
5. Cite six types of families.
6. What are the primary values of the family with European roots?
7. What are the values of the Native American family?
8. What are the values of the African American family?
9. What are the values of the Hispanic family?
10. What are the values of the Asian family?
11. What are the values of the Middle Eastern family?
12. What are the major stresses on the family today?
13. What appear to be the trends for tomorrow's family?

ACTIVITIES FOR APPLIED LEARNING

1. What were the rules in your family of origin? Make a list of these. Which were spoken and which were just assumed. If they were assumed, how did you know they were rules?
2. Create a genogram of your family of origin, tracing the family back for several generations. Are there patterns that emerge? Are these functional or dysfunctional?
3. Engage the class in a discussion of cultural variations in families. Are there class members from different cultures? How did their family role, rules, and communication differ from those in the rest of the class?
4. Look in the newspaper for articles on current events. What impact might these events have on families? Discuss this in class.
5. Plan a potluck lunch or dinner. Have class members bring a dish that was traditional in their families of origin. Discuss how these recipes originated.

SUGGESTED READING

Acock, A. C., & Demo, D. H. *Family Diversity and Well-Being.* Thousand Oaks, CA: Sage, 1994.

Berg, I. K. *Family Based Services.* New York: Norton, 1994.

Carter, B., & McGoldrick, M. *The Changing Family Life Cycle: A Framework for Family Therapy.* Boston: Allyn and Bacon, 1988.

Cowan, P. A., Field, D., Hansen, D. A., Skolnick, A., & Swanson, G. E. (Eds.) *Family, Self, and Society: Toward a New Agenda for Family Research.* Hillsdale, NJ: Lawrence Erlbaum, 1993.

Ho, M. K. *Family Therapy with Ethnic Minorities.* Beverly Hills, CA: Sage, 1987.

Hutter, M. *The Family Experience.* New York: Macmillan, 1991.

Lynch, E. W., and Hanson, M. J. *Developing Cross-Cultural Competence: A Guide for Working with Children and their Families.* Baltimore, MD: Paul H. Brooks, 1992.

McGoldrick, M. and Gerson, R. *Genograms in Family Assessment.* New York: Norton, 1985.

Walsh, F. (Ed.) *Normal Family Processes.* New York: Guilford Press, 1993.

REFERENCES

Acock, A. C., & Demo, D. H. *Family Diversity and Well-Being.* Thousand Oaks, CA: Sage, 1994.

Aerts, E. "Bringing the Institution Back In." In Cowan et al., (Eds.) *Family, Self, and Society,* 3–41. Hillsdale, NJ: Lawrence Erlbaum, 1993.

Althen, G. *American Ways: A Guide for Foreigners in the United States.* Yarmouth, ME: Intercultural Press, 1988.

Carter, B., & McGoldrick, M. *The Changing Family Life Cycle: A Framework for Family Therapy.* Boston: Allyn and Bacon, 1988.

Chan, S. "Families with Asian Roots," (181–257). In E. W. Lynch and M. J. Hanson (Eds.) *Developing Cross-Cultural Competence: A Guide for Working with Children and Their Families.* Baltimore, MD: Paul H. Brooks, 1992.

Delgado, R. "Generalist Child Welfare and Hispanic Families," (130–156). In N. Cohen (Ed.). *Child Welfare: A Multicultural Perspective.* Boston: Allyn and Bacon, 1992.

Derezotes, D. S., & Snowden, L. R. "Cultural Factors in the Intervention of Child Maltreatment," *Child and Adolescent Social Work* 7(2), (1990), 161–175.

Downs, S. W., Costin, L. B., & McFadden, E. J. *Child Welfare and Family Services.* White Plains, NY: Longman, 1996.

Freeman, D. S. *Multigenerational Family Therapy.* New York: Haworth Press, 1992.

Goldenberg, I., & Goldenberg, H. *Family Therapy.* Belmont, CA: Brooks/Cole, 1991.

Hanson, M. J. "Families with Anglo-European Roots," (65–84). In E. W. Lynch and M. J. Hanson. *Developing Cross-Cultural Competence: A Guide for Working with Children and Their Families.* Baltimore, MD: Paul H. Brooks, 1992.

Herbert, M. *Working with Children and Their Families.* Chicago, IL: Lyceum, 1989.

Hess, B. B., Markson, E. W., & Stein, P. J. *Sociology.* New York: Macmillan, 1993.

Ho, M. K. *Family Therapy with Ethnic Minorities.* Beverly Hills, CA: Sage, 1987.

Hutter, M. *The Family Experience.* New York: Macmillan, 1991.

Iglehart, A. P., & Becerra, R. M. *Social Services and the Ethnic Community.* Boston: Allyn and Bacon, 1995.

Joe, J. R., & Malach, R. S. "Families with Native American Roots," (89–119). In E. W. Lynch and M. J. Hanson (Eds.). *Developing Cross-Cultural Competence: A Guide for Working with Children and Their Families.* Baltimore, MD: Paul H. Brooks, 1992.

Johnston, J. R. "Family Transitions and Children's Functioning: The Case of Parental Conflict and Divorce," (197–234). In Cowan et al., (Eds.). *Family, Self, and Society.* Hillsdale, NJ: Lawrence Erlbaum, 1993.

Kadushin, A., & Martin, J. A. *Child Welfare Services.* New York: Macmillan, 1988.

Karpel, M., & Strauss, E. S. *Family Evaluation.* New York: Gardner Press, 1983.

LaFromboise, T. D., Trimble, J. E., & Mohatt, G. V. "Counseling Intervention and American Indian Tradition: An Integrative Approach," (145–170). In D. R. Atkinson, G. Morton, and D. W. Sue (Eds.). *Counseling American Minorities: A Cross-Cultural Perspective.* Dubuque, IA: Brown and Benchmark, 1993.

Laird, J. "Gay and Lesbian Families," (282–328). In F. Walsh (Ed.). *Normal Family Processes.* New York: Guilford Press, 1993.

Leiberman, A. F. "Culturally Sensitive Intervention with Children and Families," *Child and Adolescent Social Work* 7(2), (1990), 101–119.

Lum, D. *Social Work Practice and People of Color.* Monterey, CA: Brooks/Cole, 1992.

Lynch, E. W., & Hanson, M. J. *Developing Cross-Cultural Competence: A Guide for Working with Children and Their Families.* Baltimore, MD: Paul H. Brooks, 1992.

Mass, A. I., & Yap, J. "Child Welfare: Asian Pacific Island Families," (107–129). In N. Cohen (Ed.). *Child Welfare: A Multicultural Perspective.* Boston: Allyn and Bacon, 1992.

McCowan, W. G., Johnson, J., & associates. *Therapy with Treatment Resistant Families.* New York: Haworth Press, 1993.

McGoldrick, M. "Ethnicity, Cultural Diversity, and Normality," (331–360). In F. Walsh (Ed.). *Normal Family Processes.* New York: Guilford Press, 1993.

McGoldrick, M., & Gerson, R. *Genograms in Family Assessment.* New York: Norton, 1985.

Minuchin, S. *Families and Family Therapy.* Cambridge, MA: Harvard University Press, 1981.

Mizio, E. "The Impact of Macro Systems on Puerto Rican Families," (483–519). In A. Morales & B. W. Sheafor (Eds.). *Social Work: A Profession of Many Faces.* Boston: Allyn and Bacon, 1989.

Mollica, R. F., & Son, L. "Cultural Dimensions in the Evaluation and Treatment of Sexual Trauma," *Psychiatric Clinics of North America,* 12(2), (June 1989), 363–379.

Moorehouse, M. J. "Work and Family Dynamics," (265–286). In P. A. Cowan et al., (Eds.). *Family, Self, and Society.* Hillsdale, NJ: Lawrence Erlbaum, 1993.

Pecora, P. J., Whittaker, J. K., & Maluccio, A. N., with Barth, R. P., & Plotnik, R. D. *The Child Welfare Challenge: Policy, Practice and Research.* New York: Aldine DeGruyter, 1992.

Prater, G. S. "Child Welfare and African American Families," (84–106). In N. Cohen (Ed.). *Child Welfare: A Multicultural Perspective.* Boston: Allyn and Bacon, 1992.

Sharifzadeh, V. S. "Families with Middle Eastern Roots," (319–351). In E. W. Lynch and M. J. Hanson (Eds.). *Developing Cross-Cultural Competence: A Guide for Working with Children and Their Families.* Baltimore, MD: Paul H. Brooks, 1992.

Swanson, G. E. "The Structuring of Family Decision-Making: Personal and Societal Sources and Some Consequences for Children," (235–263). In Cowan et al. (Eds.). *Family, Self, and Society.* Hillsdale, NJ: Lawrence Erlbaum, 1993.

Thomason, T. C. "Counseling Native Americans: An Introduction for Non-Native American Counselors," (171–187). In D. R. Atkinson, G. Morton, and D. W. Sue (Eds.). *Counseling American Minorities: A Cross-Cultural Perspective.* Dubuque, IA: Brown and Benchmark, 1993.

Tower, C. C. *Understanding Child Abuse and Neglect.* Boston: Allyn and Bacon, 1996.

Walsh, F. (Ed.). *Normal Family Processes.* New York: Guilford Press, 1993.

Wells, R. V. "Demographic Change and Family Life in American History: Some Reflections," (43–62). In M. Hutter (Ed.). *The Family Experience.* New York: Macmillan, 1991.

Willis, W. "Families with African-American Roots," (121–150). In E. W. Lynch and M. J. Hanson (Eds.). *Developing Cross-Cultural Competence: A Guide for Working with Children and Their Families.* Baltimore, MD: Paul H. Brooks, 1992.

Zuniga, M. E. "Families with Latino Roots," (151–179). In E. W. Lynch and M. J. Hanson (Eds.). *Developing Cross-Cultural Competence: A Guide for Working with Children and Their Families.* Baltimore, MD: Paul H. Brooks, 1992.

3

CHILDHOOD POVERTY
IN THE UNITED STATES

Dee Whyte

She doesn't even remember all the places she has lived. At ten, she and her two sisters and her mother have become itinerants. Sometimes they were evicted, but usually they just left, trying to dodge the bill collectors. Mama would have gotten welfare but they never lived anywhere long enough. They ate whatever they could afford. Sometimes they didn't eat. Sometimes they went to school and could even get a hot lunch. That felt like heaven. The winters were the toughest though. It never seemed that there were enough coats or shoes or mittens. She thought all year long about how cold one's hands and feet could get in the winter. Sometimes she thought of her life in terms of colors. For those years, she thought of gray…just dull gray. That was what life was…shades of gray.

Childhood poverty relentlessly stalks its victims down and affects every aspect of their lives. It triggers a deluge of problems for these children—hunger, homelessness, sickness, disabilities, violence, educational failure, too-early parenthood, and family stress are often the outcomes of child poverty. Perhaps cruelest of all, it even puts these children at higher risk of dying from birth defects, fires, and diseases. Today childhood poverty is a major problem in the United States. In fact, children represent the largest group of poor—over 15,000,000 children in the United States each year—prompting some authors to refer to the current trend as the juvenilization of poverty (Gustavsson and Segal, 1994). The following chapter will consider how poverty is determined by the federal government, the causes and consequences of child poverty, and strategies needed to reduce the amount of child poverty in the United States. While all of this information is important in order to understand the complexity of child poverty, it does not humanize the issue. As you review the facts it is vital that you imagine how the lives of real children are affected by bearing the enormous burden of living in poverty.

CHILDHOOD POVERTY: THE FACTS

Nine-year-old Brenda walked slowly home from her third-grade class. She was cold, she had a sore throat, and she was pretty sure she had a fever. She was sick and anxious to get home and lie down—even though home was a small drafty trailer. Actually, Brenda knew she was sick when she went to school this morning—but she went anyway because she would be sure to get breakfast at school. And as the morning wore on, Brenda felt even sicker, but decided to stay because then she would be able to eat the school lunch, which would probably be the last good meal she would have today. Brenda was shivering. She had on a sweater, but no coat. Her mother thought that she'd have enough money for a coat next month, but the weather had turned cold earlier than usual and Brenda was cold every day as she walked to and from school.

The tiny trailer was only slightly warmer inside than the weather outside. Brenda's mother hadn't been able to afford to have the gas tank filled for the trailer's heater yet, so Brenda turned on the electric oven and opened the oven door to warm up the room. She looked in the refrigerator and realized how wise she had been to stay long enough at school for lunch—there was only a small container of milk and a small bag of french fries that her mother had brought home from her job at a fast-food restaurant.

Brenda shivered under a blanket on the couch and tried to go to sleep. She knew sleep would help her get well, and she needed to try to get well fast. She remembered the last time she was sick and needed to go to see a doctor. Her mother's job didn't come with health insurance and so they waited until she was really sick and then they went to the emergency room at the hospital. Even though her mother didn't say anything to her, Brenda knew that the cost of the visit and the medicine she needed made her mother anxious and depressed. This time she would try to will herself to get better.

Children, as a group, have been plunging deeper and deeper into poverty in the United States for the past twenty-five years, and fare worse than any other group in our society. Today child poverty in this country is twice the rate of that of adults between 18 and 64 (11.7%). Child poverty has grown by one-half since 1969, in sharp contrast to the poverty rate among Americans 65 and older, which dropped by one-half during the same period of time, from 25.3% to 12.9% (Sherman, 1994). This dramatic reduction of elder poverty is due in large part to the tremendous growth in programs such as Social Security and Supplemental Security Income.

In 1994, the number of children under the age of eighteen living in poverty was 14,610,000. This represented 21.2% of all children under the age of eighteen in our country, the third highest since 1964. The poverty rate for children younger than six was even higher—24.5%—meaning that almost a quarter of the children under the age of six were living in poverty (see Table 3-1).

Even more alarming, nearly one in two poor children (46%) lives in extreme poverty, in families with incomes well below the poverty line. This represents the highest proportion of children living in extreme poverty since 1975, the first year this data was compiled (Sherman, 1994).

Minority children are disproportionately at risk of growing up in poverty. Most startling is the fact that, while minorities represent only one-third of all children under six years, they represent 60 percent of *poor* children. While only 16 percent of all children under the age of six are African American, 33% of poor children

TABLE 3-1   Poverty Among Children*

Year	Number of Children Under 18 Who Are Poor	Child Poverty Rate	Number of Children Under 6 Who Are Poor	Poverty Rate for Children Under 6
1959	17,552,000	27.3%	n/a	n/a
1960	17,634,000	26.9	n/a	n/a
1961	16,909,000	25.6	n/a	n/a
1962	16,963,000	25.0	n/a	n/a
1963	16,005,000	23.1	n/a	n/a
1964	16,051,000	23.0	n/a	n/a
1965	14,676,000	21.0	n/a	n/a
1966	12,389,000	17.6	n/a	n/a
1967	11,656,000	16.6	n/a	n/a
1968	10,954,000	15.6	n/a	n/a
1969	9,691,000	14.0	3,298,000	15.3%
1970	10,440,000	15.1	3,561,000	16.6
1971	10,551,000	15.3	3,499,000	16.9
1972	10,284,000	15.1	3,276,000	16.1
1973	9,642,000	14.4	3,097,000	15.7
1974	10,156,000	15.4	3,294,000	16.9
1975	11,104,000	17.1	3,460,000	18.2
1976	10,773,000	16.0	3,270,000	17.7
1977	10,288,000	16.2	3,326,000	18.1
1978	9,931,000	15.9	3,184,000	17.2
1979	10,377,000	16.4	3,415,000	17.8
1980	11,543,000	18.3	4,030,000	20.5
1981	12,505,000	20.0	4,422,000	22.0
1982	13,647,000	21.9	4,821,000	23.3
1983	13,911,000	22.3	5,122,000	24.6
1984	13,420,000	21.5	4,938,000	23.4
1985	13,010,000	20.7	4,832,000	22.6
1986	12,876,000	20.5	4,619,000	21.6
1987	12,843,000	20.3	4,852,000	22.4
1988	12,455,000	19.5	5,032,000	22.6
1989	12,590,000	19.6	5,071,000	22.5
1990	13,431,000	20.6	5,198,000	23.0
1991	14,341,000	21.8	5,483,000	24.0
1992	14,617,000	21.9	5,781,000	25.0
1993	14,961,000	22.0	6,097,000	25.6
1994	14,610,000	21.2	5,878,000	24.5

*Related children in families.
Source: U.S. Department of Commerce, Bureau of the Census.

are in this minority. While Hispanic children account for only 12% of all children in this age group, they represent 23% of poor children (Jones, 1994). The number of poor non-Hispanic Caucasian children, however, still outnumbers the number of poor African American and Hispanic children.

Children are poor because they live in poor families. Just as all families are unique with their own individual characteristics and histories, poor families have diverse backgrounds and life circumstances that cause them to live in poverty. Despite a commonly held perception that the heaviest concentrations of poor people live in large cities, more poor children actually live in suburban areas, nonmetropolitan smaller cities, or rural areas. In fact, many of the popular stereotypes about poor families are not borne out by the facts.

> It's hard to characterize the average American family, but even harder not to stereotype the poor. The popular conception that most poor families are black, inner-city welfare recipients is simply incorrect: 'Ghetto Poverty' constitutes less than 10 percent of total U.S. poverty, according to Professor David Ellwood of Harvard's Kennedy School of Government (Freedman, 1993, 32).

Families living in poverty contain only slightly more children than the average family, 2.2 children compared to 1.9 children (Sherman, 1994). Poor families tend to be headed by single mothers more than their nonpoor counterparts, however. This is important to note as children living in these families are five times more likely to be poor and about ten times more likely to be extremely poor (O'Hare, 1995).

Not all families that are poor are on welfare. In fact, in 1993, 61% of poor children lived in families in which someone worked and almost one in four poor children, 23%, lived in families in which parents worked full-time throughout the year (Finlay, 1995). These families are part of the "working poor" in our country. As we shall see later in this chapter, employment no longer guarantees that a family will live above the poverty level.

POVERTY DEFINED

What is poverty? Officially, poverty is defined by the U.S. government in its "index of poverty." A poverty line is established as the means of separating those who are considered poor from those who are not. This measurement is important because it is used to compute whether people are eligible for many government programs.

To arrive at this estimate of a poverty line, the food budget thought to be the minimally adequate for a family's subsistence is "multiplied by 3 on the assumption that food should constitute one-third of a family's budget" (Huston, 1991, 7). Adjustments are then made for the number of children under eighteen, family size, and the age of the head of the household. This method of defining poverty was first developed in 1963 when Mollie Orshansky of the Social Security Administration determined, as a baseline, the minimal diet necessary to survive. The first official poverty line was set for the year as $3000 (Sidel, 1986). According to the latest poverty thresholds, families with less than the following amounts of annual cash income in 1992 were considered poor:

One person (not in a family)	$7,143.
Family of two people	9,137.
Family of three people	11,186.
Family of four people	14,335.
Family of five people	16,952.

It is important to note that poor families' incomes are usually far below these thresholds—an average of $6,289 below these thresholds in 1992 (Sherman, 1994).

While the federal poverty line provides a useful tool for defining and measuring poverty, it is criticized on several accounts. Some believe that the criteria to determine the poverty level distort the complexion of poverty by only including cash and not taking into consideration such in-kind resources as food stamps, housing assistance, and medical programs. They claim that if the noncash benefits poor families receive (which have expanded dramatically over the past thirty years) were included in the formula that there would be fewer people officially declared as living below the poverty level. They also point out that the poverty measure does not take into account assets such as a house. However, while it is true that using an assets test as well as an income test would decrease the number of poor, it is also true that most poor people have few assets.

Others believe that the index of poverty is outdated, that it is based on the average expenditure of family income on food for three people thirty years ago, before the advent of more expensive processed and fast food, and calculated during a time when women were usually home all day to bake and cook meals from scratch. Further, they argue that the poverty level should be set in relationship to the status of others in contemporary society. They believe that poverty is best identified by comparing income groups within society and call for the development of a poverty standard that is equal to one-half of the median income (the midpoint in the range of family incomes, at which 50% of families have income above that point and the other 50% have less). When the poverty thresholds for a family were first adopted, they were roughly equal to what was then 50% of median family income. Since that time the poverty level has dropped far below 50% of median income. (Blong and Leyser, 1994). If this criterion were used, many more children would be living below the poverty line today.

Still others point out that the formula to compute the poverty line is outdated, that American families now spend one-fifth of their income on food because of rising costs in other budget items such as housing and child care (Freedman, 1993).

Public opinion seems to support the belief that the poverty definition is too low. The Gallup polling organization asked Americans where they thought the poverty line should be for a family of four. The average response was that a family of four should have an additional $3000 (in 1992 dollars) in order to live above the poverty line. This is 24% higher than the current poverty line (Sherman, 1994).

The reality is that, no matter how poverty is computed, a large number of children are living in families unable to afford adequate food, shelter, medical care, and other basic necessities. As you will see later in this chapter, the burden of living in poverty reduces a child's chances to grow up to be a healthy, well-adjusted, and contributing adult in our society and, at the same time, increases a child's chances of suffering the negative outcomes associated with growing up in poverty.

WHY CHILD POVERTY IS EXPANDING

Why are increasingly larger numbers of children living in poverty in our country? Why does almost one out of every three American children experience at least one year of poverty before they turn sixteen?

Experts cite several factors that contribute to growing childhood poverty. It is clear that the reasons are complex and interrelated, involving changes in our economic structure, the reconfiguration of society, as well as other factors, such as the individual characteristics of parents.

A major reason why more children are living in poverty today is because *real wages have been falling* for most Americans since 1973 (Coontz, 1995). This means that the value of wages in terms of buying power, what a family can actually purchase with a paycheck, has declined steadily for over twenty years. Family historian Stephanie Coontz wrote the following about this long-term trend of income inequality in our country.

> *Most poverty…comes from our changing earnings structure, not from our changing family structure. Between 1969 and 1989 the number of young white men earning less than the poverty figure for a family of four rose from one in ten to almost one in four. For African American men the comparable figure rose from 26% to 37%; for Hispanics, from 25% to 40% (Coontz, 1995, 9).*

The number of low-wage workers, or the "working poor," continues to expand, proving that work alone will not necessarily keep an individual or family out of poverty. We also know that the median income of young families with children plunged 34% between 1973 and 1992, after adjusting for inflation (Sherman, 1994).

A second factor in the explanation of the increase of poverty among children is that, as the real value of wages shrink in our country, *more resources are going to a smaller number of people in our country.*

> *Even after taxes, the top 20% rake in 44% of total income (not counting capital gains from the sale of homes, cares, stocks, and bonds); the bottom 20% must get*

by on 3.9%. And this astonishingly small share includes the cash value of food stamps and other benefits for the poor! In fact, the top 1% of the population has as much income as the entire bottom 40% (Coontz, 1995, 11).

Another reason for growing childhood poverty is that *there has been a decline in the real value of government assistance to families.* Current AFDC (Aid to Dependent Children) benefits are worth less than 1975 benefits in every state and the annual cost-of-living increases in food stamp benefits have not offset the loss in AFDC benefits. Between July 1972 and 1992, the combined value of AFDC and food stamps for a three-person family dropped 26% on average (Blong and Leyser, 1994).

Even so, *families eligible do not use all services available to them.* This may be because they do not know they are eligible for assistance, because the administrative barriers are too cumbersome to overcome, or for other reasons, such as the placement of welfare offices in locations difficult to reach.

The *reconfiguration of families* in U.S. society has also contributed to the increase in childhood poverty. As the number of one-parent households grows, so does the chance that children will grow up in poverty. Since 1950, the percentage of American children living in mother-only families had climbed from 6% to 24% in 1994, when approximately 19 million children were living in families with no father (O'Hare, 1995). As noted earlier in this chapter, children living in single-parent families are almost five times more likely to be poor. In 1993, only 7% of married-couple families lived in poverty, in contrast to 36% of the mother-only families. This growing number of single-parent families is attributable to both increased divorce rates and to the tenfold increase since 1950 in the number of births outside marriage. The vast majority of single-parent families (about 90%) are headed by women. Female-headed families often receive little or no financial help from the child's father. Nationwide, only 50% of divorced fathers contribute financially to their child's support (Carnegie Corporation, Starting Points, 1994). The *failure of absent parents to financially contribute to the support of their children* is seen as another major cause of child poverty today. In addition to the failure of the absent parent to provide child support, the historically lower earning power of women contributes to the likelihood that female-headed families will live in poverty. This "gender-segregated division of labor" is often referred to as institutionalized sexism (Heffernan et al., 1997).

The difficulties of a single-mother family are often compounded when the mother is a teen (see Chapter 11). In fact, we know that children born to unmarried teen mothers are more likely to drop out of school, to give birth out of wedlock, to divorce or separate, and to be dependent on welfare. And when the mother of these families does not complete high school, the children in these families are ten times more likely to be living in poverty by the ages eight to twelve as one born to a non-adolescent, married mother with at least a high school education (O'Hare, 1995).

Family poverty is also linked to the *level of education of the parents.* People without a high school diploma will earn only about 75% as much as high school graduates, and less than half of what college graduates are likely to make during their lifetime (O'Hare, 1995). As we move into the twenty-first century, economists believe that it will be increasingly more important for adults to have skills and technical knowledge in order to hold jobs that can support a family. Other *personal characteristics of parents,* such as mental retardation or emotional illness, can also increase the likelihood that families will live in poverty. Additionally, since minority families are more likely to be poor than white families, *racism* plays a role in determining the likelihood of poverty.

Advocates for children also believe that more children live in poverty each year because *children are too young to vote, lobby, and speak up for themselves.* They point to the dramatic reduction of poverty in elders in our country since the inception of AARP (American Association of Retired Persons), which provides a vehicle for the elderly to lobby for improved living conditions. Children, on the other hand, must rely on others who are old enough to vote and lobby to speak out for them. Although there are several advocacy groups that work on behalf of children, they have not established the power base necessary to force public policy-makers to make the changes required to lift children out of poverty.

THE HUMAN CONSEQUENCES OF GROWING UP IN POVERTY

Regardless of the causes of poverty, increasing numbers of American children are growing up in environments that put them at high risk of adverse outcomes. Growing up in poverty places a child at a profound disadvantage and greatly lowers the chance that the child will mature into a well-adjusted, productive, and contributing member of society. Research today reveals that just about every part of a child's life is affected by poverty. Further, growing up in the adverse conditions created by poverty increases the chance that such children will cost the taxpayers more money as they will require more expensive publicly-funded services throughout their lives.

> David's mother, Suzanne, was not quite twenty-six when she conceived him. He was the third of Suzanne's children; the other two were two and five. David's father worked as a construction worker, making just slightly more than necessary to keep the family above the poverty level. The family constantly struggled to make ends meet and, no matter how hard they tried, never seemed to be able to save much money and barely managed to rent a small house on the outskirts of a small city.
>
> During the second month of Suzanne's pregnancy, her husband had a car accident and died after almost two weeks of hospitalization in intensive care. The little savings that they had accrued were quickly gone

to pay for hospital bills and funeral expenses, and still there were bills left to be paid. Suzanne began to receive AFDC and tried to learn how to live even more frugally. Since she had been about twenty pounds overweight before her pregnancy, she reasoned that dramatically reducing her food input would be both advantageous to her figure and help with her food budget. Suzanne only managed to keep two prenatal visits as she could not afford a sitter to watch her other children, did not own a car, and lived miles from the health clinic.

Suzanne's son, David, was a low birthweight baby. He weighed only 4.9 pounds at birth and needed all of the special hospital and aftercare necessary for an infant born at low birthweight ($21,000). From the very beginning of his life, he was colic, easily irritated, and seemed to his mother to always be awake and moving. David needed more attention and care than her other children and Suzanne began to resent her newest child. The stress of living in poverty and having a difficult child made it harder for Suzanne to nurture David. Just after his first birthday, Suzanne lost control and hit David harder than she ever had before. Despite her promises to herself to never lose control with David again, David increasingly suffered beatings from his mother.

David entered kindergarten at age five and his teachers quickly referred him for an evaluation. David was diagnosed as having severe learning disabilities and hyperactivity, conditions often associated with children born with a low birthweight. Although David was receiving special education services from the school system ($6,000 per year), he fell so far behind that he needed to repeat first grade (cost to repeat).

Meanwhile, David's mother found him harder to control at home as he got older and physically larger. She had made some attempts to work and get off AFDC, but could never make enough money to buy all of the necessities for her family and pay for health insurance. Also, it was hard to arrange for child care for David while she worked because he was so hard to manage. Eventually, Suzanne stayed on AFDC and became increasingly angry and resentful toward David.

David's third-grade teacher noticed several large bruises on both of his arms and reported suspected child abuse to Child Protection Services. This agency conducted a thorough investigation and ordered a number of services for David and Suzanne, including counseling and after-school child care ($20,000). By now, however, David's siblings were adolescents who had also lived for years in poverty and were acting out their own anger and frustrations. The stresses on Suzanne continued to increase, as did the beatings on David.

When David was ten he was removed from his home and placed in a foster home for four years ($20,000). David had trouble getting along with his foster parents and was moved several times. When he was fourteen, he rejoined his family. By then David was an angry and frustrated adolescent who could not succeed at school or maintain healthy peer relationships. When he was sixteen he dropped out of school and decided to work full time. However, because he was a high school dropout with learning disabilities and poor reading skills, David could only find minimum-wage jobs. Soon he realized that the only way to make money was through a life of crime and began dealing drugs and breaking into houses. At eighteen David was caught and brought to trial and was found guilty. He served a ten-year jail sentence ($350,000). By the time David was twenty-eight, he had consumed over $417,000 in publicly-funded services, not to mention the cost of payments to his mother on AFDC.

David's story illustrates some of the human misery and economic cost of an early life spent in poverty. Poverty puts children at a higher risk for poor outcomes and increases life stressors that place heavy burdens on them as they travel through childhood. Further, the longer a child lives in poverty the more impact it is likely to have on the child's development. Poverty is often present with other risk factors, such as low parental education or adolescent parents, making it difficult to judge how much of an impact poverty by itself makes on the life of a child. However, when research has held constant other factors that might lead to negative outcomes for children, sizable impacts remain that can only be attributed to poverty (Sherman, 1994). For many children such as David, the stress of living in poverty is greatly magnified as risk factors interact.

INCREASED LIFE STRESSORS

Living in poverty places extraordinary stresses on families that can lead to isolation, tension, anger, and hopelessness. These families must worry about how to attain the basic necessities—food, clothing, medical care, and shelter—that other Americans take for granted. Further, poverty often forces them to live in inadequate and crowded housing, to send their children to inferior schools, and to be exposed to more crime and violence than a nonpoor family. Jonathon Kozol, author of *Savage Inequalities: Children in America's Schools*, described his two-year research on public schools in poor communities throughout the United States.

> *With few exceptions, [wrote Kozol] they reminded me of "garrisons" or "outposts" in a foreign nation. Housing projects, bleak and tall, surrounded by perimeter walls lined with barbed wire, often stood adjacent to the schools I visited. The schools were surrounded frequently by signs that indicated DRUG-FREE zone. Their doors were guarded. Police sometimes patrolled the halls. The windows of the schools were often covered with steel grates. Taxi drivers flatly refused to take me to some of these schools and would deposit me a dozen blocks away, in border areas beyond which they refused to go (Kozol, 1991, 5).*

Almost always the stressors of poverty interact and compound problems for poor children. Lisabeth Schoor discusses this phenomenon in her book, *Within Our Reach.*

> *The child in a poor family who is malnourished and living in an unheated apartment is more susceptible to ear infection; once the ear infection takes hold, inaccessible or inattentive health care may mean it will not be properly treated; hearing loss will do long-term damage to a child who needs all the help he can get to cope with a world more complicated than the world of most middle-class children. When this child enters school, his chances of being in an overcrowded classroom with an overwhelmed teacher further compromise his chances of successful learning. Thus risk factors join to shorten the odds of favorable long-term outcomes (Schoor, 1988, 30).*

POOR HEALTH OUTCOMES

Table 3-2 clearly illustrates the impact that poverty has on the health conditions of children. Poor children are more likely to begin life at a disadvantage as they are 1.2 to 2.2 times more likely to be born with a low birthweight (less than 2,500 grams, or 5.5 pounds). Low birthweight babies are more likely to die in infancy, have a doubled risk of learning problems (such as learning disabilities, hyperactivity, emotional problems, and mental illness), significantly greater risk of neurodevelopmental problems (seizures, epilepsy, water on the brain, cerebral palsy, and mental retardation), and loss of eyesight and hearing. Overall, poor children are three times more likely to suffer from fair or poor health and are much more likely to have health problems than nonpoor children.

HUNGER AND MALNUTRITION

At least one-third of poor children are hungry according to a report issued by the Food Research and Action Center in 1991. These hungry children were described by their parents in this report as two to eleven times more likely to experience fatigue, concentration problems, dizziness, irritability, frequent headaches and ear infections, unwanted weight loss, and frequent colds. An inadequate food supply causes other health problems, such as stunted growth (defined as being in the shortest 10% of children for their age), low birthweight, and iron-deficiency anemia (Sherman, 1994).

ANEMIA

Iron-deficiency anemia is three to four times more prevalent in poor preschool children than it is in the general child population (Sherman, 1994). Anemia is the most common consequence of inadequate nutrition. Slow development in infants, inattentiveness, and conduct disorders have all been associated with iron-deficiency.

TABLE 3-2   Children's Health Conditions by Family Income

	Low-income children's higher risk
Death during infancy:	1.3 times more likely
Death during childhood:	3 times more likely
Low birthweight:	1.2 to 2.2 times more likely
Stunted growth:	2 to 3 times more likely[b]
Partly or completely deaf:	1.5 to 2 times more likely
Partly or completely blind:	1.2 to 1.8 times more likely
Physical or mental disabilities:	about 2 times more likely
Mild mental retardation:	more likely
Overall injuries:	no more likely
Days in bed because of injuries:	1.8 times more likely
Hospitalization for injuries:	at least 3 times more likely[a]
Fatal accidental injuries:	2 to 3 times more likely
Hospitalization for poisoning:	5 times more likely[a]
Fair or poor health:	3 times more likely
Iron deficiency in preschool years:	3 to 4 times more likely
Frequent diarrhea or colitis:	1.5 times more likely
Pneumonia:	1.6 times more likely
Repeated tonsilitis:	1.1 times more likely
Overall asthma:	more likely
Severe asthma:	about 2 times more likely
Decayed, missing, or filled teeth:	more likely
School days missed due to acute and chronic health conditions:	1.4 times more likely

[a]Based on income data for child's neighborhood, not family.
[b]For children in long-term poor families.

LEAD POISONING

Young poor children, ages one to five, are three times more likely to suffer from lead poisoning than children in moderate-income families (Sherman, 1994). Lead contamination generally comes from lead-based paint found in older, inadequately maintained houses. Children living in these houses breathe the dust that forms after the paint deteriorates, and may eat the sweet-tasting paint chips. Lead poisoning is an especially potent health risk for young children. It can cause stunted growth, hearing loss, and put a child at risk of suffering from Attention Deficit and Hyperactivity Disorder (ADHD). It damages kidney development, blood production, vitamin D metabolism, and the brain and central nervous system. Numerous studies have shown that lead poisoning can produce verbal, perceptual, motor, and behavioral problems. Children suffering from lead poisoning are often more irritable, inattentive, have lower reading scores, and score lower on IQ tests. Very high levels of lead in blood can cause mental retardation, convulsions, coma, and even death (Sidel, 1988).

NO HEALTH INSURANCE

Another reason why poor children are at greater risk of poor health is that many poor families do not have health insurance. Employer-based insurance is the major source of insurance for children, yet the number of children covered by this benefit has decreased over the past two decades.

> *This is because employers are dropping all coverage, ending dependent coverage, or increasing employees' share of premiums for dependents; it is not because fewer parents are employed. An average of 1 percent of all U.S. children—some 750,000—have been losing insurance each year since 1987. If this trend continues, less than half of the nation's children will be covered by employer-based insurance by the year 2000 (Finlay, 1996, 19).*

POOR HEALTH CARE

Lack of adequate health insurance means that poor children rely primarily on episodic health care. They often do not have routine "well checkups," but rather rely on emergency rooms and clinics for care when they are sick. Thus, the same physician does not see them each time to do a careful family history and to get a full picture of the child's needs. The absence of a regular doctor also means that parents often do not receive information about preventive health care, such as immunizations, child-proofing their house, child safety seats, and balanced diets. Even if the parents have the information about preventive practices, they may not be able to afford the materials necessary to child-proof a home, or provide a balanced diet and other safeguards of their children's health and safety (Sidel, 1988).

LOWER EDUCATIONAL OUTCOMES

Children brought up in poverty are also much less likely to successfully finish high school and receive additional education or training, thereby making it more difficult to earn wages high enough to live above the poverty level as adults (see Table 3-3). For every year a child lives in poverty, the chance that he will fall behind in school increases by two full percentage points (Sherman, 1994).

INADEQUATE HOUSING

Poor children are more than three times as likely to live in inadequate and/or crowded housing, move about twice as much as nonpoor children, and are more likely to go without heat, or other utilities (Ellwood, 1988; Sidel, 1988; Sherman, 1994). In the past decade, homelessness has increased more among families with children than any other group. The "Status Report on Hunger and Homelessness in America's Cities: 1994," published by the U.S. Conference of Mayors, reported

TABLE 3-3   Children's Education Outcomes by Family Income

	Low-income children's higher risk
Average IQ scores at age 5:	9 test points lower[a,b]
Average achievement scores for ages 3 and older:	11 to 25 percentiles lower[b]
Learning disabilities:	1.3 times more likely
In special education:	2 or 3 percentage points more likely[a]
Below the usual grade for child's age:	2 percentage points more likely for each year of childhood spent in poverty
Being a dropout at age 16 to 24:	2 times more likely than middle-income youths and 11 times more likely than wealthy youths
Enrolling in any postsecondary education:	less likely than the U.S. average or than wealthy students
Enrolling in a four-year college:	two-thirds as likely as the U.S. average and half as likely as wealthy students
Finishing a four-year college:	one-half as likely as the U.S. average and one-fourth as likely as wealthy students

[a]Holding other factors constant.
[b]For children in long-term poor families.

that one in every four individuals reported as homeless was a child younger than eighteen (Finlay, 1995).

INADEQUATE SCHOOLS

Poor children cannot necessarily count on receiving a public education that will help them overcome the disadvantages they experience because they live in poverty. According to the National Academy of Sciences, the poorest children attend the poorest schools.

> *These schools have fewer financial and material resources, and they are often unable to retain the most skilled administrators and teachers. Student achievement levels in these schools are significantly lower on virtually all measures than for students in suburban schools (National Research Council, 1993, 117).*

Kozol's *Savage Inequalities* (1991) provides striking testimony to the lack of resources and attention to safety given to poor children in schools across the country today.

UNSAFE, ISOLATED NEIGHBORHOODS

Poverty restricts a family's choices of neighborhoods where they can raise their children. Poor children are more likely to live in crowded, noisy, and crime-ridden neighborhoods. The lower quality of life in these neighborhoods means that poorer families have less access to good jobs, safe play areas and parks, and positive role models for their children (Sidel, 1988).

INCREASED VIOLENCE

All of these factors contribute to increased life stressors for families bringing their children up in poverty. These stressors and inequalities can breed violence. Thus, poor children are more likely to live in neighborhoods with a high crime rate, and are more likely to experience violence firsthand.

> *Many social science disciplines, in addition to psychology, have firmly established that poverty and its contextual life circumstances are major determinants of violence...Violence is most prevalent among the poor, regardless of race...Few differences among the races are found in rates of violence when people at the same income level are compared. But beyond mere income level, it is the socioeconomic inequality of the poor—their sense of relative deprivation and their lack of opportunity to ameliorate their life circumstances—that facilitates higher rates of violence. ...Not only do the poor in America lack basic necessities, but they are aware that they do not have those things most other Americans have and that they lack other opportunities needed to obtain them in the future. Media depictions of other Americans who are living the 'the good life' serve to compound the already untenable conditions of poverty with a heightened sense of deprivation...(Sherman, 1994, 38).*

INCREASED CHILD ABUSE AND NEGLECT

All of these stressors on poor families decrease the capacity of parents to nurture their children and increase the risk that they may abuse or neglect them. Poverty often increases parental stress, isolation, and depression. It can even lead to family instability and marital breakups. Poor two-parent families are twice as likely as nonpoor families to divorce (Coontz, 1995). The stress of living in poverty can also lead to alcohol and drug abuse. Risk factors such as stress, reactive/difficult children, parental depression, marital breakup, and substance abuse increase the risk for child abuse and neglect.

Although child abuse and neglect occurs in families of all socioeconomic levels, poverty is a strong predictable risk factor for child maltreatment. According to Sherman (1994), poor children are about four times more likely to be abused as nonpoor children and nine times more likely to be neglected or at least reported.

Poverty also plays a pivotal role in defining the parent most likely to inflict severe injury to a child leading to death.

> *What sort of parent would attack or severely neglect a child in a manner that leads to death? In recent years we have learned that the average abusive parent is in his or her mid-20's, lives near or below the poverty level, often has not finished high school, is depressed and unable to cope with stress, and has experienced violence firsthand (U.S. Advisory Board on Child Abuse and Neglect, 1995, 13).*

Unfortunately, poverty often perpetuates the cycle of abuse. Numerous studies have shown that abused children are more likely to drop out of school, commit crime, become adolescent parents, abuse substances, and to abuse or neglect their own children.

NEGATIVE IMPACT ON EARLY BRAIN DEVELOPMENT

There is a growing body of scientific evidence that reveals that the early brain development of the child is negatively affected by stressors often inherent with poverty, and that these deficits may not be reversible. Researchers have documented the effect of malnutrition on brain development over the past twenty years. The Carnegie Corporation's report, *Starting Points: Meeting the Needs of our Youngest Children* (1994), emphasized this point.

> *We have long understood that factors other than genetic programming affect brain development. Nutrition is perhaps the most obvious example: we know that inadequate nutrition before birth and in the first years of life can so seriously interfere with brain development that it may lead to a host of neurological and behavioral disorders, including learning disabilities and mental retardation (20).*

This report also went on to say that brain development takes place more rapidly and extensively at an earlier age than scientists had previously thought.

> *Scientists are also learning that the brain is very vulnerable to environmental influences, making the environment a child lives in extremely important. Thus a baby that lives in a family that does not provide adequate stimulation and nurturance, or in a family living with the stresses of poverty, homelessness, or violence may suffer long-term cognitive deficits. These deficits may result in behavioral or emotional difficulties and may not be entirely reversible. Research has also shown that children who suffer from child abuse or neglect experience changes in brain chemistry that make them more likely than others to be violent teenagers and adults (Goleman,* New York Times, *October 3, 1995).*

Complete reversal of the cognitive deficits of people raised in poor environments during infancy and childhood may not be possible.

CURRENT EFFORTS TO FIGHT POVERTY

One problem with outlining the current financial assistance programs available for families is that they are changing almost weekly. As new reforms are instituted, programs change their form and focus and it is difficult to project what programs will look like by the year 2000. Suffice it to say that social insurance programs have existed for numerous years and some form of social insurance will probably be with us for years to come.

Poor families are most likely to be eligible for some forms of social assistance such as Aid to Families with Dependent Children (AFDC) (now called Transitional Assistance in some states), Supplemental Security Income (SSI), or Earned Income Tax Credit (EITC). A number of other programs such as food stamps (coupons with which food can be purchased for less), public housing (whereby poor families may receive aid for rent or have rents reduced), Women Infants and Children (WIC—a program providing prenatal care and diet supplements for poor women with children), Head Start (early education and social start for young children), and a variety of social services are also available.

CASH BENEFITS FOR FAMILIES (FORMERLY AID TO FAMILIES WITH DEPENDENT CHILDREN OR AFDC)

Instituted in 1962, Aid to Families with Dependent Children (AFDC) was a cash benefit program devised to assist poor families financially in the hope of giving them a push to become self-supporting. Although all states still have cash benefits for families, the name given the program has changed and differs state to state. There are two eligibility criteria for applying for cash benefits: (1) that the family has minor children (under eighteen years old) who are *deprived of the support of at least one parent* due to death, incapacitation, or absence through separation or divorce; (2) the family meets financial eligibility though a *means test*. This test consists of the application of a formula that takes into consideration family size, income (including under employment), savings, expenses (including rent and utilities), and several other factors that differ from state to state. Once deemed eligible, the family is given cash assistance, the amount of which again differs from state to state. Medicaid, a state/federal health assistance program, funds medical care for recipients of cash assistance.

No program of financial assistance has been more criticized than the old AFDC program. Critics argue that the program breeds dependency rather than encourages self support and that mothers on AFDC would prefer to remain home and continue to have children. The reality is that the typical AFDC family is relatively small and the amount of the cash allowance does not provide an easy life for recipients. The rumored fraud present in the system has actually been found to be a myth by numerous studies (Heffernan et al., 1997; Johnson and Schwartz, 1991; Zastrow, 1996). The argument for dependency has been much-studied. Studies have shown that many AFDC recipients are the children of former recipients. This may in fact be a drawback of the program but new reforms seek to offer greater incentives to break the cycle of poverty and assistance (Zastrow, 1996).

Welfare reform is greatly changing the provision of financial aid to families. States have now changed not only the program requirements but the names of such programs to reflect an emphasis on the intent of such help to be temporary. For example, Massachusetts now terms its program Transitional Assistance, and with the new name have come a myriad of changes. How aid to families will change and be administered in the future is a subject of much debate. Many have suggested that welfare for work age adults be eliminated all together. Others, suggesting that the welfare system has encouraged women to give birth to more children, feel that mothers should be denied welfare if they have additional children. Some states have enacted such reforms. After the 1994 elections, numerous reforms to the welfare system were suggested by political leaders including that aid be denied to pregnant teens, who should be expected to return to the homes of their parents. In addition, it was proposed that a recipient should be eligible for welfare for no more than five years, with the possibility of reducing this time to two years. Critics of such changes feel that these regulations hurt innocent children (Zastrow, 1996).

President Bill Clinton promised to "end welfare as we know it." He emphasized increased work incentives, better child-support enforcement, and rewards for families choosing to leave welfare. Some reformers have suggested that family allowances, available in every other industrialized Western country, may be a solution. The next few years may see numerous changes for poor families.

SUPPLEMENTAL SECURITY INCOME (SSI)

Supplemental Security Income (SSI) is a federally administered and funded income maintenance program that was instituted in 1971 by an amendment to the Social Security Act. SSI provides aid to anyone who is blind, disabled, or aged and fits the criteria for eligibility. Such supplements may be used by eligible children or their families.

EARNED INCOME TAX CREDIT (EITC)

In 1975, the earned income tax credit was legislated to help to offset Social Security taxes for low-income families. Only those who are *working* are eligible, which encourages young people who might otherwise be on welfare to go to work. This is the fastest growing poverty program to date.

THE ECONOMICS OF POVERTY

It makes sense in both humane and economic terms to make the changes necessary to raise children out of poverty. Adults who have grown up in poverty are more likely to require costly public assistance and programs, and they also earn less and produce less economic output.

> *The estimated future costs range as high as $192 billion in lifetime earnings for each year of the current high child poverty level. Looked at another way, ending child poverty is estimated to add as much as $192 billion per year in long-term*

worker earnings and production in the economy. Even the lowest estimates (which are intended to capture only one piece of child poverty's total effects on productivity) are about $35.4 billion in lost lifetime earnings for each year we allow the current 14.6 million children to be poor (Sherman, 1994, 28).

How much would we save in program costs if we could eliminate most child poverty? Prevention experts estimate the savings would be substantial. If we invested in programs now, we would need to fund fewer programs later on to address the outcomes of growing up in poverty. The extent of savings would be in direct proportion to the effectiveness of prevention programs. In *From Cradle to Grave* (1993), Jonathan Freedman estimates that, even if only a fraction of the programs were effective, they might save at least $15 to $60 billion each year.

REDUCING CHILD POVERTY

Mollie Orshansky, the creator of the Poverty Line, has retired from government. She says, 'Why don't we stop doing research on the right poverty number and do something about poverty?' (Freedman, 1993, 231–232)

Indeed, why don't we do something? Are there steps our country can take to reduce child poverty? Yes, it is possible to dramatically lower the number of children who grow up in poverty in our country. Child poverty is not an unavoidable consequence of modern society. Other industrialized nations with fewer resources and similar economic and social problems have put public policies in place that insure that children are protected and have a better chance to reach their full potential. In fact, American children are twice as likely to be poor as Canadian children, three times as likely to be poor as British children, four times as likely to be poor as French children, and seven to thirteen times more likely to be poor as German, Dutch, and Swedish children (Sherman, 1994). Lower levels of government assistance are usually attributed to the higher rate of child poverty in the United States.

ATTITUDINAL CHANGES

In order to make significant progress in lifting children out of poverty, our country needs to undergo both important underlying attitudinal shifts toward children and families and implement important programs to address the causes of poverty. These new attitudes about children and families will create the public will to make the changes necessary to reduce child poverty.

Americans need to value *all* children and *develop a collective responsibility for all of our children*. Poor children, middle-class children, and wealthy children—we must feel responsible for them all, and not view them as "other people's children." If we do not make this important attitudinal shift, we run the risk of more and more

children growing up in poverty each year. Second, we need to *value the role of the family and the job of parenting.* Our nation should view parenting as the highest priority job while children are growing up. The family is the most important institution shaping the lives of children and parents must be strengthened and supported in their job of raising and nurturing them. This means that we will need to take a two-generational approach to reducing poverty. Lastly, we need to *value and fund prevention programs,* and move away from our current crisis orientation that forces us to invest in more programs designed to deal with problems *after* the damage has been done. These three important attitudinal shifts will create the public and political will to eliminate child poverty. It will also lead us to understand that effective solutions must be two-generational, affecting both the child and the child's caretakers.

COMPLEX COMBINATION OF TWO-GENERATIONAL STRATEGIES

Just as the reasons why so many children and families live in poverty are complex and interwoven, so are the solutions needed to eliminate child poverty. As well as creating the public and political will to end child poverty and funding family-friendly prevention programs, it will be necessary to implement a complex combination of strategies. To be truly effective, these must be two-generational and include income security as well as service and support programs. The following are the solutions to child poverty most often mentioned by experts.

   1. *Implement effective welfare reform.* The current welfare system should be replaced with policies that treat the causes of poverty. The new system must be geared toward providing the supports necessary to reinforce family and economic independence.
   2. *Strengthen child-support enforcement.* There should be a national system in place to more effectively collect child-support payments so that noncustodial parents bear financial responsibility for their offspring.
   3. *Implement child-support assurance.* Even if they are contributing child support, noncustodial parents earning low wages cannot contribute enough to bring their children out of poverty. In order to protect all children, a national child-support assurance system should be put into place. This would guarantee reasonable levels of child support by the government if an absent parent cannot support the child above an established minimum, or if the parent avoids payment altogether. This method of assuring that children have adequate financial support has several advantages: The government would collect revenue from the absent parent; there would be no stigma attached to the program because the program would collect money for families from all income brackets; it would not be considered public assistance and therefore would not prevent mothers from working.
   4. *Increase the minimum wage.* The minimum wage should be increased so that working parents can earn enough to keep their family out of poverty. Over the past

several years, there has been a growing number of workers who are ill-paid, who are the "working poor." A parent earning the current federal minimum wage of $4.25 an hour would barely gross enough money to be at 72% of the federal poverty level for a family of three.

5. *Create more jobs.* Public policies should be implemented (such as tax credits) that encourage job growth in the private sector. Government can also create additional jobs in the public sector.

6. *Invest in schools and training programs.* Experts project that occupations that require specialized education and training will grow the fastest in the future. In fact, it is estimated that a college degree will be necessary for one-third to two-thirds of the new jobs by the year 2000 (National Commission on Children, 1991). Children should have an equal opportunity to receive a good education, regardless of the neighborhood they live in. More Americans must also have access to job-training programs and higher education that will provide them with the marketable skills necessary to secure a job that pays adequate wages. A high school education alone no longer guarantees a living above the poverty level.

7. *Implement family-centered policies.* Flexible work schedules, family medical leaves, and assistance with quality child care, including after-school and summer child care, will make it easier for poor families to care for their children.

8. *Improve the Earned Income Tax Credit.* This is a refundable credit, which subsidizes the earnings of employed parents in low-wage jobs. It provides cash to poor working families with children, regardless of their tax liability, thereby moving these families closer to a "living wage." This should be distributed to families through advance payments that are available throughout the year.

9. *Prevent teen pregnancies.* Programs need to be expanded to discourage too-early childbearing, which dramatically increases the chance that the mother and child will live in poverty for an extended period of time.

10. *Implement health care reform.* Americans need a program that assures quality care from before birth until death. Preventative health care should be funded as well as treatment.

11. *Insure adequate housing for families.* Families currently making minimum wages must pay more than half their wages for rent in most states. The government should make subsidies available to prevent homelessness and ease this economic pressure on families.

12. *Expand programs to support and strengthen families.* Parents who are supported in their caretaking role are better able to nurture their children, and these children have a better chance to grow up to be productive, contributing members of society. Research has demonstrated that programs such as parenting education, support groups, and home visiting are effective and produce positive, significant results for parents and their children.

13. *Insure that emergency services are in place.* Emergency assistance programs that provide food, clothing, and shelter to families in time of crisis must be available and have adequate funding.

AN IMPORTANT FOOTNOTE

Advocates for poor children should remember that it is not necessary to implement all of the above strategies at once (a daunting and unlikely task in any event). Prevention of poor outcomes for children is not an "all or nothing" proposition. Even removing some of the risk factors can increase a child's chances to avoid damaging outcomes (Schoor, 1988).

Finally, it is important to note that a child growing up in poverty is not necessarily doomed to failure. Indeed, stories abound in our country of people who grew up in adverse conditions who matured to become happy, successful, and contributing members of society. Sometimes these children are especially resilient, and often they've been lucky enough to have the encouragement of a parent, or a teacher, or some other adult in their community. However, even if it is sometimes possible to beat the odds and overcome the adverse conditions associated with poverty, it is simply unfair of us to place the relentless burden of poverty with its inherent risks on the most vulnerable in our society.

SUMMARY

Children represent the largest population living in poverty in the United States today. These numbers have increased alarmingly over the last twenty years. Minority children make up a large percentage of this population. Other than this, it is difficult to draw an accurate picture of the typical poor family in spite of popular stereotypes.

Poverty is defined by the U.S. government in terms of the "poverty line," a calculated formula that assesses a family's minimally adequate budget. Despite criticisms of this formula as being outdated and too restrictive, this mechanism is still used.

The increase in poverty among children can be attributed to several factors, including economic changes over the last few years, the reconfiguration of the family unit, the use of services by families, the personal characteristics of parents, and the fact that children do not vote and so cannot lobby for themselves.

Children in poverty are subject to many life stressors, including a variety of health concerns, no health insurance, poor educational opportunities, inadequate housing, and increased violence, both at home and in the streets.

Currently there are several programs to address the needs of poor children and their families. The most widely used of these is Aid to Families with Dependent Children (AFDC), the cash assistance program to families with young children

who have been deprived of the support of one parent and who are income eligible. Children or their parents may also receive Supplemental Security Income (SSI) if they are disabled or blind. And some low-income working youths may be eligible for Earned Income Tax Credit (EITC), which offsets the Social Security taxes on their wages. Other programs such as food stamps, Women Infants and Children Program, Medicare, and Head Start are also available.

There has been much discussion about how we can reduce the incidence of poverty. Many feel that we need to value children more as well as supporting and strengthening the family. In addition, changes must be made in economic programs, schools, family-centered policies, housing, and emergency services. No simple solution will change the increasing trend toward the juvenilization of poverty.

EXPLORATION QUESTIONS

1. How is poverty defined? How is the poverty line determined?
2. How would one characterize the child growing up in poverty?
3. What are the reasons for the increase in child poverty?
4. How did the effects of growing up in poverty most likely affect David's life? What could have been done to change David's poor outcomes?
5. What are the stressors under which children in poverty must live?
6. What are some of the programs available for poor children and their families today? What is provided by each?
7. What are some ways to reduce poverty among children?
8. What is meant by "two-generational strategies"?

ACTIVITIES FOR APPLIED LEARNING

1. Imagine that you are a mother at the poverty line. You have three children, two of whom are in diapers and one of whom uses formula. By looking at apartment ads in the newspaper and price shopping in the market, construct a family budget within the allotment to a family at the poverty line. Remember to include rent, food, paper goods, diapers, and formula. After you have constructed this budget, discuss what it feels like to do so.
2. How do you believe the poverty line should be defined? Defend your answer.
3. Design your own set of solutions to reduce child poverty. What solutions do you feel should be implemented first? How? Are there others that you believe should be implemented?
4. President John F. Kennedy said, "If a free society cannot help the many who are poor, it cannot save the few who are rich." Do you agree? Disagree? Why? Discuss your opinion with a group of students.

SUGGESTED READING

Blong, A. M. and Leyser, B. *Living at the Bottom: An Analysis of 1994 AFDC Benefit Levels.* New York: Center on Social Welfare Policy and Law, 1994.

Ellwood, D. *Poor Support: Poverty in the American Family.* New York: Basic Books, 1988.

Finlay, B. (Ed.). *The State of America's Children Yearbook.* Washington, DC: The Children's Defense Fund, 1995.

Freedman, J. *From Cradle to Grave: The Human Face of Poverty in America.* New York: Atheneum, 1993.

Golden, R. *Disposable Children: America's Welfare System.* Belmont, CA: Wadsworth, 1997.

Huston, A. C. *Children in Poverty: Child Development and Public Policy.* New York: Cambridge University Press, 1991.

Jones, J. E. *Child Poverty: A Deficit that Goes Beyond Dollars.* New York: National Center for Children in Poverty, 1994.

Katz, M. B. *The Underserving Poor.* New York, Pantheon Books, 1989.

Kozol, J. *Savage Inequalities: Children in America's Schools.* New York: Crown, 1991.

Sherman, A. *Wasting America's Future: The Children's Defense Fund Report on the Costs of Child Poverty.* Boston: Beacon Press, 1994.

Sidel, R. *Women and Children Last: The Plight of Poor Women in Affluent America.* New York: Penguin, 1986.

Williams, T. & Kornblum, W. *Growing Up Poor.* Lexington, MA: Lexington Books, 1985.

REFERENCES

Blong, A. M., & Leyser, B. *Living at the Bottom: An Analysis of 1994 AFDC Benefit Levels.* New York: Center on Social Welfare Policy and Law, 1994.

Carnegie Corporation. *Starting Points: Meeting the Needs of Our Youngest Children.* New York, 1994.

Coontz, S. "The American Family and the Nostalgia Trap," *Phi Delta Kappan,* (March 1995).

Ellwood, D. T. *Poor Support: Poverty in the American Family.* New York: Basic Books, 1988.

Finlay, B. (Ed.). *The State of America's Children Yearbook,* Washington, DC: The Children's Defense Fund, 1995.

Finlay, B. (Ed.). *The State of America's Children Yearbook,* Washington, DC: The Children's Defense Fund, 1996.

Food Research and Action Center. *Community Childhood Hunger Identification Project: A Survey of Childhood Hunger in the United States.* Washington, DC: Food Research and Action Center, 1991.

Freedman, J. *From Cradle to Grave: The Human Face of Poverty in America.* New York: Atheneum, 1993.

Goleman, D. "Early Violence Leaves Its Mark on the Brain," *New York Times,* October 3, 1995, 15.

Gustavsson, N. S., & Segal, E. A. *Critical Issues in Child Welfare.* Thousand Oaks, CA: Sage, 1994.

Heffernan, J., Shuttlesworth, G., & Ambrosino, R. *Social Work and Social Welfare.* Minneapolis/St. Paul: West Publishing, 1997.

Huston, A. C. *Children in Poverty: Child Development and Public Policy.* New York: Cambridge University Press, 1991.

Johnson, L. C. & Schwartz, C. L. *Social Welfare: A Response to Human Need.* Boston: Allyn and Bacon, 1991.

Jones, J. E. *Child Poverty: A Deficit that Goes Beyond Dollars.* New York: National Center for Children in Poverty, 1994.

Kozol, J. *Savage Inequalities: Children in America's Schools.* New York: Crown, 1991.

National Commission on Children. *Beyond Rhetoric.* Washington, DC: U.S. Government Printing Office, 1991.

National Research Council, Commission on Behavioral and Social Sciences and Education. *Losing Generations: Adolescents in High Risk Settings.* Washington, DC: National Academy Press, 1993.

O'Hare, W. P. *Kids Count Data Book.* Baltimore, MD: Annie C. Casey Foundation, 1995.

Schoor, L. B. *Within Our Reach.* New York: Anchor Books, 1988.

Sherman, A. *Wasting America's Future: The Children's Defense Fund Report on the Costs of Child Poverty.* Boston: Beacon Press, 1994.

Sidel, R. *Women and Children Last: The Plight of Poor Women in Affluent America.* New York: Penguin Books, 1986.

U. S. Advisory Board on Child Abuse and Neglect. *A Nation's Shame: Fatal Child Abuse and Neglect in the United States.* Washington, DC: U.S. Government Printing Office, 1995.

Zastrow, C. *Introduction to Social Work and Social Welfare.* Pacific Grove, CA: Brooks/Cole, 1996.

4

VIOLENCE, ADDICTION, AND HOMELESSNESS
Current Societal Problems and Their Impact on Children

Child Killed in Crossfire of Police/Gang Shootout

Drug Addicted Mother Leaves Newborn in Trash Can

Homeless Parents Seek Shelter in Abandoned Church

Newspaper headlines serve as painful reminders of the fact that the welfare of children is greatly influenced by the social problems plaguing us today. As the numbers of homeless become startling, experts report that the fastest growing population of homeless today are women and children. Increasingly, drug-addicted parents come to the attention of child welfare systems across the country. And all the while the gunfire in our streets takes its toll not only on children but on the psyches of those who remain alive. Any exploration of the child welfare system must take into consideration the backdrop against which today's children live. This world is filled with many problems, but we will focus on three of the major issues that threaten the healthy development of many children: violence, addiction, and homelessness.

CHILDREN AND VIOLENCE

It would seem that today, more than ever before, our children are exposed to violence on a daily basis. Kotlowitz (1991) observed the world of two brothers, Lafeyette and Pharaoh Rivers, as they fought to survive amidst the turbulence of their home in Henry Horner, a crime-ridden Chicago housing project. Gunfire was an all too familiar sound that caused their concerned mother to count her children for fear one of them would be the victim. Plagued by rival gangs, the young project dwellers were often caught in the middle of the violence perpetrated by them. Bird Leg, the fourteen-year-old friend of the Rivers's brothers, was one such victim.

In the summer of 1986, while shooting dice with some friends he [Bird Leg] was approached by a man with a shotgun demanding his money, and Bird Leg, in his youthful defiance, ran. The man emptied a cartridge of buckshot into Bird Leg's shoulder. That incident added to the intensifying war between the gangs, [and] caused his mother to move her family into an apartment on the city's far north side. But, as is often the case when families move, Bird Leg and his brothers kept returning to Horner to visit friends.... (45)

Later that summer, Bird Leg was shot in the arm with buckshot while visiting his friends. The very next night, he returned to the project and, while watching his friends play basketball, he was taunted by a gang member. His sister begged him to take no heed and go into the building but he sent her inside:

> [B]y the time she climbed the six floors to her cousin's apartment, a single pistol shot had echoed from below. Twenty-four-year-old Willie Elliott had stepped from between two parked cars and aimed a pistol at Bird Leg.... The bullet, which had hit him at point blank range, entered his chest and spiraled through his body like an out-of-control drill, lacerating his heart, lungs, spleen, and stomach. Bird Leg, struggling to breathe, collapsed beneath an old cottonwood, where, cooled by its shade, he died (46).

So common are deaths in Henry Horner that a protocol has already been established. "When someone at Henry Horner is killed, mimeographed sheets go up in the buildings' hallways, giving details of the funeral" (Kotlowitz, 1991, 47).

WAR IN THE STREETS

Life for the two boys of Henry Horner and their friends is not unlike the lives of many other children in the United States today. The Children's Defense Fund (CDF) (1996) reports that a child is killed by gunfire every 98 minutes (55). In fact, homicide is the number one cause of death among Hispanic and African American youths and the third leading killer of white young people (56). It is not only adults who are killing our children. The rate of those who are under eighteen committing these acts has increased 158% between 1985 and 1994, with 125,000 youths arrested for crimes of violence in 1994 (55). The majority of those in court for these crimes have never committed them before. Yet, there has been a 75% increase in juvenile arrests for violent crimes over the last decade. The Department of Justice predicts that arrests of ten- to seventeen-year-olds for violent crimes will double by the year 2010 if the trend continues (57). The majority of crimes committed by youths involve weapons, most often guns. The problem is of enough concern that President Clinton, at the end of 1995, cited juvenile crime by minors as the most serious crime problem today.

It was not only crimes against others that are of concern. The accessibility to guns has produced an increase in the suicide rate as well. In 1992, more than 2,100 young people committed suicide. Between 1980 and 1992, among fifteen- to nineteen-year-olds, 81% of the suicides were gun-related. While most of those who commit suicide are white, there has been an increase in the incidence of deaths among minority children as well (57).

Influences on Youth Violence

In what context does violence in the streets occur? Certainly, as we become a more violent society, our children are increasingly aware of it. There is not a single news broadcast aired on television or radio that does not have at least one account of violence perpetrated against an individual or group. Fiction mirrors reality as prime-time shows feature a myriad of crimes and acts of violence; even situation comedies depict people being victimized by others, as though there were humor in it. Some critics of modern TV and movie entertainment suggest that violence depicted in the media actually increases violence by desensitizing us to it.

The concern over promoting violence through the media is not new. As early as 1954, congressionally authorized studies looked at the influence of TV violence on human behavior. In 1968, a group of mothers in the Boston area, concerned over their children viewing too much violence and being influenced by certain commercials, founded Action for Children's Television (ACT) to try to influence what their children watched. Dr. Anne Somers reported in 1976 that children between five and fifteen would have observed, by the time they were eighteen, 200,000 violent acts during the 15,000 hours plus that they watched television (Kinnear, 1995, 23). By 1982, the National Institute of Mental Health had concluded that "excessive levels of television violence lead to aggressive, even violent behavior in children" (Kinnear, 1995, 24).

Why does TV violence promote violence in society? The most obvious answer is that when children see violent acts committed by heroes and villains alike, they tend to want to emulate them for the risk and the thrill. But critics tell us that the effects go beyond this simple explanation. Constant exposure to violence not only desensitizes individuals to the commission of it but increases the indifference one feels as the acts take place. This, in turn, decreases the ability to feel empathy with the victims. Psychoanalyst Denise Shrine feels that there are three elements found in the makeup of juvenile violent offenders: lack of respect, inability to understand or empathize with another person, and impatience (Kinnear, 1995; Hoffman, 1996).

In addition to television, some experts also blame today's sports for the increase in violence among young people. Although sports are usually thought to be played for enjoyment and relaxation, an intense emphasis on winning can elevate competition to violent behavior. How many children observe hockey players on television club each other with sticks, football players use more force than necessary, and baseball players spit in the faces of umpires? While there has always been some degree of highly charged emotions in sports events, the price tag placed on winning now creates an intense and even violent atmosphere (Phillips, 1983; Kinnear, 1995; Hoffman, 1996).

Gangs on the Streets

Gangs have been the subject of sociological and psychological study for decades. The popular musical *West Side Story* romanticized the violence of gang warfare, but the reality is not as appealing. Today, gangs are responsible for a great deal of the violence perpetrated against other teens. They exist not only in urban areas, but in suburban and rural areas as well. Los Angeles, for example, is thought to have the most gangs currently with estimates of between 300–500 gangs (Morales, 1989).

What constitutes a gang? A youth gang is a group of teens who band together for a variety of reasons, usually including a sense of belonging and protection (McWhirter et al., 1993). Miller (1980) proposed the following definition of gangs:

> *A youth gang is a self-formed association of peers, bound together by mutual interests, with identifiable leadership, well-developed lines of authority, and other organizational features, who act in concert to achieve a specific purpose or purposes which generally include the conduct of illegal activities and control over a particular territory, facility, or type of enterprise (121).*

Morales (1989) disagrees with Miller's generalizations and describes four types of youth gangs: criminal gangs, conflict gangs, retreatist gangs, and cult/occult gangs (419–421). *Criminal gangs* are dedicated primarily to such illegal activities as theft, fencing stolen articles, and drug trafficking. *Conflict gangs* defend their turf against rival gangs. Their organization is often based on racial lines (e.g., Latino gangs, Asian gangs), and they often inhabit specific neighborhoods that then become their *turf.* Invading another gang's turf can result in gang warfare. *Retreatist gang* members dedicate themselves to getting "high" on a variety of drugs. They tend not to be involved with the drugs for financial gain as criminal gangs are, but they retreat to use the drugs. *Cult* or *occult gang* members join with each other in devil worship or belief in some cult dogma. The Charles Manson family is one well-known cult gang. These gangs may or may not be involved in criminal activity or use drugs (Zastrow, 1996). Other authors suggest that gangs cannot be as clearly defined as to purpose and that their reasons for existing often include a variety of activities (Huff, 1990).

Gangs offer youths a great deal in a time of family breakdown and social anonymity. In addition to a sense of belonging, gangs can offer status and a feeling of importance. They offer social situations and opportunities to take risks in the company of others who are also taking these risks. With the element of combined power, gangs, more than individuals, can exercise more power and have access to more resources.

The Diablos were a Hispanic youth gang in an old, predominantly Italian neighborhood. While individually the Mexican boys involved in the gang were not accepted by the old-time residents, collectively they had made their mark. When the gang entered the local grocery store, the owner knew that it was easier to ignore their shoplifting of candy bars and soda than to repair the damage done when the gang members chose to retaliate because their shoplifting was prohibited. The store owner figured into his budget the loss of his merchandise and the arrangement persisted for a number of years.

There is some debate as to how much of an increase in violence among gangs there has been over the years. It does seem clear, however, that the character of the violence has intensified. As this society becomes increasingly violent, so do the acts committed by gangs become more brutal and less comprehensible. More guns are involved and the rate of homicides has skyrocketed (Maxson and Klein, 1990).

Many communities not previously affected by gang activity are finding that the gangs from nearby cities have moved into their area. Hispanic, African American, and white Gangs are joined by Asian gangs. Los Angeles, for example, has become increasingly concerned about its Vietnamese gangs in which over 1,000 Vietnamese youths are involved (Vigil and Yun, 1990). Vigil and Yun (1990) suggest that gangs of minority groups are based on their frustration with their inability to readily integrate into the dominant culture. Not only is English a major stumbling block for newly immigrated youths, but they often do not understand the cultural mores.

> [T]he youths cited their inability to understand what is going on as their primary problem in school...Comments such as "I was too scared to talk to the teacher" are common when talking to these youths. Even the simplest act of asking for permission to go to the bathroom became a degrading ritual (152).

Traditionally, in Asian cultures, problems are handled by the family. But as youths find themselves trying to fit into new world traditions they become increasingly at odds with the traditions of the family. Hence they look for belonging elsewhere and often find it with their peers, who are experiencing similar conflicts. In addition to belonging, Asian youths find that gangs can bring in money. As they remember the poverty that many of them experienced in their families of origin and observe their parents' financial struggles, because they lack the skills recognized in this new culture, and get caught up in the U.S. emphasis on financial success, it is not surprising that easy money would have an appeal. Auto theft, drug selling, armed robbery provide quicker returns than hard work. Even the risks involved have an allure for teens. War is not foreign to them and many spent their early years absorbing the skills necessary to survive in a war-torn environment. Gang wars and the risks inherent in crime feel old and familiar (Vigil and Yun, 1990; McWhirter et al., 1993).

The role of girls in gangs has also evolved over the years (Molidor, 1996). Campbell (1990) suggests that the image of the female delinquent "has been depicted as isolated and inept; a pitiful figure trying to assuage her loneliness through brief, promiscuous liaisons with boys" (163). Early accounts of female gang involvement were based on the girl's dependence on male gang members. They were largely portrayed as sexual objects who were cajoled, tricked, or forced into sexual relations for the enjoyment of male gang members. The characteristics of the typical female gang member can be gleaned from the description of an African American gang in Chicago in the 1960s.

> Their principal roles were traditional—sexual objects, drinking partners, weapons carriers, and lookouts. They fought other female gangs, but took particular pride in exploiting their femininity to instigate inter- and intragang fights among the boys. By reporting 'passes' made by members of rival gangs, they manipulated the Vice Kings [gang to which they were affiliated] into fighting for their honor. Their raison d'etre was the male group, and they had 'little function outside the mating-dating complex.' They competed, often violently, for the attention of the male gang

members, and status within the group was largely dependent on relationships with particular boys. Going steady or having a baby by a high-status boy was prestigious, but there was no anticipation by either sex of long-term commitment or marriage (Campbell, 1990, 170).

In the early 1970s girls took on new roles in terms of gang involvement. Contemporary female gang members appear to be organized in one of three ways: as units functioning independently from male gang members; as regular members of "coed" gangs; and as auxiliary members of male gang groups. Unlike the boys, the girls are usually not pressured into joining a gang but rather do so as a result of friendships or network connections. These girls are responsible for their own affairs. They are usually closely knit as a sisterhood and resent the efforts of male gang members to interfere. Girls exert peer influence over the sexual behaviors of their sisters. Unlike the reports of their forerunners, contemporary female members tend to choose one male as a partner and remain faithful to him for the duration of the relationship. They are also as likely as male members to engage in fights, violence, and illegal acts (Campbell, 1990).

VIOLENCE IN RELATIONSHIPS

The violence among teens in dating relationships has increased in the last decade (Ageton, 1985; Aizenman and Kelly, 1988; Struckman–Johnson, 1988; Carlson, 1996; Zastrow, 1996). Although much of the research has been done among the college student population, there is evidence that violence in relationships happens at younger and younger ages (Olday and Wesley, 1988). Date or acquaintance rape appears to be related to specific attitudes and accepted behaviors among adolescents. The first attitude is that girls should be submissive. Romance novels and popular television shows perpetrate the image that females desire to be overpowered sexually. In addition, the popular assumption that males cannot control their sexual urges adds fuel to the fire. When a girl "leads a boy on" sexually, the myth is that he has the "right" to continue the sexual encounter (Miller and Dyk, 1993; Zastrow, 1996). Goodchilds et al. (1988), in a study of 432 adolescents, found that 82% of the sample felt that it "was okay for a boy to hold a girl down and force her to have sexual intercourse." The participants were then given a series of case-specific examples and responded that force was the most acceptable when a "girl gets a guy excited" (females 42%, males 51%) (Miller and Dyk, 1993, 112).

The use of substances, especially alcohol, also has an influence on aggression between adolescents. Not only does alcohol lower inhibition, which might otherwise prevent both sexual and aggressive behavior, but it can also be used as a rationalization for the occurrence of the aggression.

In addition to sexual violence, teens are now more likely to physically abuse each other by slapping, pushing, and grabbing in relationships (Bethke and DeJay, 1993). Contrary to popular opinion, studies have shown that females are more likely than men to aggress against their partners, but less apt to cause severe harm when they do (Riggs, 1993). Female aggression was viewed less negatively, however, than that of their male counterparts (Bethke and DeJay, 1993). Acting out aggressively was often based on jealousy or the inability to successfully negotiate disagreements.

Why is there more violence in peer relationships? Some feel that because dating is an opportunity to rehearse later marital roles, the increase in domestic violence has an impact on the current rate of dating violence (Bethke and DeJay, 1993; Zastrow, 1996; Falchikov, 1996). In addition, the predisposition in this culture to use violence instead of negotiation is mirrored in intimate and peer relationships. Peer mediation in schools is one technique that appears to be having some impact on the incidence of peer violence (Zastrow, 1996).

THE HOME AS A WAR ZONE

Kadushin and Martin (1988) postulate that an estimated 50 million people annually in the United States will fall victim to violence perpetrated on them by another member of their family. In addition, in 20% or more of all child abuse cases, an adult is also abused. Although child abuse and neglect is covered extensively in Chapter 9, family violence cannot be avoided when discussing the violent society the United States has become. There are actually four types of abuse in families today: spouse abuse, child abuse, parent abuse, and elder abuse.

Spouse abuse has been tolerated for many years. The implications of this type of violence for not only the spouse, but the children as well, was most dramatically exemplified in the case of Nicole Brown Simpson and her well-known abusive husband and sports figure, O. J. Simpson. The 1994 trial of Simpson for the murder of his former wife brought to light the fact that battered wives often seek help on numerous occasions before the violence ceases or the wife is dead. Shelters for battered wives also report that women leave and return to their husbands numerous times before they are able to break the bond between them. Although men can also be battered, males as batterers tend to do more harm. Studies show that nearly 11% of males who batter their wives end up murdering them (Dutton, 1988; Zastrow, 1996).

Men batter their wives for a variety of reasons. Many share the stereotyped view of women as permissive individuals who should do their bidding. When the woman resists, the man cannot tolerate it. Most have poor self-images and having power over another enhances their own esteem. The cycle of violence is well-known. When a spouse batters, he usually escalates from verbal assaults, such as finding fault and name-calling, to actual physical aggression. Following the beating episode, he is usually guilty and contrite, often apologizing and "trying to make it up" to the victim. It is this inconsistency that causes many women to assume things will be better and remain in the relationship. In addition, battered women often come from backgrounds in which abuse was the norm. Violence in their marriages seems all too familiar to them. But, seemingly paradoxically, the familiar gives comfort. Women may also be financially dependent on their husbands. And, trained by society to be the peacemakers, women often strive for harmony rather than confront the impossibility of their situations (Dutton, 1988; Zastrow, 1996).

It is the effect, not only on the victim, but also on her children, that concerns child welfare experts. From watching their mothers battered children learn that this is an acceptable way to treat women (Falchikov, 1996). Some children identify with the aggressor, a less threatening stance than becoming a victim themselves. This may put them at risk to abuse when they later become involved in intimate relationships. This may also cause them to criticize the victim or even abuse her when they become older and stronger. Other children identify with the victim, feeling fearful, withdrawn, and depressed. Children from families fraught with domestic violence grow up to exhibit low self-esteem, depression, developmental delays, acute anxiety, rage, conduct disorders, chronic fear and rage, self-blame, heightened suicide risks, and are more prone to be violent toward others. These children learn poor boundaries and how to use deceptiveness, lying, and cheating as protection. These behaviors often spill over into their dealings with others, especially at school (Jaffee et al., 1990; Tower, 1996).

The Cordovas were typical of the family in which violence is the norm. Will Cordova, trained as a military police officer, expected that his family would respect him. With a history of violence in his own parents' home, Cordova had had no other model. Tess Cordova, his wife, had also grown up in an abusive household, but when Will showered her with attention between his bouts of anger and abuse, she came to believe that she had married a good man who, just occasionally, was "a bit demanding." The Cordova children, Matt, ten, and Belle, seven, cowered in the corner when their father began to shout and hit his wife. But soon Belle, always her father's pet, saw that siding with her father against his mother met with more approval from her powerful parent and earned her special attention. When Will was out of the house, Belle began to criticize Tess and eventually began to hit her as well. Matt, on the other hand, felt protective of his mother, but was too fearful to oppose his father. It was not until he was fifteen that Matt found the gun with which his father had threatened his mother and shot his father. Although Will was not seriously injured, the incident served to cause the family finally to seek help.

For a discussion of the *abuse of children,* see Chapter 9. Although obvious aggression toward children is easily labeled as child abuse, Graziano (1994) suggests that there is a phenomenon he calls "subabuse," which cannot be as readily characterized as abusive, but is nonetheless harmful. *Subabuse* includes acts of violence that do not reach the proportions of being categorized as abuse. These include various forms of corporeal punishment such as spanking, whipping, and hitting. He suggests that these seemingly acceptable forms of child-rearing may also convey to children that violence is condoned and cause them to replicate this behavior with their own children. Graziano urges researchers to continue to study the effects of subabusive behavior on children.

Parent abuse is also exemplified in the Cordova scenario. When children observe a parent being abused by another, they will often identify with the aggressor and adopt the battering behavior themselves. *Elder abuse* occurs when an adult child batters his/her elderly parent, grandparent, aunt, or other elder. For children this can also have an impact. When the child sees a weaker person being subjected to abuse, that child may either identify and feel threatened or take on the aggressive behavior as well. Even if a child adopts neither of these stances, witnessing the abuse of an elder can have a significant effect on the child's relations with the family or view of interpersonal relationships.

The home should be the child's haven of safety. When violence permeates the home environment, the effects on children cannot help but be significant.

CHILDREN AND SUBSTANCE ABUSE

Interwoven in the mosaic of violence are the statistics about the increase of substance use and abuse among not only adults but children and adolescents as well. The dimension of substance use and abuse as it affects children can be seen on two levels: the effects of addicted parents and addicted children.

ADDICTED PARENTS

In the United States today, substance abuse has become an alarming reality. When parents abuse drugs or alcohol the impact on their children is profound. There are over 28 million children whose parents are alcoholic (Rivinus, 1991). A significant number of parents have also used some form of illegal drug, and many are addicted (Glick and Moore, 1990). The use of drugs and alcohol can greatly diminish one's parenting ability. Substance abusing parents can neglect, emotionally and physically abuse, sexually abuse, and even abandon their children, not to mention presenting a model of someone who cannot control their own lives. The correlation between substance abuse and family violence is significant (Jaffe et al., 1990; Johnson, 1991). In addition, research on the children of alcoholics indicates that there is a biological risk for alcoholism passed from parents to children (Johnson, 1991). And, mothers addicted to both drugs and alcohol, may well pass the effects on to their newborns.

While addicted parents come from all socioeconomic levels, it is often the additional factor of poverty that brings them to the attention of child welfare agencies. Parents at higher income levels are often able to pay for outside child care when their addiction prohibits them from parenting adequately. How many prominent community figures have been stopped for driving under the influence but have not been referred to children's services for neglecting or endangering their children?

Fetal Alcohol Syndrome

Studies done on infants born to alcoholic mothers point to the possibility that alcohol abuse during pregnancy can leave the child with fetal alcohol syndrome (FAS) or fetal alcohol effects (FAE). FAS involves a variety of physical and psychological defects in children, including low intelligence or mental retardation, physical abnormalities (including characteristic facial features), hyperactivity, impaired development, and failure to accurately distinguish cause and effect (Johnson, 1991; Baer et al., 1993; Zastrow, 1996). These symptoms result from the fact that when a pregnant woman drinks, the alcohol crosses the placenta, creating in the fetus the blood alcohol levels present in the mother. FAS babies are also more likely to be born prematurely, have low-birth-weight and neurological defects and extreme irritability. The greater the amount of alcohol the pregnant woman drinks, the greater her chance of producing a baby with FAS. Studies indicate that five drinks or more at a given time produce a 10% chance that the baby will be FAS. Even an ounce per day can result in a 10% chance, while two ounces results in a 20% possibility and so on (Zastrow, 1996). The difficulty is not only in the effects on the infant but drinking alcohol may also affect the mother's ability to deal with her child.

Ellen drank heavily during her pregnancy. She and her live-in boyfriend, Greg, had been drinking partners before her pregnancy and her fear was that she would lose him if she did not go out drinking with him. Their relationship had been a fairly satisfying one until she became pregnant, but now Greg's annoyance about her getting pregnant was putting pressure on their interactions. Barbie was born prematurely and weighed only four pounds. She had "a funny little face" with her eyes far apart. Her first few weeks were spent in the neonatal intensive care unit with her anxious parents looking on. When they were not with her, however, they would drink to drown their fears and upset. Ellen had heard that she should not drink during pregnancy and she blamed Barbie's sickly first weeks on herself. When the infant finally did come home she was fussy and ate often. Ellen was exhausted and Greg soon grew tired of the routine. Barbie's poor muscle tone and constant crying sent Ellen to the clinic in tears. When the clinic diagnosed a heart defect, Ellen could not be consoled. She cried constantly and drank continuously. Greg left them and a neighbor, hearing the baby's cries and finding Ellen drunk and asleep as she had many times before, called the protective services agency.

For Ellen, the reality of her drinking manifested in Barbie's fetal alcohol syndrome greatly affected her ability to parent and made her want to drink more to escape her problems.

Fetal alcohol effects (FAE) are less dramatic symptoms and may indicate that the mother ingested less alcohol or that, for some reason, the child escaped the full effects of the alcohol (Baer et al., 1993).

Due to the high incidence of FAS and FAE, a federal law was passed in 1989 that mandated manufacturers to put warnings on the labels of alcohol products that they can adversely affect fetuses. Yet, the responsibility still remains in the hands of the mother to protect her unborn infant. This may change in the future, as some child welfare advocates, as well as lawmakers, feel that abusing substances, drugs as well as alcohol, during pregnancy should be considered a form of child abuse.

Effects of Parental Drug/Alcohol Addiction on Newborns and Infants

Recent statistics tell us that the number of babies exposed to crack or cocaine ranges from 30,000 to 158,000 each year. The number of marijuana-exposed infants is estimated to be more than 611,000. Over 43,500 newborns' mothers have used hallucinogens, 92,400 have used stimulants, and 38,300 sedatives. An estimated 2.6 million infants have been exposed to their mother's use of alcohol (Schmittroth, 1994). Although not all of the mothers using alcohol abused the substance, the effects of alcohol on the development of the human brain have been documented (Rivinus, 1990).

Drugs and alcohol not only affect children in utero, but can have a significant effect on the newborn infant. Nurses in neonatal facilities can describe the heart-wrenching experience of watching newborns go through withdrawal symptoms from the drugs or alcohol that were present in their first environment—their mother's body. The effects of such withdrawal are still being researched. There is evidence that some types of drugs leave long-term effects, while others exit the system within hours or days (Rivinus, 1991; Zastrow, 1996). For example, babies born to mothers who are addicted to crack cocaine experience significant effects at birth.

> *Cocaine causes the blood vessels in a pregnant woman to constrict, thus reducing the vital flow of oxygen and other nutrients to the fetus. Because fetal cells multiply swiftly in the first months, an embryo deprived of proper blood supply by the mother's early and continuous use of cocaine is likely to suffer an adverse cognitive impact. At birth such babies may look quite normal, but they are likely to be undersized, and the circumference of their heads tends to be unusually small—a trait associated with lower IQ scores. Only the most intensive care after birth will give these babies a fighting chance to have a 'normal' life (Zastrow, 1996, 247).*

So called "crack babies" can have a myriad of deformities from which they will never recover, and they require extensive treatment and a variety of services to survive.

Children whose parents are addicted to other narcotics may go through withdrawal soon after birth. Withdrawal symptoms often include chills, severe cramping, sweating, nervousness, vomiting, dilated pupils, respiratory problems, and muscle aches. Hallucinogens can cause genetic damage in children that, in the case of the female whose eggs for a lifetime are present at birth, may cause abnormalities for the next generation (Zastrow, 1996).

In addition to the chemical aspects of parental substance abuse, parents who abuse drugs or alcohol are less able to care for their infants. Children whose parents are chemically addicted may have difficulty bonding as the care they receive may be inconsistent. Their basic needs may not be met in infancy as their parents pursue their habit. As they grow older, they may become the caretakers for younger siblings and take on the role of *parentified child* (the child who meets adults' needs) (Rivinus, 1991).

At seven, Marcy became her mother's caretaker. Early in the morning, she would awaken to find that her mother had already given herself a shot of heroin and was drifting in her own world of fantasy. Marcy would bathe her, try to get her to eat, and prepare for her own day. She got herself off to school and got herself dinner in the evening with food that a neighbor brought in. Only rarely was her mother not "strung out." If she tried to "kick the habit," she would become very sick and Marcy would take care of her. It was the only life Marcy knew.

Marcy is not unlike many children of addicted parents. When Marcy's mother began to prostitute to support her habit, the child was exposed to a variety of men and sexual acts. It was not surprising that, at nine, she was sexually abused by one of her mother's johns.

Frustrations inherent in caring for babies can lead to further substance abuse, feeling overwhelmed, resenting the baby, abusing or neglecting the child, or withdrawing from the parenting experience altogether (Levoy et al., 1991). Nellis (1980) suggests that many young women are totally unprepared for motherhood. Especially if she comes from a substance-abusing family, she may have no healthy models of parenting to follow. Her hormone imbalance after childbirth may make her emotions volatile and the chemical effects of her abuse during pregnancy may create a fussy baby who further challenges her.

Addicted Parents and Preschool Children

Toddlers need to explore their world but have a safe place to which to return. Substance abusing parents may not be able to provide the consistency and nurturance that translates into a "safe harbor" for their toddlers. The child who is just about to enter school has already begun to engage in internal dialogues about his/her view of the environment and the ability to cope with it. Inconsistency and a parent who is out of control or constantly criticized by the other parent for his/her addicted behavior does not provide the safety or the modeling to help the young child develop the internal controls to cope with the environment. The child who has two drug/alcohol-addicted parents has even fewer resources with which to work. This ability to put his/her experiences into perspective becomes affected and his/her reality testing is impaired (Bepko, 1985; Levoy et al., 1991; Krestin and Bepko, 1993).

Addicted Parents and Older Children and Adolescents

A child whose reality testing is impaired will have difficulty accepting and abiding by rules, and will not have the skills necessary for learning. His/her peer relations may also be impaired. Being a parentified child is not uncommon, and it is likely that he/she will be diagnosed in school as learning disabled, hyperactive, acting out, or even having a borderline personality. Because domestic violence and child abuse and neglect are strongly correlated with substance abuse, the child may also carry the scars of these problems as well (see Chapter 9). Sleepiness in class may belie the fact that the child has had little sleep as he/she hears drunken parents fight or cringes in bed wondering when she/he will next be physically or sexually abused (Levoy, 1991; Tower, 1996).

For adolescence, a major developmental task is the consolidation of identity, which involves planning for the future and separating from the family of origin. It is difficult to complete these tasks effectively when besieged by the family problems brought on by substance abuse. The adolescent may also have developed survival skills that are not necessarily functional in other parts of his/her life (Bepko, 1985; Levoy et al., 1991).

Callie was the eternal caretaker. She had learned early in the home of two drug-addicted parents that to stay out of the way, unless one or the other parent needed something, was the best course of action. As her parents began to deteriorate, she took on more and more responsibility. It was actually due to her ability to cover up their addiction that the school and the protective agency did not recognize the full extent of the problem. In school, she was described as "bossy." "Callie is a real manipulator," said one teacher, "and she often antagonizes others by her need to be in control all the time. In addition, when the other children do something they should not, she is always there to 'clean up' after them. We used to think she just wanted so much to be helpful and liked but it seems like more than that. She really doesn't seem to care if she's liked. It just seems like a compulsion to do 'everything for everybody.'"

Practicing Alcoholic/Addicted Parent (PAAP) Syndrome

The children of addicted parents are seen in many social agencies for a variety of reasons. Jesse (1989) refers to these children as being victims of the Practicing Alcoholic/Addicted Parent Syndrome (PAAP). The alcoholism/addiction of their parents creates in them a wide number of symptoms, some physiological, some emotional, and some perceptual. Jesse (1989) summarizes these problems as: (1) perceptual (e.g., "tunes out" or doesn't hear information properly); (2) cognitive (e.g., gets distracted or doesn't remember well); (3) affective (e.g., flat affect or, conversely, overreaction); (4) motor (e.g., hyperactivity or coordination problems); (5) social (e.g., poor peer or sibling relationships); (6) motivational (e.g., apathetic or, conversely, driven or compulsive); (7) self-development/regulation (e.g., gets fragmented under stress, poor self-esteem, poor ability to care for self); (8) stress barrier (e.g., somatic complaints, sleep problems, tension, easily distracted, enuresis/encopresis) (150).

Children of Addicted Parents and the AIDS Epidemic

There are two ways in which children of chemically dependent parents are affected by the HIV/AIDS (human immunodeficiency virus) epidemic: as bystanders watching their parents who are victims of the disease and through contracting the disease either at birth or from an infected parent. Parents may have contracted the disease themselves either through intravenous drug use (from the small amount of blood left in shared needles) or sexual contact with someone who was infected. There are also a small group of people who developed the disease as a result of a transfusion in the early years when the testing of blood was not as yet perfected.

The virus known as AIDS was first brought to light in the early 1980s when it appeared to be affecting primarily homosexual men and intravenous drug users. Now the virus has become a household word and has affected millions of people. Estimates in 1994 are that 1 out of 250 people are infected with the virus and that about twenty thousand of these are children (Forsyth, 1995, 20). The epidemic appears to be increasing among ethnic minorities and women. Today AIDS is the leading cause of death among Hispanic and African American children (Anderson, 1990; Forsyth, 1995). A study of women giving birth in New York City found that one in one hundred and fifty was infected with the virus. There is a possibility that these women passed the infection to their babies (McCarroll, 1988; Forsyth, 1995; Gabelle et al., 1995). In addition, parents who are HIV positive have the potential for passing the disease on to their offspring when they do not protect against transmission. The disease is spread through the sharing of blood from one person to another as well as through sexual contact. Although most parents do not have sexual contact with their children (except in the case of sexual abuse), they may come in contact with their children's blood and vice versa. Breast milk is also thought to transmit the virus (Anderson, 1990; Oleske, 1990; Forsyth, 1995). Unlike adults, for whom the onset of AIDS can take time, children tend to develop symptoms very quickly. Of children exposed at birth, 70% will develop symptoms by about one year and 17% of those will die within the first year (Forsyth, 1995, 26).

Contracting the AIDS virus in utero means that the infection in the mother's system has crossed the placenta. The virus attacks the white blood cells in the baby's system and impedes the development of the baby's immune system. The immune system is activated by what are called T cells or sometimes "helper cells." These vital cells impede the reproduction of unhealthy cells that might harm the body. The AIDS virus attacks the T cells to give itself an opportunity to reproduce. Once weakened, the T cells are incapable of doing their work and the AIDS cells become stronger. When babies are born, they first have B cells, small cells that are present for only the first few days of birth. When the AIDS virus attacks the B cells, the immune system is weakened. When, several days after birth, the T cells begin to develop, they may already be impeded in their strength and growth. The baby may then be said to be HIV positive when tests for AIDS come up positive. It is possible for some babies' immune systems to recover, however, and the baby who is diagnosed positive at birth, later has shaken off the virus. For other babies, the damage has been done, and they often die within the first year. Death is not actually from AIDS, but rather from other infections that take hold as a result of an inefficient or inactive immune system. For example, PCP (or pneumocystis carinii pneumonia) is a frequent killer of individuals with AIDS (McCarroll, 1988).

Contracting AIDS in childhood is less likely but certainly possible. There are an increasing number of children who contract the virus because they were sexually abused by someone with AIDS.

Effects in Later Life of Having a Substance-Abusing Parent

Some children of addicted parents are not strangers to sexual and physical abuse, violence, and being used to carry or buy drugs or alcohol. Many of these develop a variety of survival strategies that protect them against a world that has not treated them kindly. They may hoard, lie, steal, and physically assault others as they imitate what they have seen. Seeing their parent's addicted behavior, they may decide to try drugs or alcohol for themselves. Others react in the opposite way and become almost phobic about not using substances. Many carry the scars of their parents' addictions into later life.

Seixas and Youcha (1985) talk about the "hangovers from childhood" and identify them as: the need to control, denial of feelings, the lack of trust, guilt, fears or difficulty with intimacy, depression or sadness, "black and white" thinking, an excessive need to please, and an exaggerated sense of responsibility (47ff). These traits may cause the adult children of substance abusing parents (ACOSAP) to have problems in their intimate relationships, difficulty finding, keeping or enjoying a job, and regulating their lives in general. It is not uncommon for ACOSAPs to turn to chemical dependency as a way of escaping or coping with their feelings of inadequacy or lack of control. In addition, there is much research to suggest that the chemical predisposition adds to the emotional need to become drug dependent (Seixas and Youcha, 1985; Rivinus, 1991; Levoy et al., 1991; Baer et al., 1993; Zastrow, 1996).

ADDICTED CHILDREN AND ADOLESCENTS

According to the U. S. Substance Abuse and Mental Health Services Administration's statistics of 1994 (as cited in Schmittroth, 1994), 18% of all children between the ages of twelve and seventeen were using alcohol, 4.9% were using marijuana, and 1.4% were using some type of inhalant. Less than 1% were involved with such drugs as cocaine, hallucinogens, stimulants, or sedatives (142). Of these users, males were slightly more likely to use substances and white youths were more apt than African American or Hispanic youths to drink alcohol, while African American youths had a higher incidence of drug use (143). Glick and Moore (1990) and Kandal (1995) , on the other hand, felt that the statistics for Hispanic youths (between twelve and seventeen) using crack and cocaine was higher than the incidence of white and African American teens (4.6% Hispanics using cocaine and 1.3% using crack compared to 3.6% and .9% whites and 2.1% and .9% African Americans respectively) (23). While these statistics apply to adolescents, the rates of drug and alcohol use among younger children is usually only anecdotal. Yet teens or adults who drink or use drugs often report beginning at a very early age.

Dominic began drinking alcohol when he was eight. "My friend's old man used to buy us six packs," he reports. "He thought it was a riot to see us get wasted [drunk]. We used to try and hold it just to get at him. Then over the years we could drink a lot more." His drug habit began soon after. A neighbor offered him a bag of marijuana and later got him hooked on cocaine so he could "study better." By fifteen, Dominic had a serious drug and alcohol problem.

While some children become addicted to drugs at birth, as a result of their mother's addiction, many become addicted later as children. Johnson (1992) found that 12.3% of children began their alcohol use as early as the fourth grade, 8.95% in the fifth, 15.5% in the sixth, 20.2% in the seventh, and 12.4% in the eighth grade. The seventh grade saw the highest incidence in the beginning of marijuana, cocaine, and hallucinogen use than any other grade (134). It is also clear from studies that many children do not perceive that the use of drugs or alcohol will be addictive or harmful to them. For example, only 58% of Johnson's sample felt that having two to five drinks per weekend would put them at risk for becoming alcohol-dependent (176).

What causes children and adolescents to become chemically dependent? Rhodes and Jason (1988), in speaking of young children, cite social isolation as a factor that can predispose them to addiction to substances. These authors also suggest that poor self-concept may lead both young and older children to find compensation through drugs. Certainly, these factors also play a role in the substance abuse of adolescents, but there are other important factors as well.

For adolescents, a number of developmental tasks as well as societal influences affect their likelihood of becoming dependent on drugs or alcohol. Developmentally, teens are going through a great many changes. The peer group becomes increasingly important as adolescents strive for autonomy from authority figures. Thus *they rebel against the attitudes of their elders,* paradoxically mirroring the behavior they may have observed.

Jan's parents were both alcoholics during her younger years. When she was six her father was laid off and forced to attend an alcohol rehabilitation program before he could be reinstated. He began to attend AA and put pressure on his wife to become sober. Finally, when Jan was nine, her mother too started her recovery. During the early part of her teens, Jan watched both her parents conscientiously attend AA meetings and work hard at their sobriety. This effort was combined with their lectures to their daughter about the evils of drink and how she should never drink lest she become addicted. Jan promised that she would not drink, but was constantly frustrated by the taunts of her peers. She convinced herself that a few smokes of pot would feel good and would not betray her promise to her parents. But the more they nagged against drinking, the more involved she became in drugs, first pot and later cocaine. By seventeen, Jan was as addicted to drugs as her mother had been alcohol-dependent at that age.

Even teens whose parents do not themselves have a substance abuse problem may find themselves becoming involved with substances as a way of asserting their independence.

"I knew my parents didn't want me drinking" reported Ernie, "but it made me feel like a big deal...like an adult. By the time I realized what was happening, I was throwing up like the drunk on the street corner. Real adult, huh?"

One thing that adds to teen's perception that using substances makes them more important is *the influence of the media.* The prominent message on television and in the movies is that substances are fun and give one a macho or powerful appearance. Even the efforts made by drug prevention programs do not serve to obliterate these strong subliminal messages (Towers, 1987; Rhodes and Jason, 1988; Gullotta et al., 1994).

Adolescents are also *influenced by their peers,* many of whom use substances. Some studies conclude that teens actually select their peers depending on the amount of drug use they find comfortable (Rhodes and Jason, 1988; Muisener, 1994). Preoccupation with acceptance by others is paramount in the teen years and if one's peers choose to do drugs, the other teens feel compelled to go along (Towers, 1987; Botvin et al., 1995). For some, their peer group is the gang and the gang may be involved in taking or selling drugs (Glick and Moore, 1990; Botvin et al., 1995).

Drugs and alcohol also become *antidotes for the pain and stress of growing up.* Minority children who face discrimination on a daily basis, the children of the poor and children from dysfunctional homes, soon learn that a "high" is more pleasurable than dealing with the realities of their lives. Besides major life crises, all manner of issues can be stressful for the vulnerable adolescent, from failing a test in school, being shunned by a member of the opposite sex, moving to a new town or school, to having one's parents go back to work (Towers, 1987).

And finally, many adolescents are *attracted to the thrill and risk* of taking drugs. For those under the legal drinking age, alcohol is illegal. And illegal drugs, especially marijuana, cocaine, crack, and hallucinogens, are the substances most likely used by youths. With all these chemicals, there is a risk to getting them, possessing them, and sharing them. There may also be a profit motive if the teen sells them to others.

At nine, Sean started taking one beer at a time out of his father's supply. This he would sell to a teen down the street. He experimented with taking two and drinking one himself. When a friend asked to share with him, Sean suggested that he would sell half the can for twenty-five cents. As he grew older, his friends were able to get alcohol themselves and his trade lost its appeal. When a local drug dealer suggested to thirteen-year-old Sean that he sell bags of drugs, the boy agreed. By this time, it felt good to have his own money. He reasoned that the market for his product had dried up so he needed another product.

Society's emphasis on chemicals is obvious: There are television ads for every type of substance to heal or alleviate every type of condition. From this teens learn that substances can have a miraculous effect. This, combined with the culture's need for the "quick fix" and the emphasis on power and control, conveys the message that if substances help in these areas, they are well worth the risks (Resnik, 1990).

EFFECTS AND TREATMENT OF ADOLESCENT DRUG ABUSE

Adolescents who are chemically dependent are usually experiencing problems in many aspects of their lives. Brown (1993) suggests that the problems occur in the following areas: attendance and discipline problems in school; withdrawal and conflict from the family; fights or withdrawal from the peer group; stealing, absenteeism, decreased participation in work-related activities; and anxiety, injury, accidents, or suicidal ideation that affect their health (165). As the adolescent's addiction progresses, a variety of factors influence the addiction pattern and therefore the type of treatment that will be most effective. Influencing factors are such environmental variables as drug availability, drug cost, and the models (other teens or adults) who also use drugs/alcohol. In addition, the teen's own personality characteristics, such as family history, and the youth's personal traits and developmental issues will also be important (Brown, 1993).

Less attention has been paid to the definition of types of treatment needed for adolescents than has been given to assessing and documenting the problem of adolescent substance abuse. Part of this problem is related to the fact that there has been little differentiation between the treatment needs of adolescents versus adults when adolescents are at a significantly different developmental level or levels (Rickel and Becker–Lausen, 1994). Treating adolescent abuse also involves telling parents that their son or daughter has a problem, a fact that many parents prefer not to face.

Towers (1987) cites three types of treatments used with adolescents: (1) drug-free; (2) detoxification; (3) maintenance. Drug-free treatment refers to counseling the teen, without the use of medications. This is often used when the addiction is not so far advanced that the individual is unable to abstain him/herself. When the dependence has reached the point of chemical addiction, detoxification may be necessary. Detoxification is often undertaken in the same units that house adults. Increasingly, however, there is a recognition of the need for specialized services due to the inexperience of teen substance abusers. Maintenance refers to the use of some type of medication, such as methadone, and is usually employed only with long-term addicts.

Due to the recognition of the increased problem with adolescent substance addiction, treatment programs designed specifically for this population have increased in the last few years. Some are conducted on an outpatient basis and others require a stay in an inpatient type of setting. Self-help groups such as Alcoholics Anonymous are expanding their programs to adolescent services. And, although there is a need for continued work in this area, schools are becoming increasingly sensitive to their roles in helping to identify adolescent abusers and facilitate referral for treatment (Rickel and Becker–Lausen, 1994).

Whether the substance abuse problem is with the parent or with the child or adolescent him/herself, the issues are significant. Much additional research and attention will be needed in the years to come to combat the problems in this area.

HOMELESS FAMILIES

It is not surprising that the issue of homelessness would be housed in a chapter dealing with violence and substance abuse. Both affect homelessness just as homelessness influences the use of substances and violence. Of the total homeless population, a study published by the Massachusetts Institute of Technology estimated that, by the year 2003, 18 million Americans will be unable to find housing (Brown, 1994). While in 1980 the number of children who were homeless was relatively small, the fastest growing population of the homeless today is women and children.

It is difficult to actually count the homeless due to the transience of the life, but a 1989 study estimated that there were about 25,522 homeless children in urban shelters, 4,094 at churches, and 9,016 in public places. In suburban areas the number of homeless children had reached 14,427 and in rural areas it was 7,357. There was another population, sometimes referred to as the "marginally homeless," who were doubled up with other families and who would probably soon be out of these settings. These children numbered 185,512 (U.S. Government Accounting Office, 1989, 2).

Perhaps these statistics necessitate an explanation of the definition of homelessness. Although many think of the homeless as those who literally live on the streets, this is often not the case for families. Homeless families spend their time living with friends or relatives (marginally homeless), and in shelters and welfare hotels (hotels or apartments designed to house people for short periods while they find other accommodations). There are also some families who actually do live "on the streets" by moving from alleys to deserted buildings to other areas where they can find a place to sleep. Individual homeless teens are more likely to live either with friends or wherever they can find shelter (Tower and White, 1989).

THE CAUSES OF HOMELESSNESS

Much speculation has been focused on why the homeless problem is worse now than in years past. One possible explanation has to do with the complexity of life today. Families are faced with greater risk of poverty as well as such issues as limited housing and unemployment. Morse (1992) cites several causal factors for homelessness among families. First, the current economy places numerous families below the poverty level and constantly at risk for becoming homeless. In addition, housing has become a significant problem. Gentrification and condominium conversion mean that there is less low to moderate income housing. And the economic constraints on families mean that many families would be unable to pay for housing if they could find it.

Some families become homeless due to the substance abuse or mental illness of parental figures. When a parent is supporting a significant drug habit, there is often little money available for rent. And for some, homelessness has been passed down from a previous generation that never found roots.

HOMELESS FAMILIES AND CHILDREN

The plight of the homeless child and his/her family was exemplified dramatically when David Bright, an articulate ten-year-old, testified before the House Select Committee on Hunger in 1986. David and his family were residents of the Martinique Hotel (New York City) which, at that time, housed 1,500 homeless children and their families. David's account of the conditions at the Martinique, with its dark hallways and drug dealers, and of the families who chose between paying their rent or buying food, proved an emotional experience for the gathered lawmakers (Brown, 1994). The plight of the Martinique families was later chronicled in Jonathan Kozol's *Rachel and Her Children*, an exposé of the experiences of today's homeless families. Kozol (1988) estimated that, in New York City alone, there were 18,000 homeless parents and children in 5,000 families (4). Kozol also cited the Pitts Hotel in Washington, D.C., where 500 families nightly endured deplorable conditions and inadequate facilities because they had nowhere else to stay (90).

In addition to welfare hotels, there are several other arrangements for homeless families: congregate shelters without rooms for each family, shelters offering rooms for each family but with congregate bath and kitchen facilities, and shelters offering private apartments (Blau, 1992).

In a study done on homeless families in New York City, Blau (1992) reports that 44% of the families using emergency housing had never been (for more than a year) the primary tenants in any place that they lived. Instead they had spent their time moving from the home of one relative or friend to another until they ran out of options. In fact, of those in the emergency shelters surveyed, 71% had spent the evening before in the home of a friend or relative. These families were more likely to be African American (54%) and the parents under twenty-five years old (44%) (158). The most significant correlation with homelessness according to Blau (1992) was the variable of pregnancy. Twenty-five percent of those looking for shelter were pregnant mothers (158).

The ethnic composition of the homeless family population may well depend on the geographic area. For example, in contrast to the New York statistics, a Stanford University study found that in California, 36% of the 809 homeless families studied were Hispanics of Mexican heritage, 25% were African American, and 29% were non-Hispanics. Over half of these families were headed by single parents (Seltser and Miller, 1993).

McChesney (1992) divides homeless families into four categories: (1) unemployed couples; (2) mothers leaving relationships; (3) mothers on Aid to Families with Dependent Children; and (4) mothers who were homeless as adolescents (246). *Unemployed couples* have often found that their homelessness is a new issue. The spouses are often conservative and traditional and believe that it is the husband's role to support his family. Both partners often have minimal skills.

The Winstons were both thirty years old and had four children. Bob Winston had been employed by a large factory that had "downsized," laying off over 50% of its employees, including Bob. Gloria had not been employed since the children were born and had always expected that Bob would support her. She had never finished high school and was severely dyslexic, making it difficult for her to read or write. When Bob lost his job, the couple quickly found that they were unable to keep their apartment. Although Gloria tried to work as a waitress, her poor reading and writing skills made it difficult for her to decipher menus and take orders; after two days, she was fired. This so damaged her already poor self-concept, that she adamantly refused to try to get another job. Bob, too, had difficulties. He was a recovering alcoholic who had managed to stay sober for ten years. Now his lack of a high school education gave him few opportunities to find work and he began to drink once more. Thus, Gloria found herself, sometimes with Bob and sometimes without (when he was on a binge), moving from one shelter to another. For a time they stayed in a welfare hotel. Because they had no permanent address, they could not apply for welfare even if Bob, always a proud man, had agreed to it. For a time they stayed with Bob's brother and his family with six children. But the tensions of two families and ten children caused the brother's wife to terminate this arrangement.

It is not uncommon for parents in this group to have little education and inadequate job skills. When they lose their employment, they find that they have few options.

Mothers leaving relationships may or may not have been married to their partners. Some leave because they are battered; others leave because the relationship has broken down. Most of these women have depended on their male partner to support them and now they, with their children, find themselves without support or a place to stay. These mothers have usually worked prior to the birth of their first child but became full-time parents after that.

Frankie had lived with George for six years during which time they had had two children together, Yari, age six and Freda, age four. From the time that the couple moved in together, George had begun to beat Frankie. At first the beatings occurred only every six months or so. After such violence, George was very contrite and assured Frankie that he would never do it again. But over the years the beatings increased in both frequency and severity. Frankie left George to stay with friends but always returned when he found her and apologized. But when Yari accidentally stepped in front of a blow meant for her, Frankie took her children and vowed that she had left for good. Having exhausted the goodwill of friends and having no idea where else to go, Frankie and the children went from shelter to shelter.

Mothers on AFDC (Aid to Families with Dependent Children [now called Transitional Assistance]) depend on their welfare payments for their financial support. McChesney (1992) and Bassuk (1992) characterize these women as having less than a high school education and as being long-term recipients of financial aid. They move from crisis to crisis, often becoming homeless as a result of not being able or willing to pay their monthly rent. Eviction then leaves them without housing.

Angie's family had been on AFDC while she was growing up. A victim of sexual abuse by her uncle and her mother's constant criticism, Angie found solace with Paul at the age of sixteen. She was soon pregnant and she and Paul moved in together. But before the baby was born Paul was gone and she saw no recourse but to apply for AFDC herself. Ten years later, at twenty-six, Angie was still on welfare. With two more children she found that her benefits could not cover her expenses. She did not pay her rent for several months, hoping that she could get caught up. In the meantime, her landlord evicted her. After begging to return to her mother's to no avail, and spending several nights in various shelters, Angie took her three children to the welfare office and begged that they find her housing.

Some mothers were homeless as teenagers and know little of life that does not include homelessness. According to McChesney (1992) these moms tended to be younger and have only one child. They had usually had severely abusive backgrounds and may have lived on the street for a period as youths. Some had tried to subsist through prostitution. Now, as parents, they found that there was more involved than just looking out for themselves.

Kay was a victim of severe physical and sexual abuse while she was growing up. Her father beat her, then raped her, and then beat her again. Her mother, also a victim of similar abuse, left him on numerous occasions. When she did, she and the children moved from shelter to shelter until they once more returned to him. At fifteen, Kay ran away and lived with several other teens on the streets for several months. When one of the girls started earning money prostituting herself, Kay saw this as a way of eating regularly without stealing and approached the pimp for whom her friend worked. The pimp readily took in the attractive girl and for several more months, she worked for him. But when he began to beat her, Kay decided she had had enough. She took the money from her last john and hopped a bus to a distant city. There she once again lived on the streets until she met a man who took her in. She thought she had found someone who cared for her and when, three days after her seventeenth birthday, she realized that she was pregnant, Kay enthusiastically told him. His response was to hit her hard in the stomach; the blow sent her to a local hospital. She did not lose the baby as he had intended, but was placed in a home for unwed and parenting teens. Kay remained here until her baby was nine months old. Then she ran away and spent the next months going from shelter to shelter.

McChesney (1992) concludes that all four types of families shared poverty that led to residential instability. The duration of their homelessness depended on variables such as age, job skills, number of children, and personal resourcefulness. Bassuk (1992) adds that the families of origin of homeless families were characterized by disruption and dysfunction. In 12% of the cases of Bassuk's sample there was mental illness in the family of origin, death of a parent in 20% of the situations, divorce in 49%, and over 33% reported being physically abused (259). Seltser and Miller (1993) chronicle many stories that exemplify these statistics in their discussion of the homeless families of Los Angeles.

THE EFFECT OF HOMELESSNESS ON CHILDREN

What are the implications for children of being part of a homeless family? Tower and White (1989) suggested that the children of the homeless *feel hopeless and out of control of their lives.* They may become *preoccupied with worry,* often to the point of *developing physical symptoms.*

Timothy was an extremely nervous child, reported the staff of the shelter. Each time his family returned to the facility, he looked more tired but was more anxious and active. He developed a skin condition that he scratched until it became raw. He would often pick at the sores until they bled. He chewed his nails until there was nothing left. It was not long before the shelter staff became quite concerned about his health.

Children who endure homelessness often *learn survival skills that are not beneficial in other settings.* For example, Dean became an expert at finding and hoarding bits of food when he and his parents were on the streets. But when he began to exhibit this type of behavior in school, the teachers sent him to the principal.

Homeless children may also *feel that they must take care of their parents.* In reality, they may have developed better survival skills than the adults who are supposed to care for them. Tower and White (1989) describe just such a child and his parent.

Jane Hart was suffering from acute hypothermia and pneumonia when she was brought to the emergency room of the local hospital by a neighborhood worker and the police. The police were called more to restrain eleven-year-old Darren than to help the medics with his mother. Residents of a dumpster, mother and son had been homeless for several months. When Jane became ill, Darren had cared for her, bringing food he found in trash cans. When the weather became cold, he scavenged for rags and newspapers to cover them. Finally Darren stole a blanket. The store owner who observed the theft notified a local service center. "I thought that a kid who would steal a blanket must really need it. Most kids would steal something they could sell," the storekeeper told an outreach worker. From the merchant's description, the worker found Darren and his ailing mother. So fiercely protective was the boy of his parent that police were summoned to help (19).

A life of moving from place to place and of poverty means that most children are *poorly nourished* and may have *poor hygiene* as well. Dietary limitations can create a child who is *listless and withdrawn* or, conversely, this lifestyle of inconsistency and poor diet can give rise to *hyperactivity* and *hostile behavior* (Tower and White, 1989; Solarz, 1992). Bassuk (1992) also found that most homeless children did poorly when they did attend school with 43% repeating a grade and over 25% in special classes. One significant problem for schools dealing with homeless families is the unavailability of records from previous schools. By the time the records can be secured, the family has often moved on. This leads to inconsistency and impedes the children's education. It is also common for homeless children to have unattended medical or dental needs (Tower and White, 1989).

HOMELESS AND RUNAWAY YOUTHS

It is not only families who become homeless. Each year, numbers of children and adolescents run away or become homeless. Estimates range from 250,000 to one million annually (Robertson, 1992). Some, motivated by years of abuse and severe family dysfunction, choose to run away rather than continue to cope with their home life. Clary et al. (1992) report that 44% of the Portland youths they studied had had five or more previous runaway episodes. Of these, 66% admitted to family conflict at home; 37% were abused by a parent figure; 31% were victims of neglect; 28% reported family mental health problems; and 33% were believed to be sexually abused at home (381). Runaways may be without a home for days, weeks, or even years. In addition to those who run away, some children are "pushed out" (often referred to as "pushouts" or "throwaways") when their relationship with their parents becomes too conflictual. Rothman (1991) found that 46% of those in his sample were pushed out or asked by parents to leave. Although most agree that it is family issues that cause youths to run away, theorists (Robertson, 1992) propose that there are several types of homeless youths. The first is not unlike the adult mentally ill homeless. Such adolescents have psychiatric issues that make it difficult for them to function in a home environment.

Beaver was diagnosed as manic depressive early in his adolescence. Removed from a severely neglectful home when he was young, Beaver had resided in ten foster homes and a residential setting. When he was manic, he antagonized his caretakers. Then he would become depressed and on several occassions attempted suicide. Refusing to take his medication, Beaver finally became angry and ran away from his last foster home when he was sixteen. He lived on the streets with a group of alcoholic men for several months until the police picked the group up one night. When they learned how old he was, the police referred him to the Department of Children and Youth Services. Refusing to go back to a foster home or take medication, Beaver once again ran away.

Because adolescence is a time when people are attempting to sort out issues of autonomy, another type of adolescent needs to make an abrupt break from what may not have been a totally dysfunctional family.

Gwen felt totally controlled by somewhat overprotective parents. She was their only child and they both feared her leaving them. So they held on tightly, refusing to allow her the freedom enjoyed by her peers. Gwen found this stifling and finally ran to a friend's house intending to stay there until she could get a bus ticket. The friend's parents called Gwen's parents and Gwen took off. She bought a bus ticket and prepared to leave the city. But the bus was delayed and she ended up sleeping in the bus station. She considered calling home, but did not. The next day she took the bus to another city, but her experiences there were no better. After a week away, she returned home to her frantic parents.

Some youths are influenced by their peer groups. They may not have the courage to run away themselves, but when encouraged to do so with a group of friends, they agree.

Reena's boyfriend and two of her other friends urged her to go for a ride with them. Once out they told her that they had all "had it at home" and planned to take the car and "take off." Reena was hesitant, but remembering her frustration at always having to give up her plans to take care of her younger siblings while a drunken mother slept on the couch, she agreed to go. The group had a quantity of pot that they shared. For several days they slept under a bridge by the river, smoking pot and enjoying their freedom. When the police picked them up and returned them home, pending their hearings on possession of drugs, Reena's mother was furious. She threw her clothes at her, called her a "worthless tramp," and told her never to come home again.

CHANGING VIEW OF RUNAWAY AND HOMELESS YOUTHS

Since early in our country's history, youths who ran from their homes were frowned on, without giving much consideration to whether or not they had cause. Reform schools, the first of which began in Massachusetts in 1847, were filled with youths whose only "crime" was that they ran away. The juvenile court, first established in Chicago in 1899, saw numerous children and adolescents who were brought in for running from their homes. But in the 1950s and 1960s, child welfare advocates began to talk about how runaways were not like delinquent offenders and should not be subjected to the same punishments. In 1963, the New York Family Court Act established a new category for runaways, designating them as "in need of service." Further, this act acknowledged not only that these youths may have run for a reason, but that the only reason why they were coming before the court was due to their status as a minor. By 1974 the Federal Juvenile Justice and Delinquency Prevention Act was passed, which decriminalized "status offenses" as applied to runaways, as well as truants and children whose parents found them difficult to handle (Rothman, 1991). In 1980, a Youth Development Bureau study identified several categories of runaway and homeless youth: *runaways,* who leave home without parental permission; *push-outs,* who leave home with parental encouragement; *throwaways,* who leave with parental approval and often pressure; and *noncrisis youth,* who are living in a problematic situation but not intending to leave. The study also identified 42% of the sample to be runaways, 28% push-outs and throwaways, and 20% noncrisis youths. The majority of the youths studied were white (72%) with 16% African American and 6% Hispanic (Rothman, 1991, 20).

Today, experts indicate that there are significant changes in the types of youths they are seeing. Runaway and homeless youths in the 1990s tend to be younger, more representative of minorities, more emotionally disturbed, from more dysfunctional families, and more likely to have been abused or neglected (Rothman, 1991).

PROBLEMS AND SOLUTIONS FOR THE RUNAWAY/HOMELESS YOUTH

Conditions for the runaway or homeless youth are not ideal. More of these youths report ailments such as sexually transmitted diseases, drug and alcohol dependence, malnourishment, and other significant health problems. In a California study, 52% of the sample were drug-abusing, 51% abused alcohol, 42% had psychiatric problems, 25% had significant health problems, and 9% were pregnant (Rothman, 1991, 77). Interestingly enough, the highest percentage of a Los Angeles sample (86%) were seeking job training and placement as a solution to their problem of being homeless (80). This might indicate that running away for many youths is the only response they know to an impossible situation. It may also be a transitional step between living at home and attempting to become a functional adult.

Meeting the needs of homeless youths may require a variety of creative innovations. Petry and Avent (1992) report on a one hundred bed rehabilitation center in Los Angeles that is dedicated to helping homeless youths. Stepping Stone, which has been operating for close to a decade, sees more than 1,250 youths between seven and seventeen years old (the majority are between fifteen to seventeen years old) each year. Of these, about 44% report family violence as the cause for their coming to the program. Over 50% of these youths have already dropped out of school, while an estimated 90% are "bright" and capable of schoolwork (300). The youths stay for fourteen days, during which they receive counseling, life skills training, and attempted family reunification services. Approximately 94% of the residents have eventually been reunited with their families.

In addition to such shelters, which unfortunately are not numerous enough, various social service agencies offer such resources as food, clothing and shelter, counseling, family counseling, health services, substance abuse services, and vocational services.

Homelessness, whether it affects families or youths, continues to be a significant problem in our culture today. Many feel that the solution lies not only in alleviating the societal problems (e.g., housing, unemployment, and so on) that cause homelessness, but also in strengthening families so that children do not find it necessary to leave home and become homeless.

SUMMARY

Daily, we are reminded of the problems that face our children and youth today. Three of the most obvious problems are violence, substance abuse, and homelessness.

Increasingly, children are exposed to violence on the streets and in their homes. Some feel that the media and the violence in sporting activities play a large role in both desensitizing and normalizing violent behavior. One manifestation of violence, gangs, has become a significant problem today. Some experts break gangs into four categories: criminal gangs that are involved with criminal activities; conflict gangs, dedicated to protecting their territory; retreatist gangs, the members of which "retreat" to do drugs; and cult gangs, which are involved in cultist activities. Gangs offer youths a sense of belonging, a feeling of purpose, and often the thrill of risk-taking.

Relationships too have become violent for many teens. These abusive relationships often carry over into the home environment, creating men who physically and sexually abuse wives. This battering, in turn, has an effect on the children by making them fearful and guilty as well as causing them to repeat the cycle of abuse.

Children are affected by substance abuse in two ways: when they watch their parents abuse substances and when the children themselves become substance abusers. Children whose parents abuse alcohol or drugs may suffer physiological symptoms such as Fetal Alcohol Syndrome or Fetal Alcohol Effects or from withdrawal at birth from some kind of drug. These chemicals can leave children with permanent impairments. In addition, children whose parents are chemically dependent are affected psychologically and may end up becoming caretakers of both their addicted parents and younger siblings and having later psychological scars. Some children also contract the HIV virus from substance-abusing parents.

Chemically dependent children are often attempting to cope with lives that are less that satisfying. Still others become addicted as a result of peer influences. The thrill of a "quick fix," often perpetrated by the media, is another allure of drug-taking. For these youths, there are often limited treatment resources, although the number of such services appears to be increasing.

Homelessness, often interrelated with substance abuse and violence, is a phenomenon that affects many families today. In fact, families are the fastest growing homeless population. Families may be homeless because of unemployment, because a mother and her children are leaving an abusive relationship, because a parent is on aid and cannot afford to keep housing, or because the parent(s) have been homeless in adolescence and have difficulty finding another way of life. Homelessness affects the children by making them feel hopeless and powerless, causing them to care for their parents and affecting their health, both physical and emotional.

Youths may also become homeless by either running away from home, often as a result of severe family dysfunction, or by being encouraged to leave by their parents. Young people are more likely to spend time on the streets than are families. They may also spend time with friends or in shelters. There are a minimum of programs for homeless youth and this is an area where more work needs to be done.

EXPLORATION QUESTIONS

1. What factors influence the amount of violence among youths today?
2. What are the four types of gangs and what are their functions?
3. Why are more Asian youths becoming involved in gangs?
4. Why is there more violence in peer relationships today?
5. How does abuse in the home affect children?
6. What is Fetal Alcohol Syndrome? What causes it and what are its effects?
7. How does parental substance abuse affect children at different ages?
8. How might children contract AIDS?
9. What causes children to become chemically dependent? What types of problems does it cause for them?
10. What causes homelessness?
11. Why do families become homeless? What is meant by the term "marginally homeless"?
12. What effects does homelessness have on children?
13. Why do youths become homeless?

ACTIVITIES FOR APPLIED LEARNING

1. What are the statistics on youth violence in your community? If your community is a small one, research the statistics for the nearest city. What programs within the community or the school serve to combat violence among youths? Are these programs successful?

2. What services are available for chemically dependent individuals in your community? Are any of these directed toward parents? Are there any programs for youths? What can be done to prevent substance abuse among young people?

3. What agencies deal with homeless families and children in your community? Ask a representative from an agency or create a panel of staff from several agencies to speak before the class about homelessness and solutions to the homeless problem.

SUGGESTED READING

Anderson, G. (Ed.). *Courage to Care: Responding to the Crisis of Children with AIDS.* Washington, DC: Child Welfare League of America, 1990.

Baer, J. S., Marlatt, G. A., & McMahon, R. J. (Eds.). *Addictive Behaviors across the Lifespan: Prevention, Treatment and Policy Issues.* Newbury Park, CA: Sage, 1993.

Botvin, G. J., Schinke, S., & Orlandi, M. A. (Eds.). *Drug Prevention with Multiethnic Youth.* Thousand Oaks, CA: Sage, 1995.

Carlson, B. E. "Dating Violence: Student Beliefs about Consequences," *Journal of Interpersonal Violence* 11(1), 1996, 3–18.

Children's Defense Fund. *The State of America's Children Yearbook 1996.* Washington, DC: Children's Defense Fund, 1996.

Geballe, S., Gruedel, J., & Andiman, W. (Eds.). *Forgotten Children of the AIDS Epidemic.* New Haven: Yale University Press, 1995.

Gullota, T. P., Adams, G. R., & Montemayor, R. (Eds.). *Substance Misuse in Adolescence.* Thousand Oaks, CA: Sage, 1994.

Hoffman, A. M. (Ed.). *Schools, Violence and Society.* Westport, CT: Praeger, 1996.

Jencks, C. *The Homeless.* Cambridge, MA: Harvard University Press, 1994.

Kinnear, K. L. *Violent Children.* Santa Barbara, CA: ABC-CLIO, 1995.

Kotlowitz, A. *There Are No Children Here.* New York: Doubleday, 1991.

Kozol, J. *Rachel and Her Children.* New York: Crown, 1988.

Muisener, P. P. *Understanding and Treating Adolescent Substance Abuse.* Thousand Oaks, CA: Sage, 1994.

Rivinus, T. M. (Ed.). *Children of Chemically Dependent Parents.* New York: Brunner/Mazel, 1991.

Rothman, J. *Runaway and Homeless Youth.* New York: Longman, 1991.

Seltser, B. J., & Miller, D. E. *Homeless Families.* Chicago: University of Chicago Press, 1993.

REFERENCES

Ageton, S. S. *A Research Report for Adults who Work with Teenagers: Facts about Sexual Assault.* Boulder, CO: Behavioral Research Institute, 1985.

Aizenman, M., & Kelly, G. "The Incidence of Violence and Acquaintance Rape in Dating Relationships among College Men and Women," *Journal of College Student Development* 29 (1988), 305–311.

Anderson, G. (Ed.). *Courage to Care: Responding to the Crisis of Children with AIDS.* Washington, DC: Child Welfare League of America, 1990.

Baer, J. S., Marlatt, G. A., & McMahon, R. J. (Eds.). *Addictive Behaviors across the Lifespan: Prevention, Treatment and Policy Issues.* Newbury Park, CA: Sage, 1993.

Bassuk, E. L. "Women and Children without Shelter," (257–272). In M. J. Robertson and

M. Greenblatt (Eds.). *Homelessness: A National Perspective.* New York: Plenum, 1992.

Bepko, C., with Krestan, J. A. *The Responsibility Trap: A Blueprint for Treating the Alcoholic Family.* New York: Free Press, 1985.

Bethke, T. M. & DeJay, D. M. "An Experimental Study of Factors Influencing the Acceptability of Dating Violence," *Journal of Interpersonal Violence* 8(1) (1993), 36–51.

Blau, J. *The Visible Poor: Homelessness in the United States.* New York: Oxford University Press, 1992.

Botvin, G. J., Schinke, S., & Orlandi, M. A. (Eds.). *Drug Prevention with Multiethnic Youth.* Thousand Oaks, CA: Sage, 1995.

Brown, R. (Ed.). *Children in Crisis.* New York: H. W. Wilson, 1994.

Brown, S. A. "Recovery Patterns in Adolescent Substance Abuse," (161–183). In J. S. Baer, G. A. Marlatt, & R. J. McMahon (Eds.). *Addictive Behaviors across the Lifespan: Prevention, Treatment and Policy Issues.* Newbury Park, CA: Sage, 1993.

Campbell, A. "Female Participation in Gangs," (163–182). In R. C. Huff (Ed.). *Gangs in America.* Newbury Park, CA: Sage, 1990.

Carlson, B. E. "Dating Violence: Student Beliefs about Consequences," (3–18) *Journal of Interpersonal Violence* 11(1) (1996), 3–18.

Children's Defense Fund. *The State of America's Children Yearbook 1996.* Washington, DC: Children's Defense Fund, 1996.

Clary, B., Harrod, J., & Olney, R. "Subgroups of the Homeless: Street Kids," (373–387). In P. O'Malley (Ed.). *Homelessness: New England and Beyond.* Amherst, MA: University of Massachusetts Press, 1992.

Dutton, D. G. *The Domestic Assault of Women.* Boston: Allyn and Bacon, 1988.

Falchikov, N. "Adolescent Attitudes to Abuse of Women," *Journal of Interpersonal Violence* 11(3) (1996), 391–409.

Forsyth, B. W. C. "A Pandemic Out of Control: The Epidemiology of AIDS," (19–31). In S. Geballe, J. Gruedel, & W. Andiman (Eds.). *Forgotten Children of the AIDS Epidemic.* New Haven: Yale University Press, 1995.

Geballe, S., Gruedel, J., & Andiman, W. (Eds.). *Forgotten Children of the AIDS Epidemic.* New Haven: Yale University Press, 1995.

Glick, R., & Moore, J. (Eds.). *Drugs in Hispanic Communities.* New Brunswick, NJ: Rutgers, 1990.

Goodchilds, J., Zelliman, G. L., Johnson, P. B., & Giarusso, R. "Adolescents and Their Perception of Sexual Interaction," (245–270). In A. W. Burgess (Ed.). *Rape and Sexual Assault, vol. 2,* New York: Garland, 1988.

Graziano, A. M. "Why We Should Study Subabusive Violence against Children," *Journal of Interpersonal Violence* 9(3) (1994), 412–419.

Gullota, T. P., Adams, G. R., & Montemayor, R. (Eds.). *Substance Misuse in Adolescence.* Thousand Oaks, CA: Sage, 1994.

Herzberger, S. D. & Hall, J. A. "Children's Evaluations of Retaliatory Aggression against Siblings and Friends," *Journal of Interpersonal Violence* 8(1) (1993), 77–93.

Hoffman, A. M. (Ed.). *Schools, Violence and Society.* Westport, CT: Praeger, 1996.

Huff, C. R. (Ed.). *Gangs in America.* Newbury Park, CA: Sage, 1990.

Jaffee, P. G., Wolfe, D. A., & Wilson, S. K. *Children of Battered Women.* Newbury Park, CA: Sage, 1990.

Jesse, R. C. *Children in Recovery.* New York: W. W. Norton, 1989.

Johnson, J. L. "Forgotten No Longer: An Overview of Research on Children of Chemically Dependent Parents," (29–54). In T. M. Rivinus (Ed.). *Children of Chemically Dependent Parents.* New York: Brunner/Mazel, 1991.

Johnson, L. D. "Incidence of Use for Various Types of Drugs by Grade: Eighth Graders 1992" (134). In *National Survey Results on Drug Use from the Monitoring the Future Study, 1975–1992,* vol. 1, Secondary School Students, University of Michigan, Institute for Social Research, 1992.

Kadushin, A., & Martin, J. *Child Welfare Services.* New York: MacMillan, 1988.

Kandel, D. B. "Ethnic Differences in Drug Use," (81–104). In G. J. Botvin, S. Schinke, & M. A. Orlandi (Eds.). *Drug Prevention with Multiethnic Youth.* Thousand Oaks, CA: Sage, 1995.

Kinnear, K. L. *Violent Children.* Santa Barbara, CA: ABC-CLIO, 1995.

Kotlowitz, A. *There Are No Children Here.* New York: Doubleday, 1991.

Kozol, J. *Rachel and Her Children.* New York: Crown, 1988.

Krestan, J., & Bepko, C. "On Lies, Secrets, and Silence: The Multiple Levels of Denial in Addictive Families." In E. Imber–Black (Ed.). *Secrets in Families and Family Therapy.* New York: Norton, 1993.

Levoy, D., Rivinus, T. M., Matzko, M., & McGuire, J. "Children in Search of a Diagnosis: Chronic Trauma Disorder of Childhood," (153–170). In T. M. Rivinus (Ed.). *Children of Chemically Dependent Parents.* New York: Brunner/Mazel, 1991.

Maxson, C. L., & Klein, M. W. "Street Gang Violence: Twice as Great, or Half as Great?" (71–100). In R. C. Huff (Ed.). *Gangs in America.* Newbury Park, CA: Sage, 1990.

McCarroll, T. *Morning Glory Babies: Children with AIDS and the Celebration of Life.* New York: St. Martin's Press, 1988.

McChesney, K. Y. "Homeless Families: Four Patterns of Poverty," (245–256). In M. J. Robertson & M. Greenblatt (Eds.). *Homelessness: A National Perspective.* New York: Plenum, 1992.

McWhirter, J. J., McWhirter, B. T., McWhirter, A. M., & McWhirter, E. H. *At-Risk Youth: A Comprehensive Response.* Pacific Grove, CA: Brooks/Cole, 1993.

Miller, W. B. "Gangs, Groups and Serious Youth Crime," (120–127). In D. Schichor & D. Kelly (Eds.). *Critical Issues in Juvenile Delinquency.* Lexington, MA: Lexington Books, 1980.

Miller, B. C., & Dyk, P. A. H. "Sexuality," (95–123). In P. H. Tolan & B. J. Cohler (Eds.). *Handbook of Clinical Research and Practice with Adolescents.* New York: John Wiley and Sons, 1993.

Molidor, C. E. "Female Gang Members: A Profile of Aggression and Victimization." *Social Work* 41 (3) (1996) 251–257.

Morales, A. "Urban Gang Violence," (433–468). In A. Morales & B. Shaefer (Eds.). *Social Work: A Profession of Many Faces.* Boston: Allyn and Bacon, 1989.

Morse, G. A. "Causes of Homelessness," (3–17). In M. J. Robertson & M. Greenblatt (Eds.). *Homelessness: A National Perspective.* New York: Plenum, 1992.

Muisener, P. P. *Understanding and Treating Adolescent Substance Abuse.* Thousand Oaks, CA: Sage, 1994.

Nellis, M. *The Female Fix.* Boston: Houghton Mifflin, 1980.

Olday, D., & Wesley, B. "Dating Violence: A Comparison of High School and College Subsamples," *Free Inquiry in Creative Sociology,* 16 (1988), 183–190.

Oleske, J. "The Medical Management of Pediatric AIDS: Intervening on Behalf of Children and Families," (27–40). In G. Anderson (Ed.). *Courage to Care: Responding to the Crisis of Children with AIDS.* Washington, DC: Child Welfare League of America, 1990.

Petry, S., & Avent, H. "Stepping Stone: A Haven for Displaced Youths," (299–305). In M. J. Robertson and M. Greenblatt. *Homelessness: A National Perspective.* New York: Plenum, 1992.

Phillips, D. P. "The Impact of Mass Media Violence on U.S. Homicides," *American Sociological Review* 48 (August 1983), 560–568.

Resnik, H. *Youth and Drugs: Society's Mixed Messages.* Rockville, MD: Office for Substance Abuse Prevention, U.S. Department of Health and Human Services, 1990.

Rhodes, J. E., & Jason, L. A. *Preventing Substance Abuse among Children and Adolescents.* New York: Pergamon Press, 1988.

Rickel, A. U., & Becker–Lausen, E. "Treating the Adolescent Drug Misuser," (175–200). In T. P. Gullota, G. R. Adams, & R. Montemayor (Eds.). *Substance Misuse in Adolescence.* Thousand Oaks, CA: Sage, 1994.

Riggs, D. S. "Relationship Problems and Dating Aggression," *Journal of Interpersonal Violence* 8(1) (1993), 8–35.

Rivinus, T. M. (Ed.). *Children of Chemically Dependent Parents.* New York: Brunner/Mazel, 1991.

Robertson, J. M. "Homeless and Runaway Youths: A Review of the Literature," (287–297). In M. J. Robertson and M. Greenblatt (Eds.). *Homelessness: A National Perspective.* New York: Plenum, 1992.

Rothman, J. *Runaway and Homeless Youth.* New York: Longman, 1991.

Schmittroth, L. (Ed.). *Statistical Record of Children.* Detroit: Gale Research, 1994.

Seixas, J. S., & Youcha, G. *Children of Alcoholism.* New York: Crown, 1985.

Seltser, B. J., & Miller, D. E. *Homeless Families.* Chicago: University of Chicago Press, 1993.

Solarz, A. L. "To Be Young and Homeless," (275–286). In M. J. Robertson and M. Greenblatt

(Eds.). *Homelessness: A National Perspective.* New York: Plenum, 1992.

Struckman–Johnson, C. "Forced Sex on Dates: It Happens to Men Too," *Journal of Sex Research* 24, (1988), 234–241.

Terr, L. *Too Scared to Cry: Psychic Trauma in Childhood.* New York: Harper & Row, 1990.

Tower, C. C. *Understanding Child Abuse and Neglect.* Boston: Allyn and Bacon, 1996.

Tower, C. C., & White, D. J. *Homeless Students.* Washington, DC: National Education Association, 1989.

Towers, R. L. *How Schools Can Combat Student Drug and Alcohol Abuse.* Washington, DC: National Education Association, 1987.

U.S. Government Accounting Office, Report to Congressional Committees, *Children and Youths: About 68,000 Homeless and 186,000 in Shared Housing at Any Given Time.* Washington, DC: U.S. Government Printing Office, 1989.

Vigil, J. D., & Yun, S. C. "Vietnamese Youth Gangs in Southern California," (146–182). In R. C. Huff (Ed.). *Gangs in America.* Newbury Park, CA: Sage, 1990.

Zastrow, C. *Introduction to Social Work and Social Welfare.* Pacific Grove, CA: Brooks/Cole, 1996.

5

SERVING THE DEVELOPING CHILD
Day Care Services

Matthew Porter

A child before the age of seven years should never be subjected to any regular routine of studies; let him learn by fits and starts, as his inclination suits; and, when he appears tired, permit him to run and play. Physical development is much more important than mental at this period of life.
—GATELY, 1886, 360

INTRODUCTION

In our electronically sophisticated age, we would like to believe that issues regarding the family and, especially, the need for child care are new and unique. The needs of the working family, however, are as old as the industrial age. Throughout history, when men engaged in wars and were not available for the work force, women were pressed into service. The need then became the provision of adequate care for the children. More recently as families have increasingly felt it necessary for both parents to become wage earners, the need for a safe and developmentally sound environment for preschool-age children gave rise to the modern day care center.

This chapter will examine the social, educational, and societal factors that continue to influence the development of day care in the United States. It should be noted, however, that although it is possible to consider day care in general, policies and procedures in the day care centers across the country differ greatly. This may be due to the fact that the United States is the only industrial nation that has no national policies or standards for the welfare of young children and their families.

FAMILY NEEDS IN OUR TIME

According to the report *A Profile of Child Care Settings: Early Education and Care in 1990,* there were approximately 80,000 center-based early childhood programs in the United States serving over 5,000,000 children. The report stated that there were 118,000 family day care or in-home care by nonrelative programs serving 860,000 children (Kisker, 1991). The U. S. Bureau of the Census report, *What Does It Cost To Mind Our Preschoolers?* (1995), states that approximately 9,900,000 preschool age children needed child care because their parents were working. The numbers are staggering when we consider that most child care centers have between thirty to sixty children enrolled. There are millions of children and families who need care and the total capacity of child care programs meets only half the statistical need.

In many families, economic necessity means that both parents must work outside the home. In still others, parents choose to pursue careers as well as raising children and need child care while they do so. But there is an additional reason why parents seek out day care for their preschoolers. Today, parents are being bombarded by commercials and news reports that imply that if your child is not totally prepared for the "new technological work order" then he or she will be left

Is this really true?

behind. We have seen commercials on TV about teaching French to toddlers or the three-year-olds who can "read" by the application of rote phonetics. Parents are made to feel inadequate or uncaring if they cannot send their child to a professional child day care program. The reality is that the most important skills and values that children learn and understand come from the home. A child care center can reinforce certain family and societal values, e.g., manners, taking turns, sharing, and so on, but parenting remains a twenty-four-hours-a-day task for the rest of your life.

Families in crisis create a special set of challenges for day care programs. Most states have established a state department of social services that is responsible for investigating child abuse and neglect. When the need for protective services arises, as is the case when a suspected case is substantiated, one service provided might be a referral to day care programs that have training and experience working with families "in crisis." The role of the center is to provide a safe, consistent place where children receive love, attention, and comprehensive services to compensate for developmentally appropriate care often missing at home. In addition, parents may need the respite that having their children in day care provides. While parents may also receive services from the day care program, the primary focus is on the child.

Day care is also used by parents of special needs children, who face many difficulties as caregivers. The term *special needs* can encompass physical, emotional, psychological, developmental, cognitive, speech, hearing, motor, or other more specialized delays that cause a child to fall below a certain norm. Educators will say that, based on an understanding of developmentally appropriate practices, every child has needs that are "special." Semantics aside, a family facing a lifetime with a child who has multiple sclerosis or hearing impairment often needs some type of respite care. Industrialized, urban states have the greatest concentration of special needs services, while families that live in rural areas are often isolated from needed services.

NATIONAL ATTITUDES TOWARD DAY CARE: NO RHYME, NO REASON

Our nation's business community needs all types of workers, including qualified men and women who are of child-bearing age. Yet the care of their children is often the first priority for parents. It would therefore behoove businesses to anticipate parents' need for adequate child care and take a proactive stance in the provision of this care. Despite the models available in other industrialized countries, businesses in the United States have been sorely lacking in their response to on-site child care needs. Reisman, the Executive Director of the Child Care Action Campaign, states that "Child care in this country is seen as a problem for parents and not as an investment" (Galen, 1995, 38). The article goes on to chronicle the efforts of some enlightened corporations that have banded together to develop child care programs and services.

In order to understand today's crisis, we need to look back to other times when American business needed workers. Reeves, in *Child Care Crisis: A Reference Handbook* (1992), suggests a chronology of the development of day care services that provides important points of reference.

A BRIEF HISTORY OF DAY CARE PROVISION

1828   *First day care center opens in Boston.* The center was established to provide care for 18-month to 4-year-old children and to enable poor mothers to seek employment. The philosophy of the program was to form a religious and moral foundation for young disadvantaged children that would later enable them to escape poverty.

1933   Roosevelt's Federal Emergency Relief Act and Works Progress Administration (WPA) provided federal funds for day nurseries and nursery schools in a Depression-era effort to provide employment for preschool teachers and other personnel. Two-thirds of these programs were located in public schools. Although this was the government's first financial commitment to child care, the emphasis of the action was more on getting the unemployed off welfare than on benefiting children.

1937   Some 40,000 children were enrolled in approximately 1,500–1,900 WPA-supported child care programs.

1938   WPA support for child care was discontinued because the crisis of the Depression had ended.

1941   The Lanham Act (Public Law 137) allocated partial funding to set up child care centers in defense plants employing women. About 3,102 centers were established serving approximately 600,000 children. It is estimated that these centers served only 40% of child care needs at that time.

1943   Kaiser Industries opened the nation's first employer-sponsored child care center, serving a total of 4,019 children twenty-four hours a day.

1964   Project Head Start was launched and funded to provide compensatory education programs for environmentally and economically disadvantaged children. The program emphasized parent education and involvement.

1980   The *Dictionary of Occupational Titles,* a U. S. Department of Labor publication, classified child care workers in the same skill category as restroom attendants, porters, and dog groomers (1–7).

This short history lesson answers some of the questions about why early childhood teachers are so poorly regarded and paid.

WORKING PARENTS AND WHAT IS BEST FOR CHILDREN

At any child care facility at the beginning of September in any given year, the effects of separation between parent and child can be observed. Guilt, anxiety, and the sense of the loss of control is evidenced as many parents say good-bye to their often tearful children and head off to work. The decision to work rather than stay at home with young children is most often fueled by economic necessity and/or the need for self-fulfillment. Our society has presented working parents with a dilemma. On one hand, the modern work force requires the skills, ideas, and energy of all segments of society in order to be globally competitive. On the other hand, our long-standing tradition of a caregiver, traditionally the mother, at home caring for her young children or waiting at the door when the kindergartner comes home at midday are difficult to balance. It wasn't that long ago that an average American family could live on one income. Now, it is difficult to imagine ever returning to the one-income family.

Add to this reality the fact that, in most two-parent families, both are employed outside the home, and the startling increase in single-parent families, and the need for quality child care programs becomes more and more apparent. How have we prepared parents with the facts needed for choosing the right kind of child care? In many parts of the country child care resource and referral agencies, usually funded by state governments, provide unbiased advice for parents. Other ways that parents receive information is through the mass media. The August or September issue of any "woman's magazine" will contain basic advice on how to choose the "right" kind of child care. For instance, in the September 1994 edition of *Ebony*, readers were advised to "look for a reliable, trustworthy person or institution with a reputation for having good child rearing skills" (Whetstone, 1994, 116). This is obviously good advice, but how do parents determine reliability or trustworthiness? Most parents choose their child care by word of mouth from friends or relatives. The power of this type of trust is evident in the 1994 study conducted by the University of Colorado at Denver entitled "Cost, Quality, and Outcomes Study" (1995). The results of this study announced the overall mediocrity of the existing system of child care. This study was evaluated in the March 1995 edition of the well-regarded professional journal, *Child Care Information Exchange*, and in it the author concluded that

> *parents seem to overestimate the quality of care their children are receiving. While parents say they value the quality of care their children receive, they tend to be ineffective in evaluating quality. Ninety percent of parents rated the quality of the services their children receive as very good, while the ratings of trained observers*

indicate that most of these same programs are providing care that ranges from in-adequate to mediocre. The inability of parents to recognize good quality care im-plies that they do not demand it. Thus centers dependent on parent fees have little or no incentive to provide a higher level of quality at a higher cost (Neugebauer, 1995, 81).

The dilemma of the cost versus quality care issue is not lost on parents and pro-fessionals. Parents often pay a large percentage of their net income on child care and want the best they can afford. Yet the study indicates that it costs substantially more to produce better results. Parents are frightened by news reports, such as the February 20, 1995 issue of *Business Week* that states in bold print "73.7% of centers are mediocre, 12.3% are rated as poor, and only 14% are rated as developmentally appropriate" (Galen, 1995, 38; see also Bredekamp, 1987). If 90% of parents rated their child's program as very good, then whose children are attending the 86% of centers that are rated as poor or mediocre?

Working parents are given information regarding child care from a variety of sources and the decision as to where their child will go is often a very difficult and unsettling one. For example, the issue of child sexual abuse in the day care setting was a very real concern in the mid 1980s, though it has received less publicity in recent years. However, child care providers at all levels know and remember the atmosphere of mistrust that was fostered by the in-depth reporting of the news me-dia. This topic, as well as others, will always be a concern for parents and profes-sionals as the need for child care increases.

PARENTING THE SPECIAL NEEDS CHILD: A SPECIAL KIND OF CARE

Sue Ferguson (1995), outreach coordinator of the National Information Center for Children and Youth with Disabilities, described their supportive role in the care of special needs children for teachers:

Families of children with special needs are facing unique challenges that will re-quire your support and understanding. Many describe feeling overwhelmed at times by what lies ahead, and by the strength of their emotions. Feelings of isola-tion, inadequacy, and helplessness are not uncommon. The early years of knowing your child has a disability are like beginning an unplanned journey, and can be the most tender for families.

We may remember a time when children who acted or looked "differently" were moved to "special" rooms in public schools. This separateness was the norm until the concepts of inclusion and peer modeling (see Chapter 6) were introduced in the past few years. Parents of special needs children also remember the teasing, stares, and the atmosphere of fear perpetuated by society.

Educators play an important role in the education of young children with special needs. They can provide a safe, supportive environment where children are encouraged to discover their strengths and interests and, in addition, can be a strong support for the parents by building trust and by focusing on the positive. In this age of AIDS in children the prospect of finality helps put even severe needs into an eerie perspective. Working closely with parents, teachers can develop a plan of action that uses the law and institutions to provide for every aspect of the developing child. The federal Individuals with Disability Education Act requires states to provide public education for children ages three to twenty-one who have special needs. Early intervention services for younger children are also available in many states.

When a child enters a day care program, teachers and administrators act as the first line of action in identifying children with special needs. State laws require a physical examination and immunization before entering the program. In addition, some states require a developmental history that the parent must fill out and this is added to the child's record. Usually within the first few months of care, the child may display behavior that serves as a warning signal. Screenings of eyesight and hearing are usually held at the center so that intervention can take place in the shortest period of time. Parents become used to the particular idiosyncrasies that their child displays at home, but when children enter their first nonhome environment teachers can provide an objective analysis of the physical, social, emotional, and cognitive development they display in the day care setting. During parent–teacher conferences, held periodically during the school year, the interested parties share information that focuses on the strengths and weaknesses of the child. A referral recommendation may be made to the child's pediatrician or to the public school's special education program or both.

One role of day care personnel is to provide pertinent information regarding their observation of the child's behavior at the center. Another important function is to act as an advocate for the child and the family. Meeting with public school teachers, doctors, administrators, and others can be intimidating for parents. Day care staff are usually people the parents know and trust, and having these people in the room may lessen the parents' anxieties. The goal of such meetings is to develop a plan of action in which needed medical, educational, or psychiatric care is spelled out. The day care center also plays an important role in the carrying out of a comprehensive plan, such as providing the necessary socialization experiences that build the child's self-esteem and self-confidence.

The underlying assumption for educators is that parents are the primary educators of their children regardless of disability. Teachers who accept the special needs child into their classrooms accept the family as well. All parties working together provide a supportive atmosphere that is child-centered.

Not every child care center can provide for a special needs child. If the child's special needs are beyond the scope and skills of the center, then the appropriate course of action is to make a referral. The center's director should maintain a listing of specialized programs that will best suit the needs of the child and the family. The parents will need the support of the center in making the transition to a new program. Spinal bifida, multiple sclerosis, retardation, cerebral palsy, attention deficit disorder, and other forms of special needs require special training and equipment that the typical center may not have.

It can be frustrating to all parties when the child shows little or no progress after extensive testing, planning, and execution. Parents may feel discouraged when the first words from the child's teacher are, "Johnny had a rough day today," or "I don't know how we can cope with his biting behavior." Progress may be slow and each step should be viewed as another small success on the road to successfully educating a special needs child. Experience may be the best teacher but it is clarity of purpose and strong determination that will help all parties overcome the problems they face.

TYPES OF DAY CARE

When day care is mentioned, various ideas and concepts may come to mind. Most children under the age of five are cared for in their own homes or in the home of a relative or Family Day Care provider. According to the Fall 1991 census analysis, there were 7,650,000 children under the age of five whose parents work (Casper and O'Connell, 1994, 36). The statistics show that those children are cared for in a variety of ways:

Own Homes:	2,701,000
Provider's Home:	2,302,000
Child Care Facilities–Day Care:	1,235,000
Child Care Facilities–Nursery:	532,000
Other:	880,000

AT-HOME CARE

Many children are cared for in their own homes by relatives, such as a grandparent, aunt, or uncle who has the time or interest to care for the children. Another variation is the shared care concept in which one parent stays at home with related children from a single extended family. In some cases there is money exchanged for child care services, and usually the rate of pay is considerably lower than that of a commercial day care center. In a family with more than one infant and toddler, the $155–$200/week cost per child may be prohibitive and having a family member or friend who can provide adequate child care may be the only solution.

The issue of grandparents as primary care givers is currently under scrutiny. Young and energetic grandparents may well wish to look after the "baby" on an occasional basis. However, there may be a physical cost to the process. Coping with retirement and health issues appears to be typical for the older citizen, and the energy required to look after an active toddler may be too much for some seniors.

In families with many resources the use of a professional nanny may best serve the needs of the family. There are numerous agencies that supply nannies; some families find someone themselves who serves in this capacity. The nanny should have training in child growth and development, first aid, CPR, developmentally appropriate activities, and a patient nature with the children. Living with the family may present certain stresses, but ongoing communication and a common child-rearing philosophy should contribute to a successful venture. Nannies are usually paid a salary, provided with room and board, and given social security benefits and appropriate free time.

FAMILY DAY CARE

In many states there is a legal requirement that if you take care of someone else's child in your home, you must be licensed by the state. Most states limit the number of children allowed in the home to not more than six, including the caregiver's own children and only two children can be under the age of two. One of the concerns regarding this model of care is that the care of children is usually left to one person and if the provider is ill or unable to separate personal/family concerns from the provision of care, the quality of care may be unacceptable. In all other models there are at least two adults present and, if one of them is unable to provide quality care, then the other adult is able to cover the needs of the children.

Some states allow up to twelve children in a home if there is an approved assistant though other licensing requirements apply regardless of size. It is important to refer to the state law regarding the allowable size and scope when researching the requirements of each area.

In some larger communities there are systems of family day care homes. The system coordinator works closely with each provider through telephone contact and/or at-home visits. The system provides benefits, such as vacations, sick time coverage, training, and access to government funding sources. The advantage of this model is that the provider is not isolated from other adults and emergency situations can be handled efficiently. The provider pays a percentage of the tuitions collected for this service to the organization that has set up the system.

NURSERY SCHOOLS AND OTHER HALF-DAY PROGRAMS

One type of program, called a *parent cooperative nursery school,* has been in existence since the early 1920s. These were formed largely because parents recognized that children benefited from social and educational experiences obtained before entering school. They also recognized that costs to families could be reduced if each family shared the experience. Although professional teachers are employed, the duties of assisting the teacher, handling the finances, purchasing supplies, and other duties related to the program's operation fall to a parent board. There is usually a rotation of jobs with new families taking over from outgoing ones.

Many churches have worked with interested teachers and families to open half-day *church sponsored programs* for preschool age children three to five. When most mothers stayed home, those who could afford it sent their child to these facilities two or three days a week believing this extra time away from home helped prepare the child for the kindergarten experience. Nursery schools exist today in limited numbers due to increasing demands for full-time day care. One of the greatest misconceptions is that children go to "school" in these programs but that day care centers are primarily babysitting services. Often churches have responded to the needs of their parishioners and the community by opening such "schools" and may even recruit new members by offering these services.

Lab schools are sometimes offered in colleges or universities. These schools provide the opportunity for students to learn about child care while actually also providing this service for the community. These programs combine community relations efforts with a living laboratory for education and psychology departments. Parents who choose such programs know that college students as well as professional teachers will be interacting with their children. The opportunity to go beyond the textbook and learn from actual living subjects is an attractive feature for the college or university student. These programs usually charge a nominal tuition and are often subsidized by the college.

HEAD START

In 1964, Head Start, the first federally funded early childhood education program since World War II, designed for low income families, was established. This War on Poverty initiative recognized that unless poor children were given a "head start" they may not be able to keep up with the more fortunately advantaged child. Head Start is designed as a comprehensive child care model that provides educational opportunities for the child, social service support for the family, and health and nutritional services that assist each child to reach his/her full potential (Cromwell, 1994).

Beyond the provision of quality educational services, Head Start has other unique qualities. Social service workers conduct home visits to support each family and are in a position to assist the family in a crisis. Head Start was one of the first programs to mandate that special needs children be fully included in the classroom setting. Also, a percentage of each center's enrollment is set aside for children with special needs. Another important aspect is that Head Start is designed to provide job training for low-income parents at the center that their child attends. Many current Head Start teachers were parents of Head Start children. Ironically, the jobs that parents are trained for are some of the lowest paying professional jobs in our society.

Head Start has evolved into a multidimensional program that includes full day programs, at-home programs, and summer care. Despite the political changes since the early 1960s, Head Start has increased its funding and is a vital part of our educational system. Neugebauer (1995, 33), in the Child Care Information Exchange, states that Head Start has grown from a $96,000,000 allocation in 1965 to a $3,535,000,000 investment in 1995. He observes that Head Start will move forward with new programs that serve infants and toddlers, collaborate with public schools, and offer full day care programs. Untouchable, a rare example of bipartisan cooperation, Head Start has come under increased scrutiny as the program reached a total of 750,000 children in 1995, while the number of children still unserved has skyrocketed (Neugebauer, 1995, 33). Popular magazines such as *Parenting* have recently featured articles arguing the efficacy of the services provided by Head Start. In the November 1995 article "Is Head Start Doing Its Job?," Atkins (1995) suggests that nationwide Head Start serves only 41% of the four-year-olds and 17% of the three-year-olds who are eligible for such services. Critics of the program call for more federal reexamination of the program's effectiveness.

Although Head Start represents the only comprehensive federally funded effort in the profession, the expansion of Head Start into other early childhood services could create a backlash. Other child care providers have traditionally supported Head Start, yet intrusions into the marketplace may erode this support.

FULL DAY PROGRAMS

Every day care center is a unique entity that serves the community and its families. Most day care programs serve three, four, five, and six year olds with a combination of educational, social, recreational, physical, and other developmentally appropriate experiences. Infants and toddlers may be served in separate rooms with specially trained staff. There is a myth that day care is just a babysitting service or that children watch TV or are just entertained. In reality, a quality day care center is run by professionally trained people whose background and training is often equivalent to that of their public school counterparts. A day care center may be the culmination of one individual's dream to own his/her own program or it may be part of a chain of centers that stretch from coast to coast.

There are two types of centers: the *for-profit program* and the *nonprofit program.* A for-profit program is run like any other business, while a nonprofit program is not owned by an individual or partnership but has a board of directors that guides the program, hires the director, and sets policies. The misconception here is that it does not make money. Every program must cover all its expenses in order to survive. The nonprofit program doesn't pay sales or property taxes but must pay its staff. The for-profit program pays all expenses, and, if it is successful, will return a portion of any profits to the investors. A quality program provides quality services regardless of its organization. With approximately 80,000 early childhood programs in existence, there are literally thousands of programs that share the same designation and each one may be unique.

MONTESSORI SCHOOLS

The Montessori movement was begun by Maria Montessori (1870–1952), a medical doctor who opened the first "Children's House" in a Rome, Italy slum in 1907. Throughout her work with children, Montessori had been faced with many who were considered "uneducable." Montessori discovered that children's developmental education is affected by the considered use of natural materials and a form of self-education. She designed an educational system based on exploration, orientation, order, imagination, manipulation, repetition, precision, control of error leading to perfection, and communication (Lillard, 1996). The children were taught a variety of skills including hygiene, good work habits, and manners. The philosophy of the Montessori approach to education

> *combines freedom with responsibility, high standards of academic excellence, so-cial awareness and moral development, and a vision of humanity and its accom-plishments that inspires children to take their place in their communities, when the time comes, as responsible, contributing adults (Lillard, 1996, XXI).*

The "learning by doing" approach offered children a variety of sensory experiences designed to teach them mastery of a myriad of everyday and educational skills (Cromwell, 1994).

From these origins two forms of Montessori education emerged. Montessori International and the American Montessori Society (AMS) have similar roots and teacher preparation methods. Schools affiliated with the International movement are located primarily in Europe and India while AMS is practiced in America. AMS uses the basic Montessori concepts and adapts them, including more direct teacher interactions with children and the development of activity areas not found in the International schools. In International schools children accomplish a series of tasks with the teacher as a facilitator. Large group activities such as story time are not found in these schools. AMS programs allow children to learn by self-discovery and active participation by the teacher and other children (Lilliard, 1996).

In recent years Montessori education has expanded beyond the traditional pre-school base and offers programs for the infant/toddler years as well as children of elementary age. The Montessori approach is sometimes practiced in state-supported Charter Schools and in the Head Start program. The demand for a well-formulated, developmentally appropriate method of education has enabled the Montessori method to spread into communities throughout our country and around the world.

PRIVATE KINDERGARTENS

Many child care programs have developed an alternative to the public school model for children five to six years of age. The private kindergarten in most cases will have a much smaller staff-to-child ratio than is found in the public school and the program may be the logical extension of services for families that need a full day education program. Usually located in a day care center, the parent may select this method of care because younger siblings and kindergartners can be picked up at the same time. "One Step" care is a consideration for busy parents (Cromwell, 1994).

DAY NURSERIES

Day Nurseries have the longest history of early childhood services in America. Since the mid-1800s day nurseries have served the inner city family. Their focus on the "whole child" is based on the belief that in order to give each child the opportunity to fully develop the family must be involved. The social service needs of inner city families require a comprehensive approach that is often found in a day nursery. Day nurseries are the forerunners of the Head Start multiservice, family involved model of care. In most major cities there are some variations of the day nursery program (Cromwell, 1994).

EARLY CHILDHOOD PROGRAMS IN PUBLIC SCHOOLS

In public school systems across the country there is a new focus on the young child. In part, this effort is the result of the poor preparation that many children displayed when entering kindergarten. The wide disparity between children who have attended an educationally based preschool program and those who have spent little time with other children and adults is a much debated issue. There is also a recognition that by age five or six the child is already well on the way to the development of lifelong moral, social, and educational values and children who have not had prekindergarten training may be at a disadvantage. In addition, in many public school kindergartens there is a large staff-to-child ratio, with one teacher and twenty-six to twenty-nine children and perhaps one aide. This does not give the child new to the school experience enough attention from adults during this crucial adjustment period. Further, children need consistent care: the typical public school schedule of vacation, staff development, and assorted holidays may create service gaps in the typical public school-based program. Most public school early childhood programs are half-day and may not be a viable option for working parents, who might otherwise enroll in this low-cost alternative to day care. New variations in the public schools include contacted after-school programs and in some cases day care programs operated by the public school system itself. Over the next few years public schools may operate for longer hours and, in some cases, year-round.

In addition to city- or town-run schools, public and private partnerships may also allow entrepreneurs to develop community services within the public schools. The schools benefit by providing a location for additional services at no additional cost. The children and parents benefit by having affordable services, such as after-school care, in a convenient location. The provider benefits by serving a group of children at a well-established location.

TEACHERS' COOPERATIVES

There is a model of care that is the result of a collaborative effort on the part of early childhood professional teachers who band together to divide the workloads of teaching and administration. The "profits" are divided between the members and the hiring of new staff is also done in a collaborative fashion.

EMPLOYER-SPONSORED DAY CARE

In recent years, some large employers have offered day care services to their employees. While this effort encompasses only a small fraction of American business, the publicity surrounding the establishment of this type of employee benefit may be conducive to more and more businesses providing day care facilities.

On-Site Center

A business or consortium of businesses pool their resources and establish a building that houses the center. In most cases the business hires an outside provider to run the program. The building, its maintenance, utilities, and other materials are usually donated as part of the program subsidy. These donations keep down the cost of care to the employees.

Off-Site Center

A business may buy slots in an existing day care center that is located nearby. If a number of slots are purchased when a discount is usually available, the cost savings are passed on to the employees.

Resource and Referral Agency

A business can buy the services of a resource and referral agency to provide unbiased information for parents to use in making child care decisions. This service may include regularly scheduled employee meetings to provide information, answer parents' questions, give lists of schools, costs, and a checklist to determine program quality.

Whatever the choice that businesses make, it appears that providing for employees' children could reduce absenteeism, worries about unmonitored child care, and the costs involved. Many of these businesses allow for parents to pay tuition with pretaxed dollars, which further reduces the costs. If universal child care becomes a reality it is possible that the business community will play a major part.

A TYPICAL DAY IN A DAY CARE CENTER

On a dark winter morning, children and parents start arriving at their day care program. It's 6:30 a. m. Two teachers greet the early risers and, after the coats and boots are removed, children and parents say their goodbyes. Now it's time for breakfast and a period of quiet activity and conversation. Throughout the morning the separation of children and parents continues. Tearful eyes show that parents and children miss each other equally. By 9:00 a. m. all the morning teachers and children have arrived for the day. The three-year-olds have left the main group and have gone to their classroom area. They have a short meeting that will let everyone know that the day is Friday, November 10, and that it is already snowing outside. The teachers read books about snow and tell the children that today they will make cottonball snowmen for an art project. Taking a break from the activities, children use the bathroom, wash their hands, and eat bagels and cream cheese for the morning snack. At 10:30 a. m. the teachers help the children into their snowsuits and boots so they can play outside in the playground. Within the hour the children are inside and finishing up the morning's projects. When cleanup time is over children wash for lunch and get ready to talk with their friends over the hearty soup and sandwich on the day's menu.

After lunch all the children use the bathroom and get out their blankets and rest mats. During the two-hour rest period the quiet in the classroom is interrupted by children's snores. Then it's 2:00 p. m. and the last child has been awakened. The mats and blankets are returned to the cubby storage area as the children and the afternoon teachers prepare for a busy indoor project and another playground experience. During naptime the snow has covered the slide and everyone wants to be the first one outside. By 3:30 p. m. all the boots are put away and during the afternoon snack the children are listening to the teacher read a favorite story.

Between the free choice activities and the art project the first departing children say "Hello, MOM!!!" and goodbye to their teachers. By 6:00 p. m. the last child has left the building and the teachers have almost finished putting away the toys and equipment used throughout the busy day. Today they were fortunate that all the children were picked up on time. On Monday the last child left at 6:30 p. m.

THE ROLES OF THE DAY CARE PROVIDER

The successful, experienced day care provider fulfills many roles during the day and throughout the year. The first role is to provide a series of activities that are developmentally appropriate for the group of children served. He or she must also provide a safe, clean environment that stimulates, without overstimulating, the children, help children to settle conflicts without resorting to violence, provide an alternative method of verbal interactions, provide for the safety needs of children in regards to first aid and CPR, provide nutritious, well-balanced meals in adequate portions, and act as a social worker when a family crisis requires empathy, including knowing when it is appropriate to refer these parents to other professionals. It would be helpful for the provider to be a part of the social service community through participation in events that support the family.

A holistic view allows for the creation of a program that builds a positive self-concept for each child. The provider has a unique role in preparing each child for the society we live in. The use of manners, taking turns, accepting responsibility for one's actions, respect for the rights of others, and the development of moral values are all important aspects of providing for the whole child, whole family, and the whole society.

FROM A PARENT'S PERSPECTIVE

The majority of parents want the highest quality program for their children that they can afford. In the course of their hectic life parents want their children to be safe, healthy, educated, socially comfortable, and treated with respect. Parents want a clean center run by caring, educated adults who can be counted on to provide the nurturing that children need in order to grow into caring adults. A dilemma occurs when the parent drops off the child and goes off to work without knowing what is happening to their young, sometimes helpless, child. The younger the child the greater the need for trust and accountability. A quality center will keep parents updated about events on a daily basis, the progress or accidents/injuries that occurred. The lines of communication should be kept wide open to encourage the cooperation of parent and caregiver.

Guilt is a powerful by-product of values and economic realities in conflict. Mothers in particular are made to feel that if they really loved their child they would stay at home to care for them. Parents and their children need a supportive program that has the experience to say that when a parent drops off a child for the first time it might be dramatic and result in tears for one or both and it is a normal process, thus reassuring both child and parent. To some parents day care is a necessary evil that they must endure until the child goes to public school.

The high cost of quality care means that families may have to sacrifice other needs in order to pay for the care. The 1993 Bureau of the Census report states that between 9 and 21% of a family's monthly income is spent on child care (Casper and O'Connell, 1993).

Economic necessity and the expanding numbers of single-parent households has created the first day care generation and parents and educators alike wonder what will be the long-term effects of this phenomenon?

DAY CARE TRENDS

Day Care provision is a profession that has no national standards, no observable leadership, and consequently little or no power, at the present, to effect meaningful change. Although there is a delivery of service system that provides a wide range of care for many children, there is no guarantee of care for all children. With all that in mind, children hopefully will still be cared for today by dedicated, if underpaid and underappreciated, providers.

PROJECTIONS FOR THE NEXT DECADE

1. More centers will be built in order to accommodate the increasing numbers of child-bearing age women in the workplace. Currently there is nowhere near the amount of quality day care necessary to meet the needs of families today.

2. Public school systems will become more active in the provision of care for young children. This may include going to a full-year model that already exists in some states. The scope of service may involve a formal public (as in school) and private (as in for-profit or nonprofit) partnership that allows current private providers to continue to provide care under contract with government agencies.

3. There will be an increasing number of multigenerational programs that share administrative staff and facilities. This cost-saving model will grow when the 50 million baby boomers retire. Grandparents and grandchildren may go to the same building for appropriate recreational and educational experiences.

4. The federal government will develop national standards for the care of children and national credentials for the people who care for them and for the facilities that house them.

5. Day care centers will evolve into "one stop" family service centers that will provide medical, dental, social service, nutritional, and parent-training services.

6. Universal child care will have as its primary goal breaking the cycle of poverty and crime that threatens everyone in our society. If every child truly had a head start or equal opportunity, how would our society benefit?

7. When wages, benefits, and status rise substantially then the early childhood profession will attract the best and most motivated women and men. A strong calling to work with children has always existed but it takes more than dedication alone.

SUMMARY

During the course of this chapter we have explored the social and statistical need for the vital services that day care centers provide. We have used a historical model that provides a perspective on how the early childhood profession has evolved.

What are the components of the "quality care" that are so critical for the development of each child? There must be a balance of indoor and outdoor activities designed to challenge each child as well as a balance between quiet and active play. It is critical that the young child's activities be "hands on." For example, instead of talking about cows the class goes to a farm, reads about cows, sings songs that include cows, and has art projects that stimulate a knowledge of farms. A strong parent–program relationship provides the child with a cohesive upbringing so that children learn that when problems arise they are dealt with clearly and fairly. Every program type recognizes that parents are the primary educators of their children. In addition, the parent recognizes that a quality child care center allows for a work life without worrying about the child's safety.

We have examined future trends that will challenge our society. The early childhood education profession and its practitioners may well emerge as a critical factor in future economic growth. Children with special needs require a plan of action that involves home, school, medical personnel, and a range of other professionals. The day care center provides a stable environment that helps such children reach their full potential.

EXPLORATION QUESTIONS

1. In order to understand today's day care programs we must be aware of the past. Has the underlying need for day care changed over time? Discuss the historical similarities and differences.
2. Everyone talks about quality care; what are the critical components of quality?
3. The federal government has been involved with child care over the years. What is its current involvement and who benefits? What else can government do to ensure that each child receives equal treatment?
4. Compare and contrast the delivery of service components. Why do we need so many types of care?
5. What is a transition time and why is it so difficult to make it work?
6. Why do many parents have great difficulty sending their child to day care?
7. What are your state standards for professional child care? Do you feel that they protect the interests of child and families? If so, how? If not, why?
8. Given the poor pay and low status of child care providers, why are you considering this profession?
9. What is the National Association for the Education of Young Children? What standards have they developed for use by child care centers?
10. How does the Montessori method provide an education for children in your community?

ACTIVITIES FOR APPLIED LEARNING

1. In order to understand what early childhood education is all about you must spend the time and effort to observe many types of care within your community. Research the guidelines that organizations such as the Child Welfare League of America have regarding day care. Create a quality care checklist based on these standards. Use this checklist to evaluate each program you observe. Ask the center about their own guidelines.
2. Creating a quality learning environment for the special needs child is an important part of being a teacher. Discover how your community serves young children with special needs. For example, you could attend a local meeting of C.H.A.D.D. (Children with Attention Deficit Disorders) and listen to parents and providers discuss coping strategies.
3. Look through fall issues of popular magazines and record the messages about day care choices being presented. Are they informative or sensationalist? Discuss your findings with a day care center director and see if you both agree on your conclusions.
4. Observe a day care center for a few hours in the morning. How does the staff prepare the children for transition times? How do the children cope with interruptions to favorite activities? Do a fall, winter, and spring observation with the same group. How has the group changed and why is this applicable to groups of children year to year. Finding the right method for your teaching style will help eliminate a major cause of burnout.

SUGGESTED READING

Goodman, W. "Boom in Day Care Industry the Result of Many Social Changes," *Monthly Labor Review* (August 1995).

Schmittroth, L. *Statistical Record of Children.* Detroit, MI: Gale Research, 1994.

Tuttle, W. *Rosie the Riveter and Her Latchkey Children: What America Can Learn about Child Day Care from the Second World War.* Washington, DC: Child Welfare League of America, 1995.

Zigler, E. *Child Day Care in the Schools: The School of the 21st Century.* Washington, DC: Child Welfare League of America, 1995.

REFERENCES

Atkins, N. "Is Head Start Doing Its Job?" *Parenting* 9(9) (1995), 140–145.

Bredekamp, S. *Developmentally Appropriate Practice in Early Childhood Programs Serving Children from Birth through Age 8.* Expanded Ed. Washington, DC: National Association for the Education of Young Children, 1987.

Casper, L., & O'Connell, M. *Who's Minding the Kids? Child Care Arrangements.* Washington, DC: U. S. Bureau of the Census, 1993. Current Population Reports, P70–36, 1994.

Cromwell, E. S. *Quality Child Care.* Boston: Allyn and Bacon, 1994.

Galen, M. "Honey, We're Cheating the Kids," *Business Week* (2/20/95). 38.

Gately, M. R. *Gately's Universal Educator,* vol. I. Boston, MA: M. R. Gately.

———. *Gately's Universal Educator,* vol. II. Boston, MA: M. R. Gately, 1886, 360.

Kisker, E. (Ed.). "Profile of Child Care Settings: Early Education and Care in 1990." Washington, DC: U. S. Dept of Education, 1991.

Lillard, P. P. *Montessori Today.* New York, NY: Schocken Books, 1996.

Neugebauer, R. *Cost and Quality Study Findings Unveiled.* Redmond, WA: Child Care Information Exchange, 1995.

Reeves, D. L. *Child Care Crisis: A Reference Handbook.* Santa Barbara, CA: ABC–Clio, 1992.

Schmittroth, L. *Statistical Record of Children.* Detroit, MI: Gale Research, 1995.

"What Does It Cost to Mind Our Preschoolers?" Washington, DC: U. S. Bureau of the Census SIPP, 1993.

Whetstone, M. L. "How Career Mothers Deal with Day Care Problems," *Ebony* (9/94), 116–120.

Zigler, E. *Child Day Care in the Schools: The School of the 21st Century.* Washington, DC: Child Welfare League of America, 1995.

6

SERVING THE DEVELOPING CHILD
Services in Schools

Mary Ann Hanley and Elaine Francis

When I was in school we just learned the three Rs: reading, writing, and arithmetic. I don't know what happened to the kids with problems like my son. I guess they just fell between the cracks. It just seems that there are so many more services for kids in schools today. I don't know what our family would do if there weren't!

INTRODUCTION

All students attend school for the purpose of acquiring an education. Most parents expect that their children will do well, complete school, and acquire at least a high school diploma. The service that schools primarily provide for all students is an education. Education has traditionally been defined as the *learning of knowledge.* This learning takes place in the classroom with the teacher as the primary facilitator.

Children who face challenges in academic, social, and emotional development will require services beyond those that a classroom teacher can provide. This chapter will delineate those services that are usually available to all students as well as services provided to students who have special needs. The "ideal" in services will be described, with the problems in delivering services outlined whenever relevant.

PHILOSOPHY OF EDUCATION

One's beliefs about schools, and the mission they should be fulfilling, serve as guiding forces in the development of "good schools." Before discussing the services a school should provide, it is necessary to consider the mission of schools in general. Research on learning processes has significantly changed thinking on education and approaches to teaching. There are several major assumptions on teaching children and how they learn which guide school services.

CHILDREN LEARN IN DIFFERENT WAYS

A great deal of research has been conducted that considers the various learning styles of children and adults. Twenty years ago we could not understand why not all students were learning when provided with the same instruction. Today we see greater evidence that each child brings to the learning situation a unique way of processing information. Some learn visually, others prefer to have things spoken to them. Some require a structured, sequential approach to learning, while others feel constrained by this approach and need opportunities to think randomly before forming concepts. Some students have disabilities that require modifications in typical instruction or in expectations that will allow them to be successful. It is clear that the challenge of teachers today is to uncover their students' learning styles and learning needs and teach in ways that allow each individual to succeed.

CHILDREN LEARN BEST WHEN THEY LEARN TOGETHER

When one considers the diverse needs and learning styles of students in schools, an easy solution might appear to be to group students with similar issues together in homogeneous settings. Such an approach has been used over the years with students who have disabilities. It was not uncommon to find separate classes for students with mental retardation, emotional problems, or learning disabilities. The failure of this approach has been in the damage to the ego of students who are labeled as being "different." Separating students leads to barriers and a lack of understanding between groups. Students who are viewed as slower or less able become the objects of ridicule and are frequently labeled and stereotyped rather than valued as individuals.

The recent trend in education in general, and special education in particular, has been to educate all students together in the regular classroom, in their neighborhood schools, whenever possible. This concept has been called the "least restrictive environment" (20 U.S.C., section 1412 [5] [B]). It removes many of the restrictions placed on students who have learning needs that, in the past, kept them from being placed in the regular classroom. With effective teaching strategies and the right support that leads to individualized learning, all students can be successful and learn together. As we consider services to children, we will find that more and more of these services are being provided in the regular classroom.

This approach of grouping together all children at a particular grade level is referred to as the "inclusion" philosophy. It stems from the belief that our schools are microcosms of society—a community of learners (Stainback and Stainback, 1992; Stainback, 1995). Learning in school to respect and support one another despite our differences, enables us to bring these skills and attitudes into our adult life, hopefully making us more tolerant citizens. Regardless of one's cultural background, language learning style, or learning needs, one of the primary goals of the school should be to teach students how to understand and work with each other.

WE MUST TEACH THE WHOLE CHILD

Our view of schools is a holistic one. We believe that schools should address both the academic and the social/emotional needs of students. Students should receive a strong academic foundation that provides them with the basic skills and critical thinking necessary to be a successful citizen. We also believe that a child's self-esteem and emotional growth have to be strong in order for that child to be successful. Thus, a good school is as concerned with how a child feels about test scores as they are with the test scores themselves.

In our society, children's views of themselves are often defined by their performance in school. When meeting a family member or friend, a child is most often asked "How's school?" Parents compare notes on their children's performance in school, remarking with awe on children who are singled out for honors. Students with learning problems often only feel different or inferior when they are in school. Teachers, counselors, and other school staff must recognize the challenges students face in school and at home and provide the support and encouragement that is necessary for optimum learning to occur.

Teachers, counselors, and other school staff have a responsibility to meet both the academic and the social/emotional needs of their students. As we consider meeting the academic needs of students, most of us think of the "regular" academic program that is provided in the regular classroom with the classroom teacher as the central figure. However, sometimes children have needs that extend beyond those that the classroom teacher can address. If a student is experiencing great stress in his/her life, academic needs are a secondary focus in that child's life. For these reasons schools offer not only basic academic work but also support services to ensure that students with problems will have their primary needs met and that all children will have an opportunity to grow socially and emotionally. The next section of this chapter will describe the services that are offered to meet social and emotional needs.

SUPPORT SERVICES: MEETING SOCIAL AND EMOTIONAL NEEDS

Support services include *guidance and counseling, mental health counseling/social work, assessment,* and *health services.* They also include such indirect services as *consultation*—with parents, staff, and other appropriate personnel—and *coordination* of activities and programs. All these services, which we will be discussing here, are provided in schools for two reasons: they help remove barriers to the learning process and they help children and adolescents grow socially and emotionally. Both reasons are important, and speak to the need for these services to be available to all students. There is variation in the titles of the people who provide these services. Different states may use different names; professional organizations try to clarify roles, but much overlap still exists. The American School Counselors Association, for example, is attempting to clarify the role of school counselors (see *National Standards for School Counseling Programs,* Draft, 1997).

Schools organize support services in various ways, usually under the title of *pupil personnel services.* The structure of pupil personnel services departments will differ among states, school districts, and even the schools themselves. Staff who provide the services will also vary. We begin our discussion with the services, proceed to a possible framework, and conclude by describing the personnel who provide the services.

There seems to be general agreement (Borders and Drury, 1992) that most of the school counselor's services fall into one of four categories: *guidance, counseling, consultation,* and *coordination.* Additional services needed by children in schools are *assessment, mental health/social work,* and *health services.* Other support staff usually offer these services.

COUNSELING SERVICES

> When Corey was just beginning third grade, his parents told him they were getting a divorce and soon after his father moved out. His teacher noticed that the oppositional, moody child she had in her classroom was not the same one she had seen in school the previous year. After talking with Corey, who denied his new home situation, the teacher realized that he needed someone to help him process his feelings. She therefore referred him to the school counselor, who was just beginning a group for children whose parents had divorced.

Counseling involves meeting with students individually or in small groups to listen to their problems and provide an environment in which they can explore possible solutions. These problems range from issues dealing with their studies and career plans to interpersonal and family concerns. Small groups are often appropriate when students share a common problem or when the counselor thinks they might benefit from exchanging ideas and feelings with their peers in a protected environment. Studies have shown that small group work is effective in increasing academic achievement, school attendance, self-esteem, and more positive attitudes toward school (Borders and Drury, 1992). Individual counseling is needed when problems are very personal, complex, or serious, when many resources are needed to deal with the problem, or when students seem unable to make good use of a small group.

Working with families of students is another function of counseling. This is particularly true in elementary schools. Elementary school counselors spend much of their time helping families work on issues that may affect their children's school progress and/or the children's social and emotional growth. Family work is currently considered to be one of the major emphases in school counseling (Paisley and Borders, 1995). Referring students and their families for more extensive counseling when necessary is a function of counselors at any level.

There is much controversy regarding the provision of counseling services in schools. Those involved in providing and setting policy regarding services to children in school disagree as to who, within the school, should provide counseling or if schools should offer personal counseling at all. Some professionals believe that school counselors are not qualified, by virtue of their training, to provide personal counseling. These critics contend that all counseling, except that related to education and career planning, should be referred to another professional, either within the school setting (social worker, mental health counselor, or psychologist) or within an outside agency. Others feel that this service is a necessary role of the school counselor for several reasons. First, parents may agree to have their children seen by a counselor at school but, due to their biases about psychological services, would hesitate to seek the services of a counseling agency. And secondly, children of parents who are financially unable to afford counseling outside the school or whose insurance does not cover such services, may not be able to receive personal counseling unless the school provides it.

There are those, however, who believe that counseling is not an appropriate service to provide in schools and they would neither desire nor permit school counselors, or any other school personnel, to perform that function. Those who espouse this view would restrict counseling services to students who have a demonstrated special need, and the service would be provided by an outside agency.

GUIDANCE SERVICES

Sara knew that she wanted to go to college to study political science but had no idea where she wanted to go. She sought out the guidance counselor for help. He asked her questions about the types of environments she learned best in. He helped her use the school's computer program that provided information about a variety of colleges. When they had narrowed the choices down to several that her parents could afford, the counselor helped her to get catalogues. Finally, they researched financial aid plans and scholarships.

Guidance is a more direct form of help than counseling, offering students information or advice on developmental issues (e.g., making friends, moving from the elementary level to junior high, dating, sexual development), social topics (e.g., substance abuse, sexual abuse), and educational and career planning (e.g., planning for college or vocational training). Guidance takes place in the classroom in the form of organized units on topics of interest to the particular age group. In addition to classroom teaching, guidance may take place in small groups or with an individual. These activities will, of course, vary depending on the kind of school in which they take place and the nature of the guidance being offered. There might be a classroom presentation on interpersonal skills taught in an elementary school setting, a small group meeting on specific careers in a middle school, or an explanation of a school-to-work program to a high school student. There are, in addition, other guidance activities:

1. *Presenting classroom units* on topics such as diversity, violence, conflict resolution, drugs/alcohol, sexual development and attitudes about sexual behavior, divorce, peer pressure, career planning, educational planning, understanding test results, parenting, and general family living issues;

2. *Providing a library of pamphlets and other publications on issues related to growing up,* including the effects of smoking and substance abuse, sexual behavior, parenting skills, divorce, interpersonal effectiveness, colleges, careers, and so on;

3. *Informing/educating students individually or in small groups* about some of the above issues as well as others such as abuse, pregnancy, and other sensitive topics;

4. *Helping students with educational choices* while in school (e.g., course selection), helping students with post-school choices, including college choices, applications, and career choices and planning;

5. *Testing all students for achievement* and relating the results to educational and career planning; testing students for individual achievement and/or aptitude, and identifying students' interests.

6. *Training students* to be peer counselors, mediators, and/or tutors for their classmates or for younger children. Such training should be done by those who have been trained as mediators themselves;

7. *Providing referrals* to students for more information and/or services.

Counseling and guidance are direct services to students and are what most good programs emphasize. School counselors usually provide most of these services. However, teachers and other staff may do guidance work, and mental health counselors/social workers and/or school psychologists or psychiatric social workers often provide more in-depth, long-term counseling services for students who have serious difficulties.

MENTAL HEALTH COUNSELING AND SOCIAL WORK SERVICES

When Marty began missing a great deal of school, his teacher was concerned. He consulted the school social worker who approached the family. She learned that Marty's mother was quite ill and that Marty was afraid that if he went to school his mother would die while he was gone. Although the service is not available in all schools, this social worker was able to offer intensive counseling to Marty so he could deal with his fears rather than referring him to an outside counselor.

Social work or mental health counseling, when available in a school setting, includes working with students who have attendance problems, who are in trouble with authorities, or who need intensive counseling/therapy on specific difficulties. It also involves working with students who have behavioral problems or with those whose home environment does not provide enough help for them to develop in the major areas of their lives (social, emotional, academic, and physical). It includes arranging referrals for additional services (within and outside of the school) for some and monitoring equal opportunity and fair treatment for all students. There may be a need to deal with child abuse issues, domestic violence problems, and other violent behavior, sometimes with students who are victims and other times with students who are perpetrators. When social workers/mental health counselors are part of the school staff, they usually work with a small group of students who have been identified as having one or more of the above problems and who need a great deal of individual attention. Often, there is a need to coordinate counseling efforts with services provided by outside agencies. A critical element of any treatment plan involves working closely with the home.

In today's confrontational society, schools recognize the need and are placing more emphasis on mediation as a skill. This skill may be taught by the social worker/mental health counselor, but is often done by the school counselor. Whoever has the responsibility, teaches students to better handle their disputes by learning to resolve conflicts more effectively.

CONSULTATION AND COORDINATION SERVICES

Mrs. Hayes called the school counselor because she was worried that her daughter, Quinn, would not do her homework. When she tried to help her, Quinn would become upset and fly off in tears. The counselor brainstormed with this mother about the various reasons that might explain the child's behavior. In consultation with the counselor, Mrs. Hayes finally realized that she had been putting undue pressure on her child to achieve. When the girl did not understand her homework, she interpreted her mother's intervention as additional pressure. The counselor was able to help Mrs. Hayes find ways to deal with her concerns and with her daughter's.

Consultation is a major function in helping students develop socially and emotionally, as well as academically. School counselors, mental health counselors/ social workers, and psychologists consult with teachers and parents primarily, but also with administrators and with students themselves. Often this service focuses on classroom achievement or behavior. Sometimes working with the teacher to provide intervention strategies is more effective than long individual sessions with the student. These professionals can also help parents with overall strategies in parenting or may give concrete advice on how to handle a specific situation. Administrators may wish to work with counselors in designing an individual student's program or broader school programs. Students look to counselors for information on such things as setting up programs or developing workshops.

Coordination may not be obvious to students. However, the way in which the staff plan and carry out these services can have far-reaching effects. In addition to arranging for the standard school counseling curriculum, counselors need to organize such events as college fairs, articulation meetings with staffs of feeder schools, parent meetings, workshops, and so on. Many of these activities offer great benefits for students. One objection to the counselor doing a variety of different coordinating tasks is that he/she may spend too much time on these activities, while the direct services of counseling and guidance will suffer.

ASSESSMENT SERVICES

The Rickers were interested in why ten-year-old Harvey was doing poorly in school. The parents approached the school psychologist with the request that Harvey be given a series of assessment tools to determine his ability and interests. These tests uncovered the fact that Harvey did have a moderately high IQ but was hampered by a learning disability.

Assessment services are for all students, insofar as they monitor academic growth or offer insights into vocational interests and career direction. Typical tests or inventories would be measures of basic skills, achievement tests in subject areas, and inventories reporting general career interest areas. Social and emotional growth is not usually measured for the majority of students; however, students who have been referred because of possible problems are tested. If there is a concern about a student's medical status, medical evaluations would be completed by the school nurse or the student would be referred to a physician.

Interpreting results to students, parents, teachers and other appropriate staff is a part of assessment services; it may well be the most important one! The basis for test scores isn't completely understood by laypeople. School personnel need to explain the limitations and ramifications of test results so that students and their parents can utilize the results effectively.

Testing and assessment for special needs, whether physical, academic or social/emotional, are available only to those students who have been referred by teachers, parents, or other school personnel for evaluation. Various staff members are involved in this. School psychologists assess intelligence, academic potential, and emotional needs; counselors and/or teachers test for academic achievement and, perhaps, for social skills; the school nurse (or a physician consultant) will test for physical or health problems. When additional services for the child or adolescent are being considered, it is important to hear from parents and, when feasible, from the student themselves.

If the test results demonstrate that the student has a special need, an individual treatment or educational plan is required, spelling out in specific terms the services that the student will need. Plans are developed using the results of tests and other evaluations, parents' wishes, teachers and counselors or psychologists' recommendations and, if appropriate, input from the student. The special education teacher usually takes the primary responsibility for individual educational plans (IEPs).

The regular classroom teacher, the school counselor, the mental health counselor or social worker, and the parents contribute their knowledge as well. The school psychologist and other involved professionals from outside the school (e.g., a physician) may be included in this planning.

HEALTH SERVICES

> Betty was born with medical problems that necessitated that she be given medication throughout the day. It became the responsibility of the school nurse to keep, administer, and chart Betty's medications. She was in contact with Betty's physician whenever the medicines changed.

The role of the nurse or other health professional in the school is varied. Some health professionals assist children who need medication or other medical procedures such as changing bandages, monitoring catheters, or other such issues. In some schools, the regular sight and hearing evaluations are done by in-house staff.

Health services are becoming more important in middle and high schools, particularly because of an increase in adolescent sexual activity. Students need to have information regarding possible pregnancy, sexually transmitted diseases (especially AIDS), and child care. The school nurse is usually the person providing these services. The increase in substance abuse, violent behavior, and medically involved children in schools has led to an increased demand for health services. In both elementary and high schools, students may have classes on health or hygiene topics, which the nurse or other health professional teaches. School nurses are also available for consultation and help with health-related problems.

STRUCTURE FOR PROVIDING SUPPORT SERVICES

Traditionally, the school counseling program has housed many of the services discussed in this section. In a well-run school, there should be serious planning in order to develop and coordinate the services that provide appropriate support to students. In an extensive review of school counseling programs, Borders and Drury (1992) identified the core principles of school counseling programs as: (1) independent, (2) integrative, (3) developmental, and (4) equitable (488–489).

School counseling and guidance programs are independent in that they can and should have a comprehensive curriculum to help students meet the goals of academic, social, and emotional growth for all age groups and at all levels of development. The curriculum should clearly relate the types of interventions to the goals, and the program should be evaluated on how well specific services help students meet those goals.

Counseling programs are integrative in that they interrelate with other areas of the schools, including regular curricula and special needs. They offer a support system for all students. Developmental programs are necessary in order to tailor services to the physical, cognitive, social, and emotional level of the age group and of the individual student. Counseling programs must be equitable in order to meet the needs of all students.

> *All students refers to those who are average, gifted and talented, low achieving and to those with handicaps and disabilities; those in all ethnic, cultural, and sexual orientation groups; those who speak English as a second language; migrants; boys and girls; athletes and non-athletes; and any other "special students" in the school (Borders and Drury, 1992, 489).*

As was stated in the introduction to this chapter, school programs must address the whole child and all children. Students with disabilities present unique challenges that may require special services, which an effective program will provide.

SERVICES FOR CHILDREN WITH SPECIAL NEEDS

Before discussing the services provided to students with special needs, it is important to define what constitutes a *special need*. A special need typically refers to a disability that requires modified instructional strategies or additional support in order for a child to learn effectively. These disabilities are identified as mental retardation, learning disabilities, behavioral disorders, speech and/or language impairment, visual impairments, hearing impairments, physical disabilities, and health impairments. Historically, students who are considered gifted and talented have also been included among those with special needs due to the fact that they may also need modifications in their instruction to learn effectively.

Mental Retardation and Developmental Delays
Children with mental retardation, more recently referred to as developmentally delayed, are those with cognitive impairments that result in generally poorer intellectual functioning (an IQ of 70 or below) and their ability to perform life skills such as personal independence or social responsibility typically seen in other individuals of a similar age (adapted from American Association on Mental Retardation definition, Grossman, 1983).

Learning Disabilities
Learning disabilities refers to a heterogeneous group of disorders manifested by significant difficulties in the acquisition and use of listening, speaking, reading, writing, reasoning, or mathematical ability. Even though a learning disability may occur concomitantly with other disabilities, it is not the direct result of those conditions or influences (National Joint Committee on Learning Disabilities, 1981).

Behavioral and Emotional Disorders
"Excessive and chronic" (Bullock, 1992) behaviors that "interfere with a student's learning, relationships with others, or personal satisfaction to such a degree that in-

tervention is necessary" are often referred to as behavioral or emotional disorders (Smith and Luckasson, 1995, 357).

Sensory Deficits

Sensory deficits, such as vision and hearing problems that require special teaching techniques or adapted materials, are also considered disabilities that result in a child being eligible for special education.

Speech and Language Problems

Services that address language difficulties are provided for children who have difficulty understanding oral language, or whose speech is so impaired that it interferes with communication.

Physical and Health Impairments

Some children may be affected by physical challenges (such as spina bifida or cerebral palsy), but may not necessarily have any learning or cognitive deficits. In addition, health problems such as asthma, AIDS, or diabetes may affect a child's attendance at school and result in their need for special support in order to be more productive at school. These children may require assistance from physical therapists, occupational therapists, or the school nurse during the school day.

Gifted and Talented

The term *gifted* refers to individuals with high levels of intelligence, outstanding abilities, and a capacity for high performance. *Talented* refers to someone with unusual traits or abilities who does not necessarily possess a high degree of intelligence (Smith and Luckasson, 1995).

Although being gifted is not a disability, schools often see these programs as requiring additions to the budget. Therefore, they may be seen as a "special need" that some children have.

Each of the types of special needs identified above refer to students who have similar issues and characteristics. It is important, however, not to overgeneralize about any disability or need. Each child should be considered an individual with unique characteristics and needs.

Special Education Legislation

Special education services have become such an integral and accepted part of our educational systems that it is difficult to imagine that students with special needs might have ever been excluded from these services or from school. Prior to 1975, that was, in fact, the case. Many students with special needs were not identified. Many who were identified were excluded from school programs, especially those with significant disabilities. Public school programs for students with special needs were in separate classrooms, or, in many cases, separate buildings.

In 1975, PL 94–142 was passed to ensure that free and appropriate educational services are provided to children with special needs. In 1990, PL 94–142 was amended by PL 101–476, which, among other things, changed the name of the legislation to the Individuals with Disabilities Education Act, or IDEA (National Information Center for Children and Youth with Disabilities, 1993). Some of the guiding principles of IDEA include:

- *Zero Reject:* All students with special needs must be provided with a free and appropriate education, regardless of disability;
- *Nondiscriminatory Evaluation:* Evaluations determine if a child has a disability. Care must be provided to ensure that students are not inappropriately identified as having a special need (as in the case of students who are bilingual);
- *Appropriate Education:* Education must meet the needs of students with special needs, including related services, such as physical therapy, counseling, speech therapy, and so on;
- *Least Restrictive Environment:* Whenever possible and appropriate, students with special needs must be a part of the regular education program and educated alongside their "typical" peers;
- *Due Process:* Parents must be provided with notification if their child is to be determined as having a special learning need. Children cannot be placed in special education programs without parental consent;
- *Parental Participation:* Schools must collaborate with parents in the design and implementation of educational services (Bullock, 1992).

One of the major components of this federal legislation is the concept of the *Individualized Educational Plan* or *IEP*. Each plan outlines a description of the child's current level of performance, the specific special education and related services to be provided, the child's annual goals, and short-term objectives. It also delineates when services are to begin, how long they are expected to last, and how the school district will determine whether the short-term objectives are being achieved.

The Continuum of Services

Once a child has been identified as having a special need, there are a range of services that can be provided to him/her. These include:

- *Regular education classes with consultation* from the special education teacher or other professional staff (therapists, consultants, etc.);
- *Special classes* that are designed to meet the unique learning needs of students on a one-to-one or small group basis;
- *Special schools* for students with intensive special needs who cannot be adequately served in the public school;
- *Home instruction* that may be necessary for the child who cannot attend school, particularly those with health needs;
- *Hospital or institutional settings* for students with intensive special needs that require twenty-four-hour services.

Although IDEA specifies that special education services must be available in special schools or home and hospital settings when necessary, it also clearly states that these services must be provided only when the child cannot be educated in the regular classroom, even with specialized strategies and supports.

ROLES OF SCHOOL PERSONNEL

The personnel necessary to meet the various needs of students in schools are varied and numerous. Each professional will be listed in this section followed by a brief description of the educational role.

Classroom Teacher

The classroom teacher's role involves providing for the educational needs of all children in the classroom. Students with special needs may require that lessons be modified. Teachers may also require the assistance of other school personnel.

Special Education Teacher

The special education teacher's role is very much dependent on the school in which s/he is employed and the school's view of inclusion as well as the severity of the disability of the child with whom s/he is working. In schools where inclusion is not viewed as a favorable philosophical approach to instruction, the special education teacher may be involved in more of a "pull-out" model, in which students receive special education services in a separate, special education classroom. At times, the special education teacher may serve in a more collaborative role, in which s/he assists the classroom teacher in modifying instruction so that the student with a disability can be successful in the regular classroom. If a child has a significant disability or, in particular, a challenging behavior disorder, they are more likely to receive services from the special education teacher outside the regular classroom.

School Counselors

School counselors provide most of the counseling services in schools. The American School Counselors Association sees school counselors as the "vital link within the school that integrates the social and emotional components of school life with the academic and vocational aspects" (Jennings, 1995). They also see themselves as the "natural conduits to connect students, teachers, and administrators with the business community and world of work" (2). While the training and philosophy of counselors is similar regardless of the level at which they work, the role of counselors varies widely, depending on whether they serve an elementary, a middle/junior high, or a senior high school population.

Elementary school counselors probably do more actual counseling than counselors at the other levels. They see the parents more often and work more with home-school relationships. They do what is essentially play therapy with the children who demonstrate some problem behavior (e.g., overactive, withdrawn, not seeming to understand the school environment). They take an active role in classrooms, presenting teaching units, observing students, and working with students who need attention. School counselors need training in play therapy, general listening skills, family therapy, group counseling, and report writing. They need a background in child development, counseling theories, assessment, research, child abuse and neglect, legal and ethical issues, and multicultural issues.

Middle-school counselors do much work with interpersonal skills, either individually or with groups. They help students understand the changes of puberty and the need to do some educational planning. They help students choose classes and understand what is often a new system of school organization. It is usually the first time students have had choices in their class work. Middle-school counselors also need training in the skills of the elementary school counselor (with the possible exception of play therapy), and they need additional background in educational and career planning.

High school counselors spend much time with educational and career planning. They also counsel students who are having interpersonal problems with friends or family. High school students may seek help in dating situations, with substance abuse problems, with pregnancy, and with any number of other teenage problems. High school counselors process course selection planning, college applications, school-to-work planning, and monitor academic progress. They need training similar to that of the middle-school counselor, but with more emphasis on post-high school planning.

According to Paisley and Borders (1995), school counselors need to

prepare themselves to deal with increasing numbers of single-parent and low-income families, women in the workforce, and students from minority and immigrant groups; greater use of technology in schools and the workplace; more frequent career changes; and increasing violence in schools, families and communities (151).

They suggest that adjustments in programs will be necessary to address these changes.

Mental Health Counselors and Social Workers

Mental health counselors and/or social workers work with students who have serious problems. The problems may be family related, behavioral issues, or they might be a result of poor attendance. These counselors usually see students regularly in order to help them deal with their issues. In most cases the counselors need to work with the family as well as with the student. They may also need to work with the student's teachers and with outside agencies. The background required for this position includes not only a solid preparation in counseling and therapy but also knowledge of how schools operate. There is a need to understand serious pathology, as well as a need to be familiar with social service agencies and the juvenile court system.

Not all schools have counselors prepared or able to do in-depth counseling. For these schools, children are referred to outside agencies. The problem sometimes arises when parents or children familiar with school personnel might accept counseling from them but feel labeled and hesitant when asked to see an outside counselor.

School Psychologists

School psychologists do individual testing and appraisals for students who have been identified as having serious problems. They may chair committees that determine the most productive program for such students. In some schools, the psychologist will also see students in individual or small group settings. School psychologists must have a background in testing and appraisal and they must also understand psychological diagnosis and treatment.

School Nurses

In addition to monitoring the health records of all children, the school nurse must distribute medication, conduct routine procedures for children with health problems (such as catheterizations), and be available to assist in medical crises (Bullock, 1992).

> *School health nursing makes an important contribution to the support of the educational process for children and adolescents. In one of the most cost-effective community settings for the delivery of health services to the school-age child and families, professional school nurses provide an important link between the school and the community health system (Smith and Maurer, 1995, 753).*

The school nurse's role has expanded for several reasons. Changes in health care coverage, changes in laws that have brought students back into the public schools who previously might have been educated in another setting, changes in society that make it a dangerous place for children and adolescents, all contribute to that expanded role. The nurse may be the primary caregiver for some, the monitor for students with medical conditions, or the advocate for adolescents' safety in their interpersonal behavior.

Physical Therapist

Physical therapists are required to have a physician's prescription in order to work with a child, and are considered to be medical professionals. Their main goal is to assist the children in improving their motor function, including increasing their strength, mobility, and balance.

Occupational Therapist

An occupational therapist is also a medical professional who needs a prescription from a physician in order to treat a child. Occupational therapists tend to focus on upper body motor skills, most often in the context of daily living skills.

Speech and Language Therapist

This professional is responsible for treating children with language and speech problems that interfere with the student's ability to communicate on a daily basis.

The Parent's Perspective

Although they are not usually considered to be "personnel," parents play an important role in their child's education. Parents who support their child's efforts in school are helping to promote their child's social, emotional, and academic growth. Parents who are uninterested or inattentive to their child's schoolwork are communicating that neither an education nor the child is valued.

For a student to succeed in school, it is imperative that parents and school personnel work together. If a child has a learning problem, strategies need to be developed that can be implemented at home and at school. If a child has met with great success on a project in school, recognition from parents and teachers should be provided.

Often, schools and parents may not be working in concert with each other. Through misconceptions or miscommunication, distrust may grow between parents and school staff (Turnbull and Turnbull, 1990). As an example, when a student who is truant is called into the office with his/her parent(s) to discuss the matter, the school may feel that the parents are in part to blame for their child's misbehavior. Their assumption may be that the parent has not done an adequate job in disciplining the child. The parents may, perhaps because of their own negative experiences at school, be very reluctant to attend this meeting. They may feel they are to be blamed for their child's conduct or that the school personnel are not doing a sufficient job of making the school a welcoming place for their child. Many assumptions may be in place before the meeting begins, none of which may be accurate.

Schools need to work to provide an environment that provides understanding and support for parents who may be facing many challenges in raising their children. A message must be sent from school to home that parents play an important role in the educational process and that they are valued members of the educational team.

CONTROVERSIAL ISSUES AND DILEMMAS IN THE PROVISION OF SERVICE

There are a number of issues, arguments, and disagreements regarding the delivery of the services presented in this chapter. They relate to what the goals for students are and what services should therefore be provided, who provides which services, what is the best way to provide them, and how all of this will be paid for.

We would like to think that the school's goals for students would be to have them grow and develop in both the academic and social/emotional spheres. This would require academic programs designed so that all students, of varying abilities and with varying challenges to their progress, could learn to the best of their abilities. It would also require programs to deal with the social and emotional problems of some, but also to help all students grow in these areas. While legislation does protect some services for children and adolescents with special needs, many programs and staff that provide for social and emotional growth are often cut in the name of economy. In some cases this is because of a philosophy that believes that schools are only for academic growth. In others such staff are cut because they have a lower priority than other services.

WHO PROVIDES SERVICES?

Who provides the services is an ongoing debate. Traditionally, most of the services outside of the classroom have been provided by a school counselor. However, with more specialized preparation for the different professionals and because the problems students face in today's world are more complicated and more serious, other professionals are often hired (or their services are contracted for) by school districts. Teaching functions are still the province of the classroom teacher. Special education teachers may act as consultants or may be in charge of a resource room. Generally, guidance functions are still the responsibility of the school counselor, but teachers also often fulfill this function. In fact, in a comprehensive, progressive system, counselors often teach teachers how to present certain guidance-related material.

SHOULD COUNSELING BE PROVIDED IN SCHOOLS?

One argument is that counseling is not properly a function of schools. This view suggests that counseling, at least personal counseling, should be done outside the school. Even those who believe that we need to provide this service in schools, find confusion over whose role it is to do so. Increasingly, school have hired mental health specialists to work with students who have serious emotional problems. School counselors work with all students to enhance their academic, career, and personal growth. However, either by definition within the school, or by necessity because of lack of other personnel, school counselors may do more in-depth counseling than their role would suggest. School psychologists sometimes handle more serious problems; however, in many cases they are too busy doing student evaluations. Some specialists' skills, such as those of school nurses and physical therapists, are clear and unique enough that there is no argument as to who should perform the task.

HOW SHOULD SERVICES BE PROVIDED?

How services should be provided is also a much discussed topic. Partly this is because of philosophical differences, but it is also because of financial constraints. Sometimes school districts are looking for the least expensive way to provide a service, whether or not it is the best way. The "best" way, of course, is a subject of much disagreement within and among the various professions. The return of many special services to the school is an example. Legislation requires that these services be available to children with special needs. The question of whether these services are better delivered in the school or through an outside agency often centers around cost rather than meeting the child's needs in the most productive ways. Even when in-school service is recommended (as is often the case under the philosophy of inclusion), funding can still be a problem.

In terms of guidance and counseling, some think the cognitive, classroom approach is most efficient and most effective for most issues. Others feel that small groups and individual work are more productive. There is some agreement that certain sensitive interpersonal and family issues are best dealt with individually. Then, again, the issue is whether this ought to be done by school staff or should be referred to an outside agency.

FINANCING SERVICES

Finances, as we have said, tend to drive many of these decisions. There is a constant concern about balancing and prioritizing the services offered according to the available monies. While most school districts believe they need more money to provide all of these services, many in the local state and federal governments question that need. The funding of public schools is an ongoing debate.

However, the total budget is only one issue. The prioritizing of the spending for services is another. It is in this area where the arguments about the role and goals of schools come into play. This will be a continuing discussion, and those who believe, as we do, that schools need to teach the whole child, need to make sure that our voices continue to be heard.

TRENDS IN THE PROVISION OF SERVICES IN SCHOOLS

As schools strive to address the issues raised in previous sections of this chapter, several trends emerge that schools must take into consideration in developing future programs.

DELIVERY OF SERVICES WITHIN THE SCHOOL

For many reasons, schools are being asked to provide more services for their students. Students who in the past may have been referred out for assessment, treatment, or their entire education are more likely today to be assessed, treated, and educated in their local schools. This puts more burden on school staff, who must be prepared to help these students. Schools need to hire well-trained professionals and they need to provide in-service education for their present staffs. The pressure to provide more and more services comes largely from three sources: (1) the changing health care reimbursement system, (2) the financial crunch many schools are facing that forces them to find ways to avoid expensive contracted services, and (3) the increasingly complex and violent society that puts so many more pressures on students.

MORE PROGRAMS TO ADDRESS CHILDREN AT RISK

As mentioned above, an increasingly violent society, especially as it affects children, requires schools to help students understand these forces and learn to protect themselves. Unfortunately, much of that violence occurs within the students' homes and they may need to be protected from their own families. They also need help in avoiding self-destructive behaviors such as substance abuse. Depression, juvenile delinquency, and suicide are other consequences of living in dysfunctional families, neighborhoods, or society in general.

Children may live in homes where drug use, abuse, and emotional trauma take place on a daily basis. Oftentimes, children living in the poorer areas come to school lacking the nourishment to perform effectively. Schools are seeing their roles expanded beyond the classroom to provide services to meet the physical and emotional needs of children. Social skills training is a part of the regular curriculum—considered by some schools to be as important as the three Rs. An increase in ancillary staff (school counselors, mental health counselors, and social workers) should be a result.

HEALTH CARE ISSUES

Because of the epidemic growth of teenage pregnancy, schools have become the center for sex education. Students are receiving more in-depth and, at times, controversial instruction on sexual development, contraception, and pregnancy care. Condoms are being offered to students in many schools. Some schools offer day care for the children of teenage mothers and often parenting programs for the young parents. AIDS education has become another major part of the school curriculum.

These issues bring new challenges to the role of schools and will continue to be subjects of controversy.

COUNSELING AND GUIDANCE EMPHASIS ON DEVELOPMENTAL ISSUES

The emphasis in comprehensive counseling and guidance programs today is a developmental one, based on such theorists as Erikson, Piaget, Kohlberg, Gilligan, Loevinger, Dupont, Hunt, and Selman (Borders and Drury, 1992; Paisley and Peace, 1995). Counselors, or whoever is planning classroom activities, present students with information and challenges that relate to their developmental level. Guidance units for adolescents, for instance, might deal with identity issues; for older elementary students one might plan programs that teach practical skills. The goal is to help students better understand what they are experiencing and to aid them in coping with the challenges that accompany growth.

Developmental school counseling programs are intentional, educational experiences specifically designed to encourage the development of more complex meaning-

making structures. Outcomes associated with such movement would include more complex structures for processing experience and higher levels of cognitive, ethical, and interpersonal maturity (Paisley and Peace, 1995, 92).

The American School Counselors Association (National Standards for School Counseling Programs, Draft, 1997) has suggested standards for student development in three areas: academic, career, and personal/social. The academic goals relate to helping the student become a more effective learner. In career development, the goals include learning to relate personal skills and interests to the world of work. Counselors working in the personal/social area aid students to understand and appreciate themselves and others, including families. Further, the counselors promote responsible citizenship and effective goal settings and decision making. These laudable goals require that all professionals collaborate and cooperate toward the implementation and monitoring of the experiences that will produce these results.

PLANNING FOR DIVERSITY IN THE STUDENT BODY

We are becoming more aware of how diverse our society really is, and how this diversity is likely to become more pronounced as we enter the next century. Schools have had to deal with many issues related to the multiplicity of cultures from which their students come, often before society and funding sources have provided funds for programs to meet these needs. On the issue of language alone, there is an ongoing debate about the teaching of English as a second language or as the only language taught. We also have a long-standing and continuing debate on how best to deal with the issue of racism and ethnicity. We have seen evidence of how lack of sensitivity to race and gender (Noddings, 1992) lead to bias in teaching. We are currently trying to find ways to meet the needs of gay and lesbian youth, who suffer great discrimination both in and outside of schools.

INCLUSIVE PROGRAMS

More and more, schools are considering ways that they can serve all children in the regular classroom. This philosophy is being advanced through legislation at the state and national level and litigation, with several cases being won in the courts, that will allow students with disabilities to participate fully in the regular classroom with support. At issue is the amount of support (which can be costly) school systems must provide before placing a child in a separate classroom. A concern for some is the appropriateness of the curriculum in the regular classroom for students with disabilities. Proponents of inclusion suggest that curriculum modifications can be made and that the most important lifelong benefit is that the student with a disability has membership in the community of the school and thus has a sense of belonging.

COLLABORATION BETWEEN PARENTS AND PROFESSIONALS

It is increasingly apparent that school personnel and parents need to work together in order to best serve the students. Because of the trend toward more services in the schools, an individual child's or adolescent's needs may cross over the typical divisions of home and school. This is particularly true in relationship to classroom teachers, special education teachers, and school counselors. Schools need to adjust their organizational structures to facilitate this interaction.

Traditionally, classroom teachers taught in their classrooms alone, often with the door closed. With the complex issues children bring to school that extend beyond their academic needs, and with the inclusion movement described above, teachers are learning to work together and with parents and other professionals (counselors, therapists, special education staff) to meet the needs of heterogeneous groups of children. This requires all school staff to develop skills in collaboration and teamwork that may not have been necessary in earlier years.

SUMMARY

Schools face many challenges in meeting the needs of a diverse student population. Societal problems place pressures on students that were not experienced by previous generations. Services beyond the actual teaching of basic subjects are necessary to enable students to become full members of society. To achieve this goal an array of services and personnel must be available to treat the total child and help them to feel positively about themselves and their accomplishments. To maintain these services will require a huge investment from our communities—a worthwhile investment, for our children are our best resources and our future.

EXPLORATION QUESTIONS

1. How has the role of schools changed in recent years?
2. What importance does social/emotional development play in a student's education?
3. How have the laws changed in the last twenty years to provide more appropriate education for students with disabilities?
4. What does inclusion mean? What ramifications does it have for teachers? for students with and without special needs?
5. What does "least restrictive environment" mean? What are the most to least restrictive placements for students with special needs?
6. What is the recent trend in school guidance programs and what are the implications of this trend?

7. Discuss the debate on who should provide counseling services in the schools.
8. Describe the role of the various personnel in schools.
9. In what ways do counseling services and special education services overlap?

ACTIVITIES FOR APPLIED LEARNING

1. Visit your local school and ask to meet with some of the personnel listed for you in this chapter. Ask them to describe their role to you. You may want to consider asking them the following questions:

   - What are their greatest concerns about schools today?
   - Why did they choose their profession?
   - What rewards do they experience in their work?

2. View some videotapes that present inclusion as a model for teaching. Consider the tapes "Regular Lives" or "Educating Peter." Talk to a teacher or parent of a child who has gone to school under this model. Consider what your own position on this issue would be, given a choice of an inclusive placement.
3. Interview someone with a disability. What were the biggest challenges they faced in school? What do they wish had been done differently for them?
4. View movies such as *Dangerous Minds* or *Stand and Deliver*. What do schools need to provide to meet the challenges of today's inner city youth?
5. Debate the role of schools in providing services to pregnant teens or teenage parents. Should schools provide programs to keep these students in school?
6. Interview school counselors individually or invite a panel of various professionals to class to describe their roles and discuss the challenges they face in their work.
7. Write about your own experiences with school personnel, including teachers and school counselors. How has your development been affected by them?
8. Discuss ways in which teacher sensitivity can be raised regarding race and gender issues.

SUGGESTED READING

Borders, L. D., & Drury, S. M. "Comprehensive School Counseling Programs: A Review for Policy Makers and Practitioners," *Journal of Counseling and Development* 70 (1992), 487–498.

Bullock, L. *Exceptionalities in Children and Youth.* Boston: Allyn and Bacon, 1992.

Ferrara, J. M. *Peer Mediation—Finding a Way to Care.* York, ME: Stenhouse Publ., 1996.

Gibson, R. L., Mitchell, M. H., & Basile, S. K. *Counseling in the Elementary School.* Boston: Allyn & Bacon, 1993.

Jennings, M. "A New Vision of School Counseling," *The Counselor* 33, #1 (1995), 190–195.

National Information Center for Children and Youth with Disabilities (NICHY), "Questions and Answers about the IDEA." Washington, DC: Interstate Research Associates, 1993.

Paisley, P. O., & Borders, L. D. "School Counseling: An Evolving Specialty," *Journal of Counseling and Development* 74 (1995), 150–153.

Pederson, P., & Carey, J. C. *Multicultural Counseling in Schools.* Boston: Allyn & Bacon, 1994.

Schmidt, J. J. *Counseling in Schools.* Boston: Allyn & Bacon, 1996.

Smith, D., & Luckasson, R. *Introduction to Special Education.* Boston: Allyn and Bacon, 1995.

Stainback, W. *Controversial Issues Confronting Special Education.* Boston: Allyn and Bacon, 1995.

REFERENCES

Borders, L. D., & Drury, S. M. "Comprehensive School Counseling Programs: A Review for Policy Makers and Practitioners," *Journal of Counseling and Development* 70 (1992), 487–498.

Bullock, L. *Exceptionalities in Children and Youth.* Boston: Allyn and Bacon, 1992.

Education for All Handicapped Children Act (EHA). 20 U.S.C. sections 1400 et seq. and amendments.

Grossman, H. J. (Ed.). *Classification in Mental Retardation.* Washington, DC: American Association on Mental Deficiency, 1983.

Jennings, M. "A New Vision of School Counseling," *The Counselor* 33(1) (1995), 2.

National Information Center for Children and Youth with Disabilities (NICHY). "Questions and Answers about the IDEA," Washington, DC: Interstate Research Associates, 1993.

National Joint Committee on Learning Disabilities. "Learning Disabilities Definition," *Learning Disabilities Quarterly* 6 (1983), 42–44.

National Standards for School Counseling Programs, (Draft), American School Counselors Association, 1997.

Noddings, N. "The Gender Issue," *Educational Leadership* vol. 49(4) (1992), pp. 65–70.

Paisley, P. O., & Borders, L. D. "School Counseling: An Evolving Specialty," *Journal of Counseling and Development* 74 (1995), 150–153.

Paisley, P. O., & Peace, S. D. "Developmental Principles: A Framework for School Guidance Programs," *Elementary School Counselor* (December 1995), 85–93.

Smith, D., & Luckasson, R. *Introduction to Special Education.* Boston: Allyn and Bacon, 1995.

Smith, C., & Maurer, F. *Community Health Nursing: Theory and Practice.* Philadelphia: Saunders, 1995.

Stainback, W. *Controversial Issues Confronting Special Education.* Boston: Allyn and Bacon, 1995.

Stainback, W., & Stainback, S. *Curriculum Considerations in Inclusive Classrooms.* Baltimore: Brookes Publishing, 1992.

Turnbull, A., & Turnbull, R. *Families, Professionals and Partnerships.* Columbus, OH: Merrill Publishing, 1990.

7

COUNSELING FOR FAMILIES AND CHILDREN

Lloyd T. Williams

"I don't want to go into child welfare" explained one student, *"I want to study counseling."* From the perspective of someone who has worked in a variety of child welfare agencies, I found this declaration amusing. A large part of child welfare services involves counseling. It is counseling when a worker helps a distraught mother cope with the fact that her children have just been removed. Counseling is involved when a family is being helped to understand how to deal with their difficult child. A young adoptee who seeks to find his/her biological parents is coun-

seled. In fact, counseling represents the framework of the provision of services to children and their families.

This chapter seeks to explain the concept of counseling for children and families. Counseling is certainly inherent in other types of services, such as foster care, adoption, or protective services. Sometimes, however, as a part of coping with specific issues, families or children are referred to agencies whose primary service is that of counseling. These agencies might be family service centers, child guidance clinics, mental health centers, or even private therapists, such as psychiatric social workers, psychologists, mental health counselors, psychologists, or others trained in the field. It is counseling as a specific psychotherapeutic service and how families are served by this service, that will be primarily addressed in this chapter.

WHAT IS COUNSELING?

Counseling is a process of interaction between human beings, the goal of which is to improve the quality of life for those being counseled. Counselors act on behalf of their clients in such a way as to facilitate adjustment to something, self-discovery, healing, and positive change. Since all human beings, including those in the counseling professions, struggle throughout their lives with personal problems, emotional wounds, nagging anxieties, and self-limiting fears, it is important to understand that counseling is a contractual process. It is an agreement between people that, in a designated place at a designated time, certain roles will be assumed.

The role of counselor is taken on by a person who, for the duration of each counseling session, puts aside his/her own life challenges, and attends to the needs of others. The role of the people being counseled is assumed by those who, for the duration of each session, put aside the ways in which their lives are successful and satisfying to look instead at aspects of life that are painful or disappointing. Ideally, in the process of taking up these roles, both counselor and counseled deepen their experience of life.

BASIC ASSUMPTIONS

At the core of the counseling professions, certain basic assumptions are operative:

1. Human beings, by nature, strive towards wholeness (Singer, 1972). This striving occurs across every level: physically, mentally, emotionally, and spiritually. By "wholeness" is meant more than problem-free happiness. Wholeness implies an integrity of being that embraces fragmentation, tension, and conflict as ingredients crucial to the process of growth and the enjoyment of life.

2. Central to psychological health and well-being is the ability to make meaning out of one's life experience.

3. In the search for wholeness and meaning, people create or encounter obstacles in their path. These obstacles can be external or internal.

External obstacles include people, things, situations, or events that act on us, or appear to act on us, from outside ourselves. For example, a child, adolescent, or adult may be substantially set back in his/her development by injuries sustained in an automobile accident. A person's goals may be thwarted in some significant way by the deliberate interference of other people with opposing values. Illness may strike at an inopportune time. Or perhaps one's efforts in a particular endeavor do not get the hoped for results because a family crisis occurs at a critical moment. Whatever the particular circumstances, external factors seem to play a deciding role.

Internal obstacles include conflicts and complexes, fears, inhibitions, hang-ups, limiting belief systems, and maladaptive thought and behavior patterns. These obstacles are often much more difficult to come to terms with ultimately precisely because they operate within us and tend to be rooted in formative childhood experiences.

4. Finally, in almost every model of counseling it is assumed that change is possible. Human beings can learn to think, feel, and behave in different ways. The birth that brings us into this world and the death that ultimately leads us out of it are mirrored throughout life in real and equally profound experiences of death and rebirth wherein old ways of being are left behind, making way for the unfolding of new possibilities.

WHEN A FAMILY MIGHT SEEK COUNSELING

REFERRAL SYSTEM

Families generally come to a counseling agency either by way of a self-referral or via a referral made by an outside agent. Self-referred families recognize that a problem exists that needs attention and that is more than the family can cope with on its own. Such circumstances include difficulties that continue to cause distress despite the family's attempts to respond to them, as well as crisis situations that occur without warning and overwhelm family resources. Some families familiar with counseling, who have had successful past counseling experiences, also seek counseling services as a preventive measure, hoping thereby to address problems in their early stages, before things become more serious.

Examples of problems for which a family might refer itself for counseling cover the gamut of possible difficulties: A child or teenager may be noticeably depressed, without meaningful friendships, performing poorly in school, or have recurring thoughts of suicide. A mother or father may themselves struggle with depression, with adverse consequences for the children. A family member may suffer with a serious mental or physical illness, with stressful repercussions for the rest of the family as well. A trauma may have occurred, such as a rape, murder, automobile accident, sexual molestation, or incident of domestic violence, leaving the family devastated and needing support and assistance.

Family dynamics such as marital strife often create ongoing tensions within the home, with children acting out the conflict in negative ways. Divorce issues can throw a family into crisis, creating a situation that calls for containment and direction. Stepfamily issues are another stumbling block for many families: Children frequently resent the intrusion of a "stranger" into their lives when their divorced mother or father remarries. If the new partner has children of her or his own, the picture is further complicated and stress may intensify. Substance abuse is a common focus for counseling services also, a parent's or a child's drug or alcohol use often causing considerable disruption and/or dysfunction within the family.

For children and adolescents, behavior problems often motivate a family to seek outside intervention. Temper tantrums, oppositional and defiant behaviors at home or at school, hyperactivity, aggressive interactions with peers, and general disregard for family and/or community rules and expectations are among the many concerns presented by parents during an initial counseling session. For younger children, separation anxiety (excessive distress whenever out of sight of primary parenting figures), prolonged toilet training problems, inability to relate positively with other children, unexplained obsessions and/or compulsions, aggressive or cruel behavior towards animals, prolonged thumb-sucking, excessive whining or clinging behaviors, as well as various developmental delays or complications are also regularly brought to counseling professionals as areas calling for assistance.

The above listed examples by no means exhaust the many reasons families choose to refer themselves for counseling. Indeed, the important point is to underscore the enormous variety of situations for which counseling may offer families a means of support during difficult times. It should also be noted that counseling services can be employed by families to provide family members with a vehicle for self-exploration, to support them through demanding developmental phases, such as adolescence or mid-life, or simply to assist them in the ongoing process of learning about themselves and making sense of their lives.

Referrals by Outside Agencies

For many families, counseling services are arranged as a result of pressures or recommendations coming from outside the family circle. Families unable or unwilling to respond to the needs of a troubled child or adolescent often find themselves contacted by school personnel, police officers, or other local authorities about their youngster's behavior. In the case of child neglect or abuse, child protection organizations are empowered by the state to mandate counseling for families as part of comprehensive service plans implemented to protect victimized children or children at risk (Tower, 1996). For delinquent youth, the juvenile court system frequently recommends or orders counseling as a condition for avoiding more serious legal consequences, especially in the case of first-time minor offenders.

While families coming to counseling agencies via outside referrals frequently present exactly the same kind of core issues as do self-referred families, problems have often reached a more critical stage, involve a more serious degree of intensity, have led to legal proceedings, and/or have come to the attention of child protective service agencies. Examples might include the following situations:

1. A teenage boy and his family are referred to counseling by the juvenile court following an incident at school in which the boy pulled a knife on another student.

2. A family is referred to counseling by the treatment team of a hospital mental health unit following a suicide attempt by an adolescent girl.

3. A six-year-old child is in temporary foster care because of substantiated physical abuse charges against her father. The parents are required to begin family counseling as a condition for having their child returned to their home.

4. Repeated school suspensions for aggressive behavior, chronic truancy, and recent threats made to peers about gang retaliation result in a family meeting arranged at school. At this meeting, school personnel make it clear to the parent(s) that if their thirteen-year-old son's behavior does not improve immediately, placement in a more restrictive educational setting will be recommended. The parents are referred to a local counseling center to get help for the boy.

5. Teachers discover marijuana in the desk of an eleven-year-old girl. Inquiry results in the child's disclosure that her mother and her mother's "boyfriend" frequently allow her to smoke pot with them. The disclosure is reported to the local authorities. An investigation is conducted, and the family is referred for counseling as part of a service plan put into place to protect the child.

6. A concerned family doctor calls the parents of a seventeen-year-old boy after discovering numerous self-inflicted cigarette burns on the boy's body. The doctor refers the parents to a local counseling agency and encourages them to seek professional help for their son.

The specific circumstances that compel a person, agency, or social institution to recommend, pressure, or require a family to seek counseling services are virtually infinite in variety. The important point is that many families find themselves in counseling, at least initially, not because they recognized a situation needing attention, but because someone outside the family recognized it for them.

ATTITUDES ABOUT RECEIVING COUNSELING

SELF-REFERRED CLIENTS

Families who take it upon themselves to seek out services in response to recognized needs tend to approach counseling with positive expectations, or at least with an open mind toward the possibility of change. The fact that a problem or area of distress motivates a family to self-refer implies that at least some degree of denial has already been worked through. A certain readiness exists to look the problem in the eye and to grapple with it. The counselor is viewed as someone who has the training and experience to be of assistance to the family, someone with whom the family can cooperate for its own benefit.

CLIENTS REFERRED FROM OUTSIDE AGENCIES

For children and parents directed to counseling services by outside agencies, attitudes towards counseling run the range from cooperative and appreciative to cautious and suspicious, to resentful, resistant, and even hostile. Though it is risky to make generalizations, it is safe to say that children and/or families *mandated* to go to counseling by outside sources often adopt a defensive attitude, at least initially.

Alex was a sixteen-year-old boy referred to counseling by the juvenile court. He was involved with the court due to an assault he had made on a teacher. When he came to his first counseling meeting, he sullenly made it clear to his therapist that the only reason he was there was because he had to be. He told his counselor, "The court says I have to come to this place for the next six months. I'll come, 'cuz I have no choice, but forget it if you think I'm gonna talk about anything."

The Baxter family was referred to counseling by a child protective service agency as a prerequisite for being reunited with their thirteen-year-old daughter, T., following eight months of placement in a foster home. T. had been removed from her parent's home after a school gym teacher noticed and reported bruises on her back and legs. An investigation uncovered a history of physical beatings given to T. by her father whenever she disobeyed family rules. T. and her mother showed up at the first meeting, explaining to the counselor that Mr. Baxter refused to come with them because, in his words, "I don't need people sticking their noses into my personal business." When, several meetings later, the father succumbed to pressure and attended his first session, he told the counselor, "If you think you're going to tell me not to hit my kids when they have it coming, I'll tell you right now this whole therapy thing isn't going to go too far."

The defense mechanism of "denial" is often operative for families brought to counseling via outside referring agents. If a family is not actively seeking help for itself or one of its members in response to a recognized need, it frequently means the need itself, or the severity of it, is being denied. In essence, the family chooses "ignorance" as a way of coping. When outside interests pressure the family to confront a problem, a degree of resistance is expectable.

ATTITUDES ABOUT HAVING A PROBLEM

Most families bring to counseling a degree of anxiety about having a problem in the first place, and especially about giving an outsider (the counselor) detailed information about personal issues. Particularly for first-time consumers, but for people with previous experience in counseling as well, the idea of talking to a therapist produces anxiety because it implies vulnerability and exposure. The tender, not-so-successful areas of life may be revealed. A tremendous pressure exists in Western industrialized society to present oneself to the outside world in as positive a light as possible, as successful, happy, healthy, autonomous human beings in control of life. Conflicts, inhibitions, hang-ups, fears, insecurities, traumas, habits, addictions, pain, weakness, mistakes, failures, dysfunction, and so on, are viewed as undesirable. Instead of being valued as potential and powerful teachers, such "shadow" areas of life are seen as shameful (Zweig and Abrams, 1991). To let down the mask that is presented outwardly so that the inner, more private world can be explored raises anxiety and directly influences the attitude families have about seeing a counselor.

"Therapy Is for Crazy People"

The still common opinion that therapy is for "crazy" people inhibits many from considering counseling as a possible means of assistance during times of crisis or enduring family distress. Again, the stigma related to getting help in this particular form reflects the pervasive idea that having problems is not acceptable. In a society that places supreme value on productivity and autonomy, not being able to produce solutions to problems without outside help places one in the same camp as "crazy" people because it implies breakdown and dependence.

Mr. Henderson scheduled three intake appointments for his eight-year-old son, Michael, at a local youth guidance center. Each appointment came and went, with Mr. Henderson and his son failing to show up at the designated hour. Follow-up calls made by the counselor to the home resulted in explanations about transportation problems, scheduling conflicts, illness, and other extenuating circumstances. After the third "no-show," Mr. Henderson called to ask if the counselor could come to his home for the meetings. After careful questioning, the counselor learned that Mr. Henderson was troubled by the fact that the guidance center was located on the same grounds as the local state hospital. "We're not crazy," he told the counselor. "We're just looking for some help with a normal problem."

Mrs. Brandeis called a counseling agency in her area to get help for her thirteen-year-old daughter, Angela, who was acting out defiantly at school and at home. On the phone with an agency intake worker, Mrs.

Brandeis said, "It's nothing serious, just the usual thing with teenagers. Nobody's got, you know, mental problems, or anything."

"What Will the Neighbors Think?"

Preoccupation with the opinions of others is, for some populations, an anxiety related to counseling. It is somehow assumed (usually erroneously) that the neighbors (whether these be literally neighbors or "other people" in general) have no problems and that therefore one's own difficulties make one less by comparison. Being less in the eyes of others is a matter of shame for many families because it leads to a perceived diminishment of self.

Evan Johnston, Ph.D., opened a private practice for counseling in a small quiet town in Connecticut. In spite of extensive outreach to the community, Dr. Johnston's services were used by very few people in the area. Commenting on this disappointing situation to a friend one day, Dr. Johnston was told, "Evan, the reason you're not getting business is that your office is right in the downtown area. Everybody knows everybody in this town, and no one wants to be seen turning into your driveway, with that big sign in front telling the whole world that it's a Family Counseling Center." When Dr. Johnston later moved his office to a less public location in the same community, with no sign publicizing the type of services offered, business developed steadily.

"It's His/Her Problem, Not Mine"

An attitude frequently observed in family therapy is the stance that "it's *his/her* problem, not mine." The so-called identified patient, e.g., an acting-out son or daughter, is the problem and the rest of the family is fine. Parents can sometimes be stubbornly insistent that they have nothing to do with a child's distress. A defensive attitude is presented, nourished by a fear that blame may be attributed to the parents. Fear of blame has to be defended against only to the degree that parents believe it is not OK for them to be less than perfect.

"We Have a Problem, You Fix It"

Some parents come to counseling with the attitude, "Here is the problem; now you fix it." This attitude provides adult caretakers with a measure of distance from the discomfort they feel about having a child who is experiencing problems. If the child can be dropped off at the therapist's office to be fixed, parents can more easily maintain the fantasy that they are not responsible for their children's circumstances. When a car breaks down, it is taken to a garage, left for a period of time in a professional's skillful hands, and repaired. Parents with child-related problems often act as if they wish their difficulties could similarly be given over to someone else's skillful expertise to be resolved.

Jacob's mother brought her fourteen-year-old son to counseling because he was depressed, failing school, and giving her a hard time at home. After three sessions talking with Jacob, it became clear to the counselor that the boy received limited structure, encouragement, or direction at home from either his mother or his stepfather, and that the parents had significant problems of their own that were affecting Jacob negatively. With Jacob's permission, the counselor called his mother and suggested that the next several meetings include her and Jacob's stepfather. The mother agreed, but proceeded to miss every meeting subsequently scheduled. Sending Jake to counseling by himself was never a problem. Involving herself was obviously too threatening, because it implied that she might have something to do with the difficulties Jacob was experiencing.

To approach a child's unhappiness responsibly means parents must be open to the possibility that they play a part in that unhappiness. It requires parents to cut through their own denial, to look at ways in which they might be contributing to their child's distress, and to accept the fact that time, effort, and a willingness to change themselves may be required if difficulties are to be overcome.

ETHNIC AND CROSS-CULTURAL CONSIDERATIONS

Cross-cultural counseling with children and families, i.e., counseling situations where one or more members of the family hold strongly to cultural values and traditions significantly different from those held by the counselor, present unique challenges to the counseling process. Working with an ethnically diverse clientele requires a counselor to be sensitive to cultural differences, respectful of unfamiliar customs, and open to perspectives of life quite different from his/her own. Beyond sensitivity and openmindedness, active study and comprehensive knowledge of different cultures, together with specialized skills in counseling, are demanded of counselors who are engaged primarily in cross cultural work (Atkinson et al., 1993).

Attitudes towards counseling vary notably between ethnic groups, with strong beliefs and subtle differences in values complicating and coloring each individual case. While the subject of cross-cultural counseling is a vast and complex topic that can only be briefly mentioned in the present context, it is hoped that some examples may serve to give the student an appreciation for the many kinds of issues involved.

The Dega family, of Jamaican origin, was referred to counseling by a state child protection agency following the placement of the family's sixteen-year-old son, Matthew, in a foster home due to substantiated physical abuse. Mr. and Mrs. Dega came to the first meeting furious, humiliated, and determined to make it quite clear to the counselor that they resented the intrusion of outsiders into their private affairs. As counseling proceeded, the counselor learned that, in Jamaica, families settle their problems internally, without professional intervention. Such intervention is felt to be invasive, offensive, and unnecessary. In addition, the parents and grandmother of the family were outraged that a practice of child discipline common and accepted in their native country was viewed as "abusive" in the United States.

The Yamiko family came to counseling for help with problems centering around the defiant behavior of teenaged children. Mr. and Mrs. Yamiko held to traditional Japanese values in which the authority of parents was never openly challenged by the children. The adolescents in the family (James, David, and Irene), raised in the United States since early childhood, were rebellious, directly confrontational, and angry that their parents did not understand their need for independence, self-expression, and peer acceptance. The parents looked to the counselor for back-up, fully expecting that their values would be reinforced during counseling sessions.

The examples cited above present situations occurring in the United States in which therapists with North American values work with families from other cultures. It should be recognized, however, that cross-cultural counseling "refers to any counseling relationship in which two or more of the participants are culturally different" (Atkinson et al., 1993). The same kind of issues that must be attended to when a white counselor from the United States works with an African family from Nigeria are present and in need of sensitivity when an African, Puerto Rican, Japanese, or Haitian counselor works with an American family from Boston. (Very similar kinds of concerns are involved when a hearing counselor works with a family that has deaf family members, when a gay or lesbian counselor works with a family valuing a heterosexual lifestyle, or when a counselor from the Jewish faith works with a Catholic family.) In all cases, respect for difference (in attitude, orientation, belief system, and behavior) must underpin the counseling endeavor if effective work is to be accomplished.

CHANGING ATTITUDES ABOUT COUNSELING

Beginning in the late 1960s and gaining increased momentum throughout the 1970s, a notable development could be observed in the United States relative to the mainstream public's attitude towards psychotherapy. Among other factors, the influence of mind-altering drugs, the political unrest of the times, and the impact of the Vietnam War turned the attention of individuals, and the nation, inward. Self-reflection and self-exploration became primary interests. An entire generation of concerned and thoughtful individuals began delving into the workings of the human mind, with an emphasis on personal development, and psychological and spiritual growth. The stigma of psychotherapy, which once caused people to be ashamed to see a therapist, began to shift towards an appreciation of "inner work" as a vehicle for positive change, a pathway to self-knowledge, a catalyst for the realization of human potential.

In the 1980s and 1990s, emphasis on individual self-exploration in psychotherapy has been challenged on the grounds that preoccupation with strictly personal growth, unbalanced by equal time and effort given to local and global needs, contributes to the birth, intensification, and tenacity of problems on the collective level. As an increasingly connected and globally more sophisticated world community moves towards the end of the first millennium, changing attitudes towards counseling will no doubt continue to reflect the complex dynamics of internal and external developments on the micro and macro levels.

MEDICAL MODEL VERSUS HOLISTIC MODEL

As increasing numbers of individuals from the mainstream of society began to value psychotherapeutic and counseling services as valid means for personal growth, the traditional medical model of mental health also began to evolve. The old hierarchy of "helpless sick patient" treated by "powerful healthy doctor" could not maintain itself in the face of an expanding consciousness about the nature of health in general. "Health" came to be understood as operating along a continuum, the positive end of which moved into the arena of human potential and knew no limits. The traditional medical view of mental health as a condition free of categorized psychological symptoms was supplemented by a more holistic understanding of health that began to challenge the equation "symptomless = healthy" (Weick, 1983).

The holistic model opened up the entire investigation of mind/body integrity, and posed the questions, "Are symptoms necessarily bad? Could symptoms be seen as communications, as motivators for change, lessons, or as flags for conditions needing attention below the level of manifest sign? Could symptoms sometimes simply be part of an individual's life, adding color and hue, individuality and peculiarity to one's experience?" (Hillman, 1991).

Emphasis on the "whole person" has led to careful consideration of such factors as the quality and depth of a person's relationships with others, the extent to which one's creativity is free to express itself, the effectiveness of one's communications, the degree of meaningfulness that operates in one's life, one's relationship to death, and to such concepts as god, spirituality, joy, purpose, and so on. Whereas the medical model tended to view human beings primarily in terms of pathologies to be cured, the holistic model called attention to human beings as evolving selves challenged by life and life's circumstances to stretch themselves towards ever more expansive ways of being. From this perspective, the doctor–patient relationship becomes more a matter of role, rather than a statement about relative health. Even when a clear and marked discrepancy exists between level of functioning of doctor and patient, the holistic view understands that both are engaged by life with possibilities for becoming increasingly whole, however differently that wholeness may express itself (Dossey, 1994; Cassidy, 1994; LeShan 1992; Budd, 1992).

THE IMPACT OF FEMINISM

A growing and significant movement within the field of psychology calls attention to issues of gender, questioning assumptions and core beliefs about human nature that have historically been proposed and developed predominantly by male thinkers. The supremacy of traditional masculine values such as autonomy, detachment, productivity, and rationality is now being challenged by feminist theorists who wish to achieve a more balanced understanding by emphasizing the importance of relatedness, involvement, stillness, and feeling (Sullivan, 1989).

As the impact of such thinking permeates the culture, changes can be observed in prevailing attitudes towards counseling. Increasingly, men come to counseling actively seeking to better understand problems of intimacy and relationship in their lives. The ability to adequately express feelings and to communicate on deep levels is also a more commonly heard goal. Counseling itself, as a context for openly and directly expressing one's inner thoughts and feelings, is arguably less threatening today for men than it was forty years ago, due in large part to the contributions of feminist thought (Zastrow, 1993).

As feminist concepts and analyses continue to be developed and refined, and as men specifically and the culture in general absorb and respond to these new understandings, it is likely that the counseling professions will continue to see a gradual evolution in consciousness on the part of men and women, boys and girls, and adolescent youth. That this evolution has already begun is affirmed by the notable changes observable in societal attitudes towards rape, domestic violence and battering, incest, workaholism, child support, fathering, sexual orientation, gender roles, and intimacy.

TYPES OF COUNSELING

THE PROFESSIONS

Psychiatry: Psychiatrists are medical doctors who specialize in treating pathologies of the mind and emotions. Training requirements include medical school, residency in psychiatric medicine, and licensure by the medical community. Psychiatrists are the only counseling professionals who can legally prescribe psychotropic medications (i.e., medications that act on mental processes) for their patients.

While there is an enormous variety in the actual work that psychiatrists do, including in-depth short- and long-term psychotherapy/counseling with individuals, couples, families, and groups, a significant number of psychiatrists work in their practices primarily to prescribe and monitor the effect of psychotropic drugs. Due to the length, demand, and cost of their training, psychiatrists are generally the highest paid workers within the counseling field.

Psychology: Training to be a clinical psychologist includes graduate study for a master's and doctorate degree in psychology, clinically supervised internship, and licensure by the American Psychological Association. Psychologists receive extensive training in administering, scoring, and interpreting the full battery of recognized psychological tests. Because these tests are often requested by schools, courts, hospitals, clinics, and other institutions, some psychologists are able to make testing the core practice of their careers. While most psychologists do a combination of testing and psychotherapy (counseling) with clients, some prefer to concentrate on the counseling aspect of treatment, and opt for doing as little testing as possible. Like psychiatry, there is a great variety in the work that psychologists can do, in the areas of expertise they can specialize in, and the settings in which they can practice.

Social Work: Training in clinical social work includes two years of graduate study towards the completion of an MSW (Master of Social Work) degree. Graduate study requires both classroom work and field placement internship for on-the-job experience. Licensure for social work involves two years of full-time postgraduate employment under the direct supervision of a licensed social worker, and the passing of a nationally standardized board examination. While psychiatric training includes a focus on medication, and psychologists are trained to do testing, clinical social work training places an emphasis on understanding the psychological/emotional struggle of individuals and groups within the context of the greater social environment. As with the other two professions, social work is a versatile field, offering a wide variety of opportunities for employment, including private practice.

Mental Health Counseling: To work professionally as a mental health counselor, graduate study is required for a master's degree in counseling. In addition, a documented two-year period of full-time clinically supervised postgraduate work experience is required as a prerequisite for taking the certification examination. In most states, master's level mental health counselors are not permitted to take third-party reimbursement for services rendered. This means they can work in certain clinical settings, but cannot do private practice. Recently, a large and increasingly organized group of professional mental health counselors have lobbied successfully (in some states) for full licensure and recognition as third-party providers.

Art Therapy: To work as a certified art therapist, a person must complete a master's level degree in art therapy and an internship in a recognized and approved clinical setting. Art therapists, like mental health counselors, are working diligently at present to have their profession recognized and licensed under state regulation. Art therapists work in private practice, in clinics, and in hospitals.

SETTINGS

The counseling professions are carried out in a great variety of settings, each environment defining its own parameters for the work accomplished, and each exerting influence on the precise nature of the counseling process. Counseling with children and families is done in schools, outpatient clinics, private practice offices, in-patient hospital units, local parishes, synagogues, mosques, residential treatment programs, the juvenile courts, detox centers, prisons, half-way houses, homeless shelters, private homes, on the street, and on the phone, to name just some of the possibilities.

THE COUNSELING PROCESS

ASSESSMENT, DIFFERENTIAL DIAGNOSIS, AND TREATMENT PLANNING

All types of counseling services involve a process of assessment, diagnosis, and treatment planning, whether or not this process is conducted formally or informally. When a child or family comes to treatment, the counselor must evaluate a multitude of factors to ascertain the nature of the presenting concerns so that therapeutic work can be effective.

Assessment

The assessment process involves taking a thorough history of the child or family, a history that generally includes, but is not limited to, the following:

1. Names and ages of involved persons
2. Description of the presenting concern(s)
3. Precipitating factors
4. Why coming to treatment now?
5. Strengths and weaknesses
6. Genogram (family "map"—see Chapter 2)
7. Developmental history
8. Medical history
9. Psychiatric history
10. School and learning history
11. Work history
12. Depth and duration of family and peer relationships
13. Previous counseling experience
14. Suicide history, if any: attempts, statements, gestures
15. Abuse/trauma history: physical, sexual, emotional, ritual, and so on
16. Substance abuse history

17. Criminal/legal history
18. Extended family history: ethnic/cultural factors, abuse history, mental illness, physical illness, substance abuse, learning disability, criminality, and so on
19. Mental status exam
20. Initial hypotheses

Differential Diagnosis

Based on the nature and specific details of the information gathered during the assessment process, a tentative diagnosis is formulated. Whether done formally/ medically, or informally, skillful diagnosis is a critically important factor in counseling work, and one that directly guides the direction and course of treatment.

If a family brings a child for counseling, for example, concerned about recent and disturbing obsessive and compulsive behaviors, the clinician needs to know whether the behaviors indicate the early stages of Obsessive Compulsive Disorder, the probability of recent abuse or trauma, or acting out due to other factors. That is, what are the child's symptoms communicating about his/her condition?

If a child is brought for counseling because of depressed mood, the counselor needs to diagnose whether the problem is related to organic factors, circumstantial events, such as the death of a loved one, birth of a sibling, or peer conflicts, or perhaps parental expectations that are unrealistic for the child's developmental stage of life.

A teenage boy brought to treatment due to oppositional behavior at home and at school may be acting out frustration related to a learning disability, expressing anger over marital tension between his mother and father, reacting to his own ingestion of alcohol or drugs, or perhaps simply responding to his parents' and teachers' inability to set and maintain firm limits.

In all cases, misdiagnosis can lead to ineffective treatment or actual harm done to the client. Accurately assessing and diagnosing the problem, and its context, leads directly to appropriate treatment planning.

Treatment Planning

Once the counselor has completed an initial assessment and made a tentative diagnosis, a plan of intervention may be made and implemented. In true practice, assessment, diagnosis, and treatment planning all work together in an ongoing process, each affecting and modifying the other as the work proceeds. Treatment planning includes decisions about the following questions: (1) Who, specifically, is going to be the primary recipient of therapeutic services and in what modality? (2) What are the goals of treatment? (3) What approaches are going to be used in treatment to reach those goals effectively, e.g., cognitive, behavioral, psychodynamic, psychopharmacological, substance abuse detox, strategic family therapy, play therapy, expressive therapy? (4) What specific interventions will be made? (5) Should the counselor ideally be a man, a woman, or a co-therapist team? (6) What collateral parties, if any, must be involved? (7) Will the counseling likely be short- or long-term?

MODALITIES

Individual Therapy

Individual therapy is the treatment of choice when difficulties a child or family is having are assessed to be best treated by working one-on-one with a particular family member. Case examples may serve to illustrate some of the considerations involved when counseling is recommended for a single individual.

Eight-year-old Anna is brought to counseling for deep depression related to unresolved grief over the unexpected death of a beloved grandmother. Anna's family's attempts to help her understand and integrate the loss, including work in family therapy sessions, have not been sufficient to help Anna move through her grief. Individual therapy is recommended.

Wyatt, a thirteen-year-old boy, is angry, moody, uncommunicative. School performance is slipping. The boy spends increasing amounts of time by himself. All attempts to reach him are rebuffed. Wyatt has just been moved to his fifth foster home in two years. His foster mother is concerned about him. She cannot reach him. When individual sessions are suggested, for the boy with his own counselor, Wyatt becomes interested and more invested.

In response to a disclosure of sexual abuse made by her eleven-year-old daughter, a single mother, Jeanetta, in family therapy with her four children, reveals that she herself was a victim of childhood abuse. As the discussion unfolds, it becomes clear that Jeanetta's abuse history calls for in-depth individual work, as a first step towards helping her come to terms with past trauma.

Richard's chronic alcoholism is assessed to lie at the heart of his abuse of his adolescent son. The father is referred for individual treatment with an alcohol counselor.

Family Therapy

Family counseling is a treatment modality often recommended when children or teenagers are having difficulty in some aspect of their lives; family dynamics frequently lie at the core of problematic behaviors. A referral for family therapy is made when a child's struggles are understood to be primarily reflective of the family context within which those struggles arise and develop. Counseling a youngster individually may not be indicated when the child lives day to day within a family environment that is itself full of tension and conflict, especially when that conflict calls forth and supports the continuance of the child's symptoms (Nichols and Schwartz, 1991).

Toby, a ten-year-old boy, is referred out for counseling by the residential treatment center in which he resides. Because he is soon to be returned home, it is felt that his mother and father should be seen with him. They are concerned that his defiant, oppositional behaviors will resume when he comes home. A careful assessment brings to light intense marital conflict with the child caught in the middle of tensions between his mother and father. Further family therapy is recommended, to help the family sort out and appropriately attend to its various levels of discord. As Toby's parents become increasingly committed to working out their own problems, concurrently working with Toby on behavior issues, the boy's difficulties diminish notably in intensity, and reintegration into his home seems more promising.

Eddie, age seventeen, is living with his paternal grandparents due to intense and unresolved conflict between the boy and his mother. Eddie is referred for counseling after a suicidal gesture alerts the grandparents to serious underlying depression. Following two meetings with Ed alone, family therapy is recommended for the teenager and his mother, with hopes that a healing process can be facilitated between mother and son.

Marital Therapy

Couples therapy is often indicated whenever conflict between primary partners is determined to be a key element underlying child-related difficulties or family dysfunction. In the example of Toby above, initial family sessions might well be replaced or supplemented with marital work for the parents. It is not an uncommon therapeutic experience to see a child's problematic behaviors decrease or disappear, without direct intervention, after the mother and father successfully begin to address and resolve conflict between themselves.

Group Therapy

Many psychological and emotional issues have been found to be effectively approached within a group therapy format. In spite of the wide variety and types of therapy groups available, the healing experience common to group work is the support given and received by people struggling with similar life challenges. The group context, with time, care, and skillful facilitation, can reduce isolation and stigma, increase connection and depth of relationship, and provide for an environment conducive to the working through of sensitive issues. For children and families, groups can also offer straightforward information and education.

A listing for groups available at a local youth and family counseling center might include the following entries:

Group for Children of Divorce, ages 8 to 11
Group for Adolescents Whose Parents Are Living with AIDS
Group for Parents Whose Children Are Living with AIDS
Social Skills Groups for Children, ages 4 to 7, 8 to 12, and 13 to 17
Group for Adolescent Girls with Abusive Boyfriends
Group for Pregnant Teens
Group for Boyfriends of Pregnant Teenage Girls
Parenting Skills Group for Single Mothers with Young Children
Parenting Skills Group for Parents of Teenagers
Group for Teenage Fathers
Group for Teenagers Who Have Been Sexually Abused
Group for Adolescent Male Sexual Offenders
Groups for Children and Teens Whose Parents Are Substance Abusers
Anger Management Group for Children, ages 7 to 11
Group for Anorexic/Bulimic Teens

Case Management/Advocacy

Counseling services for children and families often require substantial collaborative work with key personnel outside the family circle. It is frequently necessary to speak with teachers, school adjustment counselors, school principals, family doctors, juvenile court officials, police officers, protective child care workers, lawyers, group residence staff, hospital intake workers, inpatient psychiatric staff, public assistance workers, landlords, employers, and other counselors/therapists, to mention just a few of the possibilities. To manage a difficult and complicated case successfully, and to advocate effectively for the best interests of a child or family, a counselor must be ready and able to network with the key figures and institutions involved. In this area, particularly, issues of confidentiality must be handled with great care and attention. It should also be mentioned that the end goal of all advocacy work (and, ideally, all counseling work in general) is to empower the family, not to do things for them that they can do, or learn to do, for themselves.

Technique, Schools of Thought, Theoretical Approaches

For the student intern or beginning counselor sitting with a troubled child or distressed family, a degree of anxiety and confusion is perhaps inevitable when faced with the questions, "What do I do, and how do I do it?" A profusion of techniques and theoretical approaches available for study and practice is complicated further by ongoing research and development in the field, refining and modifying established theories, and giving rise to new discoveries, approaches, and methods. To make matters more confusing, controversy enlivens the counseling professions, with differences of opinion often feverishly debated between proponents of opposing schools of thought.

Developing skill as a counselor involves many factors over and beyond formal academic training and practice experience. The counselor's personality style, belief system, assumptions about change, personal history, and experiences of healing all play an integral role. Perhaps unlike any other field, artistry as a counselor demands work on oneself, in addition to and as a counterpart to work with other people. When an individual of any age, or a family, comes to counseling for assistance with some kind of troublesome life dilemma, a counselor's efforts are given considerable power by the extent to which he or she has honestly grappled with his/her own problems in life. Because human development entails transformations and challenges throughout life that are universal to people everywhere, inevitably the issues brought to counseling by a family, sooner or later, are going to touch on some issue the counselor knows from his or her own experience.

With time, training, practice, and the deepening of one's own personal life experience, a particular style of working as a counselor evolves, with techniques and specific methods pulling together around the counselor's history, personality, interests, and natural talents. For most counselors, this is a process that unfolds slowly, and brings together the meeting ground between helping others and developing oneself. A well-known Jungian analyst and pastoral counselor was once asked what he thought about Freudian dream interpretation. He replied, "If you are reasonably competent, love what you do, have a genuine passion for it, and believe in it because of your own experience, then you are going to do good work regardless of what approach you use" (Holmes, 1993).

THE EXPERIENCE OF COUNSELING

CONSUMER PERSPECTIVE

What is it like to be in counseling? Does counseling help? The success of the counseling experience, and the degree of satisfaction derived from it by children and families, is conditioned by several key factors.

Counselor/Client Chemistry

Counseling entails a relationship between human beings. Like all human relationships, personal chemistry plays a role in determining the depth and intensity of connection between people. Having the "right" chemistry between counselor and the child and/or family favors the establishment of trust and greatly facilitates the work in progress.

Timing

Timing is an important element when it comes to counseling because it implies a certain readiness for the work involved. Issues, life dilemmas, and personal challenges tend to energize as time passes, with a certain critical tension often building before people make the decision to seek professional assistance. Life circumstances also play a role when it comes to readiness, events often times occurring in response to which people turn to the counseling professions. The "right" timing favors the counseling process because internal tension and/or external life circumstances present optimal opportunity and motivation for change.

Attitude and Expectation

A child's or family's attitude towards counseling, and the nature of their expectations, often have a direct impact on the degree of success experienced. An open and cooperative attitude, combined with positive and realistic expectations about change, favor success and client satisfaction.

Level of Functioning

"Level of functioning" is a phrase that refers to internal and external resources available to a child or family, including physiological, cognitive, emotional, social, and economic factors. A relatively high level of functioning favors a positive experience in counseling because individuals and families are able to more quickly and effectively use the support, direction, information, and specific tools provided through the counseling endeavor.

Counselor Skill

As in all professions, a continuum exists among counselors in skill level, energy, creativity, dedication to the work, passion for the profession, and willingness to "go the extra mile." Well trained, experienced, skillful, and dedicated counselors contribute in a major way to the likelihood that a child or family will have a productive and satisfying experience in counseling.

Benefits

Perhaps the best way to consider the experience of being in counseling, and the benefits derived from the process, is to listen to the words of children and families who have used counseling services for themselves.

I felt like someone really listened to me, like my words were not only heard, but what I meant and what I felt were understood and somebody cared. (Fifteen-year-old girl in individual outpatient therapy while in foster care)

It's great to have someone on my side, for once. I feel like I've got someone in my corner, like when my dad comes at me with one of his criticisms, I don't have to struggle with it all by myself. It's also great because my counselor makes my father listen to me. If Dad interrupts me, my counselor cuts him off and asks him to let me finish. He also does the same to me when I want to interrupt my dad. He makes me try to see things from different perspectives. (Fifteen-year-old boy in family counseling)

I like going there. I get to play with the toys. Sometimes Mommy plays too. Mrs. Peterson (counselor) told my daddy he couldn't hit my mommy any more. I never saw Daddy cry before. (Seven-year-old girl in individual play therapy and family counseling)

It was productive. We got coached on using the police and the courts to back up our rules at home. My son didn't like it, but he's doing better, has learned that he can't do exactly what he pleases without consequences. And my wife and I are now in therapy ourselves, working out some problems between us. This seems to be helping also. (Father of a fourteen-year-old boy, in family treatment and marital counseling after his son was involved with juvenile court)

The best part is realizing that there are other people who really care about what I am going through. And sometimes I'll say something to someone else, and it turns out that it makes a big difference to this person. That's the thing that really makes me feel good. Like I have something important I can bring to other people. (Mother in group for drug addiction)

As these comments illustrate, counseling is an experience that can include being carefully listened to, having one's feelings accurately reflected and validated, having one's emotions contained, receiving information, being constructively challenged and confronted, receiving support, giving support, being coached, learning new skills, expressing one's feelings, communicating effectively, and discovering new things about oneself.

PROFESSIONAL PERSPECTIVE

What is it like being a counselor? For the vast majority of people who work as professionals within the counseling fields, the direct person-to-person aspect of the work can be immensely rewarding and challenging, though not without its own unique frustrations and aggravations. Requirements of the job that involve work only tangentially related to direct service are often those that are experienced most negatively. An honest appraisal of counseling as a profession reveals both positive and negative considerations.

Negative Aspects of Counseling as a Career
Burnout. Professional "burnout" is a common occurrence in the counseling professions due to a variety of factors. Working with psychological trauma, emotional crisis, relational dysfunction, substance abuse, domestic violence, behavior and conduct problems, depression, family conflict, and the gamut of difficulties daily presented to workers in the counseling fields can be an emotionally draining expe-

rience. In many settings, counselors are expected to work directly with a large number of cases on a weekly basis, and to keep track of even more via case management and paperwork requirements. Problems often feel overwhelming, and endless, and unsolvable (Zastrow, 1984).

Multi-Problem Families. When poverty, lack of education, substance abuse, domestic violence, out-of-control children, delinquent adolescents, depression, and other difficulties all combine to overwhelm a single family and cause problems in the community, workers in the counseling field are often called in to help. Working with such families can be a particularly frustrating experience for counselors especially when, on top of everything else, families are hostile to outside intervention. Internal (psychological/emotional) and external (money, friendships/support network, opportunities) resources are often so limited in such families that counseling seems an inadequate and ineffective response.

Failure. All counselors experience numerous cases in which the best of efforts results in little or no positive change. Particularly when working with children and teens, efforts made with little noticeable results can be a discouraging experience.

Paperwork. Increasingly, third-party payers (insurance programs) are becoming more and more stringent in their requirements, demanding substantial record-keeping procedures relative to accounting and clinical review. The business/financial component of the counseling professions requires time, careful management, and frequent adjustment to third-party policy changes. The paperwork involved, in addition to the demands of the therapeutic work itself, can often lead to extra hours and the feeling that "catching up" is an impossibility.

Liability. Counseling professionals are often summoned to court to testify in cases involving their clients. The legalities and ethical parameters of client confidentiality can add stress to already demanding work. Written court reports are often required. In addition, careful documentation of counseling sessions and other case-related communications can be requested for review.

Income. Although counseling professionals with highly successful private practices and/or high-level administrative positions can earn substantial incomes, earnings as a human service provider generally fall far short of those possible in the business world. Counseling professionals often feel frustrated that the value and difficulty of their work is not recognized or rewarded on a level commensurate with the importance of the services provided.

Ethical Dilemmas. Counselors, on a regular basis, find themselves in the middle of situations that present ethical dilemmas relative to decision-making. It is not uncommon, for example, for a counselor's input to result in children being taken away from their parents. What this feels like for the counselor, for the parents, and for the child, and the long-term effect it has upon the family, are all factors counselors must grapple with in the course of doing their job. A variety of decision-making choices present themselves to counselors that directly and profoundly influence the lives of the children and families they work with. Making these decisions, and living with their consequences, pull counselors into the middle of ethical questions that have no easy answers.

Positive Aspects of Counseling as a Career

Counseling is a field in which burdensome elements of the work must be weighed in contrast to elements that are deeply rewarding. Counselors are known not only to complain about the demands of their profession, but also to sing its praises.

What I love about my work is the opportunity it gives me to make some small positive difference in the lives of my young clients. The greatest resource any society has is its children. It is a great blessing to be able to assist the development of young people and to beneficially influence the home environments in which they are raised. (Social worker in a community family counseling center)

You know, it's a chance to contribute something positive to the world. These kids are sent to me expecting more adult discussion and direction. Instead, they find a person and a space where they feel safe to express who they are, how they feel, what they think. There is a lot of pressure on children to conform. Kids have to meet expectations and standards, follow rules, do assignments in school, control their behavior, and so on. All of this is good and necessary. But children also need to be respected and valued as children, to let themselves go, to be creative and spontaneous in the way that only children can be. I try to provide a setting in which they can do this. (School counselor and art therapist)

The children here are ill, seriously. Some of them are dying. They have a tremendous need to connect with the significant people in their lives about what they are experiencing. My work is profoundly meaningful to me. I am involved every day with these young patients and their families. I witness their struggles, join in their victories and defeats, suffer their pain, and celebrate their courage and love of life. (Hospital social worker)

I feel like there is the work, the day-to-day sessions with people and problems, and then there is the Work, with a capitol "W." The Work is somehow bigger than individual therapists and clients. For me it entails something approaching the spiritual. It has to do with some invisible and tireless striving in the Universe towards greater fullness of being. (Social worker in private practice)

I am always moved by what children communicate to us if we just learn to understand their language. They are profoundly wise, and will almost always tell us what they need, or point us in the right direction. We only need to listen to them, and tune into the symbolic and metaphorical meaning of their behavior, artwork, play fantasies, and symptoms. (School psychologist)

Counseling keeps me honest. It often happens that a couple brings me one of my own issues. Here I am, supposedly in a position to assist people with a matter of concern, and it turns out I also struggle with this particular "problem." So I have a choice: I can either refer the couple to another therapist, or I can up the ante on my own personal growth, make some headway in my own life. If I choose the latter, then I feel I can legitimately be a guide for my clients. You can't do this work if you don't take seriously your own life. (Marriage counselor)

What most inspires me is actually witnessing change. Being part of that process is truly awesome. The combination of fragility, vulnerability, strength, and courage within human beings is what makes life soulful. (Psychotherapist working with adolescents and families)

Counseling as a profession is full of rewards and frustrations. As in all professions, it is the dynamic tension between what is inspiring in the work and what is discouraging that keeps the field alive, creative, and growing.

TRENDS IN COUNSELING SERVICES

As we near the end of the millenium, powerful forces from within and without the counseling professions are pushing and pulling the field in new directions, challenging counselors in every setting to respond creatively. The successes and failures of this response will largely shape the possibilities and parameters for counseling in the future. A brief overview of the most influential of these forces must include consideration of the significant external and internal forces at work.

EXTERNAL FORCES

Economic Factors
Deficit Reduction. National policy is immersed in efforts to reduce the federal deficit. As efforts towards this end unfold, funding is being cut or substantially reduced for a multitude of programs. After-school programs for children and teens, community day care, sports and the arts in the public schools, summer work programs for adolescents, city and town recreation programs, special programs for minority and underprivileged youth, community health care clinics, and many other projects that rely on state and federal support are finding they must drastically scale down their operations or close their doors due to lack of money. As this trend continues, overburdened families, bored and frustrated youth, lack of adult supervision and direction for teenagers, and increasingly limited opportunities for lower income families all contribute to an intensification of already pressing

societal crises. It is to the ongoing repercussions of national budget cutting that counselors in most settings will inevitably have to respond, at the same time as they must contend with vanishing resources for their own efforts in this regard (Keigher, 1994).

National Health Care Crisis. The escalating cost of health care provision has prompted a revolution in the insurance industry over the past ten to fifteen years, with major changes occurring over the last decade and continuing unabated at present. As market pressures and dollar efficiency increasingly guide and determine the delivery of care, one notable trend is that more and more people appear to be getting less and less in terms of services in the area of mental health. Of particular concern to professionals in the counseling fields, third-party reimbursement for mental health care services has seen the rise of large "managed care" companies.

The managed care industry, unlike traditional commercial insurance companies, seeks to directly intervene in the provision of mental health care services to consumers by providers, efficiently managing and thereby limiting the expenditure of dollars. While a heated debate rages currently as to the pros and cons of managed care, the appearance and influence of these companies has unquestionably resulted in dramatic changes in the way many counselors do and think about their work.

Managed care favors brief, in the present, goal-oriented, solution-focused, behavior- and symptom-directed psychotherapy. A major shift away from long-term depth work in counseling is promoted. Self-exploration, in-depth childhood trauma processing for adults, long-term relationship building between counselor and client, transference- and countertransference-based therapies, existential and/or spiritual questing, and all other nonspecific, nonsymptom or present behavior related concerns and approaches are discouraged. While the managed care industry asserts that it does not pass judgment as to whether such approaches are valid or useful, decisive policy has been implemented that vigorously resists paying for them (Bagarozzi, 1995; Mone, 1994; Cornelius, 1994).

In the same way that financial considerations have stripped many public primary school curriculums down to bare-boned academics, wholly or partially eliminating sports, music, art, and the humanities, so too have economic pressures resulted in a severe restriction as to what many third-party reimbursors are willing to cover under mental health benefits.

Social Factors

Social ramifications follow directly from decisions pertaining to money. The social welfare system is perhaps the best example of this relationship. No one argues against changes in the welfare system. What changes, how to implement them, and what to do about poverty and all its related social ills remains a quandary for those currently wrestling with the problem. Unquestionably, overwhelmed, broken, impoverished, and chaotic families and their children show up in schools, counseling centers, hospitals, courts, residential treatment programs, detox centers, 12-Step programs, homeless shelters, battered women's groups, sexual offender programs, and so on. While wealthier, less burdened, intact, and higher functioning families can show up in the same places, lack of resources is arguably a predisposing element for family dysfunction and mental/emotional disturbance.

As economic decisions on the federal, state, and municipal levels continue to affect lower income families negatively, phenomena such as single-mother households, fatherless adolescents, teenage pregnancy, child and adolescent suicide, juvenile delinquency, substance abuse, domestic violence, violence by children and teens against other children and teens, gang involvement, the high school dropout rate, and child neglect/abuse continue to increase. When these trends are combined with the trend toward managed care, brief therapy, and restricted mental health care dollars, counseling efforts begin to feel increasingly like Band-Aid responses taped over conditions calling for more radical treatment.

Political Factors
Politics inevitably enters the picture whenever major economic decisions are made. Based on allocation of resources, it appears clear that political leaders do not place families, women, or children high on the list of national priorities, especially those who are uneducated, poor, and non-white. A conservative trend in government lobbies diligently for legislation that slashes funding for social programs, deregulates environmental protection, and places the interests of corporations and wealthy Americans over those of other citizens. Native Americans, African Americans, Hispanics, other minority groups, and the poor find themselves ill-equipped to access the same opportunities taken for granted by more prosperous and privileged segments of the population. Policy-making at the macro level does not seek to remedy this discrepancy in any meaningful way, as the distribution of funds reflects. Rhetoric from politicians, liberal and conservative alike, speaks of cracking down on crime and violence without so much as a passing comment about unequal access to resources or opportunities for advancement.

INTERNAL FORCES

Notwithstanding the somewhat discouraging trends touched upon above, from within the counseling professions some notable and exciting developments can be discerned.

Mind–Body Connection
Within the counseling community, beginning back before the 1960s, but gaining increasing steam from the 1960s onward, a fringe group of practitioners has incorporated into their work techniques based on a holistic understanding of mind–body integrity. In recent years, massage therapies, bioenergetics, Rolfing, therapeutic touch, breath work, meditation, relaxation and visualization techniques, and a host of other methods that have historically been looked down on by mainstream counseling professionals have gained greater acceptance. Eastern meditation practice, yoga, deep breathing, and visualization exercises are now standard fare at many hospitals and clinics working with stress, phobias, panic disorders, chronic pain,

depression, and other conditions. As the medical and scientific communities slowly, and often begrudgingly, show cautious approval of such approaches, the general public has gained greater exposure to them as well, with considerable benefit for many people, including children and families.

Spirituality

Hand in hand with a deeper understanding and appreciation for the body–mind connection, many counselors have begun to reassert the place of psyche (soul) in psychological work, no longer so sharply distinguishing between psychotherapy, "soulmaking," or spirituality (Hillman, 1991). If a pattern of thought can actually create a problematic physical condition that in turn changes or modifies thinking, such that the physical symptom begins also to heal, it is difficult not to wonder at the inherent intelligence of such a system, or to speculate as to the possibility of some purpose or intention behind symptoms.

Questions of meaning, purpose, intention, and healing lead naturally to wondering about human potential. As counselors employ meditation techniques in their practice, this, too, opens a door to spiritual experience, to the experience of being part of something greater than, but inclusive of, human life. As medicine, physical science, and psychology explore the human psyche, it is perhaps inevitable that the mind–body connection will be mirrored by an equally profound connection between psyche, soul, and spirit.

ETHICAL CONSIDERATIONS IN COUNSELING

Counselors can, in subtle and dramatic ways, directly influence the lives of the children and families with whom they work. Counseling professionals are seen as experts, knowledgeable about psychology, development, and behavior, experienced in intervention, and qualified to give guidance. As such, they are entrusted with private and highly personal information. Their opinions, comments, and perspectives are taken seriously by clients, by courts of law, and by child protection agencies. Their suggestions, direct or implied, are often followed. Such a position inevitably involves questions of ethics, because authority and influence can have serious repercussions in the lives of those it touches. The following areas of ethical concern include those that are well-known stumbling blocks of the trade, as well as more controversial categories presented as food for thought for interested students.

CONFIDENTIALITY

Counselors receive information daily about the private lives of children and families. Some of this information can be disturbing. How the information is handled, with whom it is shared, and what decisions follow from it do not always have simple, clear-cut answers.

If a sixteen-year-old boy develops a trusting relationship with his individual counselor, and finally shares with the counselor that he has been experimenting with marijuana, alcohol, and LSD on the weekends with some of his friends, should the counselor necessarily notify the boy's parents?

If the single mother of three young children confides to her counselor that she has, on a couple of recent occasions, left the house at night for two hours while the children were asleep, does the counselor report her to the local authorities for child neglect?

What is the ethical duty of a counselor who hears from a teenager that a friend who is HIV-positive is regularly having unsafe sex with uninformed partners?

When parents from a minority culture innocently reveal to their counselor a routine child discipline technique that is common and accepted by the culture but judged to be excessive and too punitive from the American perspective, should the parents be reported to a child protection agency?

If a client reveals to her counselor that she committed a serious but nonlethal crime, does the counselor report her to the authorities?

The above confidentiality dilemmas, and countless others, come up daily in the practices of counselors in many different professions. In spite of careful parameters set forth by civil law and professional codes of ethics, many situations arise for counselors in the course of their work that fall between the lines of established protocols, and/or force a decision about what is acceptable by the profession and what is not. In these numerous cases, counselors sometimes have to struggle to come to their own conclusions, make their own decisions, and respond to the consequences.

THE DILEMMA OF DIAGNOSIS

Formal, medical diagnosis for mental/emotional problems entails assigning a recognized medical label to a carefully assessed profile of human behavior. Labels such as *Attention Deficit Disorder, Borderline Personality Disorder, Bi-Polar Disorder, Conduct Disorder,* or even *Major Depression,* often carry with them negative social implications for the people so categorized.

Aside from the more obvious ethical questions pertaining to misdiagnosis, the entire issue of labeling people is one worthy of careful consideration. What will the person diagnosed be told about the diagnosis? What does the diagnosis mean to that person and/or to the family? Who else will have access to records where that diagnosis is made? What will the diagnosis mean to *those* people?

One readily observable danger of using diagnostic labels is the tendency to lose track of individual human beings in favor of medical categories of disorder. "My borderline client," "my conduct disordered kid," "my PTSD boy," "the ADD group," "my group of heroin addicts," and so on are commonly heard terms used by practitioners in reference to counseled individuals. When, and by what process, does a person, with a personal name, an identity, a developed personality, thoughts, feelings, hopes and fears, become a "heroin addict," or a "borderline"? Does such a process insulate counselors from the problems that are brought to them? Does it protect them from seeing their own human condition reflected in their clients' lives? Does it set up and maintain a hierarchy between counselor and those being counseled?

TRAINING *for trainer*

In notable contrast to the training of psychiatrists, psychoanalysts, Jungian analysts, and other established professions that require neophyte practitioners to go through a prolonged in-depth form of psychotherapy as a critical part of their formal training, many professions, including social work, mental health counseling, and psychology, make no such demand of their trainees. What are the ethical implications for professionals who engage their clients in a process they themselves have not experienced? Is it even possible to competently guide a child or family through a psychotherapeutic process if one has never gone through such a process oneself?

VALUE SYSTEM DIFFERENCES

One of the most common types of ethical dilemmas, perhaps especially for beginning or student counselors, arises when working with families who hold to value systems markedly different from their own. For example, how does one work with a family whose religious beliefs prohibit their adolescent children from dancing, going to movies, or wearing the latest teenage fashions? If these prohibitions are at the root of parent–child conflict, and if the parents' belief system allows no room for compromise, how does a counselor proceed? If the counselor's belief system is closer in substance to the adolescent's in this case, how is collusion with the child against the parents, subtle or overt, avoided?

For counselors working with cases involving cross-cultural issues, value system conflicts can complicate and/or inhibit the therapeutic work. To take one example, families from certain ethnic backgrounds do not value direct and open communication among family members. Private thoughts and feelings are considered just that, private. If a counselor trained in the United States and raised in a very open and expressive family environment pressures a minority family to be self-revealing and openly communicative, what are the ethical considerations involved when this pressure results in significant psychological distress for the family?

COUNSELOR–CLIENT BOUNDARIES

A long-standing and well recognized ethical stumbling block for the counseling professions concerns "doctor–patient" boundaries. Counselors listen to highly personal life stories on a daily basis. Transference and countertransference dynamics, whereby the intimate nature of therapeutic work triggers family of origin issues for both counselor and client, can sometimes lead to a misplacement of feelings. A counselor who was himself abused by an alcoholic father may find himself wanting to *be* a father for an adolescent client who himself lives with an abusive and alcoholic parent. Instead of working to help the boy and his father come closer together, the counselor unconsciously allies himself with the son against the father. The counselor's deep personal feelings, relative to his own father, get mixed up in his professional work.

Writings on transference/countertransference dynamics, sexual attraction between doctor and patient, boundary confusion between counselor and counseled, and the related ramifications for both professionals and their clients abound in the psychological literature. Though the subject is too complex to consider at length in the present context, it is important for students to understand that boundary issues exist, with important and serious ethical implications.

POWER

Professional counselors are generally seen by their clients as experts, with all the authority brought by higher education, advanced training, and long-term direct experience. When the position of "expert" interfaces with the vulnerability of families in distress, dynamics of power often enter into the therapeutic process. A counselor's thoughts, feelings, suggestions, innuendos, admonitions, warnings, and praises can carry tremendous influence with children and families in crisis (Courtois, 1988).

When perceived power differentials are great, the possibility that such influence will be misused, or received in an unintended way, needs to be recognized. Take, for example, an adolescent who tells her counselor that she feels uncomfortable when her father kisses her. She may decompensate quickly if the counselor prematurely suggests intentional sexual impropriety on the part of the father. For the adolescent, the fact that the counselor mentions such a possibility means it must be true because the counselor *knows*. Because counseling involves working with children and families at varying levels of cognitive functioning, developmental maturity, and emotional stability, counselors must be acutely aware of the power their statements and actions carry if they are to avoid misunderstandings with potentially grave consequences.

COUNSELING AS A HEALING ART VERSUS THE BUSINESS OF MENTAL HEALTH

Productivity Requirements

As the counseling professions have had to respond to market conditions, national economic policy, health care reform, and other fiscal realities, ethical questions around the interface of money and therapy have proliferated. In most outpatient child and family counseling centers, where third-party reimbursement covers a substantial portion of the operational expenses of the clinic, counselors have "productivity" requirements. This means that each counselor is required to see a given number of children or families each week, as prerequisite to receiving their salaries.

When quantity of clients becomes a financially driven issue for counselors, there are inevitable implications for the quality of care, as well as ethical dilemmas for counselors who must "make their numbers" each week. This becomes increasingly problematic as productivity requirements and counselor caseloads expand. Meeting one's productivity requirement can too easily become an unstated goal of therapeutic work. Into the pool of factors determining length of treatment can occasionally enter the question of how many hours a counselor needs to satisfy productivity requirements for a given week. With many mental health clinics incorporating "incentive policies," whereby a counselor is rewarded, financially, for clients seen over and above the productivity requirement, and penalized financially for being below productivity, counselors are pressured to consider quantity as a motivating force in their work.

Linking Diagnosis to Length of Treatment

With the advent of managed care, some third-party reimbursers have begun to categorize diagnoses, allowing more sessions for certain types of disorders than for others. Again, this poses ethical questions for the practitioner. If it is assessed that a given family needs more counseling, over and above the number of sessions allowed by the insurance company for the stated diagnosis, one way around the problem would be to change the diagnosis. If the original diagnosis more accurately describes the family's situation, the counselor is in an ethical dilemma: Does he tell the family he can no longer work with them unless they wish to pay for sessions with their own money, or does he change to a less accurate diagnosis that enables work to continue under third-party coverage?

Clients without Insurance

Federal and state deficit reduction measures over the past two decades have gone hand in hand with the virtual disappearance of "free care dollars." Many counseling centers no longer have the financial support to see even a limited number of clients who cannot pay, or who cannot pay much. No ability to pay translates into no services provided. This equation poses ethical questions for all the counseling professions.

Out-of-pocket fee-setting scales also can be challenged on ethical grounds. For families with no insurance coverage, fees are often set by counseling facilities at levels tied to family income, with a minimum payment policy in place. Families who cannot meet the minimum payment are often out of luck, no matter how badly they need services. The demands and realities of keeping a counseling center financially solvent frequently mean preferential treatment for families with insurance coverage and/or independent resources.

Money Management versus Confidentiality

Tighter management of mental health care dollars has been accompanied by increasing intrusiveness on the part of third-party payers. In contrast to traditional commercial insurance company reimbursement, which simply requires a medically recognized diagnosis for a given problem, managed care companies now ask for details about presenting concerns. A written description of problems, goals, and a specific treatment plan are routinely required. Additionally, if a particular managed care review board does not feel a counselor's written request for authorized sessions is justified, the counselor may be required to discuss the case in greater detail with a company representative on the phone. Such practice continues to be hotly contested by many on the grounds that it violates consumers' rights to confidentiality.

With insurance companies "on line" and engaged in extensive computer processing of records and files, and with the "information superhighway" a reality linking computer data bases within a colossal internationally plugged-in information network, questions about who has access to what kind of information suggest possibilities with disturbing implications.

BAND-AIDS VERSUS COMMITMENT TO SOCIAL CHANGE

For many counselors, especially those who work for agencies serving lower income families, an area for sober reflection in the arena of professional ethics involves the relationship between problems faced by children in the United States and societal conditions that directly or indirectly contribute to the creation and maintenance of those problems. For these counselors, therapeutic work with the micro realities of families in distress must constantly be evaluated against the macro realities of societal structures. If national priorities do not appear to place a high value on children, women, the plight of the poor, education, or equal opportunity to resources for all citizens, what becomes the ethical response of professionals who earn an income counseling the disenfranchised? Do middle-class professional counselors benefit from the same hierarchy of priorities that keep them supplied with a steady and inexhaustible clientele? What kind of political action commitment might be ethically demanded of those who counsel?

SUMMARY

Counseling is an interactive process that seeks to facilitate positive change for those being counseled. That such change is possible is an assumption central to the counseling professions. Families come to counseling either by way of self-referral or via a referral made by an outside agency. Self-referred families actively look for professional attention in response to recognized problems or potentially problematic situations. In contrast, families referred to counseling by outside parties have often failed to notice or to respond adequately to difficulties experienced by family members.

Attitudes toward receiving counseling vary widely among individuals and between cultures and tend to mirror an individual's or culture's feelings about having a problem in the first place. For many, societal pressures to present a strong and positive face to the outside world conflict with the need in counseling to openly acknowledge and talk about painful and disappointing aspects of life. Instead of being valued as potential teachers, these "shadow" areas of life are frequently hidden, judged as shameful, or denied.

Counseling with families and children involves a process of assessment, diagnosis, treatment planning, and intervention. Intervention takes place within distinct modalities: individual, family, marital, and/or group therapy. Case management and advocacy work often accompany and support counseling sessions. The goal of all counseling modalities is to enable families and individuals to successfully manage and respond to the many demands and challenges of life.

Developing skill as a counselor demands work on oneself, in addition to and as a counterpart to work with other people. In addition to self-exploration, counseling as a profession involves complex questions of ethics, because counselors are often perceived by their clients to be in positions of considerable power and influence. Issues concerning confidentiality, client–counselor boundaries, medical diagnosis, value system differences, parental rights, child protection, money, insurance, poverty, discrimination, and the inequities of social institutions present counselors with ethical dilemmas that have no easy answers.

At present, domestic policy-making in the United States is being shaped largely by efforts to reduce the federal deficit. Economic pressures radically influence policy decisions affecting the delivery of services to families and children. In an effort to cut government spending, many programs designed to aid and support families have been curtailed or eliminated. At the same time, a crisis in national health care has seen the rise of large "managed care" companies determined to limit the expenditure of dollars significantly paid to professional providers for the provision of mental health services. As pervasive belt-tightening decisions continue to be made, lower income families suffer the consequences increasingly, with serious repercussions for the counseling professions and for the society as a whole.

EXPLORATION QUESTIONS

1. What is meant by counseling? What are some basic assumptions of counseling?
2. Cite some situations in which a family might seek counseling.
3. What attitudes might people have about receiving counseling?
4. What should a counselor consider when working with people from different ethnic or cultural backgrounds?
5. What is the difference between the medical model and the holistic model of counseling?
6. How has the feminist movement influenced counseling?
7. What is meant by assessment? By differential diagnosis? By treatment planning?
8. What are some different treatment modalities?
9. What factors can influence the success or failure of the counseling experience?

10. What are some of the negative aspects of counseling as a career?
11. How does the current political climate in the United States affect the future of the counseling profession?
12. What is meant by the term *managed care*?
13. What are some of the ethical dilemmas a counselor might face?

ACTIVITIES FOR APPLIED LEARNING

1. Invite counselors from a variety of different settings to speak with the class. How does their training differ? What approaches do they use? What are their feelings about the work that they do?
2. Role-play typical counseling situations: troubled teen with family; couple with marital problems; abuse victim; family with disabled child; family with alcoholic father. Have one person play the counselor, one (or several) the client(s), and one the observer. Change roles.
3. Visit a variety of sites where counseling is done (e.g., hospital, social service agency).
4. Interview a referring professional (e.g., physician, teacher). Find out the usual circumstances when they refer someone for therapy.

SUGGESTED READING

Atkinson, D. R., Morten, G., Wing Sue, D. *Counseling American Minorities.* Dubuque, IA: WCB Brown and Benchmark, 1993.

Bagarozzi, D. A. "Evaluation, Accountability and Clinical Expertise in Managed Mental Health Care: Basic Considerations for the Practice of Family Social Work," *Journal of Family Social Work* 1(2), (1995): 101–116.

Cornelius, D. S. "Managed Care and Social Work: Constructing a Context and a Response," *Social Work in Health Care* 20(1), (1994): 47–63.

Hillman, J. *A Blue Fire.* New York: Harper Perennial, 1991.

Nichols, M. P., & Schwartz, R. C. *Family Therapy.* Boston: Allyn and Bacon, 1991.

REFERENCES

Atkinson, D. R., Morten, G., Wing Sue, D. *Counseling American Minorities.* Dubuque, IA: WCB Brown and Benchmark, 1993.

Bagarozzi, D. A. "Evaluation, Accountability and Clinical Expertise in Managed Mental Health Care: Basic Considerations for the Practice of Family Social Work," *Journal of Family Social Work* 1(2), (1995): 101–116.

Budd, M. A. "New Possibilities for the Practice of Medicine," *Advances* 8(1), (1992): 7–16.

Cassidy, C. M. "Unraveling the Ball of String: Reality, Paradigms, and the Study of Alternative Medicine," *Advances* 10(1), (1994): 5–31.

Cornelius, D. S. "Managed Care and Social Work: Constructing a Context and a Response," *Social Work in Health Care* 20(1), (1994): 47–63.

Courtois, C. *Healing the Incest Wound.* New York: Norton, 1988.

Dossey, L. "Antonovsky's Perspective May Not Go Far Enough," *Advances* 10(3), (1994): 13–15.

Hillman, J. *A Blue Fire.* New York: Harper Perennial, 1991.

Holmes, R. Personal Communication; Jamaica Plains, MA: 1993.

Keigher, S. M. "The Morning after Deficit Reduction: The Poverty of U.S. Maternal and Child Health Policy," *Health and Social Work* 19(2), (1994): 143–147.

LeShan, L. "Creating a Climate for Self-Healing: The Principles of Modern Psychosomatic Medicine," *Advances* 8(4), (1992): 20–27.

Mone, L. C. "Managed Care Cost Effectiveness: Fantasy or Reality?" *International Journal of Group Psychotherapy* 44(4), (1994): 437–448.

Nichols, M. P., & Schwartz, R. C. *Family Therapy.* Boston: Allyn and Bacon, 1991.

Singer, J. K. *Boundaries of the Soul.* New York: Doubleday, 1972.

Sullivan, B. S. *Psychotherapy Grounded in the Feminine Principle.* Wilmette, IL: Chiron Publications, 1989.

Tower, C. C. *Understanding Child Abuse and Neglect.* Boston: Allyn & Bacon, 1996.

Weick, A. "Issues in Overturning a Medical Model of Social Work Practice," *Social Work* 28(6), (1983): 467–471.

Zastrow, C. "Understanding and Preventing Burn-Out," *British Journal of Social Work* 14(2), (1984): 141–155.

Zastrow, C. *Introduction to Social Work and Social Welfare.* California: Brooks/Cole Publishing, 1993.

Zweig, C., & Abrams, J. *Meeting the Shadow.* New York: G. P. Putnam's Sons, 1991.

8

FAMILY-CENTERED SERVICES FOR CHILDREN

Jennifer J. Savage

HISTORICAL DEVELOPMENT

Throughout history, families have sought emotional and physical support for raising children. Since the Old Testament days of King Solomon, parents have been admonished about proper ways to raise children. All cultures throughout the world have had similar admonishments for families, and for parents in particular. The method of raising children, as well as the debate over the value of children, has been constantly addressed. Children provided no socioeconomic worth to a larger society until becoming physically and, in modern times, cognitively able to contribute through physical labor (Zelizer, 1985).

Children have traditionally been (and continue to be) regarded in social policy circles as the property of parents. However, history has also shown children and childhood to be revered, particularly by mothers, but also fathers, as a fulfillment of the universal human need to make one's mark on society. Children can provide the ultimate source of gratification for a parent by an occasional self-indulgence of doting on or "spoiling" a child (Aries, 1962). Similarly, society as the larger parent has recognized, at least in political rhetoric, the importance of childhood as the orientation period, or training ground, for perpetuation of the society itself. This is the essence of the common phrase "children are our future." Children, as future adults, will either embrace or discard the societal norms, mores, customs, and government of a civilization.

How, then, can parents actually gain the knowledge and the skills necessary to raise their children into productive adults? How do families in the process of parenting teach children to value those things that will assure maintenance of an entire cultural or social heritage? And how can families be helped to better perform their parenting roles?

Child development theorists and family therapists are quick to point out that there are no training manuals for raising children. These professionals remind us that "parenting is the hardest job for which one gets the least training" (Chynoweth and Dyer, 1991; Daro, 1988; Schorr, 1989; Weissbourd and Musick, 1988). Parents initiate and facilitate the child's socialization process. This comprehensive training by parents is complemented by other educational, governmental, and religious institutions. Sometimes these institutions change so rapidly that traditional generation-to-generation methods of parenting are insufficient. The literature, from a variety of professional and academic disciplines, cites the following as areas in which child well-being is being compromised:

1. Teenage pregnancy, low-birth-weight infants born to teen mothers, and single teen mothers parenting;
2. Infant mortality;
3. Juvenile delinquency;
4. Homicide and suicide among all age groups, but particularly among older juveniles;
5. Substance abuse among children and/or their parents or guardians;
6. Poverty and homelessness among children and their families;
7. Child maltreatment, including physical and sexual abuse;
8. Poor health care for school-age and older children;
9. Poor school performance and increased high school dropouts (Chynoweth and Dyer, 1991; Hewlett, 1991; Kadushin and Martin, 1988; Melaville, Blank, and Asayesh, 1993; National Center for Children in Poverty, 1990; National Commission on Children, 1991).

Experts studying the well-being of children today predict an increase in negative indicators when support remains lacking, inconsistent, or inaccessible to families in times of rapid social change (Zill, 1994; Schorr, 1989).

Currently, U. S. standards for families raising productive citizens are still based on an "Ozzie and Harriet" version of the nuclear family. However, this modern American family has failed to be the norm for the past three decades (Zill, 1994; Weick and Saleebey, 1995; Schorr, 1989; Sachar, 1992; Pooley and Littell, 1986; Pinderhughes, 1995; Ooms and Beck, 1990; Hewlett, 1991; Kadushin and Martin, 1988; Chynoweth and Dyer, 1991; Cole, 1995). Moreover, the influence of the idealized stereotypical American family is often seen by Americans as the worldwide model for family structure. This ethnocentric view may maintain and reinforce resistance to a quick response families need to raise children in changing times. While in the minority, the United States and other technologically advanced, economically stable countries share similar stressors in modern life that create a need for family-centered services.

Stress-inducing effects on families include a decline in family purchasing power, an increase in dual-earner households, in an effort to maintain the middle-class standards of the 1950s, a stabilized divorce rate of approximately 50%, an increase in single-parent households, and a host of associated social problems resulting in a variety of combinations of families (Hewlett, 1991; Zill, 1994). Examples include "sandwiched" families raising children and providing care for aging parents (a new "old" version of the extended family), gay and lesbian parents, single-parents by choice, and homeless families.

Now we must recognize that there are a variety of family structures. There may be other cultural group norms for family structure and child-rearing techniques present in Native American, Latino, Asian American, and African American families (Dodson, 1983; Mannes, 1993; Wares et al., 1994; Pinderhughes, 1995) (see also Chapter 2).

STRESSES ON THE FAMILY UNIT

Whatever the shape and form of a family, most appear to deal with changing circumstances with fewer and fewer resources. Parents are faced with both "time" and "resource" deficits (Hewlett, 1991), working harder to provide less in material needs for their children and finding themselves robbed of both the opportunity to provide "quality" and "quantity" time with them. Parents are sometimes unable to nurture children adequately (even with two parents in the home) because one or both must engage in a second shift of full-time household and childcare management (Chynoweth and Dyer, 1991).

Rapidly changing times contribute to stress in families. Historically, however, many have sought to help themselves and others according to need. An example of this self-determination was the development in the late 1950s of breast-feeding support groups for mothers (La Leche League International, 1981). This self-help movement was a result of the social trend to bottle-feed infants. A countertrend had emerged with the recognition that breast-feeding was a healthier nutritional form for developing infants, but few mothers had access to proper breast-feeding methods. Modern mothers, then and now, had few extended family members encouraging breast-feeding. The resulting support group, La Leche League, still exists as one of the earliest forms of an outside extended family, mutual aid support group for mothers. La Leche League, supported by public health awareness, has been responsible for establishing a balanced ratio of nearly one-for-one bottle-fed to breast-fed babies today. It also has quietly maintained its roots of family support. Today, La Leche League provides information about all forms of parenting and family life, in addition to the basics of breast-feeding techniques.

Other issues, often hidden behind closed doors, have threatened family life. Over the years many families have existed in the shadows of secreted domestic violence and child maltreatment. Some were unaware of the severity of problems and the need to seek help. But as child and family advocates sought to protect the powerless a variety of services emerged. With the passage of the 1935 Social Security Act, public child welfare services uniformly resulted in various intervention methods. The Act sought to respect the civil liberty and right of parents to raise children by reasonable means in whatever way they deemed appropriate (Pecora, Whittaker, and Maluccio, 1992). American public child welfare services resulted in the expansion of foster care and adoption services for poor children and families with roots in the Children's Aid Society in the 1890s. But families severely stressed by changing times were not universally served, even by governmentally intrusive means, until the passage of the federal 1974 Child Abuse Prevention and Treatment Act. This Act provided a formal public child protection service (CPS) in each state to protect vulnerable children from all types of physical and emotional maltreatment. CPS focused on maintaining the children with their biological parents whenever the children's well-being could be safely assured. Unlike some highly motivated families who might recognize and seek self-help voluntarily, families served by CPS completely lacked the ability to recognize their need. Moreover, these parents often lacked basic social and extended familial supports for their jobs as parents.

Parents seeking help for the job of "good" parenting, in contrast to families being forced by the government to assure "minimal" parenting, illuminates the current polarization in family-centered services for children. With the convergence of family-centered services, families might find themselves in the midst of a cultural and social storm, parenting only well enough to meet minimal acceptable societal standards.

DEFINING FAMILY-CENTERED SERVICES FOR CHILDREN

Family-centered services for children are all-encompassing, and represent a wide range of services delivered to children and their families within a multidisciplinary, multiservice context. The term *family-centered* is generally attached to any service that attempts to overcome threats to family stability that can, in turn, compromise the healthy development of children.

FAMILY-CENTERED SERVICES FOR MALTREATED CHILDREN

Linda Gately and her five children live in a run-down apartment amidst others in similar need of repair. The Gately family came to the attention of the public child welfare agency after six-year-old Lester was found locked in a discarded refrigerator in the back yard. The other children were poorly clad and malnourished. Subsequent intervention with Mrs. Gately consisted of helping her to develop a schedule to feed her children, helping her to budget her AFDC check, and impressing on her the need to adequately supervise her children. For this, a social worker came to the Gately home on a weekly basis.

Family-centered services that are mandatory due to child maltreatment are referred to as *family-preservation services,* and are usually home-based. The Child Welfare League of America (CWLA), in its *Standards to Strengthen and Preserve Families with Children* (1989b), uses the concept family-centered to identify the characteristics of primarily mandatory public child welfare services. These services are delivered in the home when significant risk to a child's well being has been determined and when the family's deficiencies indicate a need for intensive home-based public services. In this category of public child welfare service delivery, family-centered services are focused on intervention.

FAMILY-CENTERED SERVICES FOR HEALTHY CHILDREN

When sixteen-year-old Maggie brought her newborn baby home from the hospital, the services of a community health nurse were offered to her. The nurse came to the home several times a weeks to help Maggie and her eighteen-year-old husband, Jed, become more comfortable with the care of their infant. The couple welcomed the help and grew fond of the nurse. Both parents had come from abusive families and they wanted very much to be good parents to this baby.

Family-centered, as a concept of voluntary service to children and their families, also implies a prevention focus. The goal of voluntary prevention-focused, family-centered services is generally the same as in mandatory intervention-focused services. This approach attempts to promote the well-being and healthy development of children by increased parental skills and healthy family interactions (CWLA, 1989b). The methods do differ because prevention family-centered services may be community-based or home-based. These services are identified as community-based family support and education (CBFSE) or as family resource, support, and education (FRSE). This identifies the expansive variety of supports provided to families (Weiss and Halpern, 1991; CSSP, 1990; CWLA, 1989b). As a way of understanding the myriad of services available through both CBFSE or FRSE, the concept of family-centered services applies to a broad range of family support services.

DIFFERENCES IN FAMILY-CENTERED SERVICES

Family-centered services have historically been considered to be either in the area of family preservation or family support. Family preservation services are mandated, usually after a crisis of child maltreatment has entered the CPS directly or through a law enforcement agency. Family preservation attempts to keep families together by direct, formal intervention, usually in the home of the child and his/her family. Family support services are sought voluntarily and are generally categorized as the prevention of negative indicators of child well-being in a given family, community, or society.

The differences in the two approaches are separate and distinguishable, yet alike and overlapping. The differences in family-centered services touch on concepts that continually are sources of conflict in a democratic society: social support and social control (Daro, 1988). Can family-centered services be truly voluntary and accessible to families before their child or children are at-risk for impaired well-being? Does a child need someone to help him or her keep his family together so that he or she can be raised effectively to become a healthy, productive adult? The answers to these questions, the differences between social support and social control, lie at the heart of the debate in family-centered services to children.

OVERLAP IN FAMILY-CENTERED SERVICES

Figure 8-1 shows the overlap of family preservation and family support services, with the continuous flow of services in and out of mandatory and voluntary consumption of services (Zalensky, 1994).

Whether aimed at prevention or intervention, family preservation or family support, the characterization of services as family-centered has led to a gradual recognition of the overlap of both types of services. Until the federal passage of the 1993 Family Preservation and Support Services Program (FPSSP) guidelines, both family preservation and family support services seemed to be evolving in isolation from one another, although both services shared many characteristics in values, knowledge, and techniques (Allen, 1993).

ROLE OF THE U. S. CHILDREN'S BUREAU

For the first time, the U. S. Children's Bureau contributed impetus through the FPSSP for the two services to begin overlapping and complementing one another for the betterment of children and families. For nearly a century, the Children's Bureau has been the largest neutral overseer of the well-being of children and families. One of its greatest accomplishments for all children and their families was

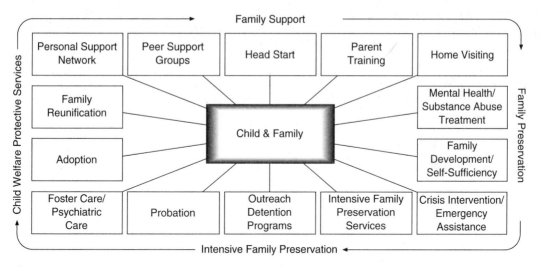

FIGURE 8-1   Spectrum of Supports and Services

inclusion of a state mandate under FPSSP to identify and coordinate family preservation and family support services. The Children's Bureau and other children's advocates have witnessed a continuing development of family-centered services over the past three decades. Recognition of a family development continuum of family-centered services, although not yet universal, provides the greatest opportunity for a swift response to sweeping the social changes that have created the cultural and social upheaval for families. A recent speaker at the 1995 National Child Welfare Conference in Washington, D.C., stated that the FPSSP is an opportunity to craft a "lifeboat for families as they are swept down that swelled river of social change." This opportunity, more importantly, is geared towards the needs of families instead of the needs of public agencies.

Indeed, families and public agencies have both been embroiled in a frantic attempt to create their own crafts as a response to the storm of social changes affecting children. Whether delivered voluntarily or mandated by an outside source and whether in the home or outside, family-centered services have historically been the norm in human services. From the beginning of the settlement house movement in the late 1800s and "friendly visitors" for the urban poor (Bremner, 1970, 1971) to the first Mother's Congress in 1902, families have eagerly sought and even created their own support when in need. From the advent of the foster care system in America in the 1800s to the 1974 Child Abuse Prevention Act (Bremner, 1971; DePanfilis and Salus, 1992), public child welfare services have sought to protect children. Necessary or attempted removal from abusive or poor families was called for by the First White House Conference on Children in 1909 as an attempt to find a secure, loving, and permanent home for children affected by child maltreatment (Bremner, 1971).

EVOLUTION OF FAMILY DEVELOPMENT PROGRAMS

Although events can be identified throughout history that illustrate the separate but parallel development of family-centered services, the two forms of these services developed in isolation from one another (Allen, 1993; Pecora, Whittaker, and Maluccio, 1992; Dalder, 1994; Adams and Nelson, 1995). The charted timeline in Figure 8-2 shows the potential for overlap of family-centered services in both family support and family preservation programs, and the overlapping in the area of family development.

FAMILY-CENTERED SERVICES AS A CONTINUUM OF FAMILY DEVELOPMENT

Families now seek and sometimes create services themselves in response to needs while raising children. These are family support services that were previously identified. Families are also being served involuntarily for the same or similar needs by family preservation services. The range of these services creates a continuum of family development and family development services (see Figure 8-3). In the middle of this continuum are services that border on voluntary and coerced consumption. To understand the full range of the continuum, it is important to identify the specific service components of each type of family-centered service, beginning with family preservation services, which are the domain of public child welfare agencies.

FAMILY PRESERVATION PROGRAM CHARACTERISTICS

Family Preservation services are usually delivered in the home with the specific purpose of preventing the removal of a child. The potential threat of child maltreatment, either physical abuse or physical neglect, must have occurred to necessitate cause for the child to be removed to protect his or her physical safety. The families, once investigated by crisis intervention (CI) specialists in public child protection service agencies (CPS), are identified by specific criteria as potential candidates for intensive home-based services (IHBS). The usual delivery method of family preservation family-centered services is instituted only when the CI worker has sufficiently determined that the family system, which has caused the well-being of the reported child to be at risk, appears amenable to brief, intensive in-home therapy. Frequently, this amenability leads to "windows of therapeutic opportunity" for the family preservation worker.

Family preservation services are sometimes referred to as intensive family-centered crisis services (IFC) or intensive home-based services (IHBS). The Child

FIGURE 8-2 Historical Overlap in Development of Family-Centered Public and Private Child Welfare Services

Family Support	Family Development	Family Preservation
1800s "Friendly Visitors"—church and social groups visit poor families		1853 Children's Aid Society begins first family foster care
		1866 Children's Aid Society pioneers family reunification
1877 Charity Organization Society continues serving poor families		
1899 Settlement House movement helps families adjustment in communities		
1902 "Congress of Mothers" meeting in New York—first mutual-aid group for parenting issues		1954 St. Paul MN Family-Centered Project—mental health program to help multi-problem families stay together
1909 First White House Conference on Children—lays groundwork for creation of U.S. Children's Bureau	1970 Parents Anonymous groups begun—self-help for abusive parents to help overcome child maltreatment	
1972 Mothers' Centers—New York		
1970s Office of Economic Development creates Parent Centers with Head Start Programs		1973 Project Kaleidoscope—Chicago, IL. Takes children other FP programs reject
1972 Avanca—Texas 1974 Parents' Place—California 1976 Family Focus—Illinois 1977 PACT (Parents & Children Together)—Michigan Services for Minority Single-Parent Families 1978 Birth-to-Three—Oregon	1977–1978 National Clearing-house on Home-Based Services established—Iowa	1974 Homebuilders—Tacoma, WA
1978 Black Family Development, Inc., Detroit—individual & family counseling to African-American families		
1978 Indian Child Welfare Act, PL 95–608, provides family support, family development, and tribal child protection for Native Americans		
1981 National Family Resource Co-alition established in Chicago, IL.	1981 National Resources Center on Family-Based Services established—Iowa (evolution of National Clearinghouse on Home-Based Services)	
1982 National Institute for Responsible Fatherhood & Family Development—Charles Bullard		

(Continued)

FIGURE 8-2 *Continued*

Family Support	Family Development	Family Preservation
	1984 Children and Adolescent Services Project (CAASP) begun (Mental Health Family Development Effort)	
1986 Maryland's Friends of the Family—statewide family support and family development project begun	1985 Hawaii's Healthy Start Program begun (Maternal/ Child Health Family Development Effort)	
1988 Kentucky Integrated Delivery System (KIDS)—comprehensive family support programs for families, on school sites	1988 Wallbridge Caring Communities—St. Louis (Community Development/ Substance Abuse Effort)	
	1988 National Association of Family-Based Services— Iowa (professional membership association of family-based service providers for at-risk and crisis-impacted families)	
	1988 Comprehensive Child Development Projects (5-year research projects in collaborative family development)	
1991 Individuals with Disabilities Education Act (I.D.E.A. PL 192–119b)—includes mandates for inclusion of parent concerns and collaboration with parents as consumers of services for disabled children	1991 Alliance for Respite Care & Health of Children (A.R.C.H.) provides daycare for at-risk families	
1993 Family Preservation and Family Support Services mandate included with Ombudsman Budget Reconciliation Act of 1993—encourages state child welfare agencies to link family preservation and family support.		
1994 Parents Anonymous develops National Parent Leadership Teams to assist all parents before abuse occurs and after	1994 National Resource Center on Family-Centered Services established (name change for NRC on Family-Based Services)	
1994 Crime Bill—includes provisions for wide range of family support and family development programs		

Welfare League of America characterizes such services as having several components in common. These intensive family services are centered around the family in a manner that seeks to empower them. The services seek to be accessible, taking into consideration the family's needs, building on their strengths and providing service in their own homes (CWLA, 1989b).

Beyond these basics, many family preservation programs provide immediate response to families who are referred for a specific crisis such as threatened removal of a child. The focus then becomes short-term crisis resolution during which the family has 24-hour access to the worker who has between two to ten families on his/her caseload. The worker provides in-home concrete, emotional, and advocacy support services for a time-limited period (an average of six months) until the family has resolved the crisis. Family preservation workers are trained (ideally) to respect and appreciate the cultural context of the family and to enable the family to decide which members will be involved in treatment and who will not (CWLA, 1989b; Kinney and Haapala, 1994).

CONSUMERS OF FAMILY-CENTERED FAMILY PRESERVATION SERVICES

A variety of types of families might receive these intensive services. Families experiencing an emergency threatening family stability such as eviction, shutoff of utilities, homelessness or a lack of food might be good candidates. Sometimes abusive or neglectful families, those abusing alcohol or drugs or even families in which there

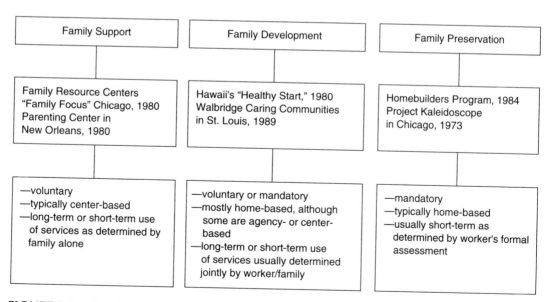

FIGURE 8-3   Continuum of Family-Centered Services

BOX 8-1   Walbridge Caring Communities: A Parent's View

Octavia Anderson had just turned 31 when she hit rock bottom. She had three children, but the love of her life was cocaine. She had quit a couple of times. In March, she even went into detox to please her mother. She stayed clean for 45 days until she got blitzed to celebrate her birthday. She could not stop celebrating. She cashed her $342.00 welfare check and $260.00 in food stamps, gave her mother $90.00, and spent the rest on crack cocaine. The next day, her mom, Margaret Carr, put her out of the home they shared in St. Louis' Walbridge community. Octavia went back home a few days later, but she could not stop smoking.

Then, Bernice Trotter King, a substance abuse counselor with Walbridge Caring Communities, came to the rescue. Octavia's three children attended Walbridge Elementary School, and King had worked with Octavia on and off for over a year ever since her youngest child had started having trouble in kindergarten. When Durrell Anderson's teacher referred him to Walbridge Caring Communities, the first thing Director Khatib Waheed did was meet with Octavia.

Walbridge's approach is a family one. So, with Octavia's permission, Waheed put the children into tutoring, the latchkey program, behavior therapy, and a codependency group to help them deal with their mother's drug abuse. He also sent a case manager to Octavia's home. Eventually, Octavia got into counseling with Bernice King. Like many other Walbridge Caring Communities staff members, King was on call 24 hours a day. She had responded to Octavia's calls on weekends and at night. She visited

Octavia in places that scared her. She had seen Octavia at her worst, and she had stuck around. This time, it was Margaret Carr who called King. After years of caring for Octavia and her three children, Margaret was at her limit. She had watched Octavia go from marijuana to cocaine to crack. She had seen her daughter's marriage disintegrate and Octavia lose jobs because of her addiction. It seemed to keep getting worse, and finally, Margaret had seen enough. She told Octavia to get out. Mother and daughter were screaming at each other. King was the peacemaker. "She said, 'Come on, let's go,'" Octavia remembers, "'cause your Momma don't want you here.' I was crying. And she said, 'I have a place I can take you.'" King drove Octavia to Archway Communities, Inc., a drug rehabilitation center. "When I walked through the Archway doors, I said, 'I'm through. I surrender,'" Octavia recalls. "I gave up all of my drinking, my drugs...all that insanity s---. I decided that's not the life for me."

Octavia celebrated her 32nd birthday sober. She attends Narcotics Anonymous and Alcoholics Anonymous meetings, and she has restored her relationship with her mother. "We get along 100 percent," she says. Her children still have behavior problems, and Octavia acknowledges they have been through a lot. "They suffered," she says. "I wouldn't want to take my kids through that no more." Still, they are doing better. Durrell, for example, seems to be more aware there are people who care about him, believes Norma Jones, who taught him in kindergarten. "He didn't know that before," Jones says.

(Reprinted by permission, Melaville, *Together We Can.*)

is a parent-child conflict resulting in such acting out behavior as running away, promiscuity, or delinquent acts might benefit from such services. Teen parents or adoptive parents might also be able to use the extra support (CWLA, 1989b).

Deborah, in Box 8-3 below, is a parent who made good use of family preservation services.

BOX 8-2   Case from Family Preservation Worker in Louisiana

A public child welfare worker recently assigned to an IHBS Unit experienced the "point of optimal intervention" in a subtle but dramatic way. Contact was established with the family referred from CI as a result of presentation of a 6-month-old child in a local hospital emergency room with severe dehydration. CI had investigated and found the infant indeed suffered from inadequate physical care by its single parent, a 25-year-old mother. This was her youngest of 4 children.

Finding the mother overwhelmed and incapacitated by poverty, lack of extended family support, and more children than the mother had the ability and skill to care for, CI referred for IHBS. The new IHBS worker readily engaged the mother, but had difficulty engaging her children, particularly her oldest child, an 11-year-old son. The IHBS worker had arranged a comprehensive range of services for the mother, including respite day-care for her 18-month-old and 3-year-old child, after school tutoring program for the 11-year-old child, an educational program for the mother to achieve a GED, while engaging her child in therapeutic developmental play and parenting instruction. The IHBS worker found herself, beyond the counseling in the home with the mother and service linkages she had established, moving toward other activities to assist the family in "nontraditional" ways, such as showing the mother and her 11-year-old son how to trim bushes outside the window of their home which were causing a mosquito problem for the family. During the activity, the IHBS worker finally reached the 11-year-old in therapeutic intervention when he asked casually, as he was clipping the bushes, "Mom, why didn't you get help like this when I was a baby?"

The boy had opened a "window of therapeutic opportunity" to begin dialogue with his mother and the IHBS worker in coming to terms with his mother's unintended neglect and other family circumstances which he had not understood.

SERVICE DELIVERY MODELS OF FAMILY PRESERVATION

The intervention methods of family preservation services are usually brief and concentrated. They are most often delivered by CPS, or the public child welfare agency in a state. They may also be delivered by private child welfare agencies contracted by the state CPS. Whoever delivers the services, the goal is to provide a concentrated effort at behavior change in the family, create a safe environment for the child, and prevent removal from his or her parents.

Family preservation may also be used when a child has already been removed from the home due to child maltreatment. However, the ultimate goal of CPS is to return the child to the biological family. Where family preservation services are deemed appropriate in these cases, application of family-centered, home-based services is known as family reunification efforts. These efforts are carried out by a team of child welfare professionals, including foster parents, foster care workers, and case managers, in the domain of foster care (Williams, 1994). (Foster care is discussed fully in Chapter 12.)

BOX 8-3   Statement of Deborah, a Parent, Intensive Family Services Program

"Before Intensive Family Services came into my life, my life had become unmanageable. I was drinking most of the time. I was forgetting things and being negligent toward my child. I can tell you I was a very unhappy woman for a number of reasons.

The school started to complain that my child was unhappy. So they called in Intensive Family Services for help. I can tell you they helped me a lot. Miss Laura Cover and Miss Peggy Dickers came out to talk to me about my life and my child and the problems we were having. She asked me if I was willing to take in some meetings like Alcoholics Anonymous and parenting classes. I really learned a lot from those classes. Alcoholics Anonymous helped me to learn that you don't have to drink to be loved by other people, and drinking don't do nothing but ruin your life, and make things worse.

Parenting learned me to listen to my child and to be patient with my daughter and to listen her and to understand her life is not just fun and games. At home I didn't have people to listen to me.

Miss Laura and Miss Peggy understood and listened. I like them very much and I know I couldn't have got my life back together if I didn't have their support."

(Reprinted by permission from "Preventing Out-of-Home Placement: Programs that Work," 1987, Hearing before the House Select Committee on Children, Youth, and Families.)

Common goals of family preservation services are sometimes described by the following program models:

- Crisis Intervention Model: Intensive, short-term, completely home-based services with strong emphasis on behavioral and skill-building interventions. The *Homebuilders Model,* in Tacoma, Washington, developed by Haapala and Kinney, is the standard of practice for this model.
- Home-Based Services Model: Longest term, less psychotherapeutic in intervention methods, whether behavioral or cognitive, with methods sometimes even described as "pretherapeutic"; emphasizes family systems, concepts, and interventions. Project Kaleidoscope in Chicago, Illinois, is the model standard.
- Family Treatment Model: Short-term or long-term, depending on ongoing assessment of the family system and updating of family goals; coordinates agency-based and home-based services; may contract a separate case manager for the family; developed by Oregon CPS (Ooms and Beck, 1990).

Family preservation services have been touted as "something new" in public child welfare services. For many child welfare professionals, success is achieved when publicly served children and families are kept together. Family preservation, with a comprehensive focus on the whole family system's strengths and empowerment, is simply "good social work." The rights of the family are weighed against society's obligation to intrude on those rights when necessary on behalf of the safety of children.

FAMILY SUPPORT PROGRAM CHARACTERISTICS

If family preservation represents "good social work at last," family support services have been "good social work from the beginning." The history of the settlement house movement and the Charity Organization Society in the United States includes many examples of neighbor-supporting-neighbor activities in raising healthy children and maintaining functional family life. Buzzwords in human services professions, *empowerment, cultural sensitivity,* and *strengths perspective,* can be put into practice by reviewing the efforts of settlement house workers who sought to help immigrants assimilate into a new world (Kinney, Strand, Hagerup, and Bruner, 1994). These efforts sought not only to preserve families, but to preserve the culture of those families (Zinn and Eitzen, 1990).

Family support services have been (and continue to be) the arena for assisting parents and children admonished by Mary Richmond, "with patience and sympathy [to] strive to remove the causes of need" (Richmond, 1899; Richmond, 1994). More recently, Lisbeth Schorr, encourages the same approach by recognizing that "all families rearing children need support" (Schorr, 1989). Many professionals agree that voluntary family support will assist not only individual children and families, but also the larger society to achieve and to maintain healthy functioning in a time of rapid social change (Allen, 1993; Bowen and Sellers, 1994; Family Resource Coalition, 1991; Hamburg, 1991; Morton, 1991; National Commission on Children, 1991; Sachar et al., 1992).

According to the most recent legislation by the U. S. Children's Bureau, family support services are community based, offering programs that prevent family stress and promote family unity and health. In addition, these programs help families use other resources needed to care for their children and provide opportunities for families to overcome social isolation.

Family support services have traditionally been offered as family resource, support, and education services (FRSE) through a combination of home visitation and center-based services. Center-based services that support the development of healthy families are often referred to as CBFSE, or community-based family support and education programs (Weiss and Halpern, 1991; Farrow, Grant, and Meltzer, 1990). The evolution of family support services since the 1974 Child Abuse Prevention and Treatment Act has resulted in a blending of these programs.

Family support programs may blend a multitude of characteristics, determined primarily by the goals of the sponsoring agencies. All have in common a basic belief in the potential and right to self determination of families. These programs build on the existing strength of the families encouraging competence instead of dependency and respecting their cultural and other individual characteristics. Workers enhance family members' self-esteem and teach them to become self-advocates, linking them with the existing community resources. These services support all stages of child and family development, from the earliest stages. In the process of service provision, the programs provide an informal support network among the families served (Poyadue, 1991; CWLA, 1989b).

SERVICE DELIVERY MODELS OF FAMILY SUPPORT

Family support programs are extremely diverse. This variation stems from a multitude of disciplines, agencies, methods, and reasons for family support programs. For example, public and private health care agencies offer parent education or infant care instruction in an effort to prevent infant mortality. Educational institutions, such as Head Start, offer school-based or home-based services to low-income families of preschool-age children to increase their learning abilities and to prevent high school dropouts. Public and private child welfare organizations such as day care, respite care nurseries, and CPS may offer family support programs, including parent education and after-school programs, at centers or in the home for the primary goal of preventing child abuse. Law enforcement and juvenile justice programs may provide similar programs. These include youth activities, such as midnight basketball at a neighborhood community center located in a public housing project, that attempt to prevent juvenile crime. Economic development programs might offer family support programs for families, including parent education and day care, for the purpose of reducing welfare dependency. Indeed, large private corporations are offering family support programs to employees, recognizing that healthy families help create a healthy company bottom line. Examples include day care on the premises, parent programs, and family programs at family resource centers, often located within large office buildings.

Family Support programs offered in the home may be similar to the Hawaii Healthy Start Program. This particular program began in the early 1980s and quickly became a national model for other states. It attempts to prevent the increase in infant mortality and child abuse as a primarily home-based visitation program for first-time mothers. Beginning in the hospital at the time of delivery, a mother and her family are identified by screening them for stress, which could result in poor infant care and possible child maltreatment. After screening for potential participation, family service workers administer the family stress test, which further measures areas of possible stress in the first-time mother and/or father. There are some factors which are seen as generating particularly high stress levels and families are assessed for potential risk by measuring these (see Table 8-1).

The responses of first-time mothers and the extended family create a home visitation plan in which the mother voluntarily agrees to participate. Healthy Start, as a family support service, is more efficient than most other types of family-centered services because it follows the family for five years (Daro, 1988; Breakey and Pratt, 1991). An entry point to preventive services is provided for many families who may have the potential to maltreat their infants, yet would not be likely to recognize stress that could cause them to act on that potential. These multiproblem families do not traditionally seek out such services on their own (Daro, 1988; Breakey and Pratt, 1991; Hamburg, 1991; Johnson, 1993; Bowen and Sellers, 1994). Healthy Start provides a safety net until the child reaches the age of five years, at which time the educational system continues family support (Breakey and Pratt, 1991).

TABLE 8-1   Factors Increasing Potential Risk in Families

- A parent abused as a child
- A parent with a history of criminal behavior, mental illness, or substance abuse
- A parent suspected of child abuse in the past
- A parent with low self-esteem or poor coping or problem-solving skills
- Multiple crises or stresses within the family
- Violent temper outbursts by mother and/or father
- Unrealistic expectations of a child's behavior
- A belief in harsh punishment of the child
- A child is (or is perceived as) difficult or provocative
- A child is unwanted or at risk of poor bonding

(Hawaii State Department of Health, 1992)

Family support programs may offer many services that help support healthy family life and child development. These services might encompass such issues as support or parent education groups, children's play groups, peer support or peer counseling, or recreational services. There may be home visitation with early developmental screening. Day-care or after-school programs are sometimes provided for children and adolescents while adults might take advantage of educational and job skill training, or intergenerational programs to engage elderly family members in day care and provide relief for caregivers (CWLA, 1989; Pooley and Littell, 1986; FPFSS Program Announcement, 1993).

Whether offered at a neighborhood center in a public housing project, such as Walbridge Caring Community in St. Louis, a school such as Families and Schools Together (FAST) in Kentucky, or a hospital-based home visitation program in Denmark, family support programs have been quietly and systematically responding to the social and cultural changes affecting all families worldwide. In the United States, family support programs are gaining momentum. An evolution towards institutionalization appears with the growing overlap in family preservation programs and family-centered services common to both.

ETHICAL ISSUES IN FAMILY-CENTERED PRACTICE

COMMON GOOD AND COMMON PROBLEMS

Family-centered services, whether offered in family preservation or family support programs, have several commonalities. These include a focus on *family self-determination, respect for the family,* and *belief in the ability of the family to develop and achieve the potential for healthy functioning and child-rearing.* Both programs seek to provide *immediate and concrete services* through a caseworker who provides link-ages to community services based on the family's needs. All family-centered ser-vices are *holistic,* considering the needs of each individual family member as they affect other members of the family. Finally, all types of family-centered services *seek to involve the community* in the recognition that communities have a responsibility to the larger society to see that future citizens (that is, children in families) are raised in a healthy environment (Allen, 1993).

Family-centered services, along the continuum of family development pro-grams, also share common problems. First among them is finding the common link between family support and family preservation programs. While a continuum of services can be clearly identified in a study of the two program types, the reality is that the continuum is not supported by a strong link between voluntary and man-datory services for families. Family preservation programs, for example, are largely provided in the context of public child welfare agencies. While these ser-vices are growing in number, they are still grossly underfunded in many states. There are many families who could stay intact with children utilizing family pres-ervation programs, but they are not served due to underfunded programs.

Struggles with underfunding and overworked staff often prevent a fruitful search by public child welfare agencies seeking an overlap with private, commu-nity-based family support programs. These struggles, unfortunately, contribute to the weak link between programs that enhance, support, and possibly expand the wide array of services offered by public child welfare agencies.

Like family preservation programs, family support programs are plagued by funding issues. Family support programs often rely on temporary grant funding (sometimes only available for a year) or public fund-raising activities and contri-butions. While family preservation programs may not be fully funded and face possible elimination, families served by these programs still have access to services when children have been maltreated. When lack of funding eliminates a family support program, all prevention services become unavailable for a potentially dys-functional family.

CREAMING FOR THE MOST COOPERATIVE

As a result of funding crises, both family preservation and family support programs place greater emphasis on program evaluation. Outcomes of program evaluation supporting the effectiveness of the family-centered service often determine the con-tinuation of a service. This has created a situation in which families are selected who are most likely to succeed in or make direct and visible use of family-centered ser-vices. This practice, called "creaming of clients" (Schuerman, Rzepnicki, and Littell, 1994), allowed program evaluations to indicate a high level of "success" determined by such measures as pre- and post-tests to measure retention of information gained in a parent education or home visitation training program. When participants were measured on a selected basis due to cooperativeness, as determined by family-centered caseworkers, pre- and post-tests, as well as any other type of program evaluation, the results were automatically skewed (Schuerman et al., 1994; Pecora, Whittaker, and Maluccio, 1992). This phenomenon, also referred to as overselection, can also result in a skewed consumption of services. Less resourceful families, most in need of the family-centered services, whether family-support or family-preservation, may not receive them due to the overselection of families who have greater potential for positive outcome (Kadushin and Martin, 1988).

GUILT BY POTENTIAL TO ABUSE

A final ethical concern of family-centered services is the level of voluntary consumption by families. Public child welfare agencies have forever struggled with their unique power of intrusion on the natural rights of parents to raise their children as they see fit (Bremner, 1971). When family preservation services were instituted as a means of keeping families together, the time-limited focus helped maintain the balance between the rights of the parents and the rights of the child. Family preservation services allow workers to develop a strengths-focused approach to service delivery. Families are empowered to help themselves, becoming less dependent on the worker. By doing so, they provide a healthy and safe environment for their children. When services are ended, the case is closed. Families do not re-enter services unless and until a child is again clearly identified as harmed or at significant risk of harm.

Family support services are entirely voluntary, and are sought out as the need arises. Families are only bound to use services as they wish to and may choose not to use a service after privately paying for it, as may be required by some family support services. Only when family support services move along the family-centered continuum toward family preservation services do families begin to lose the ability to determine their participation.

The Healthy Start Program model and demonstration family development services, called Comprehensive Family Development Programs, are based on the voluntary participation of families. The families selected for these programs are usually identified as having a higher risk of maltreating a child. Services are usually instituted at the birth of a child and extend over five years. The services are maintained, although diminished in intensity, over the five-year period on a voluntary basis. Programs frequently report that families continue in programs over the duration, based solely on the risk assessment that caused entry into the program. Families are monitored closely for signs of increased risk and decreased voluntary cooperation. When signs are evident, the family no longer is voluntary. They become involuntary and mandated participants of public child welfare services with an investigation of child maltreatment. This can be the most ambiguous, but important, ethical question in the link between family support and family preservation services. Can families be forced to receive services to prevent child maltreatment based solely on a potential to abuse?

THE FAMILY-CENTERED WORKER

Qualifications of family-centered workers are as varied as the spectrum of family-centered services themselves. Family-centered workers in some community-based family resource, support, and education programs (CBFRSE) may only need an interest in shared parent support or be indigenous to the community where the CBFRSE is located. Such workers are cited as only needing "warmth, flexibility, ability to organize, commitment, and ability to act as an appropriate role model," with these qualifications being "more important than professional training" (Pooley and Littell, 1986). Family-centered workers delivering family preservation services to multiproblem families are cited as needing not only professional training, but often professional credentials. Background is critical to service delivery, with training including a demonstrated competence from family counseling to recognition of symptoms of child maltreatment. All family-centered workers, whether delivering family support or family preservation services, must have adequate training to fully embody the strengths perspective that is at the heart of family-centered services. Failing this, families will often be ill-served by underprepared workers. According to Mary Bricker–Jenkins, an advocate for a strengths perspective in all public social services, "inadequately trained workers result in an incoherent, inconsistent, unintegrated practice system" (1992). Since family-centered services seek to deliver in a consistent and competent manner a comprehensive array of coordinated services, training of workers beyond a simple interest in shared support seems necessary.

SETTINGS OF FAMILY-CENTERED PRACTICE

The family-centered worker is engaged in a number of settings and agencies helping families enhance daily living and child-rearing skills. For example, a family-centered worker may be assigned to a Pediatric Social Service Unit to conduct parent support groups for parents caring for ventilator-dependent children. In a public health unit, a family-centered worker might provide family planning information to first-time teen parents. An advocacy group for parents to visit schools might be developed by a family service coordinator with a community-based family support program sponsored by a public housing project. Many public and private hospitals and clinics include family-centered workers who conduct screening for family stress. Their job is to implement and carry out home visitation as a means of encouraging hands-on parent education in infant and child care. Workers in a family resource center might coordinate and regularly conduct a variety of parent education programs and support groups, including teaching infant care to toilet-training, and responsible fatherhood to effective stepparenting. Those family-centered workers who are in public child welfare agencies may find themselves doing some (or all) of these activities in a coordinated effort to help keep children and parents together.

These home-based services are usually delivered to families in which child mal-treatment has actually occurred. Public child welfare workers who are involved in family-centered practice to reunite a child in foster care with his or her biological parents may also engage in a similar array of professional activities.

COMMON CHARACTERISTICS AND COMPETENCIES

Wherever family-centered workers find themselves along the family development spectrum, all share common characteristics. They must recognize the inherent dig-nity of all people, regardless of individual situations, beliefs, or cultures, while be-ing non-judgmental. Workers must keep their own personal values and attitudes separate from the client-family situation and strive to learn about the cultural dif-ferences that families bring with them. Part of this may be a need to respect the sta-tus of family roles and nontraditional beliefs. These programs are built upon family strengths and the worker must learn to recognize these no matter what form they may take. Creativity may be necessary in tailoring the services to the individ-ual needs of each family (Kinney et al., 1994; Daro, 1988).

The commonalities of all family-centered workers in basic characteristics in-dicate commonly held values. These values are based on the emphasis on recog-nizing family system strengths. According to Marcia Allen from the National Resource Center on Family-Based Services (1993), specifically held values among all family-centered workers evident in services delivered include:

1. Viewing the family as a whole and as part of a community;
2. Believing that families who receive support are more capable of supporting themselves;
3. Providing services that are culturally sensitive and culturally competent;
4. Giving parents respect;
5. Promoting a nurturing relationship between the provider and family;
6. Believing in self-determination, the family's right to speak for itself;
7. Empowering families by
   - helping families move from a passive to an active role;
   - giving families/communities the tools necessary to meet their needs;
   - allowing them to set their own agendas;
   - strengthening the family within the context of legitimate community stan-dards, morals, and civic responsibilities;
8. Keeping families together, healthy, and safe;
9. Recognizing that *all* families need support;
10. Recognizing that *all* families have strengths;
11. Recognizing that *all* families want what is best;
12. Recognizing that the community has a responsibility to families to help develop capacity and strengths; they also are responsible for the community in which they live.

All family-centered workers should possess specific experience, knowledge, and skills according to the *Standards for Services to Strengthen and Preserve Families with Children* (1989) established by the Child Welfare League of America. These include a thorough integration of the strengths-based philosophy and values common to family-centered services, whether family support or family preservation. There are other areas specified in the CWLA standards for family-centered workers that are important for those interested in working in this field. Workers should have knowledge and skills in crisis intervention, in counseling of individuals, families, and groups, and in accessing community resources. It is vital that family workers be able to recognize and deal with different developmental stages but also be able to assess the family at each stage and provide help in goal setting and life-training skills as appropriate to particular age levels. One must be able to develop a service plan especially within the context of multicultural awareness. And finally, workers must learn to deal with a whole range of client affect from the hostile or withdrawn client to the depressed or suicidal one (Salee and Mannes, 1991; CWLA, 1989).

While the values and primary tasks are shared among family-centered workers, the goals of the professional activities vary with the type of family-centered service delivered along the family development continuum. For example, goals for the family preservation worker may focus on keeping together families threatened by removal of a child from the home. When a child has been removed due to maltreatment, the goal of a family-preservation worker may be to reunite the family and child if at all possible. Focused home-based attention, increased availability of the worker, and a time-limited intensive approach may be the answer to reaching such a goal (CWLA, 1989b).

Child Welfare League of America standards also address family-centered services midway along the family development spectrum, such as those delivered by the Hawaii Healthy Start Program and many Comprehensive Child Development Program demonstrations. CWLA states that services delivered by family-centered workers should include similar goals and the same training as that provided for family-preservation workers. It specifies in its standards that family-centered workers outside of the public child welfare agencies should develop competence in working cooperatively with child protective services.

Family support services must be delivered by the family-centered worker with the same values and characteristics as other services along the family development spectrum. The primary difference in the delivery of services in family support is the worker's ability to understand the basic components of family support. Family support services are delivered with an emphasis on family strengths, with a strong emphasis on the type of relationship developed between the parents and professionals. This relationship is typified in the competent family support worker by collaboration and shared decision-making with the parents. Parents may determine the services the family support worker delivers rather than the worker offering selected services to a parent based on a thorough assessment of a presenting family crisis or changing life situation, such as the delivery of a newborn. Family support workers should view parents as partners in providing family enhancement services. This could include a self-help group, which a parent might establish and conduct, assisted by the family support worker. In a 1991 report from a Wingspread Conference entitled "Training in Family Support: Towards a Conceptual Framework," the Family Resource Coalition also specifically identified the following competencies specific to family support workers:

- Confidence in using optimal practices related to his/her position within the overall family support framework;
- The potential and desire to engage in personal growth and critical self-reflection;
- Possession of the necessary degree of energy and persistence when working with families;
- The ability to engage the families for whom they are a resource meaningfully;
- Development of the knowledge, values, and skills that will enhance their ability to create positive and productive relationships with families.

The Wingspread Conference was very specific about the cultural competence all family support workers should possess. Such competencies are applicable to all family-centered workers, as are the general competencies specified by the CWLA. They include the development of cultural competence that allows families to celebrate and value their own diversity. The culturally competent family-centered worker will allow services for families, especially in family support programs, to be created in congruence with the dominant cultural traditions and beliefs. Furthermore, the culturally competent family-centered worker will assure that services delivered celebrate and honor the dominant culture of those families who use family-centered services.

SUMMARY

Family-centered services for children resurface periodically and newly packaged. The start of such services cannot be historically identified when they are considered within the natural tendency of families to seek help from an extended family, churches, or the larger communities in raising healthy children. In the United States, the settlement house movement and Children's Aid Societies of the late 1800s are the most identifiable "beginning" of family-centered services. Currently, family-centered services are provided along a wide spectrum of professional family development activities. These range from supporting families before a crisis can occur, called *family support,* to those in which the crisis of child maltreatment has already occurred, called *family preservation.* In between are family-centered services sometimes referred to as *family development,* with delivery based on a family's assessed potential or risk to harm a child. Throughout the spectrum of family-centered services lies the common thread of family empowerment and an emphasis on family strength. Even when children have been separated from parents, focus on family strength through family reunification should be maintained. All family-centered services, from family support to family preservation, share the belief that children are best reared by their own parents or most familiar legal guardians. There are also common problems in the continued evolution of family-centered services that are not yet resolved, such as the overselection of the most cooperative families or the persistence of unmanageably high caseloads. In spite of these issues, however, family-centered services promise the best supports for all families in a time of intense social, economic, and cultural change.

EXPLORATION QUESTIONS

1. What social, economic, or cultural changes might affect all families, regardless of class, culture, or religious beliefs? List at least three.
2. What strains are families experiencing that can cause the need for family preservation services?
3. Describe an "optimal therapeutic moment" in family preservation services.
4. What name could be given to services in the mid-range of family-centered services, such as the Hawaii Healthy Start Program?
5. What civil rights issue is possibly threatened in the family-centered services that are provided based solely on potential to abuse?
6. What might cause families to resist using family support services?
7. Describe how family support programs and family preservation programs might collaborate.
8. In what ways would a family-support worker master the ability to work cooperatively with child protection services?

ACTIVITIES FOR APPLIED LEARNING

1. Identify family-centered services in your community or state. Categorize those that are family support and those that are family preservation according to the type of agency that delivers the service. How do the categorizations differ?
2. Retrieve the child abuse reporting and investigation law in your state. What are the criteria for mandatory services?
3. Contact your local child protective services agency and inquire about Intensive Home-Based Services. Invite a public child welfare worker who delivers family preservation services (IHBS) to speak to your class. Find out what model of family preservation services they use. Also, find out what the family preservation worker knows about family support services in your community.
4. Contact a state legislator or an official with the state's public child welfare agency and find out what your state's Family Preservation Support Services (FPSS) plan is.

SUGGESTED READING

Hamburg, David A. *Today's Children: Creating a Future for a Generation in Crisis.* New York: Times Books, 1992.

Hewlett, S. A. *When the Bough Breaks: The Cost of Neglecting Our Children.* New York: Basic Books, 1991.

Hochschild, A., & Machung, A. *The Second Shift: Working Parents and the Revolution at Home.* New York: Viking, 1989.

Kaplan, Lisa, & Girard, Judith L. *Strengthening High-Risk Families: A Handbook for Practitioners.* New York: Lexington Books, 1994.

Morton, E. S., & Grigsby, R. K. (Eds.). *Advancing Family Preservation Practice.* Newbury Park, CA: Sage, 1993.

National Commission on Children. *Beyond Rhetoric: A New American Agenda for Children and Families.* Washington, DC: National Commission on Children, 1991.

Richards, Keith N. *Tender Mercies: Inside the World of a Child Abuse Investigator.* Chicago, IL: Nobel Press, 1992.

Schorr, Lisbeth B. *Within Our Reach: Breaking the Cycle of Disadvantage.* New York: Anchor Books, 1989.

Zill, N., & Nord, C. W. *Running in Place: How American Families Are Faring in a Changing Economy and an Individualistic Society.* Washington, DC: Child Trends, 1994.

REFERENCES

Adams, Paul, & Nelson, Kristine. *Reinventing Human Services, Community and Family Centered Practice.* New York: Aldine de Gruyter, 1995.

Allen, Marcia. Conference Material for the Second Annual Child Welfare Conference, Washington, DC, March 21–24, 1993. Prepared for the National Resource Center on Family-Based Services (November 1993).

Aries, Philippe. *Centuries of Childhood: A Social History of Family Life.* New York: Vintage Books, 1962.

Barnet, W. Steven. "Economic Evaluation of Home Visiting Programs," *The Future of Children* 3(3) (Winter 1993), 99.

Billingsley, Andrew. *Black Families in White America.* New York: Simon & Schuster, 1968.

Bowen, Linda K., & Sellers, Sherrill. *Family Support and Socially Vulnerable Communities: Three Case Studies and Lessons Learned.* Chicago, IL: Family Resource Coalition, 1994.

Breakey, Gail, & Pratt, Betsy. "Healthy Growth for Hawaii's 'Healthy Start': Toward a Systematic Statewide Approach to the Prevention of Child Abuse and Neglect," *Zero to Three,* a National Center for Clinical Infant Programs 11 (4) (April 1991).

Bremner, R. H. (Ed.). *Children and Youth in America: A Documentary History, 1600–1865.* (Vol. 1). Cambridge, MA: Harvard University Press, 1970.

Bremner, R. (Ed.). *Children and Youth in America: A Documentary History, 1865–1965.* (Vol. 2). Cambridge, MA: Harvard University Press, 1971.

Bricker–Jenkins, Mary. "Building a Strengths Model of Practice in the Public Social Services," (122–135). In Saleebey, Dennis (Ed.). *The Strengths Perspective in Social Work Practice.* New York: Longman, 1992.

Center for the Study of Social Policy. *Helping Families Grow Strong: New Directions in Public Policy.* Washington, DC: Papers from the Colloquium on Public Policy and Family Support, 1990.

Cernoch, J., Kagan, J., & Smith, Nancy. *Understanding the 'Temporary Child Care Act'.* ARCH Factsheet Number 31, Jan., 1994. Chapel Hill, NC: Access to Respite Care and Help, National Resource Center Coordinating Office, 1994.

Child Welfare League of America. *Standards for Service for Abused or Neglected Children and Their*

Families. Washington, DC: Child Welfare League of America, 1989a.

Child Welfare League of America. *Standards for Services to Strengthen and Preserve Families with Children.* Washington, DC: Child Welfare League of America, 1989b.

Chynoweth, J. K., & Dyer, B. R. *Strengthening Families: A Guide for State Policymaking.* Washington, DC: Council of Governors' Policy Advisors, 1991.

Cole, Elizabeth S. "Becoming Family-centered: Child Welfare's Challenge." *Families in Society: The Journal of Contemporary Human Services,* 76 (1995), 163–72.

Dalder, Greg S. "In-Home Versus In-Office Family Based Services: Determining Site of Service through Differential Diagnosis." *National Association for Family-Based Services.* University of Iowa (Fall 1994).

Daro, Deborah, D. S. W. "Intervening with New Parents: An Effective Way to Prevent Child Abuse." The National Center on Child Abuse Prevention Research, a program of the National Committee for Prevention of Child Abuse. Working Paper #839. Skillman Foundation (February 1988).

DePanfilis, D., & Salus, M. K. *Child Protective Services: A Guide for Caseworkers.* Washington, DC: U. S. Department of Health and Human Services, Administration for Children and Families, Administration on Children, Youth, and Families, National Center on Child Abuse and Neglect, 1992.

Dodson, J. E. *An Afrocentric Educational Manual: Toward a Non-Deficit Perspective in Services to Families and Children.* Atlanta, GA: The Atlanta University School of Social Work, 1983.

Family Resource Coalition. "Training in Family Support: Towards a Conceptual Framework." A Wingspread Conference, Family Resource Coalition, Chicago, IL: A. L. Mailman Family Foundation and the Johnson Foundation, 1991.

Hamburg, D. A. *The Family Crucible and Healthy Child Development.* New York: Carnegie Foundation, 1991.

Hawaii State Department of Health. Report to the 16th Legislature, State of Hawaii, House Bill No. 139, D.D. 1, Requesting Review and Recommendations from the Director of Health on the Healthy Start Program, 1992.

Hewlett, S. A. *When the Bough Breaks: The Cost of Neglecting Our Children.* New York: Basic Books, 1991.

Hubbell, R., Cohen, E., Halpern, P., Desantis, J., Chaboudy, P., Titus, D., DeWolfe, J., Kelly, T., Novotney, L., Newbern, L., Baker, D., & Stec, R. *Comprehensive Child Development Program—A National Family Support Demonstration.* First Annual Report. Washington, DC: Head Start Bureau, ACYF/ACF, U. S. Department of Health and Human Services, 1991.

Johnson, Harriette C. (Ed.). *Child Mental Health in the 1990s: Curricula for Graduate and Undergraduate Professional Education.* Washington, DC: U. S. Department of Health and Human Services, Public Health Service, Substance Abuse and Mental Health Services Administration, Center for Mental Health Services, 1993.

Kadushin, A., & Martin, J. A. *Child Welfare Services,* 4th Edition. New York: Macmillan, 1988.

Kinney, J., & Haapala, D. "Preserving Families through the Homebuilders Program." *Building Bridges: Supporting Families across Service Systems.* Vol. 13, nos. I & II. Chicago, IL: Family Resource Coalition, 1994.

Kinney, J., Strand, K., Hagerup, M., & Bruner, C. *Beyond the Buzzwords: Key Principles in Effective Frontline Practice.* A working paper of the National Center for Service Integration. New Haven, CT: Yale University, 1994.

La Leche League International. *The Womanly Art of Breastfeeding.* Franklin Park, IL: La Leche League International, 1981.

Mannes, M. "Seeking the Balance between Child Protection and Family Preservation in Indian Child Welfare," *Child Welfare* 72(2), (1993), 141–152.

Melaville, A. I., Blank, M. J., & Asayesh, G. *Together We Can: A Guide for Crafting a Profamily System of Education and Human Services.* Washington, DC: U. S. Department of Health and Human Services and U. S. Department of Education, U. S. Government Printing Office, April 1993.

Morton, T. D. "Partnerships in Parenting: A Framework for Services to Children and Their Families." A paper presented for the Child Welfare Institute, 1991.

National Center for Children in Poverty. *Five Million Children: A Statistical Profile of Our Poorest Young Citizens.* New York: School of Public Health, Columbia University, 1990.

National Commission on Children. *Beyond Rhetoric: A New American Agenda for Children and Families.* Washington, DC: National Commission on Children, 1991.

National Resource Center on Family-Centered Practice. "News from the Center," *The Prevention Report.* Iowa City, IA: University of Iowa, School of Social Work, 1995.

Ooms, T., & Beck, D. "Keeping Troubled Families Together: Promising Programs and Statewide Reform." Center for the Study of Social Policy, Background Briefing Report, The Family Impact Seminar (FIS). Washington, DC: The AAMFT Research and Education Foundation, 1990.

Pecora, P. J., Whittaker, J. K., & Maluccio, A. N. *The Child Welfare Challenge: Policy, Practice, and Research.* New York: Aldine De Gruyter, 1992.

Pinderhughes, E. "Empowering Diverse Populations: Family Practice in the 21st Century," *Families in Society: The Journal of Contemporary Human Services* (1995), 131–140.

Pooley, L. E., & Littell, J. H. *Family Resource Program Builder: Blueprints for Designing and Operating Programs for Parents.* Chicago, IL: Family Resource Coalition, 1986.

Poyadue, F. S. *Steps to Starting a Family Resource Center or Self-Help Group.* PHP, The Special Children's Family Resource Center, National Center on Parent Directed Family Resource Centers, 535 Race Street, San Jose, CA 95126, 1991.

Richmond, M. E. *Friendly Visiting among the Poor.* New York: Macmillan, 1899.

Richmond, M. E. "The Family—What Are You Thinking?" in 75th Special Issue, "Revisiting Our Heritage," *Families in Society* (January 1994).

Sachar, S. F., et al. "From Homes to Classrooms to Workrooms: State Initiatives to Meet the Needs of the Changing American Family." Washington, DC: National Governors' Association, 1992.

Salee, A. L., & Mannes, M. "National Trends in Family Preservation: Implications for Region VI." The Working Paper Series, Paper 2. Las Cruces, NM: Family Preservation Institute, Department of Social Work, New Mexico State University, 1991.

Saleebey, D. (Ed.). *The Strengths Perspective in Social Work Practice.* New York: Longman, 1992.

Schorr, L. B. *Within Our Reach: Breaking the Cycle of Disadvantage.* New York: Anchor Books, 1989.

Schuerman, J. R., Rzepnicki, T. L., & Littell, J. H. *Putting Families First: An Experiment in Family Preservation.* New York: Aldine de Gruyter, 1994.

U. S. Department of Health and Human Services, Administration on Children, Youth, and Families, Administration for Children and Families, Children's Bureau. Program Instructions: Implementation of New Legislation: Family Preservation and Support Services, Title IV-B, Subpart 2. Washington, DC, 1994.

Wares, D. M., Wedel, K. R., Rosenthal, J. P., & Dobrec, A. "Indian Child Welfare: A Multicultural Challenge," *Journal of Multicultural Social Work* 3(3), (1994), 1–15.

Wasik, B. H. "Staffing Issues for Home Visiting Programs," *The Future of Children* 3(3), (Winter 1993), 140.

Weick, A., & Saleebey, D. "Supporting Family Strengths: Orienting Policy and Practice toward the 21st Century," *Families in Society: The Journal of Contemporary Human Services* (1995), 141–149.

Weiss, H., & Halpern, R. *Community-Based Family Support and Education Programs: Something Old or Something New?* New York: Columbia University, 1991.

Weissbourd, B., & Musick, J. S. *Guidelines for Establishing Family Resource Programs.* National Committee for Prevention of Child Abuse, 1988.

Williams, C. "Toward Family Supportive Child Welfare Systems," *Building Bridges: Supporting Families across Service Systems.* Vol. 13, Nos. I & II (Spring/Summer 1994). Chicago, IL: Family Resource Coalition.

Zalensky, J. "The Family Preservation and Support Services Program: A Retrospective," *National*

Association for Family-Based Services Newsletter (Fall 1994).

Zelizer, V. A. *Pricing the Priceless Child: The Changing Social Value of Children.* New York: Basic Books, 1985.

Zill, N., & Nord, C. W. *Running in Place: How American Families Are Faring in a Changing Economy and an Individualistic Society.* Washington, DC: Child Trends, 1994.

Zinn, M. B., & Eitzen, D. S. *Diversity in Families,* 2nd Edition. New York: Harper Collins, 1990.

9

PROTECTING CHILDREN
WHEN FAMILIES CANNOT
Child Abuse and Neglect

HISTORICAL VIEW

SOCIETAL ROLE OF CHILDREN

The concept of children as small, developing individuals who must be nurtured and guided is relatively new. In early history, children were viewed as the property of their parents who could do with them as they, the parents, saw fit. Children were dependent on their parents for their very existence. Parents could kill their children, sell them into slavery, maim them, or abandon them (Levine and Levine, 1992). An early form of population control or solution to an unwanted pregnancy was *infanticide,* the killing of infants and very young children. Children might even be sacrificed to God, as in the Biblical account of Abraham's intent to sacrifice his son, Isaac. DeMause (1995) reports that archaeological findings of an abundance of skeletons of infants and toddlers suggest that child murder and sacrifice was all too common. He comments:

> *I have estimated that about half of all children born in antiquity were killed by their caretakers, declining in medieval times, and dropping to under one percent only by the eighteenth century (31).*

Other writings supported the parent's right to beat children as a means of discipline or even redemption. One much-quoted Biblical passage charges parents to: "Withhold not correction from the child for if thou beatest him with the rod he shall not die; thou shalt beat him with the rod and deliver his soul from Hell" (Proverbs 23: 13–14, as cited in Kadushin & Martin, 1988).

Parental circumstances also dictated the way in which children were treated. Destitute parents found some relief in selling children as workers or as slaves to wealthier individuals. Other poor parents were placed into *almshouses,* taking their children with them. These houses for the poor offered little in the way of sustenance or escape and the weaker members of the family, often the children, died (Tower, 1996). By 1601, the Elizabethan Poor Law offered some hope for the treatment of poor children. This plan separated the poor into three categories: the able-bodied poor, who were sent to work; the impotent poor, who were old, disabled, or mothers and for whom aid was provided by the state; and dependent children, for whom aid was also provided (Tower, 1996). Still the fate of children was dependent on their parental circumstances and the indulgence of the adults in their communities.

In the United States children who arrived as immigrants worked alongside their parents and did much to shape this country. African American children came originally as slaves who were at the mercy of not only their parents, but their masters. It was not unusual for them to be beaten or separated from their families according to the needs of those who owned them. Asian and Pacific Island children may have fared somewhat better. Their parents' cultural values insured that these children were absorbed into and protected by the family, when in fact the family was able to do this. Hispanic and Native American children too had the benefit of the family or the greater community. The fact that families were not also well treated impacted the children as well (Tower, 1996).

By the late 1800s, some children from poor families found placement in so-called *orphan asylums*, a misnomer, as many of these children still had at least one living family member. Conditions in these institutions varied, but incidences of physical and sexual abuse are well documented (Smith, 1995). Even if these orphanages had not been settings in which maltreatment could be hidden from the eyes of the public, children suffered from being institutionalized.

CHILD NEGLECT THROUGHOUT HISTORY

Neglect is a concept alluded to rather than fully discussed in historical contexts. Early images of neglect conjure up street waifs, cold, hungry, and destitute. To sustain themselves, these children resorted to theft, begging, and loitering to the annoyance of the upper-class passers-by. In fact, such scenes were a contributing factor to the child-saving movement. In reality, such children reflected the social conditions of their time, when poverty was largely unaddressed. Swift (1995) contends that it was the mother at whom fingers were pointed for the neglect of these children. Rarely, she says, was the father's role considered. These mothers were felt to be "morally wanting," and often it was assumed that they were under the influence of alcohol or guilty of "loose living." Early case records describe these mothers as "mentally limited" and immature. Rarely were circumstances other than their own ineptitude given weight. For example, Swift (1995) recounts that in one case of wife abuse the mother was described as "…self-centered, does not think of the children, complains constantly, and takes no responsibility for the house" (82).

Only recently have such societal issues as poverty and housing been considered. Yet, even today, individual characteristics of maternal figures are seen as the primary reason why their children are neglected (Swift, 1995).

CHILD LABOR AND MALTREATMENT

Childhood, as we know it, is a relatively new concept. Children of previous centuries were expected to be as useful as their parents. Many parents sought to insure their children's future through a practice known as *indenture*: apprenticing children to tradesmen or masters to learn a trade. Indenture began when the child was quite young and lasted into adolescence or early adulthood. Although seemingly a good way to learn a future vocation, reports tell us that masters were not always benevolent and that some children suffered from a variety of abuses.

As the industrial revolution dawned, children began to find employment in factories. They were expected to work long and hard, often beyond their endurance. Child advocates became concerned about the abuses to children in the work force and voiced these concerns about the need for reform. One such critic was Jane Addams of Chicago's Hull House. Hull House, a settlement house established in the Chicago slums on the model of New York's Toynbee Hall, strove to help immi-

'I don't think so!

grants integrate into their new society. Economic need found immigrant children working in factories along with their parents, but without the strength or endurance of their elders. Often the conditions under which they worked were also dangerous. These conditions became a special concern of Jane Addams. She recounts these concerns in her memoirs, *Twenty Years at Hull House:*

> *During the…winter three boys from the Hull House club were injured at one machine in a neighborhood factory for lack of a guard which would have cost but a few dollars. When the injury of one of these boys resulted in death, we felt quite sure that the owners would share our horror and remorse, and that they would do everything possible to prevent the reoccurrence of such a tragedy. To our surprise they did nothing whatever, and I made my first acquaintance then with those pathetic documents signed by the parents of working children, that they will make no claim for damages resulting from 'carelessness' (Addams, 1910, 148).*

Although the staff of Hull House fought valiantly for the rights of children, it would be some years before laws protecting children from unfair labor practices would be passed. Stadum (1995) suggests that an accurate picture of such reforms must include a recognition that some families were actually dependent for their survival on the income brought in by their children (see Chapter 1). Thus poverty must be viewed as an important contributor to early child labor.

SEXUAL MORES AND ABUSES

Children have been sexually exploited throughout history, though the definition of sexual exploitation has changed. In ancient times, female children especially were seen as the property of the father who could do with them what he chose. A daughter was something that could be used for barter to gain lands, money, and prestige. Such practices are still evident in some parts of the world. Betrothal might also be sealed through intercourse if the father and tradition should dictate. Daughters given in betrothal or marriage might be as young as twelve years. Other girls entered the convent at as young an age as nine, sometimes to later be used sexually by the monks associated with the convent (Rush, 1980).

deMause (1991, 1995) reports that mothers often masturbated their sons to increase penis size or handed them over to other adult men to be indoctrinated into sexuality. For example, the ancient Greeks are known to have practiced *pederasty,* the use of young boys by adult men. Families of these boys might seek out a wealthy benefactor to whom they would offer their son for sexual training and pleasure. The rationale was that such practices turned boys into better warriors and prepared them more effectively for adult life (Rush, 1980; deMause, 1991). But the sexual use of children, sanctioned by and large by society, has continued to occur into modern times.

One often thinks of the Victorian era as staid and proper. On the surface, Western society frowned on sexuality; masturbation was considered a precursor to insanity, promiscuity, and even death, and women saw sexual behavior in the marital bed as an odious duty they had to perform. Yet, the sexual abuse of children flourished. Child pornography and prostitution were the alternatives sought by men who felt they could not prevail on their wives. Slave owners in the Southern United States sought their sexual pleasures by "breaking in" their young slave girls at eleven, twelve, thirteen and even younger (Olafson et al., 1993).

The Victorian era also was the setting of a debate over sexual abuse that would be written about until the end of this century. Sigmund Freud, the father of modern psychoanalysis, found that many of his female patients reported that they had been sexually molested by fathers, uncles, and brothers. Fleetingly, he considered the magnitude of the incidence of incest that the reports must represent. Yet, soon after disclosure, the women would flee treatment or recant their allegations. (Modern therapists now see this practice as typical of survivors of incest.) For this reason and because he found little sympathy or precedent for this thinking in the medical community of his day, Freud eventually dismissed the women's reports as the "hysterical symptoms [which] are derived from fantasies and not from real occurrences" (Freud, 1966, 584). Critics would later criticize Freud for not having developed his early theories, which might have provided help for survivors who would not be fully believed until late in the twentieth century.

Although in Western culture, sexuality seems like an adult activity and one in which we should not involve children, deMause (1995) believes that the practice of sexually using children continues today in many other parts of the world.

EFFORTS TO CONTROL CHILD ABUSE

Sagatun and Edwards (1995) suggest that two reform movements, the Refuge Movement and the Child Saver Movement, influenced the exposure of children to abuse in the nineteenth and twentieth centuries. The Refuge Movement began in the early 1800s by seeking to remove children from the almshouses and place them in institutions designed for their care. Unfortunately, the conditions in these refuge houses often rivaled those of the almshouses and children rarely fared better than they might have if left with their parents. Abuse and neglect were rampant at the hands of overworked staff and other residents. In 1838, a Pennsylvania court also set a precedent by removing children from the custody of their parents, thus establishing a practice that would continue until today (Sagatun & Edwards, 1995; deMause, 1988). There is some question as to whether the early practices of the Refuge Movement were designed to protect children or to keep them away from the rest of society. However, in 1874, a case in New York City would change the history of helping children.

Mary Ellen Wilson lived with Francis and Mary Connelly and was the daughter of Mary Connelly's first husband. It was not uncommon for neighbors to see the poorly clad figure of the eight-year-old shivering, locked out in the December cold. But it was her cries as she was beaten with a leather strap that made one neighbor alert a neighborhood church worker, Etta Wheeler. After getting no help from the police, Wheeler finally turned to the Society for the Prevention of Cruelty to Animals and its director Henry Burgh, arguing that animals had more protection than little Mary Ellen. Whether Burgh acted on behalf of the SPCA or as a private citizen is unclear but history does record that the case was prosecuted by Burgh's good friend, attorney Elbridge Gerry. From this trial and the controversy surrounding it came the Society for the Prevention of Cruelty to Children, headed by Gerry, in early 1875. From New York City, the SPCC spread to other major cities as the first agency designed to intervene on behalf of abused and neglected children (Tower, 1996). By 1881, the SPCC was given authorization to make investigations and place magistrates in courts to protect the rights of children. At that time, the purpose of the society was not only to protect children but to prosecute their abusive parents (Sagatun & Edwards, 1995). Today, as we understand more about the psychology of those who become abusive, the trend is toward the protection of children and the rehabilitation of their parents.

The Child Saver Movement was founded chiefly by middle- and upper-class women whose aim it was to protect children from abuse, at the same time influencing child labor practices and legal practices affecting children. It was these efforts that gave rise to the founding of the juvenile court system through the Juvenile Court Act of 1899 (Sagatun & Edwards, 1995). (See Chapter 10 for more detail.) The juvenile court system is the primary legal entity that deals with child abuse and neglect. The use of this system will be discussed later in this chapter.

Another significant milestone in the protection of children from maltreatment was the work of C. Henry Kempe and his colleagues. In the late 1940s, Columbia University radiologist, John Caffey, led his colleagues in the recognition that multiple unexplained and often improperly healed fractures in children could be indicative of abuse by their caretakers. As Caffey made his theory better known through medical conferences and writings, C. Henry Kempe, then chairman of the Department of Pediatrics at the University of Colorado Medical School, began his own study of the phenomenon. In a subsequent article providing the early definition of child abuse, Kempe coined the term "The Battered-Child Syndrome," which he and his colleagues defined as "a clinical condition in young children who have received severe physical abuse, generally from a parent or foster parent" (Kempe et al., 1962, 17). Clearer definition of this phenomenon brought it to the attention of a variety of professionals who sought to intervene through their own disciplines. By 1972 the National Center for the Prevention of Child Abuse and Neglect was established, through financial aid from the University of Colorado Medical Center, for the purpose of training, research, and the sponsorship of training programs in the area of child abuse and neglect. In 1974, one hundred years after Mary Ellen Wilson endured the beating of her caretakers, the Child Abuse Prevention and Treatment Act (PL 93–247) was passed. This act established the National Center on Child Abuse and Neglect (NCCAN), which would administer funding for a variety of programs and research to help abused and neglected children. Since that time great strides have been made in the interest of maltreated children. In 1980 Congress passed the Adoption Assistance and Child Welfare Act (PL 96–272), which was designed to discourage long foster-care placements and encourage permanency planning for all dependent children, including those who were abused and neglected in their own homes. And in 1986 The Child Abuse Victims' Rights Act was passed to improve investigation, court intervention training, victim protection, and treatment for maltreated children. Finally, improvements in record-keeping and more stringent penalties for offenders were mandated by the Child Protection and Penalties Enhancement Act of 1990.

Over the years child protection has been the focus of much controversy and the subject of extensive research. Although some say that the upsurge of societal violence and the higher incidence of drug abuse has caused figures to escalate, the reality is that, with heightened awareness on the part of professionals and the general public alike, there is a much higher percentage of recognition and reporting. This trend, one hopes, can only serve to aid families in getting the help they need. It is up to future professionals to insure that that help meets the best interests of children.

MALTREATMENT DEFINED

Child abuse and neglect falls into specific categories with different symptoms and often different etiologies. The four categories most often used are: *physical abuse, physical neglect, sexual abuse,* and *emotional or psychological maltreatment.* Some authors break down neglect into physical neglect, emotional neglect, educational neglect, and medical neglect.

PHYSICAL ABUSE

The physical abuse of children can be defined as a *nonaccidental injury inflicted on a child.* The abuse is usually at the hands of a caretaker but can be perpetrated by another adult or, in some cases, an older child. Some protection agencies add the proviso that the abuse needs to have caused disfigurement, impairment of physical health, loss or impairment of a bodily organ, or substantial risk of death (Stein, 1991).

In the consideration of what constitutes physical abuse two dilemmas arise. The first is related to cultural context. Some cultures have customs or practices that child protection would consider abusive. For example, some Vietnamese families, in a ritual called *cao gio,* rub their children with a coin heated to the point that it leaves burn marks. It is an intentional act, but designed, in that culture, to cure a variety of ills. Do the good intentions of the parents therefore exempt this practice from being considered abusive? Similarly, the use of corporal punishment is sanctioned in many Hispanic cultures, but is seen as abusive in this culture when it becomes excessive. Some child protection advocates adopt the "when in Rome do as the Romans do" attitude that says that minorities must abide by the laws of the culture in which they now reside. One Puerto Rican social worker, working in a predominantly Hispanic section of New York City, vehemently disagreed.

> 'Yes, there are laws,' he said, 'but those laws were made by anglos. Is it fair to deprive new immigrants of everything including their customs? Maybe the laws should be changed!'

The reality is that, if a child is reported as being harmed for whatever reason, a child protection agency will usually investigate. If the reason is one of culture, this will be considered.

Another dilemma for society is: What constitutes discipline and how is that differentiated from abuse? The physical punishment of children as a form of discipline has been practiced extensively throughout history in the United States. While more recently many parents are seeking alternatives to physical punishment in the raising of their children, there is still a significant number of parents who hit as a way to discipline. Some argue that what separates this type of discipline from abuse is a matter of degree. If bruises are left on the child and those bruises last for a prolonged period, the act is considered abusive.

Symptoms

Children who have been physically abused display a variety of symptoms. Bruises are frequently what come to mind when one thinks of abuse and indeed these constitute the most frequent symptoms. Children may acquire bruises over time and one can often discern this when the bruises are at different stages of healing. For example, on lighter skins, when bruises are first made they are usually red in color, but turn blue about six to twelve hours later. During the next twelve to twenty-four hours the site will become blackish purple, eventually taking on a greenish tint in six days and healing to a pale green or yellow by five to ten days. Thus a child who is observed to have bruises in various stages of healing may have been abused on different occasions (Tower, 1996).

Bruises may also be in the shape of objects such as ropes, cords, belt buckles, or coat hangers, indicating that the child has been hit with force using one of these instruments. Bruises that are inflicted on areas of the body that are less likely to sustain accidental injuries are also suspect; such areas are the face and head, upper arms, back, upper legs, and genitalia. Certainly it is possible for a child to be bruised by accident, but if there is an unusual quality to the bruise, poor supervision and abuse should be considered.

Another classic abuse symptom is the burn. Infants and small children may be especially vulnerable to being burned in the heat (literally) of a parent's anger. Burns may be inflicted by cigarettes, pokers, irons, scalding liquids, heating grates, or radiators. Abuse burns often appear on such unusual places as the palms of the hands, soles of the feet, abdomen, or genitals.

Fractures are one of the recognizable signs of abuse to the medical community. From Caffey's early work (mentioned above) to the present, physicians are especially vigilant for signs of certain types of fractures. For example, a spiral break is particularly indicative of abuse. A parent who, in his or her anger, grabs a child and twists the leg or arm, may cause this type of break. Previously untreated fractures, which can be detected by X rays of the calcium deposits surrounding these improperly healed breaks, suggest a situation in which the parent was hesitant to seek medical treatment. When healthy children receive a fracture, there is swelling and pain, which usually prompts the parent to seek medical advice. But a parent who has inflicted the trauma may feel hesitant to do so. Head injuries or skull fractures are especially dangerous. In addition, blood can collect around the surface of the brain, causing a condition known as a subdural hematoma. Children experiencing this injury may vomit, have seizures, lose consciousness, or even die.

Physical indicators are not the only clues to abuse. Children will often act out their cries for help in their behaviors. As infants, children cry as a way to communicate with the world. Different cries mean different things. But a baby who has learned through being abused that the world is a threatening place may develop a shrill undifferentiated cry. As abused children become older their development may not progress as it should. They may be slow to reach milestones in social and physical development. The school years may find them unable to concentrate or doing poorly without the necessary energy to learn. On the other hand, some abused children throw themselves into school as a way of coping with an unhappy homelife. This child is the chronic overachiever, the child to whom a grade of B seems like the end of the world.

Some abused children shrink from contact and withdraw into themselves. Some wet the bed or soil themselves in their anxiety. Still others fight their world by becoming pugnacious or acting out in other ways. The source of the behaviors of many delinquent children is a background of abuse. Children who have experienced abuse may also be physically hurtful toward others, especially younger children or animals. Some run away in a desperate attempt to escape their pain. (See Figure 9-1.) There are as many ways for children to cry out for help as there are individual children, and every symptom here may not spell abuse by itself. It is the cluster of symptoms that gives one cause for suspicion.

Profile of the Abuser

Who physically abuses children? Hurting a child seems so foreign to many of us that we question how any parent could be capable of such harm. Yet everyone has the potential, under certain circumstances, to harm another and especially a child. Parents who abuse may feel overwhelmed, and depressed or angry with their own lives. In order to understand such behavior, try doing the following exercise.

Answer these questions and, if possible, discuss your answers with someone else.

What is the angriest you have ever been?

What did you want to do about it?

What did you do about it?

At any point did you feel out of control?

If so, what helped you to regain control? If you did not, what helped you to maintain control? (Tower, 1984)

Most people discover that it is possible to feel out of control. When one is out of control anything can happen. It depends on how hard one is pushed.

In addition to poor control or anger, many abusive parents have never had their own needs met. They may not have been parented by stable, caring individ-

**FIGURE 9-1   Physical and Behavioral Indicators of Child Abuse and Neglect:
Clues to Look for in Detection***

Type of Child Abuse/Neglect	Physical Indicators	Behavioral Indicators
PHYSICAL ABUSE	Unexplained bruises and welts: • on face, lips, mouth • on torso, back, buttocks, thighs • in various stages of healing • clustered, forming regular patterns • reflecting shape of article used to inflict (electric cord, belt buckle) • on several different surface areas • regularly appear after absence, weekend, or vacation • human bite marks • bald spots Unexplained burns: • cigar, cigarette burns, especially on soles, palms, back, or buttocks • immersion burns (sock-like, glove-like, doughnut-shaped on buttocks or genitalia) • patterned like electric burner, iron, etc. • rope burns on arms, legs, neck, or torso Unexplained fractures: • to skull, nose, facial structure • in various stages of healing • multiple or spiral fractures Unexplained lacerations or abrasions: • to mouth, lips, gums, eyes • to external genitalia	Wary of adult contacts Apprehensive when other children cry Behavioral extremes: • aggressiveness, or • withdrawal • overly compliant Afraid to go home Reports injury by parents Exhibits anxiety about normal activities, e.g., napping Complains of soreness and moves awkwardly Destructive to self and others Early to school or stays late as if afraid to go home Accident prone Wears clothing that covers body when not appropriate Chronic runaway (especially adolescents) Cannot tolerate physical contact or touch
PHYSICAL NEGLECT	Consistent hunger, poor hygiene, inappropriate dress Consistent lack of supervision, especially in dangerous activities or long periods Unattended physical problems or medical needs Abandonment Lice Distended stomach, emaciated	Begging, stealing food Constant fatigue, listlessness or falling asleep States there is no caretaker at home Frequent school absence or tardiness Destructive, pugnacious School dropout (adolescents) Early emancipation from family (adolescents)

FIGURE 9-1   *Continued*

Type of Child Abuse/Neglect	Physical Indicators	Behavioral Indicators
SEXUAL ABUSE	Difficulty in walking or sitting	Unwilling to participate in certain physical activities
	Torn, stained or bloody underclothing	Sudden drop in school performance
	Pain or itching in genital area	
	Bruises or bleeding in external genitalia, vaginal or anal areas	Withdrawal, fantasy or unusually infantile behavior
	Venereal disease	Crying with no provocation
	Frequent urinary or yeast infections	Bizarre, sophisticated, or unusual
	Frequent unexplained sore throats	Anorexia (especially adolescents) sexual behavior or knowledge
		Sexually provocative
		Poor peer relationships
		Reports sexual assault by caretaker
		Fear of or seductiveness toward males
		Suicide attempts (especially adolescents)
		Chronic runaway
		Early pregnancies
EMOTIONAL MALTREATMENT	Speech disorders	Habit disorders (sucking, biting, rocking, etc.)
	Lags in physical development	Conduct disorders (antisocial, destructive, etc.)
	Failure to thrive (especially in infants)	
	Asthma, severe allergies, or ulcers	Neurotic traits (sleep disorders, inhibition of play)
	Substance abuse	Behavioral extremes: • compliant, passive • aggressive, demanding
		Overly adaptive behavior: • inappropriately adult • inappropriately infantile
		Developmental lags (mental, emotional)
		Delinquent behavior (especially adolescents)

*From Cynthia Crosson Tower, *Child Abuse and Neglect: A Teacher's Handbook for Detection, Reporting, and Classroom Management*, pp. 82–83. Copyright 1984 by the National Education Association of the United States. Reproduced with permission.

uals who knew how to model good parenting. If they were abused, they may assume that that is how one raises children. They may be bitter about the alcoholism that racked their childhoods or the inconsistency that moved them from place to place. Most abusive parents do not intend to hurt their children. Granted, there are a few who have been so damaged by their life experiences that they strike out to hurt others, but luckily they are in the minority.

Helfer (as cited in Tower, 1996) sums up the profile of abusive parents as people who have not learned five basic childhood tasks and as a result are unable to nurture either themselves or their children. These tasks are:

1. *Learning how to get needs met appropriately.* If one does not know what he or she feels or needs, it is difficult to ask others to help meet these needs. For example, Mary is tired and frustrated and feels the need of a hug. She may not even realize, beyond feeling vulnerable, that a hug or a kind word would help. She has grown up with others who were so filled with their own needs that rejection was all they had for Mary. So Mary is afraid to ask for the nurturing that would ease her mood. The result may be that Mary acts in an inappropriate way, i.e., becoming ill or trying to hurt herself, which brings attention to her. A more appropriate method would have been to say that she felt tired and needed some attention.

For abusive parents, this may translate into using inappropriate behavior with their children. For example, instead of saying to her children, "Mommy is very tired. Could you keep down the noise and do what I ask?" Mary hits. Her extreme frustration at this point might even cause her behavior to escalate into being quite abusive.

2. *Learning how to make decisions.* Remember the last time you could not make a decision? You probably felt powerless, frustrated, and perhaps even angry at yourself for your indecisiveness. Abusive parents, who have not learned to make decisions, may feel crippled by this inability. They may not have had the opportunity to make decisions as children and do not even know how. They see people making decisions around them and this makes them feel that there is something wrong with them. They become angry and strike out at others, often their children.

3. *Learning how to delay gratification.* As children we "want it NOW!" Experience and maturity teaches most of us that saving for tomorrow is more rewarding. Granted, our present society, based on "buy now, pay later" makes it difficult to learn this task. But if life seems unpredictable and even unfair, an individual may learn to live for the moment afraid that what he/she wants will not be available in the next moment. For example, Peter's father drank heavily. When he was sober, he would often give Peter money. Peter wanted to save for a basketball he had seen, but his father would always find the money again and take it. It was not long before Peter learned that he had to spend the money immediately if he wanted to use it himself. Later in life, Peter expected his children to respond immediately to what he said. If they hesitated, he would assume they were defying him and beat them into compliance.

4. *Learning to take responsibility.* Many children from dysfunctional families grow up with the echoes of "If it hadn't been for you…": "If it hadn't been for you, your father and I wouldn't have had to get married!" "If it hadn't been for you, I could have done what I wanted with my life!" And so goes the refrain as the child begins to feel totally at fault for all the ills of the world. All this becomes overwhelming. Eventually the individual begins to feel like a victim who is controlled by outside forces. He/she denies that anything is his/her fault. In turn, this parent will give his/her child the same message passed down from his/her childhood: "If it hadn't been for you, I wouldn't have gotten angry and hit you."

5. *Learning to separate feelings from actions.* Some people cannot distinguish between how they feel and how they behave. For example, if a parent is angry, he/she may handle it in a variety of ways. But some parents see hitting as synonymous with anger. They have never learned that feelings are one thing and actions are another.

The self-esteem of many abusive parents is dependent on their children's behavior. If their children "look good," they feel like good parents. When their children misbehave, these parents often see themselves as failures. Some parents see their children as people who can nurture them when their own parents did not. And there are parents who were raised with corporeal punishment and are only repeating the patterns with their children that they learned in their own childhood homes.

Fortunately, there are only a few parents who, caught up in their rage over their own unmet needs, abuse their children sadistically. These parents may get high on the power they feel from hurting others, sometimes even to the point of killing them. Obviously, the prognosis for this type of abuser is poor.

Another type of abuse, known as Munchausen-by-proxy, has gained more attention in the last few years. *Munchausen-by-proxy* is found predominantly in mothers of young children and is a variation of Munchausen syndrome, which affects adults. Adult Munchausen involves an adult who is so desperately in need of attention that she/he induces some form of medical condition so as to necessitate a hospital stay. The patient then basks in the attention of hospital staff while proving a very demanding patient. The psychological community has concluded that this syndrome is based on the internalized rage felt by the patient toward parents he or she feels have abandoned him/her emotionally (Schreier, 1992).

Munchausen-by-proxy is a syndrome manifested predominantly by mothers, though a few rare cases of fathers suffering from the condition have been recorded. These mothers, who may have been Munchausen patients themselves, appear to be caring and concerned about their hospitalized children, almost to a fault. The children come to the attention of the medical community for a variety of reasons and the etiology of their condition is often not discovered until well into their hospital stay. The mothers provide a picture of a concerned parent who is always involved in the resolution of the child's health problem. At the same time this mother may have induced severe vomiting by giving the child large doses of ipecac, produced diarrhea by administering phenolphthalein, interfered with the blood sugar level or contaminated the blood by injecting insulin or fecal matter, or even have smothered the child to simulate Sudden Infant Death Syndrome or respiratory problems (Stone, 1989).

It is difficult to understand this type of pathology, but experts now say that this mother needs to use

> ...*her child to forge a relationship with the physician in which lying is the essential mode of interaction... The mother becomes the 'perfect' mother in a perverse, fantasized relationship with a symbolically powerful physician, in which the harm that she inflicts on her infant is but a by-product of the needs of her relationship (Schreier, 1992, 442).*

The impact on the child who survives Munchausen-by-proxy has not been fully studied as yet because the syndrome is too newly recognized as a form of child abuse.

PHYSICAL NEGLECT

The concept of neglect differs from culture to culture. In general, it is the role of parents to meet the physical and emotional needs of their offspring. These needs usually encompass: shelter, food, clothing, medical care, educational needs, protection, and supervision and moral guidance. The manner in which these needs are met may differ, but failure to meet these basic human needs in some acceptable manner constitutes neglect. Polansky et al. (1975) expand this definition further:

> *Child neglect may be defined as a condition in which a caretaker responsible for the child either deliberately or by extraordinary inattentiveness permits the child to experience available suffering and/or fails to provide one or more of the ingredients generally deemed essential for developing a person's physical, intellectual and emotional capacities (5).*

Various cultures interpret this definition differently. For example, protection and supervision in the Native American culture is a community rather than an individual responsibility. A parent in this culture would feel comfortable allowing even a fairly young child out of his/her sight because of the knowledge that the neighbors will not let harm come to the child. In other cultures, it is the role of the extended family to assume supervision in the absence of the parents. It is therefore difficult in many cases to intervene in neglect situations when there is not a uniform definition of what is neglectful that covers all cases.

Symptoms

While it may be difficult to be clear in all situations, protective services must have some guidelines to determine what symptoms to look for in children. Practice and research have developed a list of symptoms that can be found in children who are deemed neglected.

Neglected children may demonstrate consistent hunger and even malnutrition. Very young infants who have been neglected may withdraw from their environment and waste away, demonstrating a syndrome known as Nonorganic Failure to Thrive (NFTT). Older children may also become listless and have little energy. They may not be appropriately clothed to protect them during cold weather. They may be dirty, with body odor and lice, although the latter is highly contagious and does not always suggest neglect. Neglected children often demonstrate unattended physical or medical problems.

George's teeth were badly decayed. He and his three-year-old brother, Tag, were often left alone and subsisted on the snacks that eight-year-old George could beg or steal from the package store near their apartment. Their mother, a heroin addict, had tried numerous times to "kick her habit" but to no avail. An "aunt" watched George and Tag while their mother attended rehabilitation programs, but when mother came home they were once again left to her inconsistent care. Tag had developed a cough, possibly due to the fact that his light clothes offered little protection against the weather. It was not until George's sporadic school attendance was noticed that the family came to the attention of protective services.

Like George, children who are victims of neglect may steal either to get food or because they have learned not to trust that their next meal will be there when they need it. Neglected children are often tired and listless. Developmentally, they are usually significantly delayed, lacking the stimulation, consistency, and encouragement that has benefited other children.

Many neglectful parents do not value education for their children. Or if they do feel that school is important, they lack the ability to get them there consistently. For this reason, school attendance may be sporadic. In later years, the adolescent drops out of school because school says little to him/her about the struggles of life.

Neglectful Parents

Parents who neglect were often neglected themselves as children. For them, it is a learned way of life. Their childhoods have produced in them nothing but anger and indifference. Their adult lives are dedicated to meeting the needs that were not met for them as they were growing up.

Eulalia Gibbons is a slight woman with a quiet, indifferent manner. She seems oblivious to the bits of food on the cluttered table, the flies coming in from the broken windows, the stench of urine, and the children fighting and screaming in the background. She puffs absentmindedly on a cigarette, hardly seeming to hear as the social worker explains about the complaint they have received about her children's vandalism of a local school. Eulalia has learned to tune it all out. She has heard it before.

Pregnant at thirteen, Eulalia followed her itinerant boyfriend to the city where she now resides. There was nothing for her at home. The middle child of ten children, Eulalia had tired of taking care of the younger ones and being beaten up by the older ones while her parents were away working as field hands. There had been little to eat and less to do at home and she longed to be on her own. But after dumping her with friends, her boyfriend left her, pregnant again. She drifted from relationship to relationship, each promising her some stability. But now Eulalia, at twenty-one-years-old and with five children, has an apartment in a rundown housing development. She is too involved in the goings-on of the neighborhood to find time for the children. Even if she did, she would not know how to mother them adequately. Don't children just raise themselves? That is what happened in her family.

For Eulalia, life held little meaning. For her children, life would not be much different without intervention.

Throughout the years it has been mothers who have been described when the discussion of neglectful parents has emerged. Polansky and his colleagues (1975, 1991) have created the best known profile of neglectful mothers. They defended their one-gender profile by pointing out that fathers were usually unavailable in neglectful households. Swift (1995) suggests that abandonment on the part of these fathers is the ultimate neglect.

Polansky and colleagues studied neglectful mothers in both urban and rural settings and categorized them into five types:

1. The apathetic futile mother *demonstrates little or no affect to the point of seeming numb. Burdened by her own unmet needs, she has little energy and finds that nothing is worth doing. Why put diapers on the baby when he will only get them wet? Why do dishes when they will only be dirty again? It is difficult to reach her as her thinking is very concrete and she communicates on only the most basic level, referred to by Polansky et al. as verbal inaccessibility (1991). Her seeming depression is infectious and social workers describe this mother as a very difficult client with whom to work.*

2. The impulse-ridden mother *is impulsive and inconsistent. She may have the energy to meet life expectations, but it is instead directed toward defiance, restlessness, and manipulation. She cannot tolerate stress and frustration. This is the mother who has never learned inner controls and who is therefore not capable of performing the tasks required by consistent mothering.*

3. **The mother in reactive depression** *is one who is responding to life circumstances by giving up rather than fighting. She is intensely depressed or overwhelmed by grief.*

Leanna had been a fairly consistent mother with her first child. She found her second more difficult but she settled into the task of mothering nonetheless. She took pride in her parenting and saw her children as important extensions of herself. Her young husband too found parenthood to his liking. The couple managed to weather several financial and emotional storms in their early marriage, but their future promised to be bright.

One hot summer day, Leanna took three-year-old Sam and two-year-old Jessie to the beach. She had hardly looked away when she noticed that Sam was gone. Frantically she searched for him, screaming for others to help. He was found caught between two rocks, face down in the water. Efforts to revive him were fruitless and Leanna became hysterical. Once calmed she slipped into an almost catatonic depression. No amount of coaxing by her husband or professionals could bring her out of her passiveness. She was hospitalized and put on antidepressants. Her husband, feeling they were making her worse, insisted she be taken off them. "She'll be okay," he assured. "Her brother was drowned when he was a baby too. It's just too much for her." But Leanna never fully emerged from her depression. She could not care for her remaining child, a fact that her concerned husband denied. Again and again he would return home to find that his wife had not moved from her bed. His own immaturity and frustration finally drove him away and Leanna was left alone until protective services finally intervened.

---

4. **Mothers who are mentally retarded** *may neglect their children but not all mentally retarded mothers do so. When these mothers do neglect, it is usually because they lack the necessary supports to compensate for their own impaired functioning.*
5. **Mothers who are psychotic** *may be hampered in their ability to parent by their thought disturbances, severe anxiety, withdrawal, or bizarre behavior.*

All of these categories produce mothers who, for whatever reason, are unable to meet the needs of their children. Many lack the insight into their own actions that is required in order to use the help they might be given. It should also be noted that although neglect spans all socio-economic levels, it is the lower socio-economic groups that tend to be identified. This may be because higher groups have the resources to mask their neglect of their children. By the same token, it is often assumed that minorities make up a higher proportion of neglectful parents. This too is untrue, although it is often the minority parents who are reported.

SEXUAL ABUSE

Sexual abuse refers to "contact with a child where the child is being used for sexual stimulation by the other person" (Sagatun and Edwards, 1995). It is assumed that the abuser is older than the child and therefore has more power and resources. Due to this difference in power, it is assumed that the child is enticed, cajoled, entrapped, threatened, or forced into the abuse. The abuse is progressive, beginning from the least intrusive behaviors, such as observation, or exposure, to more intrusive behaviors, such as actual penile or rectal penetration. During this progression, the abuser gauges the reactions of the child and grooms her/him for further abuse. In addition to being touched sexually or being compelled to touch the abuser, sexual abuse also includes in its definition the use of a child in the production of pornography or encouraging the child to view pornography or other sexual acts (Stein, 1991).

Types of Sexual Abuse

Sexual abuse may be divided into several categories: *incest* or *familial abuse, extrafamilial molestation, exploitation through pornography, prostitution, sex rings, or cults,* and *abuse within institutions.*

Incest has been much in the media as survivors recount their stories and experts caution that most children are abused by family members rather than strangers as once supposed. In fact, an estimated 60–70 percent of all abuse is perpetrated within the family (Faller, 1990). Abusers might be fathers, older siblings, mothers (although less common), or stepfathers. Finkelhor (1984) suggests that girls who have stepfathers are statistically more likely to be sexually abused even if the abuse is not perpetrated by the stepfather. The most common type of incest is usually thought to be between father and daughter, although new studies suggest that older siblings perpetrate much more abuse than was previously assumed (Wiehe and Herring, 1991; Laviola, 1992).

Incestuous relationships within families have usually gone on for years before they stop or are discovered. The sexual contact has progressed from seemingly benign tickling or observing the child in the bath to more obvious sexual activities such as mutual masturbation or vaginal or rectal intercourse. Children have usually been compelled to secrecy by admonishments ranging from "this is our special relationship and no one would understand or believe you" to "they will send me (or you) away if you tell." Sometimes children are threatened or physically hurt to prevent them from telling.

The perpetrator in an incestuous situation usually lacks the social and communication skills to negotiate an effective relationship with another adult, in this case, his wife. In father–daughter incest, he therefore seeks a nonconflictual partner and finds this in his daughter. In his child he finds someone over whom he can feel power in order to mold her into a sexual partner. This father, a master at denial and manipulation, can rationalize away the inappropriateness and illegality of this arrangement, often telling himself and his daughter that he is "teaching" her lessons for later life (Hanson et al., 1994).

Extrafamilial abuse is abuse that is perpetrated outside the immediate family. This can be by a friend, an acquaintance, or a stranger. Although it is a common myth that most abuse is perpetrated by strangers, children are more often abused by someone they know. Children may be abused individually or become part of *prostitution rings*. In these children are bribed, blackmailed, or forced to participate in sexual acts for money. The money is then kept by those who have involved them. Or some sex rings are dedicated to the production of *child pornography*. These groups create photos, films, and videos that are then sold at a significant profit.

Many people wonder how perpetrators outside the family gain access to children to abuse them. Newspapers are often filled with tales of coaches or priests who have abused children right "under the noses of parents." And yet sexual abuse has been, until fairly recently, so far out of the frame of reference of most people that they don't think it will happen. Sometimes the perpetrator has a bond with the parent, such as in the case of a family friend. Or the parent may need services from the perpetrator, such as a day care provider. Parents may not be supervising closely and the child wanders off or is home alone, or parents may be otherwise occupied (Tower, 1996). For example, one survivor recounted that she used to help her mother in the family bookstore. A customer used to come in and ask her (the child) for certain books. Invariably they would be on top shelves. While her mother waited on customers, the child would go in search of the books, followed by the customer. "The first time he put his hand up my skirt when I was on the stepladder, I was very surprised. I jumped down but he smiled and I thought it must have been my imagination." The stranger continued to fondle the child over the next few weeks. He threatened that if she told her mother she would never work in the store again. Liking her job, the girl kept quiet. "Finally, he just stopped coming in," she continued, "but I was afraid that he would and the job lost much of its enjoyment for me."

In the last few years, increased attention has been given to the abuse of children in cults. *Michelle Remembers* (1987) chronicles the case of a young girl's memories about being abused by a satanic cult. In these instances the perpetrators are usually multiple and the techniques used to confuse the victim often render her/his story suspect by anyone she/he tells. As more and more of these cases emerge, clinicians seek answers as to how to deal with them. Hayden's *Ghost Girl* (1992), the story of a special education teacher faced with a child who chooses elective mutism as a way to cope with the abuse, gives an excellent portrayal of the dilemma of the professional faced with the prospect of the cult-abused child.

Institutional abuse has gained increased attention over the last few years. Day care centers and child care institutions provide an excellent opportunity for a perpetrator to have access to children. One of the most publicized day care cases was in Manhattan Beach, California where the McMartin trials stimulated numerous legal proceedings and much debate. Such situations have inspired institutions to screen staff more effectively and to take precautions so that staff do not have many opportunities to be alone with children.

Symptoms

Sexually abused children demonstrate a variety of symptoms, some of which may also be associated with other types of problems. Physically, sexual abuse may not always be visible. When children do have physical symptoms they take the form of rectal or vaginal tears, urinary tract or yeast infections, and burns or bruises in the genital or rectal area. Children may also have sexually transmitted diseases such as gonorrhea, syphilis, genital warts, herpes, chlamydia, and AIDS, as these can only be contracted through contact with infected mucous membranes.

Behaviorally, sexually abused children may seem secretive or withdrawn. Their school work may suffer or, conversely, they may see school as the only safe place in which they can excel. They may suffer mood swings, cry without provocation, or engage in such self-injurious behavior as bulimia, anorexia, maiming or cutting, or suicide attempts. Some sexually abused youths used drugs or alcohol to dull the pain. These behaviors can also be indicative of nonsexual disorders and must be seen as possible indicators rather than definite signs. By the same token, not all sexually abused children demonstrate symptoms. In a recent study, Conte and Berliner (1988) found that 20 percent of the children studied did not manifest observable symptoms of their abuse. When there are no symptoms, it usually means that either the reaction is delayed or the child has repressed the material to the point that he/she is unable to feel it (Faller, 1990).

There are a few symptoms that in and of themselves point strongly to the fact that the child has been sexually abused. It is not unusual for molested children to act out their inappropriate sexual knowledge in their behavior by sexually molesting younger children. Usually this acting out will demonstrate knowledge that they would not normally have. Chronic and compulsive masturbation too can be indicative of a disturbance of a sexual nature. Older children may become extremely promiscuous. These types of sexual acting out, as well as fire-setting and mutilation of animals, should always raise one's suspicions about the presence of sexual abuse.

Perpetrators

There are three predominant theories about what motivates someone to sexually abuse a child: the *Groth typology,* the *Addiction Theory,* and the *Precondition Model.*

A. Nicholas Groth, a psychologist working with incarcerated offenders, first created the fixated/regressed typology. He contended that offenders could be separated into two categories: *fixated,* or those who were emotionally "stuck" in childhood with respect to their sexual interests, and *regressed,* those whose sexual interests reverted back to childhood due to the stresses of their life in the adult world.

The fixated offender is primarily interested in male children and he comes down to the child's level in his engagement of that child. His primary orientation is toward children and he has little interest sexually in age mates. His first sexual offense is premeditated and there is a compulsive nature to his acts. This is a man who is not motivated by stress nor is he probably under the influence of drugs or alcohol. Instead he is someone who demonstrates a sociosexual immaturity and has failed to resolve his life issues (Groth, 1979).

The regressed offender, on the other hand, is someone who may appear to function fairly well as an adult. In reality he finds that his adult life is too conflictual, especially his relations with peers. He therefore turns to a nonconflictual female partner in a female child with whom he has a sexual relationship. In the process he elevates this child to the level of an adult by treating her like one. While he may continue to participate in peer relationships, perhaps even sexually, he depends on the child to feel powerful. He may be under a great deal of stress and his first offense is often impulsive in nature. This is the father who goes a bit too far in washing his daughter's genitals or the grandfather who ends up fondling his granddaughter when she sits on his lap. Neither may have planned the event initially, but after the first incident they may engineer circumstances to give them the opportunity to abuse again. This man may also use or abuse substances, but these are not the cause of his behavior. Rather, he uses them as an excuse to abuse children (Groth, 1979).

The problem with Groth's typology is that offenders do not always fit neatly into one category or another. Carnes (1983) suggests that sexual abuse is an addiction. In this addiction, the addict develops a faulty belief system that leads to impaired thinking. As part of this thinking he denies, rationalizes, and blames others for his actions and thoughts. He becomes preoccupied with his fantasies and ritualizes his behavior. Therefore, the offender who uses one strategy on a child will probably continue that strategy with others. Finally his behavior becomes compulsive and he feels that he has to abuse children. Some child sexual abusers feel despair afterwards and some do not. Again, not all offenders fit neatly into the addiction category.

Probably the most widely used theory today is that of Finkelhor's Precondition Model. Finkelhor (1984) theorizes that in order for the sexual abuse of a child to happen, four factors must be operating. The perpetrator must be *motivated to abuse*, the *internal inhibitors that would tell most people not to abuse would not be working*, the *external inhibitors that normally protect children would not be in place*, and the *child's resistance would not be sufficiently strong* (see Figure 9-2).

Motivation to sexually abuse involves three components. First, the perpetrator must feel an *emotional congruence toward children*. This is more than a simple attraction to or desire to be with children. Rather, it is based on a pathological phenomenon in which being around children satisfies the perpetrator's emotional needs. He may feel this way because he needs to feel power over someone, because his own emotional development is arrested, or because of some childhood trauma that he feels compelled to reenact. Secondly, the perpetrator is *sexually aroused by children*. Once again, it may be a childhood trauma that is the root of this response. Or he may have grown up observing another's sexual involvement with children. For example, research tells us that an increasing number of brothers of victims in families in which father–daughter incest is present are modeling the behaviors of their fathers by themselves abusing their sisters or, later in life, their own children. Some sexual abuse perpetrators are aroused by child pornography, often misinterpreting the behavior of children as sexual and therefore inviting sexual contact. Finally, perpetrators are motivated to turn to children because their own *normal outlets for sexual expression are blocked*. Blockage may be a result of marital problems, inadequate social skills, fear of adult females, or some previous traumatic sexual experience with an adult (Finkelhor, 1984).

FIGURE 9-2   Preconditions for Sexual Abuse

	Level of Explanation	
	Individual	*Social/Cultural*
Precondition I: Factors Related to Motivation to Sexually Abuse		
Emotional congruence	Arrested emotional development Need to feel powerful and controlling Re-enactment of childhood trauma to undo the hurt Narcissistic identification with self as a young child	Masculine requirement to be dominant and powerful in sexual relationships
Sexual arousal	Childhood sexual experience that was traumatic or strongly conditioning Modeling of sexual interest in children by someone else Misattribution of arousal cues Biologic abnormality	Child pornography Erotic portrayal of children in advertising Male tendency to sexualize all emotional needs
Blockage	Oedipal conflict Castration anxiety Fear of adult females Traumatic sexual experience with adult Inadequate social skills Marital problems	Repressive norms about masturbation and extramarital sex
Precondition II: Factors Predisposing to Overcoming Internal Inhibitors	Alcohol Psychosis Impulse disorder Senility Failure of incest inhibition mechanism in family dynamics	Social toleration of sexual interest in children Weak criminal sanctions against offenders Ideology of patriarchal prerogatives for fathers Social toleration for deviance committed while intoxicated Child pornography Male inability to identify with needs of children
Precondition III: Factors Predisposing to Overcoming External Inhibitions	Mother who is absent or ill Mother who is not close to or protective of child Mother who is dominated or abused by father Social isolation of family Unusual opportunities to be alone with child Lack of supervision of child Unusual sleeping or rooming conditions	Lack of social supports for mother Barriers to women's equality Erosion of social networks Ideology of family sanctity
Predisposition IV: Factors Predisposing to Overcoming Child's Resistance	Child who is emotionally insecure or deprived Child who lacks knowledge about sexual abuse Situation of unusual trust between child and offender Coercion	Unavailability of sex education for children Social powerlessness of children

Source: *Child Sexual Abuse: New Theory and Research* by David Finkelhor. Reprinted with permission of Free Press, Copyright, 1984.

Most of us have an internal voice that lets us know that certain behavior is unacceptable. These *internal inhibitors are not operating efficiently* for sexual abuse perpetrators. They may be hampered by the influence of alcohol, senility, an impulse disorder, or psychosis. More likely, perpetrators have not developed these internal voices because they have seen sexual abuse in their own childhood. From a societal perspective, they may also not be compelled to develop internal inhibitors. With the availability of child pornography and the fact that our culture tolerates advertising that presents children in a seductive manner, the individual with a shaky set of inner controls finds little reason not to be interested in children. Further, most perpetrators know that intoxication provides an excellent excuse for a wide variety of deviant behaviors. And while patriarchy is still accepted, incestuous fathers feel justified in their abuse of their daughters (Finkelhor, 1984).

There are also external inhibitors that can protect children, but when these *external inhibitors are not operating* children are placed at risk. External inhibitors are those things that keep a child safe or rob a perpetrator of the opportunity to abuse. For example, mothers are often in key roles to protect their children. When mothers are absent or unavailable either physically or emotionally or are dominated by an abusive husband, they may not be able to protect their children. Many mothers lack social supports. The societal concept of family sanctity, while functional for the autonomy of a healthy family system, leaves the abusive family isolated and the children at risk for the continuation of abuse (Finkelhor, 1984).

Finally, in order to abuse a child, the perpetrator must *overcome the child's resistance.* Children who are emotionally needy or who are unaware of the potential for being sexually abused are usually easier targets. Society's view of children as powerless individuals with few rights renders them especially vulnerable to being victims (Finkelhor, 1984).

The correlation between abuse in childhood and perpetration in adulthood is well known. We also know that not all sexual abuse perpetrators had sexual abuse in their backgrounds, nor do all who were sexually abused as children become abusive as adults. What then predisposes an individual to become a perpetrator? Gilgun (1990) studied sexual abusers and a control group of nonabusive men in an effort to determine why some men abuse and some do not. She found that there were differences in four areas. The perpetrators were more likely to have had childhood problems in the areas of *confidant relationships,* having few confidants and feeling isolated from and excluded by others. Abusers also differed in the area of *sexuality.* Most abusers began masturbation prior to the age of twelve and used it to maintain their equilibrium. Further, they reported repetitive, coercive sexual fantasies. Controls masturbated later in adolescence and used the act to release tension. They also had peer-related (e.g., imagining appropriate sexual acts with peers) and noncoercive fantasies.

Gilgun found that the *families of abusers were characterized by domestic violence and child maltreatment.* Those who had not been abused themselves had watched the abuse of siblings or their mothers. Finally, the *peer relationships* of offenders were more likely to be centered around antisocial activities that equated masculinity with power and sexual conquest.

Most of the research done on perpetrators refers to males. Does this mean that women do not abuse children? Unfortunately, this is not the case. Women, too, have been found to be abusive, often in larger numbers than we realize. In 1984, Finkelhor postulated that women were not as often abusive because of their enculturation. Our culture taught them to prefer older and stronger partners while men learned to look for smaller and weaker partners; women are more closely aligned with nurturing and therefore more capable of relating to the whole child; women are less likely than men to sexualize affection, and, because women themselves have for centuries been victimized, they are more likely to empathize with the victim and therefore less likely to put others in a victim role.

Since this theory that somewhat exonerated women as perpetrators, reports of female abusers have increased. Little research has been published on female offenders. Mathews et al. (1990) felt that women were motivated to abuse for several reasons: (1) they were repeating the abuse they had experienced themselves as children; (2) they were going along with the abuse perpetrated by their male partners; (3) they were seeking closeness, affection, attention, or acceptance from their victims; (4) they were displacing anger, a need for power, or feelings of rejection onto their victims; or (5) they saw children as safe targets for their displaced feelings.

Kaufman et al. (1995) compared the motivations and other factors between perpetration by male and female offenders. They found that females were more likely than male offenders to engage in abuse with another perpetrator, thus supporting Mathews's hypothesis that women act as accomplices in the abuse. Males and females just as often use threats, pornographic materials, and coercion to compel their victims, but women are more prone to use devices or foreign objects in the abusive act. There was little difference in the genders in regard to their relationship to the victim and the location of the abuse, although 31 percent of the females (compared to only 8 percent of the males) were the teachers or baby-sitters of the victims (Kaufman et al., 1995, 331). Despite the similarities in the methods of male and female offenders, Kaufman et al. postulated that the motivations were different. These authors felt that men more often abused for sexual satisfaction, while women abused to get nonsexual needs, such as emotional gratification, met.

Other Family Members in Incestuous Families

The nonabusive parent in an incestuous family is often held partially responsible for the abuse. Some authors feel that, instead of blaming the nonabusive parent, usually the mother, for not knowing about the abuse, we should support her efforts to intervene once she does know. Yet, not all mothers feel able to intervene.

Johnson (1992) categorizes mothers in father–daughter incest situations as: the *collusive mother* or one who is withdrawn, cold, or psychologically absent and who pushes her daughter into her own role in the family; the *powerless mother*, who feels victimized, powerless, defeated, and unable to protect herself, let alone her child; and the *protective mother*, who does provide protection once she learns of the abuse. Many theorists now contend that the mother should not be blamed for the abuse within her family. She is already the victim of the societal expectation that women are responsible for maintaining family balance. Often devoid of adequate nurturing in her own background, these mothers are usually ill-equipped for this task. They are often either financially or emotionally dependent on their perpetrator husbands and are therefore unable to perceive that they have choices (Schonberg, 1992; Peterson, et al., 1993).

Nora grew up the youngest of ten children. Her next oldest sibling was ten when she was born and her mother made it clear that she had not planned on Nora's birth. As a child, Nora was withdrawn and her siblings nicknamed her, with some derision, "the mouse." When at five one of her uncles began to sexually abuse her, Nora told no one. She was sure no one would believe her. Nora drifted through school with few friends. When in high school a boy, Jake, began to ask her out, she was immediately enthralled with him. He seemed to be everything she wanted. When he told her that his family had had problems too, Nora felt even closer to him. They were married when they graduated from high school and Jake went to work at the local mill. Their son, Tim, was born within the year. From his birth Nora knew that there was something wrong. When the doctors told her that he had Down syndrome, she was not surprised. Jake, on the other hand, was very upset and refused to believe that their son would not be normal. He urged Nora to have another child, which they soon did. This girl's birth was followed by the births of two more girls. In the meantime, Nora strived to care for Tim while Jake virtually ignored their son. He chided Nora for coddling him and making a baby of him. Nora felt angry that Jake could not see how much Tim needed her. She withdrew more and more from her husband and her other children.

Sally, her third child, was eight when a social worker came to the house and said that Sally had told her teacher that her father was sexually abusing her. Nora was horrified and accused Sally of lies until the oldest daughter confirmed that she too had been sexually abused by her father.

Nora, plagued by her own insecurities, was ill-equipped to handle the needs of her family. Despite the care she gave her son, her daughters described her as cold and unavailable. She was, however, eventually able to believe her daughters and stood by them as the family sought help from the social service system.

The nonabused siblings in the incestuous family are often forgotten as the family copes with the crisis of disclosure. Yet they too are in crisis. The boys in a father–daughter incest family may perceive that there is something amiss but may also be too fearful either to face the situation or to intervene. They often do not recognize that, as children, it is not their place to intervene. They may instead feel very guilty. Many male siblings handle their guilt by either total denial or by what is referred to as *identification with the aggressor*. These children, too fearful to oppose their abusive father, join in the abuse either by targeting their sister, by abusing other children, or by molesting their own children when they become adults (Tower, 1996). Sisters in situations of father–son or mother–son incest often appear either to be unaware or to deny that the abuse is occurring.

When a father abuses one son or one daughter, the other siblings of the same sex, who are old enough to suspect the sexual abuse, may wonder why they were not "chosen." As Donna explained:

> I knew Dad was after my younger sister. It was not that I wanted to be abused too; I didn't. But Dad and my sister seemed awfully close and I really resented it. Dad had actually approached me a year or so before. I thought he was kidding and laughed at him. He was hurt and never bothered me again. Then when I saw him being so chummy with my kid sister, I was at first horrified and then jealous, as awful as that may sound.

For other siblings, recognition that abuse is occurring is too threatening a concept with which to deal. Instead, they live with the cloud of family dysfunction hanging over their heads. Some survivors feel that it was actually as difficult for their siblings as it was for them (Tower, 1988).

EMOTIONAL OR PSYCHOLOGICAL ABUSE

Emotional abuse refers to undermining the self-esteem of a child, or humiliating, belittling, rejecting, isolating, or terrorizing a child. Garbarino, Guttman, and Seeley (1986) suggest that the term *emotional abuse* be amended to *psychological abuse* as this type of abuse is a pattern of psychically destructive behavior. Although psychological abuse is an integral part of neglect and physical and sexual abuse, it is one type of assault that can also stand alone.

> Sandy remembers that he felt that his parents never had time for him. They both worked and Sandy was what was commonly referred to as a latch-key child. Sandy didn't really mind. He actually liked being alone better than having anyone else at home. When they were at home, they always yelled at him. Nothing he did seemed to please them. "You are so stupid!" his father told him. "Can't you ever learn?" his mother screamed. But the punishments were the worst. Sandy dared not tell them if he was fond of something. He knew that it would mean that that thing would be gone. At the first infringement, he knew that his father would destroy anything that Sandy loved. Like the baseball cards he had saved for over a year. He loved their shiny pictures. He had some that were quite rare. But one day he had not cleaned his room fast enough and his father had burned the cards. "This will make a man out

of you!" his father had said. No, Sandy thought. It will just make me hate you more.

The definition of emotional/psychological abuse is sometimes complicated by cultural variations. For example, many Asian families use shame to socialize their children to do what is expected of them (Mass and Yap, 1992). Shame may be seen as belittling a child in other cultures. And some Native American and African American families employ the cultural equivalent of the "bogeyman" to frighten children into compliance (Garbarino, Guttman, & Seeley, 1986). Such practices are construed by others as terrorizing children.

Symptoms

Emotionally or psychologically abused children demonstrate a variety of different behaviors. Burdened by low self-esteem, they may belittle themselves or engage in self-destructive behaviors either passively, through using drugs or alcohol, or actively through suicide attempts or eating disorders (O'Hagan, 1993). Some exhibit physical symptoms, such as headaches, asthma, ulcers, hyperactivity, or hypochondria. Children may withdraw or they may fight back by being openly aggressive.

Abusive Parents

Parents who abuse their children psychologically are often disillusioned with their own lives. They may be frustrated by unmet needs and unfulfilled expectations. In response, they lash out at the most vulnerable of their family members—their children (O'Hagan, 1993). Some parents abuse drugs or alcohol and some have learned their abusive patterns at the hands of their own parents.

Today, in an era when the incidence of divorce is extremely high, children sometimes suffer. Some children become symbols of one parent to the other and are emotionally battered by that person. Even well-meaning parents, embittered by divorce proceedings, can forget that the child should not be compelled to take sides, and that criticizing the child's other parent reflects on the child.

Finally, some adolescents who are ill-prepared for and overwhelmed by parenthood may find themselves emotionally abusing their children.

Dinah had had no idea how demanding a baby could be. She found that she was unable to do any of the things she enjoyed. The baby cried and cried until Dinah wanted to cry too. "Shut up, you stupid little jerk!" she found herself screaming. It wasn't long before her frustration made itself known to her infant daughter, who cringed when her mother touched her.

REPORTING CHILD MALTREATMENT

As a result of the 1974 Child Abuse Prevention and Treatment Act, every state in the United States requires that instances of child abuse and neglect be reported to the state's child protective agency. Some states name specific *mandated reporters*— that is individuals who, in their professional capacity, are obligated to report suspected abuse. For example, the law in Massachusetts lists certain professionals, such as physicians, dentists, social workers, police, educators, and so on who are considered mandated reporters. Other states are more general in their requirements, dictating that any individual must report. In addition, state laws indicate *to whom the report should be made* (child protective services, police, and so forth); *under what conditions the report should be made* (suspicion, reasonable cause to believe, and so on); *the time period during which the report must be investigated by the child protection agency* (between two hours to thirty days, depending on the state and the degree of emergency of the situation); *the action taken if a mandated reporter does not report* (anything from imprisonment to a fine); and *the type of immunity provided to mandated reporters who do report* (Tower, 1996).

The question always arises: Does a reporter have to give his/her name? It is always helpful for an agency to know the identity of the reporter. This enables the worker to contact the reporter for additional information. In states where there is a penalty for not reporting abuse, the mandated reporter who reports anonymously may not be protected from the penalty if his/her identity is unknown. If a reporter does so in good faith and identifies him/herself, he/she cannot be held liable.

INTAKE

Once the report has been made to a child protection agency, by phone and sometimes in writing, the situation is screened. Most agencies use a risk factor formula. They determine, by looking at certain factors, how much danger the child is in. For example, a situation in which there is alcohol involved, in which there has been a previous report of abuse, and in which the child is especially young might be considered a higher risk than a situation in which the child is older, the abuse has never been reported before, and the parents are substance-free. The intake social worker will look at patterns in the risk factors rather than just one variable. If the intake worker feels that there is sufficient indication that there was abuse and the child is at further risk, the case will usually be substantiated or screened into the system (see Figure 9-3). If there are concerns about the family functioning or services the family needs, but the case is not appropriate for protective services, a referral will be made to a more appropriate agency. For example, a family might need counseling or require assistance with housing issues and would be directed to someone who could help them. Although not the procedure in the past, more and more children's protective agencies are screening in situations of domestic violence. Although a child might not have been hit in a violent home, witnessing a parent being hit has significant impact.

For the Farmer children, watching their mother being battered was a way of life. The call that there was yet another bout of abuse by Mr. Farmer came in to Children's Protective services from a concerned neighbor. She had called the police earlier in the week, but was concerned that "nothing had been done." Ironically, the CPS office had received a call earlier that day from Gail Farmer's first-grade teacher, who was concerned that the girl was being sexually abused. After considering the reports, the intake worker, in conference with his supervisor, felt that there was enough evidence to screen in the report.

ASSESSMENT

If a case is screened in by the intake worker or team, the next step is diagnostic assessment or investigation. The assessment worker uses this time to gather pertinent data through interviews, previous reports, or piecing together facts to determine if the maltreatment has in fact occurred and how serious the risk is for the child for future maltreatment (Wiehe, 1992).

Once the report had been screened in, a worker was sent to the Farmer home. Because there was a potential for violence on Mr. Farmer's part, the police accompanied the worker. Had Mr. Farmer still been in the act of abusing his wife, he might have been removed by the police. He was not, however, at home. Mrs. Farmer was badly bruised and three-year-old Laura and five-year-old Jake were cowering in a corner. The worker talked with the mother, encouraged her to seek medical attention, and also talked with the children. Mrs. Farmer tearfully recounted that she suspected that her husband had sexually abused at least Gail if not Laura, but she had been too frightened of him to tell anyone. Now, she agreed to go to a shelter until plans could be made for her and her children.

Now it was the role of the assessment worker to gather additional information. Toward this end, she spoke with Gail's teacher, interviewed Gail at school, and talked with the concerned neighbor. Further, she checked with the police department and found that, although there had been other complaints of abusive behavior, Mr. Farmer had never been arrested. She also discovered that he had a drinking problem that seemed to have become worse since he was laid off his last job. For this assessment worker, the Farmer case began to evolve into a readable pattern that told her that the children were in danger.

As in this case, law enforcement officers may be involved from the onset. Most states encourage or mandate law enforcement involvement in cases of domestic violence, sexual abuse or very serious injury. It is the primary role of officers to con-

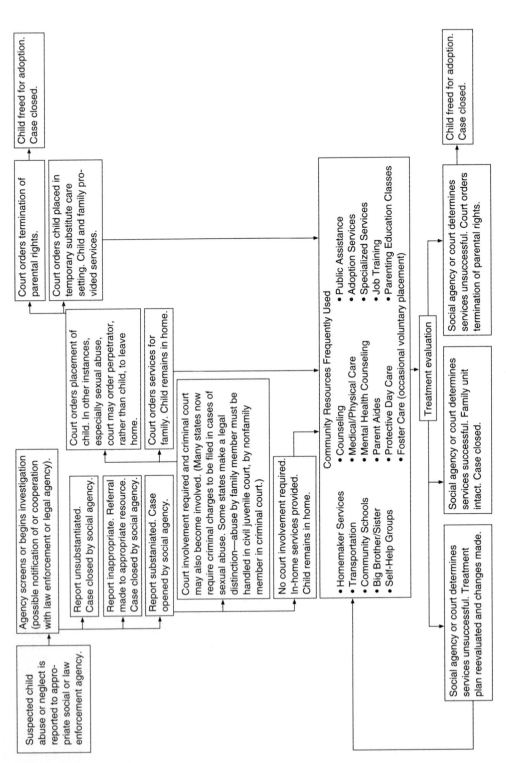

FIGURE 9-3   What Happens When Suspected Child Abuse or Neglect Is Reported

Source: National Education Association, 1984 Reprinted with Permission. (Adapted from "Open Door on Child Abuse and Neglect: Prevention and Reporting Kit." Ohio Dept. of Public Welfare, Children's Protective Services, under grant from NCCAN, n.d.).

duct criminal investigations, remove children, or offer protection for social workers in volatile situations.

Cooperation between a variety of agencies dealing with protective situations is crucial. Toward this end, some states have established child advocacy centers. Such centers are multidimensional, providing, often under one roof, such services as social service and criminal investigation, legal intervention, counseling, case management, and other treatment needs. Instead of being taken from place to place and seen by a wide variety of people, children are seen for validation of the abuse, counseling about court involvement, and treatment in one area by fewer professionals (Wiehe, 1992).

Once the assessment worker creates a picture of the family through facts and impressions gleaned from those involved in the case, she/he determines whether or not the family needs additional intervention or service. Some agencies require the formation of a treatment plan, which is a blueprint of the problems manifested by the family, the services they need, and the services that can be provided by the agency.

The assessment worker on the Farmer case concluded that the children as well as Mrs. Farmer continued to be in danger. She learned that Mr. Farmer did work steadily and, when he was not drinking, was amenable to help. Initially, he did not admit that he had sexually abused Gail or Laura, but when questioned by the police, he finally broke down and admitted the abuse. The police referred the case to the District Attorney's office pending prosecution for sexual abuse. The assessment worker realized, however, that this father would soon be released on bail, leaving his wife and children again vulnerable. She encouraged Mrs. Farmer, who after her husband's arrest had returned home, to seek a restraining order against him. This she agreed to do.

Not all cases assessed by protective services continue to be serviced by the agency. It is certainly possible for the case to be closed as a result of inconclusive evidence or the recognition that the situation was not as serious as was first assumed. Maltreatment may be unsubstantiated at this time and the case closed.

CASE MANAGEMENT AND TREATMENT

The Farmer case was then transferred to a case manager who would work with the family and oversee the provision of service to them.

Provision of service for the Farmers involved support for Mrs. Farmer and her children, legal aid, job training for this mother, and finding day care services while she trained or worked. In the meantime, the case

> manager kept in contact with the District Attorney's office to determine what was happening with Mr. Farmer. It was finally decided that Mr. Farmer would be put on probation while he sought treatment for his alcoholism and attended group and individual treatment for sexual offenders. His supervised visits with his children were also monitored by the protective agency.

The case manager's role differs from agency to agency. In some agencies the case manager is no more than a referral person who coordinates the various services provided. Other agencies expect their case managers to have clinical skills with which they can provide supportive counseling. The term *treatment* can refer to any service, from counseling to contracting with another agency for the provision of some service. The services provided can be medical services, legal services, day care, remedial help, parent aids, counseling, substance abuse treatment, or a variety of others (Tower, 1996).

COURT INTERVENTION IN PROTECTIVE CASES

Chapter 10 will discuss the court system in depth. For the purposes of our discussion of protective services cases, it is important to know how a situation might become involved with the court system.

Child protection cases might become involved in either the civil or criminal court or sometimes with both. The difference between the two courts is that the civil court, usually the juvenile or family division, is designed to protect children when parents are either abusing them or are not able to care for them. The emphasis is not on the guilt or innocence of the parents but rather on how the children can be protected from further harm. Criminal court, on the other hand, seeks to prove that someone, usually the abuser, is guilty "beyond a reasonable doubt." While the children and their needs are paramount in juvenile court, criminal court considers only proving whether or not the offender is at fault (Wiehe, 1992).

In both types of courts, everyone involved (children and parents) are entitled to "due process rights," which include:

1. *The right to formal notice of the hearing;*
2. *The right to legal counsel;*
3. *The right to a hearing in which evidence is presented;*
4. *The right to present a defense and cross-examine witnesses (Wiehe, 1992, 75).*

JUVENILE OR CIVIL COURT

A protective services case might become involved with the juvenile or family division of the civil court system at any point in its progress through social services.

When a situation is first reported to protective services the intake worker makes a determination of whether or not the parents will work with the agency. If they seem to be amenable, the CPS may investigate and provide services without court involvement. However, if the parents are unwilling to cooperate with the investigation or treatment plan, and/or the children are in imminent danger, court involvement might be sought. Sometimes it appears that the parents will cooperate, but further along in the investigation this cooperation ceases. An investigative social worker or even a case manager might feel it necessary to involve the juvenile court. A few states automatically refer cases to the juvenile court. This, they feel, gives them more control over protecting the children. If, during the investigation, the children appear to be in immediate danger, they can be removed without going back to court.

Initially, Mrs. Farmer agreed to work with CPS while they completed their investigation. She was confident that Mr. Farmer was of no threat to her due to the restraining order, which she believed he would respect. But as time went on, she became lonely and contacted Mr. Farmer herself. She begged him to come home. Knowing that continuing with his treatment meant staying out of jail, Mr. Farmer at first refused her requests. The worker soon learned, however, that the couple was meeting secretly, often in the company of the children. When confronted with this, Mrs. Farmer became angry and said that she would not stop seeing her husband. She began missing appointments with her social worker and the worker became concerned that the children were again being placed at risk. The decision was then made to file a petition on the children's behalf in juvenile court.

Filing a petition necessitates that a social worker, or other concerned party, sign a petition on behalf of the children. The petition is reviewed, usually by the clerk of court, to determine if there is enough evidence to go forward. A hearing may be scheduled to review evidence and determine what will be required. (See Chapter 10 for a more in-depth explanation.) Involvement of the juvenile court ceases when either the conditions set down by the court are met or there is insufficient evidence to continue.

CRIMINAL COURT

Criminal court involvement is sought most often in the following situations:

When the parent is found to be criminally negligent or neglectful;
When the parent has severely injured a child physically or killed a child;
When a parent has sexually abused a child.

Criminal negligence is exemplified in the following case:

Roxanne was a twenty-five-year-old woman who had been prostituting for the last ten years. She had had a variety of different "business managers" or pimps, several of whom had fathered her three children. Her children, now three, two, and three months, were left in the next room while she "entertained" her clients. She also drank heavily and had used various drugs. She often left her children alone while she went out to get new supplies. The three-year-old had taken to wandering down the hall while Roxanne was out. The neighbors complained. The next time Roxanne went out, she tied the child to a chair and the two-year-old in his crib. In her absence a grossly overloaded electrical socket caught on fire. The fire department was summoned and they found the children alone. By the time the children were rescued, the two- and three-year-olds were badly burned and the baby had died of smoke inhalation. Roxanne was charged with criminal neglect.

Some parents abuse their children to the point of severe injury or even death.

Four-year-old Jeremy's father had high standards for his children. He expected them to mind him immediately and would not tolerate any "fresh talk." Jeremy, an active child, taxed his father's minimal patience. On several occasions, his father struck him with such force that he left bruises. Neighbors noticed the bruises but could not believe that a "nice family like Jeremy's" could have caused them. One particular night Jeremy talked back to his father. Angered by an especially bad day at work and a fight with Jeremy's mother, the irate father slapped his son hard in the head. The blow sent the small body into the wall and left the child unconscious. Frantic, his mother rushed him to the hospital. The child was diagnosed with a subdural hematoma (blood collecting on the brain) and brain damage. The boy lapsed into a coma and died soon after admission. His father was charged with his death.

In the Farmer case, Mr. Farmer was charged with sexual abuse. In that situation the court agreed to put Mr. Farmer on probation while he attended treatment. When he violated probation by seeing his wife and children secretly, he was eventually incarcerated.

Criminal procedures differ depending on the court. In some instances agreements are made between the parties (called *plea bargaining*) to minimize the charges, sometimes allowing the accused, like Mr. Farmer, to become involved in treatment instead of being incarcerated. Obviously the accused is hoping for the "best deal" and it may require vigilance to insure that the children's interests are not neglected as this "deal" is being made.

Criminal court does provide leverage in dealing with the offender. Because power is an issue, especially for violent offenders and sexual abusers, such leverage may be what is needed. For the children and family, however, involvement in criminal court can seem to permeate their lives.

THE EFFECT OF COURT INVOLVEMENT ON CHILDREN

When children are abused and neglected the damage can be profound. One hopes that the intervention will be swift and competent. Unfortunately that is not always the case. Court involvement can seem like one more assault to traumatized children. How children are able to cope with court procedures depends largely on the type of support systems available to them. Victim witness advocates now provide families with the support they need to survive the legal process. *Guardians ad litem* (discussed in Chapter 10) are often assigned to children to protect their interests. Fortunately, many more attorneys and judges assigned to juvenile and criminal court cases involving children are becoming aware of the need to shelter children from additional trauma (Tower, 1996).

An interesting approach to protecting the psyches of children in court cases was described in the book *Unspeakable Acts,* by Jan Hollingsworth. Hollingsworth (1986) writes of the so called Country Walk Case in Miami, Florida in which a group of children were sexually abused by the owners of the baby-sitting service their parents used. So traumatized were the children that child psychologists, Joe and Laurie Braga, were called in to help both parents and children deal with the court process. The case set a precedent for the protection of children in such situations.

THE ROLE OF THE PROTECTIVE SERVICES WORKER

A protective services worker might provide one or more of a variety of services. It is the role of this individual, along with the agency employing him/her, to provide protection for children but also to seek family preservation whenever possible. A child's family is the best place for him/her if that family is able to meet the child's basic needs and protect him or her. For new workers especially, it sometimes feels like a child would be better off removed from a family that is less than ideal. But separation is another form of trauma for children. Thus, the decision to remove must be considered with great care.

The role of the child protection worker depends on the particular agency in which he/she is employed, and perhaps on the regulations of that state. Child protection agencies are usually state- or county-run and are therefore influenced by the political climate.

"Every time there's a new governor, things change a bit," explained one protective services worker. "Sometimes we find ourselves trying to protect our clients' best interests amidst these changes."

Some workers are assigned to intake, which means that they screen cases as they come in. This can be a high stress role as referrals often peak at certain times of the year. For example, the holidays seem to correlate with more reports of abuse as parents and children both become more stressed as the contrast between the pain they are feeling and the happiness they perceive that everyone else is feeling becomes more pronounced. Intake requires that one think quickly and not be afraid to be assertive in situations in which it is necessary. Both intake and assessment require that a worker be creative in discovering information and skilled in putting that information together. These roles do not allow the worker to form long-term relationships with clients.

The role of ongoing worker or case manager does allow one to get to know clients. Workers learn to support clients and help them to capitalize on their strengths rather than their weaknesses. It can be a challenging and frustrating job as clients may not be able to maintain their growth and watching them slip back into old patterns sometimes makes one wonder why the effort was made in the first place. But there are success stories too, and these tend to sustain one in protective services work.

Richards, in his *Tender Mercies: Inside the World of a Child Abuse Investigator* (1992), provides an excellent view of the joys and frustrations of protective services work. He captures the essence of protective work when he says:

I'm not supposed to take the cases home with me; I'm not supposed to get emotionally involved. Yet there are people's lives I touch that touch me right back. Now and then a case rears up that I can't stop thinking about, coiling itself around me like a boa, refusing to let go, squeezing me until I stagger. For these cases especially, I go the extra yard and make sacrifices because I see the potential for positive change on my hands, and I know that I can make a difference that may still be felt long after I'm gone (Richards, 1992, 4).

REFLECTIONS OF AN ABUSED CHILD: CONSUMER PERSPECTIVE

When I was asked to write this for a book to be read by potential social workers, I wondered what I could possibly say. But when I thought more about it, I realized that I had a great deal to say.

I was the oldest of five kids and the only girl. Sometimes I think my mother had me just so she would have someone to take care of us, because that is what I did from as early as I can remember. Someone once asked me if I was neglected as a child. Neglect? How does one define that? Did we have enough to eat? No. Did anyone care about us? No. Did we have what kids need to grow up emotionally healthy? No. If that's neglect, I guess I was but I never really thought about it. I was too busy surviving.

We had a lot of contact with the social service system; some good, some not so good. My father left us when I was three. I never asked who was the father of my youngest three brothers. I am not sure my mother knows. She had a lot of boyfriends when I was younger. She worked as a waitress in a bar and she often brought guys home. They would just sort of move in. Some were great and I liked them. But some were creeps. Like Jasper who used to beat my mother and me and tell my little brothers that that was what men did to women. And another guy, I can't even remember his name, who messed with me sexually until my mother found out and kicked him out.

I can't really blame my mother, I guess. I think she was always looking for someone to love her. She got pregnant with me at fifteen. I think she hoped I would love her. But I found out when I had my baby at sixteen that babies aren't like that right away.

Right after Jasper beat me up, I was ten I think, a social worker started coming to our house. It really scared my mother. She did love us and was afraid we would be taken away. The social worker said that Jasper had to leave and my mother had to see her on a regular basis. So for a while she did. But then one weekend, my mom took off with Harry (I think that was his name), a guy she met at work. I was eleven and she left me with the other kids. The next thing I know, the social worker came and told us we were abandoned and had to go to a foster home. They put me and my oldest brother in one home and the three littlest ones in another. That really upset me because I worried about them. I was so used to taking care of them. I cried and cried and the foster mother thought I "wasn't adjusting to foster care." So then they put me in a group home for girls. That was okay I guess, but I still missed the other kids. My mom used to visit and we'd cry together. Finally she must have convinced them she could take care of us because we all went back home again.

That lasted for a few years. When I was fifteen, my brother, who was thirteen, stole our landlord's car. The guy pressed charges and my brother went to court. He ended up in a home for "delinquent kids" and my mother got real upset. She took off again and we all went to juvenile court. Again, we ended up in foster homes. I was in six, because by this time I was really mad at the whole deal. I dated this guy while I was at one home and got pregnant. So they put me in another home where the foster mother was great. She helped me through my pregnancy and showed me how to take care of the baby. I stayed there until I was eighteen.

Now my son and I live on our own. He's five and I'm twenty. I work at a diner but I don't take guys home with me like my mom did. I haven't seen her for years. I don't know where my younger brothers are, but I see my oldest brother once in a while. I still call my last foster home my home. I don't know what I would do without Pam (my foster mother).

What would I say to people who are going to be social workers? Maybe I'd say "be careful not to judge." My mom did the best she could and I still love her. She didn't have the breaks I had. She thought men would solve her problems. And I'd say "listen to kids. We know what's happening and we'll tell you if you listen." I had a couple of good social workers. I've actually thought of going to college to be one. Wouldn't that be something? If I became a social worker?

FUTURE TRENDS IN PROTECTIVE SERVICES

As resources become less available, child advocates stress the need to improve the effectiveness of services within the existing framework. If more funds are not immediately available, how can families and children be best served with the existing funds?

UNIFICATION OF SERVICES

One improvement that could be made in protective services is more comprehensive provision of services. Agencies providing similar services are recognizing the need to prevent duplication and communicating with each other in order to enhance service. For example, in one particular community there were five agencies that provided counseling services as part of contracts with the child protection agency. As a result, none of these agencies had an abundance of cases. At the same time, no one within the immediate area was providing follow-up services or adequate prevention services. An interagency group tackled the problem of the increase of protective services cases in the area and discovered the duplication of services. The area agencies then worked together to coordinate the provision of service. While some agencies took over the role of prevention, others continued to contract for treatment while still others offered follow-up. In this way clients received better service and agencies were able to put their resources into a specialized service that brought them clients.

Another way to improve services to abused children is to increase the number of child advocacy centers. These centers provide, under one roof, the services needed for children and their families. Not only is the provision of services under this model more cost-effective, but it can serve to produce less trauma for the children involved.

IMPROVEMENT OF STAFF TRAINING

Protective services workers come from a variety of different types of educational backgrounds. While most social agencies require a bachelor's degree or at least an associate's degree, these degrees may be in any field. Once hired by an agency the training that new workers receive can vary from almost none to some initial training. Many agencies feel that on-the-job training is the best teacher. Yet to place a young worker in the field with a minimum of knowledge in the psychology of the individual, case-management skills, and even self-protection is to do an injustice to both client and worker. Training, not only initially but periodically, is essential for protective services workers. Periodic training not only improves skills but can help workers gain insight into seemingly insurmountable problem cases. Learning raises morale and keeps workers abreast of an ever-changing field.

In addition to agency training, colleges and universities must become more active in providing skill-based training in child protection services. While at one time only a handful of academic institutions offered courses in child abuse and neglect, an increased number are recognizing the need to do so. It is quite likely that the social services worker will find child maltreatment at the root of a variety of service needs, from corrections to mental health services to job retraining. Individuals trained at the college level will be more valuable as employees in many fields. In addition to training students in child protection skills, colleges and universities should provide instruction in community analysis, political systems, and the workings of local, state, and federal government in order to help future professionals meet the demands of tomorrow.

PREVENTION

One cannot talk about the improvement of child protective services without stressing the importance of prevention. Prevention must be seen not only as consciousness-raising through school and community awareness programs, but also as primary prevention, including parenting programs and mediation programs for children in schools. Children can be taught skills that will prevent them from being the abusive parents of tomorrow. Through learning to build self-esteem, cope with crises, make decisions, and negotiate with others, children are given tools to make them better functioning individuals. The parent who feels good about him/herself and is proud of his/her accomplishments is not likely to be one who abuses or neglects children.

A NEW ERA?

One cannot predict the effects of the attitudes of the twenty-first century on the provision of protective services. As states propose to cut off welfare benefits to teen parents and reduce the provision of welfare to other recipients as well, what impact will this have on dependent children? Will these changes further tax the already overstressed families? What programs will be funded to protect children and help their parents to better meet their needs? Are the best interests of children in fact on the new conservative agenda?

These are questions that may not be answered in the near future but ones which will be of primary importance to children.

SUMMARY

Historically, children were seen as the property of their parents. Practices such as infanticide and the sexual misuse of children were a painful part of early history. Children often worked and suffered along with poverty-stricken parents. Significant relief of these conditions did not come until late in the nineteenth century when Mary Ellen, a neglected and abused child in New York City, prompted intervention and gave rise to the first child protection agency. In 1974 the Child Abuse Prevention and Treatment Act shaped the services to maltreated children that we know today.

Maltreatment can be divided into four categories: physical abuse, physical neglect, sexual abuse, and emotional or psychological abuse. Each of these categories has a separate set of symptoms and etiology. Perpetrators of each type of abuse do so for a variety of reasons.

When child abuse and neglect is detected, it must be reported to the child protection unit of the local social service agency. This agency screens and assesses the case and determines if additional services are needed. Treatment, in the form of services, counseling, or other resources may be offered to families. In some instances, Child Protective Services will seek out court intervention through either the juvenile (civil), criminal, or probate court.

Although we have come a long way in the provision of services to abused and neglected children, much can still be done. The streamlining or unification of services, improvement in staff training, and increased prevention services are just a few of the innovations needed.

It is difficult to determine the direction in which this new political era will take the provision of services to maltreated children. Only by understanding the impact that abuse and neglect have on children and their families can we hope to work in the best interests of all concerned.

EXPLORATION QUESTIONS

1. Throughout history how have children been perceived? What examples of this view do we have?
2. Who was Mary Ellen? What impact did she have on the history of helping abused children?

3. What two reform movements influenced the response to abused and neglected children in the last two centuries?
4. What are the three types of child maltreatment?
5. What are the symptoms of physical abuse? Why do people physically abuse children?
6. What are the symptoms of neglect? What are the typologies of neglectful mothers? Why are mothers the ones primarily studied in neglectful situations?
7. What are the symptoms of sexual abuse? What are the types of sexual abuse?
8. What three typologies explain sexual abusers? What characterizes each type?
9. What happens when a case of abuse or neglect is reported? Draw a diagram of the process involved.
10. What three types of court services might be involved in maltreatment? How?

11. What are the current trends in the provision of abuse and neglect services?

ACTIVITIES FOR APPLIED LEARNING

1. Research the history of child maltreatment in more depth. What factors influenced how children were treated?
2. Invite a representative from the local child protection agency to speak to the class. Ask him or her to explain the process a case goes through once it is reported.
3. Read *Ghost Girl* (Hayden, 1992). What symptoms did Jadie exhibit? Why might this have been cult abuse?
4. Ask the local child protection agency if there is an agency in your area that treats sexual offenders. If there is, contact the agency and ask if they have offenders who speak in the community. Many agencies see community awareness as an integral part of offender treatment. Meeting and hearing an offender speak often provides more insight into the offender as a person.

SUGGESTED READING

deMause, L. *The History of Childhood: The Untold History of Child Abuse.* New York: Peter Bedrick, 1988.

Faller, K. C. *Understanding Child Sexual Maltreatment.* Newbury Park, CA: Sage, 1990.

Garbarino, J., Guttman, E., & Seeley, J. *The Psychologically Battered Child.* San Francisco: Jossey–Bass, 1986.

Hanson, R. F., Lipovsky, J. A., & Saunders, B. E. "Characteristics of Fathers in Incest Families," *Journal of Interpersonal Violence,* 9(2), (1994): 155–169.

Hayden, T. *Ghost Girl.* New York: Basic Books, 1992.

Hollingsworth, J. *Unspeakable Acts.* New York: Congdon and Weed, 1986.

O'Hagan, K. *Emotional and Psychological Abuse of Children.* Toronto: University of Toronto Press, 1993.

Polansky, N. F., Chalmers, M. A., Buttenwieser, E., & Williams, D. P. *Damaged Parents: An Anatomy of Child Neglect.* Chicago: University of Chicago Press, 1991.

Richards, K. *Tender Mercies: Inside the World of a Child Abuse Investigator.* Chicago and Washington, DC: Noble Press and The Child Welfare League of America, 1992.

Tower, C. C. *Understanding Child Abuse and Neglect.* Boston: Allyn and Bacon, 1996.

REFERENCES

Addams, J. *Twenty Years at Hull House*. New York: Signet, 1910.

Carnes, P. *Out of the Shadows: Understanding Sexual Addiction*. Minneapolis: CompCare, 1983.

Conte, J., & Berliner, L. "The Impact of Sexual Abuse." In L. Walker (Ed.), *Handbook on Sexual Abuse of Children*. New York: Guilford Press, 1988.

deMause, L. *The History of Childhood: The Untold History of Child Abuse*. New York: Peter Bedrick, 1988.

deMause, L. "The Universality of Incest," *Journal of Psychohistory* 19 (1991), 123–164.

deMause, L. "The History of Child Abuse," *Spirit of Change Magazine*, (May/June 1995), 28–34.

Faller, K. C. *Understanding Child Sexual Maltreatment*. Newbury Park, CA: Sage, 1990.

Finkelhor, D. *Child Sexual Abuse*. New York: Free Press, 1984.

Freud, S. *The Complete Introductory Letters of Psychoanalysis*. New York: Norton, 1966.

Garbarino, J., Guttman, E., & Seeley, J. *The Psychologically Battered Child*. San Francisco: Jossey–Bass, 1986.

Gilgun, J. F. "Factors Mediating the Effects of Child Maltreatment." In M. Hunter (Ed.), *The Sexually Abused Male*, vol. 1, (pp. 177–190). New York: Lexington Books, 1990.

Groth, A. N. *Men Who Rape*. New York: Plenum Press, 1979.

Hanson, R. F., Lipovsky, J. A., & Saunders, B. E. "Characteristics of Fathers in Incest Families," *Journal of Interpersonal Violence* 9(2), (1994): 155–169.

Hayden, T. *Ghost Girl*. New York: Basic Books, 1992.

Hollingsworth, J. *Unspeakable Acts*. New York: Congdon and Weed, 1986.

Johnson, J. T. *Mothers of Incest Survivors*. Bloomington, IN: Indiana University Press, 1992.

Kadushin, A., & Martin, J. *Child Welfare Services*. New York: Macmillan, 1988.

Kaufman, K. L., Wallace, A. M., Johnson, C. F., & Reeder, M. L. "Comparing Female and Male Perpetrators' Modus Operandi," *Journal of Interpersonal Violence* 10(3) (1995): 322–333.

Kempe, C. H., Silverman, F., Steele, B., Droegemueller, W., & Silver, H. "The Battered-Child Syndrome," *Journal of the American Medical Association* 181 (1962), 17–24.

Laviola, M. "Effects of Older Brother-Younger Sister Incest," *Child Abuse and Neglect* 16(3), (1992): 409–421.

Levine, M., & Levine, A. *Helping Children: A Social History*. New York: Oxford University Press, 1992.

Mass, A. I., & Yap, J. "Child Welfare: Asian Pacific Island Families." In N. Cohen (Ed.), *Child Welfare*, (pp. 107–29). Boston: Allyn & Bacon, 1992.

Mathews, R., Mathews, J., & Speltz, K. "Female Sexual Offenders." In M. Hunter (Ed.), *The Sexually Abused Male*, vol. I (pp. 275–293). New York: Lexington Books, 1990.

O'Hagan, K. *Emotional and Psychological Abuse of Children*. Toronto: University of Toronto Press, 1993.

Olafson, E., Corwin, D. L., & Summit, R. "Modern History of Child Abuse," *Child Abuse and Neglect* 17 (1993) 7–24.

Pecora, P. J., Whittaker, J. K., & Maluccio, A. N., with Barth, R. P., & Plotnick, R. D. *The Child Welfare Challenge: Policy, Practice and Research*. New York: Aldine De Gruyter, 1992.

Peterson, R. F., Basta, S. M., & Dykstra, T. A. "Mothers of Molested Children: Some Comparisons of Personality Characteristics," *Child Abuse and Neglect* 17(3) (1993): 409–418.

Polansky, N. F., Chalmers, M. A., Buttenwieser, E., & Williams, D. P. *Damaged Parents: An Anatomy of Child Neglect*. Chicago: University of Chicago Press, 1991.

Polansky, N. F., Holly, C., & Polansky, N. A. *Profile of Neglect: A Survey of the State of Knowledge of Child Neglect*. Washington, DC: Department of Health, Education and Welfare, 1975.

Richards, K. *Tender Mercies: Inside the World of a Child Abuse Investigator*. Chicago and Washington, DC: Noble Press and The Child Welfare League of America, 1992.

Rush, F. *The Best Kept Secret: Sexual Abuse of Children*. New York: McGraw-Hill, 1980.

Sagatun, I. J., & Edwards, L. P. *Child Abuse and the Legal System*. Chicago: Nelson Hall, 1995.

Schonberg, I. J. "The Distortion of the Role of Mother in Child Sexual Abuse," *Journal of Child Sexual Abuse* 1(3), (1992): 47–61.

Schreier, H. A. "The Perversion of Mothering: Munchausen Syndrome by Proxy," *Bulletin of the Menninger Clinic* 56(4), (1992): 421–437.

Smith, E. "Bring Back the Orphanages? What Policymakers of Today Can Learn from the Past," *Child Welfare* 74(1) (1995), 115–142.

Smith, M. *Michelle Remembers*. New York: Pocket Books, 1987.

Stadum, B. "The Dilemma in Saving Children from Child Labor: Reform and Casework at Odds with Family Needs (1900–1938)," *Child Welfare* 74(1) (1995), 33–55.

Stein, T. *Child Welfare and the Law*. New York: Longman, 1991.

Stone, F. B. "Munchausen-by-Proxy: An Unusual Form of Child Abuse," *Social Casework* 70(4), (1989): 243–246.

Swift, K. "An Outrage to Common Decency: Historical Perspectives on Child Neglect," *Child Welfare* 74(1) (1995), 71–91.

Tower, C. C. "NEA Training Package in Child Abuse and Neglect for Teachers," Washington, DC: National Education Association, 1984.

Tower, C. C. *Secret Scars*. New York: Viking/Penguin, 1988.

Tower, C. C. *Understanding Child Abuse and Neglect*. Boston: Allyn and Bacon, 1996.

Wiehe, V. R. *Working with Child Abuse and Neglect*. Itasca, IL: F. E. Peacock Publishers, 1992.

Wiehe, V. R., & Herring, T. *Perilous Rivalry: When Siblings Become Abusive*. Lexington, MA: Lexington Books, 1991.

10

COURT SERVICES
ON BEHALF OF CHILDREN

Judy A. Noel
with David Whelan

> *What is it that hampers the effectiveness of the function and operation of the juvenile court today…The problem is one basic to most large social institutions. It is that juvenile courts are continually given more duties and responsibilities than resources with which to perform those duties and responsibilities. Often, social institutions are abused simply because they exist. The juvenile court is a perfect example. It has to bow to the capricious nature of those who wish to use it. Thus its autonomy has been gravely undermined, and it is held in low esteem by judges, lawyers, and other professionals in the corrections field (Simonsen, 1991, 230).*

The juvenile court is the primary part of the judicial system that serves children and their families today. Although some cases involving the abuse or custody of children are seen in criminal or probate court, it is the juvenile or family court that, by design, protects the best interests of minor children. Court services are provided in the context of the civil court, because the emphasis is on protection and rehabilitation rather than on proving guilt or innocence as is required in a criminal court. In reality, juvenile courts are expected not only to orchestrate rehabilitation for wayward youth, but also to protect society from them (Simonsen, 1991). In addition, juvenile courts are given the task of protecting children whose parents cannot adequately do so. It is no wonder that the system is hard-pressed to perform these conflicting obligations in a manner that pleases everyone involved.

How juvenile court services are offered varies throughout the United States. In some areas, a specialized juvenile court provides services to alleged delinquent, dependent, and neglected and abused children. Additional needs that children may have for court intervention come under the jurisdiction of several other court systems (i.e., probate and district courts). Other communities have established more extensive services through a family court system. In addition to the services provided in juvenile courts, family courts may also be involved in custody cases due to divorce, child support, paternity cases, and all situations concerning minors that require court intervention.

The function and structure of court services are established through legislation. Although all must be in compliance with federal legislation, court services in each state are controlled by state statutes. The result has been major differences in the implementation of court services to juveniles.

AN HISTORICAL PERSPECTIVE

Specialized court services to meet the needs of children are a relatively new phenomenon in the United States. Until the early twentieth century, juveniles who committed crimes were treated as adults in the criminal justice system. Societal values supported the ultimate authority of parents, particularly fathers, over children. Dependency issues, including abuse and neglect, were deemed private issues and not public concerns.

Several events beginning in the first half of the nineteenth century have been identified as precipitating the development of separate court services for juveniles. The first of these is the combined impact of immigration, industrialization, and urbanization during the first half of the nineteenth century. This time period is characterized by unprecedented immigration from Europe. Many early immigrants worked as apprentices. Eventually apprentice programs were not able to absorb this rapidly growing new labor supply. This, and periodic recessions, resulted in poverty and high rates of unemployment.

Strangely enough in this social climate, one of the first cases in which a court ruling made reference to what was best for a child occurred. In 1813, the case of *Commonwealth v. Addicks and wife* involved a custody dispute between the biological parents of two minor children. The father considered the mother's behavior to be immoral, and he wanted the custody of the children. Although the court recognized that the mother's behavior was "highly improper," the children were being well cared for and well educated. The court's decision to leave the children in the custody of the mother against the father's objections was made based on the best interests of the children (Stein, 1991, 27).

In most instances, poor, dependent children were placed in almshouses or poorhouses if they were too ill or too young to work. Older, able-bodied dependent children were placed in workhouses. Those who committed minor offenses were placed in community asylums or homes, while those involved in serious crimes received the same punishment as adults—imprisonment and sometimes death (Siegel and Senna, 1997; Simonsen, 1991).

As industrialization and urbanization accelerated so did the number of destitute children. Young children were left to care for themselves because their parents did not want to take care of them, could not afford to support them, or were unable to supervise them while they worked long hours. Many children resorted to committing petty crimes to survive on city streets. The increasing number of destitute and delinquent children could no longer be ignored, which led to the child saving movement, the second event leading up to the development of a juvenile court system (Siegal and Senna, 1988, 363).

THE CHILD SAVERS

The *child savers* were primarily, but not exclusively, middle-class women interested in providing care for neglected and delinquent children and protecting society from their activities. For the first time, services specifically intended to meet the needs of children were developed, including shelter homes, educational opportunities, and social activities. The child savers were instrumental in developing governmental control over parental authority by promoting legislation that gave states legal jurisdiction to "control and protect" children (Siegal and Senna, 1997).

An outcome of these legislative efforts was the establishment of specialized institutions, houses of refuge, in several states for the placement of delinquent and uncontrollable children. The purpose of these institutions, which were privately funded and publicly supported, was to prevent future poverty and crime by separating these children from their undesirable environments, including their natural parents, and reforming them through training and a "family-like" environment (Siegal and Senna, 1997).

REFORM SCHOOL MOVEMENT

The reform school movement was another effort leading to the development of a juvenile court system in the United States. During the mid-1800s, the child savers used their influence on local and state governments to develop institutions exclusively for delinquent and homeless children. The first of these state-supported reform schools opened in Massachusetts in 1848 and others were established in several states soon after (Siegel and Senna, 1997; Binder et al., 1997).

Opposition to houses of refuge and reform schools to protect neglected and delinquent children continued to grow throughout the mid-nineteenth century. Charles Brace, a minister and social reformer, developed an alternative to institutionalization in houses of refuge or reform schools. Under the auspice of the Children's Aid Society, which he helped to establish, delinquent and dependent urban youth were placed with rural farm families in the West who wanted additional children to help with the chores. Brace's thought, it appears, was for moral reform as well as the provision of homes for children. In one of his much publicized speeches, Brace quoted one of the New York City newsboys he placed in the Western United States addressing others of his kind.

> *Do you want to be newsboys always, and show blacks, and timber merchants in a small way selling matches? If ye do you'll stay in New York, but if you don't you'll go West and begin to be farmers, for the beginning of a farmer, my boys, is the making of a Congressman, and a President (Simonsen, 1991, 22).*

This practice of "placing-out," the forerunner of foster home placement, was highly criticized and eventually was discontinued. One major objection was raised by the Catholic Church. Urban children, who were predominantly Catholic, were placed almost exclusively in rural Protestant homes where they were unable to actively participate in their religion. Others objected on the basis that the failure to complete extensive home studies would result in the exploitation of children. Some institutions protested being deprived of child labor. Despite these critics, later research did suggest that, for the most part, these placements were successful.

THE CONCEPT OF PARENS PATRIAE

The concept of *parens patriae* was the final development leading to the creation of the juvenile court. *Parens patriae* was a term that originated in English common law and assumed that children could be made "wards of the state." In the United States, the philosophy of *parens patriae* was extended to houses of refuge, giving them complete parental control over both delinquent and dependent children committed to these institutions. Initially, the authority of the state to intervene in parent–child relationships was legally tested and supported. At the same time, stronger objections were being made about the commitment of children under the doctrine of *parens patriae* without due process of law. This concern was reflected in the *O'Connell v. Turner* court case, which restricted admissions to only those children who had committed delinquent acts (Siegel and Senna, 1997).

THE EMERGENCE OF THE JUVENILE COURT

Several child savers and early social workers involved in the settlement house movement had a significant influence in the development of court services for juveniles. Jane Addams, who founded Hull House during the late 1800s, Julia Lathrop, and several other residents of this settlement house used their political influence to develop and implement the legislation establishing the first juvenile court in Chicago on April 2, 1899. Their concerns involved inadequate treatment in institutions for delinquent and dependent children and the placement of delinquent children with adults in jails and prisons (Siegal and Senna, 1997; Dziech and Schudson, 1991; Downs, Costin, and McFadden, 1996).

These proponents of separating juveniles from the adult court system believed that the rational for this move was threefold:

> *(1) Children committed crimes not from a sense of evil or malice, but rather from a sense of need. A child's crime was an expression of pain, a signal that something was not right with the individual or family. The child needed help, not criminal court punishment. (2) Children suffering from abuse or neglect might have to be removed from the family, an action that required special procedures to evaluate the circumstances of the family and the needs of the child in order to balance their respective rights. (3) Those responsible for decisions about delinquent, abused, or neglected children should have the special inclination and expertise needed to understand the young (Dziech & Schudson, 1991, 25).*

The initial legislation establishing the juvenile court, the Juvenile Court Act, made clear distinctions between delinquent and dependent children, although both groups came under the jurisdiction of the juvenile court. Also, it established a specific court for juveniles, provided for a juvenile probation system, permitted the commitment of children to institutions under the control of state laws, and established juvenile delinquency as a legal concept (Siegal and Senna, 1988; Simonsen, 1991).

The purpose of the newly formed juvenile court was to prevent crime and rehabilitate the juvenile offenders. The philosophy of the court stressed the best interests of the child (Stein, 1991). Because treatment rather than punishment was the focus of this specialized court, the need for protection of constitutional rights was minimized. The functions of juvenile court judges and probation officers were to identify problems and provide the necessary individualized treatment in a benevolent manner. Attorneys were not provided, hearsay evidence was admissible, trial by jury and the right to an appeal were often not available, and only a preponderance of evidence was needed for a conviction (Siegal and Senna, 1997; Binder et al., 1997).

Incorrigibility and truancy from school had come under the jurisdiction of the juvenile court in many states by 1920. In addition to probation officers, new professions were created to provide treatment services for both delinquent and nondelinquent children who came under the jurisdiction of the juvenile courts, including social workers, sociologists, criminologists, and psychologists. Once established, the specialized court services for juveniles spread across the country and by 1925 juvenile courts had been established in all but two states. By 1945, the last two states—Maine and Wyoming—had also added juvenile courts. Today there are over 2,700 juvenile courts, with many dissimilarities, in the United States (Siegal and Senna, 1988; Simonsen, 1991). During the 1960s, legislation was passed to establish the first family court in New York. The broader focus of this court includes not only delinquent, dependent, and neglected children but paternity, adoption, and child support cases as well.

One set of issues dealt with by the newly established family court were children who ran away, were truant from school, or were difficult for their parents to manage. These "offenses" were soon identified as problematic only because the offenders were underage or had the "status" of children. Thus, they became known as *status offenses,* and a new set of criteria under the term Person in Need of Supervision was developed to address the needs of the families involved. States addressed these issues differently, even adopting different names such as Children in Need of Services (CHINS), Minors in Need of Services (MINS), and Families in Need of Services (FINS). These new categories necessitated that family and juvenile courts increase the social services available to meet the needs of the growing numbers of nondelinquent status offenders (Siegel and Senna, 1988, 372).

Although family courts have received support by the American Bar Association and the National Council on Crime and Delinquency, they have not been a growing force in the provision of court services to juveniles and their families. Resistance to change by juvenile court staff and judges and the massive litigation involved have been identified as possible reasons for the limited growth of family courts (Costin, Bell, & Downs, 1991; Downs, Costin, & McFadden, 1996).

Several events occurred during the 1960s that influenced a change in the direction of the juvenile court system. Long-term concerns about the informal juvenile court processes, particularly the constitutional rights of children in the judicial system, came to a head in several U. S. Supreme Court decisions beginning in the mid-1960s (Siegal and Senna, 1988). In 1966 *Kent v. United States* established uniform procedures for waiving children from juvenile to adult court. The Supreme Court decision, *In re Gault,* reinstated many of the constitutional rights children lost with the development of the juvenile court system including the right to legal counsel, the right to cross-examination of witnesses, the right to adequate notice of charges, and the privilege against self-incrimination (Siegal & Senna, 1988). *In re Winship* in 1970 established that evidence in delinquency cases in juvenile courts must meet the more stringent criterion of beyond a reasonable doubt rather than the lesser test of preponderance of evidence or clear and convincing evidence required in most courts throughout the country (Siegel & Senna, 1988).

Not all Supreme Court decisions in the 1970s reinstituted the due process rights guaranteed to adults. In a 1971 ruling, the Court ruled in *McKeiver v. Pennsylvania* that juveniles do not have a constitutional right to a jury trial (Stein, 1991). In recent years, rehabilitation has continued to be the primary focus of the juvenile courts, while more recent Supreme Court decisions have required that these activities take place within the context of due process more so than in the past (Siegel & Senna, 1988; Binder et al., 1997).

Federal legislation enacted in the 1970s and early 1980s also reflected growing recognition of abused and neglected children. In addition, these statutes influenced the types of services to be provided by child welfare agencies for these children.

In 1974, the Child Abuse Prevention and Treatment Act was passed, establishing a National Center on Child Abuse and Neglect as well as providing federal funds for the demonstration programs on the prevention, identification, and treatment of child abuse and neglect. In an attempt to strengthen statutes in this area, states had to provide for:

1. *The reporting of known or suspected instances of child abuse;*
2. *Investigations of reports of child abuse or neglect, including procedures for protecting children if abuse or neglect are found;*
3. *The confidentiality of all records concerning child abuse and neglect;*
4. *A guardian ad litem to represent the child in any court proceedings;*
5. *Public education on child abuse and neglect; and*
6. *Immunity for persons who report in good faith (Stein, 1991, 44).*

This legislation was amended by Congress in 1984 to require reports of suspected abuse or neglect of children in state custody, including foster home and residential care settings as well as institutions.

The move toward family reunification and away from long-term foster care was evident in the enactment of the Adoption Assistance and Child Welfare Act. This federal legislation did not designate the implementation of specific reunification services, but it did stipulate that: (1) reasonable efforts be made to reunify children with their biological parents; (2) specific, written case plans for reunification are required; (3) periodic case reviews and an eighteen-month dispositional review must be done; and (4) due process safeguards for parents must be in place (Stein, 1991).

Today juvenile courts continue to develop and function in accordance with state statutes within the due process guidelines established by earlier U. S. Supreme Court decisions. Variation in state laws has resulted in court services being delivered in several diverse organizational structures. Most often juvenile courts are part of a lower court (district court, city court, recorder's court) with jurisdiction limited to delinquency issues. A growing number of states are establishing juvenile courts at the highest court of general trial jurisdiction. Some have a statewide independent juvenile court system, while still others provide juvenile court services as part of a larger family court system (Siegel & Senna, 1988, 379–380).

SITUATIONS WARRANTING JUVENILE COURT INTERVENTION

Since court services are established by state legislatures, statutes involving juvenile court practices and procedures are far from standardized. The age range of juvenile court jurisdiction varies from sixteen years of age and under to eighteen years of age and under in the United States (Siegel and Senna, 1988). At one time, gender influenced the age range for jurisdiction under the juvenile courts, with a lower maximum age for males than females. This practice was discontinued in the 1970s after being found unconstitutional (Binder et al., 1997). Delinquency, dependency, abuse, and neglect are defined somewhat differently in state statutes as well. Even so, there are many commonalities in the types of situations that come under the jurisdiction of court services to juveniles. Simonsen (1991) breaks the services provided by juvenile courts into two categories: deed, when a child has committed an act requiring court intervention, and need, when a child is in need of the court's protection.

DELINQUENCY

> Darryl was fourteen when he and two friends stole a car. The car, a flashy late-model sports car, had been parked outside a local bar each evening for the last several weeks. "The guy will be too sloshed to even know we took it!" joked Ralph, sixteen, when they discussed the plan to steal it. "It'll buy us some great grass," added Willie, fifteen. Darryl couldn't believe how easy it was when they finally wired the car and took off. Had Ralph not tried to see how fast it could go and been stopped by the police, the boys might have gotten the car to the drug dealer who had promised his juvenile customers free drugs if they brought him cars. Instead, the three boys found themselves in juvenile court.

Juvenile courts throughout the country have jurisdiction in instances of alleged delinquency. Delinquency consistently is defined as the violation of any federal, state, or local law and involves behavior that would be considered a crime if committed by an adult. State statutes do vary on how individual cases are handled. For instance, severity of offense and the age of the offender generally determine whether a case is even heard in juvenile court. Often distinctions are made between misdemeanors and felonies committed by those under and over the ages of fifteen and sixteen. Minor offenses (i.e., loitering, vagrancy) may or may not come under the jurisdiction of the juvenile court. There are also variations in how traffic violations are handled. In some instances, these cases are heard in traffic court while the juvenile court has jurisdiction in others (Downs, Costin, and McFadden, 1996).

Statutes in most states allow for the waiver of jurisdiction from juvenile court to criminal court. Again, the seriousness of the crime and the age of the offender at the time the crime was committed are factors in this decision. In all cases, the protection granted by the U. S. Supreme Court in *Kent v. United States* must be taken into consideration before a waiver to adult court takes place (Costin, Bell, and Downs, 1991).

STATUS OFFENSES

When fifteen-year-old Guido had missed ten days of school in the first month, the school became concerned. The school counselor contacted his mother only to discover that she had no idea of her son's whereabouts. "He's gone days at a time!" she admitted tearfully. "I don't know what to do with him." After numerous efforts to reach Guido in the past, the school felt it was time to file a CHINS petition in juvenile court, identifying him as a status offender.

Status offenses, which often include running away from home, truancy from school, sexual misconduct, uncontrollable behavior, curfew violation, and the use of substances such as drugs or alcohol, often come under the jurisdiction of court services to children. These offenses are illegal only because the child has not reached the status of adulthood. There is much debate about the way in which status offenders should be dealt with.

In the original legislation establishing a juvenile court, there was no separation between delinquency and status offenses. During the 1960s and 1970s, concern about the frequent long-term incarceration of status offenders in the place of treatment prompted the passage of the Juvenile Justice and Delinquency Prevention Act of 1974. Under this legislation, federal funds were made available for states that provided separate detention facilities for adults and juveniles. Also, secure detention could not be used for status offenders. In 1980 this legislation was amended to allow secure detention of status offenders, if a valid court order was violated (Sagatun and Edwards, 1995).

A few remaining states continue to define status offenses as delinquent behavior. Statutes in four states incorporate status offenses under the classification of abuse, neglect, or dependency (Binder et al., 1997). The others have developed a separate category for status offenses, generally called "persons in need of supervision" (PINS), "minors in need of supervision" (MINS), "juveniles in need of services" (JINS), "children in need of supervision" (CHINS), and "families with service needs" (FWSN).

Including status offenses under the jurisdiction of the juvenile court was controversial even before the legislation establishing this court was enacted, and it continues to be a controversial issue today. Opposition has been based on the constitutionality of the vague terms used in the statutes to define status offenses and the misuse this may lead to in the court system. Court cases challenging the constitutionality of juvenile court jurisdiction over status offenses have been defeated based on the premise that the implementation of these statutes are in the best interest of the child. Those who support the continued involvement of the court in status offenses do so on the basis that, without these legal protections, many children and their families will not get the services needed to prevent future problems (Binder et al., 1997; Simonsen, 1991; Siegel and Senna, 1997).

In recent years federal legislation has been enacted mandating the separation of status offenders from delinquents in detention facilities (Siegel and Senna, 1997; Binder et al., 1997). The American Psychiatric Association has recommended that courts also establish services for nondelinquency offenders. The reality, however, is that status offenses continue to be a perplexing problem for both the courts and social service agencies.

DEPENDENCY, ABUSE, AND NEGLECT

Amber (five years), Arthur (two years), and Candy (9 mos.) were found in a condemned factory building where their mother had set up housekeeping. The children were dirty and, from what the police could discover from Amber, they had been alone for several days. Baby Candy was severely dehydrated and the other children had apparently survived on chocolate bars and potato chips. They were taken to the hospital and then to a foster home. In the meantime, the social worker assigned to their case filed a petition on their behalf in juvenile court.

Children who have been neglected or abused come under the jurisdiction of court services for juveniles. Some state statutes classify and define dependency, abuse, and neglect separately. In others, either dependency is classified with abuse and neglect or abuse and neglect are categorized under dependency. Generally, children are defined as dependent if their guardians cannot or are not providing adequate care. Dependency may occur in cases of abandonment, when both parents are deceased, or when both parents are incarcerated for extended periods of time. A finding of dependency and the transfer of guardianship must occur to free a child for adoption. The number of children who are classified as dependent may significantly increase in the future as more children outlive both parents who die from AIDS.

Definitions of abuse and neglect differ somewhat from state to state (see Chapter 9). In general, neglect involves the failure of parents, guardians, and caretakers to adequately provide for or protect a child through acts of omission. Such behaviors commonly include failure to provide necessary physical care, supervision, a proper home environment, adequate food and clothing, basic medical care, financial support, and education as prescribed by law. Abandonment by guardians or caretakers and the failure to provide a safe environment for a child are frequently defined as neglect in the statutes (Downs, Costin, and MCFadden, 1996). In contrast, the definition of abuse involves the use of nonaccidental physical force by a parent, guardian, or caretaker.

RELATED SITUATIONS INVOLVING COURT INTERVENTION

Several other situations involving the legal status or rights of children and/or their parents often come under the jurisdiction of court services to children. Included are termination of parental rights, paternity determinations, child support, adoption, appointment of a *guardian ad litem*, determination of legal status, granting of legal custody of a minor for purposes of institutional placement, and domestic violence matters (Stein, 1991).

FACTORS INFLUENCING COURT INTERVENTION

Winston LeBlanc was a newly assigned police officer in a gang-ridden area of the city. A fairly young foot patrolman, LeBlanc tried to develop a rapport with the gang members. He became particularly fond of Chico, a fifteen-year-old youth who LeBlanc was hopeful could finish high school and leave the area. The officer was angered when an arrest following a robbery brought in Chico among the group of boys involved. Still convinced that the boy could be helped, LeBlanc testified in juvenile court on Chico's behalf.

Several other factors affect whether court intervention will take place and, if so, the type of action initiated. The police have considerable authority in determining court action because most juvenile court referrals for delinquency are made by the police, while status offense complaints generally are made by parents to the police. State statutes provide only vague guidelines for interaction between police and juveniles. Results of studies suggest that the severity of the offense, the frequency of delinquent behavior, prior arrest records, community attitudes toward the behavior, and the behavior of juveniles in interaction with the police also are decisive factors in determining what action will be taken by the police (Binder et al., 1997; Simonsen, 1991). However, the tendency for police to make subjective decisions from a parental perspective rather than as law enforcement officers is supported in findings of recent studies, which show that status offenders are more likely to be detained and referred to juvenile court than delinquents, and girls are more likely to be detained than boys (Cheney–Lind, 1988). These studies also suggest that many status offenders may enter the court system mislabeled as delinquents (Binder et al., 1997).

Once a case has been referred to the court for action, a lawyer representing the child, the parents, or the court may determine if the statutory definitions of dependency, neglect, or delinquency have been adequately met (Duquette, 1990).

Judges also have an influence on determining court action in juvenile cases. Ideally their actions must be based on statutory definitions. However, legislation often is worded in general terms, which leaves considerable interpretive discretion (Dziech and Schudson, 1991).

THE RIGHTS OF JUVENILES

The rights of those involved with the juvenile court system have been much debated over the years. One of the most influential cases establishing rights for children in court was that of *In re Gault* (387 US, 1967). In 1967, sixteen-year-old Gerald Gault made an obscene phone call to a neighborhood woman and was adjudicated delinquent by the court. Protest over the handling of the case and the way in which Gault was treated during the proceedings brought about the decision by Supreme Court Justice Abraham Fortes that children alleged to be delinquents have the following rights:

- The right to notice of charges in time to prepare for trail;
- The right to counsel;
- The right to confront and cross-examine the accusers;
- Privilege against self-incrimination, at least in court (Simonsen, 1991, 257).

Since the Gault decision, other rights have been given to youths in juvenile court settings. Today, youths brought before the court for delinquency have these additional rights:

- The right to a judicial hearing;
- The right to proof beyond a reasonable doubt that they are guilty;
- The right to trial by jury (Simonsen, 1991, 260–261).

While there is no legal requirement for a trial by jury in juvenile court, an advisory jury is an option. The option is rarely ever used, but does remain available.

ADVOCATING FOR CHILDREN

Sometimes in the court process, it is necessary for an advocate to be appointed to protect the rights and interests of the children involved. Although originally appointed in cases where there was money or property at stake, the practice of having an advocate may now be to protect the psychological as well as financial interests of children (Duquette, 1990). The Child Abuse and Neglect Prevention and Treatment Act of 1974 required that states appoint a *guardian ad litem* or special advocate to represent children in abuse and neglect proceedings. The advocate could be an attorney or another professional trained to assume this role. Advocates are also used in situations where the child is a delinquent.

In 1977, Seattle established its special court advocate program under the name of CASA (Court Appointed Special Advocates) using trained volunteers to act on behalf of children in court cases. About the same time, a similar program began in Minnesota. Today, there are over 200 local chapters in every state (Duquette, 1990).

The concept of child advocacy in court arose from the fact that attorneys did not always feel comfortable being the sole representatives of children's interests. Many did not feel adequately trained in child welfare issues and welcomed another voice.

How the advocate, whether a CASA volunteer, an attorney appointed as *guardian ad litem* (GAL), or someone from another advocacy model, serves the child differs from state to state. For the most part, advocates attempt to see the situation in light of the best interests of their clients. They may interview the child, do home visits, or generally assess what is the best plan for the child. Many advocates also provide guidance or preparation to their young clients about what will happen in court proceedings.

While for the most part victim–witness or child advocacy programs have been successful, some attorneys still have questions about the use of volunteers who are expected, after a brief training, to function effectively in the court setting. Volunteers, on the other hand, often complain that they are not taken seriously enough. The fact remains that court advocacy is important for children, both victims and offenders, and seems likely to continue.

JUVENILE COURT PROCESS AND PROCEDURES

Juvenile court processes and procedures are implemented based on state statutes that vary across the United States, although they must be within the boundaries of federal legislated guidelines. Even so, the process generally includes an intake stage (initial screening process), an adjudication stage (fact-finding process), and a disposition stage (decision-making) (Costin, Bell, and Downs, 1991, 80–81; Stein, 1991, 29).

INTAKE STAGE

The intake stage involves the screening of cases to eliminate those that do not require court action from those that do early in the process (Duquette, 1990).

Intake procedures may be initiated in several ways, depending on the circumstances. In cases of alleged delinquency or status offenses, it may begin when a minor child is taken into custody by the police, or when a parent or someone in the community files a complaint about the minor's behavior (Binder et al., 1997).

Dependency or neglect and abuse situations generally begin with a petition being filed on behalf of a minor child due to the inability of a parent, guardian, or caretaker to provide proper care, failure to provide adequate care or protection, or intentional injury of a child. A petition may be filed by the police, social workers, representatives of other community institutions (e.g., school personnel, day care staff, medical staff), neighbors, relatives, or anyone suspecting child abuse or neglect.

Whatever the initial intervention, the juvenile probation department usually becomes involved. It is often the probation officer who decides what route the case will take. This preadjudication assessment may determine whether or not the child continues in the judicial process. Among the options available at this point are:

- Referral to another jurisdiction: When the juvenile lives somewhere other than the court in which the petition or complaint is filed, the case may be transferred to the court in that jurisdiction;
- Referral to a social service agency: When a probation officer feels that another social agency can adequately deal with the case instead of having the child involved with the court;
- Counseling and dismissal: When the probation officer deems that brief counseling rather than lengthy court involvement will remedy the problem;
- Informal supervision: When the probation officer, with the consent of the parent(s), determines that supervision under probation without further court intervention is justified (Simonsen, 1991, 196–197).

ADJUDICATION STAGE

If the case does proceed, fact-finding is the primary goal of the adjudication stage. The initial phase of the adjudication stage begins with the filing of a complaint or petition that provides information about the allegations and requests of a particular finding from the court. Complaints are reviewed to establish the authority of the court by statute to intervene and to determine if the facts sufficiently support the allegations (delinquent, dependent, neglected, status offender), and then a decision is made either for dismissal or for further action by the court. Additional information may be provided by a variety of outside sources to assist the court in making a determination in this phase. When the decision is to involve the court further, a social study, the final phase of the adjudication stage, is ordered and a dispositional hearing is scheduled.

The purpose of the social study is to provide evaluations and factual information for consideration by the court during the dispositional phase. Probation staff or social workers assigned to the juvenile court, protective services, or other social agencies generally are responsible for completing the social study (Duquette, 1990).

DISPOSITION STAGE

Information provided in the social study is used to determine an appropriate treatment plan for the child. Although there are variations on a state by state basis, this stage of the process is limited by federal requirements that mandate that the best interests of the child be met in the least restrictive environment (Downs, Costin, and McFadden, 1996; Stein, 1991).

In the disposition stage, if a minor child is found to be delinquent, a status offender, dependent, neglected, or abused, a plan is devised. When the delinquent or status offense behavior is a first offense and of a minor nature, the case may be closed with no further court action. If found to be delinquent or a status offender, the court may permit the child to remain at home on probation under the supervision of the court. A child found to be neglected or abused may remain at home under the supervision of a social service agency.

Finally, the court may decide that placement outside of the home for a child found to be a status offender, delinquent, dependent, neglected, or abused is justified. This decision has the most serious consequences for the child and his or her parents. Depending on the circumstances, the purpose of placement may be for adoption, protection, treatment, or rehabilitation. Out-of-home placements often include foster homes, adoptive homes (permanent placement), group homes, residential treatment institutions, or correctional institutions (state training schools). When placement out of the home is the decision of the court, the disposition stage often includes the process of transferring custody or guardianship of the child (Binder et al., 1997).

THE ROLE OF THE SOCIAL WORKER AND THE COURT

To be effective in any role associated with the juvenile court, social workers must be knowledgeable about the federal and state statutes. These statutes provide the guidelines for practice. For example, statutes define if a child is abused, neglected, dependent, or delinquent. They determine if the court should intervene, outline the processes and procedures to be followed, and decide what interventions can be used.

Social workers are involved in obtaining and organizing evidence for the juvenile court. In the role of investigator, the social worker may interview the parents, the child, other relatives, and collateral resources, including school personnel, medical staff, and police. Evaluation by psychiatrists or psychologists may be requested. At the intake stage, this information is used in screening cases to determine if court involvement is necessary. During the dispositional stage, the material, presented in the form of a social history, will assist the court in developing a treatment plan for the child. Those involved primarily in the investigative role may be employed by law enforcement agencies, child welfare agencies, or family and juvenile courts (Johnson, 1995).

Historically, social workers have provided direct services for children with problems and their families. Child welfare workers have supervised children found to be dependent, neglected, or abused in their own homes or in foster homes, as directed by the court. Social workers employed by community agencies or by the court have counseled minors needing rehabilitation or experiencing mental health problems as a consequence of parental abuse or neglect.

Occasionally those with a social work background are employed as juvenile probation or parole officers. Roles of probation and parole officers are similar in that the goal is rehabilitation and prevention. The purpose of probation is to prevent incarceration in a juvenile correctional institution, whereas the goal of parole is to prevent the return to an institution.

It is not uncommon for social workers to provide testimony in court. Child welfare workers are called on to describe indications of abuse and neglect as well as home environments that they judge to be below standards of safety and cleanliness, in the course of working with children and their families. Social workers with a master's degree and experience now qualify as expert witnesses and frequently are called on to testify in divorce cases involving contested child custody, child abuse and neglect cases, termination of parental rights situations, and delinquency cases (Downs, Costin, and McFadden, 1996). More recently the role of the social worker has been expanded to include assessing a defendant's mental state and competency to stand trial (Gothard, 1989).

CONSUMER PERSPECTIVE

Britta was fifteen when she became involved with the juvenile court. She lived with her mother who found her increasingly difficult to handle.

My father left when I was really little. I don't even remember him. We lived with my Mom's dad for awhile. He was really old and would do things like forget where he was and wander around. I kind of had to watch him a lot. It was a pain. When he died, it was almost a relief, you know. I mean, that sounds awful but it was. I thought, "Okay, now we'll be okay." But then my Mom started seeing this guy and he moved in with us. He was a real jerk. He used to beat her up. She didn't think I knew that. She'd hide the bruises and stuff, but I did. So I used to stay out a lot. My Mom got on my case about that. Then I met Renardo. He was cool. He did pot and crack and got me using the stuff. I sold a little for him, but was afraid to do that too much. My friend Angie got in big trouble selling and I didn't want to.

When I was high, my Mom would hassle me and it bugged me. We got into a few real screaming matches. When we did, I would cut out and go stay with Renardo. He was twenty-four and had this apartment with some other guys. He had his mattress on the floor and we'd sleep there. It was fun, sort of like camping inside. But one day my Mom had her creepy boyfriend follow me. I mean, can you believe it! He followed me! He found out where I was and my Mom really lit into me about that. I was skipping school too and she got really mad. I told her what did she expect with her boyfriend beating her. I couldn't take it. She cried and said that she'd get rid of him and she did. But she still hassled me and I stayed out more and more. Renardo wanted me to run away, but I really didn't want to.

My Mom went to a counselor and the guy told her to go to court and take out this thing called a CHINS on me. It's what parents do I guess when they just can't handle their kids. The next thing I know I get dragged into juvenile court. There's a judge and a lawyer and a bunch of people working for the court. This lady, a probation officer, was "assigned to our case" as they put it and told me I had to come see her. It kind of scared me a little bit. I mean here was this big deal in court, like I had a record or something. Renardo said it was no big deal. It was then that he told me he'd done time. I didn't like that. Being in jail didn't seem like where I wanted to be. He said that I was getting to be a wimp and he kind of disappeared. He just didn't come around anymore.

The court also made me see a social worker at the Department of Social Services. She was nice and I liked her. We made up a plan. I had to go to school and I couldn't do drugs and I couldn't run away. That was okay for a while but then one night my Mom and I had a big fight. I blew up and left the house. I had no place to go so I just walked. Then the next thing I know, the police picked me up!! I couldn't believe it. I figured they'd take me home but they took me to this detention center. There were kids there who had done all kinds of stuff. I was afraid they'd beat me up and I just stayed in bed. They kept me there all night. The next day they took me back to court. My Mom was there and the judge told me that if I did that again they'd put me in a foster home. Angie was in a foster home and she hated it! I said "No way!"

So for the next year I saw my social worker and I went to this after school group for kids who had done the stuff that I did. My Mom and I went to a counselor too. I knew that if I pulled anything, she'd take me back to court. I didn't want that!

Now I am almost seventeen and we're doing okay I guess. I met this guy at school who is really nice to me. It's just easier not to hassle my Mom and not get hassled. I think that if I hadn't gotten involved with the court, I might be in bigger trouble. It kind of woke me up!

Fortunately for Britta, court intervention was early enough to make a difference. There are others for whom the system does not work as well. It is not uncommon for such juveniles to be seen later in the adult criminal system.

ALTERNATIVE APPROACHES TO COURT INTERVENTION

Even before the first juvenile court was established in Illinois in 1899, there was controversy over the loss of due process in juvenile court proceedings and concern about the legitimacy of court intervention, particularly in status offense cases. Rapid growth in the number of juveniles entering the juvenile justice system and discontent with the court throughout the years has resulted in the development of an alternative to judicial intervention—diversion.

DIVERSION

Concerns about the constitutionality of juvenile court jurisdiction in status offenses and the failure of many states to carry out the federal mandate separating alleged delinquents from nondelinquents have prompted the development of diversion programs. The purpose of these programs is to involve status offenders and their families in relevant community services and divert them from the juvenile court system (Binder et al., 1997).

The Office of Juvenile Justice and Delinquency Prevention has defined diversion as "a process by which youth who would otherwise be adjudicated are referred out of the juvenile justice system sometime after apprehension and prior to adjudication" (De Angelo, 1988). The primary goal of diversion is to direct referrals from the attention of the juvenile court and link status offenders and first offenders with a variety of community-based services. A secondary goal is to reduce the stigma caused by court involvement, and a third is to free the courts to focus on the increasing number of serious juvenile cases requiring attention (Barton, 1995).

Services offered through diversion programs are not standardized and vary considerably in different communities. In some areas, individual, group, and/or family therapy by psychologists or social workers is provided through private, not-for-profit, community-based organizations as opposed to traditional mental health agencies. Others offer alternative school programs, recreational programs, job counseling, training, and placement. Some have a community service component that requires juveniles to "volunteer" to work a designated number of hours in a service agency. These services generally are offered through traditional, public or nonprofit agencies that have extended their services to include diversion programs or by nonprofit community-based organizations that have been developed to meet a specific need in a given community (Siegel and Senna, 1997).

Research on the effectiveness of diversion programs in circumventing juvenile court involvement is inconclusive at this time. Some studies have shown a decrease in court appearances of status offenders referred to diversion programs in comparison to those referred to juvenile court (Stewart et al., 1986), while others have found no difference between the two groups (Gensheimer et al., 1986).

TRENDS

SHOULD THERE BE A SEPARATE JUVENILE COURT?

The concern of some over guarantees of due process through the juvenile court, an issue since this court was established, continues today. For many who believe that this court has not met the goals of protection and rehabilitation, the solution is to do away with the juvenile court system completely. Although this has been a relatively strong movement at times, it does not seem feasible in light of several Supreme Court decisions since the 1960s reaffirming due process protection within the context of a specialized court system for juveniles (e.g., *Kent v. United States, In re Gault,* and *In re Winship*). Developing national guidelines that assure due process procedures are implemented in a standardized way throughout the country may be a more satisfactory solution.

SHOULD STATUS OFFENDERS COME UNDER THE JURISDICTION OF THE JUVENILE COURT?

Much concern has been voiced over whether there should be a separate bureaucracy to handle status offenses. Critics of the current procedures argue that intervention through juvenile court relegates these youths to the same status as their delinquent counterparts. Some argue that status offenders are more likely to be older children who are reacting to being abused or neglected and should not be treated as if the fault is with them. By the same token, many feel that it is the family who should be responsible for children's misbehavior. Does giving this task to the courts weaken the family's already dwindling power?

To compound this argument Costin, Bell, and Downs (1991) point to research that suggests that status offenders are, in fact, "more similar than different from delinquent youth" (97). Although the delinquent behavior in which status offenders appear to be involved is not usually as serious as the quality of crimes committed by their delinquent counterparts, the fact remains that this research disproves the idea that status offenders are merely older dependent children.

WHAT SHOULD BE DONE WITH SERIOUS OFFENDERS?

As the violence in our society escalates, the crimes committed by youth are becoming more and more serious. According to the Statistical Abstracts of the United

States (1990; as cited in Hess et al., 1993), of those arrested for serious crimes in 1988, 11.1 percent were under fifteen years of age and 28.2 percent were under eighteen (433). Of these, 10.8 percent arrested for murder were under eighteen and 14.5 percent arrested for forcible rape were also under eighteen. Heide (1993), in her study of children who kill their parents, found that one in eleven of all family murders involve children who kill their parents. Of these a significant percentage of the murderers were under eighteen at the time of the crime (531, 541). The fact that an increased number of these serious offenders are under the influence of one or more drugs compounds the implications for treatment.

In the past, a small number of juveniles who had committed serious crimes were bound over to be tried as adults. Due to the increase in such crimes, however, the juvenile court system must seek more innovative ways to deal with these offenders.

SUMMARY

The role of the juvenile court is a complex one. The services provided by these courts evolved as people began to realize that the offenses of children did not warrant the same treatment as those of adults. In addition, some parents could not adequately care for their children and it fell to the legal system to make provisions for them. The juvenile court emerged largely under the influence of the settlement houses, most notably Hull House in Chicago, and the first juvenile court was established on April 2, 1899. Once established the concept spread and by the early 1900s all but two states had juvenile courts. The last two had established such a system by 1945. The subject of the rights juveniles are entitled to has been debated for some time. The case of *In re Gault* did much to establish a firm set of guidelines.

There are three types of situations that would bring a youth before the juvenile court: delinquency, a status offense, or being dependent, abused, or neglected. Delinquents commit crimes that might also be committed by adults: assault, robbery, theft, drug-dealing or possession, or murder, and so forth. Status offenders are those who have been accused of running away from home, being truant from school, of sexual misconduct, curfew violation, using substances, or of uncontrollable behavior. These are acts or behaviors that would not be seen in court if the individual had reached the status of adulthood. Abused or neglected children may come before the juvenile court so that plans can be made to insure their welfare.

When a child enters the juvenile court system in intake, he/she is often screened by the probation department. The probation officer has a great deal of influence about what happens next. The child may then proceed to adjudication, which is basically a fact-finding stage. The disposition determines what type of services will be offered to the juvenile and, possibly, the family. It is possible that, instead of being seen in court, the child might become part of a diversion program and be referred to services in agencies other than the court with the hope of preventing further court intervention.

Today there are several questions that plague those professionals involved with the juvenile court system. First, should there be a separate juvenile court? Should status offenders continue to be seen along with delinquents in the juvenile court system? Finally, what provisions should be made for the increasing number of juveniles committing serious crimes? These are questions that will probably be debated well into the next century.

EXPLORATION QUESTIONS

1. What is the role of the juvenile court?
2. How did court services for children become specialized?
3. What is meant by the "child savers"?
4. What are family courts?
5. What influence did the 1974 Child Abuse Prevention and Treatment Act have on the juvenile justice system? What did it mandate?
6. What is meant by *parens patriae*? Where did the term originate?
7. What did the Juvenile Court Act mandate?
8. What situations might warrant juvenile court intervention?
9. What are status offenders?
10. What are the rights of juveniles when they become involved with the juvenile court system?
11. Outline the juvenile court process.
12. What is the role of the social worker in the juvenile court?
13. What are the trends in the juvenile court system today?

ACTIVITIES FOR APPLIED LEARNING

1. Visit a juvenile court. Interview personnel about their roles.
2. Research major court decisions influencing the juvenile court (e.g., *In re Gault; In re Winship*).
3. Invite a juvenile probation officer to speak to the class about his/her role in the juvenile court and how this role interfaces with others.
4. Research the early initiators of the juvenile court system. (You might start with Hull House or Julia Lathrop, for example.)

SUGGESTED READING

Crnich, J. E., & Crnich, K. A. *Shifting the Burden of Truth.* Lake Oswego, OR: Recollex Publishing, 1992.

Duquette, D. N. *Advocating for the Child in Protection Proceedings.* Lexington, MA: Lexington Books, 1990.

Dziech, B. W., & Schudson, C. B. *On Trial: America's Courts and Their Treatment of Sexually Abused Children.* Boston: Beacon Press, 1991.

Flicker, B. D. *Standards for Juvenile Justice: A Summary and Analysis,* 2nd ed. Cambridge, MA: Ballinger Publishing Company, 1982.

Gibelman, M., & Demone, H. W. "The Social Worker as a Mediator in the Legal System," *Social Casework* 70(1) (1989): 28–36.

Lipinsky, J. A. "The Impact of Court on Children," *Journal of Interpersonal Violence* 9(2), (1994): 238–257.

Perry, N. W., & Wrightman, L. S. *The Child Witness.* Newbury Park, CA: Sage, 1991.

Platt, A. M. *The Child Savers: The Invention of Delinquency,* 2nd ed. Chicago: The University of Chicago Press, 1977.

Sagatun, I. J., & Edwards, L. P. *Child Abuse and the Legal System.* Chicago: Nelson Hall, 1995.

Senna, J. J., & Siegel, L. J. *Juvenile Law: Cases and Comments,* 2nd ed. New York: West, 1992.

Stein, T. J. *Child Welfare and the Law.* New York: Longman, 1991.

REFERENCES

Barton, W. H. "Juvenile Corrections," (pp. 1563–1577). In NASW (Eds.), *Encyclopedia of Social Work,* 19th ed. Washington DC: NASW Press, 1995.

Binder, A., Geis, B., & Bruce, D. D. *Juvenile Delinquency: Historical, Cultural and Legal.* Cinncinati, OH: Anderson, 1997.

Cheney–Lind, M. "Girls in Jail," *Crime & Delinquency* 54 (1988): 151–168.

Costin, L. B., Bell, C. J., & Downs, S. W. *Child Welfare Policies and Practice,* 4th ed. New York: Longman, 1991.

De Angelo, A. J. "Diversion Programs in the Juvenile Justice System: An Alternative Method of Treatment for Juvenile Offenders," *Juvenile & Family Court Journal* 39 (1988): 21–28.

Dorne, C. K. *Crimes against Children.* New York: Harrow and Heston, 1989.

Downs, S. W., Costin, L. B., & McFadden. *Child Welfare and Family Services.* New York: Longman, 1996.

Duquette, D. N. *Advocating for the Child in Protection Proceedings.* Lexington, MA: Lexington Books, 1990.

Dziech, B. W., & Schudson, C. B. *On Trial: America's Courts and Their Treatment of Sexually Abused Children.* Boston: Beacon Press, 1991.

Gensheimer, L. K., Meyer, J. P., Gottschalk, R., & Davidson, W. S. "Diverting Youth from the Juvenile Justice System: A Meta-Analysis of Intervention Efficacy," (pp. 39–57). In S. J. Apter and A. Goldstein (Eds.), *Youth Violence: Problems and Prospects.* Elmsford, NY: Pergamon Press, 1986.

Gothard, S. "Power in the Court: The Social Worker as an Expert Witness," *Social Work* 34 (1989): 65–67.

Heide, K. M. "Parents Who Get Killed and the Children Who Kill Them," *Journal of Interpersonal Violence* 8(4) (1993): 531–544.

Hess, B. B., Markson, E. W., & Stein, P. J. *Sociology.* New York: Macmillan, 1993.

Johnson, H. W. "Criminal and Juvenile Justice," pp. 199–222. In Johnson, H. W. (Ed.), *The Social Services: An Introduction,* 4th ed., Itasca, IL: F. E. Peacock, 1995.

Sagatun, I. J., & Edwards, L. P. *Child Abuse and the Legal System.* Chicago: Nelson–Hall, 1995.

Siegel, L. J., & Senna, J. J. *Juvenile Delinquency: Theory, Practice, and Law.* St. Paul, MN: West, 1997.

Simonsen, C. E. *Juvenile Justice in America.* New York: Macmillan, 1991.

Stein, T. J. *Child Welfare and the Law.* New York: Longman, 1991.

Stewart, J. J., Vockell, E. L., & Ray, R. E. "Decreasing Court Appearances of Juvenile Status Offenders," *Social Casework* 67 (1986): 74–79.

11

OUR CHILDREN'S CHILDREN
Teen Parents and Their Children

Pamela Higgins Saulsberry

HISTORICAL PERSPECTIVE

'It is a matter of context,' wrote Marian Wright Edelman, Executive Director of the Children's Defense Fund. 'Adolescent parents have always been with us, but the devastating and economic consequences associated with adolescent parenthood *are new. The majority of all teen parents raise their children as single parents facing almost certain poverty. We no longer live in an America in which eighteen- or nineteen-year-old men can earn enough to support a family, and because we never have had an America in which the average single woman with children would earn a decent wage at any age. Adolescent parenthood is a problem because young men, unable to fulfill their traditional "breadwinner" role, are less willing to accept their responsibilities as teen fathers, and because young women, continuing in their traditional role of childbearer in spite of changed times, are unable to support their families alone' (Children's Defense Fund, 1986, 3).*

The issues faced by teen parents in today's society are myriad. Because the vast majority of adolescent parents are unmarried, the attitude of society has been tinged by attitudes toward premarital sex and this has often dictated the services offered. Despite these overtones, however, the principle concern, today and in the past, remains on economics rather than circumstances of conception.

The primary needs of adolescent parents continue to be financial support, a place to live (especially when the reaction from the family is punitive), medical care, a continuation of education, and an opportunity for employment. The most historically pressing need that precipitates most others is that of financial support. More recently, the ability or inability to adequately rear offspring has become as important a consideration as financial support.

A historical view of services needed by adolescent mothers reveals a division involving sociotherapy and psychotherapy. *Sociotherapeutic* services include income maintenance, housing (sometimes away from the mother's family), prenatal and obstetrical medical care, legal counseling, vocational counseling, and educational counseling. *Psychotherapeutic* services were also provided to help with emotional disturbance, conflict, and tensions occasioned by out-of-wedlock pregnancy. These services included counseling and emotional support for the adolescent female's changing relationship with her family, her relationship with an adolescent father, her changing relationship to peers, her reaction to pregnancy and the anticipated birth experience, her plans for the child, her changes in self-concept, and the total emotional configuration that may have initially led the girl to become pregnant (Kadushin and Martin, 1988).

Historically, teen pregnancy has been regarded as primarily a female problem. The expectant teen father has generally been ignored or regarded only as a source of financial support for the mother and child. More recently, this perception of the expectant father has neglected to view him as a person in his own right who may be troubled about a difficult situation in which he has become a principal participant.

In the 1970s and 1980s, concern about a teenage pregnancy epidemic gave rise to an enormous increase in systematic study on the subject, having both positive and negative results. Chilman (1980) outlines these effects as follows: Positively, the study increased public awareness and acceptance of a need for contraceptive services and education about sexuality. Further, it stimulated federal funds for services and research in these areas. Negatively, however, the "crisis" approach appeared sexist in its focus on a problem-laden, sexually active female. It clouded the realities of birthrate statistics and "directed attention away from the more fundamental social and economic problems that warped the lives of so many teenagers during the 1970s, especially if they came from the minority low income group backgrounds."

A QUESTION OF MORALITY

Over the years, concepts of morality have colored the way people view teen pregnancy. The attitude that teen pregnancy would not be an issue if young adolescent females would "just say no" to sex or exhibit higher morals still appears pervasive today. This attitude became especially apparent in a recent Teen Pregnancy Forum:

> *A school principal with one boy and one girl was asked for his solutions to the problem of adolescent parenthood in his community. While serving as a panel member he remarked, "All a girl has to say is no when asked for sexual favors and we have no problem, no chance of a baby." When asked if he taught his son not to ask girls for sex his reply was "No! I'm not raising a sissy. It is different for boys."*

Both male and female participants at the forum agreed with the principal's response, appearing to reflect the notion that it is perfectly normal for boys to be sexually active. If a girl becomes pregnant, it is her fault and, thus, her (and her family's) responsibility.

This common attitude can be traced back to English poor laws that formed the basis for the double standard concerning adolescent fornication and illegitimacy (out-of-wedlock births) held today in the United States. The English poor laws led to harsh treatment by Puritan colonists who punished extramarital fornication and required parents to support the illegitimate.

In 1658, Anne Williams petitioned the court for maintenance from Richard Smith "for a child the defendant hath got by her." The court "ordered that the said Richard Smith maintain the child and that the woman for her act committed, be whipped and have thirty lashes well laid on" (Bremner, 1970, 52).

ECONOMICS AS A CONCERN

Although sociotherapeutic and psychotherapeutic services have been historically offered to teen parents and their children, the main social service that continues to draw more attention is economic maintenance. When scrutinizing the issue of adolescent parenthood and economic maintenance, the question of public welfare inevitably surfaces.

The issue of welfare's effect on teen pregnancy is well examined in the Children's Defense Fund's publication, *Welfare and Teen Pregnancy: What Do We Know? What Do We Do?* (1986a). The question, "Does AFDC (Aid to Families with Dependent Children), commonly known as welfare, encourage births to unmarried teenagers?" was specifically addressed. The report notes:

> *The argument that welfare contributes to teen pregnancy has two permutations: first, that "generous" benefit levels encourage young women to bear children because it is financially attractive to do so; second, that the availability of any welfare benefits—without regard to how generous they are—encourages out-of-wedlock births... [M]ost critics do not claim that welfare plays a significant role in encouraging pregnancy. Rather, they say, it encourages a pregnant teen to bear the child and leaves her free not to marry (Children's Defense Fund, 1986, 5).*

Chilman (1980), addressing the issue of financial aid for adolescent mothers, observes:

> *The availability of public assistance appears not to cause out-of-marriage pregnancy; but it may affect what the young woman does about this pregnancy (1980).*

And Plotnick, emphasizing a negative side effect of such help, points out that:

> *Entitlement programs may influence teenage childbearing as an unintended side effect of their primary objective. The most widely mentioned example is Aid to Families with Dependent Children (AFDC). The main objective of AFDC is to provide income support to needy single parents with children. However, the availability of an independent source of income, which is generally contingent on being unmarried, may induce some pregnant women and their partners to forgo marriage (Plotnick, 1993).*

Although the prevailing conclusion appears to be that there is no evidence to suggest that AFDC "causes" out-of-wedlock pregnancies, the question has been much debated. Analyzing relationships between the levels of grant payments and the access barriers to AFDC as these relate to legitimacy rates to 1965, Cutright (1971) found that AFDC was *not* an incentive to an out-of-wedlock pregnancy. Janowitz (1976), however, analyzing somewhat similar factors for a later period, found that for nonwhite younger women, larger welfare payments were associated with higher illegitimacy rates. Moore and Caldwell (1976) studied a 1971 national probability sample of fifteen- to nineteen-year-old women, and found that "high state AFDC benefit levels and acceptance rates were not found to be associated with greater probability of pregnancy." They concluded that benefits did not "increase the likelihood that an unmarried virgin would have intercourse" and that "there was no evidence that AFDC benefits serve as an evident incentive to child-rearing outside marriage" (2–3).

Can the availability of welfare to unmarried mothers and their children provide a disincentive to marriage as an unintended side effect? (Recent proposals designed to link welfare eligibility or benefit levels more closely with "responsible" behavior may result in policies designed to encourage marriage.) Analysis of marriage behavior suggests that such disincentives affect behavior. White, unmarried, pregnant teenagers are less likely to marry if they live in states with relatively high

AFDC benefits. However, no such disincentive for African American women has been found (Lundberg and Plotnick, 1990a, 1990b; South and Lloyd, 1992).

Hoffman, Duncan, and Mincy (1991) reported that higher AFDC benefits were associated with lower rates of marriage among African American and white women. The findings of these two studies are consistent with the view that AFDC tends to increase out-of-wedlock births, although neither focused directly on the marriage behavior of premarital pregnant women. Other researchers have examined whether AFDC benefits affected teenage premarital childbearing but did not identify the specific behavior (abortion, marriage, and so on) on which the program had an effect (Duncan and Hoffman, 1990; Plotnick, 1990; Ellwood and Bane, 1985; Moore, 1991).

None of these studies found a relationship between AFDC and premarital childbearing for African American or Hispanic teenagers. For white teenagers, only Plotnick (1990) found that more liberal welfare benefits and administrative policies were associated with a greater likelihood of premarital childbearing. On balance, current research is inconclusive regarding AFDC's effects on teenage premarital childbearing. However, AFDC benefits may affect marriage rates.

Even if higher welfare benefits were to discourage marriage and are associated with premarital childbearing, cutting benefits would not be a wise policy response for reducing unwanted side effects when one considers other consequences of benefit reductions. Benefits in most states currently fall well below the poverty line. Cuts would increase the deprivation of millions of children and parents, further eroding the central income support function of AFDC. Alternatives to AFDC that offer opportunities for a minimally decent income, while mitigating marriage disincentives, offer more promise for policy reform (Ellwood, 1988).

More recent studies on the subject conclude that AFDC encourages single mothers to live independently rather than as part of a larger household (Ellwood and Bane, 1985; Hutchens, et al., 1989). Its impact on living arrangements does not increase the number of teenage parents. However, because single parents and their children are more likely to be poor if they live independently than if they live in a larger family (typically with the child's grandparents), this unanticipated effect of AFDC is a matter of concern (Plotnick, 1993, 325–326).

The Children's Defense Fund report on *Welfare and Teenage Pregnancy* (1986) also concluded that:

> *Although the availability of welfare and the level of welfare benefits in a state do not appear to have an impact on the decision of young unmarried women to have children, higher benefit levels do appear to increase the likelihood that a young mother will establish her own independent household (7).*

The report also states that consideration has to be given to policies that allow for adolescent mothers to make these choices. Adolescent mothers who choose to keep their children and establish independent households are allowed to do so by policies that they did not create, but elected to use.

One such policy, proposed in 1984 by President Reagan and later adopted by Congress, put additional pressure on young parents to live apart from their own parents. The 1984 policy changed how a minor parent's AFDC eligibility was determined by requiring that a portion of his or her own parent's income (if that grandparent was not receiving AFDC) must be counted as available to the minor parent and the grandchild when they are living in the parent's home, regardless of whether the parent's income was actually available to and being used to help the minor parent and child. Prior to 1984, the parent's income had to be counted as available only to the minor child but not the grandchild, unless the grandparent actually was contributing to the grandchild's support. Another 1984 change in the AFDC program placed increased pressure on a young teen in an AFDC family to move out after having a child. Under that change, the teen was not eligible for a separate grant for herself and her baby. Her family of origin's already inadequate AFDC grant had to be (and still has to be since this policy is still in effect) stretched further to meet her infant's needs as well. Even though having a baby in adolescence may not be the wisest choice for a teen to make, welfare policies instituted pressuring teens to forego supports and opportunities that may be available to them by choosing to live at home may prove to be counterproductive.

According to information compiled in *The State of America's Children Yearbook*, published by the Children's Defense Fund in 1995, seventy-six prominent economists and social scientists examined the relationship between welfare and out-of-wedlock childbearing. A joint statement, issued in June 1994, stressed that no significant correlation existed between births to unmarried women and the amount of welfare benefits provided by various states. Moreover, the large and troubling increase in the proportion of children born to never-married mothers rose from 17 percent in 1979 to 30 percent in 1992, during a period in which the value of the average AFDC benefit (adjusted for inflation) was reduced by nearly half (86).

Also included in this report were the findings of a 1994 study by the Center for Law and Social Policy (CLASP) that confirmed that the precarious economic circumstances of many teenage mothers often forces them to turn to AFDC for at least temporary help. In 1990, slightly more than half (51 percent) of all mothers receiving AFDC had their first child when they were younger than twenty. Yet the CLASP study challenged the myth that most teen parents remain on AFDC for extended periods. Analyzing data from the National Longitudinal Survey of Youth (NLSY), CLASP found that 40 percent of unmarried teenage mothers leave AFDC within one year, and 70 percent leave within four years (Children's Defense Fund, 86).

In response to public concerns about teen parents on welfare, the Clinton administration incorporated tough new provisions in a 1994 welfare reform plan. Some of the new conditions for receiving AFDC benefits (now referred to as cash benefits; see Chapter 3) include:

1. All minor parents are required to live at home or in a supervised group setting, and are required to stay in school;

2. Unmarried minor mothers are required to identify their child's father, and teen fathers are responsible for child support;
3. On reaching their eighteenth birthdays, mothers who have received benefits for two years are required to work fifteen to thirty-five hours per week.

In 1995, the Children's Defense Fund contrasted Clinton's provisions to those proposed by Republicans:

> *In contrast, House Republican welfare reform proposals unveiled in the fall of 1994 would have eliminated completely welfare benefits to unmarried teen mothers younger than 18 and permanently denied aid to children born to such mothers. The House leadership relented slightly early in 1995—apparently responding to public concern about the consequences for children—proposing instead to deny benefits to children of mothers younger than 21 (87).*

Additional information supports the contention that availability of public assistance appears not to cause out-of-marriage teenage births. *Facts at a Glance* reported data on teen birth rates collected by the National Center for Health Statistics (Moore et al., 1995), and commented that "more generous welfare benefits are typical in Europe, yet rates of teenage childbearing are only one-eighth to about one-half of the U. S. rates." The much lower rates achieved by European nations casts doubt on the contention that welfare benefits represent an incentive to teenage childbearing.

SOCIETAL ATTITUDES AND CURRENT DILEMMAS

Present-day attitudes regarding adolescent parents are a direct result of the dilemmas facing most teenage parents. There are no advocates for adolescent parenthood because very few adolescent parents, given their age and inexperience, can deal with the responsibilities that parenthood brings. This is true even when the teen parents are married. However, the vast majority of teen parents do not marry. The pervasive social attitudes regarding adolescent parenthood are generally negative. These seem to stem from the many negative consequences adolescent pregnancy and parenthood carry. Among these are such factors as reduced educational achievement and earning potential for adolescent parents, the risk of adverse health consequences for both mother and baby, and the poor socioeconomic prospects for the entire teen family.

EDUCATIONAL OPPORTUNITIES

The major repercussions of early childbearing include a lower likelihood of school completion or advancing education, and a lower likelihood of working in the future with adequate wages. Information compiled by the National Longitudinal Survey of Youth (as cited in Ahn, 1994) suggests that

> *merely having a teenage birth leads to a 50% reduction in the likelihood of high school completion, compared with not having a teenage birth. Individual heterogeneity accounts for a 42% reduction in the likelihood of finishing high school among those who have a birth before age 17, and a 30% reduction among those who have a birth between ages 17 and 19, compared with those who do not have a teenage birth. However, individual heterogeneity accounts for less than 30% of the difference in the likelihood that black teenage mothers will complete school, compared with more that 50% among Hispanics and whites. Family background variables, such as maternal education and parental marital stability, also have positive effects on school completion (19).*

If a teen mother does not have at least a high school diploma or the equivalent, the likelihood that she will be able to find employment that adequately provides for herself and her offspring without assistance are slim.

Young, unmarried fathers often have characteristics that make it difficult for them to assume the responsibilities of their paternal role. In comparison to all young men, those who are unmarried fathers tend to have less education, and are more likely to have dropped out of high school. They more frequently have been involved in illegal activity, been suspended from school, and have exhibited other problem behaviors. They are more likely to be unemployed and, if working, to be in low-paying jobs. Many live with extended family members, perhaps because of their reduced financial circumstances (Adams and Pittman, 1988).

Ced is a seventeen-year-old unmarried father. He became a father at sixteen. He lives with his mother and three brothers. He says he learned about sex on his own from the things he saw on TV "while watching programs on HBO and Cinemax." He said he never talked with any adults about any aspect of sex including responsibility and he began exploring sexually at the age of five or six. The mother of his child was fourteen when she gave birth to his daughter. "I guess the baby is mine, I never questioned it," he commented. Her mother allowed him to spend the night with her at her home. Ced's mother "adopted" the mother of his child after the baby was born. Presently Ced, his baby, the baby's mother, Ced's mother, and his brothers all live together. Ced said he is very attached to his child. A school dropout, Ced has had several encounters with the juvenile justice system, some resulting in detention. He is presently enrolled in a community-based social service program aimed at assisting him in receiving his G.E.D., staying out of trouble, and finding employment.

HEALTH ISSUES

Health risks and health disadvantages associated with teen pregnancy add to the negative attitudes connected with this issue. Pregnant adolescents are at risk for a number of health complications having serious consequences if left untreated. The most serious of these health complications are *anemia* and *pregnancy-related hyper-tension*. Table 11-1 shows rates of selected complications for live births in 1989 (the most recent year available) among adolescents younger than twenty, women ages twenty to twenty-four, and all women. As this table indicates, adolescents are at risk for some serious complications, and at a reduced risk for others. It should also be taken into account that adolescents are the least likely to get early prenatal care. The earlier prenatal care is obtained, the more likely complications can be detected and managed and prepared for in delivery.

Low birth weight (LBW) is another health area of concern in teen pregnancy. Maternal education, maternal age, and marital status are all reflective of socioeconomic status and predictive of LBW. Teenage mothers are at greater risk of having a low-birth-weight baby than mothers aged twenty-five to thrity-four. It is not always clear, however, that the risk of teenage childbearing and LBW is due to young maternal age or to the low socioeconomic status often accompanying teenage pregnancy. It *is* clear that most teenage pregnancies are likely to involve both of these variables.

There are two reasons for infants being born at a birth weight falling below 2500 grams (approximately five and one-half pounds). LBW is primarily caused by:

TABLE 11-1   Rates of Medical Complications of Pregnancy for Adolescents and Older Women, 1989

Complication	Younger than 20 years[a]	20–24 years[a]	All women
Anemia	30.3	22.9	19.1
Cardiac disease	2.3	2.9	3.6
Lung disease	3.5	2.9	3.0
Diabetes	7.4	13.6	21.1
Genital herpes	5.3	6.8	8.1
Pregnanacy-related hypertension	35.4	29.4	28.2
Renal disease	4.1	3.2	2.7
Eclampsia	7.3	4.6	4.4
Uterine bleeding	6.7	8.1	9.1

Adapted from National Center for Health Statistics. (1992). *Monthly Vital Statistics Report, 40*(12-S), 11.
[a]Number of births with complication per 1,000 live births.

1. Prematurity, conventionally defined as delivery before thirty-seven weeks of gestation; and
2. Intrauterine growth retardation (IGR).

Low birth weight increases the risk of cognitive deficit, morbidity, and death during the first year of life (McCormick, 1985). Adolescents are at excess risk for LBW infants due to both causes (Malinson, 1985). The risk is particularly high for very young adolescents (younger than 15). The distribution of LBW babies by mother's age indicates increased risk for adolescents, shown in Table 11-2.

Infant mortality is another health consideration associated with teenage pregnancy. Two components of infant mortality are neonatal death (within the first twenty-eight days of life) and postneonatal death (occurring between twenty-nine days and twelve months of life). Neonatal mortality generally results from perinatal conditions such as LBW, whereas postneonatal mortality is correlated with socioeconomic factors. (See Table 11-3.)

Letha is a fourteen-year-old who gave birth to a stillborn baby after twenty-two weeks of gestation. Letha lives with her mother and seven siblings ranging in age from three to twenty-two. Letha is repeating the

TABLE 11-2   Low Birth Weight by Maternal Age

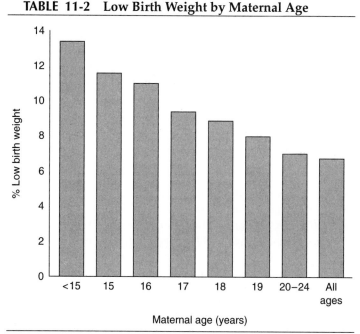

Adapted from National Center for Health Statistics. (1991). *Monthly Vital Statistics Report,* 40(8-S), 28.

TABLE 11-3   Infant Mortality by Maternal Age, 1987

Unpublished data adapted from the Centers for Disease Control, Public Health Service, U.S. Department of Health and Human Services, Washington, DC.

seventh grade due to poor performance in classes and mostly poor attendance at school. She would often miss school because she had to baby-sit for her mother. Before Letha gave birth to the stillborn infant, she received no prenatal care. Letha's family was in no way able to take on the responsibility of another child, nor was the father or his family.

POVERTY

Besides the above-mentioned health consideration for teen pregnancy, it also must be taken into consideration that women who begin to bear children in adolescence are highly likely to bear more children over their lifetimes than will women whose first birth occurs later in life. Consideration has to be given to the negative socioeconomic circumstances that result when women have large numbers of children beginning in adolescence. The primary risk for infants of adolescent parents is the poor socioeconomic prospects for the family. Adolescent mothers and their infants (and fathers who live with their families) are more likely to have lower incomes than older families, and thus suffer the consequential disadvantages of low income: poor and unsafe housing, fewer cultural and social advantages, poorer quality nutrition, and fewer goods and services of all kinds. In many cases, the young family lives with an extended family in a large, crowded dwelling.

One study that speaks to the negative long-term socioeconomic effects of teenage childbearing provides the following statistics.

> *Hardy and Zabin's (1991) three-month follow-up of adolescent mothers and their infants in Baltimore confirmed these disadvantages. In their study, 80% of African American and 57% of white adolescent mothers lived in female-headed households. Six percent of the total (1% of African Americans and 25% of whites) were married and living with their husbands, and 6% of white and 12% of African American adolescent mothers lived with their boyfriends. Many of these mothers had moved several times, often living in large households. Most of these adolescents lived in poverty (45% of whites and 58% of African Americans had a total income below $10,000). After 15 to 18 months, little change had occurred (Combs–Orme, 1993, 347).*

The issue of out-of-wedlock children is regarded as morally negative due to the perception that it threatens U. S. society's idea of "family." The belief prevails that mature adults should be the heads of families and that two parents assume the emotional, social, and economic needs of their child. Unwed teenagers giving birth and attempting to rear children has been a disturbing trend in recent years. As has been illustrated in the case example of Letha, pregnant teenagers often lack adequate nutrition and prenatal care, and bear offspring susceptible to numerous health risks, including low birth weight, birth defects, infant death, and a host of serious illnesses. There is mounting evidence that bearing children at a young age is a major deterrent to escaping the cycle of poverty. What emerges from the above facts and figures is a vivid picture showing those in the most precarious position to bear and raise children—those who are unschooled, unskilled, and inexperienced in life—creating a frighteningly large number of the U. S.'s new families. What this spells for the future should trigger an alarm.

THE UNITED STATES COMPARED TO OTHER COUNTRIES

Adolescent pregnancy is far more prevalent in the United States than in most other Westernized nations. Indeed, the United States leads other developed countries in adolescent pregnancy, abortions, and births.

> *Birth rates among teenagers in other industrial nations are much lower than rates in the United States. International comparisons show that Japan has the lowest birth rate with 4 births per 1,000 females aged 15–19, Sweden has 13 per 1,000, Canada has 26, and the United Kingdom's birth rate of 33 per 1,000 ranks second to the United States' birth rate which is 61 per 1,000 females aged 15–19. The birth rate among U. S. non-Hispanic whites was 42 per 1,000 females 15–19 in 1992. While lower than the overall U. S. teen birth rate of 61, the birth rate among white teens is*

still high compared to other nations. Of all pregnancies to teens in 1987, 35% ended in abortion, 14% ended in miscarriages, 37% ended in unintended births, and only 14% ended in births that were intended at conception. Of all pregnancies among females aged 15–19 in 1987, 71% occurred to teens who were not using contraception when they became pregnant (National Center for Health Statistics, 1995, 2).

What are some of the reasons that the American teens of all races are much more likely than teens from other industrialized countries to experience pregnancy (and abortion or childbirth) as part of their adolescence? The Children's Defense Fund (1986), in its "Alan Guttmacher Institute Report," reports that, in a comparison of the United States to five other wealthy industrial countries, each of the five comparison countries appeared to be more tolerant of teenage sexual activity and more open about sex in general. It appeared that these occurrences made it easier for teens to acknowledge their sexual activity and seek appropriate counseling and services. In each comparison country there was a broad consensus that teenage pregnancy is undesirable and that teenagers need help to avoid pregnancy. The government in each comparison country perceived its role as helping sexually active teenagers avoid pregnancy, not as helping teenagers delay sexual activity. No comparison country attempted to place restrictions on confidential access to contraceptives. All comparison countries make confidential and free or nearly free contraceptive services that are easily accessible to teenagers. Only in the United States are free or reduced-cost contraceptive services to teens offered through a system that is designed to service only poor women and is thus sometimes stigmatized. All of the countries offer free or subsidized abortion services to teens regardless of income. Abortion rates in the five comparison countries were about half the U. S. rate. The report also noted that in England, Wales, and Sweden, national policies encourage sex education in the schools. In Sweden, the only one of the countries studied in which abortion rates have been going down in recent years, sex education is required and there is a closely established link between the schools and the clinics that provide contraceptive services to adolescents.

The authors of the "Alan Guttmacher Institute Report" concluded:

American teenagers seem to have inherited the worst of all possible worlds regarding their exposure to messages about sex: movies, music, radio, and TV tell them that sex is romantic, exciting, and titillating; premarital sex and cohabitation are visible ways of life among the adults they see and hear about; their own parents or their parents' friends are divorced or separated but involved in sexual relationships. Yet, at the same time, young people get the message good girls should say no. Almost nothing that they see or hear about sex informs them about contraception or the importance of avoiding pregnancy (Children's Defense Fund, 1986, 5).

Although the United States has begun to address the issues of teenage sex education and contraception, controversy surrounding the methods of delivering this information still exists, making it difficult to address a particular issue and adolescent sexuality as a whole.

Every person in our society should be interested in drastically reducing the numbers of births to teen parents, not only because of the economic costs, but for the social costs as well. One social problem society faces is violence, especially among young Americans. Since teens are ill-equipped to handle the medical and economic responsibilities that they face when pregnancy occurs, it is highly unlikely that they will do an adequate job of teaching their offspring how to restrain anger or control violent impulses. In her book *Deadly Consequences* (1991), Dr. Deborah Prothrow–Stith stated that boys who grow up in poverty and in homes that lack nonviolent male role models, are vulnerable to the deadly lesson of violence with which they are constantly bombarded in the media.

Emmett Folgert, a youth worker in Boston's Dorchester Youth Collaborative who is close to scores of young, poor fatherless males has elaborated on this... Boys without fathers who grow up in impoverished, female-headed households, Folgert believes, identify with the violent heroes on television to a degree that other young boys do not. Folgert, trained as a social worker, labels this kind of identification "clinical." The imaginary relationship such boys have with their TV heroes has great emotional meaning. Desperately hungry for fathering, such boys transform their television heroes into imaginary fathers. They talk to these pretend fathers. They make up long stories about what their TV heroes would do if they lived in Boston in a poor neighborhood. They ask their imaginary heroes for advice. What should they do? How should they handle themselves? Folgert says the answer they receive is always the same. Their heroes tell them to be tough. Their heroes tell them to fight (47).

It would be interesting to see how many of these young men live in homes where the first birth to their mothers occurred while she was in her adolescent years.

Following are some of the similar experiences of this author during her practice as a school social worker:

Tony, a fourteen-year-old overage sixth-grade elementary student, was continuously suspended from school for fighting. He would either pick fights or choose to fight as his way of solving any dispute, no matter how slight. Tony was the oldest of six children. His mother had Tony when she was sixteen. Tony knew who his father was, but he never really had a relationship with him.

Nic, a thirteen-year-old sixth-grade student, never went to junior high school. He was sent to one juvenile detention center after another and suspended from school for fighting, bringing weapons to school, cutting tires, threatening to sexually assault school personnel's children, and so on. Nic, who stated he wanted to be a criminal, lived with his mother and four siblings. His mother began having children when she was fifteen.

Joe, a fifteen-year-old seventh-grader, didn't attend school until he was eight years old. He was born to a fifteen-year-old mother. Joe came to school only "to eat" after which he very often would leave school. He was involved in several types of illegal activities, often including violent fights.

Mack, a sixteen-year-old seventh-grader, was the oldest of ten children. He often fought with other kids who called him dumb for being sixteen and in the seventh grade. Many times he would come to school and fall asleep. Often, Mack would eat his breakfast and lunch, then leave school and hang out for the rest of the day and into the night. His mother, who had him when she was sixteen, said she was tired of fooling with him and his siblings because she was still a young woman who had "her" life to live. Mack never knew his father.

These are but a few of the stories of young people born to adolescent parents. How often these scenarios will be repeated can be predicted from the number of teens creating families before they are able to handle the inherent responsibilities of child-rearing.

EXTENT OF TEEN BIRTHS

Teen birth rates have begun to decline slightly. According to information included in the Children's Defense Fund's *The State of America's Children Yearbook* (1995), the teen birth rate dropped 2.3 percent from the 1991 level. However, the proportion of births to unmarried teens reached the highest level ever recorded (81).

The report also stated that in 1992 there were 505,419 births to girls ages fifteen to nineteen, for a rate of 60.7 births per 1,000 girls, down from the 1991 rate of 62.1. The drop follows a steady increase between 1986 and 1991, and there is no way to know whether it is a one-time event or the beginning of a downward trend. The rate is still considerably higher than those experienced throughout most of the 1980s. Virtually all of the decline occurred among teens ages fifteen to seventeen (82).

The Alan Guttmacher Institute (AGI) and the Center for Disease Control (CDC) data suggest that sexually active teenagers are increasingly likely to use some form of contraception on a regular basis, a trend that may be contributing to a decline in both teenage pregnancy and childbearing rates. There is also some evidence that the proportion of teenagers who are sexually active may no longer be rising. This information, as well as a number of recent studies, suggests that family life education may be beginning to make a positive difference in teens' sexual behavior.

When looking at the sexual activity of adolescents, sexual abuse has to be taken into consideration. Sexual abuse plays a significant role in a high number of situations in which girls become pregnant as teens. Emerging research indicates that much of the teen pregnancy problem in America is tied to older men.

Debra Boyer (1992), a research assistant professor at the University of Washington, conducted a study of 535 young women who had become pregnant as adolescents, and found that 66 percent had been sexually abused as children. Judith Musick, author of *Young, Poor and Pregnant* (1995), during her experience directing Chicago's "Ounce of Prevention Program," a social service group, found that 61 percent of 445 teen mothers reported sexual abuse.

The proposed solution to America's teen pregnancy problem—withdrawing cash payments to unmarried teens as the most expedient and productive way to change female adolescents' sexual behavior—seems more complicated than welfare reform. When considering the connection between sexual abuse and teen pregnancy, punishment is an ineffective way to stop adolescent parenthood.

SERVICES TO TEEN PARENTS AND THEIR CHILDREN

According to the Child Welfare League of America (1986),

> *achieving a coordinated delivery system for pregnant and parenting adolescents is not simple, and is often blocked by a scarcity of resources. Few communities have the necessary full array of services. Developing these services requires a long-term commitment by community agencies, and an investment of resources by policymakers and public officials (11).*

The roadblocks to developing coordinated service delivery systems for pregnant and parenting adolescents stem from the pervasive objections to teen parents in particular and parents in general who cannot take care of their offspring without public assistance. However, services must be provided for the benefit of the offspring of teen parents so that they can have the best chance possible to maximize their potential in life. Services to teen parents will have the same result. All services that are available should be community-based and linked together to be cost-effective.

An essential coordinated service system for pregnant adolescents, young parents, and their children should include prevention services, educational services, health care services, social services, employment and training services, child care, financial assistance, and case management.

PREVENTION SERVICES

As with any situation that has more negative ramifications than positive ones, a community service system established to deal with the issue of adolescent pregnancies should emphasize prevention through a variety of strategies. Some of these involve direct services to adolescents; others should be directed at increasing the awareness of adolescents, families, and the community at large of the negative consequences that frequently accompany adolescent pregnancy.

Though effective strategies for preventing adolescent pregnancies are still developing, there are several characteristics of effective approaches. These include early identification of at-risk family situations and at-risk children, especially younger siblings in families where adolescent births have already occurred; absentee rates at school, along with recognition of poor reading skills and dropping grades, indicates high-risk adolescents. Services should be provided where adolescents are most comfortable and in large numbers, i.e. schools, neighborhood community and recreation centers, churches, and so on. Services should be culturally specific and economically feasible.

Services aimed at preventing pregnancy should be situation-specific. For example, adolescents who are not sexually active should be supported in remaining so. Those who are already sexually active can be helped to manage their sexuality in a responsible way.

Adolescent parents (both male and female) can be provided services that will assist them in preventing additional pregnancies. Specific services that should be included in a community-based service system to help prevent and/or reduce adolescent pregnancies include:

- Positive self-esteem development
- Family life and sex education for youth
- Family planning services
- Family support and preservation services
- Adolescent health care services
- A range of education, employment, recreational, and social activities aimed at offering opportunities, options, and hope for adolescents (especially at-risk adolescents) other than pregnancy and parenting

EDUCATIONAL SERVICES

A primary goal for pregnant adolescents and young parents should be to continue and complete their education. Failure to achieve a high school diploma or its equivalent can limit an adolescent's long-term prospects for independence.

Components of educational services should include a continuum of educational programs for pregnant adolescents and young parents. These include, but are not limited to: enrollment in a standard educational program or a General Equivalency Diploma (GED) program, or its equivalent; vocational education and training during or after standard educational programs and/or equivalency programs is an essential educational service that will help prepare these adolescents for employment; home schooling programs for teen mothers, particularly for the weeks immediately following the birth of the baby. Both male and female teen parents need post-high school educational and vocational training opportunities.

In any such array of programs, the guiding principle should be to allow adolescent parents access to the educational programs available to any other adolescents, while recognizing that some adolescent parents will do better in alternative or specialized programs.

To build a continuum of educational services that serve pregnant adolescents and young parents adequately requires the involvement of local school systems, including the general education program, the vocational education program, and in some communities special education programs. The support of the entire community is an essential ingredient.

HEALTH CARE SERVICES

Adolescent parents not only have all the regular health care needs of their peers, but also require high quality, regular health care for the well-being of the adolescent mother and her child. Attention has already been given to the problems faced by a pregnant teen mother who fails to receive proper prenatal care. The most important health-related issues for adolescents and their children that must be addressed include:

- Prenatal care for the pregnant woman
- Health services for the young mother after the birth of the baby
- Family planning, support, and preservation services
- Specialized assessment, diagnostic services, and pediatric care for the child
- Dental services
- Ongoing primary care for the adolescent mother, father, and their child

Assuring that adequate health care services are in place for pregnant and parenting adolescents requires the involvement of community health care practitioners and organizations. Access to and the receipt of health care for adolescents is a critical area of concern. One model of service that is being documented as effective in reducing pregnancies is the provision of health care services in or near public high schools as well as in neighborhood community and recreation centers. Evidence indicates that the setting in which primary health care is provided can have a significant impact on adolescents' use of that health care.

SOCIAL SERVICES

With the multiple demands of their own development, responsibilities as parents, and relationships with their own parents, siblings, and peers, pregnant adolescents and young parents need a variety of social services.

These social services can be provided by traditional sources or new, community-based settings for services. All services should have as their goal the building of self-esteem and a sense of competence on the part of the adolescent. A strong self-esteem promotes the adolescent's pursuit of, and success with, other goals, including completion of education, effective parenting, obtaining employment, and maintaining strong relationships with family members and friends. Strong self-esteem can empower adolescents to perceive a wider range of options available to them, allowing them to exercise wise choices among available alternatives.

Primary types of social services that should be considered include:

- Counseling services
- Homemaker and parent aide services
- Family preservation and support services
- Recreational programs
- Parenting support and education programs
- Peer counseling and support services

For these social services to be provided in the manner in which they are needed, a variety of community agencies must be involved in their provision. Some of the most innovative programs for young parents are those that provide wide-ranging parenting and family support. These programs often have goals that are similar to those of more traditional programs. Services that prevent repeat pregnancies, foster the return to school, and develop parenting skills are especially important. Recreational activities, parenting support and education, and peer counseling cannot be minimized when developing programs to provide social services for pregnant teens and adolescent parents.

EMPLOYMENT AND TRAINING SERVICES

Services that offer vocational preparation or training must be provided as essential elements of a service system for young parents. It is now recognized that the most important assistance provided to an adolescent mother and/or father is a marketable skill. Adolescent parents, like all adolescents, are best served by preparation for long-term independence.

The components of employment and training programs for many adolescent parents should be based on the fact that the pathway to eventual employment will require several years and a continuum of vocationally oriented services including:

- Vocational counseling and job orientation
- Programs that promote exposure to a range of job options and opportunities to facilitate vocational or career decisions
- Skill training
- Job placement

As with education and health, the importance of work opportunities during adolescence cannot be overemphasized. Not only does job consistency teach important lifelong lessons, it also provides young people with an opportunity to make a positive contribution to their families.

CHILD CARE PROGRAMS

Child care services must be available if pregnant and parenting adolescents are to return to school or participate in employment-related activities or jobs. In addition, quality child care programs can offer other services designed to ease the pressure of parenting for an adolescent who is unprepared for this role, and to teach important child-rearing skills through such means as role-modeling of parenting behavior. Finally, child care programs can help to identify developmental problems of the children participating in the program, and stimulate healthy development. Child care used by adolescent parents may be informal, as through family and friends, or formal, as from licensed child care providers.

The range of community child care services available to adolescent parents should include:

- Infant care programs
- Child care center programs
- Care before and after school
- Child care programs for children with special needs, including handicapped children
- Child care programs that emphasize developmental experiences for the mother and mother–child bonding experiences
- Respite child care

Child care arrangements should be determined by the needs of the child and in the context of the mother's support program. Child care should be integral to the overall plan for meeting the parent's and the child's developmental needs. Child care services can be a base for parenting education that leads to improving relationships between the parent and child.

FINANCIAL ASSISTANCE

It is important to distinguish between those who need financial aid and those who need both money and specialized services. For some parents, the method of help may be to supply supplemental income only. These parents would be the ones who have solid family support with guidance through pregnancy, child care, and parenting. Others may need assistance in assessing or planning better use of their own financial resources, such as budgeting, managing money, or obtaining better housing. Many parents may need both money and support in caring for their children, or in resolving or coping with physical, social, emotional, and financial problems that interfere with parental functioning and well-being.

CASE MANAGEMENT SERVICES

Case management services often are essential to meet the diverse health, social service, child care, educational, employment, and financial needs of adolescent parents and their children. Case management assures that community services, even though administered by varying service agencies and different service systems, are part of a coherent service plan for an individual client.

Case management can be provided as a separate service or in close association with other services, and should include: a full assessment of an individual's or a family's needs, including more specialized diagnostic services as necessary; the development of a plan of services and implementation of the plan; arrangement for the delivery of a variety of public and private services; follow-up and assessment of the effectiveness of services, with a change in the service plans as appropriate; advocacy on behalf of the individual or family, verifying that services or benefits are received.

The list of services outlined and strongly recommended by the Child Welfare League of America (CWLA, 1986) demonstrates the complexity of the issues faced by pregnant adolescents and adolescent parents. If and when any one of the services is not available and, therefore, not provided to pregnant teens and teen parents, the results can be devastating, especially to the teen parents' offspring.

GRANDPARENT INVOLVEMENT

The majority of teens who have children need assistance in caring for them. The source usually called on to provide help is the grandparents. Maternal grandparents most often assume the responsibility for the offspring of a teenage daughter. Teen mothers, especially the youngest, often live at home during pregnancy and the first part of their children's lives, if not longer. Under this arrangement, grandparents become the primary caretakers of the grandchildren, assuming the role of the parent.

> It is estimated that 3.2 million children in the United States live with their grandparents. An increase of almost 40 percent in the past decade, according to the U. S. Census Bureau. Some 4 percent of all white children in the United States and 12 percent of black children now live with grandparents. Of these, half the families have both grandparents and most of the rest live only with the grandmother. Beyond them are the millions of grandparents who have assumed important part-time child-rearing responsibilities because of the growth of single-parent households and the number of families where both parents work (Creighton, 1991, 80).

When a teen mother lives with her parents and the grandmother is involved in rearing the grandchild, friction between the teen parent and her mother may develop. The teen is faced with juggling two roles within her family, that of being her mother's daughter and that of being the parent of her own child. This is a difficult situation for both the teen as well as the grandparent. The younger the teen parent, the more likely it is that the grandmother will become the primary caregiver of the child, totally replacing the teen mother as parent and leaving no place for the teen father in his child's life.

Even when the teen mother is an older teen, there is a good chance that this may occur, or that the mother and grandmother (or grandparents) will have conflicts over the child-rearing methods the teen uses. This can lead to teen mothers seeking to leave their parents' home and trying to establish an independent living situation.

Having family support when a teen gives birth provides the best possible opportunity for the mother and the baby's survival by having their security needs met. However, many grandchildren become extremely attached to their grandparents. By the time the adolescent parent develops educationally, socially, and psychologically to the point where she can assume the total responsibilities of parenting, her offspring has grown so attached to the grandparents that he or she may choose to remain with them.

Rhonda had Mark when she was sixteen and lived at home with her mother next to her grandparents. She finished high school, got a job and, after working for several years, was able to move out on her own. By this time, Rhonda had another child and was involved with that child's father. When she decided to move into her own apartment, Mark refused to move with her, though he would visit and spend the night. Mark had become attached to his grandmother and great-grandparents. Their homes were where he had spent the first seven years of his life and he didn't want to leave his familiar surroundings. Mark never lived with his mother after she left her mother's house.

Nita also found it difficult to establish a home with her son once he had begun life with his extended family.

Nita, seventeen, stopped taking birth control pills because they made her ill. She became pregnant only a few weeks after she stopped. At that time, she lived with her maternal grandparents, who had raised her. After she had another child, Nita was able to move out of her grandparents' home and maintain a home on her own. Her first son, age four at the time, refused all attempts to have him live with her. His great-grandmother continued to care for him, but insisted that Nita take her younger son with her immediately because "I'm just too old and tired to try and raise another baby."

The emotional pull is as difficult for the grandmother as it is for the teen.

Frankie was "heartsick" when her eighteen-year-old daughter gave birth to her granddaughter. From the beginning Frankie and her daughter Tina clashed over Tina's child care skills. Frankie felt that Tina treated the baby like she was a doll and Tina felt that her mother should mind her own business and let her raise her child the way she wanted to. Tina would often threaten to move out if her mother did not get off of her "case." Their conflicts continued to grow, and Tina did move out with her baby.

Because she is not in the position to care for herself without help, not to mention a child, she lives from friend to friend, coming back home for short intervals only to leave again when her mother suggests regular feeding or bed times for the baby. Frankie states that, even with Tina's attitude, she will always be there for Tina when she "gets over being angry with her and wants to come home" because her granddaughter needs her. Frankie's ultimate desire is for her granddaughter to have a stable home life.

A DAY IN A CENTER FOR TEEN PARENTS

Very few comprehensive teen parent programs exist in the United States. Those available too often have inadequate funding and are frequently in danger of having their funding cut or lost altogether. Ideally, centers providing social services for pregnant teens and teen parents offer health care services, planned parenthood advice, as well as nutritional and educational counseling. These services meet the essential daily needs of a teen parent, including food for both the teen and the child to begin the day. The teen parent and the child may need public or private transportation to get to their destinations, including the child care facility, the teen parent's educational setting, and perhaps a job after school. Transportation would also pick up the child after school and/or work. Assistance with homework may be provided, as well as assistance with child care after school or work. Daily attention assists the teen parent with personal development and enhancement of parenting skills, thereby learning to cope with being a teen parent (or an expectant teen).

It would be extremely difficult for a center to meet all the service needs every day for even a small number of teen parents. Given the number of teen parents in our society and the cost of funding comprehensive teen parent centers, it is highly unlikely that these services will be pervasively provided for those in need. Most teen parent programs focus on the daily provision of health care services, educational and vocational counseling, planned parenthood services aimed at reducing the likelihood of repeat teen pregnancies, and some emphasis on the development or enhancement of parenting skills.

A TEEN PARENT'S VIEW

"If my family had not been in the position to help me out as much as they did, I don't know what I would have done," reports Augusta, who at sixteen gave birth to her son, Tommy. For Augusta, there were no teen parent centers or programs in the area she lived in at the time she became pregnant and gave birth. She did not know of any program that existed in the city where she lived nor anyone (teen parent) who had received such services.

> I was turned down for services when I applied for food stamps and the Women Infants and Child (W.I.C.). They told me that because of my family's income I didn't qualify. If my family had been really poor, or if I had of wanted to move out on my own, or did not have the family support I did, I guess my son and I would have been really bad off. It was like everybody at these programs wanted to punish me for having had my son, not to help me deal with the situation. I already knew that I had made a mistake, and what I needed was help in making the best of the situation, you know, someone to help me learn what I needed to know to be a good mother, and help me with the needs that me and my baby had. Instead, they just seemed to be down on me, like here is another teen parent, why don't they learn. That attitude is a real turnoff when you really need some help.

Augusta was later informed about some programs offered, which included "First Steps." This particular program provides teen parents (as well as other first-time parents) with emotional support, parenting education, and referral to services that assist the families of newborns in the hospital and in early months of parenting. Programs like "Healthy Families," a program similar to "First Steps," also offer parenting education, support, and help with connecting to other social service programs for new parents. Augusta was asked if she believed programs such as this would have been beneficial to her while she was pregnant and after she delivered her son. Her response was:

> You better believe it! Money wasn't the major need for me, but I sure could have used the other things programs like these offer. I didn't know programs like that existed.

Augusta was one of the fortunate teen parents who had a family able to deal with the financial needs resulting from teen pregnancy and parenting. Even with financial stress, her family members worked together to deal with their problems. However, money is not the only pressing need that teen parents or their family members face. Programs must be made available to teen parents and their families offering comprehensive services to deal with the myriad issues brought about by teen pregnancy and parenthood.

Augusta and her son still live with her family, and Augusta has been offered a four-year basketball scholarship to college.

TRENDS IN SERVICE PROVISION

Trends in service provision for pregnant teens, teen parents, and their families appear to be moving to community-based comprehensive service. Pilot programs such as "Healthy Start" in Hawaii are now being duplicated in other areas. This program includes a social worker who can provide support to a teen mother beginning in the hospital, and assists the teen parent with whatever need she may have if the teen parent is willing to accept the services and responsibility of helping herself. The "First Steps" Program in Louisiana, and the "I Have a Future" Program in Nashville, Tennessee, are such programs that have been very successful by establishing a community-based, holistic approach.

"I Have a Future" is a preventative program that teaches disadvantaged teens the value of sexual abstinence and education. The program seeks to provide disadvantaged teens with reasons for waiting to engage in sex, pursuing a quality education, and waiting to bring a child into the world.

One of the most important aspects of service provision is prevention education. Community-based programs presented to adolescents in a culturally relevant manner are immeasurably valuable because they aim at the prevention of adolescent pregnancy and parenthood.

The trend for service provision appears to be the establishment of a network of community-based, family development centers, combining prevention and intervention strategies with an identified target population. These programs use a holistic approach and service integration/case management strategy to create the optimum environment for building healthy families by concentrating on prevention, self-esteem enhancement, and educational and economic empowerment.

SUMMARY

There are very few advocates for adolescent parenthood or teen pregnancy. The responsibilities of parenthood, from the provision of human consumption needs to the provision of nurturing and emotional support, are difficult, even for mature adults who have prepared for the extremely demanding job of parenting. Adolescents, due to their age and inexperience, are not emotionally prepared to assume the awesome responsibilities of parenthood.

The impact of teen pregnancy and adolescent parenthood on the lives of those involved—the offspring, the parents, the grandparents, and families—in most cases is negative. Teenage pregnancy interrupts normal adolescent development by placing additional stressors on the adolescent and parent (guardian) relationship. Additional financial demands envelop teen families and rob the teen parents' offspring of a productive family environment in which to develop.

When a seed is planted too soon, the harvest is very likely to be weak.

To reduce too-early pregnancy and childbearing, communities must make sure children grow up acquiring the motivation as well as the knowledge and capacity to prevent pregnancy. Children and their families must have access to jobs that provide a decent standard of living, adequate nutrition and housing, and services to meet special needs. Children must have access to an education that provides them with the solid academic skills on which long-term employability, self-esteem, and confidence in the future are based. For youths who are not doing well in school, nonacademic avenues for success are crucial. Children also need links to caring adults who provide positive role models, values, and encouragement. Without such comprehensive supports for children as they grow toward adulthood, there is little chance of achieving a major reduction in too-early childbearing among America's teenagers (CDF, 1995, 85).

The solutions to the problem are as complex as the ramifications. Many facets of society need to come together to reduce the numbers of children having children. A punitive approach, such as the foundational method of addressing the issue, may attract positive attention politically, but does little to address the totality of the situation. Society cannot afford to frame the issue of children having children in simplistic terms. It must look at the complexity of this issue and develop programs and services on that basis.

EXPLORATION QUESTIONS

1. What are the major problems faced by teen parents?
2. What is the usual attitude toward a teen father? What services have traditionally been offered to him?
3. Why does the United States appear to be behind other industrialized nations in dealing with the problem of teen pregnancy and parenthood?
4. What impact, if any, do family life education programs beginning in the early elementary school years have on reducing the numbers of teen parents?
5. What impact does sexual abuse have on teen pregnancy?
6. What are the health issues associated with teen pregnancies?
7. What services are available for teens?
8. What trends are there in the provision of services for teen parents?

ACTIVITIES FOR APPLIED LEARNING

1. Design a Teen Parent Prevention Program. What would be its main components?
2. With parental permission, take a survey of adolescents seeking information on their self-esteem and what role they feel that it would play in their decision to engage in sexual activity.

3. Gather information on the total amount of AFDC payments that were made in your state for the most recent year available. From the total amount of money paid to recipients, how much went to teen parents?
4. What is the birth rate for teens in your city or state? What type of services are available in your city or state for teen parents?

SUGGESTED READING

Children's Defense Fund. *The State of America's Children Yearbook.* Washington, DC: Children's Defense Fund, 1995.

Dash, Leon. *When Children Want Children. The Urban Crisis of Teenage Childbearing.* New York: Morrow, 1989.

Department of Health and Human Services, Public Health Service, Centers for Disease Control and Prevention, and National Center for Health Statistics. *U. S. Report to Congress on Out-of-Wedlock Childbearing.* Maryland: 1995.

Quint, J. C., Musick, J. S., & Ladner, J. A. *Lives of Promise, Lives of Pain. Young Mothers after New Chance.* New York: Manpower Demonstration Research Corporation, 1994.

Simons, J., Finlay, B., & Yang, A. *The Adolescent Young Adult Fact Book.* Children's Defense Fund, 1991.

REFERENCES

Adams, G. & Pittman, K. "Adolescent and Young Adult Fathers: Problems and Solutions." Washington, DC: Children's Defense Fund, 1988.

Ahn, N. "Teenage Childbearing and High School Completion: Accounting for Individual Heterogeneity," *Family Planning Perspectives* 26 (1994), 17–22.

Boyer, D., & Fine, D. "Sexual Abuse as a Factor in Adolescent Pregnancy and Child Maltreatment," *Family Planning Perspectives* 24(4) (1992), 4–11.

Bremner, R. (Ed.), *Children and Youth in America: A Documentary History.* Cambridge, MA: Harvard University Press, 1970.

Carnegie Council on Adolescent Development. *A Matter of Time. Risk and Opportunity in the Nonschool Hours.* New York: Carnegie Corp., 1992.

Children's Defense Fund. "Welfare and Teen Pregnancy: What Do We Know: What Do We Do?" Washington, DC: Children's Defense Fund, 1986.

Children's Defense Fund. "Adolescent Pregnancy: Whose Problem Is It?" Washington, DC: Children's Defense Fund, 1986a.

Children's Defense Fund. "Teen Pregnancy Prevention and Youth Development," *The State of America's Children Yearbook.* Washington, DC: Children's Defense Fund, 1995.

Child Welfare League of America. *Standards for Services for Pregnant Adolescents and Young Parents.* New York: Child Welfare League of America, Inc., 1986.

Chilman, C. S. "Feminist Issues in Teenage Parenting," *Child Welfare* 64(3), (1985), 225–234.

Combs-Orme, T. "Health Effects of Adolescent Pregnancy: Implications for Social Workers," *Families in Society* 76(6), (1993), 344–348.

Creighton, L. L. "Silent Saviors," *U. S. News and World Report,* Vol. 111, (25), (1991), p. 80.

Cutright, P. "Illegitimacy: Myths, Causes and Cures," *Family Planning Perspectives* 3(1) (1971), 26–48.

Duncan, G., & Hoffman, S. "Welfare Benefits, Economic Opportunities, and Out-of-Wedlock Childbearing among Black Teenage Girls," *Demography* 27 (1990), 519–539.

Ellwood, D. T. *Poor Support: Poverty in the American Family.* New York: Basic Books, 1988.

Ellwood, D. T., & Bane, M. J. "The Impact of AFDC on Family Structure and Living Arrangement," *Research in Labor Economics* 7, (1985), 137–207.

Hardy, J., & Zabin, L. S. "Adolescent Pregnancy in an Urban Environment: Issues, Programs, and Evaluation." Washington, DC: Urban Institute Press, 1991.

Hoffman, S., Duncan, G., & Mincy, R. "Marriage and Welfare Use among Young Women: Do Labor Market, Welfare and Neighborhood Factors Account for Declining Rates of Marriage among Black and White Women?" Paper presented at the meeting of Population Association of America, Washington, DC. March 1991.

Hutchens, R., Jakubson, G., and Schwartz, S. "AFDC and the Formation of Subfamilies," *Journal of Human Resources* 24 (1989), 599–628.

Janowitz, B. "The Impact of AFDC on Illegitimate Birth Rates," *Journal of Marriage and the Family* 38(3) (1976), 485–494.

Kadushin, A., & Martin, Judith A. *Child Welfare Services.* New York: Macmillan, 1988.

Lundberg, S., & Plotnick, R. D. "Effects of State Welfare, Abortion and Family Planning Policies on Premarital Childbearing among White Adolescents," *Family Planning Perspectives* 22 (1990a), 246–250.

Makinson, C. "The Health Consequences of Teenage Fertility," *Family Planning Perspectives* 17 (3), (1985), 132–139.

McCormick, M. "The Contribution of Low Birth Weight to Infant Mortality and Childhood Morbidity," *New England Journal of Medicine.* 312 (1985), 82–90.

Moore, K. *Policy Determinants of Teenage Childbearing.* Washington, DC: Urban Institute, 1980.

Moore, K. A. *A State by State Look at Teenage Childbearing in the U. S.* Flint, MI: Charles Stewart Mott Foundation, 1991.

Moore, K. A., & Caldwell, S. B. *Out of Wedlock Pregnancy and Childbearing.* Washington, DC: Urban Institute Press, 1976.

Moore, K., Snyder, M. A., & Dans Glei, M. A. "Facts at a Glance." Washington, DC: National Center for Health Statistics, 1995.

National Center for Health Statistics, *Advance Report of Final Fatality Statistics, 1991. Monthly Vital Statistics Report,* 42(3) Hyarrsville, MD: Public Health Service, 1993.

Plotnick, R. D. "The Effect of Social Policies on Teenage Pregnancy and Childbearing," *Families in Society,* 74(6) (1993), 325–326.

Prothrow–Stith, D. with Weissman, M. *Deadly Consequences. How Violence Is Destroying Our Teenage Population and a Plan to Begin Solving the Problem.* New York: HarperCollins, 1991.

South, S. J., & Lloyd, K. M. "March Markets and Nonmarital Fertility in the United States," *Demography* 29 (1992), 247–264.

12

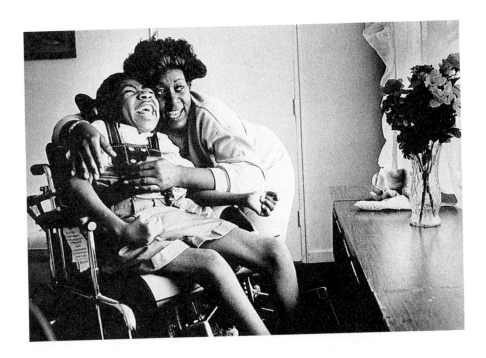

CHILDREN IN FAMILY FOSTER CARE

Debra was six when her father abandoned the family. Even at that age, Debra knew that her father sold drugs and that he had had to leave before the police found him. Her mother, an addict, was usually too strung out to care for her daughter. A younger child had died several years earlier and it was only because the family fled that Debra had not been removed by Child Protective Services (CPS). Mother and daughter drifted from place to place until they found themselves in the home of a man her mother knew. Debra begged to go to school and finally they agreed to send her. But the school recognized that the child was ill-kept and poorly fed. They became concerned that she was overtired and that she had lice. The school's report to the CPS initiated an investigation and resulted in Debra's removal from her home. At six-and-a-half, Debra found herself in a new home—a foster home—with three new siblings and a mother and father who appeared to care about her. While she missed her mother, it was kind of nice to be warm in her own bed instead of wondering where they would sleep or where the next meal would come from.

Child welfare advocates attest to the fact that the best environment for a child, especially a young one, who cannot be maintained in his/her own home, is another family setting. Although some children cannot tolerate a family atmosphere once their own has failed them, many do well in family foster care.

HISTORY OF FAMILY FOSTER CARE

EARLY BEGINNINGS

To better understand foster care today, we need to look at the origins of the foster care system. From ancient times, it was expected that children would be attached to and part of a family. Without a family, children became a problem to society. If these children could not be taken in by relatives, another solution had to be found. While indenture was a popular method of providing for children, it was not always a solution, especially with very young children who were not of an age to work. Institutions such as almshouses were often the solution for poor children, much to the detriment of their health and safety.

In the early 1800s Charles Loring Brace became concerned about the children abandoned in institutions and on the streets of New York. In 1853, he and a group of New York City clergymen founded the New York Children's Aid Society, designed to advocate for and solve the problem of dependent children. Brace initiated a program of transporting children from the city to farm families in the middle United States. His plan involved sending small groups of children—forty to one hundred per trip—by train accompanied by "agents" (nurses and social workers) to preselected spots in the rural Midwest. These children, who soon became known as "train orphans," would be greeted at the train station by families interested in caring for them. Later, churches became involved and would preselect families before the trains arrived. This practice, called "placing out," lasted well into the 1920s (Cook, 1995; Hacsi, 1995; Downs et al., 1996).

Other agencies besides Brace's adopted the practice of placing out. One woman, abandoned at the New York Foundling's Hospital in the early 1920s, recounts her experience as part of an orphan train.

> By the time I rode the train out to Nebraska, in 1923, you knew where you were going to. I was 22 months old and wore a sign with my birth name on it and the name of the family who expected me. Years earlier, my parents told me later, children used to be dropped off at stations and lined up for people to pick up which one they wanted.

A church had arranged the placement of the following child:

> My Mother and Father told me that a priest had announced in church some months before that an orphan train was coming. If anyone wanted a child, they were to tell the priest. My folks had lost six of their own children and had a boy of 19. To them, a girl sounded ideal. We arrived all dressed in white. I later learned that the clothes were made of bed sheets. A nurse handed me to my new parents and that was that.

For some children, the experience was a positive one. Some were adopted while others remained in an early form of foster care. From 1853 to 1929 there were 31,081 children placed in families through the orphan trains (Thurston, 1930, 121).

Support for the concept of foster care became stronger in the 1890s when Homer Folks, also of New York City, extolled the virtues of and importance of family life for children. It was Charles Britwell of the Children's Aid Society of Boston who instituted the concept of supervised boarding homes instead of orphan asylums. These homes were initially developed with the idea of rescuing "good" children from "bad" parents. Initially it took no more than a willingness to do so for parents to foster children. Not until the 1930s were foster parents assessed for their suitability for caring for children (Steinhauer, 1991).

Early foster homes did not expect payment for the children they housed. Agencies advocating foster care argued that payment for foster care might cause them to take children for money rather than goodwill. Later, however, in the early 1900s, the practice of paying foster parents evolved. It wasn't until this century that the government became involved in regulating and administering the foster care system (Hacsi, 1995).

Over the years, foster care became, increasingly, a more acceptable method of caring for children whose parents were unable to do so. Voluntary placement by parents, who recognized their inabilities or who sought a place for their children while they underwent a period of treatment or looking for employment or housing, became more widely practiced. Infants awaiting adoption were often placed in foster homes pending their placement.

FOSTER CARE IN RECENT YEARS

After World War II, the complexion of foster care changed considerably. With the advent of more resources within the community, families who had placed their children while they recovered from illness, received treatments, or solved financial problems were less dependent on foster care. Increasingly newborn infants were placed in adoptive homes directly from the hospital. With the advent of the Aid to Families with Dependent Children (AFDC) program, impoverished families who might have previously had to place children in asylums or homes were able to maintain them at home. By the 1950s more of the children not residing in their own homes were in foster care rather than institutions. These figures increased until the late 1960s, when three times as many children in care were in foster homes. Subsequent amendments to the Social Security Act made more federal monies available to support the practice of foster care (Hacsi, 1995).

By the 1970s the trend in child welfare became *permanency planning*. Permanency planning is the

> *systematic process of carrying out, within a limited period, a set of goal-directed activities designed to help children and youths live in families that offer continuity of relationships with nurturing parents or caretakers, and the opportunity to offer lifetime relationships (Maluccio and Fein, 1983, 197).*

The move toward permanency planning was the result of several studies that found that children placed in foster care remained there, in virtual limbo, for years. For example, Harvey was placed in a foster home shortly after his birth by a single mother. Her original intent was to release him for adoption. When the mother's social worker left before the adoption release was signed and was not immediately replaced, the mother assumed her child was cared for and went on with her life. When a new worker was assigned, he had great difficulty finding the mother and obtaining a release. By the time Harvey was finally free for adoption, he was over two years old. He was also suffering in his overcrowded foster home from lack of stimulation. Therefore what had been an alert, healthy baby at birth was now a lethargic, withdrawn two-year-old who was suspected of being mentally retarded. Thus Harvey was placed as a special needs child, further delaying his adoption process. It was not until concerned adoptive parents had him evaluated, after several months of stimulation in their home, that anyone realized that Harvey's only problem was that he had been a victim of an inefficient system that had operated too slowly.

With the emphasis on permanency planning, the mandate of child welfare agencies was to insure that a child who could not remain at home was placed with a permanent family as soon as possible. But continued research brought attention to the effect that separation had on children. The Indian Child Welfare Act in 1978 and Adoption Assistance and Child Welfare Act of 1980 both sought to place emphasis first on the preservation of the child's biological family. *Family preservation* became the new phrase in the practice of child welfare. Now efforts were made to save the family unit with a variety of services and resources so that the children would not be subjected to the pain of separation (Downs et al., 1996).

It soon became obvious that, with the advent of such problems as drug addiction, homelessness, and HIV/AIDS, it was not always possible to save the original family unit. By the 1990s, the numbers of children placed in foster care began to increase again. Terpstra (personal communication as cited in Downs et al., 1996) estimated that, in 1995, the number of children in out-of-home care was about 500,000, with 80 percent in foster care and 20 percent in residential settings.

Today, the emphasis is on family continuity or attempting to strengthen or preserve the family unit while recognizing that foster care may be a necessary alternative. Increasingly there has also been an effort to assess the availability of kinship care or the placing of children with the relatives of their natural parents. This practice may also serve to acknowledge and preserve important cultural connections for the children. Downs, Costin, and McFadden (1996) describe family continuity well when they say that this new trend

> integrates principles of family preservation into all aspects of child welfare by underscoring the necessity for continuing important relationships across the life span and acknowledging that children need to be embedded in family and community networks of caring. The evolution of services for children and families in the twentieth century has culminated in a wide-angle family focus that increases for children the possibility of family connection throughout the life course and has increased the engagement of all formal services with families and communities (267).

Today, we must see foster care as only one option in the effort to protect the best interests of the children in our society.

THE NATURE OF FOSTER CARE TODAY

The intent of foster care is to offer children care within a family environment when their own homes are temporarily unable to do so. Foster care is meant to provide the following:

- Temporary emergency care of a child
- Relief for a parent when he or she cannot manage stress
- Time for a parent to solve problems (e.g., housing, addiction, illness)
- A different home experience or protection for a child (in case of abuse, neglect, or extreme instability)
- Care until institutional treatment is available
- Care until release for adoption or adoption is approved

The National Commission on Family Foster Care (NCFFC) suggests that family foster care must fulfill five critical tasks:

1. *Protecting and nurturing infants, children and youth;*
2. *Ameliorating developmental delays and meeting social, emotional, and medical needs resulting from physical abuse, sexual abuse, neglect, maltreatment, exposure to alcohol and other drugs, and HIV infection;*
3. *Enhancing positive self-esteem, family relationships, and cultural and ethnic identity;*
4. *Developing and implementing a plan for permanence; and*
5. *Educating and socializing children and youth toward successful transitions to young adult life, relationships, and responsibilities (NCFFC, 1991, 36).*

Foster care may be voluntary or at the request of the parent. This written agreement between the parent and the agency may be terminated on either's request. In most instances, however, foster care is mandated by the situation involved, whether it be the parent's abuse or neglect of children or another type of inability to care for them.

TYPES OF FOSTER HOMES

There are several types of foster homes, designated by their various functions: crisis or emergency foster homes, family boarding homes, small group homes, and specialized foster homes. Some states use homes interchangeably while others clearly define the role of the home for one particular service.

The *crisis home* is designed to accept children at any time—day or night—and to keep them for a limited amount of time while other arrangements are being made. For example, children who have been abandoned may be placed in a home temporarily while their parents are found. Or parents who must undergo short-term medical or rehabilitation treatment may require an emergency home for their children. In some situations, the risk of severe abuse necessitates that children be placed on a short-term basis until protective services workers can diffuse the situation. Foster parents who operate emergency homes may require specialized skills. Sometimes this short respite care is used for diagnostic purposes, and it is important that foster parents have a keen awareness of crisis intervention skills. Not all foster parents are trained in these skills, however, and it may actually make their jobs more difficult. Crisis homes, like all foster homes, are paid for the care of children. Sometimes the rate reflects their crisis status or the specialized training some foster parents have received. In other states these foster parents are paid at the same rate as long-term boarding homes.

Family boarding homes are committed to taking children for longer periods, months or even years. Foster parents are expected to work as part of the therapeutic team overseeing the needs of the children in their care. For this, they are usually paid according to the numbers and ages of the children in their care. The amount differs from state to state. In addition, children usually receive a clothing allowance and receive some kind of medical benefits such as Medicaid. A *small group home* is a family that takes small groups of children—often siblings or adolescents. The home may be administered like a boarding home or a specialized foster home.

An emerging concept in the area of foster care is the *specialized foster home*. Such homes are set up to deal specifically with certain populations of children or for one or two particular children. For example, some foster parents have skills in dealing with adolescents, or with sexually abused children, or with children who are HIV-positive. As a specialized home, these parents take only these types of children. The number of children in the home usually depends on the need as well as the particular population. Theoretically, these specialized foster parents are better trained, receive more support, and are better paid than the average foster home.

The term *specialized* can also refer to foster parents who are screened by the placement agency and have been approved for a specific child or children. For example, if an adolescent runs away to the home of a friend, the friend's parents might be screened by the agency involved in the case as potential foster parents for this child. Or a teacher who befriends a child who must be placed outside of his/her home might request approval as a special foster home.

Kinship care is another type of fostering arrangement that reflects the increasing awareness that the trauma of placement may be minimized if children can be placed with extended family members. An exploratory study of the kinship homes in New York City found that 10 percent were African American and 70 percent were white protestant. In the majority of these homes (66 percent) the parents had less than a high school education, were an average age of fifty-four years old, and 45 percent had annual incomes of less than $5,000 (Gebel, 1996, 5). In addition to continuity, kinship placements offer children an opportunity to remain within their own cultural/ethnic group. These homes are also less likely than nonrelated placements to be disrupted (Berrick, Barth, and Needell, 1993). These homes are also more likely to keep the children until they reach majority. An estimated 88 percent of children in kinship care left to live on their own compared with 1 percent who returned to their parents and 10 percent who were placed for adoption, contrasted with 42 percent of the children in nonrelated homes who left for independent living, 14 percent who returned to their parents, and 38 percent who were placed in adoptive homes (NCFFC, 1991).

Although kinship care has become increasingly popular, some child advocates are concerned that the quality of care in these untrained homes be maintained. Answering these concerns, the Child Welfare League Kinship Care Policy and Practice Committee (CWLA, 1994) recommended that several factors be considered in the assessment of such homes:

1. *The nature and quality of the relationship between the child and the relative;*
2. *The ability and the desire of the kinship parent to protect the child from further abuse and maltreatment;*
3. *The safety of the kinship home and the ability of the kin to provide a nurturing environment for the child;*
4. *The willingness of the kinship family to accept the child into the home;*

5. *The ability of the kinship parent to meet the developmental needs of the child;*
6. *The nature and quality of the relationship between the birth parent and the relative, including the birth parent's preference about placement of the child with kin;*
7. *Any family dynamics in the kinship home related to the abuse or neglect of the child;*
8. *The presence of alcohol or other drug involvement in the kinship home (44–45).*

Foster homes are funded in a variety of ways. The majority of foster homes are state- or county-funded, either directly or through contracts. Most state or county protective services agencies maintain a number of foster homes that they study, approve, pay, and supervise. In other instances, privately funded agencies approve foster homes that they agree to let state agencies use for a contracted fee.

REASONS WHY CHILDREN COME INTO FOSTER CARE

Today, most of the children who come into foster care have parents who are not able to care for them for one reason or another. At one time, however, it was not unusual for children to be placed when *their parents had died.* One adult who grew up in a foster home remembers:

My father died when I was two. When my mother died three years later, my three brothers and I ended up in a foster home. I always wondered why no relatives came forward to take us, but no one did. We never were placed for adoption. We just all grew up there.

In other instances, one parent died and the other felt too overwhelmed to take on the role of parenting. One former foster child has this story to tell:

We were very, very poor. My mother, who was very small, was told not to have more children after her first five. She had a bad heart. But she continued to have them feeling that it was her duty as a good Catholic. She had five more, but during the birth of the last one, she had a heart attack. My father was left with ten children. He became an alcoholic and gave us all into foster care, but he would never release us, so we just grew up in foster homes.

Today, more effort would be expended to help children find relatives who could assume their care.

A large number of children come into care because *they are abused or neglected.*

My father was a violent, cruel man when he lost his temper. I didn't suffer from the physical abuse my brothers did. Instead he sexually abused me until we were taken from our home and placed in foster care.

Chapter 9 outlines in depth how children are placed in foster homes as a result of abuse and neglect. Usually foster care serves as a way to protect them from continued abuse. In some instances, they will return to their parents. In others, they will be released for and placed for adoption. Children who come into care as a result of maltreatment often exhibit behavior that is reactive to their abuse. Increasingly, foster parents are trained to recognize and help them with a variety of reactions and disturbances. Sometimes the abuse cannot be clearly pinpointed but it becomes obvious that the child's home is dysfunctional.

I saw my mother really torn between two men. She'd married one but she still loved her ex-husband. She used to flit back and forth between them. I was fifteen and desperate for stability. I had a boyfriend and was an honor student in school. But when we began all these moves, sometimes six times a month, my school work began to suffer. If my school records were anywhere, they were in the mail. I wanted to run away. I thought of suicide. I finally attempted it and the school called Protective Services. They knew I was really unhappy with all the moves. Because my mother was into drugs and alcohol, they put me in a foster home. It was really better. I had stability and I got to finish school.

Increasingly families are being seen with histories of *domestic violence.* When a parent is being battered the children often suffer as well. While agencies first attempt to work with the family to stop the violence, it is often impossible. If the battered parent will not leave, the children are sometimes removed and placed in foster care to protect them.

Substance abuse is a phenomenon that destroys many families today. In a recent study of African American children in foster care, about 36 percent were there as a result of substance abuse by a parent (National Black Child Development Institute, 1989, 36). Children of substance-abusing parents may come into care voluntarily or through court mandate. Some parents recognize their need for drug rehabilitation and request voluntary foster care while in a program, or children may be addicted to drugs and automatically taken into care as a result. For many other families, substance abuse results in their maltreatment of their children. Child welfare systems are reporting an increase of 50 to 80 percent in the number of substance-abusing (mostly drugs) parents on social workers' caseloads (Solomon, 1990, 24). Many of these children will end up being placed in foster homes.

Physical and mental illnesses are often a factor in the families of children who come into foster care. Parents who find themselves facing operations and who have no other resources may request foster care.

Doreen discovered that she had uterine cancer, but that the prognosis was good if she could be operated on immediately. She had no family in the area and no friends able to care for her daughter. She requested that her daughter be placed in foster care while she had her operation and got back on her feet.

Such a request would be considered carefully. Being placed in the home of strangers could compound a young child's trauma in the face of a parent's illness. Because one of a child's most profound fears is abandonment, all other avenues, other than placement, must be explored. In Doreen's case, foster care was the only alternative, but sensitive preparation of the children enabled the plan to work.

Throughout the years, mental illness has had a more significant impact on the need to place children in foster homes than physical illness. In her study of 277 former foster children in New York City, Festinger (1983) found that 20 percent of her respondents had been placed in care due to the mental illness of their caretakers, while only 8 percent were placed due to physical illness (41).

The 1989 study of African American children reported that 14 percent of these children were placed in foster care due to mental illness while only 4 percent were in foster care as a result of physical illness (NBCDI, 1989, 36). While mentally ill parents still need placement for their children during periods of acute crisis, there have been changes in the provision of long-term mental health services that have had an impact on how long children remain in care. Prior to the 1970s the chronically mentally ill were treated in institutionalized settings. Today, with the implementation of community-based treatment, whereby people live in the community and are seen on an outpatient basis with counseling and support, more mentally ill parents care for their own children.

Today, some children are given up for foster care or adoption *due to their own physical or mental problems.* Increasingly children who are HIV-positive are coming into foster care. Their parents, usually with AIDS themselves, are either unable to care for them or feel that they would have a better chance in placement. Coping with children with particular disabilities, such as cerebral palsy, mental retardation, brain damage, Attention Deficit Disorder, or Autism, may be beyond the skills of some parents. As a result they may be placed in foster care.

Mothers or single fathers who are incarcerated may also have a right to have their children in foster care. Usually, other relatives are sought who can assume this responsibility, but if no one is available, foster care may be the answer.

Finally foster care may be an *interim arrangement* while a child awaits an adoptive home or placement in a residential setting. Parents wanting to give up their children for adoption may need either a period to decide if this is the right course or an agency may need time to find the appropriate home. By the same token, children who are slated to be placed in a residence may find that there are no beds open at a given time, or that the agency placing them needs time to find the appropriate setting. In these situations, a child may be placed in foster care for days, weeks, or even months.

FOSTER PARENTS

Foster parenting is not the relatively uncomplicated task that it once was. Today, it is expected that foster parents will be part of the therapeutic team involved in children's lives. This task requires new responsibilities and brings with it many stressors. Agencies differ in their recruitment, training, and involvement of foster parents, but some standards can be found throughout the field.

RECRUITMENT

Foster parents are recruited to their job in a variety of ways. Public service announcements, newspaper ads, television spots, and personal contacts represent some methods. Which means are most effective is a much-debated question.

A Minnesota study found that the media was an extremely effective tool for recruiting. Through a series of public service announcements and newspaper ads, the agency studied received more foster parent applicants than by the use of any other method. Television public service announcements seemed to yield an especially high number of much-needed African American applicants (Moore et al., 1988). One problem with media recruitment is that many of the applicants who respond may not actually have the necessary qualities to become foster parents. One recruiter remarked:

> The media often appeals to the soft-hearted, and a soft heart doesn't help one through the real world of foster parenting. Foster parents must mix caring for kids with realistic expectations of kids who are often reacting to tough lives. They must also refine their parenting skills beyond those expected of most parents.

Critics of the Minnesota method argued that the agency wasted valuable time screening out inappropriate homes. Yet, the results of the study did prove that the number of acceptable foster homes increased significantly (Moore et al., 1988).

New York City's Salvation Army Social Services (SASSC) found what they felt was an even more effective way of recruiting than the use of the media (Smith and Gutheil, 1988). The agency used trained foster parents to recruit others. Initially these recruiters began in their own neighborhoods. Each recruiter was helped to develop a unique plan designed for their own environment. Agency social workers provided support, coordination, and supervision. As an additional incentive, the foster parent recruiters were paid $250 for their first week of work and an additional $100 for each family they recruited thereafter. Built into the process was the agency's encouragement of the foster parent recruiter's evaluation of agency policy. For example, if applicants dropped out of the process of being studied because of some restrictive agency policy, the recruiter was asked to report it. The agency then tried to remedy this situation. Throughout the process of application and selection to become foster parents, these recruits were followed closely by agency social workers. The results were positive. Foster care beds at SASSC increased by 49 percent and both recruiters and newly approved foster parents felt that the personal touch enhanced the ability for the foster parents to care for children.

Terpstra (1990), Foster Care Specialist for the Bureau for Children, commented regarding recruitment:

> *In the long haul, the most effective recruitment is foster parents who are satisfied with agency services. This is often apart from any specific recruitment effort: word of mouth reports tend to be viewed as most credible.*

Why do people want to become foster parents? Reasons vary from the altruistic motivation of identifying with unhappy children and wanting to provide a community service, to the more individual motivations of wanting to continue to parent or wanting a playmate for their own children. Increasingly, agencies are encouraging potential foster parents to assess their own motivations and determine how realistic they are.

In predicting the success of parents' ability to provide foster care, several authors (Fine, 1993; Walsh and Walsh, 1990) found that successful foster parents had a sincere liking for children, a strong sense of themselves and their own abilities, and were able to tolerate a variety of behaviors from children that some other homes might find difficult to put up with.

The shortage of foster homes, particularly for specific ethnic groups, necessitates that agencies look closer at recruiting foster homes from the children's own families or informal networks, referred to earlier as kinship care. There has in the past been some resistance to the extensive use of kinship care for several reasons. First, if natural parents abused or neglected a child, their relatives may also behave in similar ways. Yet, what drives one individual to abuse may not affect his kin in the same manner. A second issue is that children's relatives might be less easy to locate, thus requiring more social worker energy for recruitment. Yet using relatives can be more beneficial for the child.

A third issue that tended, in the past, to make agencies less likely to use informal support systems is the fact that parents considered for a particular child are less likely to see themselves as working for an agency. They are less aware of child welfare policies and may seem less interested in cooperating with agencies in the interest of the child. These same characteristics make the home a more natural atmosphere for the child, but may present difficulties for social workers who expect to have total cooperation from the foster parents (Lewis and Fraser, 1987).

There are additional advantages to kinship care. While unrelated foster homes have a median duration for one child of 6.5 months, kinship homes tend to last (median) 10.5 months. Certainly, homes studied for specific children have a greater commitment to those children perhaps lessening the feelings of isolation described by many former foster children. It may be likely that these homes might also maintain the tie more closely with natural parents (Lewis and Fraser, 1987).

The trade-off for the advantages of homes already known to the child is more ingenuity on the part of the foster care agency. Not only must the child's informal networks be explored for potential homes, but these parents must be studied, trained, and supervised with the understanding that they may only be foster homes for a single child rather than the many children taken by professional foster homes. Yet the result—the child's well-being—would seem worth the effort. In this time of scarcity of foster homes, this approach is also a way of increasing foster care resources (Terpstra, 1990).

HOME STUDY AND TRAINING

Once recruited, potential foster parents undergo a lengthy process of screening, selection, and training known as a *homestudy.* At one time, this homestudy was an individual affair between the foster parents and the social worker, known as a homefinder or family resource specialist. Now, however, most agencies favor a group approach. One reason for this is that the current emphasis is on foster parents as part of a team that strives to insure that the child is provided with the best plan possible. The *Blueprint for Fostering Infants, Children, and Youths in the Nineties* (National Commission on Family Foster Care, 1991) was the Child Welfare League of America's effort to outline the new role of foster parents as team members. With this new emphasis came revised training for potential foster parents. These trainings are based on a variety of models.

The *Model Approach to Partnerships in Parenting* (MAPP) has been adopted in numerous states and combines screening with intensive training for future foster parents. One Massachusetts family resource worker described their program:

> *Our training is completed in ten sessions. We explain to our group participants at the onset that foster parents need three things: certain information, attitudes, and skills that will enable them to be good at their job. Some people develop the attitudes and skills as they go through life and bring them to the group. Other people will learn them through the ten weeks of the group process. We, as facilitators, reserve the right to discuss with the applicants at the end of training whether we feel that they have the information, attitudes, and skills that our agency has found are needed by foster parents.*

Similar curricula are used by other states or agencies as part of their training efforts. The Child Welfare League of America's Foster Pride/Adopt Pride uses a model of training which addresses both foster and adoptive applicants. Colorado State University School of Social Work has developed a program called Fostering Families which brings foster families together with social workers to explore a variety of topics vital to foster parenting effectively. The program developed at Eastern Michigan University includes seventeen course outlines touching on such issues as problematic behavior in foster children, working with natural parents, and team work (Downs et al., 1996).

Whatever model the agency uses, through a combination of providing information, role-play, exercises, and discussion, it encourages applicants to explore their attitudes toward discipline, natural parents, loss and separation, how their own children might react to sharing their parents, the behaviors exhibited by children in foster care, and a variety of other topics relevant to parenting a foster child successfully. Participants also discuss feelings about their own upbringing, and how their pasts, or realizations about their pasts, help or hinder them in their role as parents. The social workers visit the family in their homes to determine how their thinking has evolved.

Not all applicants who begin the training finish. Some learn that foster parenting is not what they had hoped for. Others drop out for other reasons. As one woman put it:

I dropped out of the homestudy because I learned that I had a great deal of emotional housecleaning to do before I could be comfortable parenting someone else's kids. When I applied to be a foster parent I imagined saving poor little kids from abusing parents. Now I realize that part of a foster parent's job is to work with those same parents and I am not sure I could do that.

In addition to being studied, trained, and selected, foster parents must be licensed. Many states include the licensing process as a part of the homestudy. Other states have an independent process. Basically, a license will mean that the family and their home have passed specific requirements such as fire safety, health safety, cleanliness, and so forth. Potential foster parents are expected to have a physical exam and also to undergo a criminal records check. It is certainly possible for a family to meet licensing criteria, but not be approved by a homefinder because of their emotional instability or lack of readiness. The reverse is also possible.

Although the above is the typical plan for recruiting, screening, and training foster parents, agencies recognize the need for flexibility given the diverse cultural differences in the children in foster care today and the families who apply to take them in as foster children. The importance of training workers to understand ethnic and cultural variations so as not to fit families into a particular mindset, cannot be understated.

Once foster parents have been approved to take children, their file is kept until a child needs such a home. The amount of matching done between child needs and foster parent characteristics differs from state to state, but studies show that the more these factors are taken into consideration, the more successful the placement. Given the shortage of foster homes, however, foster parents are often asked to take children who do not fit the age-range or type of child they feel equipped to handle. This may not be beneficial for the child or the foster parents.

PLACEMENT AND FOLLOW-UP

When a child needs a particular type of foster home, the foster family is approached about taking him or her. The placement process can take as much as a week but more likely happens very quickly.

> *"When I go into court on a particular abuse case," said one social worker, "I know that I may need to place the child immediately after the hearing. I line up a home that will be ready to take the child. It doesn't give the foster family much time to prepare but that is the way the system works."*

Once children are in foster placement, they are visited on a regular basis by an agency social worker to provide support and monitor the placement. Foster families provide ongoing care and may also be responsible for such extras as transportation to medical appointments, therapy visits, or even visits with the child's parents. If parents are allowed to visit in the foster home, the foster parents may also supervise these arrangements. Foster families are also included in periodic case conferences to assess the progress of the child and the family. For these services, they are paid a small foster care allowance and often a sum for clothing for the children in their care.

Although it is the foster mother who usually shoulders the major part of the responsibility for caretaking and dealing with the social service agency, the role of the foster father cannot be underestimated. The support he provides his wife can make a real difference in the success of the care. If foster children are truly to be part of the family, their involvement with the foster father is equally as important as their involvement with the mother.

The inclusion of foster parents on the therapeutic team is a continually evolving concept. While at one time foster parents were seen as mere caregivers, they are now expected to be part of the child's treatment. Some agencies, like the Casey Foundation (see Walsh and Walsh, 1990), use highly trained foster parents for intense therapeutic services. Other agencies provide ongoing training and even special certification for foster parents. Certified foster parents receive higher rates of payment for their services and describe feeling more competent and able to handle the problems presented by their charges (Dawson, 1989).

STRESSES OF BEING A FOSTER PARENT

Foster parenting comes with many stressors. First and foremost is the fact that foster care is designed to be temporary. Thus, foster parents are asked to love children in their care but then *be ready to let them go.* How well they have been able to handle the losses in their own lives may determine how successful they are at letting go and preparing their foster children for return home or adoptive placement.

Foster parents are also asked to *handle a variety of behaviors* exhibited by the children who come into their care. These children may be withdrawn, destructive, abuse others, set fires, or act out in a variety of ways. Foster parents are expected to consider the underlying causes as opposed to just reacting to the behavior. In the crunch of everyday activities, this may not always be easy (Kadushin and Martin, 1988).

It may be a challenge for the foster parents to *provide foster care while still considering the needs of their own family members.* The foster parents' own children may not always understand the needs of the children in care. Or they may mimic behaviors that their parents do not appreciate. Foster couples find that they need to pay careful attention to their own relationships lest the stresses of having foster children alienate them from one another. Dedicated foster parents tell us that none of these tasks are easy and that they must be constantly aware of the dynamics of their own families.

It is not easy to have one's parenting techniques under constant scrutiny. Providing care for someone else's child under agency supervision may make people *feel that they are constantly under observation.* In addition, each social worker has his/her own method of supervision and foster parents sometimes feel that they cannot please anyone. More experienced foster parents learn to develop a personal style that will help them weather the *turnover of social work staff.*

In addition to agency scrutiny, foster parents may feel that they are being criticized by the natural parents. But this too must be understood. As one foster mother commented:

> It must not be an easy thing to have your children taken away from you. It's like a judgment that says "you weren't a good enough parent." So, if you see someone else taking care of your children, it is just human nature to want to find fault with them. I try to understand how hurt these parents must feel and it helps when I feel criticized by them.

Visits by natural parents may not always be easy on foster parents. Not only can foster parents feel criticized, but they may have to deal with birth parents who abuse alcohol or drugs. Or the visit by a natural parent may send the foster child into crisis. Foster mothers often describe the conflict felt by foster children about separation from their parents and the reactions exhibited by children after each visit. Once again, foster parents are expected to understand these problems and deal effectively with natural parents (Kadushin and Martin, 1988).

FOSTER PARENTS AS PART OF THE TEAM

With the number of profoundly disturbed children coming into foster care, more and more is expected of foster parents. Many states require foster parents to seek out or participate in ongoing training. Foster parents are often asked to observe, monitor, and record the behavior of the children in their care. They are asked to participate in foster care reviews not only as advocates for their foster children, but also as professionals with vital pieces of information to contribute to an overall assessment of the child(ren).

It is not unusual for foster parents to be asked to help natural parents by providing role models or aiding them in the understanding of their children or such parenting skills as behavior management, discipline, and the management of challenging health care issues.

Demetrius was a five-year-old child whose medical problems necessitated that he have a colostomy. The bag that collected his urine had to be changed regularly and the medical incision cleaned properly. Although well meaning, Demetrius's mother had failed to complete these procedures properly. In fact she was totally overwhelmed by the magnitude of his care. Feeling unable to cope after a drinking binge, she left her child with a neighbor and disappeared. After a week, she missed him and felt very guilty for having abandoned him. She called the neighbor who told her that she had had no idea how to care for the child's medical needs and had taken him to the hospital explaining that his mother had abandoned him. The hospital called CPS and Demetrius was placed in a foster home with a foster mother who was a nurse.

After talking with the boy's mother, CPS became convinced that she could care for her child if educated to do so. Thus, for the next three months the mother visited the foster home and received intensive training from the foster mother on how to care for Demetrius.

In this situation, it was the skill of the foster mother that provided the needed therapeutic intervention that allowed Demetrius to eventually return home.

As foster parents become more involved as members of the therapeutic team, there is more pressure on agencies to change the attitudes that formerly saw these parents as merely caretakers of children. There is also an increased emphasis on more intensive training opportunities.

BIRTH PARENTS WITH CHILDREN IN FOSTER CARE

The characteristics of parents whose children are in foster care are included in various chapters throughout this text. When we are caught up in protecting children form maltreatment and improper care, it is not always easy to recognize the impact that placement has on the birth parents.

ATTITUDES AND REACTIONS

Our society communicates the message that anyone can parent. Having children is something that most people expect to be able to do. There are no directions provided for the important role of parent, and unless individuals have had role models in their own parents, they may have no concept of what parenting is all about. Yet, this lack of knowledge can remain a carefully hidden secret until society, in the guise of CPS, intervenes and removes the children because they are being inadequately parented. Or, in some cases, parents are forced to place their children because life circumstances interfere with their ability to parent. Imagine the resentment, no matter how aware you may be of your inabilities, that your children should require the care of someone else, often a stranger. Parents often go through a variety of feelings. The first may be *shock.*

> When the loss of your child first hits you, it is like going into shock. You may cry, feel shaky, and find it hard to hear what people are saying to you. You can't think of anything except the child who has been placed… This shock usually lasts from a few days to a few weeks. Other people may try to be comforting and kind to you, but you feel distant and "outside" the rest of the world (Rutter, 1989, 17).

While some may protest that it should be obvious to some parents why they lost their children, the feelings are not diminished.

> When my kids were taken away, I just couldn't believe it. I knew I had been drinking a lot and I know I left them alone overnight, but I still loved them. It's just that no one ever told me that it would be so tough to take care of kids! As I sat in that apartment after they were gone, I just stared at the walls. I kept thinking I heard them. No, it wasn't them— just the unbearable silence. I hated myself then. I hated the drinking and drugging. I hated everything. But I missed my kids!

When parents come out of the shock they may feel *resentful and angry.* These feelings are often masks for their *feelings of failure* because they have not been able to do what, it seems to them, every other parent in the world does—care for their children. This may lead to *feelings of inadequacy* that may manifest themselves in a variety of ways (Rutter, 1989; Plumer, 1992). The manner in which parents demonstrate these feelings of inadequacy may differ. Some parents eat more, drink or drug more, or act out in other ways.

> I yelled at my social worker and told her to get out of my house. I called my kid's foster mother and told her off. I even screamed at my kids that I never wanted to see them again. And then I cried and cried. What was wrong with me anyway? I should be pleasing everyone just to get my kids back. Instead I was alienating them all!

There may also be cultural reasons for how they react. For example, some cultures become extremely hostile and threatening. Still others protest with silence.

> Poppi was a thirty-four-year-old, African American mother whose children were removed after she neglected them. Although she sincerely loved her children her drinking had created problems for her in caring for them. When they were removed she was very angry and depressed. The social workers told her that there were numerous things she had to do to have them returned. Feeling that she could never please what she referred to as "them nigger hatin' child stealers," Poppi refused to respond to phone calls or attempts on the part of CPS workers to visit her. Unfortunately, this was interpreted by the workers as this mother's lack of interest in her children.

Many natural parents get stuck in the anger stage. It is easier to be angry than to acknowledge the hurt. Unfortunately, some social workers react to the angry behavior rather than recognizing the feeling beneath it. Parental rights may actually be terminated if the parents cannot move beyond the anger stage and desire to strike out long enough to cooperate with the agency. It is often forgotten that people who lose their children due to their inability to effectively parent have usually faced failure, betrayal, and disappointment throughout their lives. The coping patterns they have developed may not seem appropriate, but for some the anger or withdrawal has enabled them to survive.

Parents who give up their anger often go into *despair* (Rutter, 1989). They become depressed and unmotivated. Nothing seems worth doing. For some there may also be *feelings of relief* that there are no children at home to force them to do daily tasks. Some parents reach out to social workers or foster parents. But many, from troubled backgrounds themselves, cannot trust others to this degree and turn inward. Again, their lack of energy and motivation is often interpreted by social service personnel as a lack of caring.

Due to feelings of inadequacy, some parents search for ways in which the present caretakers are also inadequate. Birth parents who visit their children in foster homes may look for ways to criticize foster parents. It may be difficult for the foster parent to remain sympathetic to the loss the birth parents have experienced, but for the child's sake, it is important that relations remain harmonious.

Certainly, some birth parents are able to adjust to their children's placement in foster care and can work in cooperation with the agency involved to secure the return of their children.

RIGHTS AND RESPONSIBILITIES OF BIRTH PARENTS

While their children are in foster care, and especially if the plan is reunification of the family, birth parents are encouraged to visit their children. Traditionally these visits have taken place in the foster home, although they may also be arranged at the agency. Some parents describe it as being very difficult to see their children for brief periods of time and then having to leave them again. As one parent put it:

> You see your child in a home situation where everything is apparently orderly and calm, and, quite often, materially superior to anything you are going to be able to offer them, and you wonder why the hell you are bothering to rock the boat...maybe it would be better to leave your child there. It would be a lot less upsetting for everyone involved if you just drop out of the picture (McAdams, 1970).

But therapeutically it may be better for children to maintain contact with their birth parents than to cut all ties. Studies also show that children do better in foster care and are less likely to be damaged by separation if they are able to maintain contact with their natural parents.

In reality, natural parents should be considered as an integral part of the foster care team for several reasons: First, their involvement with the foster home helps the child's adjustment. Secondly, natural parent involvement may be therapeutic to these parents as well. Through modeling the parenting skills of the foster parents they may recognize what their children need. And finally, if the children return home, the ongoing contact maintained between birth parents and children may smooth the return.

Certainly, not all natural parents end up being reunited with their children, nor should all continue to be involved with their children. But the fact is that natural parents who are encouraged to be involved with their children, while still held accountable, tend to make more effective progress toward reorganizing their lives and having their children returned.

What is meant by *parental involvement?* Parental involvement can refer to minimal contact of parents with their children in foster care. On the other end of the continuum is a more active role that may involve participation in goal-setting, attending conferences and reviews concerning their children, visiting and even caring for the children at the foster home or during extended home visits.

Natural parents are actually entitled to certain rights while their children are in foster care. Unless parental rights are terminated by the court, parents have a right to see the treatment plan (an outline of what is expected from them and what the agency will provide to them) and to attend all court hearings concerning their children. Whether or not parents exercise these rights depends on several issues, not the least of which is whether they have been informed by the agency of what these rights are. And even if parents are informed of their rights, they are not always able to act on them. Some parents are so angry that they refuse to cooperate, while others feel that nothing they do will make any difference.

WHEN CHILDREN RETURN HOME

Removing one individual from a family constellation shifts the balance of that family. Because a family is a system and all systems seek homeostasis, the family may rebalance itself without the missing member(s). Thus, when a child returns to a natural family, the transition may not always be smooth no matter how much it was anticipated by parents or children. Children will test limits. They will expect the old patterns to continue to exist and are confused when they do not. Parents who worked hard on their own issues may find that the added stress of the child's return brings up those issues again. One birth mother who had undergone therapy for drug and alcohol addiction described how she felt when her children returned home:

> The kids were so noisy that first week they were home that all I could think of doing was mellowing out with a joint and a few drinks.

It is often careful reunification planning and implementation that makes the difference between the children's ability to reintegrate into the home and their returning to foster care.

CHILDREN IN FOSTER CARE

FEELINGS ABOUT PLACEMENT AND SEPARATION

When children are placed in foster care they may not understand what is happening to them. For children, separation evokes many different feelings. For most there are *feelings of sadness.* No matter what the experiences they have had there, most children want to be at home. They may also feel *lonely and abandoned.* They may feel that they are unlovable and if their parents "didn't want them" they wonder if anyone ever will. Feeling that they are somehow to blame for being taken from their parents, children often *feel guilty.* They wonder how they could have been so bad that their parents wanted to "get rid of them." Even if children are removed because of abuse or neglect, they may feel that their parents wanted them sent away (Stahl, 1990).

Nicole was five when she came into foster care. At twelve, she was still in a foster home although she had been in seven since she first entered care. At first her mother had visited but this had been short-lived. When Nicole talked about her life she expressed resentment toward her parents for "dumping her." In reality, she had been removed from her mother's care due to severe neglect. Nicole also demonstrated what some foster children do—*hostility*. She was very angry and spat her words as she described how she felt about her mother.

The reality of being without birth families causes some children to *feel fear*. They wonder who will care for them and where they will live. And some children *feel shame*—shame at being a foster child; shame at having parents who, seemingly unlike other people's parents, cannot take care of them. And like their birth parents', children's feelings are often experienced in phases—shock, protest, despair, and detachment (Kadushin and Martin, 1988; Steinhauer, 1991; Plumer, 1992).

Being with one's own parents seems like such a fundamental part of childhood that foster children begin to *wonder why they are different from other children*. But it is too threatening to attribute the blame to adults; the result is that children *internalize the guilt*. As one teen put it:

I used to lie in bed in my foster home and think about every lousy thing I had ever done when I was with my parents. It never occurred to me that the fact that both of my parents were drug addicts could have been the cause of my placement. I was convinced that if I had been good enough, they would have kept me.

This feeling of being different and unworthy causes foster children to *devalue themselves*. For each child, these feelings of inferiority are expressed differently. While some children become withdrawn, compliant, and even self-abusive or suicidal, others act out in anger. A few are able to question the injustice of the fact that for their parents' problems they, the children, must leave home. Even if the child is able to recognize the injustice, there is not always a good explanation provided to them.

Bonnie spent a good deal of time letting everyone know how angry she was at being placed in foster care. "My father had sexually abused me [she recounted] and *I* had to leave home. I felt betrayed and abandoned by my own family. I wanted to strike out and hurt them and everyone else because I was hurt. So I would get into fights with everyone. I had so much anger bottled up inside that I didn't know what to do with it."

Some children may feel, in addition to the hurt and anger, a sense of *sadness*. Former foster child, Lisa, described this sadness in her life.

> I think I did a lot of crying that people never knew about. I suppose I was scared. I never let my mother see me cry when she visited. I always felt that I had to be strong for her. I knew that she hadn't wanted us taken away but she just couldn't kick her problems long enough to take care of her kids. I cried alone in bed at night and just wished sometimes that the world would end.

Not only are children separated from their parents but they may also be separated from their siblings as well. For many, who are taken into care with their siblings, their overwhelming desire is to protect younger brothers and sisters. Lisa recounted:

> Even though there was only a year between my brother and I, I felt like I was his mother. It seemed like he was always a nuisance to everyone and I tried to protect him from their anger. When we were separated, I was devastated. I felt like I had lost my purpose.

It is not unusual for older siblings to care for younger in dysfunctional families. Separation from each other may increase the impact of separation on both siblings. The caretaking role has given the older child a sense of purpose and even a feeling of some degree of control. This separation robs the older child of not just his/her home but of the responsible role he/she may have needed. Separation of siblings may also make the younger child feel more vulnerable and alone. Certainly there are exceptions, but for the most part, when siblings can be placed together, it may ease their transitions.

FEELINGS ABOUT NATURAL PARENTS

The ability of foster children to attach to their new caretakers is often related not only to their previous experiences with natural parents and how they separated from them, but also to their contact and relationship with these parents while they are in foster care. While it might seem that the less contact with natural parents the better the child's ability to adjust, this is not the case (Steinhauer, 1991). In addition, the attempt of foster parents or agency personnel, however well-meaning, to discredit natural parents makes placement more difficult for the child. When foster parents convey that they do not approve of natural parents, it sets up conflicting loyalties for the child. As one former foster child explained:

My parents were part of me. I guess I knew that they would never get me back, but I needed closure, I guess. At first they visited and then they didn't, but it helped me to adjust. My foster parents were great about the visits. That was good because no matter what my parents had done to me, I cared about them. If anyone had knocked them, I would have felt that they were knocking me.

Some children, hurt by abuse at the hands of their birth parents, are angry and do not want contact. Although this is usually respected, the child may deal with this issue in later life.

FEELINGS ABOUT FOSTER PARENTS

The feelings that foster children have about their foster parents are varied. Some are hampered from their experiences at home so that they are unable to trust and bond with others. For them, the foster parents may seem like a threat or perhaps just someone else who has the potential of letting them down. Some learn from their foster families how to trust again. For young children, foster care may represent the first consistent care they have experienced.

Certainly the chemistry that affects any type of relationship is important in the bond or lack thereof between foster parents and foster children. Children who have had an abundance of foster homes recount that some "felt right" and some did not. Today foster parents are trained to understand what their charges are experiencing in the hope that the relationship can be as strong as possible.

LIFE IN FOSTER CARE

What is it like for a child who is residing in a home that was totally strange to him/her at placement? As one former foster child recounted:

Every family has different rules—not just the spoken ones like when to come in at night or who takes out the trash. It's the unspoken rules that are hardest. For example, it may not seem like a big deal, but everyone sets the table somewhat differently. That shouldn't matter, but when you're new in the home and you're asked to set the table and you do it wrong, it can seem monumental. Like you have failed when you are really trying to fit in and please these people. It may sound silly, but when you don't have a home you can really call your own, it is important to fit in.

It is not only family rules, routines, and relationships that may be difficult for a foster child. There continues to be stigma attached to being "in care" and foster children can feel it profoundly. In school, children often feel like the "foster kids" and may perceive a separation from their classmates. They may also recognize that foster care is designed to be a temporary arrangement and wonder when they will be asked to move again. It is small wonder why permanency planning has been considered to be an important move in the provision of services to children (Plumer, 1992).

LEAVING FOSTER CARE

Children leave foster care for a variety of reasons. For some, their parents are able to readjust their lives and welcome their children home. Some foster children, who are not able to adjust to a foster home, move to institutions designed to cope with behavior that the foster home could not handle. But some children, though fewer in number in recent years, "age out " of foster care by turning eighteen. There may be provisions for continuing the support of a child if he/she seeks more education or has a physical or mental disability, but for others, eighteen is the cutoff age. After this, it remains the choice of the foster parents and the child as to how and if the relationship will continue.

Until recently, the preparation for the emancipation of youth from foster care has been informal. The picture is now beginning to change. In the ninety-ninth Congress, states were mandated (under the Title IV-E Foster Care Program) to provide transitional independent living programs for foster children sixteen years of age and older who are "aging out" of the foster care system. Since 1987 funds have been reauthorized to continue this practice (CWLA, 1989).

When we think of living on our own, rarely do we consider all the implications of this independence. Our complex society mandates that we have specific skills and resources. Usually, children are prepared for independence by their parents, who then maintain ties with them to help them along the way. How many people can honestly say that they have not called their parents for extra money, for advice on budgeting, career choices, or moves, or for child care? For many people, their first apartment is furnished by excess or cast-off furniture, eating utensils, and dishes from the family household. But foster children do not have this luxury, nor have they been able to watch parents balance the checkbook or make everyday decisions. The responsibility for their emancipation education rests in the hands of their legal "parents," the state or county agency. Thus programs have been set up to enable these foster children to develop the skills they need to leave care (Barth, 1989).

Canada's concerns for youths leaving care are much like those in the United States. In 1988, newly emancipated foster youth, Brian Raychaba, expressed his concerns for his Canadian peers in his book, *To Be on Our Own with No Direction from Home* (1988). The report, done for the National Youth in Care Network, was a culmination of Raychaba's research on youth who had recently left foster care. Raychaba pointed out that youths leaving care need not only practical information, but also help in addressing their own personal needs. Abuse may have been part of their experience either prior to or during foster care, resulting in residual scars. Their years in foster care may have failed to address these issues and even possibly augmented them. When faced with emancipation, these issues of emotional conflict do not disappear.

While preparation for leaving care is usually considered to be an orientation to independent living, Raychaba's study clearly attested to the fact that foster youths need a whole range of services. He recommends that a full assessment be made of the psychological, emotional, and health-related needs of each foster child about to leave care. Once these needs are identified, they can be more adequately addressed. The youths in Raychaba's study also felt the need for a "mentor" to follow them after care. Raychaba suggested that "after-care workers" or alumnae workers be created to carry a caseload of youths who are out of care but who are still resolving issues to help them to live more independently. The financial feasibility of such a plan might make it difficult to undertake, but it is clear that agencies need to pay even more attention to the needs of children who become independent after being in foster care.

THE ROLE OF THE FOSTER CARE SOCIAL WORKER

Being a foster care caseworker demands intelligence, fairness, good judgment, empathy, and determination. The job entails being responsible for the safety of foster children, being the target of angry or bewildered biological parents, consoling confused or anxious children, and handling the demands and irritations of foster parents…Endless reams of paperwork accompany all tasks (Hubbell, 1981, 110).

The description of the foster care worker has not changed much since Hubbell's description in 1981, except perhaps that the endless paperwork is now done on computer in many agencies. The foster care social worker enters the child's life during a troubled, volatile period and must assess the situation with understanding and expertise. Often this worker makes the recommendation that leads to the decision to place a child in foster care. It may be that the foster care worker follows the child through foster care until either the child returns home or is placed for adoption or the worker leaves the unit or the agency. The latter often happens first. Every day, a social worker may witness pain and loss. And every day, the decision that the worker must make alone or in conjunction with his/her supervisor must be covered by an immense paper (or computer) trail of forms to document that decision. It is not surprising that workers can feel overwhelmed.

What exactly does a foster care worker's job entail? There are at least two and often three types of workers involved in foster care. The first, usually referred to as a homefinder or family resource specialist, recruits and assesses foster parents for approval (see section on home study). Often homefinders keep in touch with approved parents until they receive children. Sometimes these workers perform a supportive role to insure some degree of continuity for the foster parents. The average day for a homefinder might be filled with group meetings with foster parents, home visits, case recording, or supportive counseling with foster parents. Group meetings necessitate a good deal of preparation, supervision, and consultation, which also takes time.

The foster care caseworker is responsible for *case management*. Some agencies use their protective services workers to monitor the homes in which they place children. Other agencies use protective services workers (see Chapter 9) to do intake and the placement of children and then transfer the case to a foster care worker for ongoing case management. While larger agencies use a variety of workers in various roles, smaller agencies might require a social worker to follow a case from start to finish. Both these models of service have advantages. While fewer workers may provide more consistency and continuity of services, having multiple workers allows for specialization and fresher, more objective viewpoints.

The day of the case manager varies greatly, depending on what is happening in individual cases. One day might involve fairly leisurely, routine visits to foster homes or to schools to monitor a child's progress. Another day might be punctuated with the problems generated by a disrupted foster home or a foster child who has run away or acted out in some other way. Plans that have been made for a day might change with the needs of the children and the foster home.

Caseworkers not only work with natural parents and foster parents but also with foster children. One particularly difficult task is helping children sort out the feelings about the people in their lives. No matter what they have suffered in their natural homes, children have feelings for their parents. The social worker must be skilled in listening to children's feelings and in allowing them their ambivalence without being judgmental. Children must know that their parents' problems predated them. They must also be helped to deal with their disappointments when the hopes they have about being with their parents are not realized. As one social worker put it:

It used to kill me every time we arranged for Jody's mother to visit her. The foster mother would get Jody all ready. I would prepare her emotionally for the visit and then we'd wait—and wait. Most of the time the mother never came. But we never knew, because sometimes she would come full of smiles and gifts and promises. But when she didn't come, I could feel Jody's pain. It hurt her so much that it hurt me too. So we'd talk about the hurt. No matter how angry I was at her mother, right then I had to remember that Jody loved her and that she was an important part of Jody's life.

Children may also feel torn by divided loyalties—loyalty on one hand to the parents they love and, on the other hand, to the foster parents with whom they live. It is the worker's role to accept that confusion and help children recognize that there is room for both in their lives.

Leaving a foster home or moving from one home to another can be a traumatic event for which children must be prepared. Not only must the foster care worker arrange for the logistical elements of any move, the children, foster parents, and often natural parents must also be prepared. Each individual must be helped to deal with the impending loss and guided through the grieving process following it. Counseling children around the time of the move becomes more intense and a social worker involved in several moves at one time can be constantly on call. If the children go to another foster home, the adjustment must be carefully monitored. If children return to their natural parents, supervision may be necessary to ensure that the reunification will be successful. And of course, every move must be documented by reams of paperwork. Forms authorize the payment of foster parents. Forms keep track of the children through the system. Forms open cases and close cases. As one social worker put it: "I felt as though I couldn't even breathe unless I did it in triplicate!"

Another important aspect of the role of the foster care worker, which often gets overlooked, is the need to do grief counseling with foster parents. Losing children to which one has become attached is not an easy task. In the past, agencies have not always recognized the need for foster parents to process their grief. Yet, the inability to grieve makes for difficulty with the next child and can hasten burnout for foster parents. Social workers now realize that it is important to do visits following children leaving to enable foster parents to adjust.

While not always an easy role, the job of the foster care case manager can have a great many rewards. Watching children gain stability and direction for their lives can be energizing. Seeing a child return home because of the effective casework done by the agency gives the worker a sense of accomplishment.

A FORMER FOSTER CHILD RECALLS LIFE IN CARE

Yvonne Barry Cataldi, currently a professor in the field of Human Services, shares her experience of what it was like to be in foster care.

I was a young adult, approximately twenty-six years old, when I read my file and learned that I had been placed in foster care when I was three years old. This was quite a surprise to me. I remembered being in elementary school and being in foster care but nothing younger than that. Unfortunately I also have no memory of a lot of the experience. I think that many foster children who have been in more than one placement lose pieces of their memories. We often don't know things like what illnesses we had, what schools we went to, whether we were with our siblings or not. We wondered what had really happened to our parents. And little questions made us think. When did we lose the first tooth? Did anyone save it? Did we ever take music lessons or play sports? Were we good at some things? I have no answers to those questions. Most children have the oral tradition of their families to fill in gaps. I did not. I didn't even remember the names of the foster families who had sheltered me. Sometimes I recall faces, but I don't know if those faces had any significance in my life. Most of the time I felt like a "yoyo," repeatedly having to leave home and then come back.

I remember not wanting to go home sometimes and at other times wanting to return to my parents. These feelings often had more to do with the foster family I was with than my parents. When I was with the family who washed my sister's mouth out with soap, I wanted to return home. Often we were expected to be playmates for the foster parents' children even if we didn't like them. We had to adapt to the different ways people did things. I was told that I should feel "at home" when I didn't even know where the bathroom or the kitchen was. Sometimes it wasn't clear to me where I was expected to sleep. It certainly didn't feel like home and by the time it did, I was returned to my parents once again. No one ever asked me what I wanted. It just happened.

I do recall that the placements I was fondest of were the ones in which I was placed with other foster children, like in group foster homes. I finally felt like I fit in. There were others in the same boat and I felt that I fared well. The toughest placement was when I was separated from my sister because neither home had two beds available. I felt a tremendous loss being away from her. I was thirteen and she was twelve and that was the last time we would ever be together. She died of cancer when she was eighteen years old.

I finally did have a set of foster parents in a group home who are still in my life today. Their acceptance and compassion and understanding gave me a view of what family life really could be. I regarded their son as my "brother." When my mother was again discharged from the hospital a worker finally asked me if I wanted to return. I said no. I liked where I was.

My sister and I talked about how unstable living with our mother was. When we finally had an opportunity to make some choices about where we lived, we were able to benefit from placement. It allowed us to begin to develop the skills we needed in order to become responsible, productive adults. I know that living with my family was not good for me, but parts of my experience in foster care had negatives too. Once I had some choice, my view of foster care changed and I believe that I felt more positive about it.

THE FUTURE OF FOSTER CARE

The future trends in the provision of foster care services are influenced largely by the political climate in which those services will be provided.

POLITICAL INFLUENCES

Policies related to foster care are based primarily on four major laws enacted by Congress in the last twenty years. The Child Abuse Prevention and Treatment Act (PL 93–247), passed in 1974, changed the provision of services for children who were abused or neglected. In so doing, it influenced how alternative home care was provided for them. The Indian Child Welfare Act (PL 95–608) of 1978 mandated that more concern be given to the placement of Native American children when foster care was the only alternative. The Adoption Assistance and Child Welfare Act (PL 96–272) in 1980 gave increased emphasis to the need to consider permanency planning for all children who come to the attention of the social service system. Finally, The Independent Living Initiative of 1986 (PL 99–272) amended Title IV-E of the Social Security Act in such a way that youths leaving foster care would be given increased attention and support (Pecora et al., 1992). With each of these laws came significant changes in the way foster care was provided.

There is still considerable political debate focused on the termination of parental rights when abuse or neglect is an issue. Some states have streamlined court procedures to free children for permanent placements in a more timely manner. Others have mandated time frames that allow parents only a certain amount of time to rearrange their lives and resume the care of their children. Critics say that change for many of these parents is a long-term goal and the expectation that it can be accomplished in a short period is unrealistic. Still others, especially among former foster children, argue that the only way for children to lead healthy lives is to separate them earlier from dysfunctional families and place them in permanent, consistent environments.

TRENDS

There are numerous trends and alterations in child welfare policy that appear to be affecting the provision of foster care services.

Permanency Planning and Family Preservation

While, at one time, the only apparent options for permanency for a child were family reunification or adoption, new alternatives are now being considered. For example, there is now more extensive exploration of the child's extended family as a potential placement alternative. Kinship care, mentioned earlier, is a viable plan for children whose parents cannot care for them but who can find a home with relatives, godparents, or close family friends (Leashore et al., 1991). This trend may have gained strength from minority families who are connected with their own culture and extended families and who, in the past, have solved child care problems within their own familial circle. As increased stressors have been put on these families, however, and they begin to look to the dominant culture to solve more of their problems, formalized kinship agreements may become more effective.

In addition to kinship care or placement with relatives, the nature of adoption has also changed. Instead of the closed adoptions of the past, adoptions may now be arranged according to the needs of the child. Open adoption, in which the child maintains contact with either the birth parents and/or the foster parents, provides children with more consistency while still offering permanence. Subsidized adoptions by adoptive or foster parents provide children whose medical or emotional needs, and the financial obligation inherent in meeting these needs, may formerly have precluded their ability to be adopted, to find stable homes (Pecora et al., 1992).

Finally permanent foster homes or guardianship arrangements make it possible for many children to have more consistency in their lives.

Darren and Dwight were children of seventeen-year-old Heidi, by different fathers. The girl had become pregnant with Darren at fourteen and had moved from her abusive home to a foster home with a neighbor, Ellie Driscoll. After she had her baby she left and lived for a time on her own. But alcohol abuse and drug use made it impossible for her to care for Darren and he was removed from her by CPS. Still very much interested in the girl, Mrs. Driscoll and her husband had kept in touch and offered to provide a foster home for Darren. By this time, Heidi had a new boyfriend and was already pregnant with Dwight. When this child was born, she asked the Driscolls to take him as well. But, although Heidi visited, she was inconsistent and would often take the children and not return for days. Neither the Driscolls nor the CPS felt that this was good for the children and CPS urged Heidi to give them up for adoption. This she refused to do. While the agency debated about the feasibility of involving the court to terminate parental rights, the Driscolls worried that they would lose the boys. They offered to seek guardianship of the children, which would allow their continued involvement with their mother, but give the Driscolls some rights to monitor her interaction with them. It would also give the boys consistency for years to come. Heidi agreed to this arrangement. Today she sees the boys periodically but with two new children she has her hands full. Although the boys like to see their mother, they see the Driscolls as their parents and have settled down into being well-adjusted boys who feel secure in their environment.

Such arrangements might not have been sanctioned in the past, but today there is more of an emphasis on the needs of the children. By the same token, more efforts are made in the area of family preservation (see Chapter 8). Programs provide more intensive services to help natural families be able to care for their children. At the same time, families are being held more accountable so that children can be offered permanency at as young an age as possible.

Training and Professionalization of Foster Parents

While foster parents have, for some time, been seen as members of the child's therapeutic team, it was clear that some agencies merely paid lip service to this concept. As foster parents have developed more of a voice on their own behalf, through such organizations as the National Foster Parent Association, and handling of the problems of the children coming into care have required more skill, foster parents have become more involved in training and areas of therapeutic intervention. Some agencies actually see foster parents as agency employees and treat them as such (Kufeldt and Allison, 1990).

While the concept of the professionalization of foster parents is defined differently by each agency and each organization, Pecora et al. (1992) suggest that the following benefits generally characterize professionalization:

1. *Systematic evaluation and selection of foster parents;*
2. *Foster care perceived as a goal-oriented service;*
3. *Adequate compensation, benefits, and rewards for foster parents, based on training, experience, merit, and job expectations;*
4. *Training for foster parents on a continuing basis, including incentives for completion of training programs;*
5. *Careful matching of foster parents with the kinds of children whom they can most effectively help;*
6. *Participation of foster parents as members of the agency's service team;*
7. *Provisions of supports of foster parents, such as quick access to social workers;*
8. *Involvement of foster parents in helping biological parents;*
9. *Objective evaluation of individual foster placements (347).*

Although some programs, such as the Casey Family Program out of Washington, do an excellent job of providing the respect and training that foster parents feel they need to accomplish their tasks, many public agencies still lag behind. Possibly as a result, or perhaps due to other economic factors, there is a serious lack of foster parents. Increasing the number of foster homes available as well as keeping those already committed will require that agencies take a serious look at how foster parents fit into the scheme of therapeutic intervention for children.

Attention to Special Populations in Foster Care

Over the years the type of children placed in foster care has changed. As drug addiction becomes more prevalent (see Chapter 4), more children will be placed into care because of their parents' inability to overcome their addiction sufficiently to care for them. Many of these children will be born addicted to substances themselves, and many will live with the aftereffects of the addiction of their parents to alcohol or drugs. In addition, there are an increasing number of children born of HIV-positive mothers who may or may not be HIV-positive themselves in years to come. The care of all of these types of children requires special knowledge and skills. The Biennial Resolutions for Family Foster Care of the Child Welfare League of America (NCFFC, 1991) advocates that training be given to both foster parents and staff to aid them in the handling of these issues. Agencies will be called on more and more in the future to find creative solutions to the provision of services to such children. Not only education, but other support services, such as grief counseling for foster parents who have an AIDS baby die while in their care, are vital to meeting these needs.

Another population that is becoming more visible in foster care is a growing number of gay and lesbian youths.

Gene was fifteen and a foster child when he recognized that he was attracted to other boys more than girls. After talking to a youth leader he knew to be gay, Gene realized that he was too. Yet he was afraid to say anything to anyone else. He liked his foster home, but was sure that his sports-oriented foster father would reject him if he knew. And these weren't even his own parents. How could they accept him? Would they think he was a freak or crazy? Realizing that something was bothering Gene, his foster mother engaged him in conversation one day. Feeling secure in the conversation, he finally told her of his feelings. She was quiet for a moment and then told him that she had had a brother who was gay who had been badly beaten by a group of boys. The beating had caused brain damage and the brother had never been the same. The foster mother told him that she had vowed that she would somehow make it up to her brother. With a new understanding between them, Gene and his foster mother had other conversations and she was to prove a valuable advocate for him in the future.

Not every situation ends as positively as Gene's did. Increasingly foster parents and foster care workers are requiring training to understand the complex issues and feelings faced by gay and lesbian youths. A few agencies on the West Coast provide homes specifically for gay and lesbian young people (Ricketts, 1991). While this gives the foster children support and validation for their feelings, it does not always insulate them from the sentiments of the larger society. As more homosexual youths feel comfortable in identifying themselves, agencies will be pressed to respond more to their needs.

Reconceptualization and the Quality of Care

Downs et al. (1996) contend that two important trends in care require the reconceptualization of care and attention to the quality of care.

No longer the relatively simple service provided for dependent children, the provision of foster care now demands attention to a myriad of cultural, community, and family-based issues. The skill of the social worker dealing with foster children must be more finely honed. As well as a case manager, a counselor, and a broker, the worker must also be an advocate for both foster children and their caretakers. Their knowledge must be more specialized, including knowledge of cultural variations, HIV awareness, knowledge of drug issues, and a variety of other specialties. Foster parents, too, cannot be merely caretakers, but must also be able to deal with the complexity of the children who come into their care.

The provision of foster care is also affected by managed care regulations. Funding is dependent on meeting specific criteria and those providing care must be able to meet the needs of children while remaining within the guidelines set down by outside funding sources. This is not always an easy task.

Inherent in the changes in the provision of foster care is the necessity to insure that the care given to dependent children is of quality. It will be increasingly necessary to consider the best interests of the child. Issues like protecting children from maltreatment in care, insuring effective services for reunification along with termination of parental rights when necessary, will provide a more therapeutic environment for foster children. Increased emphasis must be given to preparing children to leave care both to return home but especially to become independent (Downs et al., 1996).

For many children, family foster care is a necessity. Although there are some who feel that a return to the concept of orphanages would better serve children, there is a sufficient amount of research that attests to the fact that a family environment, if healthy and sensitive to a child's needs, provides more for dependent children than an institutional environment. Our challenge as practitioners is to create the healthy environments that can be the most effective in helping children to become functioning adults.

SUMMARY

Family foster care has long been a method of providing dependent children with a nurturing environment. The origins of the placement of children with families seems to have been when apprentices, while learning their trades, were sheltered in the households of their masters. Later, in the late nineteenth century, Charles Loring Brace sent children, via orphan trains, to the Western United States to be fostered or adopted. From 1853 to 1929, there were 31,081 children placed in this manner. Eventually fostering parents were expected to undergo scrutiny in order to be surrogate parents for children, and in the early 1900s they began to be paid for this service.

Today, foster care is influenced largely by the concept of permanency planning, providing the best possible nurturing for children while moving toward the goal of a permanent environment for them. While more emphasis is now placed on family preservation, which requires more concentrated attempts to salvage the family structure, there is growing recognition that, if this plan fails, children must be provided with alternatives that help to insure their stability and protection.

There are several different types of foster homes, including *crisis homes* for short-term emergency placements, *family boarding homes* for longer periods of substitute care, *small group homes,* which provide care for several children in the same home, and *specialized homes* that provide care for certain individual children or certain types of children. *Kinship care,* or the provision of care by the child's extended family members, is an increasingly popular alternative, especially among minority populations who, before their integration into the larger society, solved many of their child care needs informally, within their own culture. Kinship homes have the advantage of providing consistency for children in that the kinship parents may already be known to them and may also share the children's cultural values.

Children come into foster care for a variety of reasons. Some have been *maltreated by their parents* and foster care is seen as a method of protecting them from further abuse or neglect. Some children come from families in which there is *domestic violence or substance abuse,* preventing the continuation of their care by their parents. *Parents who are physically or mentally ill* may also place their children or these children may be removed from them due to their inability to provide for their care. *Incarcerated parents* may require placement for their children until they are released or until another plan can be devised for the children's care. Finally, foster care may be used as an *interim arrangement* while a child awaits placement in an adoptive home.

Foster parents are recruited or become foster parents because they want to provide a service, want to continue to parent, or as a result of other personal experiences. Minority families are less likely to come forward, except in kinship situations, but there is more need for such homes. Potential foster parents undergo a screening/training process called a home study. This is usually accomplished in groups and is often based on the NOVA model, which provides an eight to twelve week intensive program that exposes the applicants to a variety of topics inherent in foster care. Once they have finished this process, children can be placed in the home and supervised by foster care social workers.

It is not always easy to have one's child placed in foster care. Birth parents often feel that they have failed in a role—that of parenting—that society expects anyone to be able to do. As a result of separation they may go through several stages, from denial, anger, and despair, to eventual acceptance, in an attempt to cope with their dilemma. Research now tells us that how effectively these parents are helped to adjust to the placement and to work with the agency and the foster parents may determine how successful the placement will be for their children.

Children who are placed in care may have feelings about separation that mirror those of their parents. They may feel guilt, shame, fear, hostility, isolation, and sadness. They may want to return to their parents while feeling abandoned and resentful toward them. Life in foster care may also be punctuated with a variety of conflicting feelings that are not always dealt with while children are in care and may surface for them in later years.

When children leave foster care, it may be to return home, be placed for adoption, or to live on their own. The writings of former foster children tell us that there is a need to improve the services provided for children who go from care to independence. Not only do they need physical and logistical supports, but they may be dealing with a variety of emotional issues that hamper their ability to live comfortably as autonomous adults. Increasingly agencies are creating programs to offer these necessary supports.

The role of the foster care worker is one that requires patience, flexibility, and stamina. One never knows exactly what a daily schedule could encompass. From routine foster home visits, supervised visits for birth parents, and attendance at school review meetings to dealing with a variety of emergency situations, the foster care worker does his or her best to keep in touch with children and foster parents and meet the needs of both, often while working with birth parents as well. It is not surprising that the turnover in such a profession is high.

Today, the provision of foster care is influenced by several trends. The balance between family preservation and permanency planning for children puts increasing pressure on agencies, courts, and child advocacy groups to devise better ways to serve the best interests of children. There is an increasing emphasis on the need to train foster parents and include them more effectively as integral members of the therapeutic team. There is also a need to redesign some foster care services to meet the needs of special segments of the child population now coming into care, such as children who have been exposed to substance abuse, who are HIV-positive, or youths who are gay or lesbian. And finally, there is a need, as we go into the twenty-first century, to fine-tune or reconceptualize the structure of foster care in a variety of ways so that the children who are in need of this vital service can be best served.

EXPLORATION QUESTIONS

1. Who was Charles Loring Brace and what was his contribution to the history of foster care?
2. What two concepts most influence the provision of family foster care today?
3. What is it expected that foster care will provide?
4. Cite the different types of foster homes and explain each one.
5. What is kinship care? What are the advantages and why has it become so popular?
6. Cite the reasons that children come into foster care.

7. What is the process one must go through to become a foster parent?
8. What are the stresses inherent in being a foster parent?
9. How might birth parents feel about having their children placed in foster care? How might they express these feelings?
10. What feelings do children have about separation and placement? About their natural parents? About being in foster care?
11. What are the needs of a child leaving foster care to go out on his or her own?
12. What trends influence the future of the provision of foster care?

ACTIVITIES FOR APPLIED LEARNING

1. Invite a homefinder or family resource worker to outline what is involved in a home study.
2. Research the current legislation affecting the provision of foster care.
3. Contact the local agency providing foster care and ask if they know of a former foster child who would be willing to speak to the class. This might be combined with an invitation to a foster care social worker. How have procedures, laws, and services changed?
4. Research the orphan trains and how they influenced the provision of foster care today.

SUGGESTED READING

Cahn, K., & Johnson, P. (Eds.) *Children Can't Wait: Reducing Delays in Out of Home Care.* Washington, DC: Child Welfare League of America, 1993.

Child Welfare League of America. *Kinship Care: A Natural Bridge.* Washington, DC: Child Welfare League of America, 1994.

Cook, J. F. "A History of Placing-Out: The Orphan Trains," *Child Welfare* 74(1), (1995), 181–197.

Dawson, R. "Improving the Quality and Status of Foster Care: The Concept of Certification for Providers," *Community Alternatives: International Journal of Family Care* 1(1), (1989), 11–12.

Hacsi, T. "From Indenture to Family Foster Care: A Brief History of Child Placing," *Child Welfare* 74(1), (1995), 162–180.

Hubbell, R. *Foster Care and Families: Conflicting Values and Policies.* Philadelphia, PA: Temple University Press, 1981.

McAdams, P. "The Parent in the Shadows," *Child Welfare* 51(1), (1972), 15–25.

Plumer, E. H. *When You Place a Child...* Springfield, IL: Charles C. Thomas, 1992.

Raychaba, B. *To Be on Our Own with No Direction from Home: A Report on the Special Needs of Youth Leaving the Care of the Child Welfare System.* Ottawa, Ontario: National Youth in Care Network, 1988.

Steinhauer, P. D. *The Least Detrimental Alternative: A Systematic Guide to Case Planning and Decision Making for Children in Care.* Toronto: University of Toronto Press, 1991.

REFERENCES

Barth, R. P. "Programs for Independent Living." In J. Aldgate, A. Maluccio, and C. Reeves, *Adolescents in Foster Care*. Chicago, IL: Lyceum Books, 1989.

Berrick, J., Barth, R., & Needell, B. "A Comparison of Kinship Foster Homes and Family Foster Homes." In R. P. Barth, J. D. Berrick, & N. Gilbert (Eds.), *Child Welfare Research Review*. New York: Columbia University Press, 1993.

Child Welfare League of America (CWLA). "Children's Legislative Agenda, 1989." Washington, DC: CWLA, 1989.

Child Welfare League of America (CWLA). "Kinship Care: A Natural Bridge." Washington, DC: Child Welfare League of America, 1994.

Cook, J. F. "A History of Placing-Out: The Orphan Trains," *Child Welfare* 74(1), (1995), 181–197.

Dawson, R. "Improving the Quality and Status of Foster Care: The Concept of Certification for Providers," *Community Alternatives: International Journal of Family Care* 1(1), (1989), 11–12.

Downs, S. W., Costin, L. B., & McFadden, E. J. *Child Welfare and Family Services*. White Plains, NY: Longman, 1996.

Festinger, T. *No One Ever Asked Us: A Postscript to Foster Care*. New York: Columbia University Press, 1983.

Fine, P. *A Developmental Network Approach to Therapeutic Foster Care*. Washington DC: Child Welfare League of America, 1993.

Gambrill, E., & Stein, T. J. *Controversial Issues in Child Welfare*. Boston: Allyn and Bacon, 1994.

Gebel, T. J. "Kinship Care and Non-Related Family Foster Care," *Child Welfare* 75(1), (1996), 5–18.

Hacsi, T. "From Indenture to Family Foster Care: A Brief History of Child Placing," *Child Welfare* 74(1), (1995), 162–180.

Hubbell, R. *Foster Care and Families: Conflicting Values and Policies*. Philadelphia, PA: Temple University Press, 1981.

Kadushin, A., & Martin, J. A. *Child Welfare Services*. New York: Macmillan, 1988.

Kufeldt, K., & Allison, J. "Fostering Children: Fostering Families," *Community Alternatives: International Journal of Family Care* 2(1), (1990), 1–17.

Leashore, B. R., McMurray, H. L., & Bailey, B. C. "Reuniting and Preserving African American Families." In J. E. Everett, S. S. Chipungu, and B. R. Leashore (Eds.) *Child Welfare: An Africentric Perspective*. New Brunswick, NJ: Rutgers University Press, 1991.

Lewis, R. E., & Fraser, M. "Blending Informal and Formal Helping Networks in Foster Care," *Children and Youth Services Review*, 9(3), (1987), 153–169.

Maluccio, A., and Fein, E. "Permanency Planning: A Redefinition," *Child Welfare* 62(3), (1983), 195–201.

McAdams, P. "The Parent in the Shadows," *Child Welfare* 51(1), (1972), 15–25.

Moore, B., Granpre, M., & Scoll, B. "Foster Home Recruitment: A Market Research Approach to Attracting and Licensing Applicants," *Child Welfare* 67(2), (1988), 147–160.

National Black Child Development Institute. *Who Will Care When Parents Can't?* Washington, DC: National Black Child Development Institute, 1989.

National Commission on Family Foster Care (NCFFC). *A Blueprint for Fostering Infants: Children and Youths in the 1990's*. Washington, DC: Child Welfare League of America, 1991.

Pecora, P. J., Whittaker, J. K., & Maluccio, A. N. *The Child Welfare Challenge*. New York: Aldine De Gruyter, 1992.

Plumer, E. H. *When You Place a Child...* Springfield, IL: Charles C. Thomas, 1992.

Raychaba, B. *To Be on Our Own with No Direction from Home: A Report on the Special Needs of Youth Leaving the Care of the Child Welfare System*. Ottawa, Ontario: National Youth in Care Network, 1988.

Ricketts, W. *Lesbians and Gay Men as Foster Parents*. Portland, ME: University of Southern Maine, National Child Welfare Resource Center, 1991.

Rutter, B. *The Parent's Guide to Family Foster Care.* Washington, DC: Child Welfare League of America, 1989.

Smith, E. P., & Gutheil, R. H. "Sucessful Foster Parent Recruiting: A Voluntary Agency Effort," *Child Welfare* 67(2), (1988), 1.

Solomon, R. "Substance Abusive Parents: A Challenge for Child Welfare Systems." In *1990 Abstract Compendium for the National Symposium on Child Victimization.* Washington, DC: Children's National Medical Center, 1990.

Stahl, P. M. *Children on Consignment.* Lexington, MA: Lexington Books, 1990.

Steinhauer, P. D. *The Least Detrimental Alternative: A Systematic Guide to Case Planning and Decision Making for Children in Care.* Toronto: University of Toronto Press, 1991.

Terpstra, J. Foster Care Specialist: Childrens' Bureau, Department of Health and Human Services. *Personal Communication,* May 1990.

Terpstra, J. "The Rich and Exacting Role of the Social Worker in Foster Care," *Child and Adolescent Social Work* 4(3–4), (1987), 160–177.

Thurston, H. W. *The Dependent Child.* New York: Columbia University Press, 1930.

Walsh, J., & Walsh, R. *Quality Care for Tough Kids.* Washington, DC: Child Welfare League of America, 1990.

13

THE ADOPTION OF CHILDREN

What is adoption? A child brought into your home? A bigger family? A new brother or sister for an only child? Not so fast! Adoption is not just an event. Adoption is a lifelong process... (Coleman et al., 1988, v)

Adoption has long been a method of providing children with both legal and emotional security. Through adoption children find permanency and parents can nurture or increase their families. Adoptive parents provide substitute, societally sanctioned, long-term care when birth parents have been unable to assume their roles adequately. Through adoption a new family is created that can, hopefully, meet the needs of all those involved.

THE HISTORY OF ADOPTION

Adoption has not always been designed to meet the needs of *all* participants; rather the practice was originally seen as a method of meeting the needs of the adoptive parents. Reasons for adopting children have varied from a desire to continue the family line or trade (especially through the male heirs), to provide for ancestor worship, to ensure additional workers, to maintain family wealth, to provide a solution for out-of-wedlock pregnancies, and to provide homes for homeless children.

Perhaps one of the best-known adoption stories was that of Moses, who was found in the bulrushes by the Pharaoh's daughter. Cognizant of the fact that he was a Hebrew child whose future was in jeopardy and being childless herself, the Pharaoh's daughter adopted Moses as her own son, thus ensuring his survival and (she thought) his future.

Early Rome had formal adoption requirements. The motivation was primarily to ensure male heirs. Female children were not eligible for placement and only men could do the actual adopting. The transaction was sealed with a judicial hearing (Howe, 1983). India and China used adoption as a formal method of providing male heirs. For Hindu men, a male child met the demands of religious ceremonials. For the Chinese family, an heir was expected to provide for the parents in their old age. In other early cultures, the adoption of children was more informally arranged (Kadushin and Martin, 1988).

European countries, throughout history, developed adoption practices based primarily on Roman law. In France, the Napoleonic Code most closely resembled Roman practices. England, a country with traditions based on blood lineage, found it more difficult to espouse the practice of adoption. In order to adopt, therefore, a family was required to seek a special act of Parliament. Only then could the adoptee be considered a legal heir. It was not until 1926 that England passed a statute that made adoption a viable option for any family (Smith & Miroff, 1987).

Much of early legislation in what was to become the United States was based on English common law. Because adoption was unknown in England, the new states were forced to devise their own standards; each did in its own way. There is some controversy about which state actually enacted the first legal statute. Whether we believe sources that cite this forerunner as Mississippi in 1846 (Sloan, 1988), Texas in 1850 (Cole, 1987), or Massachusetts in 1851 (Samuels, 1990; Downs et al., 1996), the fact remains that the Massachusetts statute was the closest to currently accepted philosophies. Both Texas and Mississippi statutes were geared more toward real estate transactions; through adoption, property could be legally passed on to the adoptee. Massachusetts law, on the other hand, provided for the "best interests of the child." The four components of the 1851 law that have remained to the present require that

- *There be written consent by the child's biological parent;*
- *Both the adoptive mother and father join in the petition;*

- *A judge must decree that the adoption is 'fit and proper';*
- *There be legal and complete severance of the relationship between biological parents and the child (Kadushin and Martin, 1988).*

While there are exceptions to and variations on these provisions in current adoption practice, the 1851 law still influences adoption policy today.

By 1929 all states in the United States had enacted some type of adoption legislation. Prior to this time state legislatures continued to adopt legislation as individual cases came to their attention. As more procedures became formalized, standardization of adoption practice seemed imminent. Yet in the late nineteenth century states still interpreted their laws differently. For example, all that was required by federal law was the legal transfer of the child from the biological to adoptive parents, and the pronouncement by a judge that all was "fit and proper," but this did not protect children from abusive adoptive situations, and some states began to look more closely at adoptive applicants. Finally, in 1891, Michigan instituted a requirement that the judge investigate the adoptive home before finalizing the adoption. Later, agencies took over this task. A 1917 Minnesota law requiring detailed investigation by a social agency was copied in numerous other states by the late 1930s (Kadushin and Martin, 1988).

Where were the children while their fate was being debated by politicians and lawmakers? During the nineteenth and early twentieth centuries most homeless children resided in orphanages. Some had been placed there by their unwed mothers or poor parents; others had been orphaned by death, substance abuse, poverty, or other problems. Some were destined to grow up as permanent orphans, while others—the younger and more appealing perhaps—would find themselves placed with adoptive parents.

The orphan trains (mentioned in Chapter 12) were also responsible for some adoptions. While Charles Loring Brace's initial idea appeared to be to provide permanency for homeless children of all ages, some of the children sent to families in the Western United States were eventually legally adopted. In 1859 close to 5,000 children had been placed "out West" (in both foster care and adoption) and 24,000 children had found homes nationwide (Brace, 1872).

Finally, in the early twentieth century more emphasis was being placed on the "best interests of the child." Minnesota, in 1917, was the first state to mandate the sealing of birth records (Gitlin, 1987). Agencies began to assess adoptive couples more rigorously. In 1938 the Child Welfare League of America published the first set of standards for adoption practice. But adoption did not become a popular form of substitute care until the end of World War II when homeless children were more visibly plentiful (Downs et al., 1996). The upsurge in the demand for children caused agencies to further reassess and redesign their policies. An adoption worker who placed numerous infants in the 1950s describes the practices of her agency.

We placed mostly white healthy infants then. Couples who applied for them were expected to be white, upstanding, moral individuals who were financially secure.

Age-wise we insisted that these potential parents could have had this child biolog-ically—in other words—we rarely took someone over forty-five for an infant. We expected them to be active in their church and placed a child with them who was of their religious faith. We also attempted to match coloring, nationality, etc. of the parents and child as closely as possible. We gave parents little information about the biological parents beyond a brief description and some health information. We were careful not to give any "negative" information. I think all our parents be-lieved that the biological mother of their child was a poor little high school or col-lege girl who "got in trouble." It was so unrealistic.

By the 1950s, the demand for healthy white infants outweighed the availability of such children. African American and mixed racial infants were also available, but usually only African American couples were considered as adoptive parents for such children. However, the numbers of African American couples seeking to adopt from agencies was small, so agencies began to look at other types of adoptive arrangements—both interracial and international (Kadushin and Martin, 1988).

In order to find suitable homes for all children, Ohio (1958) developed an adoption resource exchange that pooled statewide resources in search of homes. Other states followed and in 1967 the Child Welfare League of America established the Adoption Resource Exchange of North America (ARENA) (Pecora et al., 1992).

The 1960s and 1970s saw a significant shift in the adoption picture. Agencies recognized that children who had once been considered unadoptable might also be placed. "Special needs" adoptions—defined as those involving older, African American, and disabled children—began to be seen as possibilities. For the first time single parents were considered for otherwise "hard to place" children. Agen-cies began assessing couples in groups rather than just individually.

But as the adoption picture became more complex, more controversies arose. In 1972 the National Association of Black Social Workers took the stand that transracial placement was "a threat to the preservation of the black family" (Pecora et al., 1992). Why was more not being done to place these children within the African American community? they asked. Agencies were criticized for using white middle-class stan-dards in their recruitment and assessment of minority adoptive applicants.

At the same time researchers and reformers of the child care system found that children—many of whom were legally free for adoption (or could be with a mini-mum of work with their families)—were living in temporary foster care when they could have been given the permanency of adoption (Gruber, 1973). Foster families who were stimulating and providing well for children questioned why they could not adopt them. While the practice of foster parents adopting had been discour-aged in the past, in 1973 CWLA recognized the acceptability of this practice if the needs of the child would be best served.

Amidst the controversy over the placement of African American children in white homes, the Native American community began to question placement of its children outside the Indian community. Largely in response to the fact that between 25 and 35 percent of Native American children were being placed in substitute care (foster care and adoption), the Indian Child Welfare Act of 1978 (PL 95–608) was passed. This legislation mandated that Native American children be kept within their community whenever possible in order to maintain connections with their own tribes (Cohen, 1992).

The numerous debates and controversies made it clear to child welfare advocates that more standardization of adoption practice had become necessary. In 1980 the passage of PL 96–272 became a milestone in substitute care history. This law made state adoption programs mandatory and provided federal matching monies for subsidized adoption. Adoption subsidy meant that families who were interested in adopting children with special needs, but were unable to do so financially, would be provided with funds to supplement the child's care. These payments could not exceed the amount that would be given to a foster family for the same child. To guide states in developing their own laws to govern subsidy payments, the federal government published the "Model Act for the Adoption of Children with Special Needs" (Kadushin and Martin, 1988).

PL 96–272, the Federal Adoption Assistance and Child Welfare Act of 1980, urged agencies to have as a priority "permanency planning" for every child. Agencies were encouraged to first strengthen the child's biological family. If this was not possible agencies should place the child in an immediate long-term or permanent nurturing situation with caring adults—usually an adoptive home (Cole & Donley, 1990). Although the intent of the law was beneficial for children, agencies argue that they do not always have the funds or resources to adhere to it.

Today adoption agencies provide services for older children and special needs children in greater numbers than infants.

DEFINITIONS AND ASSUMPTIONS

The purpose of adoption is to provide a permanent home for a child whose biological parents are unable or unwilling to provide that home. Today, we assume that, although the needs of the adoptive family are important, the adoption is primarily to provide a home for a child.

Adoption is a legally sanctioned arrangement. The Child Welfare League of America describes this legal agreement as "the method provided by law to establish the legal relationship of parent and child between persons who are not related by birth" (Child Welfare League of America, 1978, 11). It is in this legality that adoption differs from foster care. While foster care is seen as a temporary living arrangement, adoption substitutes adoptive parents for biological parents—giving them all the rights and privileges of biological parents.

Adoption is based on several assumptions or values:

1. A child has a right to grow up in the safe, nurturing environment of a family;
2. If the child's biological family cannot provide him or her with what he or she needs, the child has the right to a substitute family;

3. Adoption is the preferred type of substitute care because it provides legal sanction and permanency of the relationship;

4. Children should be placed for adoption as early as possible in order to provide as much consistency as possible;

5. Adoption is expected to be a lifelong experience for all the participants;

6. Adopted children are entitled to information about their birth, their biological family, genetic information, placements, and particulars about their adoption (Kadushin and Martin, 1988; Cole and Donley, 1990).

TYPES OF ADOPTION

Kadushin and Martin (1988) divide adoptions into two types: *related* and *unrelated.* In related adoptions the child has a preexisting blood tie to some member of his or her adoptive family. In other words, a stepfather might adopt his wife's child or a couple might adopt the child of their unmarried son or daughter. A newly recognized practice that can be seen as related adoption is created by *surrogate mothering.* The term *surrogate mothering,* created by Keane, an attorney in Michigan, refers to the agreement between a couple and a surrogate mother. The mother agrees, for a fee, to be artificially inseminated and impregnated by the adoptive father's sperm, to carry the baby, and then to relinquish the child to the sperm donor and his wife. Usually this couple will then legally adopt the child (Gitlin, 1987). Although this practice is new, it has in fact been practiced since ancient times. Surrogate mothering appeared to be gaining momentum until two legal landmarks brought the practice under scrutiny. In 1988, Michigan, concerned that surrogate mothers might use this practice as a lucrative business, passed a law that limits the amount of money surrogates can receive. Further, the controversy and court battle over "Baby M" may have changed sentiments. Baby M's biological mother, Mary Beth Whitehead–Gould, was impregnated by the sperm of Stern and agreed that, once the child was born, to relinquish it to the Sterns. Once the baby had been born, however, Mrs. Whitehead–Gould decided that she wanted to keep the child. The result was the case Whitehead–Gould versus Stern, which received a lot of media coverage and gave rise to seventy bills in twenty-seven state legislatures seeking to ban, regulate, or undertake research on surrogate parenting. Currently both the Child Welfare League of America and the National Committee for Adoption (a lobbying organization representing 145 nonprofit, private adoption agencies nationally) oppose the practice of surrogate parenting (Samuels, 1990).

Unrelated adoptions are what comes to mind most frequently when the word adoption arises. In this type of adoption, the child has no blood relation to the adoptive family. Most of these adoptions are *agency sponsored;* that is the agency counsels and contracts with biological parents of the court to place the child, recruits and assesses the adoptive couple, places the child, and provides follow-up until or after the adoption is legalized. Agencies sometimes sponsor *legal risk* adoptions. In these arrangements the agency has already petitioned the court to terminate the biological parents' rights. The expectation is that the court will agree and the child will be legally free for adoption. In the meantime, instead of placing the child in yet another foster home, the agency places the child with the family that hopes to legally adopt him or her. Because the courts usually take considerable time to process the termination of parental rights, this arrangement seems to be in the best interest of the child. The problem arises, however, when the biological parents contest the termination of their rights. In addition, adoptive couples often feel insecure until they know the child is legally free.

Another type of adoption that is fairly recent is what is known as a *"special needs"* adoption. Children who might be difficult to place are placed with families who have been assessed especially for them. For example, Walter was a two-year-old boy with Down syndrome. When it became necessary for Walter to be moved from the foster home where he had been from birth, the agency decided to place him in an adoptive home instead. The Brandts had had their children when they were young and now these children were grown and married. Mrs. Brandt, a teacher, and Mr. Brandt, a nurse, felt they could give love and a home to a special kind of child. The agency studied them for a special needs child and eventually placed Walter with them. The match was a good one and until Walter's death ten years later, the family provided consistency and love for him.

George was fourteen when he was finally released for adoption. At one time George would have been placed in a foster home where, under ideal circumstances, he would have remained until he was eighteen. The reality is that most children in foster care will be in a number of homes before their eighteenth birthday. For this reason agencies have begun to place children for adoption who are considerably older and George was an excellent candidate. His new adoptive family was excellent with teenagers and the arrangement provided George with the stability he might not have otherwise had.

Currently children with disabilities and older children as well are being placed with increasing frequency. Sometimes the placement of special needs children requires subsidized adoption (discussed earlier). Parents interested in adopting a child whose care necessitates extra costs (beyond those expected in raising a child) are given a subsidy to defer the extra expense. Thus children who require expensive medication, medical procedures, or therapeutic services can still benefit from an adoptive home.

Single-parent adoptions, which gained popularity in the sixties and seventies, are still in vogue today. While the assumption is that a child should be given the opportunity for a two-parent home, some children would be better suited to a single-parent family. Tammy, for example, had been severely abused, both physically and sexually, by most of the men in her life. Now she was angry and distrustful of men and unable to bond with any of them. The agency therefore decided to seek a placement for Tammy with a mother in a fatherless home. Often teenagers in particular do better with a one-parent figure rather than in a two-parent family.

Some children require the undivided attention of the parent, leaving this person with little energy to maintain a healthy marital relationship.

When children of one race are placed with parents of another, the adoption is referred to as *transracial* or *interracial adoption*. Adoptive parents involved in these placements are guided in aiding children to understand and accept their own racial backgrounds. It is most common for children of African American or mixed parentage to be adopted by white families. At one time Native American children were also placed in the homes of white parents. The Indian Child Welfare Act of 1978 reserved the right of determining where an Indian child would be placed, with the hope and intention of placing him or her in a family of the tribe in which the biological parent was registered. Tribal governments try to place Indian children within their own Native American culture first.

International adoptions are those in which children are brought from other countries and placed with adoptive couples in the United States. The Holt Agency, founded in 1956, by Harry and Bertha Holt of Eugene, Oregon, to aid children of the Korean War, is responsible for the greatest number of international adoptions. Originally the agency brought over Korean war "orphans" who were in fact the American children of wives, lovers, prostitutes, and rape victims of servicemen. Later, Vietnamese children joined the ranks of children who needed permanent homes. By 1987, 10,097 children were being brought to the United States for the purpose of being adopted here (Register, 1991). No longer a wartime rescue mission, children are now being brought in from Central and South America as well as from Asia.

Register describes the type of children who are often brought to the United States for adoption.

Soon Young's parents brought her to an orphanage when she was six years old because they could no longer manage her care. Her muscles were atrophied as a result of polio and she had severe curvature of the spine. The orphanage outfitted her with crutches and braces so she could walk a little. She spent the next six years there, until she was adopted by an American family who had requested a handicapped child and had the resources to pay for surgery and physical therapy (Register, 1991, 4).

Register goes on to describe a five-month-old child from Honduras whose mother gave him to a lawyer to place, a seven-year-old from Guatamala who was found on the streets, and a malnourished four-pound baby placed by her young mother in an orphanage in India. All of these children were adopted by American families. As children become less available in the United States many families seek out this type of adoption.

Independent adoption refers to placements of children with parents unrelated to them without going through an agency. Downs et al. (1996) describe three types of independent placements.

> **1.** Direct placements: *biological parents give their child to someone known to them;*

2. Intermediary placement not for profit: *the person who acts as an interme-diary is well intentioned and the money exchanged is only for legal services or the mother's medical bills; the biological parent often knows the adoptive par-ents. Such adoptions are sometimes referred to as "gray market";*

3. Intermediary placement for profit: *often called "black market" adoption, these arrangements involve "selling" children for profit; the intermediary fee is as high as the participants will pay. The "service" may be connected with an abortion clinic and the intermediary is connected with mothers who have agreed to give up their child rather than abort. These placements are illegal and are outlawed in most states (Samuels, 1990; Downs et al., 1996).*

Even when adoptions are done independently, an agency may become involved. In many states the adoption cannot be legalized until an agency undertakes an adoptive home study.

ISSUES IN ADOPTION TODAY

Today's adoption literature is dedicated to the discussion of several pertinent issues:

1. The decreasing numbers of children available for adoption;
2. Changes in the types of children available for adoption;
3. The controversy of agency versus independent adoption;
4. Adoption disruptions and the need for follow-up;
5. The effects of adoption on children and families (mental health implications).

DECREASED NUMBER OF ADOPTABLE CHILDREN

During the mid 1980s the National Committee for Adoption (NCFA) estimated that there were 104,088 adoptions within the United States. Of these, 52,931 (or about 51 percent) were adoptions of children by family members (related adop-tions). These family members may have been stepfathers, grandparents, uncles and aunts, or other concerned relatives. Unrelated adoptions (children placed with families usually unknown or unrelated to them) totaled 51,157 (about 49 percent). But if we compare data published in 1982 and in 1986 we discover that the num-bers of children placed in 1982, 91,141, exceeded the numbers placed in 1986, 52,031 (NCFA, 1989). If we look further, there appears to be a pattern. The total number of adoptions (related and unrelated) increased in 1951 from 72,000 to an all-time high of 175,000 in 1970. From 1970, the rate of adoptions has fallen considerably and continues to do so (Kadushin and Martin, 1988).

What accounts for this decline? Researchers attribute the decline to several fac-tors. First, the increased acceptance of abortion, birth control, and the laws regard-ing these have influenced the numbers of children being born. Secondly, while teen pregnancy has gained more attention in recent years, more teens are actually keeping their babies. Increased societal acceptance of single parenthood may affect this decision. For example, while at one time a pregnant adolescent was forced to leave school, this is no longer the case. Birth fathers are also expected—since the 1970s—to be more involved in the adoption and decision-making process. A father's protestations over a mother's decision to place her child for adoption may influence a teen to keep her baby, whether out of concern for the father or because fighting him on her adoption decision would be too complex and overwhelming (Samuels, 1990).

The adoption story does not end for teens when their child is in its infancy, however. Often these children are released by their parents when they are older—because the teen parent finds their care too great a task. Unfortunately, by this time the children are often abused, neglected, or have developed other problems. Their age may also be a deterrent to finding an adoptive placement easily.

African American teen mothers often do not place their children for adoption for cultural reasons. According to the National Committee for Adoption (1989), a high percentage of African American children born to teens are found living in their mother's family of origin. Hispanic and Asian women too may place their babies with extended family members.

CHANGES IN TYPES OF CHILDREN AVAILABLE FOR ADOPTION

While at one time the most adopted and adoptable child, the healthy white infant, was available, this is not the case today. The National Adoption Exchange reported that in the summer of 1987, 57 percent of all adopted children were African American children with special needs, 88 percent were over six years of age, and 40 percent were over twelve years old (Marindin, 1987). Despite the fact that it is the older or minority child who needs a home, not all couples are able to parent such a child.

Some couples' hesitation in adopting special needs children may be related to the recognition of their own infertility. Studies indicate a correlation between a couple's comfort level with their infertility and their ability to accept adoption. Infertility is as much of a loss as a death in the family and some couples have never been helped to grieve. For them adoption may become a less than healthy replacement (Helweg and Ruthven, 1990). These couples feel the need to parent an infant to whom they could have given birth. According to experts, the rate of infertility is on the rise (Wingard, 1987; Register, 1991). As couples marry later their fertility rate may decrease. Resolve, Inc., a national infertility education and advocacy network, reports that one in six of the couples in the United States are experiencing infertility. In the face of these statistics, it becomes increasingly important to help couples come to terms with infertility before they adopt. While some childless couples want to parent, they may not want the extra responsibility of a special needs child (Register, 1991).

Margie, a forty-three-year-old white social worker and her husband finally concluded that the only recourse for their fertility problem was adoption. They approached several agencies about adopting an infant and, as they had expected, they were told that the wait could be from five to eight years.

"They offered us special needs children but I wasn't ready for that," Margie admitted. "I work with abuse and neglect all day long and have for years. I've seen children maimed and their emotional growth retarded. After working with it all day long, I just couldn't cope with it at home."

Some couples believe that they are able to cope with special needs children, but after adopting a disabled five-year-old, Bridgett and Bill admitted that it has been difficult. "People must really know what they're getting into," says Bill, "the doctors' visits, the bills, the attitudes of other people." Agencies cognizant of this fact are now beginning to better prepare adoptive parents for special needs children.

CONTROVERSY OVER AGENCY VERSUS INDEPENDENT ADOPTIONS

Each year numbers of couples and single adults seek to adopt children without going through a public or private agency. Whether an intermediary is involved or the mother places with the couple, there are still numerous risks to all parties. If this is the case, why then do people seek out independent adoptions?

Currently couples are being told by agencies that either they are not taking applications for healthy infants or the waiting period will be anywhere from five to eight years. On the other had, a study of independent adoptions found that of the 105 infants placed independently, two-thirds were already with their adoptive parents within four months of the parents' attempts to find the child. The remainder of the children in the study were with their new parents within eleven months of the parents' initial search (Register, 1991).

Rights of the Child

Despite the advantage of a short waiting time, there are also disadvantages for both the child and for the adoptive couple. First and foremost, independent placements do not protect the child's right to the best home possible. Because the only real eligibility criterion is that the couple can provide the necessary fee, there is no guarantee that they will be suitable parents. Granted, undergoing an agency homestudy does not guarantee that the parents will be ideal, but agencies put their years of experience into their decision about whether or not to approve an adoptive couple.

Today agency homestudies not only assess the readiness of the applicant to parent through adoption, but they also provide valuable information and education for potential adoptive parents. The intensity of today's homestudies also aids parents in sorting out their feelings about whether adoption is in fact for them. Some applicants, after participating in the home study, have realized that adoption is not a suitable alternative to their particular needs. The time involved in the study and in waiting for the child, which every potential adoptive parent hates to consider, can actually contribute to the success of the adoption. As one adoptive mother recounts:

Sam and I knew when we were married at twenty-two that I'd never be able to conceive. So shortly after we were married we approached agencies to adopt. What an eye opener! We had no idea it could take so long—up to six years they told us. We tried to find an independent adoption. We found a doctor who would arrange it for us. He knew a teenager who was due in two months. A week before the baby was due I panicked. Suddenly I realized it was too soon. We hadn't even been married a year. We'd had no time to gel as a couple, so I backed out. Sam was really angry. It actually drove us to counseling. Then we reapplied to the adoption agency. They had us complete a ten-week home study with four other couples. At those meetings we looked at a lot of stuff I'd never considered—like how we would discipline. Sam and I totally disagreed. More negotiations followed. We learned a lot about our differences as well as our similarities. After a series of home visits, we were approved. Then came the waiting. It seemed an eternity. But three years to the date that we applied, they called us about a baby girl. After I took the call, I just sat there and thought—"Yes, now I'm ready."

No Follow-Up Services

In addition to no education about adoption, parents who adopt independently receive no follow-up services. There will be no supportive social worker to answer their questions, suggest resources, or provide referrals. Increasingly, researchers are citing agency follow-up as one of the most significant contributions to a successful adoption experience (Kadushin and Martin, 1988).

No Assurance of Confidentiality

Couples who adopt independently have little or no assurance that particulars about the adoption will be kept confidential. Neither intermediaries nor natural parents are necessarily bound to keep what is told to them confidential. In addition, biological parents may be given the name and address of adoptive parents and may in some cases feel justified in seeking them out. One couple recounts:

We adopted through an attorney. He told us the mother didn't want to have any contact with us. She didn't want our name and didn't want us to have hers. But a year later I was at the Laundromat and overheard two women talking. One said, in conversation, "My niece had a baby a year ago and gave it to a foster couple over on Chestnut. I told her she should go look them up." That was us! I whisked my son out of there quickly and went home. I was petrified. Would the mother come? Would she want Aaron back? I was also extremely angry with the attorney who had arranged the adoption. He would have been the only one who could have told. Who else had he told?

Biological parents may agree to or seek out independent arrangements because they are reluctant to face the red tape and the perceived impersonal treatment afforded by an agency. They may also feel that they have more control over the people with whom their child will be placed. Yet their right for confidentiality may also be unprotected.

Marvina recounts her experiences as a biological mother who gave up her child through her doctor.

He [the doctor] must have given the couple my name and address. I hadn't wanted that. The couple paid some of my medical bills and felt I owed them. They'd call up around holidays and tell me that the baby needed this or that. Hey, I was working two jobs just to get by. They sent some pictures, which was a nice thing to do, but it made it hurt more. I just wanted to forget. I'd done what I thought was best. Then I got involved with someone and before I could tell him about the baby, they did. He answered the phone one day when he was at my apartment and they told him my daughter needed something. I was really angry and hurt.

Insufficient Information about the Child

Experience has taught agencies who place children for adoption that honesty ensures the best placements. When adoptive couples are told as much as possible about a child they are offered, they are more likely to be comfortable with their choice. Agencies give couples the right to refuse a particular child if that child does not seem right for them. On the other hand, in an independent placement couples are often told little about the child. In addition, they may fear that if they refuse a child offered them, another might not be available.

Legal Aspects of Adoption Are Not as Clear-Cut

Agencies who place children for adoption either ensure that these children are legally free or inform the adoptive parents that this is a "legal risk" adoption—that is, the biological parents have not yet legally surrendered the child or the court has not yet terminated parental rights. In independent adoptions it is not always as clear-cut. If a biological mother places her own child in an adoptive home, she may have never legally surrendered her rights. If a couple is not cognizant of the legal procedures necessary, they may not realize this. Thus, at any point, the child's mother could reclaim her child. If any intermediary is involved there is still no guarantee that the adoption is free of legal risk.

No Counseling for Biological Mother or Adoptive Couple

Agencies recognize that the decision to place one's child for adoption is not made lightly. Birth mothers often require counseling to sort out their feelings and feel comfortable with their decision. Mothers who place their own child usually have not had the opportunity for professional help with their decisions. This lack of professional support often leaves the mother in conflict and makes it more difficult for her to get on with her life. Adoptive couples also may need support and counseling. The adjustments that come with new parenthood can be great. When an agency is not involved, this help is not readily available. Recognizing that independent adoption is not agency-sanctioned, couples may also be reluctant to seek out counseling from any agency.

No Protection in Adoption Disruption

When an agency places a child and, for whatever reasons, the placement is not successful, the agency will find another home for the child and provide counseling for both the child and the adoptive parents. Without agency involvement the disrupted adoption becomes even more problematic. Where does the child go if he or she cannot remain with the adoptive couple? Who will help the child and the parents cope with the loss and feelings of failure? Currently most states discourage or prohibit independent adoptions. In many instances, however, the penalties for violations are minimal (Kadushin and Martin, 1988).

ADOPTION DISRUPTION AND THE NEED FOR FOLLOW-UP

Each year approximately 10 percent of adoptions will be disrupted (Barth and Berry, 1988; Berry and Barth, 1990). The disruption statistics increase when an older child is placed for adoption. Boyne et al. (1984) estimated that children who are twelve years or older when adopted show a disruption rate of 47 percent. Berry and Barth (1990) reported that the adoptions of 22 percent of children between the ages of twelve and fourteen will be disrupted and 26 percent of those where the children are fifteen years and older.

While placement assessment, education, and support are vital to a successful adoption, follow-up services are also crucial. Currently agencies provide placement services to adoptive families for only short periods of time. For example, infants are usually followed for three months, while older children may be visited in their adoptive homes for up to a year; few agencies offer more extensive supervision. The North American Postlegal Adoption Committee reports that postplacement services are vitally important and should be available whenever needed, throughout the life of the family (Spencer, 1985).

Lack of postplacement services can be an important factor in adoption disruption. While adoptions are most likely to fail when the child exhibits behavior problems, when the child is older, or when he or she has already had an interrupted adoption experience, adequate services once the child has been placed in the adoptive home can often prevent the adoption from ending. Increasingly, agencies are recognizing the importance of follow-up services. In reality, adoptive families receive fewer services than birth families despite the fact that they are parenting the child.

THE EFFECTS OF ADOPTION ON CHILDREN

Typical of our society's desire for happy endings, we often think of postadoption life for families and children in a happily-ever-after context. In reality, family life is never without its adjustments. When the concept of adoption is added to the already delicate balance of familial relationships, problems may arise.

Therapists report that it is not uncommon for adopted children to question why their parents gave them up. While some are told "your biological mother [parents] loved you and wanted the best for you, so she gave you up," this explanation does not necessarily quell the conflicts over being abandoned and rejected. Adoptees who struggle with these feelings may feel distrust and confusion.

Any loss creates the need for grieving. Even the individual placed as an infant recognizes that another mother, some shadowy figure of his or her thoughts, once carried him or her in her womb and gave that baby to others. Most adopted children are never given the opportunity to grieve this loss, however insubstantial it may appear to others. The result can be a profound and often deep-seated sense of sadness. When other losses occur in later life, they may be especially difficult to bear as they serve as reminders of the initial separation from birth parents. The individual may therefore provoke rejection from others as confirmation that he or she is still unlovable (Helwig and Ruthven, 1990; Rosenberg, 1992).

In addition to potential conflicts related to adoption in general, particular populations of adopted children experience problems related to their own adoptions. For example, transracial adoptees who, cognizant of their African American or Asian origins, find themselves living in a white family may experience an identity crisis. "Who am I?" "What culture is mine?" are thoughts that plague some. Older children may have been exposed to physical abuse, substance abuse, or domestic violence before they were adopted and be coping with the residual scars of these traumas. Or, adopted parents may know little of the children's background, leaving adoptees with vague, possibly distorted memories and no answers to questions about their origins. Adoptive children, assured that they were "chosen," may harbor feelings that they must live up to the expectations of those who have adopted them.

All of the above issues translate into a variety of behaviors and attitudes. While some adopted children exhibit problem behaviors for their parents, others express the fears and conflicts inherent in having difficulty with trust and therefore relationships. Others repress their conflicts, becoming the "perfect children" they feel that their parents wanted. The inner toll may be enormous. For some adopted children, it is counseling or the readiness of their adoptive parents to face issues openly and help them master developmental tasks that enables these children to cope with or resolve the conflicts of their adoptive status.

ADOPTIVE PARTICIPANTS

BIRTH PARENTS

The Reasons behind the Decision

Giving birth to a child does not guarantee the parent's ability to care for that child or to face the responsibilities of parenting fully. Such responsibilities, with the many sacrifices involved, may be overwhelming for the woman or man whose own needs have never been fully met. Some parents recognize this early and give up their children at birth. Others believe that they can parent only to discover later that they are not able to meet the needs of either their children or themselves.

"I had no idea," recounts Rosina, "what a baby would be like. I pictured this little doll that I could take care of and who would love me like no one has ever loved me before. But Antonio cried all the time and spit up a lot. I liked to dress nice and all of a sudden all my clothes smelled like baby throw-up. And when he got older he was everywhere. I'd try to talk to a friend out front and before I knew it he'd be in the street. It was just too much."

When a friend offered Rosina a job in another state she dropped her two-year-old off at a convent saying she would return. She never did.

Not every parent gives up their child voluntarily. Those who abuse or neglect their children may have the decision to release them made for them by the social service or court system (see Chapter 9).

There are three ways that children become available for adoption:

- their parents voluntarily relinquish custody
- their parents abandon them
- the court terminates parental rights

Voluntary surrender. Parents voluntarily surrender their children for a variety of reasons. When we think of birth parents who give up children, we often conjure up an image of the pregnant teen who cannot keep the baby due to her own immaturity, educational needs, or financial situation. But who exactly are these teens?

Cushman, Kalmuss, and Nameron (1993) studied 215 young birth mothers who chose to place their babies for adoption. In this study, 64 percent of these mothers were between eighteen and twenty-one years with 36 percent between thirteen and seventeen years of age. The vast majority (86 percent) were in the appropriate grades in school and 53 percent had graduated from high school. Ninety-three percent of these young women were white and 7 percent were African American. Only 6 percent of the families of these mothers received welfare while they were growing up and, in 42 percent of the sample, the girl's fathers had graduated from college. These authors took their sample predominantly from maternity residences, which might have accounted somewhat for their findings. The women did receive counseling, and of those studied, 95 percent opted to place their babies for adoption while 5 percent decided to parent.

While Cushman and her colleagues found that their sample consisted of older adolescents, we know that pregnancy is occurring at younger and younger ages. With the advent of better health care conditions and the cultural changes in views about sexuality, women are becoming sexually active much earlier than their predecessors. Kadushin and Martin (1988) estimated that, out of the teens who are sexually active, only four in ten are using any form of birth control. Of those who do become pregnant, some will opt for adoption.

Unwed teens who decide on adoption may do so because they recognize their inexperience and inability to parent effectively. Chandra was fifteen when she became pregnant. Initially, she had decided that she would carry her baby to term and raise it herself. But she soon realized that her emotional supports at home were minimal and her options were few with a young child. Raised by an abusive, alcoholic mother, Chandra wanted better for her child.

It is not only the adolescent who gives up her child for adoption. Monica was thirty-five and separated from her husband when she realized that she was pregnant. Her career was thriving and rewarding and she could not imagine herself parenting at this stage of her life. Her strong religious belief made having an abortion out of the question. Instead, Monica took a leave of absence from her job, had the baby in another state, and placed her for adoption.

What of the biological father of the child who is given up for adoption? He, too, may be young and not ready for parenthood. Or he may not be in the position to parent this particular child. The father of Monica's baby was her husband, but he saw the pregnancy as Monica's attempt to reengage him in what had been a conflict-ridden marital relationship. He had children from a previous marriage and had no desire to support Monica's having this child.

Other fathers may be concerned, but not willing to share their parenting with the baby's mother. Some putative or biological fathers have asked for custody of children their mothers intended to release for adoption. Whether or not this request is granted depends on the father's prior involvement, his plan for the care of the child, and the laws in individual states. Some states require that the biological father also be involved in surrendering the child.

Parents who give up children for adoption do so because they realize that their lives cannot accommodate the responsibility. Adoption is not a decision that can be made lightly, nor is it one devoid of future conflicts. For some parents, parenting a particular child is something they do not feel able to do.

Joshua was born with many medical problems. His young mother, Janet, already had two other children, three and four years old. Joshua required frequent hospitalizations and consistent attention to giving him his medications. When his overwhelmed mother was unable to follow through with either medical appointments or the administration of his medicine, Joshua lapsed into a coma and was rushed to the hospital by a neighbor. Janet, frightened that Joshua would die and she would be blamed, took her other children and hid out for several weeks. The local social service agency took Joshua into custody when he was released from the hospital. Janet returned and, learning that her son was in foster care, angrily called the social worker involved in the case. After counseling to see if this mother was able to have Joshua returned to her, Janet was finally able to admit that her son's care was more than she could handle. She signed adoption releases and Joshua was eventually adopted by his foster parents.

Parents who voluntarily surrender their children do so by signing an adoption surrender. This legal document is a legally binding agreement by which parents give up their parental rights. To ensure that this document is legally binding, many states have stipulations that must be followed. For example, in many states, a mother cannot sign a surrender for a newborn until she has left the hospital. The rationale for this is that she should be free of medications that might confuse her and have some distance to be sure of her decision. There is also a trend toward encouraging birth parents to see their children at the hospital to determine if they are comfortable with their decision. Birth mothers, especially, who are ambivalent are given counseling to aid them in making a decision about relinquishing their child (Samuels, 1990).

Currently, there is much more attention paid to birth fathers than in years passed. Numerous cases, such as *Stanley vs. the State of Illinois* (1972) and *Lehr vs. Robertson* (1983), brought attention to the rights of these fathers. As a result, the Supreme Court ruled that the rights of birth fathers must be protected when adoption is being considered (Gitlin, 1987). Some sources (Kadushin and Martin, 1988; Brodzinsky and Schechter, 1990; Samuels, 1990) feel that agencies' previous reluctance to consider the birth father was based on the stereotype about his lack of involvement. He was often thought to be an unworthy, uninvolved character who gave the mother little or no support and whose involvement was merely in the sexual encounter. In reality, many birth fathers are interested in and concerned, if not about the mother, at least with the child.

Abandonment.   Parents who abandon their children may do so because they feel they have no other choice. A Hmong (a Laotian sect) baby was found in the back of a church. When the young mother was finally found, it was learned that she had been ostracized by her community and saw her only choice as abandoning her baby and killing herself.

Still other parents are so disturbed themselves or caught up in their own dysfunction that they have little time or energy for their children. The police in a large city were called to an address when neighbors were concerned that three children had been left alone. The children's parents had left town for several days on a "drug run" and had left the children alone. The children were taken into the custody of the local child welfare agency. When parents abandon their children and show no inclination to resume their care, the court steps in. Often the children are placed in foster homes and sometimes for adoption.

Termination of parental rights.   When parents cannot care for their children, either because they have abused or neglected them, are using substances that hinder their ability to care for the children, or are unable to protect their children, the juvenile court may intervene (see Chapter 10). Initially these children are usually placed in foster care. At one time, they may have remained in foster homes until they were eighteen. But PL 96–272 (1980) shifted the emphasis to permanency planning—finding the children a permanent home. Thus, more children brought into foster care due to their parents' inability to care for them effectively were freed for adoption by court action.

The issue of permanency planning raises several questions. The primary goal of child welfare agencies is family preservation (see Chapter 8). Therefore, when children come into foster care, agencies stress that services will be focused on reuniting the family. The reality is that a dearth of available workers in an agency, funds, and resources may mean that sufficient services are not available to reunite families quickly. In addition, change or rehabilitation is not an easy process. Thus, children may sometimes remain in foster care for an inordinate amount of time. Many of these children, already dealing with the scars of abuse and neglect, must also learn to adjust to living in a state of limbo. To reduce the trauma of children not knowing where they belong, many states have now mandated a time period during which biological parents are helped. If the parents are not able to demonstrate stability within this proscribed period, their rights as parents are legally terminated.

Some states require an additional process beyond the termination of parental rights to free a child for adoption. Instead the agency must then petition the court, usually probate, for the further termination of right for the purpose of adoption. This extra step may mean an additional period of time before the child can find permanency.

The Emotional Aspects of Losing One's Child

Parents, especially those who voluntarily surrender their children, deal with the impact of this decision for many years to come. For many, their view of themselves is significantly changed. Plumer (1992) suggests that biological parents face the separation from their children with diverse feelings:

> *Feeling that they lack control.* Even parents who choose to place their children often feel that they had no choice. They may feel that others were telling them what to do, or that there was no other action open to them.
>
> *Feeling inadequate.* Our society assumes that parenting is something that anyone can do. To admit that one cannot parent often makes an individual feel ashamed, guilty, and a failure.
>
> *Feeling stigmatized by the community.* Because everyone "should be able to parent," someone who cannot is somehow "different" and may feel stigmatized by others.
>
> *Feeling that they would like to blame others.* It is often easier, when one is in pain, to assume that another caused it. "If the baby's father had been more supportive" or "If my parents had not abused me," are classic reasons parents may use to account for their separation from their children.
>
> *Feeling bitter or angry.* Birth parents, in their desire to not face separation, may project their feelings onto others, becoming bitter, angry, and sometimes abusive to those around them.
>
> *Feeling like they want to give up.* Losing a child is emotionally draining and, experienced with the above feelings, can seem overwhelming. Some parents do not feel they can cope. Some parents become childlike ("the agency can take care of everything for me"). Some become apathetic; some want to escape the pain though denial, or even suicide.

Jenkins and Norman (1972), in a study of the reactions to separation of a sample of 297 birth mothers, found that the predominant feelings were sadness (87 percent) worry (74 percent), nervousness (68 percent), emptiness (60 percent), anger (50 percent), bitterness (43 percent), and thankfulness (43 percent). For birth fathers, the feelings were sadness (90 percent), worry (68 percent), thankfulness (57 percent), nervousness (56 percent), anger (45 percent), and bitterness (43 percent) (Plumer, 1992, 61).

Birth parents wonder what will become of their children. Will they be loved? Will the children wonder about them? Will the children be safe? The stereotype of parents who can easily forget the experience and go on with their lives is erroneous. Numerous studies have borne this out. Rynearson (1981) studied twenty birth mothers with histories of psychosis. They had surrendered their babies when they were between fifteen and nineteen years old. All the subjects reported that, within two years of giving up their children, they had disturbing dreams about losing their babies. Even beyond the two-year period, these women described having emotional reactions when seeing children who were about the age of those they had given up.

A more significant sample of 364 birth parents was collected by Deykin, Campbell, and Patti (1984) through Concerned United Birth Parents (CUB). Of these, 280 respondents who had been married reported that the experience of relinquishing a child had had a negative influence on their marriage. Of the 219 who had later again become parents, 81 percent said that the adoption experience had had a significant impact on their parenting practices. While Brodzinsky and Schechter (1990) question the bias of the respondents in this study, because the sample was collected from CUB (an organization of birth parents who are dissatisfied with their experiences), they did feel that this and other research indicated that the separation experience does leave long-term residual effects on birth parents.

Services for Birth Parents

Despite research attesting to the significant effect that giving up a child has on the birth parent, agencies do not always provide a sufficient amount of help for those parents. As one social worker explained:

> We are a child welfare agency. Once a mother has given up her children, she is technically no longer eligible for services. We can counsel her for the period right after the placement, but then we have to close the case. It's policy. We just have to hope that she finds a counselor later who can help her grieve.

The problem is that many birth parents do not recognize that their problems or feelings are related to the loss of a child. Many find it easier to deny. Nellie Barringer, in *One Two Three: Matt a Feral Child* (Craig, 1978), laments her loss of her children for her neglect of them by overprotecting and indulging a later child, Matt. So intense is their symbiotic attachment that Matt becomes feral (animal-like) and Nellie a recluse.

If parents are able to get help with their grieving, Brodzinsky and Schechter (1990) propose that they should be allowed the space, empathy, time, and expression necessary to come to terms with the loss. They also point out that rituals can play a large part in the passages of our lives. Part of the grieving process may be acknowledging the day of separation or some other way to accept that this has been part of one's experience. It is the individual who has been helped to put his or her life back in perspective who can go on with his or her life in a healthy manner.

CHILDREN AVAILABLE FOR ADOPTION

Kadushin and Martin (1988) describe three categories of children who are available for adoption: healthy infants, children with special needs, and children adopted from foreign countries.

Healthy infants.   Today there are fewer and fewer healthy infants available for adoption. Despite the fact that adolescents have become sexually active at younger ages than in past decades, birth control and abortion are increasingly available. There has also been a trend toward young mothers keeping their babies. If these babies do come into the social service system, it is usually at an older age and often as a result of abuse, neglect, or family dysfunction. The increased incidence of substance abuse has also altered the picture of how many healthy infants are available. As more mothers abuse drugs and alcohol during pregnancy, more babies are born either addicted to drugs at birth or suffering the effects of fetal alcohol syndrome (FAS). The demand for healthy infants has always outweighed the availability of such children, but today this is especially true. It is not uncommon for a couple wanting a baby to be told that they will have to wait between five and ten years. Some agencies refuse to study couples asking for a healthy child.

Children with special needs.   *Special needs* is a term that refers to many different issues and conditions. In the context of adoption, special needs children are those whose issues necessitate either that the adoption agency look further for parents who want this type of child, or that, once adopted, the family may face more financial burdens or emotional issues. The term *special needs* can encompass: children with medical problems; children who are older than three years; sibling groups; children who are mentally retarded; or children with some emotional disturbance.

Kadushin and Martin (1988) also include African American, Hispanic, Native American, and mixed racial children in this category. During the 1960s and 1970s an increasing number of nonwhite children were placed in white homes. For example, by 1979, approximately 15,000 African American children were placed for adoption with white families (Day, 1979) amid much protest by such groups as the National Association of Black Social Workers. Members of this organization expressed the belief that African American children should grow up among those of their own racial background. Others argued that a permanent home, whether black or white, was in the best interests of the child (Samuels, 1990). This view was supported by Shireman and Johnson (1986), who found that most children placed across racial lines *did* develop a healthy sense of their own racial identity.

Native American children, too, were placed predominantly with white couples until the 1978 Indian Child Welfare Act. This act gave tribes the authority to make placement decisions for their own children. Preference was given first to the children's extended family members, then to other tribal members or Native Americans. Today there are greater numbers of children available from racial minorities than ever before.

Children with medical problems.   Children may have a variety of medical problems that range from the minor to the severe.

Lee was born with a cleft pallet, which required surgery several times during his childhood. His mother felt unable to deal with the severity of his problems and relinquished him for adoption when he was an infant.

Addison was a perky three-year-old African American child who was born deaf. His mother's drug use during pregnancy had sent him into withdrawal soon after birth. The doctors were initially somewhat guarded about his condition, but at three, Addison's only apparent problem was his deafness.

Helen was shaken by her abusive father when she was an infant. The result was that both her retinas were detached. Although surgery had been tried, the results were less than the medical community had hoped for.

Bobby was born HIV-positive. Soon after his birth, his mother and her boyfriend (Bobby's father) both died with AIDS. With no relatives willing to parent him, Bobby was placed for adoption. Some children with Bobby's diagnosis will test negative as they grow older. Others will continue to be positive for HIV and will eventually die.

Of all the medical issues, adopting an HIV-positive child is one of the newest and most uncertain. Families interested in providing a permanent home for these children must be prepared for the worst as well as the best. While there may be only a few physical adjustments to be made by a family parenting an HIV-positive child, the emotional issues are significant. There is still pronounced negative sentiment toward those who are HIV-positive. In addition, when parenting an HIV-positive child, common childhood illnesses become more significant and problematic. And, the possibility of eventually losing the child must be considered. Still, there is an increasing need for stability in the lives of these children (Skinner, 1989).

Children who are mentally retarded.   Mental retardation can present a challenge in children who are available for adoption and to the families who adopt them. Glidden (1989) looked at issues brought to their adoption by fifty-six mentally retarded children. Fifteen of the children studied were placed prior to six months of age, ten were between seven and twelve months, five between thirteen and twenty-four months, six between twenty-five and sixty months, and ten between sixty-one and one hundred twenty months. Another ten were placed at over 120 months of age. Of the sample some twenty-seven were girls and twenty-nine were boys. Fifty-nine percent of the children studied had Down syndrome (a chromosome abnormality) and were therefore (by nature of the syndrome) likely to exhibit not only mental retardation but also congenital abnormalities of the intestines and heart, decreasing their life span. The other children in Glidden's study exhibited other less common syndromes and birth defects as causes of their mental retardation.

Fifty-three percent of the birth families were considered stable with no history of abuse, neglect, substance abuse, mental illness, criminality, or mental retardation. The remainder had subjected their children to maltreatment or a severely dysfunctional family life. Thirty-five of the fifty-six children had been released for adoption because of their disability. In the case of eleven, the reason was uncertain, while ten others were available due to other factors (Glidden, 1989).

Children who are older than three years.   Children who are not released for adoption until they are older have a greater risk of having been abused, neglected, or having witnessed domestic violence or drug abuse. Children who come into care at a later age than three do so either because their parents' rights have been terminated because of the above situations or because their birth parents have determined that they are unable to care for them for some reason.

When April was a baby, her sixteen-year-old mother, Lara, found that parenting was a novelty. But by the time April was three, the responsibility weighed heavily on the young mother. Lara had a new boyfriend who drank heavily. When he wasn't beating Lara or April, he was taking them places they had never been before. Lara was jealous of his attention to April. She began leaving April home when they went out. During one two-day absence, a neighbor reported to the police that April was alone in the house. The police took April to a local social service agency. Lara's inability to work consistently with the agency over the next year led to April's release for adoption.

Lara's inability to properly care for her child is not unlike other parents whose children become free for adoption at a later age. Most of these releases are involuntary. Only infrequently do parents recognize the need to help their children find permanency.

Children who have experienced dysfunctional homes bring with them not only feelings of loss but also scars from the pain they have experienced and witnessed. For them and their adoptive parents, the adjustments may be many.

Sibling groups.   At one time siblings who were free for adoption might have gone to different adoptive homes, perhaps not being allowed to maintain contact with each other. Increasingly, agencies are trying to keep family groups together whenever possible. This sometimes presents a challenge.

The Foster children were three, five, and seven years old when the court terminated their birth parents' rights. Three-year-old Kit and five-year-old Kerry were outgoing, responsive children who would adjust well to a new home. For seven-year-old Kim, life had been dedicated to taking care of her younger siblings. She had done this well, but it had taken its toll. Angry and sullen, Kim had no use for adults. They had betrayed

> her before and she would not trust them again. It would take Kim years before she would see her adoptive parents as anything but a threat.

While sibling groups can be a challenge, some couples value the prospect of a ready-made family.

Children with some emotional disturbance.   Many of the children mentioned earlier also fit in this category. Pain takes its toll on children and that pain is made visible in children who act out behaviorally, who express their anger openly, or who have difficulty relating to others.

> Tricia, at fourteen, had been in a residential treatment center for two years. Her mother died when Tricia was ten from a drug overdose. Her stepfather, after kicking his own drug habit, could not cope with Tricia's angry outbursts. Her life had been punctuated by neglect since infancy. Now she ran away with frequency. At home she disobeyed, was sexually promiscuous, and experimented with drugs herself. An unsuccessful suicide attempt brought her to a psychiatric hospital and later into residential treatment. A time came when Tricia was discharged. The professionals working with her felt that she was ready to return to home, but Tricia's stepfather signed an adoption surrender saying he could not accept the responsibility of a fourteen-year-old. At fourteen, Tricia became available for adoption.

Children adopted from foreign countries.   The adoption of children from other countries has been practiced formally for the last four decades. Since 1956 the Holt Agency has sought to place children from a variety of countries in adoptive homes in this country. Although this was not the earliest attempt to place war orphans it has been one of the most extensive. During 1987 there were approximately 10,097 children brought to the United States to be adopted by American families (not all of these came through the Holt Agency). Although 1987 was the peak year for such adoptions, 9,120 children were admitted in 1988 (Register, 1991, 3). Latin America, as well as Vietnam, Korea, the Philippines, India, and other Asian countries have sent children to the United States, Canada, Australia, and Western Europe.

Who are the children? Register (1991) gives profiles of some of the children involved.

> David was the fifth child born to a poor woman living in Tegucigalpa, the capital of Honduras. Her husband had left her during the pregnancy and she knew it would be difficult to raise the four children she already had, let alone a new baby... (4).

> Anita was found on the street in Guatemala City after a beating by a group of older boys. She did not know her birth date but seemed about seven years old and had been living on her own for a year or so… (4).

> Asha weighed less than four pounds and was malnourished when her mother, a young, unmarried woman in northern India, left her at a clinic a week or so after her birth… (4).

All of these children remained in an orphanage or a foster home until they could be placed with adoptive families. For many of these children, international adoption is their only hope for survival. Cultural taboos, such as illegitimacy, or economic conditions may make it impossible for them to remain in the countries of their birth. Because professionals feel that these children will face less stigmatization and have more resources available to them, agencies like Holt arrange for them to be adopted in North America and Western Europe.

ADOPTIVE APPLICANTS

Recruitment

Recruitment is an important part of the adoption process. Although some applicants seek out adoption agencies, others may either not know where to start pursuing their interest in adopting or may not perceive that there is a need for agencies to find homes for children. Recruitment is especially important for special needs children. Sometimes, when potential applicants become aware of a particular child, they are more able to consider adoption. For example, a television network in Boston features a piece called "Wednesday's Child." Here children who may have some special need are introduced as viewers watch them on the TV screen. Invitations to call in often generate numerous applicants and may result in finding an adoptive home for the child.

"One Church, One Child" is another example of a recruitment effort that has been successful. In 1979, a Chicago priest, Father George Clements, challenged the African American churches in Chicago to see that at least one member of each congregation adopted an African American child. Using slide presentations about specific children, the program was instituted by more than fifty Churches and eventually supported by the federal government. Currently, over twenty states have some variation of this recruitment tool (Pecora et al., 1992).

Other innovative strategies have been implemented by corporations, newspapers, and civic groups, though undoubtedly more widespread recruitment should be done to place the children who are available.

Profile of Applicants

Kadushin and Martin (1988) divide those who apply to adopt children into two categories: traditional and preferential. The traditional applicant is the couple that has been unable to have children biologically.

Sam and Melissa married after both became established in their respective careers. In their early thirties the couple decided to add children to their satisfying relationship. After several years, they became concerned about their fertility. Melissa originally sought help and underwent a series of fertility tests. Ruling out infertility for her, Melissa's physician suggested that Sam be seen. The results of preliminary tests revealed that, probably due to a childhood illness, Sam was infertile.

"It really upset him." Melissa recounts. "He was from a family of macho men and he felt that this made him less of a man. It took a year of counseling to convince him otherwise."

No matter who is the infertile partner, or even if no cause is discovered, couples often go through a grieving process. "You don't really question being able to have children," Melissa explains. "You just expect that you will."

Infertile couples experience not only disappointment but anger and guilt. Often they describe difficulties in their relationship with each other. But couples who do not adequately grieve their inability to have their own biological children may never fully accept an adopted child. They may have difficulty accepting their child's origins and be less able to discuss adoption openly with her or him (Samuels, 1990). For this reason, during the screening process, most agencies discuss in depth the couple's feelings about their infertility.

Preferential applicants are those who choose, for whatever reason, to adopt. Some couples hope to complete an already existing family with a child of the opposite sex.

The mother of three boys, Arlene had always wanted a girl. "I worked so hard at being comfortable being female," she recounts. "I felt that I wanted a daughter with whom I could share all this."

Other couples seek to adopt children from other cultures. Bus Wagner had been in India during the service. He knew of the plight of many poor children in that country, and had always hoped to adopt one. After having a biological child, he and his wife felt ready to take a child from India into their home.

Granted, not all couples who adopt foreign-born children have biological children. Many are unable to have their own families but prefer to adopt children who are unlike the children they might have had. Register (1991) explains that, while some couples have altruistic goals for adopting internationally, others feel that children are available from other countries more quickly and at a younger age. Couples who adopt internationally also appear to fit a specific profile themselves.

A 1986 survey of adoption agencies found that parents who adopt foreign-born children are generally college-educated, suburban couples earning an average of $36,000 a year. Although most have no children of their own, the couples—who are likely to be in their mid-thirties—have been married an average of seven years (Register, 1991, 27).

Some couples who decide to adopt may do so because they perceive that there is a need. Connie and George Adams had one biological child when they applied to adopt a disabled child. They had spent a good deal of time with Connie's Down syndrome sister and felt ready to parent such a child themselves.

Couples may not always refer to heterosexual partners. Increasingly gay and lesbian couples are seeking to adopt. States and agencies differ as to their policies regarding these couples. Over the last few decades an increasing number of single people have also become adoptive parents. Knowing that she did not intend to marry, Isabella still wanted to parent. She had heard that agencies sometimes had children who have never learned to trust the relationships in their lives and might have an easier time building trust with one person than with several.

Studies show that single adoptive parents are more likely to be women who have occupations and skills that lend themselves to understanding children's special issues. For example, nurses, social workers, and teachers are highly represented among single adoptive applicants. They usually have extended family backup and a high percent were raised themselves in single parent homes (Shireman and Johnson, 1976; Feigelman and Silverman, 1983).

Foster parents are another group of adoptive applicants that is relatively recent. Although foster parents have always adopted some of their foster charges, the practice was not encouraged. "We used to call it the back door to adoption," recounts a social worker who worked with foster parents in the 1960s and 1970s. "If you wanted to adopt, we felt you should apply for adoption, not do foster care. But foster parents grow to love children in their care and the children become fond of them. Our old ideas weren't too realistic."

Today people are still not encouraged to pursue adoption by becoming foster parents. The reality is that many of the children placed in foster care are not free for adoption. However, when a child becomes available for adoption whose foster parents have become attached they are often given the option to adopt.

There are still pros and cons to this type of adoption. While the greatest advantage in undeniably the consistency for the child, foster parents who adopt must also consider the disadvantages. The foster parents' relationship with the biological parents will change if they adopt. Can all parties adjust to this? In addition, foster parents must consider whether they expect to continue fostering. If they do, can their adopted child be helped to feel secure when he or she sees other foster children leave the home? Although foster parent adoption is no longer discouraged, the child's bonding within the home, the length of the child's stay, and the availability of other potential adoptive homes are all considered before this kind of adoption is allowed.

Adoptive Siblings

One often forgotten part of the potential adoptive family are the couples' biological children. Potential siblings come in all ages, yet the wise couple will have explained their desire to adopt and be assured of some degree of enthusiasm and cooperation from their children. Biological children may be extremely worried about their contribution to the home study and the adoption placement. One anxious four-year-old refused to come out of his room when the social worker came to visit the applicants' house. Finally, the worker overheard the child's response to his mother's pleas to appear. "If you think I'm going to come out and blow this whole deal, you're crazy!" The child, knowing how much his parents wanted this adoption, was convinced that his reservations would spoil their chances.

Biological children often wonder and express, either nonverbally or outloud, their concern that they are not enough for their parents. They may fear that the new child will receive all the parents' love and worry that they will be "left out." While children facing the arrival of any new sibling may have these fears, the biological sibling may be much more aware of what his parents have been going through to get this new child. For this reason, most agencies encourage careful preparation of biological children.

THE ADOPTIVE PROCESS

THE HOMESTUDY

A child has just become free for adoption, possibly through years of court appearances and/or counseling (see Chapters 9 through 12). In the meantime, the couple or individual who will eventually adopt this child have been going through a process themselves.

> "When we initially decided to adopt," says Allison Kelly, "we called an adoption agency we had heard about. They invited us to an information meeting the next week. Here we met with ten other couples who were interested in adopting, too. We learned what types of children were available for adoption, why they became available, and what we should expect if we adopted them. Some of these children came from rough home backgrounds and might have behavior problems. The logistics of the home study was also explained to us.
>
> "After we left there, I was very excited but I also realized that things would not be as quick and easy as I had hoped."

Early meetings of this type have several purposes. First, they acquaint applicants with agency requirements. They also ask applicants to consider their suitability related to the several other factors on which they will be judged.

Motivation: Agencies are interested in applicants' reasons for wanting to adopt. If they are unable to have children, have they explored infertility issues? Are they trying to replace a child they have lost? Agencies wonder if an applicant's altruistic desire to take children ignores the fact that real children have real problems. For example, it may seem commendable to a couple to take a child who was maltreated, but can they cope with the scars that may result from this maltreatment? Most agencies expect applicants to be consciously aware of their motivations (Kadushin and Martin, 1988).

Stability of the Relationship: Couples who wish to adopt will be assessed with respect to their relationship as a couple. It is hoped that they have given their marriage/relationship a chance and that they do not hope that adopting a child will cement a faltering union.

Age: Agencies usually consider applicants who are within normal child-rearing ages. Much also depends on the age of the child the applicants are considering. While couples in their forties may be studied for an older child, they might not be considered for an infant. In situations where unmarried partners or gay/lesbian couples are considered, it is usually expected that the relationship is stable and of some duration.

Physical and Emotional Health: Since the intent of adoption is to provide permanency and a healthy environment for children, the applicants' physical and emotional health is important to agencies. Required medical examinations explore the potential adopters physical capability to care for children. Social workers also look for applicants who appear emotionally stable, mature, have a good self-concept, and are able to meet a child's emotional needs (Downs et al., 1996).

Financial Stability: Taking a child into one's home requires sufficient income to accommodate the needs of another individual. Although subsidized adoption is available, these monies are earmarked for special circumstances. In general, applicants must be employed (or at least one member of a couple) and financially secure. Mothers who intend to work are asked about child care arrangements. Some agencies still lean toward at least one parent being the primary caretaker of the child.

Despite the above requirements, agencies often find that they must be flexible, respecting cultural diversity and increasingly different family values.

Informational meetings may serve another purpose in addition to outlining agency requirements and informing applicants about the children who are available. For some, the meetings also generate self-selection. Potential adoptive parents who perceive that they do not meet agency criteria or discover that adoption does not meet their expectations may opt to discontinue the process.

After the informational meeting, Allison and Dan Kelly decided to continue in their quest to adopt and were invited to be part of a homestudy group that was to begin several months later. *Homestudy* is the term agencies use to describe the screening, education, and selection of adoptive couples and individuals. While at one time the norm was to study couples individually, home studies are now more likely to be done initially in groups. This allows applicants to gain support and learn from their peers. Allison Kelly describes the process:

"We met with five other couples with whom we became quite close. The groups met for a ten-week period, during which we were asked to explore our values and attitudes about such issues as biological parents, our infertility, disciplining children, and telling children they are adopted. Sometimes it was painful to look at our feelings. And sometimes it was funny. Danny and I discovered a lot about each other that we hadn't known after six years of marriage."

The above model, called the Model Approach to Partnership in Parenting (M.A.P.P.), is currently used by numerous agencies because it has been found to strengthen high risk placements (Barth and Berry, 1988).

PLACEMENT AND LEGALIZATION

Once adoptive applications have been approved for placement, their names are kept on file until a particular child who fits the criteria they can accept is in need of a home. Depending on the age of the child, the placement process may be fairly swift or spread over a longer period of time to insure proper adjustment on the part of all parties.

Time from actual placement to legalization differs once again. Agencies usually maintain contact with adoptive families for at least three months, although research indicates that the length of this supervised adjustment period is really not sufficient (Barth and Berry, 1988). Having a "ready-made" child placed in one's home is quite different from knowing the child from birth. The older the child, the more adjustment issues there may be.

Legalization through probate court may mean that the agency's contact with the new adoptive family will cease. The child's birth records are sealed and a new birth certificate is issued with the adoptive couple or individual shown as the parent(s).

Open Adoption

Following their release for adoption, children's contacts with their birth parents terminate. Traditionally this was felt to be best for all involved. Only then could children grieve properly for birth parents. This practice also allowed adoptive couples who were not entirely comfortable with their own infertility to deny that the child had ever had another family.

More recently, experts in adoption began to see that some children, especially those who were older when placed, needed continuity from the past. Some actually feel that the secrecy of traditional adoptions denies children their rights (Pannor and Baran, 1984; Small, 1987).

Open adoption describes what Siegel (1993) has called "a continuum of options" (16) enabling birth parents and adoptive parents to have contact or information about each other prior to and after adoption placement. At one end of the continuum, parents do not meet but exchange letters and photographs through an intermediary. In other adoptions, the parties not only meet but carry on relationships (e.g., adoptive parents become mentors for a young unmarried birth mother). Between these two extremes lies a variety of options. The underlying criterion, however, is the birth parents' ability to relinquish their claims and recognize the adoptive parents as the child's legal and emotional parents (Byrd, 1988).

Siegel (1993) studied twenty-one adoptive couples who had participated in open adoptions. None of these individuals regretted the openness of their adoptions, but collectively they generated a list of advantages and disadvantages. The adoptive parents felt more in control over which birth parents they worked with. They were comforted to know that they interviewed birth mothers firsthand rather than having to rely on information given them secondhand by an agency. They could learn more about prenatal care and issues that might affect their children's future, e.g., the genetic risk factors, substance abuse, and so forth. These parents also felt more able to answer their children's questions about their histories and birth parents. Finally, it was comforting for the adoptive parents to know that the birth parents had given up their children willingly. They also felt it would be comforting for birth parents to know that their offspring had found good homes (Siegel, 1993).

The disadvantages cited by adoptive couples related more to their own comfort than to the welfare of children or birth parents. Several parents felt it would be difficult to tolerate the birth mother's pain over her loss. One mother recognized that her discomfort with her own infertility made it difficult for her to bond with another woman's child when she knew the woman. Couples who had mentored birth mothers during their pregnancy found it difficult to adjust once the child was born. Some parents felt the need to look especially competent as parents in front of the birth family. Finally, adoptive couples worried about meeting birth parents on the street or being expected to be more involved than they felt comfortable with (Siegel, 1993).

Siegel concludes that agencies should be more open in their adoption procedures. But open adoption, like other types of adoption, requires recognition that agencies must provide continued support, education, and counseling services.

POSTLEGALIZATION SERVICES

Services available to adoptive families following placement and legalization are both formal (agency-based) and informal (parent-generated).

Agency Services
Many agencies, recognizing that adoption is a lifelong experience, make support groups and educational programs available. Developmental milestones (e.g., adolescence) are as difficult for adoptive families as any other parents, but the added

issue of adoption makes the picture even more complex. Understanding these milestones through educational seminars may help adoptive parents anticipate and deal with them. Many agencies offer workshops on parenting techniques, parenting toddlers, parenting adolescents, or even helping older children separate, and may also provide libraries of films and books for those who are interested. Support groups of other adoptive couples who are experiencing similar issues may also fill a need for families. Social events and retreats are an additional form of support for both adoptive couples and children.

The North American Council on Adoptable Children (NACAC) advocates a "buddy system" that pairs new adoptive parents with more experienced ones. Agencies initially oversee this arrangement, which may in time become more informal (Boersdarfer et al., 1986). The "buddy" may actually participate in some of the homestudy process and provide support thereafter.

Agencies today report that a significant number of adoptive families and adoptees are returning to request record reviews. While at one time families were given only a scant amount of information about their adopted children, today agencies recognize that more information is necessary. Although agencies and state laws differ, many agencies at a couple or adoptee's request, will review records and provide whatever additional health or background information is available that was not given at the time of the adoption.

Counseling is also a service that should be available for postadoption. Adopted children may have the same issues other children present in therapy, e.g., poor school performance, acting out, oppositional behavior, and poor self-esteem. Not all adoptive families remain functional. Any of these eventualities may bring adoptive families to counseling. In addition several themes seem to be more prevalent among adoptive families:

- *Powerlessness:* Often the members of adoptive families feel powerless. The couple may bring with them their initial feelings of helplessness over not being able to have children. They may feel powerless in their relations with the agency involved. Adopted children often feel that they had no decision in their placement and feel powerless over their futures. All members may feel unable to deal with the early trauma the child experienced (Hartman and Laird, 1990).
- *The "bad seed" myth:* Hartman and Laird (1990) describe how parents often fear that the child's biological past may predestine him or her to respond in negative ways. Or families worry that the child's past experiences will be unalterable. These "ghosts" become a part of family secrecy and may lead to disfunction.
- *Adoptive issues:* Some families seek counseling to enable them to handle how to explain adoption to their children. Often those sessions bring up the parents' old uncertainties about adoption. Parents may also seek help when they perceive that their adopted children may search for birth parents (Hartman and Laird, 1990; Schaffer and Lindstrom, 1990; Rosenberg, 1992).
- *Needing to be a perfect parent:* It is not uncommon for adoptive parents, who may have worked hard to become parents, to feel the need to be perfect in that role.

Caught up in a sense of failure over not being able to have children themselves these couples often seek reassurance that they are doing a good job (Hartman and Laird, 1990).

- *Identity issues:* Adoptees may seek counseling in an attempt to understand who they are and where they belong. They were born to one set of parents and are being raised by others. Children whose adoption has been the traditional, closed, secretive affair wonder about their histories. They may feel the need for loyalty to both birth and adoptive parents and wonder how to bridge the gap. This is especially true of nonwhite children placed in white families. Nonwhite children often identify with both cultures but may find it difficult to figure out where they feel comfortable (Silverman and Feigelman, 1990; Rosenberg, 1992).

Telling the Child about Adoption

There has been some controversy over the years as to how and when to tell a child that he or she is adopted. While a few psychoanalytic theorists (Wieder, 1977; Berger and Hodges, 1982) contend that discussion of adoption before the resolution of the Oedipal Complex causes psychic damage to the child, most adoption resources recommend the use of the word *adoption* early in the child's life. Brodzinsky, Singer, and Braff (1984) concluded, as a result of their study of 200 four- to thirteen-year-old adopted and nonadopted children, that children's understanding of adoption grows over time. Before they are six years old, children can accept that they are adopted but do not comprehend the significance. Statements about having "two mommies" are so far out of their frames of reference that they mean little. By the time they are close to six, children begin to worry and focus on why they may have been given up. Between eight and eleven years of age, children finally begin to understand the complex nature of adoption with its losses and changes, and some children fantasize that birth parents will appear to claim them. By adolescence, children are more able to understand the legalities, rights, and responsibilities of adoption (Berger and Hodges, 1982; Samuels, 1990; Rosenberg, 1992).

In reality, not telling children they are adopted until after they are five years old can also have negative results. Not telling them forces adoptive parents into keeping a secret, and children may later resent not being told. In addition, children may inadvertently learn from someone else before parents tell them.

"When I was twelve," Rob recounts, "my aunt, who was drinking at the time, told me I was adopted. At first I didn't believe it. When I was finally convinced it was true, I was angry. Angry that my parents didn't tell me. I had a right to know. It made me wonder what else they hadn't told me and how much I could trust them."

Parents who use the word *adoption* in a loving way early in the child's life help the child to become comfortable gradually. Adoptive parents who are not able to talk openly about adoption may have difficulty with the concept themselves. On the other hand, Samuels (1990) cautions against overemphasizing the issue of adoption, suggesting that belaboring the issue may also point to adoptive parents' discomfort. Open, honest, confident telling in age-appropriate ways appears to correlate with successful adoptions (Kadushin and Martin, 1988; Rosenberg, 1992; Downs et al., 1996).

Some agencies currently provide "life books" to enable children to understand their histories. These books consist of pictures, letters, and narratives depicting the child's life from birth to adoption. The use of "life books" is often a way to help children understand how they came to be adopted. Children are curious about why they were given up for adoption. It is important not to imply inadequacy on the part of birth parents as they are an integral part of children's perception of themselves. Children often fear that they contributed to being released for adoption by being intrinsically undesirable or misbehaving. Adoptive parents must assure adoptees that they were wanted by both sets of parents. Yet there is a delicate balance between describing as truthfully as necessary the circumstances of the birth parents' decision to give up their child and, at the same time, not portraying them as totally victimized.

There are several books out for children that aid adoptive parents in explaining adoption to their children, including *Why Was I Adopted?* (Livingston, 1978) and *How It Feels to Be Adopted* (Krementz, 1982).

ADOPTION DISRUPTION

Not all adoptions are successful. About 10 percent of all placements will be unsuccessful or disrupted each year. Some families, though at risk for disruption, will either receive counseling or find other ways to avoid it. Often, however, families do *not* seek services or alternatives until it is too late (Barth and Berry, 1988).

Several factors put adoptive families at higher risk for disruption. The seeds that grow into failed adoption relationships may have been undetected during the initial home study, may have been recognized but were not explored, or may not have been predictable.

Roland and Bev Markham felt they had a good marriage. When it became apparent that a childhood illness had rendered Roland infertile, the couple dealt with the issue openly. Several years later, the Markhams were approved for adoption and eventually received a three-month-old girl who was the picture of redheaded Bev. After several years of successful parenting the Markhams asked for a second child. This time a black-eyed, black-haired Native American boy of six months, who looked very much like Roland, was placed in their home. A Native American himself, Roland initially welcomed this addition. The child had minor medical problems, but recognizing how well the Markhams had done with their daughter, the agency felt that this was an appropriate placement. Six months after the initial placement, it became obvious that the family was in trouble. Roland, always very involved with his daughter, could not bond with this male child. Sensing the rejection, the boy had become withdrawn. After counseling the couple it became clear to the agency that this child must be removed. Roland had come to recognize that this child was too much of a reminder of his own sickly childhood in a culture that stressed strength in males. He had also been helped to realize that these memories brought up his unresolved anger and guilt over his infertility.

The risk for disruption is rooted in several areas. Certainly the adoptive parents' own issues may prevent them from being successful with adoption in general or with a specific child. The family balance may also be a factor. For example, a couple with older children may find that the family cannot sufficiently rebalance when a new child is added. This causes disharmony. While, through counseling, some families can find solutions, others cannot and the result may be disruption.

The adopted child also brings issues with which a family may have difficulty dealing. The child's age, behavioral problems, number of previous placements, and past history can influence his/her integration into the household (Pecora et al., 1992; Rosenberg, 1992; Downs et al. 1996). Children may never have resolved their conflict over loyalty to birth parents versus their adoptive parents. Kadushin and Martin (1988) suggest that the adoptive family's ability to handle destructive, aggressive behaviors (often the result of the child's abusive history or multiple moves) and the adequacy of the family's support system are also key factors.

Effective casework on the part of the placement agency is vital when the family is at risk for disruption, and indeed throughout the placement process. Festinger (1986, 1990) in her study of adopted children found that continuity from the agency lowered the risk of disruption. Families who maintained the same social worker throughout the placement process, for example, were less likely to experience disruption. Helping families work out these issues is a difficult task, but a vital one in the adoption process.

THE ROLE OF THE ADOPTION WORKER

Adoption workers perform a variety of roles. In some agencies, workers specialize (e.g., home finding, recruitment, placement) while in other agencies workers vary their assignments. Stacia Fellows, who has been in adoption for close to twenty-five years, describes her experience.

When I first got out of school I worked for a large state agency, first as a placement worker. My role was to see children in foster homes and prepare them for adoption. Often I worked closely with their family worker, the social worker who was helping the family release the child for adoption. Once the child was legally free, I'd look for a couple or individual to meet the child's needs. I'd place the child and follow up with the family until the adoption was legalized. I still have families who keep in touch with me.

My role, once I transferred to home finding, was equally as satisfying. I ran group homestudies for couples and singles and did a few individualized studies. I'd often become quite involved with these people. Their hopes for a family, so important to many of us, rested on my relationship and ultimate impression of them.

Years later I worked at a small private agency. For this agency, adoption was one service of many. We were less likely to see older children; more likely to have infants. As a worker, I worked with both children and couples. Although it was nice to see all sides of an adoption, I found specializing somehow easier.

THE SEARCH

The term *search* refers to adult adoptees' interest in finding information about themselves and about their biological parents, with the possible end of locating and meeting with them. As mentioned earlier, legal adoption results in the child's records being sealed and they become available only to the child who, as an adult, requests access and then only if the court deems the request to be justifiable.

SUPPORTERS OF THE SEARCH

Over the last few decades, several women have supported and made contributions to adoptees searching for their roots. In 1954, social worker Jean Paton, an adoptee herself, searched for and found her sixty-nine-year-old biological mother. She wrote of her experience, and founded an organization called Orphan Voyage. As an organization, Orphan Voyage gives support and guidance to adoptees. Paton lectured widely on adoption and advocated for a "reunion file" that would keep updated information on adoptees and biological parents. This file would then be available to help either party in the search (Coleman, 1988).

Florence Ladden Fisher, another pioneer of adoption searches, spent twenty years searching for her own parents. From overcoming barriers to the end of her successful search, Fisher said that she learned that everything based on her biological and genetic heritage was negative while her adoptive experience was considered positive. Her eventual reunion with her birth parents helped her to resolve her own identity crisis and strengthened her belief that sealed records are an infringement on an adoptee's rights (Coleman, 1988). The writings of numerous authors has done much to support the need for adoptees to search.

WHO SEARCHES

In reality, fewer adoptees undertake a search than one might expect. Although there are few accurate statistics on how many adoptees actually search (Samuels, 1990), females tend to be more likely to do so than males (Schechter and Bertocci, 1990). This may be, Smith and Meroff (1987) suggest, because women are trained by the culture to be more sensitive to feelings about identity issues. In addition to being female, most searchers are between twenty-six and thirty (Kadushin and Martin, 1988). Several other researchers have found that searchers are more likely than nonsearchers to have significant stressors in their lives as well as a weaker sense of identity and self-esteem (Feigelman and Silverman, 1983; Sobol and Cardiff, 1983). The search itself may be an attempt to fill what these adoptees perceive to be a void in their lives. Most adoptees are curious about their pasts but comparatively few search. African American adoptees are more likely to search than their white or Asian counterparts. Feigelman and Silverman (1988) estimated that, while 39 percent of African American adoptees will search, only 2 percent of whites and 14 percent of Koreans will (220). Those who search for birth parents may also have had more problematic relationships with adoptive parents (Stein and Hoopes, 1985; Sobol and Cardiff, 1983). Adoptive parents who are uncomfortable with the concept of adoption can actually impel their children to search. Yet, according to Feigelman and Silverman (1983), parents who support their adopted children's need for and efforts to search promote a closer and more positive relationship with these children.

SEARCH OUTCOME

Of those adoptees who search, a fairly high percentage, 80 percent (Kadushin and Martin, 1988), experienced a favorable reunion. For many, having an opportunity to search gave them a more positive view of life in general.

Andrea was a college student when she began her search. "I think it was just the typical college student's questioning mind, rather than unreal disharmony in my adoptive family that made me want to find my biological parents.

"My search was actually fairly easy, probably because I knew the agency that had placed me. The social worker was still there. She located my natural mother and asked if she'd meet with me.

"I'm a carbon copy of my mother and it was such a shock to see her. I was so nervous at our meeting! But I guess she was, too. I learned that she was a college student when she had me, had gotten into drugs and had gotten pregnant. She actually was asked to leave school! Now she's in business and seems to have done well for herself.

"I don't regret finding her, or learning that my father was just a party date. I have no real desire to find him. I rarely see my biological mother now, but I feel more self directed—like I know who I am. My parents had a tough time initially, but they're supportive. I feel more sympathetic now to what adopting meant to them."

Data in the area of favorable reunions is collected primarily from cases in which birth parents have voluntarily relinquished children. The neglect and abuse underlying situations in which the court removes children may make for more problematic reunions.

What of the effect of adoptees' need to search for their biological parents? Many of those who have given up children for adoption (or had them taken away) rebuilt their lives, and they experience various emotions when a living memory of the past comes into these lives. Yet most birth parents are agreeable to a reunion once their children have requested it (Samuels, 1990).

"I felt like it was the last chapter in a book I'd never finished," explained Elaine, a forty-year-old birth mother. "I knew I had a daughter. But I had no idea what had happened to her. Once I knew, I was content to let things rest. She was too, and it worked out."

SEALED RECORDS

It was the frustrations of both adoptees and birth parents that gave rise to organized search efforts. Orphan Voyage (mentioned earlier) aids adoptees in their searches. The Adoptee's Liberty Movement Association (ALMA), the inspiration of Florence Fisher, publishes a handbook giving advice to adoptees on how to search. Other organizations have become involved in the debate about sealed versus unsealed records. While United Birth Parents (CUB) advocated opening sealed adoption records when a child reaches a certain age, the Association for the Protection of the Adoptive Triangle (APAP), composed mostly of adoptive parents, insists that records should remain closed. The Child Welfare League of America (CWLA), the primary standard-setting organization for children, still advocates the practice of sealing records (Kadushin and Martin, 1988; Schechter and Bertocci, 1990). Today, access to sealed adoption records can be obtained in most states only if the adoptee has "good cause" to petition the court for access. "Good cause" is not, however, adequately defined; in the past matters of concern over genetic abnormalities, health, and contested inheritance have been considered. The subject of sealed versus unsealed records continues to be debated (Kadushin and Martin, 1988; Downs et al., 1996).

CONSENT CONTRACTS

Today many adoption agencies are offering the option of *consent contracts* to natural parents. These contracts assure the agency that the parents will agree to be contacted if their children should search for them in the future. Such contracts, although they are not foolproof, eliminate some of the uncertainty of past years.

Some agencies also ask adoptive parents if they would be agreeable should their adopted child choose to search out his or her roots. It is felt that these procedures will help future adoptees in their searches.

TRENDS

CHILDREN AVAILABLE FOR ADOPTION

The trend toward fewer infants available for adoption continues. Because abortion is seen as one solution to unwanted pregnancy, and young women who opt to continue pregnancies receive more support for keeping babies, the number of healthy adoptable infants continues to decrease. However, there are numerous special needs children still in need of adoptive homes.

The need for *homes for special needs children* places additional responsibilities on the adoption agency. Along with the home study, to determine if couples meet the required means to adopt, agencies also find that it is essential that couples be prepared for the magnitude of their new venture.

"Having a special needs child," recounted one adoptive mother, "requires not only the ability to parent, but also skills in advocacy and case management. Someone has to coordinate the myriad of services these children should have and advocate for them when the services are needed but not forthcoming. That role usually falls to the parents."

Parents adopting multiracial, older children, or sibling groups must also be prepared for a change in their lifestyles. While a baby means that one may not have the same freedom, children with special needs further complicate life by requiring additional doctors' or therapists' visits, an increased number of school meetings, and new stressors between adoptive parents.

Another source of children to meet the demand for adoptable infants will be through *independent adoptions*. Despite the inherent risks in nonagency-sponsored adoptions, ads continue to appear in newspapers ("couple seeks infant to adopt"), while attorneys and physicians continue to receive calls from those looking to adopt or place infants for adoption. The continuation of such practices will leave adoption open to the unscrupulous, who hope to make a profit from someone else's need. By the same token, the popularity of independently arranged adoptions may alert agencies to the need to reevaluate their own standards and practices.

As young children become less available in the United States, those hoping to adopt will more frequently seek *foreign-born children*. Feigelman and Silverman's study of white families adopting Columbian infants (1983) found that 87 percent of the parents adopting internationally did so because no infants were available in the United States (125). The Holt International Children's Fund reports that, despite the decrease in children available from Korea and other Asian countries, increasing numbers of children can be adopted from Central and South America, Mexico, and Canada. There is concern, however, about the lack of standardization of adoption practices in various countries.

The number of different types of children available for adoption has caused agencies to lean more toward *specialization in their adoption practices.*

> *"It used to be," said one adoption worker, "that we placed mostly infants. We became experts at it. But today there are few infants and many other types of children—from the disabled and mentally retarded to sibling groups and children who have experienced severe trauma. It became too complicated for us—a small adoption agency—to serve all types of children. So now we specialize. We place only single healthy children under ten. It makes it much easier to address the needs of all the parties involved. The staff also receives specific training to help us do our job more effectively."*

For the most part, public child welfare agencies continue to see children with a variety of backgrounds and needs. However, many have developed units that are dedicated to handling particular types of children. As private agencies become more specialized, larger agencies may also refer to them. Some agencies specialize in helping older adoptees with their searches rather than the actual placement of children.

PERMANENCY PLANNING

Another trend that may make more children available for adoption is the move toward *permanency planning,*

> *the systematic process of carrying out, within a limited period, a set of goal-directed activities designed to help children and youths live in families that offer continuity of relationships with nurturing parents or caretakers, and the opportunity to offer life-time relationships (Maluccio et al., 1986, 5).*

Designed to promote the best interests of the child, the permanency planning movement was assisted in its popularity by the Oregon Project, a 1973 federally funded program carried out by the Oregon State Dept. of Human Resources, aided by Portland State University School of Social Work. The Project stimulated a great push toward permanent solutions for children. Birth families received intensified services and every effort was made to keep children in their homes. However, if parents were unable to parent effectively, steps were taken to terminate parental rights (Pecora et al., 1992).

The Adoption Assistance and Child Welfare Act of 1980 now mandates agencies to follow permanency planning guidelines attempting first to reunite families and then make other plans for children. Only through compliance with these guidelines will they receive funds for services.

RESOURCES AVAILABLE

Adoption Resource Exchanges provide one more method of finding homes for children, especially those who are hard to place. The first such exchange was developed in Ohio, but the concept has become not only a statewide, but a regional and national idea as well. The Adoption Resource Exchange of North America was credited with aiding in 1,760 adoptions during its first nine years of operation. In 1978, NAIES (National Adoption Information Exchange System) was funded by the Adoption Reform Act. NAIES is a fully computerized system to identify children who need homes and the parents who wait for them.

Children in need of homes (usually hard-to-place children) are initially registered with the statewide adoption resource exchange. This exchange is, in turn, connected with the national service. In this way a child on the East Coast who has particular needs may find new parents as far away as the opposite coast. In this way, both children and adoptive parents are provided with many more opportunities for adoption placement.

Another resource that has gained increased popularity is *adoption subsidy*. This is based on data (Shyne and Schroeder, 1978) that estimated that over 100,000 children were legally freed for adoption, but their care would require more financial outlay than interested adoptive families could provide. These special financial burdens were often based on pre-existing medical problems. The states, beginning with New York in 1968, enacted legislation providing adoption subsidies. By 1976 forty-two states had enacted subsidy programs, but provisions and eligibility criteria varied widely. The Adoption Assistance and Child Welfare Act of 1980 (PL 96–272) provided more uniformity in subsidies as well as making special needs children eligible for Medicaid and, in some instances, Supplemental Security Income (Stein, 1981; Kadushin and Martin, 1988).

Despite the fact that subsidies allow many children who might not otherwise have this opportunity to be adopted, there are several drawbacks for adoptive parents. First, some states base eligibility criteria not on children's needs but on the adoptive parents' income. And some states limit the duration of subsidy to three years, with the possibility of a two-year extension (Stein, 1981).

Subsidies are based on written agreements made with the adoptive parents at the time of placement. The subsidy cannot be more than state-set foster care payments (Kadushin and Martin, 1988; Downs et al., 1996). Although subsidized adoption has made it possible for many more children to be adopted and for those who were previously unable financially to become adoptive parents, the future of subsidized adoption is constantly debated due to a lack of funds.

LIFELONG SERVICES

Today there is increased recognition that adoption is a lifelong experience. One group supporting both adoptive parents and their adopted children in a variety of ways are *parent organizations*. These groups provide education, social supports, recruitment, and advocacy for other adoptive families. Many groups publish newsletters and hold support meetings, sometimes independently and sometimes working closely with agencies. One widely known national group, OURS (Organization for United Response), publishes a newsletter that contains all types of parenting experiences. These organizations are often provided with resources by such groups as the North American Council on Adaptable Children (NACAC), which publishes a newsletter (*Adoptable*) outlining activities, resources, and adoption news across the nation (Kadushin and Martin 1988), and by the Council on Adoptive Parents (COAC).

> "Our adoptive parent group was a great deal of help to us," said one adoptive mother. "Several members spoke with us during our home-study and provided all sorts of help when we first got our child. They had a 'help line' we could call if we had a question. It felt better to call someone who'd adopted than the agency. Later the group was a great deal of support when we needed some advocacy. Now I help out new adoptive parents and it feels great. Every time I talk to a new struggling parent, I am helped to work out my own issues."

In addition to input from parent groups, agencies are becoming increasingly aware of additional *lifelong support services*. Many agencies provide adoption-specific counseling. As one adoptive mother who is also a mental health clinician put it:

> We professionals are just beginning to realize that what we thought were family problems are specifically adoption issues. We need to continue to develop our skills in counseling adolescent and adult adoptees. Adoption is not always a happily-ever-after story. It's work—like every other worthwhile relationship. But we have to learn to help adoptive families through the trials of adjustment throughout their lives!

When children are unable to adjust they may be removed from the adoptive home in later life. Only recently have theorists and clinicians begun to recognize adoption as a factor of importance in children's problems (see Goodrich et al., 1990 and Grotevant and McRoy, 1990). The already turbulent teen years, when individuals strive to find their identity, can prove overwhelming for the adopted child. Biological parents and heredity can become such preoccupations that the adolescent's quest for understanding, combined with the insecurity felt by many adoptive parents, creates a dangerous imbalance in the family. The results usually seen in the adolescent—

impulsive, provocative, aggressive, or antisocial behavior—can lead to placement outside the home (Grotevant and McRoy, 1990). Residential treatment centers across the country attest to the upsurge in the number of adolescents coming to them from adoptive families. Professionals treating these individuals are becoming increasingly aware that the experience of adoption cannot be ignored if one is to take a holistic approach to the adolescents' problem (Rosenberg, 1992).

As we consider the issues discussed in this chapter, it becomes obvious that the process of adoption is complex. There are so many variables that affect the successful outcome of this created family. Those in the field of adoption strive to improve services to all involved in the process.

SUMMARY

Adoption has its roots in antiquity. Over the years the rationale for adoption shifted its primary focus from providing heirs for the titled to acknowledging every child's right to a home. While originally based on English law, adoption laws in the United States began to take shape in the mid-nineteenth century. Different cultural groups influenced the evolution of these laws. Today adoption practice is shaped largely by PL 96–272 and the Federal Adoption Assistance and Child Welfare Act of 1980, which emphasizes permanency planning for every child.

Adoption can be divided into two categories: related and unrelated. Related adoptions encompass such arrangements as adoption by a relative or stepparent and, more recently, adoption by the biological father of a surrogate mother's child. Unrelated adoption can be agency-sponsored or independent of agency involvement. Agencies are increasingly involved in the placement of special needs children which encompasses children with disabilities, cross-cultural adoptions, the adoption of children older than five, or of sibling groups. Subsidized adoption provides adoptive couples with a stipend to help them with the support of their special needs child. Some agencies allow single-parent adoptions, placing children in the homes of unmarried adoptive parents. In international adoptions children are brought from other countries to the homes of parents in the United States.

Today there are increasingly fewer white, healthy infants available for adoption. Perhaps the increase in birth control and abortion is one set of factors. In addition, teen parents are more likely to keep their children than in years past. The focus has therefore shifted to the placement of special needs children and to couples searching out and arranging their own independent adoptions. Both of these types of adoptions involve risks and require special thought on the part of adoptive couples.

The adoption process is complex. Birth parents must be recognized as having their own motivations for and feelings about placing their children for adoption. While some lose their children through abuse and neglect, others make a conscious, often painful, choice, recognizing that adoption provides a better alternative for their children. Race and culture may also influence the biological mother's decision and her ability to act on her choice. Parents who relinquish their children may feel out of control, inadequate, stigmatized, bitter and angry, or powerless. Agencies strive to help them with these feelings and enable them to make the choice with which they can feel relatively comfortable.

The children available for adoption may be healthy infants, older children, sibling groups, children with disabilities or medical problems, children from minority groups, or foreign-born children. Depending on who they are, they will present different issues for their adoptive families.

Adoptive applicants are recruited by agencies in different ways. Increasingly agencies have used churches and other civic organizations to improve their recruitment efforts. Applicants are motivated to adopt for varied reasons, some because they want to enlarge their families, others because they believe that there is a need for homes for specific types of children.

Potential adoptive couples are screened through a home study that evaluates their motivation and eligibility criteria, as well as educating them about the children available and the issues inherent in adoption. Children are then placed with appropriate families. Sometimes the children's ties with the past are maintained—called open adoption—while in other instances these ties are severed. Legalization means that the original records are sealed and the child legally becomes the child of the adoptive parents. Despite this finality, families are encouraged to keep the issue of adoption open and talked about at home.

Increasingly agencies are recognizing that legalization is not the end of the story. Families need postadoption support, and may return for counseling around adoption issues. Occasionally adoption placements will fail, necessitating further agency intervention and counseling.

Over the last few years there has been an increase in the numbers of adoptees who have searched for their biological parents. This upsurge in the interest in biological roots has stimulated further controversy over whether or not adoption records should continue to be sealed. Today agencies often offer biological parents consent contracts, documents that state the parents' willingness to meet their offspring if that individual, as an adult, chooses to search.

Several trends can be seen in the field of adoption today. These fall into three categories: the children available for adoption, resources currently available, and adoption as a lifelong issue. The children available are increasingly special needs children. Some adoptive applicants seek foreign adoptions instead. For this reason an increased number of couples are exploring independent adoption as an alternative. Various resources aid couples and children in their search for family life. Adoption resource exchanges unite children from one geographical area with parents from another. Adoption subsidies provide funds for adoptive parents who could not otherwise afford the expenses incurred by a particular child.

Finally, adoption must be seen as a lifelong issue. More and more services are recognizing this fact. Adoption is not an easy answer to a desire to augment one's family or to provide permanency for a child. But with resources, time, and support for all those involved, adoption can be a rewarding option.

EXPLORATION QUESTIONS

1. What was the original purpose of adoption in early history? How has that view changed?
2. What is meant by "permanency planning"? What legal statute influenced our current perception of adoption?
3. On what values is adoption practice based?
4. What are the types of adoption? Explain each briefly.
5. What is meant by independent adoption? What types of placements are there in this area? Why is this type of adoption seen as problematic?
6. Cite five issues prevalent in adoption literature today. Explain each briefly.
7. Why might a birth parent give up a child for adoption? What might she feel in making this decision?
8. Who are the children who are available for adoption?
9. Why might someone want to adopt a child? Outline a profile of those who apply to adopt.
10. Explain the adoption process.
11. What is meant by adoption disruption? Why might it happen?
12. Cite the trends in adoption today. Explain each briefly.

ACTIVITIES FOR APPLIED LEARNING

1. Research the adoption laws in your state. How do they differ from other states?
2. Invite an adoption placement worker or homefinder to speak in class. What do they do in their particular agency?
3. Invite an adoptive parent to talk about his or her experiences. Or invite a panel of adoptive parents to compare experiences.
4. Check with your local chapter of a search group. Would they agree to talk about searching or would someone who has searched come to speak to the class?
   (The North American Council on Adoptable Children, P.O. Box 14808, Minneapolis, MN 55414 or Adoptees Liberty Movement Association, 853 Seventh Ave, New York, NY 10019 may provide a list of local resources in your area.)

SUGGESTED READING

Aigner, H. *Adoption in America: Coming of Age.* Greenbrae, CA: Paradigm Press, 1986.

Brodzinsky, D. M., & Schechter M. D. (Eds). *The Psychology of Adoption.* New York: Oxford University Press, 1990.

Coleman, L., Tilbor, K., Hornby, H., & Boggis, C. *Working with Older Adoptees.* Portland, ME: University of Southern Maine Press, 1988.

Festinger, T. B. *Necessary Risk—A Study of Adoptions and Disrupted Adoptive Placements.* NY: Child Welfare League of America, 1986.

Glidden, L. M. *Parents for Children: Children for Parents.* Washington, DC: American Association on Mental Retardation, 1989.

Register, C. *Are Those Kids Yours? American Families with Children Adopted from Other Countries.* New York: Free Press, 1991.

Rosenberg, E. B. *The Adoption Life Cycle.* New York: Free Press, 1992.

Samuels, S. C. *Ideal Adoption: A Comprehensive Guide to Forming an Adoptive Family.* New York: Plenum Press, 1990.

Smith J., & Miroff F. I. *You're Our Child: The Adoption Experience.* New York: Madison, 1987.

REFERENCES

Barry, M. "Preparing and Supporting Special Needs Adoptive Families: A Review of the Literature," *Child and Adolescent Social Work 7* (1990), 403–418.

Barth, R. P., & Berry, M. *Adoption and Disruption: Rates, Risks and Responses.* New York: Aldine De Gruyter, 1988.

Berger, M., & Hodges, J. "Some Thoughts on the Question of When to Tell the Child That He Is Adopted," *Journal of Child Psychotherapy 8,* (1982), 67–88.

Berry, M., & Barth R. P. "A Study of Disrupted Adoptive Placements of Adolescents," *Child Welfare* 69(3) (1990), 209–225.

Boersdorfer, R. K., Kaser, J. S., & Tremitier W. C. *Guide to Local TEAM Programs.* York, PA: Tressler-Lutheran Associates, 1986.

Boyne, J., Denby, L., Kettering J. R., & Wheeler, W. *The Shadow of Success: A Statistical Analysis of Outcomes of Adoptions of Hard-to-Place Children.* Westfield, NJ: Spaulding for Children, 1984.

Brace, C. L. *The Dangerous Classes in New York and Twenty Years' Work among Them.* NY: Wynkoop & Hallenbeck, 1872.

Brodzinsky, D. M., Singer L. M., & Braff, A. M. "Children's Understanding of Adoption," *Child Development* 55, (1984), 869–878.

Brodzinsky, D. M., & Schechter, M. D. (Eds.). *The Psychology of Adoption.* NY: Oxford University Press, 1990.

Byrd, A. D. "The Case for Confidential Adoption," *Public Welfare* 46(4) (1988), 20–23.

Child Welfare League of America. *Standards of Adoption Service.* NY: Child Welfare League of America, 1978.

Cohen, N. (Ed.). *Child Welfare: A Multicultural Perspective.* Boston: Allyn & Bacon, 1992.

Cole, E. S. "Adoption." In A. Minahan (Ed.) *Encyclopedia of Social Work* (Vol 1, 18th ed.). Silver Springs, MD: National Association of Social Workers, 1987.

Cole, E. S., & Donley, K. S. "History, Values & Placement Policy Issues in Adoption." In D. M. Brodzinsky & M. D. Schechter (Eds.) *The Psychology of Adoption.* NY: Oxford University Press, 1990.

Coleman, L. "The Search." In L. Coleman et al. *Working with Older Adoptee's.* Portland, ME: University of Southern Maine, 1988.

Coleman, L., Tilbor, K., Hornby, H., & Boggis, C. *Working with Older Adoptee's: A Sourcebook of Innovative Models.* Portland, Maine: University of Southern Maine, 1988.

Craig, E. *One, Two, Three: Matt, a Feral Child.* NY: Signet, 1978.

Cushman, L., Kalmuss, D., & Nameron, P. B. "Placing an Infant for Adoption: The Experiences of Young Birth Mothers," *Social Work* 38(3) (1993), 264–272.

Day, D. *The Adoption of Black Children.* Lexington, MA: Lexington Books, 1979.

Deykin, E. Y., Campbell, L., & Patti, P. "The Post Adoption Experience of Surrendering Parents," *American Journal of Orthopsychiatry* 54, (1984), 271–280.

Downs, S. W., Costin, L. B., & McFadden, E. J. *Child Welfare and Family Services: Policies and Practice.* New York: Longman, 1996.

Feigelman, W., & Silverman, A. *Chosen Children: New Patterns of Adoptive Relationships.* New York: Praeger, 1983.

Festinger, T. B. *Necessary Risk—A Study of Adoptions and Disrupted Adoptive Placements.* NY: Child Welfare League of America, 1986.

Festinger, T. "Adoption Disruption: Rates and Correlates." In D. M. Brodzinsky & M. D. Schechter, *The Psychology of Adoption.* NY: Oxford University Press, 1990.

Fish, A., & Speirs, C. "Biological Parents Choose Adoptive Parents: The Use of Profiles in Adoptions" *Child Welfare* 69 (1990), 129–139.

Frey, L. "Making an Impact: Post-Adoption Crisis Counseling." In L. Coleman et al. *Working with Older Adoptee's.* Portland, ME: University of Southern Maine, 1988.

Gitlin, H. *Adoptions: An Attorney's Guide to Helping Adoptive Parents.* Wilmette, IL: Callaghan, 1987.

Glidden, L. M. *Parents for Children, Children for Parents.* Washington, DC: American Association on Mental Retardation, 1989.

Goodrich, W., Fullerton, C. S., Yates, B. T., & Berman, L. B. "The Residential Treatment of Severely Disturbed Adolescent Adoptee's." In D. M. Brodzinsky & M. D. Schechter, *The Psychology of Adoption.* New York: Oxford University Press, 1990.

Grotevant, H. D., & McRoy, R. G. "Adopted Adolescents in Residential Treatment: The Role of the Family." In D. M. Brodzinsky & M. D. Schechter, *The Psychology of Adoption.* New York: Oxford University Press, 1990.

Gruber, A. R. *Foster Home Care in Massachusetts.* Boston: Governers Commission on Adoption & Foster Care, 1973.

Hartman, A., & Laird, J. "Family Treatment after Adoption: Common Themes," (221–239). In D. M. Brodzinsky & M. D. Schechter, *The Psychology of Adoption.* NY: Oxford University Press, 1990.

Helwig, A. A., & Ruthven, D. H. "Psychological Ramifications of Adoption and Implications for Counseling," *Journal of Mental Health Counseling* 12 (1990), 24–37.

Howe, R. W. "Adoption Practices, Issues and Laws. 1958–1983," *Family Law Quarterly* 17, (1983), 173–197.

Kadushin, A., & Martin, J. A. *Child Welfare Services.* New York: MacMillan, 1988.

Krementz, J. *How It Feels to Be Adopted.* New York: Alfred A. Knopf, 1982.

Livingston, C. *Why Was I Adopted?* Seacaucus NJ: Lyle Stuart, 1978.

Maluccio, A. N., Fein E., & Olmstead, K. A. *Permanency Planning for Children: Concepts and Methods.* London and New York: Routledge, Chapman, & Hall, 1986.

Marindin, H. *The Handbook for Single Adoptive Parents.* Chevy Chase, MD: Committee for Single Adoptive Parents, 1987.

Maza, P. L. "Trends in National Data on the Adoptions of Children with Handicaps," *Journal of Children in Contemporary Society* 21(3–4) (1990), 119–138.

Mica, M. D., & Vosler N. R. "Foster-Adoptive Programs in Public Social Service Agencies: Toward Flexible Family Resources," *Child Welfare* 69(1) (1990), 433–446.

National Committee for Adoption. *Adoption Factbook: U. S. Data Issues Regulations and Resources.* Washington DC: National Committee for Adoption, 1989.

Pannor, R., & Baran, A. "Open Adoption as Standard Practice," *Child Welfare* 63(3) (1984), 245–250.

Pecora, P. J., Whittaker, J. K., Maluccio, A. N. with Barth R. P., & Plotnick, R. D. *The Child Welfare Challenge: Policy, Practice and Research.* NY: Aldine DeGruyter, 1992.

Plumer, E. H. *When You Place a Child.* Springfield, IL: Charles C. Thomas, 1992.

Register, C. *Are Those Kids Yours? American Families with Children Adopted from Other Countries.* NY: Free Press, 1991.

Rosenberg, E. B. *The Adoption Life Cycle.* New York: Free Press, 1992.

Rynearson, E. K. "Relinquishment and Its Maternal Complications," *American Journal of Psychiatry* 139, (1981), 338–340.

Samuels, S. C. *Ideal Adoption: A Comprehensive Guide to Forming an Adoptive Family:* New York: Plenum Press, 1990.

Schaffer, J., & Lindstrom, C. "Brief Solution-Focused Therapy with Adoptive Families," (240–252). In D. M. Brodzinsky and M. D. Schechter, *The Psychology of Adoption*. New York: Oxford University Press, 1990.

Schechter, M. D., & Bertocci, D. "The Meaning of the Search." In D. M. Brodzinsky and M. D. Schechter, *The Psychology of Adoption*. New York: Oxford University Press, 1990.

Shireman, J. F., & Johnson P. R. "Single Persons as Adoptive Parents," *Social Service Review* 50(1) (1976), 103–116.

Shireman, J. F., & Johnson P. R. "A Longitudinal Study of Black Adoptions: Single Parent, Transracial & Traditional," *Social Work* 31, (1986), 172–176.

Shyne, A., & Schroeder A. *National Study of Social Services to Children and Their Families*. Washington, DC: DHEW, 1978.

Siegel, D. H. "Open Adoption of Infants: Adoptive Parents' Perceptions of Advantages and Disadvantages," *Social Work* 38(1) (1993), 15–23.

Silverman, A. R., & Feigelman, W. "Adjustment in Interracial Adoptees: An Overview," (187–200). In D. M. Brodzinsky & M. D. Schechter, *The Psychology of Adoption*. New York: Oxford University Press, 1990.

Silverstein, D. N., & Kaplan, S. "Lifelong Issues in Adoption." In L. Coleman et al. *Working with Older Adoptee's*. Portland, ME: University of Southern Maine, 1988.

Skinner, K. "Counseling Issues in the Fostering & Adoption of Children at Risk of HIV Infection," *Counseling Psychology Quarterly* 10 (1989), 89–92.

Sloan, I. J. *The Law of Adoption and Surrogate Parenting*. New York: Oceans Publ, 1988.

Small, J. "Working with Adoptive Families," *Public Welfare* 45(3) (1987), 33–41.

Smith, J., & Miroff, F. *You're Our Child: The Adoption Experience*. New York: Madison, 1987.

Sobol, M., & Cardiff. J. "A Socio-Psychological Investigation of Adult Adoptee's Search for Birth Parents," *Family Relations* 32, (1983), 477–483.

Stein, L. M., and Hoopes, J. L. *Identity Formation in the Adopted Adolescent—The Delaware Family Study*. New York: Child Welfare League of America, 1985.

Stein, T. J. *Social Work Practice in Child Welfare*. Englewood Cliffs, New Jersey: Prentice Hall, 1981.

Wieder, H. "On Being Told of Adoption," *Psychoanalytic Quarterly* 46 (1977), 1–22.

Wingard, D. "Trends and Characteristics of California Adoptions. 1946–1982." *Child Welfare* 66, (1987), 303–314.

14

CHILDREN IN
RESIDENTIAL SETTINGS

HISTORICAL PERSPECTIVE

Residential settings for children have evolved as society's view of children and their needs has changed. Early institutional care was based on the concept of providing homeless children with a place to stay. In France, in the fifteenth century, St. Vincent dePaul established homes for abandoned children (Kadushin and Martin, 1988). The first institution in the United States was founded by the Ursuline nuns of New Orleans to harbor children who were orphaned by the Natchez Indian Massacre (Pecora et al., 1992).

For many years, poor children resided with their parents in *almshouses*. But critics of these institutions felt that they were unhealthy for young souls and bodies and encouraged separate sections of almshouses, if not separate institutions, dedicated to the needs of children. In 1875, the state of New York mandated that children be removed from almshouses and placed in institutions specifically set up for children or in families. The movement toward the establishment of *orphanages* for children flourished and by the early 1900s there were close to 125,000 children in the United States living in orphanages (Kadushin and Martin, 1988). Most of the institutions built were designated for white children with policies excluding African American children (Billingsley and Giovannoni, 1972; Everett et al., 1991). These orphanages, or asylums, built mostly by charitable, benevolent, or religious organizations, served to house and feed children as well as instilling in them a sense of order, good moral character, and obedience. The hope was to save "children from both physical and moral degradation" (Keith–Lucas and Sanford, 1977, 6).

As child care institutions increased and flourished into the mid-1900s, there came the rumblings of criticism of the effects of institutional care on the development of young children. In 1951, Bowlby, in *Maternal Care and Mental Health*, written as a United Nations Report, discussed considerable research demonstrating that institutional care had a negative effect on children. Goffman, in 1961, wrote his well-known *Asylums*, in which he argued that children brought up in institutions learned behaviors that actually inhibited their ability to adjust once they left the institutional setting (Kadushin and Martin, 1988).

While orphan asylums were built and debated about, another type of institution for children had its inception. The first *setting for juvenile delinquents*, the House of Refuge, was built in New York in the 1800s to be followed by similar institutions in Boston in 1826 and in Philadelphia in 1928. In Massachusetts, the Lyman School, a state-funded reform or training school for delinquent boys, opened its doors in 1847 and operated until the early 1970s on the model of the German agricultural reformatory (Pecora et al., 1992). The 1800s also saw the development of *institutions for the mentally retarded, deaf, blind, and physically handicapped* (Kadushin and Martin, 1988).

Another type of institution for children, the *residential treatment center*, began between the 1930s to 1950s. These settings were based on an increased interest in mental health and the recognition that for some children the family could not meet their needs. Emotionally disturbed children became a new interest of practitioners, and techniques to treat them as groups in congregate settings became popular.

Pecora et al. (1992) suggest that the history of residential care can be divided into four phases: (1) provision of separate institutions for children as opposed to mixing them with adults; (2) the move to cottage or family-style units as opposed to barrack-style living; (3) the psychological phase, which emphasized the introduction of treatment concepts as opposed to maintenance of children in institutions; and (4) the environmental or ecological phase, which emphasized evaluation of outcomes in residential care (404–405).

The history of one large institution, the Devereux Foundation, exemplifies how institutions for children developed in the United States. In the early 1900s, while the media of Philadelphia were expounding on the quality of local schools, there was little available to address the needs of children who had "fallen behind their classmates in school." One educator cognizant of this deficit was Helena Trafford Devereux, a young teacher who began to focus on these children with special needs. Initially, she was assigned to teach mentally retarded children within the public school system. In 1912, she began a program in her own home, designing an around-the-clock program for three children in a "homelike setting." In 1918, she moved the children to a home in Devon, Pennsylvania, and a year later was ready to expand her program into an adjoining house. Parents of special children began to seek out Miss Devereux and the school/residence expanded, until in 1924 it became the Devereux Schools. As Devereux's reputation grew, the program continued to expand. Additional components offered help to young men in their late teens to train them for trades, and a camp component offered "therapeutic programming and recreation for children and adolescents who were braindamaged, mentally handicapped, and/or emotionally disturbed."

By 1938, the Commonwealth of Pennsylvania had granted a charter to the Devereux Foundation with the purpose of

> *studying, treating and carrying on research and educational work in connection with functional and nervous disorders; and educating and developing, and advancing boys and girls of any age along psychological and psychiatric lines, in addition to serving their intellectual, emotional, and vocational needs (4).*

During the 1940s the Foundation opened centers in other areas of the United States as well as several new centers in Pennsylvania. From treating the mentally retarded and emotionally disturbed child, the Devereux Foundation expanded its programs to serve the newly diagnosed condition of autism. The 1950s saw additional expansion and in 1958 the American Psychiatric Association made Helena Devereux an Honorary Fellow, the first woman without a medical degree to be so honored. By the 1970s Devereux's standards in residential treatment had become the "benchmark by which other programs were measured" (7).

Today, the Devereux Foundation offers programs for mentally retarded children, emotionally disturbed and autistic children and adolescents, and individuals with head trauma. Programs serve fourteen states and provide such services as residential treatment, group homes, supported apartment living, therapeutic foster care, day treatment, respite services, and partial and acute hospital facilities. In addition, the Foundation carries out research and provides training for those interested in therapeutic work with a variety of populations. Although not all institutional programs for children have the components of the Devereux Foundation, many provide such services on a smaller scale.

The complexion of child care institutions has changed a good deal since the nineteenth and early twentieth centuries. The orphanage, at one time the most popular child care institution, has all but disappeared as a result of the recognition of the importance of a family setting to children's healthy development. The beginnings of this extinction came when cottage settings or family-style units began to replace the sterile barrack-style buildings of early orphanages. The deinstitutional movement of the mid 1900s continued the trend toward replicating family and community whenever possible. It is interesting that today's political leaders have spoken of the reestablishment of orphanages despite the lessons of the past.

While some institutions for the handicapped do still exist, the move is toward having those who are able, live in the community as opposed to an institution. The emphasis on the least restrictive environment and the preservation of the family has significantly changed the nature of residential settings today.

ASSUMPTIONS ABOUT RESIDENTIAL CARE

Nancy was twelve when her mother was institutionalized. Before that she had been in and out of foster care from the age of four. "My mom had been sick for a long time," she recounts. "We never knew who she'd be and when. Sometimes she was like another kid and it was fun to be with her. We didn't get meals and stuff, but we got used to that. But sometimes she'd sleep all day or scream at us and curl up in a ball under the table. That was scary. It seems like every few months we'd end up in a foster home. I got sick of it."

When her mother was finally institutionalized, Nancy ran away and was gone for several days. When she returned she was once again placed in a foster home. "That was just it!" she explained. "I was sick of everyone telling me what to do, of new rules and new faces! The foster mother's kid really got to me. I couldn't stand the little brat! I got really mad one day and pulled a knife on him. I think I would've killed him, but the foster father grabbed me and the foster mother called the social worker. The next thing I know, I'm in this place with other kids who'd blown out of foster homes too."

A residential setting is seen as *the last alternative for children.* Children who are placed in such settings have either had difficulty in foster homes or demonstrate behavior that would be difficult to handle in a family setting. Children who are extremely self-abusive or suicidal, children who cannot conform to family rules, children who are dangerous to others or are exceptionally destructive to property may be candidates for residential care. In addition to behaviors, some children have physical limitations that are difficult for families to handle. Jared was born severely mentally retarded, deaf, and blind. Because of his disabilities he was minimally responsive to his environment. At first, his parents kept him at home, but as he grew they found that they were no longer able to do so.

"It was with a great deal of guilt that we placed him in the center," explained his mother tearfully. "But it got to be too much. We have four other children and we couldn't have any kind of a family life. I began to resent Jared and that wasn't fair to him either."

The trend is to place children in the *least restrictive setting.* Some settings are locked and the staff ratio is high. Others are more like a community setting and residents have a good deal of freedom. The needs of each child are considered when he or she is placed in residential care and the hope is that children will be placed in a situation where there is just enough structure to meet their needs.

What makes residential settings more beneficial than family environments for some children? First, having a staff of several people provides children with *opportunities for diluted emotional interaction with others.* Instead of one mother and one father, children in residential settings have choices as to the parenting figure to whom they are exposed. They can feel safe by knowing that there is structure with *consistent rules* that a family setting cannot always offer. For the staff, relating to the children and understanding their needs is their primary function while they are on duty. Thus, not faced with tasks of maintaining a family that foster parents have to contend with, child care *staff can be more focused on their charges' needs* (Kadushin and Martin, 1988).

Residential programs are *structured specifically to meet the needs of their residents.* The treatment environment can be orchestrated so that it addresses the therapeutic challenges of each child. The day of each child can be planned to be of maximum therapeutic benefit. If a child is having difficulty with his or her program it can be adjusted. If there are problems with roommates or cottage mates, the unit can be rearranged. These changes might not be possible in a family setting. Educational programs can be geared to the abilities of the specific child and can be monitored closely if changes are necessary (Marohn, 1993).

Residential settings *can also accommodate a wider range of destructive behaviors.* Although most foster parents learn to childproof their houses, the fact remains that they have more investment in the preservation of their furniture, house, and possessions than do staff in an institutional setting. Residences also tend to be furnished with almost indestructible furniture and a dearth of fragile items (Kadushin and Martin, 1988).

Kathy was diagnosed as ADHD (Attention Deficit Disorder with Hyperactivity), and was placed by her mother in a residential setting. "She is constantly destroying my home," recounted the mother. Kathy also had very poor boundaries, was abusing drugs, and was promiscuous. In placement, Kathy was cooperative and eager to benefit from counseling. She fit well into the cottage to which she was assigned, kept her room neat, and was a model resident. She was somewhat clumsy, but the housemother was not very disturbed by this. The treatment center began wondering why she could not return home with outpatient services. This idea the mother vehemently opposed. Puzzled, the social worker from the center did a home visit. When she walked into the house, it became clear why mother and child were having so much difficulty. The house was a showplace of priceless antiques and delicate costly figurines. The mother showed them off with a great deal of pride. These were obviously her joy. It became more obvious to the worker why clumsy Kathy with her hyperactivity would have difficulty fitting into this home.

Granted, the attributes of residential treatment settings described previously represent the conditions in the best case scenario. In reality, staff is not always consistent and there is usually a high turnover rate. Training for child care staff is often not given as much time and emphasis as would be ideal. Funding may mean that school supplies are in short supply, and vandalism still does happen. (Additional problems will be discussed later in this chapter.) But, on the whole, for some children, the comparatively impersonal structure of a group residence provides a better opportunity for therapeutic intervention.

TYPES OF RESIDENTIAL SETTINGS

Currently residential group settings serve several different populations:

1. *Children who are in need of diagnostic services;*
2. *Children who are in need of intense therapeutic services due to being abused, neglected, or abandoned;*
3. *Children who are emotionally disturbed and require residential treatment;*
4. *Children who are adjudicated delinquent and require rehabilitative services;*
5. *Children who are severely mentally retarded or multiply handicapped (Kadushin and Martin, 1988).*

Pecora et al. (1992), referring to the types of residential settings, comment that:

We must be wary of references to 'group and institutional care' as though it were a single entity. It is not. Rather, this segment of the service continuum contains a range of different kinds of residential placements that overlap considerably in terms of definition, purpose, population served, and bureaucratic responsibility (406–407).

In addition, not every type of residential service is provided by one specific agency. Many settings mix clients with various types of problems. For example, a large setting might have a cottage or program dedicated to diagnostic services, where children stay for a short period of time while a treatment strategy is being devised for them. That same center may have another section designed to treat children over a longer period of time, while working with their families and attempting to integrate them back into the community. Some centers have components that deal with children who are severely disabled and/or mentally retarded and others that deal with higher functioning children. There are also residential treatment settings that treat both the dependent child, who may be in the care of the social services agency, along with the child who has been adjudicated delinquent by the court. These centers also may see children on a short-term basis (often called an emergency placement) or on a longer ongoing basis. The combinations and possibilities are endless. There are also a few settings that specialize in certain types of problems. For example, increasingly, there are programs dedicated to the treatment of adolescent sexual offenders.

As we consider the types of services provided in residential settings, bear in mind that a center may either specialize or combine a variety of different services in one organization.

DIAGNOSTIC SERVICES

It is not always clear, when a child is in emotional distress, what has caused his or her behavior, suicide attempt, depression, or other manifestation of disturbance, or what type of treatment will be most helpful to him or her. In order to best serve the child, this information must be discovered. Diagnostic centers, or diagnostic components of programs, observe children closely while having them participate in various types of testing and assessment interviews. Children stay in diagnostic centers from a day or two to several months, depending on their needs and the availability of services for them once they leave the diagnostic center. Some agencies use diagnostic programs not only as initial screening tools, but also as evaluative services.

Jordan had been in several foster homes when his severe depression and suicidal thoughts occurred. At an early age (between one and two years) he had reportedly watched his father kill his mother. It was difficult to know how much he had seen or understood. He had had great difficulty bonding with foster parents and his social worker was unsure what would be best for him. He was placed in a diagnostic center for two weeks while he was evaluated. It was felt by the center that, due to his young age (eight years) he should be placed in a specialized foster home. This plan seemed to be working until the foster mother was killed in an auto accident. Jordan became extremely depressed and was returned to the diagnostic center to determine what was best for him in the future. Being in the center, where he had apparently been comfortable in the past, also gave him the space to grieve. Eventually it was recommended that he be placed in a residential treatment center as it did not seem that he could handle the close relationship with another mother figure.

INTENSE THERAPEUTIC SERVICES FOR DEPENDENT CHILDREN

Children who have been exposed to extreme trauma in their families may need treatment or respite before they are able to respond to another family experience such as a foster home. These children are usually young and their final plan may involve adoption.

Shannon was the oldest of four children, all of whom had been severely neglected by their natural mother. The girl was extremely protective of her younger siblings and adamant that they not be placed separately. Because a foster home could not be found for the entire group, the four children were placed in a small church-sponsored residential center. Shannon was helped to feel safe and to overcome some of the residual behaviors of her mother's neglect. Eventually, an adoptive home was found for all four siblings.

Possibly the closest modern thing to the old orphanage, these centers specialize in young children who are not so deeply affected by their abuse that they cannot return to a family setting. Often that family will not be their own.

RESIDENTIAL TREATMENT CENTERS

Residential treatment is perhaps the most common type of setting for children and adolescents today. These agencies specialize in the *therapeutic milieu,* combining therapeutic services from a residential, educational, and psychological perspective. Barker (1988) cites three reasons why children might be placed in residential treatment: (1) for the protection of the community; (2) for the protection of the child; and (3) because "the child's behavior, though not dangerous to others, is so disturbed as to be more than the community can deal with using available resources" (9). This author goes on to say that residential treatment is indicated when

1. *A self-perpetuating cycle of dysfunctional behaviors is well established, and other less draconian, and less expensive, measures have failed;*
2. *The treatment required by the child demands technical skills that the parents do not possess, and that cannot readily and quickly be taught;*
3. *The young person is psychotic and out of touch with reality to such an extent that he or she cannot be managed by untrained laypeople; or*
4. *the severity of the child's behavior disorder is so great that only skilled management by highly trained professionals can bring it under control (Barker, 1988, 9–10).*

The following descriptions illustrate the types of children who are appropriate for residential treatment:

Rosalee is a fifteen-year-old girl who will not go to school. When her parents attempt to compel her to go, she runs away and is gone for several days. She uses marijuana and has recently tried crack cocaine. She is sexually active and has many older partners. Her parents are at a loss as to what to do with her. The school suggested that she be placed in residential treatment.

Donald is thirteen and has been involved in criminal activity. He has been seen by the juvenile court for breaking and entering, assault, truancy, and possession of drugs. His mother is dead and his father is an alcoholic who wants to "wash his hands of the kid." His older brother is serving time in prison. Donald can no longer live at home and refuses to go to a foster home. In addition, foster parents fear his violent temper. Therefore, the juvenile court has mandated that he be placed in residential treatment.

Jadie is fourteen. She was severely sexually abused by her father and two of her uncles. She became pregnant at thirteen and gave up her child for adoption. Jadie is extremely impulsive and very concerned with boys. She is bulemic and is into cutting herself with knives. Although Jadie's mother is concerned, she does not feel that she can handle her daughter. This mother's hope is that a program will "knock some sense into her." Due to this mother's inability to cope with her daughter's behavior, the social service agency working with her has recommended residential treatment.

These scenarios also describe situations in which children might reach residential treatment. Usually, placement is initiated by one or more of four sources: the school, the social service agency (often CPS), the juvenile court, or the probation officer or agency dealing with delinquent behaviors or the child's parents. These referral sources are also those who may be responsible for paying for this placement.

REHABILITATIVE OR SECURE TREATMENT FOR DELINQUENTS

Harvey was a fifteen-year-old who had a long history of delinquent acts. He had been in and out of the court system since he was ten. When he pulled a knife on another student at school, he was arrested and again referred to the court. Harvey became out-of-control in the court room and threatened to "get that lousy kid who sent me here!" (the child on whom he had pulled the knife.) Feeling that Harvey was a safety risk, the judge sent him to a secure detention center until further plans could be made. From there, he was placed in a locked setting for delinquent boys.

The goal of secure treatment is to protect the community from delinquents while trying to change their behavior until it is possible to place them in a less secure setting, usually a residential treatment center. Most secure settings are locked and have a high staff-to-student ratio. Residents are closely monitored, have educational services at the facility, and receive intensive therapeutic services. The hope is that the restrictive setting, combined with the intensity of the intervention services, will help the individuals to gain sufficient control so that they can benefit from a less restrictive treatment program.

What determines if a child is placed in a secure setting or in a residential treatment setting that is less secure? There are several factors involved. First, the child's behavior must be assessed to determine how injurious it is to self or others and if it can be managed without constant attention from staff. Secondly, the child's potential for the development of inner controls is important. Can he or she monitor him- or herself to some extent or is it necessary for the controls to be totally external? And, does the child have a history of running away? Many nonsecure centers have no recourse but to let the child run away. A locked center might be more appropriate for a chronic runner. Finally, the choice of where the child is placed may not be based as much on therapeutic considerations (although it should be) as on the institution that is able to take a child at a given time (Barker, 1988; Marohn, 1993).

CENTERS FOR CHILDREN WITH SEVERE SPECIAL NEEDS

When children have severe special needs, it may not be possible for their parents to care for them. For example, one center for brain-injured children took those who could not do any of their own self-care. Usually these children had become older, larger, and were too heavy or their needs too complex for their parents to handle. Many of these parents had been well intentioned when the children were little, and had expected to keep them at home. But time had taken its toll, and as their lives began to center exclusively around these children, many parents felt they could no longer care for them. This is not to say that many parents do not feel terribly guilty about their decision to place their child in a residential setting. But many also realize that the residence may be better equipped to deal with their child's issues. In addition, having a special needs child in a family can be difficult for other siblings. Sometimes it is the needs of other children that the parents must consider, also.

Centers for mentally retarded or physically disabled children are usually staffed by a variety of professionals, including medical personnel. The facility may look like a hospital when the population is more severely disabled or it may look like any other institution, or even a large private home. Services usually include medical care, as well as residential and educational services for higher functioning clients. Some centers also have a day program in which children can spend the day, giving their parents respite to work or perform tasks for the rest of the family.

CHILDREN IN RESIDENTIAL SETTINGS

REASONS FOR REFERRAL

What might point to placement of a child in residential care as opposed to placement in a foster home? Some answers to this question were alluded to in an earlier section (Assumptions about Residential Care). Basically, children are placed in these centers because their needs are beyond the domain of the foster care system. Barker (1988) responds to this question by saying that placement decisions fit into two categories: (1) admissions for reasons other than the need for the residential program itself, and (2) admissions due to need for the residential treatment program itself.

Admissions for Reasons Other Than the Need for the Residential Program Itself
Barker (1988) includes three main groups under this heading. First, some children are placed in order to protect the community. These children may be homicidal, fire-setters, sexually abusive, or otherwise injurious to others.

> Quentin was ten when he killed his younger brother. After a brief observation period, it was felt that he must be placed in a center for severely disturbed children. He had three other younger siblings and had also threatened other children in the neighborhood. His parents admitted that even they were afraid of him.

Secondly, a child might be placed for its own protection. Some children are suicidal or abuse substances to a degree that is unmanageable in a home environment.

> Wendell was a fourteen-year-old who had been taking drugs and drinking since he was nine. At nine, he and several friends stole cough syrup containing codeine and drank it in large quantities to enjoy the effect. Later, Wendell graduated to street drugs and alcohol. By twelve, he was usually either drunk or "stoned" on some substance. A drug addict her-

self, with five other children, his mother had little control over his behavior. At thirteen, he was removed from her home due to severe
neglect. Then followed placement in seven foster homes within a year,
until finally Wendell was placed in a secure residential setting.

Sometimes a child's behavior is not necessarily dangerous to others or him- or herself but is so disturbed that neither parents nor foster parents are able to manage it.

At nine, Fanny was diagnosed as psychotic. Her severely abusive background gave her little ability to trust adults, including the therapists
who had tried to help her. She hallucinated and seemed unable to maintain touch with reality. After a series of placements in psychiatric hospitals, it seemed better, both emotionally and financially, to place her in a
center for severely disturbed children.

Admissions Due to the Need for the Residential
Treatment Program Itself

Some children can benefit from the type of treatment provided in a residential setting. For those who have demonstrated a self-perpetuating cycle of dysfunctional
behaviors that could not be dealt with in less restrictive settings, a residential program may be the answer (Barker, 1988).

Gabrielle seemed to be locked into a pattern with her parents that was
proving harmful to her. At thirteen, she had rebelled against the strict
authoritative rules set down by her father. She began staying out all
night and became promiscuous. She was picked up by the police and
taken to court. Her father, an influential man in the community, saw
that the case was dropped. This angered Gabrielle and her behavior
continued. Unconsciously she hungered for control but her father, intent on protecting his reputation, constantly intervened for her. Finally,
one juvenile officer recognized the pattern and asked the judge to place
her in a foster home. Despite the father's protests, this was done. But after antagonizing several sets of foster parents, it became clear that Gabrielle needed a more structured setting with less contact with parental
figures. She was therefore placed in a residential setting.

In some cases, a child needs treatment that requires skills that the parents do
not possess and residential placement may be the solution.

Vivienne was adopted by the Reiners when she was five years old. It soon became clear from her bizarre behavior that she was having difficulty bonding with her new parents or with anyone else. Several diagnostic screenings made it clear to the distraught Reiners that Vivienne had "attachment disorder," a condition usually associated with early trauma that renders an individual unable to bond with others. As a result the individual has little feelings or empathy for others and may actually harm them. All concerned felt that Vivienne should be placed in a residential setting that was a pioneer in the treatment of attachment disorders.

For such children, a residential setting is used when all other attempts have failed. Some children perceive this and strive to make good in this new setting. Others feel that this is the "end of the road" and have difficulty with their residential experience. Effective casework with these children can often help them to recognize that there is hope.

ADJUSTMENT TO PLACEMENT

Often, placement in residential care is abrupt and children are given little opportunity to adjust to it. Even if they are allowed to accept the fact of placement by pre-placement visits to the new site and given time to acclimate to the idea, children have feelings about the transition (Schaefer and Swanson, 1988).

The predominant feeling among children who have been separated from their parents is that they are bad. This may be especially true when the placement is in an institution. Then children feel that they may have been "too bad" to live in a family setting. They may even feel that placement is a form of punishment. It may require intensive casework to help children recognize that there are problems but that it is possible for them to change their behavior.

We can probably all remember a time when we had to go from a family environment to an impersonal setting and how that felt. Perhaps when you went to college was the first time that you were suddenly alone in a room with the bathroom down the hall and none of the little personal touches of a private home. Further, it may seem that there is no one there who cares exclusively about you. Children in residential settings may also have this isolated, impersonal feeling, but often at a much younger age. One way to help children who are placed to overcome this is to allow them to bring personal items from home, such as special toys or other objects. These are sometimes referred to as "transitional objects" (Swanson and Schaefer, 1988).

The feelings of aloneness may cause some children to isolate themselves from their peers. It may take time and help with learning to recognize their own and others' needs before the child acclimates him- or herself to congregate living. However, such living can provide valuable lessons in the development of social skills.

LIFE IN A RESIDENTIAL SETTING

Every residential setting interprets its mission differently. In general a residential setting can be seen as a "comprehensive coordinated system of services to support children and their families...with its most important role to support changes necessary to move the family as well as the child where possible, toward unification or life in the community" (Stuck, 1992, 484). Most settings are comprised of three separate components—residential, educational, and clinical—that are designed to provide a complete therapeutic program for each child. The intent of residential treatment is to be a temporary arrangement during which intensive therapy with the child is done, with the intent of preparing the child for placement in a less restrictive setting, such as his or her own home or a foster home. Certainly, the intent is that the child will eventually return to his or her own home. Residences for more chronically involved children may expect to keep them until their majority, although this is the exception rather than the rule.

COMPONENTS OF A RESIDENTIAL SETTING

Although they are designed to work together in a total program for each child, called *the therapeutic milieu,* each component of group care provides a different service. The *residential* component is made up of those staff members who interact with children in their living space and who guide them in their daily living skills. Swanson and Richard (1988) explain that staff are responsible

> *for ensuring that each child's daily needs are met, establishing and maintaining daily routines (mealtime, bedtime, etc.), providing a stable, secure environment, providing an opportunity for positive interactions among staff, children, and their peers. In order to accomplish this Herculean task, it is essential that staff establish clear, consistent guidelines for maintaining discipline and for controlling the behavior of children who often have had a history of behavior problems (77).*

Children may live in dorms with child care workers who monitor them while they are in this setting. Child care workers may continue to be with their charges at any time when they are not either with their therapists or in school. Or children may reside in smaller, more homelike settings, often referred to as cottages or houses. In these settings there may be houseparents who act almost like surrogate parents. The type of setting children reside in differs from agency to agency and is sometimes based on the children's ability to function independently. For example, one residence for disturbed girls operates on a level system. When a girl first comes to the agency, she is placed in a dorm with child care workers who monitor her progress. When the girl has integrated into the program and seems to be following the rules, she achieves a higher level and may be moved to a residential setting that is more like a cottage. Here, there are houseparents, but the girl has more freedom.

When a girl is almost ready to leave the center, she moves to a house that operates like an apartment. Although there is a housemother, the girls are expected to care for themselves as they would in an apartment setting. This prepares them for living on their own.

The *educational* component is designed to provide specialized instruction to the children to enable them to realize their scholastic potential. Many children who come to residential settings are behind educationally, because their individual problem has hindered their ability to learn, they have missed too much school, or the school they attended found them difficult to teach due to behavior problems. For this reason, children are tested scholastically and their educational plan is geared toward their own level, often requiring remedial work. Teachers also maintain close contact with both residential and clinical staff to ensure that they are aware of any nonscholastic issues (e.g., residual issues from the past, disputes with peers, and so on) that are impeding the student's learning or ability to concentrate (Marohn, 1993).

The *clinical* component is dedicated to counseling services to help children understand themselves and their needs. Children are seen, both on an individual and a group basis, by staff trained in social work and psychology. Some programs offer a once- or twice-a-week individual therapy session as well as group sessions that deal with a variety of issues. Other centers offer more intensive therapeutic services. For example, one program for latency aged boys offers individual therapy with a case worker for an hour three times a week. The boys are also involved with at least one group a day on week days. The groups address such issues as anger management and understanding their past abuse; there is a group for boys who show signs of sexually abusing others, a group that addresses substance abuse issues, and a group that helps them understand how to live and deal with each other in the residential setting. Almost all programs feature groups designed to enhance children's social skills, and an increasing number of programs have groups to help children deal with their past abuse in their homes.

TOKEN ECONOMY AND PHASE SYSTEM

Most residential centers, especially those for disturbed or delinquent children, are set up along behavior modification lines. These programs use points or tokens as rewards when children are abiding by the rules or following their treatment plans. There are also levels, usually based on how much independence children are allowed. When children have earned a certain number of points, they may progress to the next level and be given more privileges.

When a child comes to the Holyrood Center, he is on Level 1. This means that he resides in House #1 (Forrest Hall) where there is a high level of supervision and structure. While he is in this house, he cannot receive outside phone calls or leave the grounds, and is not allowed visitors. Most boys, by following the rules, progress to Level 2 fairly quickly. This enables them to move to House #2 (Sherwood Hall) where they can decorate their room with their personal items, make two outside phone calls a week, and have visits from parents and siblings. Although they may leave the grounds, they must be accompanied by a staff member. Boys who achieve Level 3 move to House #3 (Garland Hall), where they have a good deal of independence. They can make calls off-campus and receive visitors at any time when they have free time. The atmosphere at Garland House is collegial and informal and the boys learn to do a great many of the house tasks themselves. They can leave campus alone with permission.

If children in this system do not continue to make progress, they can be dropped back down a level. It is not uncommon for children to move back and forth between levels as the events in their lives put a great deal of stress on them.

Judy had been in the residential treatment center for nine months. She had done well and had progressed to the highest level. Judy had come to the center after her eighty-year-old grandmother had found her behavior too difficult to manage and Judy had been unable to adjust to two foster homes. She enjoyed the residential setting and it was expected that, due to her excellent progress, she would be returned to the last foster home. Shortly before Judy was released, her mother, who had abandoned her as a toddler, returned and wanted to resume a relationship with her daughter. Judy, angry and confused by the attention of a woman who she had always assumed "did not want her," began to act up in the residence. She fought with her peers and finally pulled a knife on one of them. Feeling that she needed much more supervision to contain her behavior, the residence dropped her back to Level 1. It took numerous family meetings between Judy, her grandmother, and her mother before Judy was able to control her behavior to the extent that she could progress again to a higher level.

Children often feel safer with a token economy because they can measure the progress they are making. Some centers use tangible rewards like chips, but more use points, which are accounted for on a chart.

THE INFLUENCE OF PEER CULTURE

A major factor in the rehabilitative process for children in residential treatment is their contact with their peers. These are usually children whose relations with others have been extremely problematic. Now they are faced with a group of other children all of whom have had similar negative experiences. These children are often hyperactive, overly aggressive, antisocial, impulsive, and have a variety of other ego deficits (Gwynn et al., 1988). Even though the peer interaction may be negative, the development of the ability to interact with these peers helps children to develop many skills.

Gwynn, Meyer, and Schaefer (1988) suggest that peer culture has a negative impact on individual children.

> [The] peer group positively reinforced anti-social talk and actions (e.g., rule-breaking, criticisms of adults, and aggressive behaviors), whereas it negatively reinforced or punished socially conforming behavior (e.g., saying they liked someone on staff, expressing cooperation with the treatment program, etc.) (110).

These authors suggest that more intensive family work, using the peer group in therapy sessions, teaching values to peers as a group, and behavior modification can be used to reduce the negative influence of the peer culture.

Other authors (Kadushin and Martin, 1988) feel that the peer culture can have a positive influence. In their peers, children find examples of others who have had similar backgrounds of abuse and family dysfunction. There is a safety in knowing that others have shared your experiences, despite the fact that children may not recognize or admit it. Further, peers give children an opportunity to try out a variety of relational styles in the relative safety of a structured environment.

Cassandra remembered fondly her housemates at the residential setting where she stayed for two years. "They were my best friends!" she commented. "I didn't have to be embarrassed with them because my Mom drank and my Dad sexually abused me. Those things happened to them, too. And living with a bunch of girls made it feel like family. I never really had a family so it was really good to have them. I still write to a couple of the other kids."

Whether the peer culture teaches children negative attitudes or behavior or provides support for them, it does play an extremely important role in their rehabilitation.

HANDLING CRISES IN RESIDENTIAL SETTINGS

What is a crisis when you are dealing with a group of disturbed or delinquent children? The term *crisis* is often used to describe when a child or children lose control. Children who feel especially vulnerable may express it by losing control. Sometimes staff can predict what might cause a child to lose control and prevent it. A crisis often occurs when staff are unprepared for the acting-out behavior.

Dillon had not had a self-abusive episode for months. The staff had begun to relax and not keep up their constant vigilance. When Henry was admitted to the center, his intake profile had not mentioned any self-abusive behavior, but Henry got into a fight with Yanus and became very angry. He grabbed a bottle someone had left in the kitchen, slammed it against the refrigerator to break it, and began cutting himself. Dillon, observing the scene, began to gouge deep cuts in his arm with his fingernails. Yanus, who was petrified of the sight of blood, began to scream and run around the room.

Clearly the two staff members who were in the kitchen area saw this as a crisis and called for help. But crises are not always as unpredictable or dramatic. Holidays, for example, often cause crises for children in residential settings. Christmas, Easter, Thanksgiving, and birthdays may not have been the happy times most of us remember. Instead, these days, surrounded by the excitement usually associated with them, may have served to point out for children who are eventually placed in a residential setting that life is not as idyllic as they perceive the lives of other children to be. This may create in them anger or sadness and these feelings are often acted out. Anniversary reactions (anniversary dates of deaths or traumas from the past) may also send children into crisis.

Everyday events may also contribute. Katz (1988) cites several instances that can increase the risk of some children going into crisis.

1. *Lack of sufficient structure:* Structure is an important part of residential treatment. When there is less structure than usual or less supervision, children may feel vulnerable, unsafe, and then lose control.

2. *Competitive situations:* Children who have a history of failures are often oversensitive to being put in positions where they feel they can fail again. Whether the event is a sports competition or doing school work and being compared to others, these fears may cause them to lose control.

3. *Contact with family:* Children in residential settings have usually had problematic relations with their family members. Seeing them again, whether it is during home visits or family sessions, can generate feelings of anger, rage, sadness, and longing. These vulnerable feelings must be denied by hurt children and the way they deny is often to act out. This out-of-control behavior can either precede or follow these contacts.

4. *Changes in relationships with staff:* Children who have finally allowed themselves to trust another, to whatever small degree, are often overly sensitive when staff leave, are not consistent, or in some way change. Sometimes staff will discover a change in the behavior of the children when they know that a staff member is getting married.

"It's like she was no longer just ours," explained one adolescent girl when her social worker returned from her honeymoon. The girls had been particularly difficult in therapy and it soon became obvious that they were jealous of the new husband.

5. *Ability to deal with stress:* It is not always easy for children in residential treatment to deal with stressful situations. Instead of being able to handle them calmly, they may overreact and lose control. The stressful events can be minor or major and even happy events can cause children's behavior to escalate.

"Not only holidays but the end of school is hard at this center," explained one child care worker. "The kids know there will be an award ceremony and they are excited to find out who got awards. And many of them will go home in the summer and these changes always create crises."

In handling crisis events, it may be necessary to physically restrain children who are so out-of-control that words cannot calm them. While not all agencies use physical restraints, most do have some preferred method. Staff are usually trained when they are hired in whatever method the center uses. Most techniques stress a continuum of restraint, teaching the worker to first try to de-escalate the problematic behavior and, if all else fails, to physically restrain in a manner that will not endanger either the child or the staff member.

Staff in residential centers learn that they can often anticipate problematic behavior. If they can recognize the child's precursors to out-of-control behavior, they can sometimes prevent it. In time, they may also be able to teach the child how to recognize what leads to crisis and seek help or activate his or her inner controls before things get out of hand (Katz, 1988).

SEXUALLY ACTING OUT IN RESIDENTIAL CARE

One of the most difficult problems for staff in residential care to handle is the issue of residents sexually acting out (see Plach, 1993; Braga and Schimmer, 1993; Northrup, 1993). Crenshaw (1988) postulates that sexually acting out should be seen in a broader Freudian psychosocial framework. In the course of their development, children experience sexuality in different ways. Psychosocial theory maintains that the first area of sexuality is the mouth, as oral gratification is the child's first contact with the world. If that contact is inconsistent or unsatisfactory, the child can develop an oral fixation. Because many children in residential treatment have experienced neglect, abuse, or a lack of attention at the hands of caretakers in their early years, food becomes an issue. Thus, the tendency to withhold food as a form of punishment (e.g., "you'll go to your room with no dinner" or "you'll miss your snack") can actually be extremely counter-therapeutic for the orally deprived child.

A child's oral deprivation may also account for the problems many centers have in enlisting his or her cooperation in taking medication by mouth. Staff may assume that a child does not want to take the drug that will help him or her with depression, hyperactivity, or seizures. Yet it is not necessarily the effect of the drug that the child is avoiding; he or she may be experiencing conflict about the dispensing of it. Medication is often dispensed by a female nurse who appears to be the mother figure from whom the child did not receive early nurturing. Thus, the anger and rage about this early deprivation is often unconsciously centered on this medical person (Crenshaw, 1988).

During later development, the bowels and elimination become the focus of psychosexual development. Thus, for children traumatized in this period of their development (between one to three years) the smearing of feces or urination or inappropriate elimination is not uncommon. In addition, control becomes paramount and children can go to seemingly extraordinary means to control child care staff (Crenshaw, 1988).

Juanita, a fourteen-year-old who had been severely abused as a toddler, was a staff favorite. She was small for her age and had leg braces that impeded some of her activities. She sought the help and attention of staff and usually got it. She did not get on as well with peers and took a particular dislike to Dawn, a new girl on the unit. After a particularly heated fight between the two girls, staff sent both to their rooms. When she was allowed to come out Juanita was at first sullen and then extremely clingy and manipulative with staff. That night at bedtime, Dawn came crying hysterically to the staff member in charge saying that "there was crap in her room!" Indeed, there was a pile of feces placed neatly on her pillow. Staff questioned everyone but could not uncover the culprit. Two days later, there was another deposit of feces. Several days after that, Juanita started another fight with Dawn. This night, Dawn's whole bed was smeared with feces and staff began to recognize a pattern. Each time, Juanita had been particularly endearing to staff after she had apparently planted the feces in Dawn's room.

In the course of psychosocial development, the years of three to six are characterized by a preoccupation with the genital area. Masturbation can be practiced often and it is not uncommon for children to masturbate openly in front of others. This may also translate into a desire for genital contact with others, usually exhibitionism, touching, or competitive activities (e.g., "my penis is bigger than yours"). Sex talk is common. For children who are fixated in this period of development, genital preoccupation is quite common. One of the most difficult tasks for residential staff is to determine what types of behavior involving exposure, mutual viewing, and touching are curiosity and exploration and what behaviors are exploitive (Crenshaw, 1988). Most residential treatment settings prohibit all interactive sexual contact. Some permit solo masturbation for teens when they are alone in their bedrooms. Other centers frown on this.

It is expected, for several reasons, that there will be some sexual acting out in residential settings. First, most of the children in these settings have had inappropriate models for sexuality or insufficient or inappropriate sexual education. Children who observe parents having sex with each other or with someone else are usually traumatized by the experience. Children who are sexually abused are not allowed to develop sexual attitudes and behavior normally. And children who are shielded from even healthy information about sex may develop their own distorted ideas and need to try them out. Secondly, children who learn about sexuality by being victimized or watching others in adult sexual pursuits become confused. This confusion may result in a need to "try out" this behavior on others (Johnson and Aoki, 1993), or they may have a psychological need to replicate the relationship they had with their parents or caretakers by setting up that same type of relationship (including the sexuality) with their current care providers (Charles et al., 1993). Also, children who have not been taught appropriate sexuality may confuse it with attention or caring or use sexuality to act out rage, control, or dehumanization. And finally, because staff do not want to "jump to conclusions," they may not intervene with debatable sexually acting out (e.g., brushing past a staff member somewhat seductively, touching other areas of the body like the hair or the back) until the behaviors are quite obviously sexual. This is often because either the staff member was abused him- or herself and cannot recognize the behavior or because the staff member has been sheltered from abusive situations and is inexperienced at the job.

The types of sexual behaviors that staff in residential settings usually identify are masturbation, especially in the presence of others, profane sexual talk, participating in sexual interactions with other residents, exhibitionism, and exploitive sexual contact with others (Powers, 1993). It is vitally important that staff be given adequate training to deal with these various behaviors. In addition, Powers suggests that the staff may actually contribute to sexual acting out by not having resolved their own sexual conflicts, breaking boundaries by talking about their own sexual prowess or pursuits to residents, being seductive with the children in their care or with other staff members in front of the children, wearing seductive clothing, and inappropriately touching children, which, although not sexual, could be misinterpreted as being so by the children (1993, 33–34).

Increasingly, the treatment of youthful sexual offenders is undertaken in group homes. Although there is some question if grouping youthful offenders together is the best method of treatment, the reality is that they usually cannot be handled at home or in foster homes. Thus, the move has been to create centers, or at least units, that specialize in their rehabilitation (Breer, 1987; Burnett and Rathbun, 1993; Ross and deViller, 1993). Certainly, placing children who have sexually abused other children with others who have done the same involves some serious considerations.

Screening, training, and supervision of staff.   It is vital that the staff working with abuse issues and youthful sexual offenders be thoroughly screened for their past involvement with sexual abuse issues and attitudes toward sexuality. Punitive attitudes or unresolved sexual conflicts in staff leave young offenders vulnerable to being revictimized, as they have themselves been early victims of abuse. In addition, staff must be well trained not only in sexual abuse issues but in behavior management. And, due to the fact that sexual abuse may well bring up personal issues for staff members, careful supervision is a must (Ross and deViller, 1993).

Managing the living space.   Sexual offenders should be housed separately from those without a history of sexual aggression. In addition, most programs for youthful offenders strive to provide single rooms whenever possible. When single rooms are not an option, careful supervision of residents is necessary (Ross and deViller, 1993).

Adequate treatment plans.   Sexual offenders require intensive treatment, including both group and individual counseling (Breer, 1987; Burnett and Rathbun, 1993; Ross and deViller, 1993). Burnett and Rathbun (1993) suggest that this therapy should include groups led by both a male and female therapist. The treatment should address such issues as denial, the offender as a victim, victim personalization (seeing the victim as a person and trying to understand how he or she might feel), social skill training, human sexuality, and relapse prevention (60–62).

Staff protection.   There are some youthful offenders who may pose a threat to staff members. Thus, in addition to screening for such offenders, the center must be careful to ensure that staff members are never placed in a vulnerable position. For example, a staff member should not be alone with a child or enter a bedroom or shower area without being "covered" by another staff member. The agency must be careful to protect staff boundaries, such as home addresses and phone numbers. And when incidents do occur, they must be dealt with immediately and staff members supported in this (Ross and deViller, 1993).

SEXUAL ABUSE OF CHILDREN IN RESIDENTIAL CARE

Although the residential care system is set up to protect children and have a therapeutic effect on their lives, it is always possible for someone who is in the role of the helper to further victimize the child (see Rindfleisch, 1988; Plach, 1993; Bloom, 1993; Braga, 1993). Bloom, Denton, and Caflish (1991) report that in the Illinois Department of Children and Family Services between 1986 and 1989 there were 211 allegations of sexual abuse among children in residential settings. Of these, 27 percent came to the point of serious investigation. Groze (1990) studied sexual abuse in institutions in one large southwestern state and found that, between 1985 and 1987, one in five of the reported cases of abuse were confirmed.

What causes someone who cares for children to sexually abuse them? First, those who have the inclination to sexually abuse will be attracted to settings that give them close proximity to children and the opportunity to have access to them. Secondly, the frustrations of the job, along with the closeness to children, may bring out tendencies in some to abuse that they did not realize they had. Also, child care workers, especially, are among the poorest paid in the mental health field. Agencies do not always have an easy time finding staff due to the low pay and long hours, and so may not do sufficient screening.

Horace Milner was sexually abused as a child by his father, a priest, and two uncles. He had forgotten much of the abuse (and was not to think of it until he ended up in therapy years later for sexually abusing two children). When Horace was in his early twenties, he knew he wanted to help kids. He had finished a stint in the army and was looking for a job he could do while he went back to school. A local home for disturbed boys had been having a difficult time finding staff for the night shift. When Horace applied they asked if he could start immediately. Horace enjoyed the contact with the boys. The dependence some of them developed on him made him feel needed.

For Horace, extremely needy himself, the neediness of these boys fed into a part of his pathology of which he was as yet unaware. Several weeks after he began working at the center, several boys reported that he was sexually abusing another boy. The reports turned out to be true.

Bloom (1993) states that centers must recognize that abuse can happen and make provisions for the safety of both children and staff. He suggests a process whereby both child and staff are heard and fair attention is given to the allegations and reports of each.

WORKING WITH FAMILIES OF CHILDREN IN RESIDENTIAL CARE

Work with the families of the children in institutional care can be one of the most frustrating and is often the least emphasized part of the therapeutic process. Yet, if we recognize that the child may well return to this family someday, the importance of such work cannot be underestimated. The focus of family work is usually three-fold: to help the family maintain a functional relationship with the child in placement; to aid the family in preparing for the return of the child (if this is the plan); and to help the family sort out and cope with the dysfunction that caused the placement of the child in residential care. All of these factors are usually intertwined.

MOTIVATION OF PARENTS

The attitudes of parents of placed children range from the very concerned and involved parents to the disengaged parents, who would prefer to forget that they have a child in placement. Before we criticize the latter parents, however, we must remember that, by the time a child gets to residential care, many other solutions have probably been tried. The parents may have invested heavily in those attempts at solving their problems but to no avail. Now the parents are most likely at the end of their patience and resources. To have someone else responsible for this child may seem like a relief.

Van Hagen (1988) divides parents into several categories: absent, ambivalent, impoverished, addicted, and abusive. The *absent parent* is not available because of mental illness or incarceration. The lack of parental visits may be a problem for the child, who feels abandoned and resentful. The child may also harbor fantasies about the absent parent and therapeutic work with that child may focus on the resolution of these fantasies. A powerful example of such fantasies was told in Hayden's *The Tiger's Child* (1995). Sheila, the tiger's child of Hayden's story, was abandoned when she was four years old by her mother, who left her at the side of the road. After several foster homes, Sheila was placed in a group home. Intermittently in touch with Hayden, a former special education teacher and mentor, Sheila has shared fantasies of finding and being reunited with her mother. While in the group home, she sends an ad to a California paper to attempt to locate her mother. A letter arrives from a woman claiming to be her mother, a woman whom Hayden quickly recognizes as being disturbed. Trying gently to alert Sheila to the danger of getting her hopes up does not work and Sheila runs away to find her mother. Defeated and disillusioned, but wiser, Sheila eventually returns to contact Hayden. The woman was indeed disturbed and was not her mother. But the fantasies had been a powerful motivator for the child.

A second type of parent identified by Van Hagen (1988) is the *ambivalent parent.* The child may have spent a good amount of time outside of the home and reunification efforts may have been tried before. The ambivalent parent feels exhausted by these efforts and is not sure whether or not she or he wants the child at home. Sometimes the placed child is scapegoated and all the family ills are attributed to him or her. The family has deluded itself into thinking that, if this child is gone, the family will be fine.

When Coraleen was placed in residential care, it was almost as if her family breathed a collective sigh of relief. The family had been dysfunctional for years. The father, now dead, had sexually abused his two daughters and physically abused his son and wife. But the family had guarded the secret of its pathology. The oldest girl had been the "good child" and had excelled in school, and the boy had remained quiet, drawing little attention to himself. Then Coraleen gave up the family secret in her attempts to deal with her own eating disorder. The family was furious with her for "tarnishing the name of the father." After years of rejection by them, Coraleen began to act out and, after a brush with the juvenile justice system, was placed in residential care. Visits to her were constantly postponed or cancelled by the mother, who found one conflict after another. Not having Coraleen at home gave the family the

> opportunity to pretend that the secret had never come out. While the mother loved her daughter and wanted to see that she was well cared for, the burden of having her home was too great.

The problem for such families is that placement is rarely permanent and they will need to come to terms with the fact that the child may come home.

The *impoverished parent* (Van Hagen, 1988) is overwhelmed by a whole set of external problems that require the family to put a great deal of effort into merely surviving.

> The Harbingers were beset by a myriad of problems. While a steady worker, Mr. Harbinger found it difficult to make enough to support his six children, who ranged in age from twenty to nine. The oldest child, Ned, had suffered a spinal injury and was now quadriplegic and living at home. Seventeen-year-old Fran had just announced that she was pregnant and that the father was HIV-positive. Fifteen-year-old Justine had recently been placed in residential care after years of running away and using drugs. Fourteen-year-old Suzie appeared not to be copying her sister's drug abuse. While twelve-year-old Gary and nine-year-old Farley appeared to have no problems as yet, the Harbingers were sure they would in time. In addition to their other problems, Mrs. Harbinger's father, who had sexually abused her as a child and who she suspected of abusing at least one of the older girls, was living with them. He had recently been diagnosed with Alzheimers and could no longer live alone.

For this overwhelmed family, the placement of Justine seemed like a respite from one small part of their problems. Although they worked diligently with the social worker at the residential treatment setting, it was clear that they had little investment in having her home.

The *addicted parent* is often too caught up in her or his addiction to be much of a resource for the child. Only after he or she is willing to deal with this problem can work with the family be effective. And the *abusive parent* may be a threat to the child if he or she is returned home. Such a parent will need additional services in order to be an appropriate resource for the child (Van Hagen, 1988).

Some parents are most interested in having their children home and work well with agencies.

> The DeRosas adopted Angela when she was three years old. As a young adolescent Angela became quite difficult. She would not go to school, was promiscuous, and generally difficult to handle. The school recom-

mended that she be placed in residential treatment. Unsure of what else to do, the DeRosas agreed. After a year of intensive family work, Angela returned home.

For Angela and her parents, family therapy proved quite effective. The more successful the work with the family, the more smoothly the child's transition from the institution to the home will be.

TYPES OF FAMILY TREATMENT

Each agency has a different commitment to family treatment and, therefore, different techniques and procedures. Some see families once a week or even once a month, depending on the needs of the family and their availability to come to the center. Families may be seen individually or with their institutionalized child. All members may be present or just one parent. Sometimes, one parent is comfortable working with a therapist while the other is not. There are also some agencies that feature group treatment for parents or parenting skills classes.

It is not only therapy sessions but also visits that are part of family work. Families are usually encouraged to visit as this means that the child will not feel abandoned. Visits may be made at the center or the child may be allowed to have supervised visits off-site or at home. When children progress in their program, they may be allowed home visits for a day, a weekend, or over a holiday or vacation.

Visits can be extremely conflictual for both parents and children. Children may harbor a variety of resentments toward their parents that have not been resolved. They may feel that they were abandoned and feel angry. If parents cancel at the last minute, children feel betrayed, or they may not want to see their parents at all. It is not uncommon for the day preceding or following visits to be difficult emotionally for children.

Parents, too, might feel some ambivalence. After all, this is the child whose problem seemed to cause them a great deal of trouble in the recent past. This is the child who has caused society to question them as parents and who has made them feel inadequate. They may feel anger toward this child or they may not trust the child and may be fearful about how the child will behave. For parents, visits may be as much of an adjustment as they are for their children. Often, much social worker time is dedicated to helping both parents and children with visiting issues.

What if a child does not have a family that is willing to visit or available for the child's return? These children are either kept in long-term residential placement or, more likely, placed in a foster home when they are ready to return home. Some agencies provide children who do not have visits from parents with a *visiting resource*. This visiting resource might be an adult friend or family member, a concerned member of the community who volunteers to do so, or a potential foster parent who may someday receive them in placement. When children will not be returning to their own homes, but rather leaving placement to be on their own, they are prepared by the agency for independent living (see Chapter 12 for discussion of independent living).

PROBLEMS IN WORKING WITH FAMILIES

Parents whose children have been placed in any type of setting may *feel ambivalence*. The fact that their child is not home with them may make them *feel as though they have failed*. They believe that people in the community will criticize them and many parents do not tell their neighbors that their child is in placement. They may *feel hurt* if their child is doing better in residential care than they were at home. For all these reasons parents might act in a variety of ways. They may *approach the agency with hostility*.

"Nothing we did for Mrs. Garnett or her son seemed right," said one social worker in a residential treatment center. "She complained about everything! We weren't giving her son enough to eat or the parent events were never scheduled when she could come. She disliked the child care staff and thought they had something against her son. This mother felt so out of control by having her son in placement that she had to make the center look bad!"

Some parents, either consciously or unconsciously, *sabotage their child's treatment*.

Kelly was extremely obese when she came to the center. One of her problems was that she was so ostracized by her peers that she became angry and would try to hurt them. At the center, she was put on a rigid diet, a plan with which she cooperated well. After a month of placement and ten lost pounds she went on her first home visit. When she returned, she came back with a large selection of sweets bought for her by her mother, who was fully aware of the treatment plan. When the mother was confronted about this she apologized saying that she had "forgotten." But after every subsequent visit, the same thing happened. Kelly, formerly motivated, but now confused about her loyalties, became difficult and would not comply with her treatment plan. It took several months of intensive casework before the social worker was able to enlist the mother's full cooperation. Having been pregnant herself at fifteen, the mother was finally able to recognize that she feared the same would happen to Kelly if she became "too attractive and desirable." The mother was helped to see that there were others ways to break the pattern.

Family work can also create difficulties for staff, whether they are working directly with the family or dealing primarily with the child. For clinical staff who work with the family, the missed appointments, the parents who arrive drunk or high, the hostility, and the sabotage can take its toll. The staff members must remember how difficult it may be for these parents to cope with the fact that they have lost control over their children's lives. For all staff who see a child who has been maltreated, rejected, or hurt in some other manner, they may have difficulty understanding the parents' motivation. Staff may feel a need to protect the child from further abuse from these parents. The reality is that the parents are an integral part of the child and it is not possible to separate the two entirely.

THE ROLE OF STAFF IN A RESIDENTIAL SETTING

The roles performed by staff members in a residential setting differ according to the department they are involved with and the agency itself. As previously discussed, most agencies are composed of three departments organized by function: residential, educational, and clinical.

RESIDENTIAL STAFF

The residential component oversees the children's everyday life, from their waking hours to bedtime and through the night. Child care workers or residential counselors are the backbone of the residential component and work in shifts similar to those of nurses. It is these staff members who help the children get up and get ready for the day. They are often responsible for preparing or serving breakfast. Some residences serve all meals in a common dining room while, in others, the children eat some or all of their meals at their living units. If not responsible for the preparation of food, they must monitor the children's behavior while they eat in the dining hall.

While the children go to school, whether on grounds or off, the residential staff either help with transitions, help the educational staff, or return to their units to do housekeeping in anticipation of the children's return. Afterschool and evening hours may be punctuated by a series of activities or groups, often led by child care workers. If the children have therapeutic activities, such as counseling appointments or therapy groups, child care staff are usually responsible for getting the children there. Although this may not sound like much of a task, the reality is that many children have difficulties with transitional periods.

Bedtime, too, can be problematic, especially for sexually abused children who do not remember their beds as being safe places. Child care workers report talking to children before they go to bed and comforting them after they wake with distressing nightmares. Night terrors can be a common occurrence for children whose early lives have been filled with trauma.

Despite the fact that child care workers spend most of their time with children and can be one of the most influential aspects of their therapeutic program, they are often the youngest, most inexperienced, and most poorly trained of all agency staff. This can be problematic for all involved. As Kagan (1988) comments:

> *Children from troubled families repeat behavioral patterns experienced in their homes and previous placements. Children in group care, in effect, reenact family dilemmas with staff. Accordingly, the child who has experienced abuse, abandonment, and neglect will often provoke the same interactions with staff members (160).*

Child care workers are usually supervised by a staff member who oversees their work. In turn, these supervisors may answer to a program director or the agency director, depending on the size and organization of the agency.

Instead of child care workers, some agencies use housemothers or houseparents, with a single woman (or man) or a married couple acting as surrogate parents. They are relieved for time off by other staff, but remain the primary resource for child care responsibilities. Although these individuals may have more life experience, they too are usually undertrained.

Wendy was in college when she found a job with a residential treatment center for disturbed girls. "Most of the girls had had some scrape with the law," said Wendy, "and some of them could be pretty tough! But when we got to know each other, we did okay." Wendy took college classes in the morning and arrived at the residence at about 3 P.M. There she stayed with a unit of seven girls and one other child care worker. "The two of us helped the girls with their homework, figured out who had to do laundry, and got them ready for the evening's activities. At 5:30, we all went down to the dining hall and ate. We broke up food fights and other arguments and made an attempt at teaching some of the kids some basic table manners. Dinner could be a really stressful time. After dinner, we usually had some kind of activity that the other worker and I planned. Sometimes we played a game, or made our own sundaes, or had discussions of things that were bothering the kids. Then we supervised who took showers while the other girls had some 'down time' in their rooms. Bedtime was always chaos. Somebody was always upset about something. The other worker and I usually took turns. One of us would work on the crisis while the other one monitored the other kids while they got ready for bed. We were trained to physically restrain out-of-control kids and once or twice we had to do that and call for a backup person. There was never a dull moment. If all was relatively quiet, I could go back to my dorm at the college around 11 P.M. I used to work on the 11 P.M. to 7 A.M. shift, but that got to be too much.

> We could sleep when the kids did, but there was always some crisis! And I really did enjoy being with the girls."

The training required for each staff position differs according to the population served, the organization and needs of the agency and, in some cases, supply and demand. Most agencies will hire child care workers with little experience or education if their need is great enough and the applicant seems qualified. Many college students have worked as evening or overnight child care staff while they pursue their degree. Increasingly, agencies are asking for workers who have had more education or experience with children. Retired people or parents can bring parenting skills to a residential setting, but without training they may not be prepared for the fact that the children placed in residential care may present many more challenges to patience than their own children did.

EDUCATIONAL STAFF

Children in residential settings are usually educated on the grounds of the agency, although there are exceptions and some children attend local schools. Those who teach them on-site are usually teachers trained in special education techniques. It is true, however, that many states do not have as stringent regulations requiring the hiring of licensed teachers for residences as they do for public schools. Teachers may also use aides, as it is important that the ratio of teacher-to-child be small enough to promote optimum learning.

Children are usually tested when they enter a residence to determine their educational level and their remedial needs, if they have any. Then teachers work with children to help them achieve their academic potential. Classes may be organized according to ability rather than age or grade level equivalent to public school.

Teaching in a residential setting is not just dedicated to academics. A significant part of a teacher's role may be removing the barriers to learning that have prevented the child from achieving on the outside. Children who come to residences often feel that they have failed and may exhibit behavioral problems in reaction to this perception. They may also have difficulty with their peers and therefore cause trouble in the organized classroom.

> Gordon Howly had taught in a public high school for ten years. "I just needed a new challenge when I took a job in a residential center for disabled and disturbed kids. I had completed most of a Master's in Special Education and thought I would really like to work with kids like this. I taught History and English and the kids rotated classes. I had about five adolescents in a class with an aide. The aide was there mostly because some of the kids needed help with manual tasks. Each child had different educational needs and I found myself working with most of them individually. For example, one child had cerebral palsy and couldn't

talk. He used a board with letters to communicate. He would spell
things by pointing to the letters. But he got frustrated very easily and
when he was not understood, he would hurl the board across the room.
I learned to duck very quickly. But all in all, I loved the job. The drive
that some of those kids had was an inspiration!"

In addition to teachers, most educational departments have administrators and
other educational staff who oversee the child's academic progress.

CLINICAL STAFF

Social workers, or counselors, psychologists, and psychiatrists make up an
agency's clinical component. These individuals may be on staff or they may operate on a consultant or part-time basis. For example, one residential treatment center had three social workers who did therapy both individually and in groups with
the children on a weekly basis. These social workers also saw the families, arranged home visits, and kept in touch with the residential and educational staff to
monitor the progress of each child. In addition, a psychologist was hired on a part-
time basis to do psychological testing and make treatment recommendations. She
came to the agency twice a week. A psychiatrist from a nearby mental health clinic
reviewed the medications of the children on a once-a-week basis and prescribed
other medications as needed. He would also see children for a screening interview
if the staff had questions about treatment.

The number of clinical staff depends largely on the mission of the agency and
the population served. As clinical staff may be the most highly trained, and therefore command higher salaries, fiscal constraints may mean that there are fewer clinicians than would be optimal.

Clinicians see children on a regular basis to help them sort out and understand
the issues that brought them into care. These issues may be their own behaviors,
family dysfunction, and/or abuse/neglect issues. In addition to individual meetings with children, clinicians may hold groups to help children with such issues as
anger management, divorced families, abuse/neglect, substance abuse, social
skills, and a variety of other concerns. In centers for juvenile offenders, groups help
them confront their problems, understand their victims, understand their own cycles, and take steps to interrupt their abusive patterns (Braga and Schimmer, 1993;
Burnett and Rathburn, 1993; Plach, 1993). Group work in these settings is an integral part of treatment.

Todd, with a Master's degree in Social Work, is a therapist in a residential setting for sexually abusive boys. Formerly, he worked for a protective services agency studying families in which abuse had occurred. "I
was always fascinated by the motivation of the offender, especially
when he or she was young. I find doing groups with these kids very en-

lightening. It is amazing that being a victim is so traumatic for some of these kids that victimizing someone else is the only way they see to escape that victim role."

Since the treatment of children in residential settings requires communication among the components, it is often the role of the clinician or case manager to facilitate this communication. He or she, with knowledge of abnormal psychology, might also consult with staff in other components to help them understand children's behaviors and problems.

OTHER STAFF FUNCTIONS

There are important functions, and therefore integral staff members, who may not fit neatly into the previously mentioned categories.

The *nurse* is extremely important in residential settings. While sometimes one person fills this role, with contracted services from the outside as needed, other agencies have whole medical units. For example, a residence for physically disabled residents might require a larger medical component than a center in which physical health is not the primary issue.

The program to rehabilitate children must be carefully planned and many agencies hire a *program director* and often other program staff to perform this function. These individuals may be part of the previously mentioned components or may make up a component by themselves. The administrative staff of an agency cannot be underestimated. It is these individuals who not only oversee the running of the agency, but may also need to raise funds for its continued existence. The *director*, especially, may set the tone of how an agency operates. Diamond (1988) comments that:

> the presence of the director will be reflected in agency practices such as the nature of specific therapies provided and prescribed roles and functions of treatment team members. In addition, the quality and nature of interpersonal relationships among children and staff will reflect the director's standards and values. Other important areas of impact include behavioral expectations, discipline, recreational activities, home visiting, dress code, and activities of daily living (e.g., meal and bedtime procedures) (148).

Some agencies also have a training component responsible for in-service training for all staff, and many larger centers have instituted quality control specialists or units to ensure that the quality of service remains consistent and high.

No residential agency could function without some form of intake. The *admissions specialist* or unit is assigned the task of reviewing applicant files, interviewing children and their parents before acceptance, and determining if the agency can meet the needs of this potential client.

Other support personnel, such as chaplains, transportation specialists, and visiting coordinators, may figure in a particular agency's plan. Other agencies operate with a minimum of staff who perform a variety of different roles.

THE FRUSTRATIONS OF STAFF

> Upon speaking to Johnny, one quickly learns that he is feeling extremely vulnerable and somewhat abused. He wants nothing more than to be accepted, appreciated, and recognized. Instead he feels victimized, exploited, and devalued. Although he seems to long for the opportunity to share more of himself emotionally, the thought of this frightens him. He feels that he has tried this in the past, but that his efforts have been at times unheard. Johnny is feeling alone and unsupported. Beneath his stoic demeanor lies an individual crying out for help.
>
> Johnny came to residential care roughly six months ago. He is twenty-eight years old, and works as a child care worker (Katz, 1988, 30).

One of the most widely discussed frustrations for staff in residential settings is the work itself. Children who are placed have had lives filled with abuse and injustices and they know nothing else but to mirror the way they have been treated in their treatment of others. In addition, it is difficult to constantly be a secondhand witness to the inhumanity that has been perpetrated on so many children. Their pain is not easy to watch and burnout is not uncommon (Corcoran, 1988).

Corcoran (1988) describes *burnout* as a phenomenon peculiar to professions that have one-to-one contact with people who have problems. A practitioner becomes burned out when he or she experiences "the depletion of emotional energies needed to perform one's job" (252). Dealing with problems daily can leave one short-tempered and emotionally exhausted. Although this can be true with any type of helping profession, residential treatment, because of the close proximity with clients on a continual basis, can make one especially vulnerable to burnout.

The *turnover of staff* in line positions (child care worker) can be especially high. Some centers estimate that they will be able to keep a child care worker for between six to eighteen months. It is not surprising, for this reason, that many centers do not invest a great deal of time in training such transient staff members. Yet, some would argue that better trained workers would not burn out as quickly (Kagan, 1988).

The high turnover rate can be a frustration for staff members as well as administration. When the work is taxing, it is important to trust and depend on one's fellow workers. When there are constantly new faces to relate to, workers feel isolated and perhaps more vulnerable.

Another issue for both staff and residents is the *inconsistency among child care practices*. Each staff member has a different idea of how children should be dealt with. As shifts change, so do the approaches of the staff. Thus, the very thing needed most by the child—consistency—is lacking (Kadushin and Martin, 1988). Consistency requires good communication as well as adequate training. When there is poor communication staff become frustrated and children feel unsafe.

While there are frustrations in residential settings, many staff say that the rewards outweigh them.

"Just to see a child who is so out of control at intake become a more stable, happier child is worth all the insults and grief you get while that's happening," reported one child care worker.

Staff often report that being prepared for the frustrations at the onset through an effective orientation program goes a long way toward helping them deal with their jobs.

TERMINATION

Where do children go when they leave a residential setting? Children leave a residence usually for one of several settings: home, a foster home, a less restrictive residence, a more restrictive residence, hospitalization, or independent living.

RETURN HOME

Children who return to their own homes may do so because the center feels that the child is now able to control his or her behavior sufficiently and/or the parents are able to handle the child's problems. This step is not undertaken without a great deal of thought. Usually, the parents have participated in family therapy and the child has progressed well in the residence. The agency social worker has met with the school and school staff feel able to provide educational services. Other therapeutic resources, such as therapists or support groups or remedial help, have been arranged. This planning has probably taken weeks or even months. The parties are motivated and feel that the child's return will be a success. This is a "best case scenario" and unfortunately does not always happen. Even when it does, the plan may or may not be successful.

There are other reasons why children return home. Residential treatment is funded by the social service agency or the child's school department and, though very rarely, the parents. If any of these parties feel that they are unable to continue funding the placement or any other out-of-home placement, the child may return home. In these situations, it is unusual for a sufficient amount of progress to have been made and the child is often the one who suffers.

Children occasionally return home because the parent does not feel that the child is being well served by the agency. This may be a reality or the parent may find that the problems are not as easy as she or he first thought.

> Mary Keller urged the school to place her daughter, Stephanie, because neither the teachers nor the mother could handle her oppositional behavior. After several psychiatric evaluations, the school agreed to fund a placement in a residential center for disturbed girls. Soon after placement, Stephanie became a model resident, obeying all the rules and complying with her treatment plan. In family sessions with Mrs. Keller, the agency social worker tried to explore the reasons why this mother and daughter had such a troubled relationship that the daughter became uncontrollable when at home. Mrs. Keller was incensed that the center was "blaming her" and immediately removed her daughter from placement.

Family work becomes an extremely important aspect of treatment if it is expected that the child will return home. Without such intervention, the problems that brought the child to placement often go unsolved. As one director of a residence explained about family work:

> "I have seen some very concerned, motivated families try their best to raise a child and find that the child ends up in placement. It might not even be what the family is doing that is the problem, but how the child interprets it. So often it is communication, or the lack of it, that is at the core of family problems."

PLACEMENT IN A FOSTER HOME OR A LESS RESTRICTIVE ENVIRONMENT

Some children progress in the residence but are not as yet ready to return home. For example, a child might be placed in a secure setting because he or she might be a danger to him- or herself or others. As treatment progresses, it becomes clear that he or she can benefit from a less restrictive setting in which internalized controls are necessary. From this new setting, the child might either return home or to a foster home. Or, if he or she is not ready for the amount of freedom given, he or she might again return to a more restrictive setting.

A child may no longer need the structure of a residential setting but cannot yet cope with the issues at home. Or some children may not have a home to return to, for whatever reason. In these instances, children may be placed in a foster home until they can return home or until they are able to live on their own. The foster parents often work with the residential center during the transition period to acclimate the child to the new foster home. The child may visit the home prior to placement to facilitate the move.

PLACEMENT IN A MORE RESTRICTIVE SETTING

As previously mentioned, some children need more structure than was anticipated when they were originally placed in a residential setting. There are several factors that might alert staff to this fact. A child may run away from the center. Less restrictive centers may have little recourse if a child decides to run away.

We are trained that if we see a child who is threatening to run, we will try to talk him out of it. If you see a kid who you know is on his way off grounds, you can call him back, but you cannot go after him. Different centers have different policies. Some actually chase the kid, but we don't. But most kids don't threaten when they are going to run. They just leave, and then it is our policy to call the police.

Children who run away may need a locked facility or an environment in which there is a higher staff-to-child ratio.

Sometimes children become so out of control that they are abusive to other residents, to themselves, or to staff. These children may require a more highly structured environment to ensure their safety. When children begin to act out their sexual abuse history by abusing other children, they may be moved to settings that provide better treatment for these issues.

The more structured settings to which children are transferred may be more secure residential facilities or even psychiatric hospital units.

HOSPITALIZATION

Children who are in residential settings may require hospitalization in psychiatric facilities. It may be that some aspect of the treatment process throws the child so off balance that they cannot cope.

Lois had been ritualistically sexually abused by her father. She had forgotten much of the abuse, but the residual effects came out in her oppositional behavior. When she was placed in the residential center, she had been in three foster homes previously. None of these families felt capable of dealing with her. Probably due to the less intensive relationships, Lois settled easily into the residential setting. She was assigned a therapist and the two began to work on helping her understand her past.

Then the memories began to return. At first they came through in terrifying dreams. Eventually Lois began remembering in therapy sessions. But these memories were too frightening, too overwhelming. Lois became so terrified that she curled up in a ball and could not be reached. After numerous unsuccessful attempts, the decision was made to hospitalize the child.

Children who are hospitalized usually stay there for only a short period of time while they are stabilized. After this, they may be returned to the same residential setting or to another.

INDEPENDENT LIVING

It may be that a child remains in a residential setting until he or she is old enough to become independent. Increasingly centers, much like foster care agencies, are developing programs for this possibility. Centers may have job readiness programs or teach specific independent living skills. They may also transfer teens who are almost ready for emancipation to small group homes that are often off the main campus of the residential center. These homes operate much like an apartment and give the teen a chance to try out such tasks as buying food and keeping house. Such programs are found to be fairly successful.

A FORMER RESIDENT REMEMBERS: JENNIFER'S STORY

"What was it like to be a kid in a residential treatment center? I guess I have a lot of responses to that!! Some parts were great but some weren't.

"When I was eight years old, my brothers [ages six and four] and I were taken away from our mother. She was always boozed up and used to bring men into the apartment. We were neglected and one of her boyfriends actually sexually abused me. One night my mom and this guy got into a fight and someone called the police. I guess when they saw our place (it was a real pigpen) the cops figured we shouldn't be there, so they took us to a foster home. We stayed in foster homes for a couple of years until my mom got her act together. Then she got us back. But that didn't last long. The guys started coming again and this time she did drugs as well as booze. But before the child welfare people could take us again, she shipped us off to an aunt. That was really bad news and I ran away. When they found me, I was put in a foster home by myself. But I was real angry and hated it and the other two after that. I wouldn't go to school and finally some kids and I stole a car but they caught us. They bailed me out and the foster parents took me back but I was real angry by then. I said I was going to kill myself and when the foster mother tried to stop me I turned the knife on her.

"There was a mess of legal and court stuff, but then they sent me off to this place for girls way out in the country. No one was going to tell me what to do and at first I guess I gave them a real hard time. I was about fifteen but I was a big kid and I think some of them were afraid of me. At first I was on this unit with about six other kids. They watched us every minute. It was awful. We had to eat in the unit and sleep there. We went to school on the grounds, too. The classes were small and we got a lot of attention, but at that point I was so angry at the world that I didn't care. There was this one teacher I liked though. She was young and could make stuff real interesting. She used to bring me books to read from her house…like her own books, I mean. That made me feel good, like someone trusted me.

"I saw a social worker once a week and we tried to figure out what had gotten me there. She was also supposed to see my mother, but Mom only came when she felt like it, which wasn't too often. She was pregnant again and sick a lot and then she had the baby and that was her excuse. The social worker also helped me learn how angry I was at Mom. We talked about that a lot.

"The director of the place was great too. He was an older guy who had had daughters, but they were grown. They came down sometimes to see the kids at the center. One of them had a little kid she used to bring, too. I played with him a lot and figured out that I liked little kids. And I made a bunch of friends there too. The kids were from all over the state. They were in there for lots of different stuff like running away and drugs and just being obnoxious to people. I still write to one of the girls.

"After I'd been there a couple of years and they couldn't get my Mom to straighten out, they transferred me to a group home. I was seventeen and it looked like I could never go home. The group home was a house with six girls, each in her own room. We were supposed to think of it like an apartment. We got jobs after school and had to pay rent. It wasn't much. It just was supposed to teach us to budget and stuff. They also made us take classes on budgeting and other things we had to do on our own, like cooking and that stuff.

"A week before I was eighteen, I found out that I was pregnant. I was going to leave the home when I was eighteen and I think I was a little scared. The guy who got me pregnant was twenty-six and I figured we'd get married. Right! When he found out I was pregnant he took off and I never saw him again. So the center helped me get welfare and an apartment until I got a job at this fast food place.

"That was five years ago. My daughter and I are doing pretty well. It's tough being a parent, but I'm going to be a better one than my mother! Looking back, the center was probably better than any of the foster homes I was in. But who knows. I don't think I gave any of them a chance."

PROBLEMS IN RESIDENTIAL SETTINGS

As in any service, there are problems associated with residential treatment. These can be both internal and external.

STAFF ISSUES

There are a variety of issues associated with staff in residential treatment that can be problematic. Many of these have been discussed earlier but it is useful to summarize them here.

The *high staff turnover* can undermine the consistency that is the objective of many residential settings. As mentioned earlier, *burnout* occurs frequently due to the complexity and intensity of the job. Even when there is not a high turnover rate, *staff members have different styles* that can confuse and frustrate the residents. These differences also make it easier for children to play one staff member against another unless the agency is dedicated to good communication.

There can also be an *overlap in staff roles.* For example, a child care worker confronted with a child at bedtime who wants to talk about his or her abuse may not feel it is appropriate to tell the child to wait to speak to the social worker the next day. Yet, child care staff are often not trained in counseling and to counsel under these circumstances might not be therapeutic. Once again, communication between the two staff components is essential.

ABUSE IN RESIDENTIAL SETTINGS

The amount of contact with children that staff members have gives ample opportunity for both physical and sexual abuse to occur. Increasingly, centers are concerned with proper screening of new staff members. Many states require potential workers to be processed through a criminal records check, but these files usually identify a sexual offender only if he or she has been prosecuted. Current antidiscrimination practices and laws also prohibit asking some of the questions that might identify someone as a person who would abuse children. Agencies are finding that it is within their authority to use case scenarios and ask applicants to respond to these. The scenarios would have to be written with a knowledge of behaviors and attitudes that correlate with abusive behavior, however, and some critics argue that there is no way to anticipate an abuser no matter what techniques of evaluation are available. And so the dilemma of how to protect children in residential settings continues to be debated.

Once staff have been hired, many agencies now safeguard their populations by insisting that no staff member be alone with a child. This may work in some situations. Better training might be given to staff to help them to avoid the temptation of using physical punishment to cope with problematic behavior. Severe penalties for abusive practices might serve as another deterrent.

COMMUNITY SUPPORT

Another issue often faced by residential centers is the lack of support within the community.

"The St. Joseph's Center used to bring the kids to community events in a big blue van," recounted one resident of a small town in which there was a forty-bed facility for disturbed boys. "When the van would drive up, everyone would whisper 'here come the St. Joe's kids.' It was as if everyone expected them to get into trouble. I felt sorry for the kids."

The mentality of "not in my community" can surround the presence of a residential treatment center in a given area. How well the center is accepted within the community can be the most challenging public relations issue for any center. Some agencies find that giving back to the community helps its public image. For example, one residence was in close proximity to a nursing home. The agency began a program in which the more high functioning of the residents would volunteer time at the nursing home to read to the elders, sort mail, do light chores, or just provide a listening ear. The program was so successful that the community awarded the agency a public service award. Unfortunately, all residential centers are not as well received. This stigma can have a great impact on children who already have lives filled with rejection.

TRENDS

POPULATION SERVED

While at one time the child served by many residential settings tended to be the child who was unmanageable in a home, the problems being seen in centers today are much more severe. Many children have been involved with the court system for years before placement. This may mean that their attitudes make treatment challenging. Substance abuse is now a common problem necessitating residential treatment. The seriousness of these problems calls for better staff training and more creative methods of handling the residents. Clinical staff as well as residential and educational staff will require more sophisticated training to deal with these children in the most effective and therapeutic manner.

In addition to the severity of problems, there is increasing recognition that there are a high percentage of children in residential settings who come from a variety of minority groups. Thus centers are called on to provide bilingual and bicultural staff to help the children in their care. Additional staff training will also be needed to understand the variety of cultural attitudes and customs that residents bring with them into care.

RESTRICTION IN FUNDING

Residential treatment is usually funded by several sources: the public child welfare agency, the school system, the mental health system, or the parents and/or their insurance. As funds become more restricted, the funding of this service is more in question. Child welfare agency budgets have been drastically cut from state to state meaning that these agencies seek the least expensive means to treat their clients. School budgets have been decreased, leaving schools to look for the most cost-effective ways of dealing with students.

Managed care has also played a role in the provision of residential services. As insurance companies become more selective and advocate the least restrictive and least expensive settings, parents find that they are unable to afford residential treatment for their children no matter how desperate their need may be.

These constraints will put a great deal of pressure on residential centers and necessitate that they do more active recruiting, cut their costs and services, and seek creative ways to continue to function.

MORE EFFECTIVE EVALUATION

As residential settings face their critics they will be called on to demonstrate the efficacy of their services. Yet, how effectively children have been treated cannot always be measured by the children's future directions. The question of "what if" is always at issue. For example, what if Jennifer (in "A Former Resident Remembers") had not been influenced by the residential setting in which she was placed. Would she have become a substance abuser, following in her mother's footsteps? Or did the fact that she became pregnant before leaving the center mean that treatment and therefore the attempt to help her live a productive life were unsuccessful?

Mordock (1988) contends that "evaluative efforts in residential treatment centers should now focus less on outcome and more on monitoring treatment environments" (243). Children from dysfunctional backgrounds may not have an easy time, but rather than looking at their life as a whole, it will be important to monitor the coping mechanisms they have developed as a result of residential treatment. It is the challenge of the future to devise evaluation techniques that are accurate in assessing the efficacy of this type of service.

FAMILY INVOLVEMENT

As the emphasis continues to shift away from institutional settings and toward community treatment, it will be necessary to develop creative ways to involve parents in the discharge planning for children in residential settings. Some feel that involving an overwhelmed parent who has given up on being able to handle a child in the planning of that child's return home is futile. And yet, the child will need to return to the community more quickly than in years past. Thus residential treatment must be seen as merely a step toward that goal. Parental involvement will be a critical part of the therapeutic picture.

As we face the twenty-first century, there will be numerous challenges inherent in the provision of child welfare services. With the increased emphasis on our nation's failure to support the family, residential treatment centers will have their work cut out for them in justifying their existence.

SUMMARY

Residential settings for children have roots that go back as far as the fifteenth century. Initially, orphan asylums met the needs of dependent children, while centers for delinquents attempted to rehabilitate and secure juveniles. There were also settings for disabled children and those who were mentally retarded. Over the years they have evolved to meet many different needs.

In considering residential care for children today, two assumptions are made: a residential setting is the last alternative and the least restrictive setting is best. Residential settings give children an opportunity for diluted emotional interaction with others and programs are structured to try to meet the individual needs of children, many of whom exhibit destructive behaviors.

Residential settings range from those designed to be diagnostic, those designed to provide treatment for both the emotionally disturbed and the disabled, and those designed to rehabilitate juvenile offenders. Children are referred to such settings as a way of removing them from the community or because their individual problems necessitate specialized treatment.

Residential settings are usually made up of three components: the residential, the educational, and the clinical. Most centers use a token economy that reinforces children for acceptable behavior. An important part of group treatment is the influence that the residents have on each other. Many centers work with the families of the children in their care. Families range from those who are invested in their children to those who either do not become involved with their children's care or who attempt to sabotage the treatment efforts made by professionals.

Children leave residential centers for a variety of reasons. Some return home, some are placed in a less or more restrictive environment, and some are placed temporarily in psychiatric facilities. In some situations, children leave residential care to live on their own.

Over the last few years the types of children placed in residential centers have been more of a challenge to take care of. In addition, funding has decreased, placing more pressure on centers to provided comprehensive programs. The future of group care must be marked by more creative ways of operating if residential centers are to meet the needs of the children of the future.

EXPLORATION QUESTIONS

1. How did residential centers begin? Outline the history of the movement.
2. Cite six assumptions about residential care.
3. What are the five types of residential settings? What is the function of each?
4. What are the three components of residential treatment? What role does each play in the therapeutic milieu?
5. What instances can induce crisis situations in residential settings?
6. What are some issues regarding sexual acting out in residential settings? How can they be handled?
7. What are some considerations when working with the parents of children in residential care?
8. What roles do staff members take in residential settings? What are some of their frustrations?
9. Why might a child leave residential care?
10. What are the problems inherent in residential care?
11. What trends characterize residential care in the future?

ACTIVITIES FOR APPLIED LEARNING

1. Visit a residential treatment center. How does it compare with the description presented in this chapter?
2. Invite a child care worker or a social worker in a residential treatment center to speak in class. What are some of the joys and frustrations they experience in their work?
3. Contact a residential treatment center and ask if they offer speakers, especially former residents or current residents. Invite these individuals to speak to the class.

SUGGESTED READING

Braga, W., & Schimmer, R. (Eds.). *Sexual Abuse and Residential Treatment.* New York: Haworth Press, 1993.

Keith–Lucas, A., & Sanford, C. *Group Child Care as a Family Service.* Chapel Hill, NC: University of North Carolina Press, 1977.

Northrup, G. (Ed.). *The Management of Sexuality in Residential Treatment.* New York: Haworth Press, 1993.

Plach, T. A. *Residential Treatment and the Sexually Abused Child.* Springfield, IL: Charles C. Thomas, 1993.

Schaefer, C. E., & Swanson, A. J. *Children in Residential Care: Clinical Issues in Treatment.* New York: Van Nostrand Reinhold, 1988.

REFERENCES

Barker, P. "The Future of Residential Treatment for Children," (1–16). In C. E. Schaefer, & A. J. Swanson (Eds.) *Children in Residential Care: Critical Issues in Treatment.* New York: Van Nostrand Reinhold, 1988.

Billingsley, A., & Giovannoni, J. *Children of the Storm: Black Children and American Child Welfare.* New York: Harcourt Brace Jovanovich, 1972.

Bloom, R. B. "When Staff Members Sexually Abuse Children in Residential Care," (89–106). In G. Northrup (Ed.) *The Management of Sexuality in Residential Treatment.* New York: Haworth Press, 1993.

Bloom, R., Denton, I. R., & Caflish, C. "Institutional Sexual Abuse: A Crisis in Trust," (48–49). *In Contributions to Residential Treatment,* AACRC, 1991.

Bowlby, J. *Maternal Care and Mental Health.* Geneva: World Health Organization, 1951.

Braga, W. "Experience with Alleged Sexual Abuse in Residential Programs: Problems in the Management of Allegations," (99–116). In W. Braga & R. Schimmer (Eds.) *Sexual Abuse and Residential Treatment.* New York: Haworth Press, 1993.

Braga, W., & Schimmer, R. (Eds.). *Sexual Abuse and Residential Treatment.* New York: Haworth Press, 1993.

Breer, W. *The Adolescent Molester.* Springfield, IL: Charles C. Thomas, 1987.

Burnett, R., & Rathburn, C. "Discovery and Treatment of Adolescent Sexual Offenders in a Residential Treatment Center," (57–64). In G. Northrup (Ed.) *The Management of Sexuality in Residential Treatment.* New York: Haworth Press, 1993.

Charles, G., Coleman, H., & Matheson, J. "Staff Reactions to Young People Who Have Been Sexually Abused," (9–21). In G. Northrup (Ed.) *The Management of Sexuality in Residential Treatment.* New York: Haworth Press, 1993.

Corcoran, K. J. "Understanding and Coping with Burnout," (251–262). In C. E. Schaefer, & A. J. Swanson (Eds.) *Children in Residential Care: Critical Issues in Treatment.* New York: Van Nostrand Reinhold, 1988.

Costin, L. B., Bell, C. J., & Downs, S. W. *Child Welfare: Policies and Practice.* New York: Longman, 1991.

Crenshaw, D. A. "Responding to Sexual Acting-Out," (50–76). In C. E. Schaefer, & A. J. Swanson (Eds.) *Children in Residential Care: Critical Issues in Treatment.* New York: Van Nostrand Reinhold, 1988.

Devereux Foundation. "The Devereux Legacy in the Seventy-Fifth Annual Report." Devon, PA: The Devereux Foundation, 1987.

Diamond, A. "The Establishment and Maintenance of the Director's Influence on a Residential Treatment Program," (147–159). In C. E. Schaefer, & A. J. Swanson (Eds.) *Children in Residential Care: Critical Issues in Treatment.* New York: Van Nostrand Reinhold, 1988.

Everett, J. E., Chipungu, S. S., & Leashore, B. R. (Eds.). *Child Welfare: An Africentric Perspective.* New Brunswick, NJ: Rutgers University Press, 1991.

Gambrill, E. & Stein, T. J. (Eds.). *Controversial Issues in Child Welfare.* Boston: Allyn and Bacon, 1994.

Goffman, E. *Asylums.* Garden City, NY: Anchor, 1961.

Groze, V. "An Exploratory Investigation into Institutional Maltreatment," *Child and Youth Services Review,* 12, 1990, 229–241.

Gwynn, C., Meyer, R., & Schaefer, C. "The Influence of Peer Culture in Residential Treatment," (104–133). In C. E. Schaefer & A. J. Swanson (Eds.) *Children in Residential Care: Clinical Issues in Treatment.* New York: Van Nostrand Reinhold, 1988.

Hayden, T. *The Tiger's Child.* New York: Avon, 1995.

Johnson, T. C., & Aoki, W. T. "Sexual Behaviors of Latency Age Children in Residential Treatment," (1–22). In W. Braga & R. Schimmer (Eds.) *Sexual Abuse and Residential Treatment.* New York: Haworth Press, 1993.

Kadushin, A., & Martin, J. A. *Child Welfare Services.* New York: Macmillan, 1988.

Kagan, R. M. "Professional Development for a Therapeutic Environment," (160–174). In C. E. Schaefer & A. J. Swanson (Eds.) *Children in Residential Care: Clinical Issues in Treatment.* New York: Van Nostrand Reinhold, 1988.

Katz, M. "Crisis Intervention in Residential Care," (30–49). In C. E. Schaefer, and A. J. Swanson (Eds.) *Children in Residential Care: Clinical Issues in Treatment.* New York: Van Nostrand Reinhold, 1988.

Keith–Lucas, A., & Sanford, C. *Group Child Care as a Family Service.* Chapel Hill, NC: University of North Carolina Press, 1977.

Marohn, R. C. "Residential Services," (453–466). In P. H. Tolan & B. J. Cohler (Eds.) *Handbook of Clinical Research and Practice with Adolescents.* New York: John Wiley and Sons, 1993.

Mordock, J. B. "Evaluating Treatment Effectiveness," (219–250). In C. E. Schaefer & A. J. Swanson (Eds.) *Children in Residential Care: Clinical Issues in Treatment.* New York: Van Nostrand Reinhold, 1988.

Northrup, G. (Ed.). *The Management of Sexuality in Residential Treatment.* New York: Haworth Press, 1993.

Pecora, P. J., Whittaker, J. K., Maluccio, A. N., with Barth, R. P., & Plotnick, R. D. *The Child Welfare Challenge.* Hawthorne, NY: Aldine deGruyter, 1992.

Plach, T. A. *Residential Treatment and the Sexually Abused Child.* Sringfield, IL: Charles C. Thomas, 1993.

Powers, D. "Some Medical Implications of Sexuality in Residential Centers," (23–36). In G. Northrup (Ed.) *The Management of Sexuality in Residential Treatment.* New York: Haworth Press, 1993.

Rindfleisch, N. "Combating Institutional Abuse," (263–283). In C. E. Schaefer & A. J. Swanson (Eds.) *Children in Residential Care: Clinical Issues in Treatment.* New York: Van Nostrand Reinhold, 1988.

Ross, J. E., & deViller, M. P. "Safety Considerations in Developing an Adolescent Sex Offender Program in Residential Treatment," (37–47). In W. Braga and R. Schimmer (Eds.). *Sexual Abuse and Residential Treatment.* New York: Haworth Press, 1993.

Schaefer, C. E., & Swanson, A. J. *Children in Residential Care: Clinical Issues in Treatment.* New York: Van Nostrand Reinhold, 1988.

Stuck, E., Forward to Special Practice Issue from the North American Out-of-Home Care Conference. *Child Welfare* 71(6) (1992), 483–485.

Swanson, A. J., & Richard, B. A. "Discipline and Child Behavior Management in Group Care," (77–88). In C. E. Schaefer and A. J. Swanson (Eds.) *Children in Residential Care: Clinical Issues in Treatment.* New York: Van Nostrand Reinhold, 1988.

Van Hagan, J. "Family Work in Residential Treatment," (134–144). In C. E. Schaefer and A. J. Swanson (Eds.) *Children in Residential Care: Clinical Issues in Treatment.* New York: Van Nostrand Reinhold, 1988.

15

OUR CHILDREN'S FUTURE

WHAT IS IN OUR CHILDREN'S FUTURE?

Our children's future depends largely on the formation of policies and programs that ensure that their rights are protected and their needs are met. The status of today's children suggests that this is not being done adequately. The number of children in poverty has increased. Our protective services agencies are seeing more and more maltreated children and teens. Our juvenile courts are overworked, and the protection of children's health is regulated largely by those who can and will pay the bills. These facts do not present a favorable picture for the future of children.

President Clinton has indicated his concern for children calling this a "time for change." In 1993 his proclamation of National Children's Day served to highlight the need for more thoughtful policy formulation. In his proclamation, Clinton affirmed that

> *America's children are at once our most precious national resource and our most weighty responsibility...Millions of America's children grow up in stable and loving families. At the same time, an alarmingly high number of our youth do not have the benefit of such security; many grow up hungry, neglected, or abused... We must take it upon ourselves to address these problems... (Clinton, 1993, as cited in Garfinkel et al., 1996, 1).*

To further underscore the national concern about children, Jesse Jackson asserted, "When a nation's children are in trouble, our nation is in trouble" (Graves, 1994).

Solutions to the problems that face children are far from easy. One impediment to finding adequate solutions is the fact that Americans are often split on a number of questions that impact our youngest citizens. For example, the controversy over welfare reform, the educational reform law, the reinstitution of orphanages, and the child abuse reporting backlash represent only a few of the difficulties we have on agreeing about the issues.

The resolution of the dilemma of how to best serve our children may fall largely on the shoulders of the next generation of citizens, policy-makers, and child welfare advocates and workers. For this reason, a text on child welfare would be remiss if it did not give consideration to the issues at hand. The issues discussed here will be children's status, poverty, children at risk, health issues, and educational concerns. This list is in no way exhaustive but does cover some of the areas in which there is currently debate.

CHILDREN'S STATUS

> *"If I was taller, bigger, and my voice had changed," my ten-year-old son told me recently, "people would listen to what I had to say. But as soon as they see a small person and recognize me as a child, my views are discounted and everyone assumes that I know nothing. I do know how I feel and what I need. In this world of consumer rights, I think adults have forgotten one group of important consumers—kids!"*

The old expression "out of the mouths of babes" comes to mind as we read the words of an articulate ten-year-old. How many times has a child dreaded unsupervised visits with a sexually abusive parent only to have the court, unable to prove beyond the child's word that the abuse has occurred, order that the visit must take place? And how many children have told their parents by their behaviors that they are not comfortable in a particular setting, but not being "heard" they are sent anyway?

Admittedly, today's world is not always a friendly place for adults either, but so often the needs of the adult come first. For example, in many families both parents must work in order to support their family's needs. But, even given this reality, the day care services provided for children across the United States are at best uneven and at worse grossly inadequate. Currently there are no national standards for centers providing day care and many states have few, if any, guidelines about teacher qualifications or group size. Not only are children as a group not "heard" in terms of their needs, but in some areas there are marked gender and cultural differences in the services available. For example, several studies found that boys were more likely than girls to commit suicide or drop out of school and yet there are no more services offered for one gender than the other (Garfinkel et al., 1996).

Why are children discounted? The most obvious answer is that, in a democratic society, they cannot vote. If one cannot vote, one's rights and needs may be overlooked. It falls to those working with and advocating for children then to bring forward their causes. This also necessitates that those advocating for children be listening to them. This is not always easy for adults who have learned that money is what drives the mechanisms to provide service and marketing is what creates the money. Thus, even if children are "heard," what they need may not be provided.

The first and most involved advocates for children can be their parents. When parents can make themselves heard, children can benefit. Thus, support groups for parents that empower parents to help their children go a long way toward making sure that children's needs are met. One neighborhood of concerned parents proved this point.

> *The street between Maple and Magnolia had become busy, but was the only route to school for neighborhood children. The children had expressed their fear of crossing the street, even when monitored by parents, but the city took no action. Finally, the concerned parents took a stand. Through an intense community awareness effort, they convinced the city of the need for a stoplight. It was a proud group of parents that watched the light being put up so that their children could cross in safety.*

Although a streetlight may seem minor in the total lives of children, it may have taken on a different emphasis if a child had been hurt or killed by oncoming traffic. For this group of low-income parents, who had never felt in control of their own lives, advocating in this manner was not only beneficial for their children but a lesson in empowerment for them. Parents must be helped to recognize that they have the power to speak for their children.

When parents are not able to speak for children, others may need to. Advocacy for children necessitates recognizing and weighing all the issues. One agency that has been especially effective in advocating for children is the Children's Defense Fund. Knitzer (as cited in Downs et al., 1996, 445–446), of the Children's Defense Fund, identifies several underlying assumptions about advocating for children:

1. *Advocacy assumes that people have, or ought to have, certain basic rights;*
2. *Advocacy assumes that rights are enforceable by statutes, administration, or judicial procedure;*
3. *Advocacy efforts are focused on institutional failures that produce or aggravate individual problems;*
4. *Advocacy is inherently political;*
5. *Advocacy is most effective when it is focused on specific issues;*
6. *Advocacy is different from the provision of direct services (Downs et al., 1996, 445–446).*

Changing the status of children will require serious attitudinal changes on the part of society. This may never happen. In the meantime it is up to child advocates to exert sufficient influence to protect children's rights.

CHILDREN IN POVERTY

Poverty among children and their families is a major problem in the United States (see Chapter 3). Not only does poverty cause health and educational problems, but some argue that it can create conditions in which maltreatment of children by parents is likely as well (see Pelton and see Milner in Gambrill & Stein, 1994). What would be involved in ending poverty? Sherman (1994) estimates that in 1992 it would have taken $39.4 billion to bring poor families with children up to the poverty line—a cost of approximately $2,800 per child (116), and that the taxpayer cost for ending child poverty would be about $62 billion per year (119).

Baker (1995) suggests the adoption of Canada's child allowances and tax concessions for families. The child allowance would give each family with children a certain amount of money for the care of each child. Administrative costs are actually lower because of the elimination of eligibility testing. Feminists argue that this gives mothers more freedom and those who chose to stay home to raise their children could do so. The disadvantage with such a program is the higher cost of providing money for all children rather than just those whose parents cannot adequately provide for them.

Instead of child allowances, some countries are increasing tax concessions (i.e., exemptions, deductions, or credits) for those who have children. These are less visible to the public and eligibility can be determined without the stigma of welfare eligibility determination procedures. The United States is one of the only industrialized countries that provides tax concessions instead of a child allowance. Baker (1995) comments that "American children fare considerably worse in terms of poverty rates than do their counterparts in Western Europe" (150).

Smith (1995) suggests that one program may break the cycle of poverty and welfare. This program is a result of the passage of the Family Support Act of 1988. The goals of this legislation were to

foster economic self-sufficiency of families through education and job training for heads of welfare-dependent families, mostly single mothers, and…increase the economic support that noncustodial parents, mostly fathers, provide to families (300).

The main reform provided by this legislation is the Jobs Opportunities and Basic Skills (JOBS) program, which makes available education, job skills training, and other types of job preparation services to parents. This model is also intertwined with Head Start and extends day care services to parents who work as part of the JOBS program and provides case management services to these families as well.

Paradoxically, while programs such as this are being instituted, other legislation may have a more deleterious influence on poverty-stricken parents and their children. Welfare reform and specifically welfare-to-work programs directed at teenage parents have not improved the economic well-being of the teens in whom proponents of the legislation had hoped to instill motivation and discourage childbearing. In fact, the program has done neither (Aber et al., 1995). The solutions to child poverty are extremely complex. New and creative solutions are the only possibilities that might interrupt the cycle (see Chapter 3 for additional solutions).

CHILDREN AT RISK

When we speak of *children at risk,* we think first of children who are at risk for abuse and neglect. Over the last few years there has been much debate over what is best for maltreated children. Costin et al. (1996) contend that current "child abuse policy contains dangerous contradictions that contribute to the breakdown of the system" (6). Further, these authors feel that the current method of protecting children is less than effective and requires revisions. The media, attracted to high spectacle events, does not help to raise the consciousness of Americans about the realities of child abuse effectively. Instead, reporters focus on the well-known perpetrator and the bizarre or sadistic case. This distorts the picture of maltreatment and almost negates the seriousness of the plight of the low-income child.

Costin et al. (1996) also criticize what they refer to as the "child abuse industry" or the network of agencies and services designed to intervene in abusive situations. Caught up in bureaucracy, political disputes, legislative rhetoric, and debates over false versus repressed memories, the mechanisms do not always serve the children. The legal system, too, can do more damage than good with court delays and grandstand courtroom tactics.

Drake (1996) points out that even the semantics can be in question. The term *substantiated* is given to a case that the Child Protective Services feels warrants further investigation because, according to the evidence available, maltreatment appears to have taken place. *Unsubstantiation* is often misinterpreted to mean that there was no abuse or neglect. In fact, the term *unsubstantiated* can indicate that there was insufficient evidence or insufficient harm to the child, without necessarily meaning that there was no such abuse. In such situations, the child may be just as much in danger but is not protected by an agency. Drake suggests that further research is needed in the areas of screening accuracy and overreporting. Giovannoni (1989) feels that *unsubstantiated* should be clearly defined and divided into two categories: *unsubstantiated,* no further action taken, and *unsubstantiated,* services provided or arranged (317). Whatever the area considered, the protection of children from maltreatment must be better addressed and researched in the future.

Maltreated children are not the only ones covered by the phrase *at risk.* The term has been broadened to include children whose dysfunctional family or whose poverty puts them at risk for a variety of social service needs. Since the late 1980s the literature has been filled with the term and proposed ways to deal with the problem of children at risk. Throughout this text, we have considered different ways that children are put at risk and possible solutions to protect them. But Swadener and Lubeck (1995) contend that the phrase has become a "buzzword" that emphasizes the negative and in no way accentuates the positive or builds on the family's strengths. These authors suggest that this "deficit model" often results in blaming the victim. When we blame someone for their own victimization, we then feel justified in not helping them. Swadener and Lubeck (1995) suggest the term *at promise* rather than *at risk.* "At promise" would consider all the possibilities for all children whatever their socioeconomic class, race, gender, or age.

> *Perhaps the time has finally come to move beyond the dominant culture assumptions and deficit-model thinking that have so separated students and educators alike, particularly as they create barriers to building the sort of culturally inclusive alliances which authentic change will require. Such alliances for children can begin to transcend the internalized oppression which is a major by-product of the deficiency model embodied in the construct 'children and families at risk' (41).*

These authors suggest that plans for children's well-being would be done in partnerships with parents, who would be empowered to meet their children's needs and seek out resources for the needs that they are unable to meet. As the authors put it: "By viewing parents and children as 'at promise' we enhance the possibilities of constructing authentic relations where we actively *listen* and learn from one another" (42).

While an attitudinal change is not a complete solution to protecting children from harm, it may well enhance our ability to find solutions. Instead of looking to "fix" broken families, would not such a reframing cause us to be more creative and proactive about services for children?

CHILDREN AND HEALTH

There is no area in need of adopting a proactive state of mind more than health care. One problem for poor children seeking medical care is finding a doctor who will accept Medicaid. A high percentage of doctors refuse to accept Medicaid due to the long delays in reimbursement (Sherman, 1994; Brown, 1994; Chase–Lansdale & Brooks–Gunn, 1995). One pediatrician from a particularly deprived low-income area commented:

> *It got so I literally could not pay my bills. With 90 percent of my patients covered by Medicaid and the very long delays before I was reimbursed, I could be seeing patients for weeks with no income at all. I am certainly not in medicine for the money. If I was, I would not be practicing where I do, but I also need to feed my family.*

Poor families who are not eligible for Medicaid may have trouble paying medical fees. Even middle-income families who have no or minimal insurance coverage may find themselves bankrupted by one medical crisis. Even regular checkups may not be done when a family has difficulty meeting the costs.

Landrigan & Carlson (1995) emphasize that it is not only routine health and organic illness that threatens children. Increasingly, environmental hazards take their toll on human beings, and children are actually more vulnerable for several reasons:

1. *Children have greater exposure to toxins than adults. As they grow, children actually take in more food and water and breathe more air than their adult counterparts.*
2. *Children's metabolic pathways, especially in the first months after birth, are immature compared to those of adults. This means that their ability to detoxify harmful substances is less than adults.*
3. *Children are undergoing rapid growth and development, and their delicate developmental processes are easily disrupted.*
4. *Because children have more future years than adults, they have more time to develop any chronic diseases that may be triggered by early environmental exposures (Landrigan & Carlson, 1995, 36).*

Attention to environmental policy-making may also be crucial to the protection of the future health of children.

Provisions under the Family Support Act of 1988 do offer some opportunity to study health issues for children thought to be at particular risk. Lear (1996) outlines a plan for a school health care center that would link "existing efforts in primary care, public health, school health, and health education with emerging systems of managed health care to ensure that the health care requirements of the neediest children are met" (176). But more could be done for all children. It will be the challenge of the next generation of child welfare professionals to advocate for primary health care for every child.

CHILDREN AND EDUCATION

Another area of much controversy has been our educational system. Innovations in the inclusion of special needs children as well as the total Educational Reform Act have sought to make the educational experience a rewarding one for every child. But we are far from that goal.

Some learning in school goes beyond reading, writing, and math. Children come to their learning environment with a set of cultural values as well as familial values. Increasingly, it has become important for educators to be sensitized to the diversity brought to the educational experience by each child. In addition, Mosteller (1995) found in a study of Tennessee schools, that children taught in smaller classes, especially in the lower grades, performed better than children in larger class groups, even when a classroom aide was present.

Children also come to school with a variety of barriers to learning. The residual effects of abuse and neglect, the conflict over domestic violence in the home, the scars of poverty, health issues, and the threat of community violence all affect a child's ability to learn. It is not until we fully address these other social issues that we can truly remove the barriers to learning for all children. In the meantime, educators must develop a sensitivity that goes beyond the ability to communicate information. As one educator put it:

When it was suggested that the teachers at our school go to a child prevention program, a number of my colleagues protested. "We don't even have time to teach the basics!" retorted one veteran teacher, "and now we have to train to detect child abuse!" My response was that she should wake up! Teaching today is not just about the "three R's"! When a child comes in hungry or hurting from the beating he got, he's not going to care about the spelling words for the day. Until you deal with his safety or hunger issues, there is no way that child will learn to his full potential!

Fortunately more teachers are recognizing their need to become aware of the whole child and to gear education toward *that* child. Increasingly, educators value and use the services provided within the school system (see Chapter 6) and within the community. Preparation for the future necessitates that educational as well as health and child welfare professionals work together for the whole child within his or her total environment.

PREPARING THOSE WHO HELP CHILDREN

The role of the child welfare worker, no matter what the discipline or the agency, is an important one. For this reason, it is vital that child welfare professionals be well trained, not only in their particular job, but also to understand every issue concerning children. The child welfare worker should have training in the following areas at the very least:

- child development
- interviewing skills (especially as they apply to children)

- child welfare services
- child abuse and neglect
- systems theory (so that there is recognition that the child is part of the family system, the neighborhood, the community, and so forth)
- formulation of social policy and grant writing
- state, urban, and federal government
- cultural diversity
- computer skills

Many of these areas should be covered in college courses. Agencies do not always train their workers in skills or knowledge beyond the definition of their particular jobs. Thus, when a worker is faced with interviewing a young child for the first time, he or she may be hampered by a lack of knowledge of either child development and/or interviewing. Or, when an agency needs a new program to better serve clients, the worker would be well advised to have knowledge in grant writing and/or the political working of the community to be in the best position to apply for or negotiate for such a program. And, most agencies are now computerized and require that workers do their own documentation on a personal computer. Thus, a familiarity with computer skills can be invaluable.

Training once one is hired by an agency may be thorough but is more likely to be brief and often incomplete.

When I started as a worker in a foster care agency, I had just graduated from college as an English major. I could do great dictation, but I didn't have a clue if a child was acting normal for his or her age or not. I started work on Monday, got a brief training in forms and policies on Monday and Tuesday, and was sent to my first foster home visit on Wednesday. I had no idea what to say or how to talk to young children. Later my supervisor told me that we were short-staffed that day or they would have let me shadow a worker for a day. Even a day would not have done it!

Smith (1993) emphasizes the importance of training, especially in the field of child abuse and neglect. She stresses that the training environment should be well organized with attention to such things as selection of the trainers, seating arrangement, timing, and group interaction.

"Good training also promotes a good team," explained one agency director. "My agency training consists of team building right at the onset. Experienced workers join new workers in training groups and we do problem-solving exercises. This helps the new workers see how the work is done without just talking at them. I have had workers come to me years after they have been with us, telling me what a valuable experience that training was."

Child welfare workers also have ongoing supervision and the quality of this supervision is extremely important. "I tell my workers that quality supervison is their right! If they aren't getting it, I'd like to know why," asserted the same agency director. It is in supervision that one learns how to prioritize difficult cases adeptly, receives support to make decisions, learns more about the agency, and has an opportunity to process one's own feelings about particular cases.

"One case was giving me a lot of trouble," said one new child welfare worker. "I couldn't figure out why. It was only after supervision that I realized that this mother was pushing old 'buttons' in me that reminded me of things I hated when I was growing up."

In addition to weekly training, many agencies provide ongoing in-service training or give workers the opportunity to take workshops, training sessions outside the agency, or courses at a local college. This is a valuable chance to keep up one's knowledge in the field. The preparation of child welfare workers cannot be taken too lightly. It is these individuals who may be responsible for major decisions in the lives of children.

CHILD WELFARE IN THE NEXT CENTURY

It would be nice if we could jump ahead and see what is facing us in the year 2000 and beyond. Only then could we fully tailor the services to children to meet their needs. But, because we cannot use a time machine, we can only guess what faces us in the future.

Schwartz (1991) expresses concern that the efforts to preserve families has not been working. Pecora (1994) argues that Intensive Family Preservation Services have been ineffective and that as a result these services should be refined and evaluated in the future. Roberts (1991) calls for new models to address child protection issues. Changes must take place not only within child protection agencies, but also within the larger community—business, churches, schools, and neighborhoods. And Finkelhor (1991), examining societal trends and their impact on child welfare issues, speculates that, despite the impact of the rising divorce rate, federal budget problems, poverty, and the threat of AIDS, there are some positive projections for the future. Demographic trends indicate that there will be fewer unwanted children, which may influence the number of children being abused or neglected. Improved medical care and biotechnology may result in fewer medical problems and developmental disabilities for children. In addition, the medical and social service community, with updated research, will be better able to deal with children who have these problems. And as women rise higher in institutions and various influential professions, more attention will be paid to the needs of children.

Whatever the demographics tell us, experience has made us aware that the only hope we have of meeting the needs of all citizens, but especially children, is through a team approach. We cannot afford the luxury of turf-ism in which each profession stakes out a territory that it fiercely guards. Only through sharing our knowledge and ideas with others who are concerned for children can we solve the problems that we all face in the provision of services for them.

If you have read this text, you are probably considering child welfare as a career goal or teaching those for whom this is an option. Providing services for children is an exciting and challenging endeavor. It falls to you and others like you to make a difference for our children. Holocaust survivor and noted writer, Elie Wiesel (1989), spoke of the future being assured by building a moral society.

> *In a moral society, people listen to each other and care about the other person. No person may be sacrificed for any goal...A primary difference between an immoral society and a moral society is that in an immoral society, people don't listen. [They] know everything, know the question, know the answer to the question. Clichés are used. But in a moral society, there is a sense of wonder at the presence of someone else. I am free because other people are free. No cliches are used...(3).*

It is up to all of us to build a moral society in which even children can be heard. As those who advocate for children, we must help children to be heard. This may involve promoting pro-child/pro-family federal legislation or searching for creative agency responses or supporting clients to empower themselves, or a variety of other responses. It will mean not seeing our clients as doomed to fail, but rather filled with promise. Only when we begin to recognize the importance of children as our future and value the strengths their families can provide for them, will today's children receive adequate services. Being a voice for the children is the only way we can help them be heard. It will be a challenge, but one well worth meeting.

SUMMARY

The future of child welfare is dependent largely on the policies and programs that are designed to protect and serve children. Responsibility for the formulation and implementation of policies that work falls on the shoulders of those about to enter the field as well as veteran advocates and policy-makers. Therefore, it is important for new child welfare workers to know the issues and begin to search proactively for solutions.

Several issues immediately present themselves in a discussion of the future of child welfare. First, how can we improve the status of children? Children are often discounted because they are unable to vote. Therefore, it will be important to develop effective advocacy on behalf of children. Secondly, how can we elevate children and their families above the poverty level? Increased financial allocations is one possibility. Unlike the United States, which depends on tax concessions, some countries give parents a child allowance to help them care for their children. Next, how can we protect children at risk? *At risk* can be seen as being at risk for maltreatment or at risk for a variety of other reasons. Some believe that the phrase *at risk* emphasizes the negative rather than allowing for the strengths that families and children have. We need also to think about how we can improve both health care and education for children.

It is also imperative that those who work with children be adequately trained, both at the college level and within the agency. Beyond training, effective supervision is also vital. It will fall to the child welfare worker of tomorrow, if not each citizen, to protect children and speak for them so that their needs will be met and the services they need will be provided.

EXPLORATION QUESTIONS

1. What are some areas of controversy among those considering services to children?
2. What accounts for the status that children have in society? How could it be improved?
3. What is meant by advocacy? What are some basic assumptions about advocacy?
4. What are some possible solutions for poverty among children and their families?
5. What is meant by "children at risk"? Why might they be at risk?
6. What is the criticism of the term *at risk*? What is an alternative?
7. Why are environmental factors such a concern with respect to children's health?
8. What needs to be considered when discussing education in the future?
9. What type of preparation should child welfare workers have?
10. What are some projections for the next century?

ACTIVITIES FOR APPLIED LEARNING

1. Research the term *child advocacy*. What does it involve? What agencies are dedicated to child advocacy? What do they do on behalf of children?
2. What legislation is pending, either on a state or federal level, that would affect children? Have a class debate on the pros and cons of the legislation.
3. Design a comprehensive child welfare system for the future. Be realistic but creative.
4. Find an unmet child welfare need in your community. Write a grant designing a program to meet this need, and present your plan before the class. You might ask them to imagine that they are a funding source. Would they give you funding based on your proposal?

SUGGESTED READING

Behrman, R. E. (Ed.). *The Future of Children, vol. 5 (2).* Los Altos, CA: Center for the Future of Children, David and Lucille Packard Foundation, 1995.

Brown, R. (Ed.). *Children in Crisis.* New York: H. W. Wilson, 1994.

Chase–Lansdale, P. L., & Brooks–Gunn, J. (Eds.). *Escape from Poverty: What Makes a Difference to Children?* Cambridge: Cambridge University Press, 1995.

Costin, L. B., Karger, H. J., & Stoesz, D. *The Politics of Child Abuse in America.* New York: Oxford University Press, 1996.

Finkelhor, D. "The Lazy Revolutionary's Guide to the Prospects for Reforming Child Welfare," *Child Abuse and Neglect* 15(1), (1991), 17–23.

Gambrill, E., & Stein, T. J. (Eds.). *Controversial Issues in Child Welfare.* Boston: Allyn and Bacon, 1994.

Roberts, D. "Child Protection in the 21st Century," *Child Abuse and Neglect,* 15(1), (1991), 25–30.

Schwartz, I. M. "Out-of-home Placement of Children: Selected Issues and Prospects for the Future," *Behavioral Sciences and the Law* 9(2), (1991), 189–199.

Sherman, A. *Wasting America's Future.* Boston: Beacon Press, 1994.

Smith, G. *Systematic Approaches to Training in Child Protection.* London: Karnac Books, 1993.

Swadener, B. B., & Lubeck, S. (Eds.). *Children and Families "at Promise."* Albany: State University of New York Press, 1995.

REFERENCES

Aber, J. L., Brooks–Gunn, J., & Maynard, R. A. "Effects of Welfare Reform on Teenage Parents and Their Children," (53–71). In Behrman, R. E. (Ed.), *The Future of Children, vol. 5 (2).* Los Altos, CA: Center for the Future of Children, David and Lucille Packard Foundation, 1995.

Baker, M. *Canadian Family Policies: Cross-National Comparisons.* Toronto: Univ. of Toronto Press, 1995.

Behrman, R. E. (Ed.). *The Future of Children, vol. 5 (2).* Los Altos, CA: Center for the Future of Children, David and Lucille Packard Foundation, 1995.

Brown, R. (Ed.). *Children in Crisis.* New York: H. W. Wilson Co., 1994.

Chase–Lansdale, P. L., & Brooks–Gunn, J. (Eds.). *Escape from Poverty: What Makes a Difference to Children?* Cambridge: Cambridge University Press, 1995.

Clinton, B. "Proclamation 6626–National Children's Day, 1993." In *Weekly Compilation of Presidential Documents,* Nov. 22, 1993, vol. 29

(46), pp. 2393–94 as cited in Garfinkel, I., Hochschild, J. L., and McLanahan, S. S. (Eds.). *Social Policies for Children.* Washington, DC: The Brookings Institution, 1996, 1.

Costin, L. B., Karger, H. J., & Stoesz, D. *The Politics of Child Abuse in America.* New York: Oxford University Press, 1996.

Downs, S. W., Costin, L. B., & McFadden, E. J. *Child Welfare and Family Services: Policies and Practice.* White Plains, NY: Longman, 1996.

Drake, B. "Unraveling 'Unsubstantiated'," *Child Maltreatment,* Vol. 1 (3), (1996), 261–271.

English, D. J., & Pecora, P. J. "Risk Assessment as a Practice Method in Child Protective Services," *Child Welfare,* Vol. 73 (5), (1994), 451–473.

Finkelhor, D. "The Lazy Revolutionary's Guide to the Prospects for Reforming Child Welfare," *Child Abuse and Neglect,* Vol 15 (suppl. 1), (1991), 17–23.

Gambrill, E., & Stein, T. J. (Eds.). *Controversial Issues in Child Welfare.* Boston: Allyn and Bacon, 1994.

Garfinkel, I., Hochschild, J. L., & McLanahan, S. S. (Eds.). *Social Policies for Children*. Washington, DC: The Brookings Institution, 1996.

Giovannoni, J. "Substantiated and Unsubstantiated Reports of Child Maltreatment," *Children and Youth Services Review* 11, (1989), 299–318.

Graves, C. "Jackson Urges Youths to Look to the Future," *Star Tribune*, Feb. 13, 1994, 7b.

Knitzer, J. E. "Child Advocacy: A Perspective," *American Journal of Orthopsychiatry*, Vol. 46(2), 200–216 as cited in Downs, S. W., Costin, L. B., & McFadden, E. J. *Child Welfare and Family Services: Policies and Practice*. White Plains, NY: Longman, 1996, 445–446.

Landrigan, P. J., & Carlson, J. E. "Environmental Policy and Children's Health," (34–52). In Behrman, R. E. (Ed.). *The Future of Children, vol. 5 (2)*. Los Altos, CA.: Center for the Future of Children, David and Lucille Packard Foundation, 1995.

Lear, J. G. "Health Care Goes to School: An Untidy Strategy to Improve the Well-Being of School Age Children," (173–201). In Garfinkel, I., Hochschild, J. L., & McLanahan, S. S. (Eds.). *Social Policies for Children*. Washington, DC: The Brookings Institution, 1996.

MacPherson, A. "Parent-Professional Partnership: A Review and Discussion of Issues," *Early Child Development and Care*, (86) (1993), 61–77.

Milner, J. S. "Is Poverty a Key Contributor to Child Abuse? No," (23–26). In Gambrill, E. & Stein, T. J. (Eds.). *Controversial Issues in Child Welfare*. Boston: Allyn and Bacon, 1994.

Mosteller, F. "The Tennessee Study of Class Size in the Early School Grades," (113–127). In Behrman, R. E. (Ed.). *The Future of Children, vol. 5 (2)*. Los Altos, CA: Center for the Future of Children, David and Lucille Packard Foundation, 1995.

Pecora, P. J. "Are Intensive Family Preservation Services Effective? Yes," (290–301). In Gambrill, E. & Stein, T. J. (Eds.). *Controversial Issues in Child Welfare*. Boston: Allyn and Bacon, 1994.

Pelton, L. H. "Is Poverty a Key Contributor to Child Abuse? Yes," (16–22). In Gambrill, E. & Stein, T. J. (Eds.). *Controversial Issues in Child Welfare*. Boston: Allyn and Bacon, 1994.

Roberts, D. "Child Protection in the 21st Century," *Child Abuse and Neglect*, Vol. 15 (1), (1991), 25–30.

Schwartz, I. M. "Out-of-Home Placement of Children: Selected Issues and Prospects for the Future," *Behavioral Sciences and the Law*. Vol. 9 (2), 1991, 189–199.

Sherman, A. *Wasting America's Future*. Boston: Beacon Press, 1994.

Smith, G. *Systematic Approaches to Training in Child Protection*. London: Karnac Books, 1993.

Smith, S. "Two-generation Programs: A New Intervention Strategy and Directions for Future Research," (299–314). In Chase–Lansdale, P. L. and Brooks–Gunn, J. (Eds.) *Escape from Poverty: What Makes a Difference to Children?* Cambridge: Cambridge University Press, 1995.

Swadener, B. B., & Lubeck, S. (Eds.). *Children and Families "at Promise."* Albany: State University of New York Press, 1995.

Weisel, E. "Building a Moral Society." Lecture at the Provost's Forum, Kent State University, Kent, Ohio, April 1989, as cited in Swadener, B. B., & Lubeck, S. (Eds.). *Children and Families "at Promise."* Albany: State University of New York Press, 1995, 41.

INDEX